ISBN: 9781313880541

Published by:
HardPress Publishing
8345 NW 66TH ST #2561
MIAMI FL 33166-2626

Email: info@hardpress.net
Web: http://www.hardpress.net

MULTIPLY PERIODIC FUNCTIONS

CAMBRIDGE UNIVERSITY PRESS WAREHOUSE,
C. F. CLAY, MANAGER.
London: FETTER LANE, E.C.
Glasgow: 50, WELLINGTON STREET.

Leipzig: F. A. BROCKHAUS.
New York: G. P. PUTNAM'S SONS.
Bombay and Calcutta: MACMILLAN & CO., LTD.

AN INTRODUCTION TO THE THEORY

OF

MULTIPLY PERIODIC FUNCTIONS

BY

H. F. BAKER, Sc.D., F.R.S.,

FELLOW OF ST JOHN'S COLLEGE AND LECTURER IN MATHEMATICS
IN THE UNIVERSITY OF CAMBRIDGE

CAMBRIDGE:
at the University Press
1907

"Sie erinnern Sich aber auch vielleicht zu gleicher Zeit meiner Klagen, über einen Satz, der theils schon an sich sehr interessant ist, theils einem sehr beträchtlichen Theile jener Untersuchungen als Grundlage oder als Schlussstein dient, den ich damals schon über 2 Jahr kannte, und der alle meine Bemühungen, einen genügenden Beweis zu finden, vereitelt hatte, dieser Satz ist schon in meiner Theorie der Zahlen angedeutet, und betrifft die Bestimmung eines Wurzelzeichens, sie hat mich immer gequält.

Dieser Mangel hat mir alles Uebrige, was ich fand, verleidet und seit 4 Jahren wird selten eine Woche hingegangen sein, wo ich nicht einen oder den anderen vergeblichen Versuch, diesen Knoten zu lösen, gemacht hätte--besonders lebhaft nun auch wieder in der letzten Zeit. Aber alles Brüten, alles Suchen ist umsonst gewesen, traurig habe ich jedesmal die Feder wieder niederlegen müssen.

Endlich vor ein Paar Tagen ist's gelungen——"

Gauss an Olbers, September 1805 (Schering, Festrede).

PREFACE.

THE present volume consists of two parts; the first of these deals with the theory of hyperelliptic functions of two variables, the second with the reduction of the theory of general multiply-periodic functions to the theory of algebraic functions; taken together they furnish what is intended to be an elementary and self-contained introduction to many of the leading ideas of the theory of multiply-periodic functions, with the incidental aim of aiding the comprehension of the importance of this theory in analytical geometry.

The first part is centred round some remarkable differential equations satisfied by the functions, which appear to be equally illuminative both of the analytical and geometrical aspects of the theory; it was in fact to explain this that the book was originally entered upon. The account has no pretensions to completeness: being anxious to explain the properties of the functions from the beginning, I have been debarred from following Humbert's brilliant monograph, which assumes from the first Poincaré's theorem as to the number of zeros common to two theta functions; this theorem is reached in this volume, certainly in a generalised form, only in the last chapter of Part II.: being anxious to render the geometrical portions of the volume quite elementary, I have not been able to utilise the theory of quadratic complexes, which has proved so powerful in this connexion in the hands of Kummer and Klein; and, for both these reasons, the account given here, and that given in the remarkable book from the pen of R. W. H. T. Hudson, will, I believe, only be regarded by readers as complementary. The theory of Kummer's surface, and of the theta functions, has been much studied since the year (1847 or before) in which Göpel first obtained the biquadratic relation connecting four theta functions; and Wirtinger has shewn, in his *Untersuchungen über Thetafunctionen*, which has helped me in several ways in the second part of this volume, that the theory is capable of generalisation, in many of its results, to space of $2^p - 1$ dimensions; but even in the case of two variables there is a certain inducement, not to come to too close quarters with the details, in the fact of the existence of sixteen theta functions connected together by many relations, at least in the minds of beginners. I hope therefore that the treatment here followed, which reduces the theory, in a very practical way, to that of one theta function and three periodic functions connected by an algebraic equation, may recommend itself to others, and, in a humble way, serve the purpose of the earlier books on elliptic functions, of encouraging a wider use of the functions in other branches of mathematics. The slightest examination will shew that, even for the functions of two variables, many of the problems entered upon demand further study; while, for the hyperelliptic functions of p variables, for which the forms of the corresponding differential equations are known, there exist constructs, of p dimensions, in space of $\frac{1}{2}p(p+1)$ dimensions, which await similar investigation.

The problem studied in the second part of the volume was one of the life problems of Weierstrass, but, so far as I know, he did not himself publish during his lifetime anything more than several brief indications of the lines to be followed to effect a solution. The account given here is based upon a memoir in the third volume of the *Gesammelte Werke*, published in 1903; notwithstanding other publications dealing with the matter, as for example by Poincaré and Picard, and particularly by Wirtinger, it appears to me that Weierstrass's paper is of fundamental importance, for its precision and clearness in regard to the problem in hand, and for the insight it allows into what is peculiarly Weierstrass's own point of view in the general Theory of Functions; at the same time, perhaps for this reason, some points in the course of the argument, and particularly the conclusion of it, seem, to me at least, to admit of further analysis, or to be capable of greater definiteness. In making this exposition I have therefore ventured to add such things as the explanation in § 53, the limitation to a monogenic portion of the construct and the argument of § 60, an examination of simple cases of curves possessing defective integrals and the argument of Chapter IX. These are doubtless capable of much improvement. But the whole matter is of singular fascination, both because of the great generality and breadth of view of the results achieved and because of the promise of development which it offers; I hope that the very obvious need for further investigation, suggested constantly throughout this part of the volume, may encourage a wider cultivation of the subject, and a more thorough study of the original papers referred to in the text, of which I have in no case attempted to give a complete reproduction, though I have endeavoured in all cases to acknowledge my obligations.

I may not conclude without expressing my gratitude, amply called for in the case of any intricate piece of mathematical printing, for the carefulness and courtesy of the staff of the University Press.

H. F. BAKER.

CAMBRIDGE,
19 *August* 1907.

TABLE OF CONTENTS.

PART I.

HYPERELLIPTIC FUNCTIONS OF TWO VARIABLES.

CHAPTER I.

INTRODUCTORY.

CHAPTER II.

THE DIFFERENTIAL EQUATIONS FOR THE SIGMA FUNCTIONS.

CHAPTER III.

ANALYTICAL RESULTS RELATING TO THE ASSOCIATED QUARTIC SURFACES.

CHAPTER IV.

THE EXPANSION OF THE SIGMA FUNCTIONS.

CHAPTER V.

CERTAIN FUNCTIONAL RELATIONS AND THEIR GEOMETRICAL INTERPRETATION.

APPENDIX TO PART I.

PART II.

THE REDUCTION OF THE THEORY OF MULTIPLY-PERIODIC FUNCTIONS TO THE THEORY OF ALGEBRAIC FUNCTIONS.

CHAPTER VI.

GENERAL INTRODUCTORY THEOREMS.

CHAPTER VII.

ON THE REDUCTION OF THE THEORY OF A MULTIPLY-PERIODIC FUNCTION TO THE THEORY OF ALGEBRAIC FUNCTIONS.

CHAPTER VIII.

DEFECTIVE INTEGRALS.

CHAPTER IX.

PROPOSITIONS FOR RATIONAL FUNCTIONS.
EXPRESSIONS OF A GENERAL PERIODIC FUNCTION BY THETA FUNCTIONS.

CHAPTER X.

THE ZEROS OF JACOBIAN FUNCTIONS.

APPENDIX TO PART II.

CORRIGENDA.

p. 121, l. 4, *for* $\wp_{222}(2w)$ *read* $\wp_{222}(w)$.

p. 121, l. 9, *for* $\wp_{2222}(u)$, etc., *read* $\wp_{2222}(w)$, etc.

p. 152, Ex. 6, l. 13 and l. 21, *for* $\Theta P_\theta - \Phi P_\phi$ *read* $\Theta P_\phi - \Phi P_\theta$.

p. 164, l. 18, *for* $m_2 n_1'$ *read* $m_1' n_2$.

PART I.

THE HYPERELLIPTIC FUNCTIONS OF TWO VARIABLES AND THE ASSOCIATED GEOMETRY.

CHAPTER I.

INTRODUCTORY.

1. LET x be a complex variable represented upon an infinite plane, regarded in the ordinary way as closed at infinity, and let

$$f(x) = \lambda_0 + \lambda_1 x + \lambda_2 x^2 + \ldots + \lambda_5 x^5 + \lambda_6 x^6$$

be any sextic polynomial. The pairs of values (x, y), $(x, -y)$, which satisfy the equation $y^2 = f(x)$, may be represented by the points of a two-sheeted surface lying upon the plane of x, the sheets crossing one another along three lines joining respectively the first and second roots of $f(x) = 0$, the third and fourth roots, and the fifth and sixth roots, where the order in which the roots are taken is indifferent; thus a closed line on this two-sheeted surface, drawn about and near to the point representing one of these roots, will make two circuits before returning on itself, and each of these roots is represented by a winding place—or branch place—of the surface; if $\lambda_6 = 0$ one of the six branch places is at infinity. We may represent any place of the surface, corresponding to a single pair (x, y), by a single symbol (x), or simply by x. If (a) be such a place, for which x is finite, and not a root of $f(x) = 0$, and (x) be any sufficiently near place, we can solve the equation $y^2 = f(x)$ by $x = a + t$, $y = P(t)$, where $P(t)$ is a series of positive integral powers of the parameter t, and every place in the immediate neighbourhood of (a) is given by one value of t. If (a) be a branch place, for which both x and y are finite, say a finite branch place, we can similarly solve by $x = a + t^2$, $y = P(t)$, an increment of 2π in the phase of t corresponding in this case to an increment of 4π in the phase of $x - a$, that is to a path on the surface which closes itself only after containing points of both sheets. If $\lambda_6 \neq 0$ we can similarly represent all points of the surface for which x is sufficiently large by two pairs of formulae of the forms $x^{-1} = t$, $y^{-1} = t^3 P(t)$, and $x^{-1} = t$, $y^{-1} = -t^3 P(t)$, corresponding to the two superimposed but distinct places of the surface; while if $\lambda_6 = 0$, all points in the immediate neighbourhood of the single place at infinity are represented by a single pair of formulae $x^{-1} = t^2$, $y^{-1} = t^5 P(t)$. In fact these various power series converge within a circular range about the place considered which excludes the nearest branch place; but it is sufficient for our purpose to assume the convergence for sufficiently small values of t. This quantity we call the parameter of the place.

It is manifest that any rational function of x and y, say $H(x, y)$, is representable about any place in terms of the parameter of the place in a form $H(x, y) = t^{-m} P(t)$, where m is an integer, positive, negative, or zero, and $P(t)$ does not vanish for $t = 0$; the number m, if positive, is then called the order of infinity of the function at the place; if m is negative, the number $-m$ is the order of the zero of the function at the place. And any integral $\int_a^x H(x, y)\, dx$, which is supposed to be integrated along a path on the surface from the place (a) to the place (x), is, in the neighbourhood of any place, of a form $t^{-m} P(t) + C \log t$, where C is a constant. It will appear that there are forms of $H(x, y)$ such that the constant C is zero at every place, finite or infinite, and the integer m everywhere zero or negative; the corresponding integrals are then said to be of the first kind: there are also forms of $H(x, y)$ such that the constant C is everywhere zero, the integer m being positive for a finite number of places; the corresponding integrals, with a finite number of algebraic infinities, are said to be of the second kind; but, whatever form $H(x, y)$ have, there can only be a finite number of places where m is positive or C other than zero, and the sum of the values of C which arise at different places for the same integral is necessarily zero, as will be proved below; thus there can be no integral having only one place where C is not zero: integrals for which there are two or more places at which the logarithmic term is present, while m is never positive, are called integrals of the third kind.

Let us restrict ourselves now, for a little, to the consideration of integrals of the first or second kind. In the immediate neighbourhood of any place, even an infinity of the integral, the integral is single-valued; but this is not the case for any path; for instance a closed path passing entirely on one sheet of the surface round two only of the branch places will give a value for the integral not generally zero. In order then to deal only with single-valued functions we restrict the paths along which integration can take place by supposing the surface cut along certain curves. First let any closed curve be drawn on the surface of such a kind as could not be continuously deformed to a point without passing over branch places, and let the surface be cut along this curve; if a definite direction be assigned to the closed curve, either of the two possibilities being taken, we can appropriately speak of the left side, and of the right side, of the cut; we call this cut the first cut, or (A_1), and speak of the edges of the cut as period-loops; taking now an arbitrary point on the left side of the cut (A_1), it will be found that a continuous curve can be drawn on the surface, not passing through any branch place, to the opposite point on the right side of the cut (A_1); let the surface be now cut along this curve, the edge of the cut which is on the left when the curve is described being called the left edge; the new cut will be called (A_3). The surface now has a continuous boundary, consisting of the left side of (A_1), followed by the left side of (A_3), then the right side of (A_1), described however in the direction opposite to that of the curve from which (A_1) was constructed, and then the right side of (A_3), also in the negative direction of the curve from which (A_3) was constructed; this boundary may then be denoted by $(A_1A_3A_1^{-1}A_3^{-1})$. Upon the surface with this boundary it is possible to make another couplet of cuts, (A_2) and (A_4), related to one another as are (A_1) and (A_3), in such a way that neither (A_2) nor (A_4) intersects (A_1) or (A_3), while the surface does not break up into separate pieces. And upon the surface as now cut, with two continuous non-intersecting boundary lines $(A_1A_3A_1^{-1}A_3^{-1})$, $(A_2A_4A_2^{-1}A_4^{-1})$, every integral

$$\int_a^x H(x, y)\,dx,$$

of the first or second kind, can be shewn to be single-valued. The value of this integral at any point on the left side of (A_1) will exceed its value at the opposite point on the right side of (A_1) by a quantity Ω_1 which is the same all along (A_1); similarly its value at any point of the left side of (A_3) exceeds its value at the opposite point on the right side of (A_3) by a constant Ω_1'; and there are similar constants Ω_2, Ω_2' for (A_2) and (A_4). These four constants are called the periods of the integral, and the general value of which the integral is capable on the original surface, before this is cut, can be shewn to be of the form

$$\int_a^x H(x, y)\,dx + h_1\Omega_1 + h_2\Omega_2 + h_1'\Omega_1' + h_2'\Omega_2',$$

where h_1, h_2, h_1', h_2' are integers.

The statement for an integral with logarithmic infinities is analogous to the foregoing, but there is the modification that a closed path about a place where the expansion of the integral involves the logarithmic term $C \log t$ leads to an increment $2\pi iC$ in the value of the integral; in the simplest case that arises, to which in fact all others can be reduced, where there are two logarithmic places with equal and opposite values of C, the integral is rendered single-valued if, in addition to the cuts already made, a cut, not intersecting these, be made between the two logarithmic places.

2. That, as remarked above, the sum of the logarithmic coefficients C, for a given integral, at all the places where they exist, is zero, may be seen in either of the two following ways.

First, if in the neighbourhood of a place $x=a$, $y=b$, of logarithmic infinity for the particular integral under consideration, both x and y be expressed in terms of the parameter t belonging to the place, the logarithmic coefficient C is clearly the coefficient of t^{-1} in the expansion, in terms of t, of

$$H(x, y)\frac{dx}{dt};$$

there may, or may not, be a term in t^{-1} in the expansion of the same expression for the neighbourhood of the conjugate place $(a, -b)$; in any case where a is finite, the sum of the logarithmic coefficients for these two places, or the unique logarithmic coefficient if they are the same (branch) place, is at once seen to be the coefficient of $(x-a)^{-1}$ in the function

$$H(x, y)+H(x, -y),$$

which is rational in x only; similarly if (a, b) be at infinity, the sum of the coefficients C for the two places $a=\infty$, or the one coefficient when this is a branch place, is the negative of the coefficient of x^{-1} in the same rational function of x; by expressing this rational function of x in partial fractions it is at once evident thence that the sum of all existing coefficients C, for places where $H(x, y)\,dx/dt$ has a term in t^{-1}, is zero.

This result follows also from the fact that the closed curves

$$(A_1A_3A_1^{-1}A_3^{-1}),\quad (A_2A_4A_2^{-1}A_4^{-1})$$

form a complete boundary of the surface; this shews that the sum of the values of the integral $\int H(x, y)\,dx$, taken once positively round these curves, is equal to the sum of the values of this integral taken, along small closed curves, once round every place of logarithmic infinity, the value of the integral round any other point being zero. The contribution from such a logarithmic infinity is $2\pi i$ times the logarithmic coefficient; on the other hand, the value of the integral $\int H(x, y)\,dx$ round the perimeter

$$(A_1A_3A_1^{-1}A_3^{-1})$$

is zero, the contribution, for instance, from (A_1) and (A_1^{-1}) being $\Omega_1\int dx$, taken once positively along (A_1), namely zero, since x has the same value at the two sides of (A_3).

3. The most general form of an integral of the first kind can be shewn to be

$$\int_a^x \frac{(A+Bx)\,dx}{y}, \quad = Au_1^{x,\,a}+Bu_2^{x,\,a}, \text{ say,}$$

where A and B are arbitrary constants. If we put

$$(x, x_1)=\frac{y+y_1}{2y\,(x-x_1)},$$

where (x, y), (x_1, y_1) are two arbitrary finite places, of which one or both may be branch places, it can be verified that

$$P^{x, a}_{x_1, x_2} = \int_a^x [(x, x_1) - (x, x_2)]\, dx$$

is an integral of the third kind with logarithmic coefficients $+1$ and -1 respectively at the two arbitrary finite places (x_1, y_1), (x_2, y_2), having no infinities but these. The case where one or both of (x_1, y_1), (x_2, y_2) is at infinity can be derived from this by a transformation of the form $x = (x' - c)^{-1}$, with the appropriate corresponding change for y. The function

$$P^{x, a}_{x_1, x_2} + C_1 u_1^{x, a} + C_2 u_2^{x, a},$$

wherein C_1 and C_2 are constants, has the same infinities as $P^{x, a}_{x_1, x_2}$; denoting the periods of $P^{x, a}_{x_1, x_2}$ at (A_1), (A_3), (A_2), (A_4) respectively by Ω_1, Ω_1', Ω_2, Ω_2', and the periods of $u_1^{x, a}$, $u_2^{x, a}$, similarly, by

	(A_1)	(A_2)	(A_3)	(A_4)
$u_1^{x, a}$	ω_{11}	ω_{12}	ω_{11}'	ω_{12}'
$u_2^{x, a}$	ω_{21}	ω_{22}	ω_{21}'	ω_{22}'

the periods of this new integral of the third kind, at (A_1), (A_2), will be

$$\Omega_1 + C_1\omega_{11} + C_2\omega_{21}, \quad \Omega_2 + C_1\omega_{12} + C_2\omega_{22};$$

it will presently be shewn that the determinant $\omega_{11}\omega_{22} - \omega_{21}\omega_{12}$ is not zero; thus the constants C_1, C_2 can be chosen so that these two periods are zero; when this is done the integral of the third kind will be denoted by $\Pi^{x, a}_{x_1, x_2}$, and called the normal elementary integral of the third kind, the former epithet referring to the fact that it has vanishing periods at (A_1) and (A_2), the latter to the fact that it has only two logarithmic infinities (x_1), (x_2), of respective coefficients 1 and -1.

4. To obtain the theorem just quoted in regard to the determinant $\omega_{11}\omega_{22} - \omega_{21}\omega_{12}$, and at the same time some other results necessary for our purpose, let $U = \int H(x, y)\, dx$, $V = \int K(x, y)\, dx$, be any two algebraic integrals, the functions $H(x, y)$, $K(x, y)$ being rational in x and y, and consider the contour integral $\int U dV$, taken in succession along the closed curves $(A_1 A_3 A_1^{-1} A_3^{-1})$, $(A_2 A_4 A_2^{-1} A_4^{-1})$; denoting the periods of U for (A_1), (A_2), (A_3), (A_4) respectively by Ω_1, Ω_2, Ω_3, Ω_4, and by V_1, V_2, V_3, V_4 the corresponding periods of V, the contribution to the integral from (A_1) and (A_1^{-1}) is $\int (U + \Omega_1 - U)\, dV$, extended once along (A_1) only, from the right side to the left side of (A_3), namely is $\Omega_1 V_3$; so the contribution from (A_3) and (A_3^{-1}) is $\Omega_3 \int dV$, extended once along (A_3) only, from the left side to the right side of (A_1), namely is $-\Omega_3 V_1$; the sum of the two contour integrals is thus

$$\Omega_1 V_3 - \Omega_3 V_1 + \Omega_2 V_4 - \Omega_4 V_2;$$

the formation of this quantity from the scheme of periods

$$\begin{array}{c|cccc} U & \Omega_1 & \Omega_2 & \Omega_3 & \Omega_4 \\ V & V_1 & V_2 & V_3 & V_4 \end{array}$$

is evident, and the remark assists the memory in writing it down.

Let now in particular, U be an integral of the first kind, and V be an elementary integral of the third kind with logarithmic infinities of coefficients respectively 1 and -1 at (z_1) and (z_2); then the previously described contour integral is equal to the counterclockwise integral along a closed curve containing the cut previously explained which goes from (z_1) to (z_2); near (z_1), however, UdV is of the form $U\frac{dt}{t}$, where t is the parameter for the neighbourhood of (z_1), and a counterclockwise integration round (z_1) gives $2\pi i U^{z_1}$, where U^{z_1} is the value of U at (z_1); so the integration round (z_2) gives $-2\pi i U^{z_2}$; the two sides of the cut, between (z_1) and (z_2), taken together, give no contribution. We thus have, in this case,

$$\Omega_1 V_3 - \Omega_3 V_1 + \Omega_2 V_4 - \Omega_4 V_2 = 2\pi i\,(U^{z_1} - U^{z_2}).$$

In a precisely similar way, if U be also an elementary integral of the third kind with logarithmic coefficients 1 and -1 respectively at (x_1) and (x_2), we infer, since $UdV = d(UV) - VdU$, that the right side must be increased by $-2\pi i\,(V^{x_1} - V^{x_2})$; while if U and V be both integrals of the first kind, the right side is to be replaced by zero.

We may apply a similar procedure when U and V are the real and imaginary parts of an algebraic integral $U + iV$, of periods $\Omega_1 + iV_1$, etc.; in case the integral $U + iV$ is of the first kind, say equal to $n_1 u_1^{x,a} + n_2 u_2^{x,a}$, the contour integral $\int UdV$, or $\int U\frac{dV}{dt}\,dt$, or $\int\left(U\frac{\partial V}{\partial\xi}d\xi + U\frac{\partial V}{\partial\eta}d\eta\right)$, where $t = \xi + i\eta$, is equal to a sum of area integrals of the form

$$\iint d\xi d\eta\left[\frac{\partial}{\partial\xi}\left(U\frac{\partial V}{\partial\eta}\right) - \frac{\partial}{\partial\eta}\left(U\frac{\partial V}{\partial\xi}\right)\right] = \iint d\xi d\eta\left[\left(\frac{\partial U}{\partial\xi}\right)^2 + \left(\frac{\partial U}{\partial\eta}\right)^2\right];$$

each one of these is necessarily positive, and has a lower limiting value greater than zero, since U and V and their differential coefficients are continuous functions of ξ and η, and U and V are not constant over any two-dimensional portion of the surface; there are as many of these integrals as is necessary to cover the whole surface (and it can be shewn that this number is finite). In this case we infer therefore that

$$\Omega_1 V_3 - \Omega_3 V_1 + \Omega_2 V_4 - \Omega_4 V_2$$

is positive, and not indefinitely near to zero.

From these general considerations various results follow:—

(1) The determinant $\omega_{11}\omega_{22} - \omega_{12}\omega_{21}$ is not zero. For then $\omega_{21}u_1^{x,a} - \omega_{11}u_2^{x,a}$ would be an integral of the first kind having zero periods at (A_1) and (A_2);

calling this $U + iV$, as in the last of the general considerations just given, we should have $\Omega_1 = V_1 = 0$, $\Omega_2 = V_2 = 0$, contrary to the necessarily positive character of the expression $\Omega_1 V_3 - \Omega_3 V_1 + \Omega_2 V_4 - \Omega_4 V_2$. And by the same proof it follows that no function, other than a constant, exists, which is single-valued on the surface save that its values on the two sides of each of two non-intersecting curves differ by a quantity constant along the curve, which is expressible about every point of the surface by a series of positive integral powers of the parameter.

(2) Hence we can form two integrals of the first kind

$$v_1^{x,a} = \frac{1}{\Delta}(\omega_{22} u_1^{x,a} - \omega_{12} u_2^{x,a}), \quad v_2^{x,a} = \frac{1}{\Delta}(-\omega_{21} u_1^{x,a} + \omega_{11} u_2^{x,a}),$$

where
$$\Delta = \omega_{11}\omega_{22} - \omega_{12}\omega_{21},$$

which have a period scheme

	(A_1)	(A_2)	(A_3)	(A_4)
$v_1^{x,a}$	1	0	τ_{11}	τ_{12}
$v_2^{x,a}$	0	1	τ_{21}	τ_{22}

;

then the theorem that the integral $\int v_1 dv_2$ round $(A_1 A_3 A_1^{-1} A_3^{-1})$ and $(A_2 A_4 A_2^{-1} A_4^{-1})$ gives zero, leads to

$$1 \,.\, \tau_{21} - \tau_{11} \,.\, 0 + 0 \,.\, \tau_{22} - \tau_{12} \,.\, 1 = 0,$$

or $\tau_{12} = \tau_{21}$. These integrals are called the normal integrals of the first kind, being unique, save for additive constants, when the period-loops are once drawn, as follows from the concluding remark of (1).

(3) If n_1, n_2 be real quantities, and $n_1 v_1^{x,a} + n_2 v_2^{x,a} = U + iV$, the consideration of the contour integral $\int U dV$ gives, if $\tau_{rs} = \rho_{rs} + i\sigma_{rs}$, the result

$$n_1(n_1\sigma_{11} + n_2\sigma_{21}) - (n_1\rho_{11} + n_2\rho_{21}) \,.\, 0 + n_2(n_1\sigma_{12} + n_2\sigma_{22}) - (n_1\rho_{12} + n_2\rho_{22}) \,.\, 0 > 0,$$

so that the real part of the quadratic form

$$i(\tau_{11} n_1^2 + 2\tau_{12} n_1 n_2 + \tau_{22} n_2^2)$$

is necessarily negative and not indefinitely near to zero.

(4) The consideration of the contour integral

$$\int v_1^{x,a} d\Pi_{x_1, x_2}^{x,a}$$

for which, respectively,

$$\begin{pmatrix} \Omega_1 & \Omega_2 & \Omega_3 & \Omega_4 \\ V_1 & V_2 & V_3 & V_4 \end{pmatrix} = \begin{pmatrix} 1 & 0 & \tau_{11} & \tau_{12} \\ 0 & 0 & V_3 & V_4 \end{pmatrix},$$

gives
$$V_3 = 2\pi i (v_1^{x_1,a} - v_1^{x_2,a}) = 2\pi i v_1^{x_1,x_2},$$

so that the periods of the elementary normal integral $\Pi_{x_1,x_2}^{x,a}$ at (A_3) and (A_4) are respectively $2\pi i v_1^{x_1,x_2}$ and $2\pi i v_2^{x_1,x_2}$.

(5) The consideration of the contour integral

$$\int \Pi_{x_1, x_2}^{x, a}\, d\Pi_{z_1, z_2}^{x, a},$$

for which $\Omega_1 = \Omega_2 = V_1 = V_2 = 0$, gives

$$\Pi_{x_1, x_2}^{z_1, a} - \Pi_{x_1, x_2}^{z_2, a} - \left(\Pi_{z_1, z_2}^{x_1, a} - \Pi_{z_1, z_2}^{x_2, a}\right) = 0,$$

or

$$\Pi_{x_1, x_2}^{z_1, z_2} = \Pi_{z_1, z_2}^{x_1, x_2}.$$

(6) We have already remarked that there is no other integral of the first kind than $v_1^{x, a}$ having periods 1, 0 at (A_1), (A_2); it follows similarly that there is no other normal elementary integral of the third kind than $\Pi_{x_1, x_2}^{x, a}$. Two integrals of the third kind, having the same two infinities and the same multipliers at these, have a difference which is expressible about every point by a series of positive integral powers of the parameter for the point; this difference will have periods at (A_1), (A_2), (A_3), (A_4); denoting the integrals of the third kind by P and P', and the periods of the difference $P' - P$ at (A_1) and (A_2) by C_1 and C_2, the function

$$P' - P - C_1 v_1^{x, a} - C_2 v_2^{x, a}$$

has periods only at (A_3) and (A_4). Hence, by the remark made at the conclusion of (1), this function is a constant.

5. From an elementary integral of the third kind we can form an algebraic integral whose expansion in terms of the parameter, in the neighbourhood of any place of the surface, contains only positive integral powers, there being exception at only one place, for which the expansion contains the single term $-t^{-1}$; and the integral can be taken so that this pole is at an arbitrary place. Such an integral is called an elementary integral of the second kind. Consider for instance

$$P_{x_1, x_2}^{x, a} = \int_a^x [(x, x_1) - (x, x_2)]\, dx;$$

let (z) be an arbitrary finite place, and t the parameter for the neighbourhood of (z); let (x_1) be in the neighbourhood of (z); let (x, x_1) be expressed in terms of t, and let $(x, x_1)_t$ denote the coefficient of t in the expression; this will be a function of (x), and of (z); the integral

$$\int_a^x (x, x_1)_t\, dx$$

is then a function of (x), infinite only when (x) approaches z, and then like $-t^{-1}$. This statement can easily be verified from the form

$$(x, x_1) = \frac{y + y_1}{2y\,(x - x_1)}.$$

For, when (z) is not a branch place, we find, putting $x_1 = z + t$ and $y_1 = s + s't + \frac{1}{2}s''t^2 + \dots$,

$$(x, x_1)_t = \frac{y + s + s'(x - z)}{2y(x - z)^2},$$

and putting herein $x = z + t_x$, $y = s + s't_x + \dots$, we find

$$(x, x_1)_t = \frac{1}{t_x^2} + A + A_1 t_x + \dots;$$

while, when (z) is a branch place, putting $x_1 = z + t^2$ and $y_1 = s't + \frac{1}{6}s'''t^3 + \dots$ we have

$$(x, x_1)_t = \frac{s'}{2y(x - z)},$$

and putting herein $x = z + t_x^2$, $y = s't_x + \frac{1}{6}s'''t_x^3 + \dots$, we obtain

$$(x, x_1)_t \frac{dx}{dt_x} = \frac{1}{t_x^2} + B + B_2 t_x^2 + \dots.$$

There exists, therefore, a function of the form

$$\int_a^x (x, x_1)_t \, dx + C_1 u_1^{x, a} + C_2 u_2^{x, a},$$

where C_1, C_2 are suitable constants, which is infinite at the arbitrary finite place (z), like $-t^{-1}$, and not elsewhere, which has vanishing periods at the period-loops (A_1), (A_2). This function is called the normal elementary integral of the second kind, and will be denoted here by $\Gamma_z^{x, a}$. There exists such a function also when (z) is at infinity, whose form can be obtained by making, in the integral of the third kind used above, a previous transformation of the form $x = (x' - z)^{-1}$. The integral can be obtained by differentiation from the integral $\Pi_{x_1, x_2}^{x, a}$. For when (x) and (x_1) are both in the neighbourhood of (z), if $x_1 = z + t_{x_1}$, $x = z + t_x$ or $x_1 = z + t_{x_1}^2$, $x = z + t_x^2$, the latter when (z) is a branch place, we can put

$$\Pi_{x_1, x_2}^{x, a} = \log(t_x - t_{x_1}) + A + A_1(t_x - t_{x_1}) + \dots;$$

now let this expression be differentiated in regard to t_{x_1}, and, afterwards, put $t_{x_1} = 0$; let this operation be denoted by $D_z \Pi_{z, x_2}^{x, a}$; we have then

$$D_z \Pi_{z, x_2}^{x, a} = -\frac{1}{t_x} + B + B_1 t_x + \dots,$$

and this is the integral denoted by $\Gamma_z^{x, a}$; the formula $\Pi_{x_1, x_2}^{x, a} = \Pi_{x, a}^{x_1, x_2}$ shews that it does not depend upon (x_2). The periods of $\Gamma_z^{x, a}$ at the loops (A_1), (A_2), (A_3), (A_4) are 0, 0, $2\pi i\,(v_1^{x_1, x_2})_t$, $2\pi i\,(v_2^{x_1, x_2})_t$, where $(v_1^{x_1, x_2})_t$ denotes the coefficient of t in the expansion of $v_1^{x_1, x_2}$ in terms of the parameter at (z), when (x_1) approaches to this place.

6. Consider now the two integrals

$$L_1^{x,a} = \int_a^x \frac{\lambda_3 x + 2\lambda_4 x^2 + 3\lambda_5 x^3 + 4\lambda_6 x^4}{4y}\, dx, \quad L_2^{x,a} = \int_a^x \frac{\lambda_5 x^2 + 2\lambda_6 x^3}{4y}\, dx.$$

It is clear that neither integral is infinite for finite positions of (x); considering the neighbourhood of $x = \infty$, the work depends upon whether λ_6 is zero or not. When λ_6 is not zero, there are two places at infinity; the neighbourhood of either of these is represented by a pair of equations such as

$$x = t^{-1}, \quad y^{-1} = \lambda_6^{-\frac{1}{2}} t^3 (1 + A_1 t + A_2 t^2 + \dots),$$

where $\sqrt{\lambda_6}$ has one of two signs; by substitution we find

$$L_1^{x,a} = \frac{\sqrt{\lambda_6}}{2t^2} + \frac{\lambda_5}{4\sqrt{\lambda_6}} \cdot \frac{1}{t} + M_1 t + \dots, \qquad L_2^{x,a} = \frac{\sqrt{\lambda_6}}{2t} + P_1 t + \dots,$$

the terms not written involving positive integral powers of t. Thus each integral is algebraically, but not logarithmically, infinite at infinity, in each sheet, the first integral to the second order, and the second integral to the first order, and it is not possible to find a linear aggregate $p_1 L_1^{x,a} + p_2 L_2^{x,a}$ which does not become infinite. When $\lambda_6 = 0$, and $\lambda_5 = 4$, we find, by substituting

$$x = t^{-2}, \quad y^{-1} = \tfrac{1}{2} t^5 [1 + \tfrac{1}{4}\lambda_4 t^2 + \dots + \tfrac{1}{4}\lambda_0 t^{10}]^{-\frac{1}{2}},$$

that

$$L_1^{x,a} = \frac{1}{t^3} + \frac{\lambda_4}{8t} + Ht + \dots, \qquad L_2^{x,a} = \frac{1}{t} + \frac{1}{8}\lambda_4 t + \dots,$$

so that the integrals are again algebraically, but not logarithmically, infinite, to different orders, at the single place at infinity.

It can now be verified, by differentiation in regard to x and z, that

$$\int_a^x [(x, z) - (x, c)]\, dx + u_1^{x,a} L_1^{z,c} + u_2^{x,a} L_2^{z,c} = \int_a^x \int_c^z \frac{F(x,z) + 2ys}{4(x-z)^2} \frac{dx}{y} \frac{dz}{s},$$

where

$$f(x) = \lambda_0 + \lambda_1 x + \lambda_2 x^2 + \dots + \lambda_6 x^6, \quad y^2 = f(x), \quad s^2 = f(z),$$

$$(x, z) = \frac{y+s}{x-z} \cdot \frac{1}{2y}, \qquad u_1^{x,a} = \int_a^x \frac{dx}{y}, \qquad u_2^{x,a} = \int_a^x \frac{x\,dx}{y},$$

and

$$F(x,z) = 2\lambda_0 + \lambda_1 (x+z) + xz[2\lambda_2 + \lambda_3 (x+z)] + x^2 z^2 [2\lambda_4 + \lambda_5 (x+z)] + 2\lambda_6 x^3 z^3.$$

We shall put

$$R_{z,c}^{x,a} = \int_a^x \int_c^z \frac{F(x,z) + 2ys}{4(x-z)^2} \frac{dx}{y} \frac{dz}{s};$$

then the form of the left side in the identity shews that $R_{z,c}^{x,a}$, as a function of (x), is an elementary integral of the third kind with logarithmic infinities of coefficients 1 and -1 respectively at (z) and (c); and its own form shews that

$$R^{x,a}_{z,c} = R^{z,c}_{x,a};$$

we have seen however (§ 4), that two elementary integrals of the third kind, having the same logarithmic infinities and multipliers, differ by a linear aggregate of integrals of the first kind; there must therefore exist an equation

$$R^{x,a}_{z,c} = \Pi^{x,a}_{z,c} - 2\sum_{r=1}^{2}\sum_{s=1}^{2} a_{r,s} u_r^{x,a} u_s^{z,c},$$

wherein the constant coefficients a_{11}, a_{12}, a_{21}, a_{22} are subject to the relation $a_{12} = a_{21}$; this leads to

$$u_1^{z,c} L_1^{x,a} + u_2^{z,c} L_2^{x,a} + 2\Sigma\Sigma a_{r,s} u_s^{z,c} u_r^{x,a} = \Pi^{x,a}_{z,c} - \int_c^z [(z,x) - (z,a)]\,dz.$$

Now let (z) be in the neighbourhood of a particular place (z_0), and express z and s in terms of the parameter of this place, and equate coefficients of the first power of this parameter; from $u_1^{z,c}$ we obtain an expression which is the limit of $\frac{1}{s}\frac{dz}{dt}$ when $t=0$; this we denote by $\mu_1(z_0)$; from $u_2^{z,c}$ we obtain the limit of $\frac{z}{s}\frac{dz}{dt}$, which we denote by $\mu_2(z_0)$; from $\Pi^{x,a}_{z,c}$ we obtain $\Gamma^{x,a}_{z_0}$; from $\int_c^z [(z,x)-(z,a)]\,dz$ we obtain the limit for $t=0$ of $[(z,x)-(z,a)]\frac{dz}{dt}$, which is a certain rational function of (x); replacing now again (z_0) by (z), we may write the resulting equation

$$\mu_1(z) L_1^{x,a} + \mu_2(z) L_2^{x,a} + 2\Sigma\Sigma a_{r,s}\mu_s(z) u_r^{x,a} = \Gamma_z^{x,a} - [(z,x)-(z,a)]\frac{dz}{dt}.$$

7. Before passing on it seems necessary to make a few introductory remarks relative to a notation which will be found of great use in the sequel.

A rectangular arrangement of mn elements, in m rows and n columns, may be added to, or subtracted from, another such array or *matrix*, of the same number of rows and columns, the meaning being that the (r, s)th element of the resulting array, namely the element in the r-th row and s-th column, is the sum, or difference, in the respective cases, of the corresponding elements $a_{r,s}$, $a'_{r,s}$, of the two original arrays; and, the whole matrix being denoted by a, and N being any number, the notation Na may be used for the matrix of m rows and n columns whose general element is $Na_{r,s}$. Or the matrix of type (m, n), that is, of m rows and n columns, with general element $a_{r,s}$, may be multiplied into another matrix of type (n, p), of general element $b_{s,t}$, the meaning being that the result is a matrix of type (m, p) whose general element $c_{r,t}$ is given by

$$c_{r,t} = \sum_{s=1}^{n} a_{r,s} b_{s,t},$$

namely given by combining the r-th row of the first matrix, a, with the t-th column of the second matrix, b. The result may be written $c = ab$; this is by no means the same as $c = ba$. In a somewhat similar way, if x denote the set of n quantities $x_1, \ldots, x_n$, we may denote by ax the set of m quantities such as

$$a_{r,1} x_1 + \ldots + a_{r,n} x_n, \qquad (r = 1, \ldots, m);$$

then, if y denote a set of m quantities $y_1, \ldots, y_m$, we may denote by axy the single quantity

$$\sum_{r=1}^{m} (a_{r,1} x_1 + \ldots + a_{r,n} x_n) y_r,$$

which is the same as

$$\sum_{r=1}^{m} \sum_{s=1}^{n} a_{r,s} x_s y_r.$$

It is usual to call the matrix of type (n, m), obtained by changing the rows, of the matrix a, into columns, the transposed matrix of a; we shall denote it by $\bar{a}$; it is manifest that $axy = \bar{a}yx$. If z, z' each denote a set of m quantities, $z_1, \ldots, z_m$ and $z_1', \ldots z_m'$, we often denote by zz', or $z'z$, the single quantity $z_1 z_1' + \ldots + z_m z_m'$; in particular if a, a' be two matrices, both of type (m, n), we may have $z = ax$, $z' = a'x'$, where x, x' each denote a set of n quantities; then $zz' = ax \, . \, z' = \bar{a}z'x = \bar{a}a'x'x$; and $z'z = a'x'z = \bar{a}'zx' = \bar{a}'axx'$; in the form $ax \, . \, a'x' = \bar{a}a'x'x = \bar{a}'axx'$, this result occurs very often in the sequel; it is in accordance with the easily verified fact that the transposed of the matrix ab is $\bar{b}\bar{a}$, obtained by reversing the order of the matrices and transposing both; the notation $\bar{a}a'x'x$, meaning $(\bar{a}a'x')x$, is not found by experience liable to confusion with $(\bar{a}a')(x'x)$, which, if used, would mean the matrix obtained by multiplying every element of the matrix $\bar{a}a'$ by the single quantity $x'x$. Very often the matrices used are square, of type (n, n); for such, the determinant of the product ab, usually written $|ab|$, is equal to the product of the individual determinants $|a|$, $|b|$; of such square matrices, the simplest is that having every element zero save those in the diagonal, all these being unities; this, so-called unit matrix, when multiplied into, or by, any other matrix of the same number of rows and columns, say a, gives a as result; the unit matrix is, thus, often denoted simply by 1; and the matrix of which every element is zero save those in the diagonal, all of which are equal to a number N, is denoted simply by N. A square matrix a, of non-vanishing determinant, has an inverse, denoted by a^{-1}, with the properties $aa^{-1} = a^{-1}a = E$, where E is the unit matrix of the proper order; in fact, if $a_{r,s}$ be the (r, s)th element of a, and $A_{r,s}$ the minor determinant of the (r, s)th element of the determinant, $|a|$, of a, it is easy to prove that the (r, s)th element of a^{-1} is $A_{s,r} \div |a|$, namely is the minor of the (s, r)th element of $|a|$, divided by $|a|$.

8. Returning now to our theory, denote the periods of $u_r^{x,a}$, $L_r^{x,a}$ at (A_1), (A_2), (A_3), (A_4), as follows:

	(A_1)	(A_2)	(A_3)	(A_4)
$u_r^{x,a}$	$2\omega_{r1}$	$2\omega_{r2}$	$2\omega'_{r1}$	$2\omega'_{r2}$
$L_r^{x,a}$	$-2\eta_{r1}$	$-2\eta_{r2}$	$-2\eta'_{r1}$	$-2\eta'_{r2}$

;

the normal elementary integrals of the first kind $v_1^{x,a}$, $v_2^{x,a}$ are necessarily linear functions of $u_1^{x,a}$, $u_2^{x,a}$; let the expressions be given by

$$\pi i v_1^{x,a} = h_{11} u_1^{x,a} + h_{12} u_2^{x,a}, \quad \pi i v_2^{x,a} = h_{21} u_1^{x,a} + h_{22} u_2^{x,a};$$

then, comparing periods at (A_1), (A_2) we have the four equations given by

$$\begin{pmatrix} \pi i & 0 \\ 0 & \pi i \end{pmatrix} = \begin{pmatrix} 2h_{11}\omega_{11} + 2h_{12}\omega_{21} & 2h_{11}\omega_{12} + 2h_{12}\omega_{22} \\ 2h_{21}\omega_{11} + 2h_{22}\omega_{21} & 2h_{21}\omega_{12} + 2h_{22}\omega_{22} \end{pmatrix},$$

which is the same as

$$\pi i \begin{pmatrix} 1 & 0 \\ 0 & 1 \end{pmatrix} = 2 \begin{pmatrix} h_{11} & h_{12} \\ h_{21} & h_{22} \end{pmatrix} \begin{pmatrix} \omega_{11} & \omega_{12} \\ \omega_{21} & \omega_{22} \end{pmatrix},$$

and is expressed by

$$\pi i = 2h\omega.$$

The product of the determinants $|h|$, $|\omega|$ is thus, numerically, $(\pi/2)^2$, and neither of these determinants is zero.

Similarly, comparing periods at (A_3), (A_4), and denoting by τ the symmetrical matrix of the periods of $v_1^{x,a}$, $v_2^{x,a}$ at (A_3), (A_4), we have four equations all expressed by

$$\pi i \tau = 2h\omega';$$

and as the determinant of ω is not zero we may write

$$h = \tfrac{1}{2}\pi i \omega^{-1}, \quad \tau = \omega^{-1}\omega'.$$

The periods of $\Gamma_z^{x,a}$ at (A_1), (A_2) are both zero; at (A_3), (A_4), they are, as has been remarked, $2\pi i$ times the values, at (z), of the integrands of $v_1^{x,a}$ and $v_2^{x,a}$, that is, in a notation explained above (§ 6), respectively

$$2[h_{11}\mu_1(z) + h_{12}\mu_2(z)], \quad 2[h_{21}\mu_1(z) + h_{22}\mu_2(z)];$$

hence the equation, which we previously had,

$$\mu_1(z) L_1^{x,a} + \mu_2(z) L_2^{x,a} + 2\Sigma\Sigma a_{r,s}\mu_s(z) u_r^{x,a} = \Gamma_z^{x,a} - [(z, x) - (z, a)] \frac{dz}{dt},$$

gives, by taking the periods at (A_i) and (A_{2+i}),

$$-2\mu_1(z)\eta_{1i} - 2\mu_2(z)\eta_{2i} + 4\Sigma\Sigma a_{rs}\mu_s(z)\omega_{ri} = 0$$
$$-2\mu_1(z)\eta'_{1i} - 2\mu_2(z)\eta'_{2i} + 4\Sigma\Sigma a_{rs}\mu_s(z)\omega'_{ri} = 2[h_{i1}\mu_1(z) + h_{i2}\mu_2(z)];$$

from these, since there exists no equation $A_1\mu_1(z) + A_2\mu_2(z) = 0$, in which A_1, A_2 are quantities independent of (z), we derive

$$\eta_{si} = 2(a_{1s}\omega_{1i} + a_{2s}\omega_{2i}), = 2(a_{s1}\omega_{1i} + a_{s2}\omega_{2i}),$$

since $a_{rs} = a_{sr}$; and the four equations contained in this are capable of the form

$$\begin{pmatrix}\eta_{11} & \eta_{12}\\ \eta_{21} & \eta_{22}\end{pmatrix} = 2\begin{pmatrix}a_{11} & a_{12}\\ a_{21} & a_{22}\end{pmatrix}\begin{pmatrix}\omega_{11} & \omega_{12}\\ \omega_{21} & \omega_{22}\end{pmatrix},$$

which we write

$$\eta = 2a\omega;$$

from the same identities we also, similarly, derive four equations of the form

$$\eta'_{si} = 2(a_{s1}\omega'_{1i} + a_{s2}\omega'_{2i}) - h_{is}$$

which we write

$$\eta' = 2a\omega' - \bar{h},$$

where $\bar{h}$ is the matrix obtained from h by transposition of rows and columns.

The equations

$$\pi i = 2h\omega, \quad \pi i\tau = 2h\omega', \quad \eta = 2a\omega, \quad \eta' = 2a\omega' - \bar{h}$$

are sixteen relations connecting the quantities; on elimination of the $3+3+4$ quantities in the matrices τ, a and h, they lead to six relations connecting the periods ω, ω', η, η', as we proceed to shew. The equations give

$$\omega' = \tfrac{1}{2}\pi i h^{-1}\tau = \omega\tau,$$

and hence

$$\omega'\bar{\omega} = \omega\tau\bar{\omega} = \omega\bar{\tau}\bar{\omega} = \omega\bar{\omega}',$$

which is equivalent to one equation; also they give

$$h = \tfrac{1}{2}\pi i\omega^{-1}, \quad \omega h = \tfrac{1}{2}\pi i,$$

and thus

$$\eta'\bar{\omega} - \eta\bar{\omega}' = 2a(\omega'\bar{\omega} - \omega\bar{\omega}') - \bar{h}\bar{\omega} = -\omega h = -\tfrac{1}{2}\pi i,$$

which is equivalent to four equations; and they give, thence,

$$\omega\bar{\eta}' - \omega'\bar{\eta} = -\tfrac{1}{2}\pi i,$$

and so

$$\eta\bar{\eta}' = 2a\omega\bar{\eta}' = 2a(\omega'\bar{\eta} - \tfrac{1}{2}\pi i) = (\eta' + h)\bar{\eta} - \pi i a = \eta'\bar{\eta},$$

because

$$\bar{h}\bar{\eta} = 2\bar{h}\bar{\omega}\bar{a} = \pi i\bar{a} = \pi i a,$$

and this equation

$$\eta\bar{\eta}' - \eta'\bar{\eta} = 0,$$

is equivalent to one relation.

These relations can be written together, as follows: let

$$A = \begin{pmatrix}\omega & \omega'\\ \eta & \eta'\end{pmatrix}$$

denote the matrix of four rows and columns, of which the elements are those of the four matrices ω, ω', η, η'; if a, b, c, d, a', b', c', d' momentarily denote any matrices each of two rows and columns, it is at once evident on consideration that the product

$$\begin{pmatrix} a & b \\ c & d \end{pmatrix} \begin{pmatrix} a' & b' \\ c' & d' \end{pmatrix},$$

of two matrices each of type (4, 4), may be written as

$$\begin{pmatrix} aa' + bc', & ab' + bd' \\ ca' + dc', & cb' + dd' \end{pmatrix},$$

where aa' denotes the product of two matrices, and is a matrix of type (2, 2), of which the elements are to be separately added each to the corresponding element of bc', to give the matrix $aa' + bc'$ of type (2, 2); this form is the same as if a, b, c, d were single quantities. Now let

$$\epsilon_4 = \begin{pmatrix} 0 & -1 \\ 1 & 0 \end{pmatrix}$$

be the matrix of type (4, 4), of which every element is zero, save the elements (1, 3) and (2, 4), each of which is -1, and the elements (3, 1), (4, 2), each of which is 1, so that, as is easily seen,

$$\epsilon_4^2 = -1, \quad \epsilon_4^{-1} = \bar{\epsilon}_4 = -\epsilon_4;$$

consider the product

$$A\epsilon_4\bar{A} = \begin{pmatrix} \omega & \omega' \\ \eta & \eta' \end{pmatrix} \begin{pmatrix} 0 & -1 \\ 1 & 0 \end{pmatrix} \begin{pmatrix} \bar{\omega} & \bar{\eta} \\ \bar{\omega}' & \bar{\eta}' \end{pmatrix} = \begin{pmatrix} \omega' & -\omega \\ \eta' & -\eta \end{pmatrix} \begin{pmatrix} \bar{\omega} & \bar{\eta} \\ \bar{\omega}' & \bar{\eta}' \end{pmatrix}$$

$$= \begin{pmatrix} \omega'\bar{\omega} - \omega\bar{\omega}' & \omega'\bar{\eta} - \omega\bar{\eta}' \\ \eta'\bar{\omega} - \eta\bar{\omega}' & \eta'\bar{\eta} - \eta\bar{\eta}' \end{pmatrix};$$

by the relations established above we thus have

$$A\epsilon_4\bar{A} = -\tfrac{1}{2}\pi i\epsilon_4;$$

and this includes all the relations connecting the periods. It shews too that the determinant of the matrix A is a square root of $(\pi/2)^4$, and not zero.

Taking then the inverse of both sides we have

$$-\bar{A}^{-1}\epsilon_4 A^{-1} = \frac{2}{\pi i}\epsilon_4,$$

and hence $$\bar{A}\epsilon_4 A = -\tfrac{1}{2}\pi i\epsilon_4,$$

or

$$\begin{pmatrix} \bar{\omega} & \bar{\eta} \\ \bar{\omega}' & \bar{\eta}' \end{pmatrix} \begin{pmatrix} 0 & -1 \\ 1 & 0 \end{pmatrix} \begin{pmatrix} \omega & \omega' \\ \eta & \eta' \end{pmatrix}, = \begin{pmatrix} \bar{\eta} & -\bar{\omega} \\ \bar{\eta}' & -\bar{\omega}' \end{pmatrix} \begin{pmatrix} \omega & \omega' \\ \eta & \eta' \end{pmatrix} = \begin{pmatrix} \bar{\eta}\omega - \bar{\omega}\eta & \bar{\eta}\omega' - \bar{\omega}\eta' \\ \bar{\eta}'\omega - \bar{\omega}'\eta & \bar{\eta}'\omega' - \bar{\omega}'\eta' \end{pmatrix},$$

$$= -\tfrac{1}{2}\pi i\epsilon_4,$$

so that the relations among the periods may also be written

$$\bar{\eta}\omega = \bar{\omega}\eta, \quad \bar{\eta}\omega' - \bar{\omega}\eta' = \tfrac{1}{2}\pi i, \quad \bar{\eta}'\omega' = \bar{\omega}'\eta';$$

these are of different form from those originally obtained, but may also be deduced directly from the equations

$$\tfrac{1}{2}\pi i = h\omega, \quad \tfrac{1}{2}\pi i\tau = h\omega', \quad \eta = 2a\omega, \quad \eta' = 2a\omega' - \bar{h}.$$

Let p_1, p_2, q_1, q_2 be any four variables; write

$$(P_1, P_2, Q_1, Q_2) = \begin{pmatrix} \overline{\omega} & \overline{\eta} \\ \overline{\omega}' & \overline{\eta}' \end{pmatrix} (p_1, p_2, q_1, q_2),$$

namely

$$P_1 = \omega_{11} p_1 + \omega_{21} p_2 + \eta_{11} q_1 + \eta_{21} q_2,$$
$$P_2 = \omega_{12} p_1 + \omega_{22} p_2 + \eta_{12} q_1 + \eta_{22} q_2,$$
$$Q_1 = \omega'_{11} p_1 + \omega'_{21} p_2 + \eta'_{11} q_1 + \eta'_{21} q_2,$$
$$Q_2 = \omega'_{12} p_1 + \omega'_{22} p_2 + \eta'_{12} q_1 + \eta'_{22} q_2,$$

so that P_1, P_2, Q_1, Q_2 are the periods of the integral

$$\tfrac{1}{2}(p_1 u_1^{x,\,a} + p_2 u_2^{x,\,a} - q_1 L_1^{x,\,a} - q_2 L_2^{x,\,a}),$$

respectively at (A_1), (A_2), (A_3), (A_4); then if P_1', P_2', Q_1', Q_2' be the same linear functions of p_1', p_2', q_1', q_2', the equation

$$A\epsilon_4\overline{A} = -\tfrac{1}{2}\pi i \epsilon_4$$

gives

$$A\epsilon_4\overline{A}\,(p_1, p_2, q_1, q_2)(p_1', p_2', q_1', q_2') = -\tfrac{1}{2}\pi i\epsilon_4\,(p_1, p_2, q_1, q_2)(p_1', p_2', q_1', q_2'),$$

or

$$\epsilon_4\overline{A}\,(p_1, p_2, q_1, q_2)\,.\,\overline{A}\,(p_1', p_2', q_1', q_2') = -\tfrac{1}{2}\pi i\epsilon_4(p_1, p_2, q_1, q_2)(p_1', p_2', q_1', q_2'),$$

that is

$$\epsilon_4(P_1, P_2, Q_1, Q_2)(P_1', P_2', Q_1', Q_2') = -\tfrac{1}{2}\pi i\epsilon_4(p_1, p_2, q_1, q_2)(p_1', p_2', q_1', q_2'),$$

or

$$(-Q_1, -Q_2, P_1, P_2)(P_1', P_2', Q_1', Q_2') = -\tfrac{1}{2}\pi i(-q_1, -q_2, p_1, p_2)(p_1', p_2', q_1', q_2'),$$

or $$P_1Q_1' - P_1'Q_1 + P_2Q_2' - P_2'Q_2 = -\tfrac{1}{2}\pi i\,(p_1q_1' - p_1'q_1 + p_2q_2' - p_2'q_2);$$

and conversely the relations among the periods are those which are necessary in order that the linear substitutions

$$(P_1, P_2, Q_1, Q_2) = \overline{A}\,(p_1, p_2, q_1, q_2), \quad (P_1', P_2', Q_1', Q_2') = \overline{A}\,(p_1', p_2', q_1', q_2')$$

should multiply the form $p_1q_1' - p_1'q_1 + p_2q_2' - p_2'q_2$ by $-\tfrac{1}{2}\pi i$, for all values of the variables $p_1, \ldots, q_2'$.

Finally, in view of subsequent work, it is desirable to notice in more detail the relations affecting ω and ω' only. The relation $\omega'\overline{\omega} = \omega\overline{\omega}'$ is equivalent with

$$(\omega, \omega')\,\epsilon_4 \begin{pmatrix} \overline{\omega} \\ \overline{\omega}' \end{pmatrix} = (\omega, \omega') \begin{pmatrix} 0 & -1 \\ 1 & 0 \end{pmatrix} \begin{pmatrix} \overline{\omega} \\ \overline{\omega}' \end{pmatrix} = (\omega', -\omega) \begin{pmatrix} \overline{\omega} \\ \overline{\omega}' \end{pmatrix} = \omega'\overline{\omega} - \omega\overline{\omega}' = 0.$$

Let now ω_0, ω_0' denote the matrices whose elements are the conjugate complexes of those of ω and ω', and let $z = (t_1, t_2)$ be a set of two arbitrary quantities, and z_0 the set of their conjugate complexes; put then

$$s = (s_1, s_2) = \overline{\omega}t = (\omega_{11}t_1 + \omega_{21}t_2,\ \omega_{12}t_1 + \omega_{22}t_2),$$

so that the quantities s are the periods at (A_1), (A_2) of the integral

$$\tfrac{1}{2}(t_1u_1^{x,\,a} + t_2u_2^{x,\,a}),$$

and let s_0 be the two conjugate complexes of s_1 and s_2; further, let $\tau = \rho + i\sigma$, so that ρ, σ are two symmetrical matrices, each of type (2, 2), of entirely real elements; then if $s_1 = p_1 + iq_1$, $s_2 = p_2 + iq_2$, or say $s = p + iq$, where p_1, p_2, q_1, q_2 are real, we have, since $\omega' = \omega\tau$,

$$(\omega, \omega')\,\epsilon_4 \begin{pmatrix}\overline{\omega}_0\\ \overline{\omega}_0'\end{pmatrix} t_0 t = (\omega', -\omega) \begin{pmatrix}\overline{\omega}_0\\ \overline{\omega}_0'\end{pmatrix} t_0 t = (\omega'\overline{\omega}_0 - \omega\overline{\omega}_0')\, t_0 t = (\omega\tau\overline{\omega}_0 - \omega\tau_0\overline{\omega}_0) t_0 t$$

$$= \omega(\tau - \tau_0)\,\overline{\omega}_0 t_0 t = 2i\sigma\overline{\omega}_0 t_0 \,.\, \overline{\omega} t = 2i\sigma s_0 s = 2i\sigma\,(p - iq)(p + iq)$$

$$= 2i\,(\sigma p - i\sigma q)(p + iq)$$

$$= 2i\,(\sigma p^2 - i\sigma qp + i\sigma pq + \sigma q^2) = 2i\,(\sigma p^2 - i\overline{\sigma} pq + i\sigma pq + \sigma q^2) = 2i\sigma\,(p^2 + q^2);$$

we know that $\sigma p^2 > 0$, $\sigma q^2 > 0$ for all real sets p_1, p_2 and q_1, q_2, whose elements are not zero; hence we have

$$-i\,(\omega, \omega')\,\epsilon_4 \begin{pmatrix}\overline{\omega}_0\\ \overline{\omega}_0'\end{pmatrix} t_0 t > 0,$$

where t denotes a set of two arbitrary quantities not both zero; and we have proved also that

$$(\omega, \omega')\,\epsilon_4 \begin{pmatrix}\overline{\omega}\\ \overline{\omega}'\end{pmatrix} = 0.$$

9. We consider now certain properties of integral functions of two variables.

(*a*) If for the continuum of values of two complex variables ξ_1, ξ_2 which is expressed by the conditions

$$r_1 < |\xi_1| < R_1, \quad r_2 < |\xi_2| < R_2,$$

where r_1, R_1, r_2, R_2 are real positive quantities, there exists a function $F(\xi_1, \xi_2)$, developable about every point $\xi_1 = \alpha_1$, $\xi_2 = \alpha_2$ of this continuum as a power series in $\xi_1 - \alpha_1$, $\xi_2 - \alpha_2$, of presumably limited range of convergence, the function being single-valued in the continuum, then there exists a series of positive and negative powers

$$\sum_{-\infty}^{\infty}\sum_{-\infty}^{\infty} A_{n_1, n_2}\, \xi_1^{n_1}\xi_2^{n_2}$$

converging for, and representing the value of the function in the whole continuum. This can be proved, in the manner of Laurent's Theorem, by considering the repeated integral

$$\frac{1}{(2\pi i)^2}\int d\tau_1 \int \frac{F(\tau_1, \tau_2)}{(\tau_1 - \xi_1)(\tau_2 - \xi_2)}\, d\tau_2,$$

taken, for τ_1, clockwise round the circle $|\tau_1| = r_1$ and counterclockwise round the circle $|\tau_1| = R_1$, and, for τ_2, clockwise round $|\tau_2| = r_2$ and counterclockwise round $|\tau_2| = R_2$. As in that case we have

$$A_{n_1, n_2} = \frac{1}{(2\pi i)^2}\int d\tau_1 \int \frac{F(\tau_1, \tau_2)}{\tau_1^{n_1+1}\tau_2^{n_2+1}}\, d\tau_2,$$

where, now, the integration for τ_1 is counterclockwise round a single circle concentric with and lying anywhere between $|\tau_1|=r_1$ and $|\tau_1|=R_1$, and similarly for τ_2.

(*b*) If an integral function of v_1, v_2, say $Q(v_1, v_2)$, satisfy the conditions

$$Q(v_1+1, v_2)=Q(v_1, v_2), \quad Q(v_1, v_2+1)=Q(v_1, v_2),$$

that is, have the period unity for each argument independently of the other, then the function can be expressed by a series

$$\sum_{-\infty}^{\infty}\sum_{-\infty}^{\infty} A_{n_1, n_2}\, e^{2\pi i(n_1v_1+n_2v_2)},$$

converging uniformly and absolutely for all finite values of v_1 and v_2. For if we put

$$\xi_1=e^{2\pi i v_1}, \quad \xi_2=e^{2\pi i v_2},$$

the function

$$Q(v_1, v_2)=Q\left[\frac{1}{2\pi i}\log \xi_1, \ \frac{1}{2\pi i}\log \xi_2\right], \quad =F(\xi_1, \xi_2), \text{ say},$$

is a single-valued function of ξ_1, ξ_2, developable about every point for which ξ_1 is not zero or infinite, and ξ_2 not zero or infinite; we can thus apply the preceding result (*a*), and obtain

$$A_{n_1, n_2}=\frac{1}{(2\pi i)^2}\iint \frac{F(\tau_1, \tau_2)}{\tau_1^{n_1+1}\tau_2^{n_2+1}}\,d\tau_1 d\tau_2, \quad =\iint Q(v_1, v_2)\,e^{-2\pi i(n_1v_1+n_2v_2)}\,dv_1 dv_2,$$

where, putting $v_1=x_1+iy_1$, $v_2=x_2+iy_2$, the integration in regard to v_1 is, for an arbitrary constant value of y_1, in regard to x_1 from $x_1=0$ to $x_1=1$; and similarly for v_2; thus we may write

$$A_{n_1, n_2}=\int_0^1\int_0^1 Q(x_1, x_2)\,e^{-2\pi i(n_1x_1+n_2x_2)}\,dx_1 dx_2,$$

and if, for arbitrarily chosen constant values of y_1 and y_2, the function $Q(v_1, v_2)$ remains in absolute value less than a real positive quantity M, we have

$$|A_{n_1, n_2}|<Me^{2\pi(n_1y_1+n_2y_2)}.$$

(*c*) There can exist no equality of the form

$$\sum_{n_1=-\infty}^{\infty}\sum_{n_2=-\infty}^{\infty} A_{n_1, n_2}\, e^{2\pi i(n_1v_1+n_2v_2)}=\sum_{n_1=-\infty}^{\infty}\sum_{n_2=-\infty}^{\infty} B_{n_1, n_2}\, e^{2\pi i(n_1v_1+n_2v_2)}$$

in which the series converge for all finite values of the variables v_1, v_2; or there would exist an equation

$$\sum_{-\infty}^{\infty}\sum_{-\infty}^{\infty} C_{n_1, n_2}\, e^{2\pi i(n_1v_1+n_2v_2)}=0$$

in which the series converges uniformly for all finite values of v_1, v_2. But multiplying this equation by $e^{-2\pi i(n_1v_1+n_2v_2)}$, and integrating in regard to v_1 from 0 to 1, and in regard to v_2 from 0 to 1, we could then infer $C_{n_1, n_2}=0$.

Hence for an integral function $Q(v_1, v_2)$ with the properties

$$Q(v_1+1,\ v_2) = Q(v_1,\ v_2) = Q(v_1,\ v_2+1)$$

there can exist no pair of constants ω_1, ω_2 such that

$$Q(v_1+\omega_1,\ v_2+\omega_2) = Q(v_1,\ v_2),$$

or even a pair such that

$$Q(v_1+\omega_1,\ v_2+\omega_2) = CQ(v_1,\ v_2),$$

where C is a constant; for, taking the latter, which includes the former, this would give

$$\frac{1}{C}\Sigma\Sigma A_{n_1, n_2}\, e^{2\pi i(n_1\omega_1+n_2\omega_2)}\, e^{2\pi i(n_1v_1+n_2v_2)} = \Sigma\Sigma A_{n_1, n_2}\, e^{2\pi i(n_1v_1+n_2v_2)},$$

and hence $$e^{2\pi i(n_1\omega_1+n_2\omega_2)} = C,$$

for all values of n_1, n_2.

There can however exist a pair of constants ω_1, ω_2 leading to an equation of the form

$$Q(v_1+\omega_1,\ v_2+\omega_2) = Ce^{\mu_1v_1+\mu_2v_2}\, Q(v_1,\ v_2),$$

where C, μ_1, μ_2 are constants, and, indeed, simultaneously, another pair ω_1', ω_2' leading to an equation

$$Q(v_1+\omega_1',\ v_2+\omega_2') = C'e^{\mu_1'v_1+\mu_2'v_2}\, Q(v_1,\ v_2),$$

where C', μ_1', μ_2' are also constants. This will appear abundantly in the sequel: in order to be as brief as is consistent with our immediate object we shall proceed at once to the following proposition, leaving till subsequently the verification that this is the most general theorem that need be considered for integral functions.

(*d*) Let d_1, d_2, be two positive integers, of which d_2 is a multiple of d_1; let σ be a symmetrical matrix of two rows and columns such that the real part of the quadratic form $i\sigma n^2$ is necessarily negative, and not zero, for all real values of the elements n_1, n_2, of n, other than both zero; let r be a positive integer divisible by d_2, and therefore by d_1; let $\phi(w)$, or $\phi(w_1, w_2)$, be an integral function of the variables w_1, w_2, with the properties (wherein σ_{11}, $\sigma_{12}=\sigma_{21}$, σ_{22} are the elements of the matrix σ)

$$\phi\left(w_1+\frac{1}{d_1},\ w_2\right) = \phi(w_1,\ w_2) = \phi\left(w_1,\ w_2+\frac{1}{d_2}\right),$$

$$\phi(w_1+\sigma_{11},\ w_2+\sigma_{21}) = e^{-2\pi ir(w_1+\frac{1}{2}\sigma_{11})}\,\phi(w_1,\ w_2),$$

$$\phi(w_1+\sigma_{12},\ w_2+\sigma_{22}) = e^{-2\pi ir(w_2+\frac{1}{2}\sigma_{22})}\,\phi(w_1,\ w_2);$$

it can then be proved by induction that if m_1, m_2, m_1', m_2' be any, positive or negative, integers,

$$\phi\left(w_1+\frac{m_1}{d_1}+m_1'\sigma_{11}+m_2'\sigma_{12},\ w_2+\frac{m_2}{d_2}+m_1'\sigma_{21}+m_2'\sigma_{22}\right) = e^{-2\pi irH}\,\phi(w_1,\ w_2),$$

where

$$H = w_1 m_1' + w_2 m_2' + \tfrac{1}{2}(\sigma_{11} m_1'^2 + 2\sigma_{12} m_1' m_2' + \sigma_{22} m_2'^2),$$

while conversely this last equation includes the previous four. By employing the notation of matrices we can put this definition-equation into a form in which it is much more easily grasped; denoting by d the diagonal matrix $\begin{pmatrix} d_1 & 0 \\ 0 & d_2 \end{pmatrix}$, the two elements of $d^{-1}m + \sigma m'$ or

$$\begin{pmatrix} d_1^{-1} & 0 \\ 0 & d_2^{-1} \end{pmatrix} m + \begin{pmatrix} \sigma_{11} & \sigma_{12} \\ \sigma_{21} & \sigma_{22} \end{pmatrix} m'$$

are $\quad d_1^{-1}m_1 + \sigma_{11}m_1' + \sigma_{12}m_2'$ and $d_2^{-1}m_2 + \sigma_{21}m_1' + \sigma_{22}m_2'$;

thus the function on the left side of the definition-equation may be denoted by $\phi(w + d^{-1}m + \sigma m')$; also

$$H = m'w + \tfrac{1}{2}\sigma m'^2 = m'w + \tfrac{1}{2}m'.\sigma m' = m'(w + \tfrac{1}{2}\sigma m');$$

the definition-equation is thus

$$\phi(w + d^{-1}m + \sigma m') = e^{-2\pi i r m'(w + \frac{1}{2}\sigma m')}\,\phi(w).$$

Since now $\phi(w)$ has the periods d_1^{-1}, d_2^{-1} for the arguments w_1, w_2 separately, it follows, from (*b*) above, that we may write

$$\phi(w) = \sum_{k=-\infty}^{\infty} A_k e^{2\pi i k d w},$$

where A_k stands for A_{k_1, k_2} and kdw stands for $k_1(dw)_1 + k_2(dw)_2$, that is for $k_1 d_1 w_1 + k_2 d_2 w_2$, and the summation is in regard to the integers k_1, k_2, each from $-\infty$ to $+\infty$ independently of the other. When we put for w the values $w + d^{-1}m + \sigma m'$, the expression kdw becomes $kdw + km + kd\sigma m'$, so that, since $km = k_1 m_1 + k_2 m_2$ is an integer, the defining equation gives

$$e^{-2\pi i r m'(w + \frac{1}{2}\sigma m')} \sum_k A_k e^{2\pi i k d w} = \sum_k A_k e^{2\pi i k d \sigma m'} e^{2\pi i k d w};$$

now denote dw by x, so that $x_1 = d_1 w_1$ and $x_2 = d_2 w_2$; further let

$$h = k - rd^{-1}m',$$

so that h is a set of two integers, rd^{-1} being a diagonal matrix of two integers rd_1^{-1}, rd_2^{-1}; then the whole exponent of the general term on the left is

$$-\pi i r \sigma m'^2 + 2\pi i k x - 2\pi i r d^{-1} m' x, \quad = -\pi i r \sigma m'^2 + 2\pi i h x,$$

and the equation is

$$e^{-\pi i r \sigma m'^2} \sum_h A_k e^{2\pi i h x} = \sum_k A_k e^{2\pi i k . d\sigma m'} e^{2\pi i k x},$$

where, on the left, the k in the suffix of A_k stands for $h + rd^{-1}m'$. To every integer pair k corresponds, by $h = k - rd^{-1}m'$, a definite integer pair h, and conversely; we may thus on the right replace k by h throughout; then comparing coefficients of $e^{2\pi i h x}$ on the two sides, we have

$$A_{h + rd^{-1}m'} = A_h e^{\pi i r \sigma m'^2 + 2\pi i h . d\sigma m'};$$

as $$h \,.\, d\sigma m' = d\sigma m' h = \sigma d h m' = \sigma m' \,.\, dh,$$
this is the same as
$$A_{h+rd^{-1}m'} = A_h e^H, \quad \text{.................................(i)}$$
where $$H = \pi i r \sigma \left(m' + \frac{1}{r}\, dh\right)^2 - \frac{\pi i}{r}\, \sigma\, (dh)^2,$$

and this holds for arbitrary integer pairs h and m'. Now any pair of integers (n_1, n_2) can be uniquely written in the form $(h_1 + rd_1^{-1}m_1', h_2 + rd_2^{-1}m_2')$ by choosing the integers m_1', m_2' suitably, with the condition $0 \leqq h_1 < rd_1^{-1}$, $0 \leqq h_2 < rd_2^{-1}$; the terms of the doubly infinite series $\sum_{n=-\infty}^{\infty} A_n e^{2\pi i n d w}$ can then be arranged in a finite number of sets according to the appropriate values of h_1 and h_2; namely, we have
$$\sum_{-\infty}^{\infty} A_n e^{2\pi i n d w} = \sum_h \sum_{m'} A_n\, e^{2\pi i (h + rd^{-1}m') \,.\, dw};$$
and
$$(h + rd^{-1}m') \,.\, dw = d\,(h + rd^{-1}m')\, w = r\left(m' + \frac{1}{r}\, dh\right) w = rw\left(m' + \frac{1}{r}\, dh\right);$$
thus, from (i), above,
$$\sum_{-\infty}^{\infty} A_n e^{2\pi i n d w} = \sum_h A_h e^{-\frac{\pi i}{r}\sigma (dh)^2} \sum_{m'=-\infty}^{\infty} e^{2\pi i r w \left(m' + \frac{1}{r} dh\right) + \pi i r \sigma \left(m' + \frac{1}{r} dh\right)^2};$$
we introduce now the notation
$$\Theta\left(v,\ \tau;\ \begin{matrix} q' \\ q \end{matrix}\right) = \sum_{\lambda=-\infty}^{\infty} e^{2\pi i v (\lambda + q') + \pi i \tau (\lambda + q')^2 + 2\pi i q (\lambda + q')},$$
where v, $= (v_1, v_2)$, denotes two independent variables, τ is a symmetrical matrix of type (2, 2), q is a row of any two constants, as is also q', and λ stands for two integers, each of which independently of the other takes all integer values from $-\infty$ to $+\infty$; it will be proved that if, when x_1, x_2 are any two real quantities, the quadratic $i\tau x^2$ has its real part essentially negative and not zero, this expression represents an integral function of v_1, v_2, and is uniformly and absolutely converging; in terms of such functions, the integral function $\phi(w)$ is now shewn to be expressible in the form
$$\phi(w) = \sum_h B_h \Theta\left(rw,\ r\sigma;\ \begin{matrix} r^{-1}dh \\ 0 \end{matrix}\right),$$
where h_1, h_2 are limited only by $0 \leqq h_1 < rd_1^{-1}$, $0 \leqq h_2 < rd_2^{-1}$, so that the number of terms on the right is $r^2 d_1^{-1} d_2^{-1}$, the unknown constant B_h replacing
$$A_h e^{-\frac{\pi i}{r}\sigma (dh)^2}.$$

(*e*) As our defining equation was hypothetical it is necessary to shew that the expression $\Theta\left(v,\ \tau;\ \begin{matrix} q' \\ q \end{matrix}\right)$ represents a function. Consider first the case when q and q' consist of zeros, namely the expression

$$\Theta(v, \tau) = \sum_{n_1=-\infty}^{\infty} \sum_{n_2=-\infty}^{\infty} e^{2\pi i (v_1 n_1 + v_2 n_2) + \pi i (\tau_{11} n_1^2 + 2\tau_{12} n_1 n_2 + \tau_{22} n_2^2)},$$

wherein v_1, v_2 are the variables, and τ_{11}, τ_{12}, τ_{22} are any constants subject to the condition that if $\tau_{r,s} = \rho_{r,s} + i\sigma_{r,s}$ the quadratic form

$$\sigma_{11} n_1^2 + 2\sigma_{12} n_1 n_2 + \sigma_{22} n_2^2$$

is necessarily positive and greater than zero for all real values of n_1, n_2 other than the single pair $n_1 = 0$, $n_2 = 0$. Writing $\kappa_{r,s}$ for $\pi\sigma_{r,s}$ and $a_r + ib_r$ for $2\pi v_r$, the modulus of the general term of the series is e^{-H}, where

$$H = \phi + \psi, \quad \phi = b_1 n_1 + b_2 n_2, \quad \psi = \kappa_{11} n_1^2 + 2\kappa_{12} n_1 n_2 + \kappa_{22} n_2^2;$$

now let μ be any real fixed positive quantity greater than unity; we have

$$e^{\frac{H}{\mu}} > 1 + \frac{H}{\mu}, \quad e^{-H} < \left(1 + \frac{H}{\mu}\right)^{-\mu};$$

the series of moduli of the terms of $\Theta(v, \tau)$ will therefore converge if the series whose general term is $(1 + H/\mu)^{-\mu}$ converges; but when one or both of n_1, n_2 is large, H has the sign of ψ, and is positive, and the ratio $\left(1 + \frac{H}{\mu}\right) : \psi$ approaches to the constant limit μ^{-1}; the series of moduli will therefore converge if the series whose general term is $\psi^{-\mu}$, or

$$(\kappa_{11} n_1^2 + 2\kappa_{12} n_1 n_2 + \kappa_{22} n_2^2)^{-\mu},$$

converges, which is known to be the case when $\mu > 1$. The series for $\Theta(v, \tau)$ thus converges absolutely for any finite values of v_1 and v_2, and, ψ being independent of v_1 and v_2, it converges uniformly over any finite range of values of these variables. It is thus capable of being replaced by a power series in these, converging for all finite values, and represents an integral function.

This function has certain properties which are fundamental, following at once from the form of it. Denoting it by $\Theta(v)$, or $\Theta(v_1, v_2)$, we have

(α) $$\Theta(v_1 + 1, v_2) = \Theta(v_1, v_2 + 1) = \Theta(v_1, v_2),$$

as is evident because the addition of $2\pi i n_1$ or $2\pi i n_2$ to the exponent of any term does not alter the value of that term.

(β) $$\Theta(v_1 + \tau_{11}, v_2 + \tau_{21}) = e^{-2\pi i (v_1 + \frac{1}{2}\tau_{11})} \Theta(v_1, v_2);$$

for if $E(x)$ denote $e^{2\pi i x}$, the left side is

$$\sum_n E(vn + \tfrac{1}{2}\tau n^2 + \tau_{11} n_1 + \tau_{12} n_2),$$

while the single term here written is

$$E[v_1(n_1 + 1) + v_2 n_2 + \tfrac{1}{2}\tau_{11}(n_1 + 1)^2 + \tau_{12}(n_1 + 1) n_2 + \tfrac{1}{2}\tau_{22} n_2^2]\, E(-v_1 - \tfrac{1}{2}\tau_{11}),$$

of which the second factor is independent of n_1, n_2, and the first is the general term of $\Theta(v)$, with the unessential change of n_1 into n_1+1. The result is then obvious. We similarly have

$$\Theta(v_1+\tau_{12},\ v_2+\tau_{22}) = e^{-2\pi i(v_2+\frac{1}{2}\tau_{22})}\,\Theta(v_1,\ v_2).$$

(γ) From (α) and (β) we at once deduce by induction that if m_1, m_2, m_1', m_2' be any integers

$$\Theta(v_1+m_1+m_1'\tau_{11}+m_2'\tau_{12},\ v_2+m_2+m_1'\tau_{21}+m_2'\tau_{22}) = e^{\lambda}\,\Theta(v_1,\ v_2),$$

where $\lambda = -2\pi i\,[v_1m_1'+v_2m_2'+\tfrac{1}{2}\tau_{11}m_1'^2+\tau_{12}m_1'm_2'+\tfrac{1}{2}\tau_{22}m_2'^2]$.

This result we write in the form

$$\Theta(v+m+\tau m') = e^{-2\pi i m'(v+\frac{1}{2}\tau m')}\,\Theta(v).$$

(δ) More generally, if

$$q, =(q_1,\ q_2),\quad q', =(q_1',\ q_2'),\quad p, =(p_1,\ p_2),\quad p', =(p_1',\ p_2'),$$

be any four couples of constants, and qq' denote $q_1q_1'+q_2q_2'$, etc., we have

$$\Theta(v+q+\tau q') = e^{-2\pi i q'(v+\frac{1}{2}\tau q')-2\pi i qq'}\,\Theta\left(v;\ \begin{matrix}q'\\ q\end{matrix}\right)$$

and $$\Theta\left(v+q+\tau q';\ \begin{matrix}p'\\ p\end{matrix}\right) = e^{-2\pi i q'(v+\frac{1}{2}\tau q')-2\pi i qq'-2\pi i pq'}\,\Theta\left(v;\ \begin{matrix}p'+q'\\ p+q\end{matrix}\right),$$

of which the former is included in the latter.

To verify this, compare the general exponent on the left with the general exponent on the right; we require, dividing by the factor $2\pi i$,

$$(v+q+\tau q')(n+p')+\tfrac{1}{2}\tau(n+p')^2+p(n+p')$$
$$= -q'(v+\tfrac{1}{2}\tau q')-qq'-pq'+v(n+p'+q')+\tfrac{1}{2}\tau(n+p'+q')^2+(p+q)(n+p'+q'),$$

and this is at once seen to be an identity.

(ϵ) Since the alteration of the summation numbers n_1, n_2 respectively into n_1+m_1', n_2+m_2', where m_1' and m_2' are definite integers, does not affect the sum, we clearly have, if m_1, m_2 be also integers,

$$\Theta\left(v;\ \begin{matrix}p'+m'\\ p+m\end{matrix}\right) = \sum_n E\,[v(n+p'+m')+\tfrac{1}{2}\tau(n+p'+m')^2+(p+m)(n+p'+m')]$$
$$= E(mp')\sum_k E\,[v(k+p')+\tfrac{1}{2}\tau(k+p')+p(k+p')],$$
$$= e^{2\pi i mp'}\,\Theta\left(v;\ \begin{matrix}p'\\ p\end{matrix}\right),$$

and the second formula of (δ) gives

$$\Theta\left(v+m+\tau m';\ \begin{matrix}p'\\ p\end{matrix}\right) = e^{-2\pi i m'(v+\frac{1}{2}\tau m')+2\pi i(mp-m'p)}\,\Theta\left(v;\ \begin{matrix}p'\\ p\end{matrix}\right).$$

In particular

$$\Theta\left(v_1+1,\, v_2\,;\, \begin{matrix} p' \\ p \end{matrix}\right) = e^{2\pi i p_1'}\,\Theta\left(v\,;\, \begin{matrix} p' \\ p \end{matrix}\right), \quad \Theta\left(v_1,\, v_2+1\,;\, \begin{matrix} p' \\ p \end{matrix}\right) = e^{2\pi i p_2'}\,\Theta\left(v\,;\, \begin{matrix} p' \\ p \end{matrix}\right),$$

$$\Theta\left(v_1+\tau_{11},\, v_2+\tau_{21}\,;\, \begin{matrix} p' \\ p \end{matrix}\right) = e^{-2\pi i\,(v_1+\frac{1}{2}\tau_{11})-2\pi i p_1}\,\Theta\left(v\,;\, \begin{matrix} p' \\ p \end{matrix}\right),$$

$$\Theta\left(v_1+\tau_{12},\, v_2+\tau_{22}\,;\, \begin{matrix} p' \\ p \end{matrix}\right) = e^{-2\pi i\,(v_2+\frac{1}{2}\tau_{22})-2\pi i p_2}\,\Theta\left(v\,;\, \begin{matrix} p' \\ p \end{matrix}\right).$$

(ζ) In case the couplets $2q, = (2q_1,\ 2q_2)$, $2q', = (2q_1',\ 2q_2')$ consist of integers, we have

$$\Theta\left(-v_1,\, -v_2\,;\, \begin{matrix} q' \\ q \end{matrix}\right) = \sum_n E\,[-v\,(n+q') + \tfrac{1}{2}\tau\,(n+q')^2 + q\,(n+q')],$$

and, by writing, as a new summation letter, $m = -n - 2q'$, or $m_1 = -n_1 - 2q_1'$, $m_2 = -n_2 - 2q_2'$, this becomes

$$\Theta\left(-v\,;\, \begin{matrix} q' \\ q \end{matrix}\right) = \sum_n E\,[v\,(m+q') + \tfrac{1}{2}\tau\,(m+q')^2 + q\,(m+q')]\,E\,[-2q\,(m+q')],$$

$$= e^{-4\pi i q q'}\,\Theta\left(v\,;\, \begin{matrix} q' \\ q \end{matrix}\right);$$

thus the function $\Theta\left(v\,;\, \begin{matrix} q' \\ q \end{matrix}\right)$, when q, q' each consists of half integers, is either even or odd, being even when $4qq'$ is an even integer, and odd when $4qq'$ is an odd integer. Putting $2q = x$, $2q' = x'$, and noting that the addition of integers to the numbers q, q' only multiplies the function by a constant, as in the first formula of (ϵ), we see that the number of even functions obtainable by taking q, q' to be half integers is effectively the number of solutions of $x_1 x_1' + x_2 x_2' =$ an even integer in which each of x_1, x_2, x_1', x_2' is zero or unity, and is thus easily found to be 10; similarly the number of odd functions is found by solving $x_1 x_1' + x_2 x_2' =$ odd integer, and is effectively 6. It can be shewn without difficulty that $\Theta\left(v\,;\, \begin{matrix} q' \\ q \end{matrix}\right)$ can only be an odd or even function when $2q$ and $2q'$ consist of integers.

(ι) For many purposes it is convenient to modify the notation as follows. Let a be any symmetrical matrix of type (2, 2); let h be any matrix of type (2, 2), of not vanishing determinant; let τ, as heretofore, be a symmetrical matrix of type (2, 2) such that the quadratic form $i\tau n^2$ has its real part essentially negative when n_1, n_2 are not both zero; let q, q' be any two couples of constants; and let u_1, u_2 be the variables. The series

$$\vartheta\left(u\,;\, \begin{matrix} q' \\ q \end{matrix}\right) = \sum_n e^H,$$

where $\quad H = au^2 + 2hu\,(n+q') + i\pi\tau\,(n+q')^2 + 2\pi i q\,(n+q'),$

becomes, by putting

$$\pi i v_1 = h_{11}u_1 + h_{12}u_2, \quad \pi i v_2 = h_{21}u_1 + h_{22}u_2,$$

or, say,

$$\pi i v = hu,$$

simply

$$\vartheta\left(u;\, \begin{matrix} q' \\ q \end{matrix}\right) = e^{au^2}\, \Theta\left(v;\, \begin{matrix} q' \\ q \end{matrix}\right),$$

and so differs essentially from $\Theta\left(v;\, \begin{matrix} q' \\ q \end{matrix}\right)$ only in the multiplication by an exponential of a quadratic function of v_1 and v_2. Now let ω, ω', η, η' be matrices such that, as before (p. 14),

$$\pi i = 2h\omega, \quad \pi i\tau = 2h\omega', \quad \eta = 2a\omega, \quad \eta' = 2a\omega' - \bar{h};$$

and, when $p, = (p_1, p_2)$, $p', = (p_1', p_2')$, are any two couples of constants, write

$$\Omega_p = 2\omega p + 2\omega' p', \quad H_p = 2\eta p + 2\eta' p',$$

so that Ω_p, H_p each consists of two quantities, and we have

$$H_p = 4a\omega p + 4a\omega' p' - 2\bar{h}p' = 2a\Omega_p - 2\bar{h}p', \quad h\Omega_p = \pi i\,(p + \tau p'),$$

and also

$$\begin{aligned} a\,(u + \Omega_p)^2 - au^2 &= 2au\Omega_p + a\Omega_p^2 = 2a\Omega_p u + a\Omega_p^2 = 2a\Omega_p\,(u + \tfrac{1}{2}\Omega_p) \\ &= (H_p + 2\bar{h}p')\,(u + \tfrac{1}{2}\Omega_p) = H_p\,(u + \tfrac{1}{2}\Omega_p) + 2\bar{h}p'u + \bar{h}p'\Omega_p \\ &= H_p\,(u + \tfrac{1}{2}\Omega_p) + 2hup' + h\Omega_p p' \\ &= H_p\,(u + \tfrac{1}{2}\Omega_p) + 2\pi i v p' + \pi i\,(p + \tau p')\,p' \\ &= H_p\,(u + \tfrac{1}{2}\Omega_p) + \pi i p p' + 2\pi i p'\,(v + \tfrac{1}{2}\tau p'); \end{aligned}$$

put $\lambda_p(u)$ to denote the expression

$$\lambda_p(u) = H_p\,(u + \tfrac{1}{2}\Omega_p) - \pi i p p';$$

then by (δ) above we have

$$\vartheta\left(u + \Omega_q;\, \begin{matrix} p' \\ p \end{matrix}\right) = e^{H}\,\vartheta\left(u;\, \begin{matrix} p' + q' \\ p + q \end{matrix}\right),$$

where

$$\begin{aligned} H &= \lambda_q(u) + 2\pi i q q' + 2\pi i q'\,(v + \tfrac{1}{2}\tau q') - 2\pi i q'\,(v + \tfrac{1}{2}\tau q') - 2\pi i q'\,(p + q) \\ &= \lambda_q(u) - 2\pi i p q'; \end{aligned}$$

when m, m' consist of integers we have, as before,

$$\vartheta\left(u;\, \begin{matrix} p' + m' \\ p + m \end{matrix}\right) = e^{2\pi i m p'}\,\vartheta\left(u;\, \begin{matrix} p' \\ p \end{matrix}\right);$$

from this

$$\vartheta\left(u + \Omega_m;\, \begin{matrix} p' \\ p \end{matrix}\right) = e^{\lambda_m(u) + 2\pi i\,(mp' - m'p)}\,\vartheta\left(u;\, \begin{matrix} p' \\ p \end{matrix}\right);$$

in particular when p, p' both consist of zeros,

$$\vartheta\,(u + \Omega_q) = e^{\lambda_q(u)}\,\vartheta\left(u;\, \begin{matrix} q' \\ q \end{matrix}\right),$$

and, if m, m' consist of integers,

$$\vartheta(u + \Omega_m) = e^{\lambda_m(u)} \vartheta(u);$$

thus we have, for $r = 1, 2$,

$$\vartheta\left(u_1 + 2\omega_{1,r},\ u_2 + 2\omega_{2,r};\ \begin{matrix} p' \\ p \end{matrix}\right) = e^{H_r} \vartheta\left(u;\ \begin{matrix} p' \\ p \end{matrix}\right),$$

$$\vartheta\left(u_1 + 2\omega'_{1,r},\ u_2 + 2\omega'_{2,r};\ \begin{matrix} p' \\ p \end{matrix}\right) = e^{K_r} \vartheta\left(u;\ \begin{matrix} p' \\ p \end{matrix}\right),$$

where
$$H_r = 2\eta_{1,r}(u_1 + \omega_{1,r}) + 2\eta_{2,r}(u_2 + \omega_{2,r}) + 2\pi i p_r',$$
$$K_r = 2\eta'_{1,r}(u_1 + \omega'_{1,r}) + 2\eta'_{2,r}(u_2 + \omega'_{2,r}) - 2\pi i p_r.$$

In subsequent applications of theta functions to the Riemann surface we shall suppose the matrices a and h (and τ) to be those arising in connexion with the algebraic integrals (p. 13).

10. We return now to the Riemann surface, and consider upon it the function of (x) expressed by

$$\Theta(v_1^{x,m} - e_1,\ v_2^{x,m} - e_2),$$

where e_1, e_2 are arbitrary constants, and $v_1^{x,m}$, $v_2^{x,m}$ are the normal integrals of the first kind, integrated from an arbitrary place (m) to the variable place (x). If we dissect the surface by the cuts (A_1), (A_2), (A_3), (A_4), so rendering the integrals single-valued, the function is a single-valued function of the position of (x), which never becomes infinite; it has the same value at any point on one side of the cut (A_1) as at the opposite point of the cut, for we have $\Theta(v_1 + 1, v_2) = \Theta(v_1, v_2)$; and the same is true of the cut (A_2); but the value of the function at any point on the left side of the cut (A_3) is obtained from its value at the opposite point on the right side by multiplication with the factor

$$e^{-2\pi i (v_1^{x,m} - e_1 + \frac{1}{2}\tau_{11})},$$

where $v_1^{x,m}$ denotes the value of the integral at that point on the right side, so that $v_1^{x,m} - e_1 + \frac{1}{2}\tau_{11}$ is the mean of the values, $v_1^{x,m} - e_1$ and $v_1^{x,m} - e_1 + \tau_{11}$, taken by $v_1^{x,m} - e_1$ at the right and left sides of (A_3); a similar statement holds for (A_4). The function $\Theta(v^{x,m} - e)$ is an integral function of $v_1^{x,m}$, $v_2^{x,m}$, and therefore analytical on the Riemann surface, capable, that is, of representation about any place of the surface by a series of integral powers of the parameter for that place, there being no negative powers; hence, the number of places (x) where the function vanishes to the first order, if any, or the sum of the orders with which it vanishes, is given by taking the integral

$$\frac{1}{2\pi i}\int \frac{d\Theta}{\Theta}$$

round the closed curves $(A_1 A_3 A_1^{-1} A_3^{-1})$, $(A_2 A_4 A_2^{-1} A_4^{-1})$. Of the former contour the two sides of (A_1) give no contribution; the two sides of (A_3) give

$$-\int d\,(v_1^{x,m} - e_1 + \tfrac{1}{2}\tau_{11}),$$

taken once along the positive or left side of (A_3), from the left to the right side of (A_1); this is equal to $+1$. Similarly the contribution from $(A_2 A_4 A_2^{-1} A_4^{-1})$ is also $+1$. There are thus two places (x) where $\Theta(v^{x,m} - e)$ vanishes to the first order, or one place where it vanishes to the second order.

An analytic function of two independent variables has manifestly, as values of the variables for which it vanishes, not a set of discrete values, but vanishes for an arbitrary value of one of its variables when the other is suitably chosen to correspond; this at least is true, for a function which vanishes at all, for a suitable range of variation of the one variable which is taken arbitrarily. Thus, when the two variables are both replaced by functions of a single third variable, whose elimination establishes a relation between the two original variables, it may happen that the function vanishes identically for all values of the single third variable. The previous investigation might therefore fail for particular values of e_1, e_2; but it does not fail for all values of these, in particular not for $e_1 = 0$, $e_2 = 0$; for then the function reduces to $\Theta(v^{x,m})$, which even when $(x) = (m)$ and $\tau_{11} = i$, $\tau_{12} = 0$, $\tau_{22} = i$, does not vanish, being equal to $\left(\sum_{n_1} e^{-\pi n_1^2}\right)\left(\sum_{n_2} e^{-\pi n_2^2}\right)$.

Let then (m_1), (m_2) denote the positions of (x) for which $\Theta(v^{x,m})$ is zero; we proceed to shew that, if (x_1), (x_2) denote the zeros of $\Theta(v^{x,m} - e)$, we have

$$e_1 = v_1^{x_1, m_1} + v_1^{x_2, m_2} + M_1 + M_1' \tau_{11} + M_2' \tau_{12},$$

$$e_2 = v_2^{x_1, m_1} + v_2^{x_2, m_2} + M_2 + M_1' \tau_{21} + M_2' \tau_{22},$$

where M_1, M_2, M_1', M_2' are certain integers; and, as, by the addition of periods to the arguments of the function Θ, the function is reproduced multiplied by a non-vanishing factor, it is sufficient to write these equations as congruences

$$e_1 \equiv v_1^{x_1, m_1} + v_1^{x_2, m_2}, \quad e_2 \equiv v_2^{x_1, m_1} + v_2^{x_2, m_2}.$$

To prove this result we use two properties of rational functions. Firstly, a function which is single-valued on the undissected Riemann surface, and is capable of expression about every point as a series of integral powers of the parameter for the neighbourhood of this point, there being only a finite number of negative powers of the parameter, if any—so that, as can be shewn to be a consequence of this, there is only a finite number of points for which negative powers enter at all—is necessarily capable of representation as a rational function of x and y. For if R_1, R_2 be the two values of the function for the conjugate places (x, y), $(x, -y)$, the functions $R_1 + R_2$ and $y(R_1 - R_2)$ are at once seen to be rational functions of x only. Secondly, it is not possible to construct a rational function R with poles of the first order at two arbitrary places (x_1, y_1), (x_2, y_2), unless these be conjugate places having $x_1 = x_2$ and $y_1 = -y_2$, in which case $(x - x_1)^{-1}$ is such a function. For otherwise $R+A_1\Gamma_{x_1}^{x,a}+A_2\Gamma_{x_2}^{x,a}$, wherein A_1 and A_2 are suitably chosen constants, could be taken to be a function without infinities, single-valued and analytical on the surface, save for the periods (cf. p. 9)

$$2\pi i\,[A_1(v_1^{x_1})_{t_1}+A_2(v_1^{x_2})_{t_2}],\quad 2\pi i\,[A_1(v_2^{x_1})_{t_1}+A_2(v_2^{x_2})_{t_2}]$$

at the period-loops (A_3), (A_4); this function would then be a constant (p. 7, (1)), and both these periods zero, so that $y_1^{-1}/y_2^{-1}=x_1y_1^{-1}/x_2y_2^{-1}$, or $x_1=x_2$. Take then (x_1), (x_2) different from one another and consider the function of (x)

$$\frac{\Theta\,(v^{x,m}-v^{x_1,m_1}-v^{x_2,m_2})}{\Theta\,(v^{x,m})}\,e^{-\left(\Pi_{x_1,m_1}^{x,c}+\Pi_{x_2,m_2}^{x,c}\right)};$$

this function is analytical and single-valued on the dissected surface, its values at the two sides of the loop (A_1) being the same, as they are also at the two sides of (A_2); its value at the left side of (A_3) is obtained by multiplying its value at the right side by $e^{2\pi i H_1}$, where

$$H_1=-(v_1^{x,m}-v_1^{x_1,m_1}-v_1^{x_2,m_2}+\tfrac{1}{2}\tau_{11})+(v_1^{x,m}+\tfrac{1}{2}\tau_{11})-(v_1^{x_1,m_1}+v_1^{x_2,m_2}),$$

which is zero; similarly at the loop (A_4). The function is thus single-valued on the undissected surface. Next, at (m_1) the function $\Theta\,(v^{x,m})$ vanishes to the first order, and $e^{-\Pi_{x_1\,m_1}^{x,c}}$ also vanishes to the first order; the Θ-function in the numerator has no infinities; the function $e^{-\Pi_{x_1,m_1}^{x,c}}$ becomes infinite to the first order at (x_1). On the whole then the function is a single-valued analytic function on the undissected surface, with at most two poles, at (x_1) and (x_2), and with zeros where $\Theta\,(v^{x,m}-v^{x_1,m_1}-v^{x_2,m_2})$ vanishes. For general positions of (x_1) and (x_2) no such function exists, as we have proved. Thus the function is in fact a constant, and the function $\Theta\,(v^{x,m}-v^{x_1,m_1}-v^{x_2,m_2})$ vanishes to the first order at (x_1) and (x_2). Therefore, if e_1, e_2 be two constants, such that the function $\Theta\,(v^{x,m}-e)$ does not vanish identically, and (z_1), (z_2) be the zeros of this function, the ratio

$$\phi=\Theta\,(v^{x,m}-v^{z_1,m_1}-v^{z_2,m_2})/\Theta\,(v^{x,m}-e)$$

is a single-valued analytic function on the dissected Riemann surface, with neither zeros nor poles; it has the same value at opposite points of the loop (A_1), and of the loop (A_2); its values at the left sides of the loops (A_3), (A_4) are obtained from those at the right sides by multiplication by the respective constants $e^{2\pi i B_1}$, $e^{2\pi i B_2}$, where

$$B_1=v_1^{z_1,m_1}+v_1^{z_2,m_2}-e_1,\quad B_2=v_2^{z_1,m_1}+v_2^{z_2,m_2}-e_2;$$

the function $\log\phi$ is thus single-valued on the dissected surface; let its values at the left sides of the loops (A_1), (A_2), (A_3), (A_4) exceed its values at the right sides respectively by

$$2\pi i M_1',\quad 2\pi i M_2',\quad 2\pi i\,(B_1-M_1),\quad 2\pi i\,(B_2-M_2),$$

where M_1', M_2', M_1, M_2 are integers; then the function

$$\log \phi - 2\pi i (M_1' v_1^{x, m} + M_2' v_2^{x, m})$$

will also be single-valued on the dissected surface, and analytic, and finite, and its values on the two sides of the loops (A_1), (A_2) will be the same. We have seen that such a function is a constant (p. 7, (1)). Thus the increments of this function for the loops (A_3) and (A_4) are zero; these are

$$2\pi i (B_1 - M_1 - M_1'\tau_{11} - M_2'\tau_{21}), \quad 2\pi i (B_2 - M_2 - M_1'\tau_{12} - M_2'\tau_{22}),$$

and that these vanish is the proposition we set out to prove.

It thus appears also that, arbitrary values of e_1, e_2 being given, places (z_1), (z_2), and integers M_1, M_2, M_1', M_2' are determinable uniquely, so that, on the dissected surface

$$v_1^{z_1, m_1} + v_1^{z_2, m_2} = e_1 + M_1 + M_1'\tau_{11} + M_2'\tau_{12},$$
$$v_2^{z_1, m_1} + v_2^{z_2, m_2} = e_2 + M_2 + M_1'\tau_{21} + M_2'\tau_{22},$$

there being exception only for a connected sequence of values of e_1 and e_2 of one dimension, those namely for which $\Theta(v^{x, m} - e)$ vanishes for all positions of (x); these values will be expressed below in terms of one arbitrary parameter. For such exceptional values the equations are still soluble in fact, but by an infinite number of sets of positions of (z_1) and (z_2).

Incidentally we see that if we consider the pairs of values of the two expressions

$$u_1 = v_1^{x_1, m_1} + v_1^{x_2, m_2}, \quad u_2 = v_2^{x_1, m_1} + v_2^{x_2, m_2},$$

for all independent pairs of positions of (x_1) and (x_2) on the dissected surface, not only does the pair (u_1, u_2) not occur twice, but two pairs do not arise satisfying equations

$$u_1' - u_1 = M_1 + M_1'\tau_{11} + M_2'\tau_{12}, \quad u_2' - u_2 = M_2 + M_1'\tau_{21} + M_2'\tau_{22},$$

wherein M_1, M_2, M_1', M_2' are integers. This can also be proved independently by noticing that if these equations were possible, and (x_1'), (x_2') the positions of (x_1), (x_2) corresponding to the values u_1', u_2', the function

$$\exp\left[\Pi_{x_1', x_1}^{x, c} + \Pi_{x_2', x_2}^{x, c} - 2\pi i (M_1' v_1^{x, c} + M_2' v_2^{x, c})\right]$$

would be an analytic function on the surface, single-valued on the surface dissected by the cuts (A_3), (A_4) where it would have the respective factors

$$\exp\left[2\pi i (v_1^{x_1', x_1} + v_1^{x_2', x_2} - M_1'\tau_{11} - M_2'\tau_{12})\right],$$
$$\exp\left[2\pi i (v_2^{x_1', x_1} + v_2^{x_2', x_2} - M_1'\tau_{21} - M_2'\tau_{22})\right],$$

that is

$$\exp\left[2\pi i (u_1' - u_1 - M_1'\tau_{11} - M_2'\tau_{12})\right], \quad \exp\left[2\pi i (u_2' - u_2 - M_1'\tau_{21} - M_2'\tau_{22})\right],$$

which are both unity; the function would thus be a rational function with two poles of the first order, at (x_1), (x_2), which we have proved to be impossible unless (x_1), (x_2) are conjugate places on the surface, a hypothesis at once seen to lead to $u_1 = \text{constant}$, $u_2 = \text{constant}$. The result may be interpreted by putting

$$v_1^{x_1, m_1} + v_1^{x_2, m_2} = t_1 + it_2, \quad v_2^{x_1, m_1} + v_2^{x_2, m_2} = t_3 + it_4$$

and speaking of t_1, t_2, t_3, t_4 as the coordinates of a point in a real space of four dimensions. Whatever t_1, t_2, t_3, t_4 may be we can determine real quantities $\mu_1, \mu_2, \mu_1', \mu_2'$ so that

$$t_1 + it_2 = \mu_1 + \mu_1'\tau_{11} + \mu_2'\tau_{12}, \quad t_3 + it_4 = \mu_2 + \mu_1'\tau_{21} + \mu_2'\tau_{22},$$

for we have proved that if $\tau_{rs} = \rho_{rs} + i\sigma_{rs}$ the determinant $|\sigma|$ is not zero, and the equating of the real and imaginary parts in these equations determines $\mu_1, \mu_2, \mu_1', \mu_2'$ uniquely; speaking of two sets $\mu_1, \mu_2, \mu_1', \mu_2'$ and $(\mu_1), (\mu_2), (\mu_1'), (\mu_2')$ as congruent when each of the differences $(\mu_1) - \mu_1$, $(\mu_2) - \mu_2$, $(\mu_1') - \mu_1'$, $(\mu_2') - \mu_2'$ is an integer, we have proved that if we put

$$v_1^{x_1, m_1} + v_1^{x_2, m_2} = \mu_1 + \mu_1'\tau_{11} + \mu_2'\tau_{12}, \quad v_2^{x_1, m_1} + v_2^{x_2, m_2} = \mu_2 + \mu_1'\tau_{21} + \mu_2'\tau_{22},$$

and allow (x_1), (x_2), independently of one another, to take all positions on the dissected Riemann surface, every set $\mu_1, \mu_2, \mu_1', \mu_2'$ or else a set congruent thereto, but never both, arises, just once. In order not too far to interrupt the prosecution of our immediate purpose we defer the proof of the theorem which is suggested, that in fact the sets arising form a continuum of non-congruent values of four dimensions.

We may similarly consider the aggregate of values for $\mu_1, \mu_2, \mu_1', \mu_2'$ obtained by putting

$$v_1^{x, c} = \mu_1 + \mu_1'\tau_{11} + \mu_2'\tau_{12}, \quad v_2^{x, c} = \mu_2 + \mu_1'\tau_{21} + \mu_2'\tau_{22},$$

and allowing (x) to describe the whole dissected Riemann surface. As before, equations

$$v_1^{x_1', x_1} = M_1 + M_1'\tau_{11} + M_2'\tau_{12}, \quad v_2^{x_1', x_1} = M_2 + M_1'\tau_{21} + M_2'\tau_{22},$$

in which M_1, M_2, M_1', M_2' are integers, are impossible, leading as they would to the existence of a rational function

$$\exp\left[\Pi_{x_1', x_1}^{x, c} - 2\pi i\,(M_1'v_1^{x, c} + M_2'v_2^{x, c})\right]$$

of only one pole and one zero; but it is not now the case that all values of $\mu_1, \mu_2, \mu_1', \mu_2'$ arise.

Returning to the vanishing of the theta function, we have shewn that if (m_1), (m_2) be the zeros of $\Theta(v^{x, m})$, the function $\Theta(v^{x, m} - v^{x_1, m_1} - v^{x_2, m_2})$ vanishes at (x_1) and (x_2); thus if (m') be any other position, and (m_1'), (m_2') the zeros of $\Theta(v^{x, m'})$, the function expressed by the quotient

$$\Theta(v^{x, m} - v^{x_1, m_1} - v^{x_2, m_2}) / \Theta(v^{x, m'} - v^{x_1, m_1'} - v^{x_2, m_2'})$$

is analytical and single-valued on the dissected Riemann surface, but with no zeros or poles, having factors at the loops (A_3), (A_4) respectively

$$\exp\left[2\pi i\,(v_1^{m_1', m_1} + v_1^{m_2', m_2} - v_1^{m', m})\right], \quad \exp\left[2\pi i\,(v_2^{m_1', m_1} + v_2^{m_2', m_2} - v_2^{m', m})\right];$$

it follows therefore, as in the argument above, that the quotient is a constant multiple of a function of the form

$$\exp\left[2\pi i\left(M_1' v_1^{x,c} + M_2' v_2^{x,c}\right)\right],$$

where M_1', M_2' are integers, and that we have equations

$$v_1^{m_1', m_1} + v_1^{m_2', m_2} - v_1^{m', m} = M_1 + M_1'\tau_{11} + M_2'\tau_{12},$$
$$v_2^{m_1', m_1} + v_2^{m_2', m_2} - v_2^{m', m} = M_2 + M_1'\tau_{21} + M_2'\tau_{22},$$

wherein M_1, M_2 are also integers; and therefore, that a rational function exists capable of the form e^T where

$$T = \Pi^{x,c}_{m_1', m_1} + \Pi^{x,c}_{m_2', m_2} + \Pi^{x,c}_{m, m'} - 2\pi i\left(M_1' v_1^{x,c} + M_2' v_2^{x,c}\right),$$

having poles at (m_1), (m_2) and (m'), and zeros at (m_1'), (m_2') and (m). Now a rational function can easily be seen to be determined save for a multiplying constant when its Q poles and all but two of its zeros are given—being capable of the form

$$\frac{(x, 1)_Q + y\,(x, 1)_{Q-3}}{(x - x_1)\ldots(x - x_Q)},$$

wherein $(x, 1)_Q$, $(x, 1)_{Q-3}$ denote polynomials of orders respectively Q and $Q-3$ in x, the $Q + 1 + Q - 2 = 2Q - 1$ homogeneously entering coefficients of the numerator having their ratios determined by the vanishing of the numerator at the Q places $(x_r, -y_r)$ conjugate to the prescribed poles (x_r, y_r), as well as at the $Q - 2$ assigned zeros; thus if (m), (m_1), (m_2) be determined, for an arbitrary position of (m), and (m') be arbitrarily assigned, then (m_1'), (m_2') can be determined as the remaining zeros of the easily constructed rational function which has (m_1), (m_2), (m') as poles and (m) as one zero.

We now shew that one possibility for the set (m), (m_1), (m_2) consists of three branch places, which may in fact be any three, provided the dissecting cuts be taken appropriately. For this, let the branch places in any order be named c_1, a_1, c_2, a_2, c, a, these symbols being also used occasionally for the values of x for which the fundamental sextic vanishes, with the proviso that

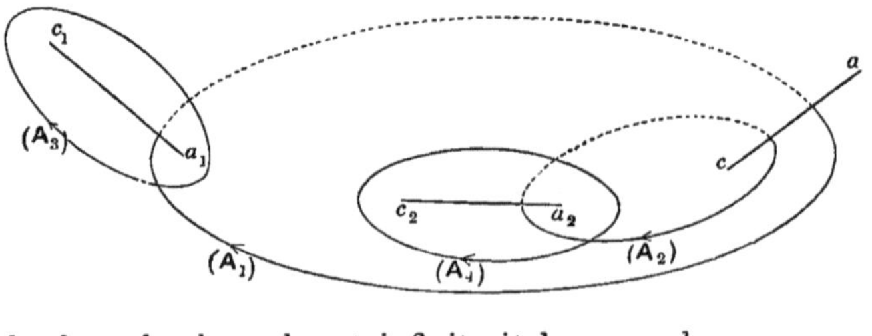

if one of the branch places be at infinity it be named a; suppose there are cross lines of the sheets between c_1 and a_1, between c_2 and a_2, and between c and a; let the loops along which the surface is cut in order to give the cuts

(A_3), (A_4) be such that when projected upon the plane of x they enclose respectively the pair of points c_1, a_1 and the pair of points c_2, a_2, these cuts being in the upper sheet; in a similar sense let (A_2) enclose a_2 and c, and (A_1) enclose a_1, c_2, a_2 and c, and also the loops (A_2) and (A_4); we can then prove that

$$\Theta(v^{a_1, a}) = 0, \quad \Theta(v^{a_2, a}) = 0.$$

For this we prove that, if θ, ϕ denote any two of the branch places, and the integral be taken on the dissected surface,

$$v_1^{\theta,\phi} = \tfrac{1}{2}(M_1 + M_1'\tau_{11} + M_2'\tau_{12}), \quad v_2^{\theta,\phi} = \tfrac{1}{2}(M_2 + M_1'\tau_{21} + M_2'\tau_{22}),$$

wherein M_1, M_2, M_1', M_2' are integers determinable at sight from the diagram, by the following rule: If this diagram, and a path on the surface from ϕ to θ, be projected on to the plane of x below, and if this path cut the projection of any period-loop, μ times from the right side to the left side, where μ is positive, or $-\mu$ times from the left side to the right side, where μ is negative, then we are to take, as the corresponding contribution to the sums on the right sides of these equations, μ times the half period associated with that loop. For instance, to explain first the rule, suppose we consider $v_r^{c_1, a_1}$: in going from a_1 to c_1 we cross from the right to the left side of (A_1); we are thus to reckon $\frac{1}{2}$ towards $\frac{1}{2}M_1$ for $v_1^{c_1, a_1}$ and zero towards $\frac{1}{2}M_2$ for $v_2^{c_1, a_1}$. To prove the rule, notice that we can go from ϕ to θ on the dissected surface entirely in the lower sheet; consider the path lying above this in the upper sheet; it will be broken at various points by the necessity of a detour to reach the other side of a cut; suppose these detours give on the whole respectively, M_1 times the period associated with (A_1), M_2 times that associated with (A_2), M_1' times that associated with (A_3) and M_2' times that associated with (A_4); then since y has opposite signs, and therefore $dv_r^{x, c}$ opposite signs in the two sheets, we have

$$v_1^{\theta,\phi} = -v_1^{\theta,\phi} + M_1 \quad + M_1'\tau_{11} + M_2'\tau_{12},$$
$$v_2^{\theta,\phi} = -v_2^{\theta,\phi} + \quad M_2 + M_1'\tau_{21} + M_2'\tau_{22},$$

where the integrals on the right are evaluated on the lower sheet, and those on the left on the upper sheet of the surface; these are the equations stated.

It is convenient to denote these equations, for the present, by putting

$$v^{\theta,\phi} = \tfrac{1}{2}\begin{pmatrix} M_1' & M_2' \\ M_1 & M_2 \end{pmatrix};$$

then in particular we find

$$v^{c,a} = \tfrac{1}{2}\begin{pmatrix} 0 & 0 \\ -1 & -1 \end{pmatrix}, \quad v^{a_2,c} = \tfrac{1}{2}\begin{pmatrix} 0 & -1 \\ 0 & 0 \end{pmatrix}, \quad v^{c_2,a_2} = \tfrac{1}{2}\begin{pmatrix} 0 & 0 \\ 0 & 1 \end{pmatrix}, \quad v^{a_1,c_2} = \tfrac{1}{2}\begin{pmatrix} -1 & 1 \\ 0 & 0 \end{pmatrix},$$

so that

$$v^{a_2,a} = \tfrac{1}{2}\begin{pmatrix} 0 & -1 \\ -1 & -1 \end{pmatrix}, \ = \tfrac{1}{2}\begin{pmatrix} p_1' & p_2' \\ p_1 & p_2 \end{pmatrix}, \text{ say}; \quad v^{a_1,a} = \tfrac{1}{2}\begin{pmatrix} -1 & 0 \\ -1 & 0 \end{pmatrix}, \ = \tfrac{1}{2}\begin{pmatrix} q_1' & q_2' \\ q_1 & q_2 \end{pmatrix}, \text{ say},$$

giving $\quad pp', = p_1p_1' + p_2p_2', = \text{odd}; \quad qq', = q_1q_1' + q_2q_2', = \text{odd};$

now we have previously shewn (pp. 23, 24) that

$$\Theta(v + \tfrac{1}{2}\Omega_q) = e^{-\pi i q'(v + \frac{1}{4}\tau q') - \frac{1}{2}\pi i q q'}\, \Theta\left(v;\ \begin{matrix}\frac{1}{2}q' \\ \frac{1}{2}q\end{matrix}\right),$$

and that, if $qq' = q_1q_1' + q_2q_2'$ be odd, the function Θ on the right of this equation is an odd function, and therefore vanishes for $v = 0$; thus when qq' is odd, we have $\Theta(\frac{1}{2}\Omega_q) = 0$. This shews that $\Theta(v^{a_1, a}) = 0$, and $\Theta(v^{a_2, a}) = 0$, and therefore that the zeros of the function $\Theta(v^{x, a})$ are $(x) = a_1$, $(x) = a_2$. Hence, by what has preceded, the function

$$\Theta(v^{x, a} - v^{x_1, a_1} - v^{x_2, a_2})$$

vanishes for $(x) = (x_1)$ and $(x) = (x_2)$.

It follows thence, by putting (x_1) for (x), and then (x) for (x_2), that the function

$$\Theta(v^{a_1, a} - v^{x, a_2})$$

vanishes for all positions of (x). As the function

$$\Theta(v_1 + m_1 + m_1'\tau_{11} + m_2'\tau_{12}, \quad v_2 + m_2 + m_1'\tau_{21} + m_2'\tau_{22}),$$

or say $\Theta(v + \Omega_m)$, where m_1, m_2, m_1', m_2' are integers, has the same zeros as $\Theta(v)$, and we have proved that

$$2v_1^{a_1, a} = m_1 + m_1'\tau_{11} + m_2'\tau_{12}, \quad 2v_2^{a_2, a} = m_2 + m_1'\tau_{21} + m_2'\tau_{22},$$

or say $v^{a_1, a} = v^{a, a_1} + \Omega_m$, and as $v^{a, a_1} - v^{x, a_2}$ is the same as $v^{a, x} + v^{a_2, a_1}$, it follows that $\Theta(v^{x, a} + v^{a_1, a_2})$ vanishes identically in regard to (x). In other words $\Theta(u)$ vanishes when u_1, u_2 are replaced by functions of the same independent variable of the form

$$u_1 = v_1^{x, a} + v_1^{a_1, a_2}, \quad u_2 = v_2^{x, a} + v_2^{a_1, a_2},$$

for all positions of (x).

We prove conversely that every pair of values of u_1, u_2 for which $\Theta(u)$ vanishes can be put into this form, save for the addition of integral multiples of the periods. Suppose $\Theta(u) = 0$; suppose also, if possible, that $\Theta(v^{x, z} + u)$ vanishes for every position of (x) and (z). Consider $\Theta(v^{x, z} + v^{x_1, z_1} + u)$; for $(x) = (z)$ this reduces to $\Theta(v^{x_1, z_1} + u)$, which vanishes by hypothesis; for $(x) = (z_1)$ it reduces to $\Theta(v^{x_1, z} + u)$ which also vanishes; and as $v^{x_1, z_1} = v^{\zeta_1, \xi_1}$, where (ξ_1), (ζ_1) are the places respectively conjugate to (x_1), (z_1)—for the change in the sign of y involves a change in the sign of dv_1 and dv_2—the function $\Theta(v^{x, z} + v^{x_1, z_1} + u)$ reduces for $(x) = (\xi_1)$ to $\Theta(v^{\zeta_1, z} + u)$, which again vanishes, by hypothesis. The function $\Theta(v^{x, z} + v^{x_1, z_1} + u)$, regarded as depending on (x), has thus three zeros, and therefore, by what was shewn (p. 26), vanishes identically. Next consider $\Theta(v^{x, z} + v^{x_1, z_1} + v^{x_2, z_2} + u)$, as a function of (x); it has, with others, the three zeros (z), (z_1), (z_2), and therefore also vanishes identically. So more generally the function

$$\Theta(v^{x,z}+v^{x_1,z_1}+\ldots+v^{x_m,z_m}+u),$$

for $m=1,2,3,\ldots$, vanishes identically; from this, by supposing (x_m) taken in the infinitely near neighbourhood of (z_m), we infer that the first partial derivatives, $\partial\Theta(w)/\partial w_1$, $\partial\Theta(w)/\partial w_2$, vanish identically for

$$w=v^{x,z}+v^{x_1,z_1}+\ldots+v^{x_{m-1},z_{m-1}}+u;$$

a similar inference is possible as to the second partial derivatives, for the values

$$v^{x,z}+v^{x_1,z_1}+\ldots+v^{x_{m-2},z_{m-2}}+u$$

of the arguments, by supposing, in the first partial derivatives, x_{m-1} to approach to z_{m-1}; and so on. On the whole then, from the hypotheses made, that $\Theta(u)=0$ and that $\Theta(v^{x,z}+u)=0$ for all positions of (x) and (z), would follow that $\Theta(u)$ and all its partial derivatives of every order, were zero. Hence we deduce that if $\Theta(u)=0$ there are positions of (z) for which $\Theta(v^{x,z}+u)$, regarded as a function of (x), has only two zeros; of these zeros, one is manifestly (z), and if (t) be the other, we can write, save for multiples of the periods,

$$u^{x,z}+u=v^{x,a}-v^{z,a_1}-v^{t,a_2},$$

and therefore

$$u=v^{a_1,a}-v^{t,a_2},$$

(t) being, as we see, perfectly definite. This is the result enunciated above; if (x) be the position conjugate to (t) we have, save for periods,

$$u=v^{a_1,a}+v^{x,a_2}=v^{x,a}+v^{a_1,a_2}.$$

With the dissection of p. 31, we have

$$v_1^{a_1,a_2}=-\tfrac{1}{2}\tau_{11}+\tfrac{1}{2}\tau_{12},\quad v_2^{a_1,a_2}=\tfrac{1}{2}(1-\tau_{21}+\tau_{22});$$

if then we write

$$\begin{pmatrix}\lambda'\\ \lambda\end{pmatrix},=\begin{pmatrix}\lambda_1' & \lambda_2'\\ \lambda_1 & \lambda_2\end{pmatrix},=\tfrac{1}{2}\begin{pmatrix}-1 & 1\\ 0 & 1\end{pmatrix},$$

the result is that $\Theta\left(u;\begin{matrix}\lambda'\\ \lambda\end{matrix}\right)$ vanishes if, and only if, u be of the form $v^{x,a}$.

11. Recall now that we have (p. 25)

$$\vartheta(u)=e^{au^2}\Theta(v),$$

and hence

$$\frac{\vartheta(u-u')}{\vartheta(u-u'')}\bigg/\frac{\vartheta(u^{(0)}-u')}{\vartheta(u^{(0)}-u'')}=e^H\frac{\vartheta(v-v')}{\vartheta(v-v'')}\bigg/\frac{\vartheta(v^{(0)}-v')}{\vartheta(v^{(0)}-v'')},$$

where

$$\begin{aligned}H&=a(u-u')^2-a(u-u'')^2-a(u^{(0)}-u')^2+a(u^{(0)}-u'')^2\\&=-2a(u'-u'')(u-u^{(0)})\\&=-2\sum_{r=1}^{2}\sum_{s=1}^{2}a_{r,s}(u_s'-u_s'')(u_r-u_r^{(0)});\end{aligned}$$

also (p. 11),

$$R^{x,\mu}_{x_1,\mu_1}+R^{x,\mu}_{x_2,\mu_2}-\Pi^{x,\mu}_{x_1,\mu_1}-\Pi^{x,\mu}_{x_2,\mu_2}=-2\sum_{r=1}^{2}\sum_{s=1}^{2}a_{r,s}u_r^{x,\mu}(u_s^{x_1,\mu_1}+u_s^{x_2,\mu_2})$$

if, in particular,

$$u=u^{x,a},\quad u'=u^{x_1,a_1}+u^{x_2,a_2},\quad u''=u^{\mu_1,a_1}+u^{\mu_2,a_2},\quad u^{(0)}=u^{\mu,a},$$

then we have

$$H=-2\sum_{r,s}a_{r,s}u_r^{x,\mu}(u_s^{x_1,\mu_1}+u_s^{x_2,\mu_2}).$$

Recall also the equation (p. 10)

$$R^{x,\mu}_{x_1,\mu_1}=R^{x_1,\mu_1}_{x,\mu}=P^{x_1,\mu_1}_{x,\mu}+u_1^{x_1,\mu_1}L_1^{x,\mu}+u_2^{x_1,\mu_1}L_2^{x,\mu}$$

which gives

$$R^{x,\mu}_{x_1,\mu_1}+R^{x,\mu}_{x_2,\mu_2}=P^{x_1,\mu_1}_{x,\mu}+P^{x_2,\mu_2}_{x,\mu}+(u_1^{x_1,\mu_1}+u_1^{x_2,\mu_2})L_1^{x,\mu}+(u_2^{x_1,\mu_1}+u_2^{x_2,\mu_2})L_2^{x,\mu}.$$

These notations being made clear, consider the function

$$\frac{\Theta(v^{x,a}-v^{x_1,a_1}-v^{x_2,a_2})}{\Theta(v^{x,a}-v^{\mu_1,a_1}-v^{\mu_2,a_2})}e^{-\Pi^{x,\mu}_{x_1,\mu_1}-\Pi^{x,\mu}_{x_2,\mu_2}},$$

wherein a, a_1, a_2 are branch places, as before, but (x_1), (x_2), (μ_1), (μ_2), (μ), are arbitrary places. This function is analytical and single-valued on the dissected surface; it has, on account of the theta quotient, zeros of the first order at (x_1), (x_2), and poles of the first order at (μ_1), (μ_2); but, on account of the exponential it has poles of the first order at (x_1), (x_2) and zeros of the first order at (μ_1), (μ_2); at the two sides of each of the period-loops (A_1), (A_2) its values agree, but at (A_3), (A_4) it has factors $e^{-2\pi i H_1}$, $e^{-2\pi i H_2}$, where

$$H_1=(v_1^{x,a}-v_1^{x_1,a_1}-v_1^{x_2,a_2}+\tfrac{1}{2}\tau_{11})-(v_1^{x,a}-v_1^{\mu_1,a}-v_1^{\mu_2,a}+\tfrac{1}{2}\tau_{11})+v_1^{x_1,\mu_1}+v_1^{x_2,\mu_2},$$

is zero, as also, similarly, is H_2. The function is thus equal to the constant value taken by it for $(x)=(\mu)$. Thus, putting

$$v_r'=v_r^{x_1,a_1}+v_r^{x_2,a_2},\quad v_r''=v_r^{\mu_1,a_1}+v_r^{\mu_2,a_2},$$

we have $$\Pi^{x,\mu}_{x_1,\mu_1}+\Pi^{x,\mu}_{x_2,\mu_2}=\log\frac{\Theta(v^{x,a}-v')}{\Theta(v^{x,a}-v'')}\Big/\frac{\Theta(v^{\mu,a}-v')}{\Theta(v^{\mu,a}-v'')}.$$

From this, by the lemmas just preceding, we obtain

$$R^{x,\mu}_{x_1,\mu_1}+R^{x,\mu}_{x_2,\mu_2}=\log\frac{\vartheta(u^{x,a}-u')}{\vartheta(u^{x,a}-u'')}\Big/\frac{\vartheta(u^{\mu,a}-u')}{\vartheta(u^{\mu,a}-u'')}.$$

We have proved (p. 29) that we may regard the arguments (u_1', u_2'), and the arguments (u_1'', u_2''), as the independent variables, the places (x_1), (x_2) and (μ_1), (μ_2) being functions of these; hence, from the equation

$$\log\frac{\vartheta(u^{x,a}-u')}{\vartheta(u^{x,a}-u'')}\Big/\frac{\vartheta(u^{\mu,a}-u')}{\vartheta(u^{\mu,a}-u'')}=P^{x_1,\mu_1}_{x,\mu}+P^{x_2,\mu_2}_{x,\mu}+(u_1'-u_1'')L_1^{x,\mu}+(u_2'-u_2'')L_2^{x,\mu},$$

which is another form of that last obtained, we obtain, by differentiating in regard to u_r', for $r = 1, 2$,

$$-\zeta_r(u^{x,a}-u')+\zeta_r(u^{\mu,a}-u')=[(x_1,x)-(x_1,\mu)]\frac{\partial x_1}{\partial u_r'}+[(x_2,x)-(x_2,\mu)]\frac{\partial x_2}{\partial u_r'}+L_r^{x,\mu};$$

therein we employ the notations expressed by

$$\zeta_r(u)=\frac{\partial}{\partial u_r}\log\vartheta(u), \qquad \wp_{rs}(u)=-\frac{\partial^2}{\partial u_r \partial u_s}\log\vartheta(u),$$

so that, from (p. 26) $\vartheta(u+\Omega_m)=\exp[H_m(u+\tfrac{1}{2}\Omega_m)-\pi i m m']\,\vartheta(u)$, we have

$$\zeta_r(u+\Omega_m)-\zeta_r(u)=(H_m)_r=2\eta_{r1}m_1+2\eta_{r2}m_2+2\eta'_{r1}m_1'+2\eta'_{r2}m_2',$$

and
$$\wp_{rs}(u+\Omega_m)=\wp_{rs}(u).$$

Now, by means of

$$du_1'=\frac{dx_1}{y_1}+\frac{dx_2}{y_2}, \qquad du_2'=\frac{x_1dx_1}{y_1}+\frac{x_2dx_2}{y_2},$$

the partial derivatives $\partial x_1/\partial u_r'$, $\partial x_2/\partial u_r'$ can be expressed; when this has been done, let (x_1), (x_2) be replaced by their conjugate places, by changing (x_1, y_1) into $(x_1, -y_1)$ and (x_2, y_2) into $(x_2, -y_2)$; thereby $u_r'=u_r^{x_1,a_1}+u_r^{x_2,a_2}$ is changed to

$$-u_r'+2\omega_{r1}m_1+2\omega_{r2}m_2+2\omega'_{r1}m_1'+2\omega'_{r2}m_2',$$

where m_1, m_2, m_1', m_2' are certain integers; as $\zeta_r(u+\Omega_m)-\zeta_r(u)$ depends on these integers and not on u, the left side of the equation at the top of this page becomes

$$-\zeta_r(u^{x,a}+u')+\zeta_r(u^{\mu,a}+u');$$

thence the equation is found to have the form

$$L_r^{x,\mu}+L_r^{x_1,\mu}+L_r^{x_2,\mu}+\zeta_r(u^{x,a}+u')-\tfrac{1}{2}f_r(x,x_1,x_2)$$
$$=L_r^{x_1,\mu}+L_r^{x_2,\mu}+\zeta_r(u^{\mu,u}+u')-\tfrac{1}{2}f_r(\mu,x_1,x_2),$$

where the two functions $f_r(x, x_1, x_2)$ are those given by

$$f_1(x,x_1,x_2)=\frac{y(x-x_1-x_2)}{(x-x_1)(x-x_2)}+\frac{y_1(x_1-x-x_2)}{(x_1-x)(x_1-x_2)}+\frac{y_2(x_2-x-x_1)}{(x_2-x)(x_2-x_1)},$$

$$f_2(x,x_1,x_2)=\frac{y}{(x-x_1)(x-x_2)}+\frac{y_1}{(x_1-x)(x_1-x_2)}+\frac{y_2}{(x_2-x)(x_2-x_1)};$$

the left side of the equation is thus symmetrical in (x), (x_1), (x_2), and the right side is obtained from the left by putting (μ) for (x). It follows that the left side is independent of (x), (x_1), (x_2), and we have therefore

$$L_r^{x_1,a_1}+L_r^{x_2,a_2}+\zeta_r(u^{x,a}+u^{x_1,a_1}+u^{x_2,a_2})=C_r+\tfrac{1}{2}f_r(x,x_1,x_2)-L_r^{x,\mu},$$

where C_r is independent of (x), (x_1), (x_2). In this equation allow (x) to approach indefinitely near to the branch place a, which we now suppose to be at infinity; the limit of the left side is perfectly definite; so therefore is that of the right side; the right side may be regarded as the sum of two parts; for $r = 1$ these parts are

$$A_1 = C_1 + \tfrac{1}{2}\frac{y(x - x_1 - x_2)}{(x - x_1)(x - x_2)} - L_1^{x,\mu}, \quad B_1 = \tfrac{1}{2}\frac{y_1(x_1 - x - x_2)}{(x_1 - x)(x_1 - x_2)} + \tfrac{1}{2}\frac{y_2(x_2 - x - x_1)}{(x_2 - x)(x_2 - x_1)},$$

and for $r = 2$ they are

$$A_2 = C_2 + \tfrac{1}{2}\frac{y}{(x - x_1)(x - x_2)} - L_2^{x,\mu}, \quad B_2 = \tfrac{1}{2}\frac{y_1}{(x_1 - x)(x_1 - x_2)} + \tfrac{1}{2}\frac{y_2}{(x_2 - x)(x_2 - x_1)};$$

the limits of B_1 and B_2 when (x) approaches the branch place at infinity are respectively

$$(B_1) = \tfrac{1}{2}\frac{y_1 - y_2}{x_1 - x_2}, \qquad (B_2) = 0;$$

as to the limits of A_1 and A_2, we know them to be finite, and it can be shewn that they are independent of (x_1) and (x_2): the fundamental equation being taken in the form $y^2 = \lambda_0 + \lambda_1 x + \ldots + \lambda_4 x^4 + 4x^5$, we put $x = t^{-2}$, $y = \frac{1}{2}t^{-5}(1 + \frac{1}{4}\lambda_4 t^2 + \ldots)^{\frac{1}{2}}$, and expand in powers of t; the negative powers in $\frac{1}{2}y(x - x_1 - x_2)/(x - x_1)(x - x_2)$ and $\frac{1}{2}y/(x - x_1)(x - x_2)$ will, of course, as may also be verified by computation, cancel the negative powers respectively in $L_1^{x,\mu}$ and $L_2^{x,\mu}$; the positive powers of t will vanish with t; the terms independent of t are the limits required; but both

$$\tfrac{1}{2}y(x - x_1 - x_2)/(x - x_1)(x - x_2) \quad \text{and} \quad \tfrac{1}{2}y/(x - x_1)(x - x_2)$$

are changed in sign when the sign of y is changed—the expansions of these thus contain only odd powers of t and no terms independent of t; if λ_1, λ_2 be the terms independent of t in $L_1^{x,\mu}$ and $L_2^{x,\mu}$, the limits of A_1 and A_2 are thus $C_1 - \lambda_1$ and $C_2 - \lambda_2$, and these are independent of (x_1) and (x_2): in fact they are both zero; for, being the values of

$$L_1^{x_1, a_1} + L_1^{x_2, a_2} + \zeta_1(u^{x_1, a_1} + u^{x_2, a_2}) - \tfrac{1}{2}\frac{y_1 - y_2}{x_1 - x_2}, \quad L_2^{x_1, a_1} + L_2^{x_2, a_2} + \zeta_2(u^{x_1, a_1} + u^{x_2, a_2}),$$

and being independent of (x_1) and (x_2), they may be obtained from these expressions by writing herein $(x_1) = (a_1)$ and $(x_2) = (a_2)$; as $\vartheta(u)$ is an even function of u, the functions $\zeta_1(u)$, $\zeta_2(u)$ are both odd functions, and vanish for $u = 0$.

If then we put

$$u_r = u_r^{x_1, a_1} + u_r^{x_2, a_2}, \qquad (r = 1, 2)$$

we have proved that

$$-\zeta_1(u) = L_1^{x_1, a_1} + L_1^{x_2, a_2} - \tfrac{1}{2}\frac{y_1 - y_2}{x_1 - x_2}, \qquad -\zeta_2(u) = L_2^{x_1, a_1} + L_2^{x_2, a_2}.$$

We now differentiate these expressions in regard to u_1 and u_2; the fundamental equation having the form

$$y^2 = \lambda_0 + \lambda_1 x + \lambda_2 x^2 + \lambda_3 x^3 + \lambda_4 x^4 + 4x^5,$$

as we suppose, we have

$$\frac{\partial x_1}{\partial u_1} = -\frac{x_2 y_1}{x_1 - x_2}, \quad \frac{\partial x_1}{\partial u_2} = \frac{y_1}{x_1 - x_2}, \quad \frac{\partial x_2}{\partial u_1} = \frac{x_1 y_2}{x_1 - x_2}, \quad \frac{\partial x_2}{\partial u_2} = -\frac{y_2}{x_1 - x_2},$$

$$L_1^{x,\,a} = \int_a^x \frac{\lambda_3 x + 2\lambda_4 x^2 + 12x^3}{4y}\,dx, \quad L_2^{x,\,a} = \int_a^x \frac{x^2 dx}{y};$$

putting $$F(x_1, x_2) = \sum_{r=0}^{r=2} x_1^r x_2^r \left[2\lambda_{2r} + \lambda_{2r+1}(x_1 + x_2)\right],$$

and, as before, $$\wp_{rs}(u) = -\frac{\partial^2 \log \sigma(u)}{\partial u_r \partial u_s},$$

we thus find

$$\wp_{22}(u) = x_1 + x_2, \quad \wp_{21}(u) = -x_1 x_2, \quad \wp_{11}(u) = \frac{F(x_1, x_2) - 2y_1 y_2}{4(x_1 - x_2)^2}.$$

From these, if $$\wp_{rst}(u) = \frac{\partial \wp_{rs}(u)}{\partial u_t},$$

we obtain

$$\wp_{222}(u) = \frac{y_1 - y_2}{x_1 - x_2}, \quad \wp_{221}(u) = \frac{x_1 y_2 - x_2 y_1}{x_1 - x_2}, \quad \wp_{211}(u) = -\frac{x_1^2 y_2 - x_2^2 y_1}{x_1 - x_2},$$

and $$\wp_{111}(u) = \frac{y_2 \psi(x_1, x_2) - y_1 \psi(x_2, x_1)}{4(x_1 - x_2)^3},$$

where

$$\psi(x_1, x_2) = 4\lambda_0 + \lambda_1(3x_1 + x_2) + 2\lambda_2 x_1(x_1 + x_2) + \lambda_3 x_1^2(x_1 + 3x_2) + 4\lambda_4 x_1^3 x_2 + 4x_1^3 x_2(3x_1 + x_2).$$

Thus we have

$$y_1 = x_1 \wp_{222}(u) + \wp_{221}(u), \quad y_2 = x_2 \wp_{222}(u) + \wp_{221}(u),$$

and these, together with the fact that x_1, x_2 are the roots of the equation

$$x^2 - x\wp_{22}(u) - \wp_{21}(u) = 0,$$

give the solution of the inversion problem expressed by the equations

$$u_1^{x_1,\,a_1} + u_1^{x_2,\,a_2} = u_1, \quad u_2^{x_1,\,a_1} + u_2^{x_2,\,a_2} = u_2.$$

It can be shewn, from the values of $\wp_{22}(u)$, $\wp_{21}(u)$, $\wp_{11}(u)$ in terms of the two places (x_1), (x_2), by elimination of these, that there exists the equation

$$\begin{vmatrix} -\lambda_0 & \tfrac{1}{2}\lambda_1 & 2\wp_{11} & -2\wp_{12} \\ \tfrac{1}{2}\lambda_1 & -(\lambda_2 + 4\wp_{11}) & \tfrac{1}{2}\lambda_3 + 2\wp_{12} & 2\wp_{22} \\ 2\wp_{11} & \tfrac{1}{2}\lambda_3 + 2\wp_{12} & -(\lambda_4 + 4\wp_{22}) & 2 \\ -2\wp_{12} & 2\wp_{22} & 2 & 0 \end{vmatrix} = 0;$$

further, from the values of $\wp_{222}(u)$, $\wp_{221}(u)$, $\wp_{211}(u)$, $\wp_{111}(u)$, that these functions are in the ratios of the minors of the elements of any row of this vanishing determinant, and that their squares and products, such as $\wp^2_{222}$, $\wp_{222}\wp_{221}$, are all rational integral polynomials of the third degree in $\wp_{22}$, $\wp_{21}$, $\wp_{11}$; in particular

$$\wp^2_{222} - \lambda_2 - \lambda_3\wp_{22} - \lambda_4\wp_{22}^2 - 4\wp_{22}\wp_{21} - 4\wp_{22}^3,$$

$$= (y_1 - y_2)^2/(x_1 - x_2)^2 - \lambda_2 - \lambda_3(x_1 + x_2) - \lambda_4(x_1 + x_2)^2 + 4x_1x_2(x_1 + x_2) - 4(x_1 + x_2)^3,$$

is at once found to be $(x_1 - x_2)^{-2}[F(x_1, x_2) - 2y_1y_2]$, or $4\wp_{11}$; thus it is easy to see that $\wp^2_{222}$ is one-quarter the minor of the element $-\lambda_0$ in the first row and column of the determinant above; thus we have, for arbitrary values of l_0, l_1, l_2, l_3,

$$(l_0\wp_{222} + l_1\wp_{221} + l_2\wp_{211} + l_3\wp_{111})^2 = -\tfrac{1}{4}\begin{vmatrix} -\lambda_0 & \tfrac{1}{2}\lambda_1 & 2\wp_{11} & -2\wp_{12} & l_0 \\ \tfrac{1}{2}\lambda_1 & -(\lambda_2 + 4\wp_{11}) & \tfrac{1}{2}\lambda_3 + 2\wp_{12} & 2\wp_{22} & l_1 \\ 2\wp_{11} & \tfrac{1}{2}\lambda_3 + 2\wp_{12} & -(\lambda_4 + 4\wp_{22}) & 2 & l_2 \\ -2\wp_{12} & 2\wp_{22} & 2 & 0 & l_3 \\ l_0 & l_1 & l_2 & l_3 & 0 \end{vmatrix}.$$

We shall however obtain these results from a somewhat different and more interesting point of view, as follows in the next chapter.

Note. It may add to simplicity to anticipate later discussions by the following remarks. If we write $x = \wp_{22}(u)$, $y = \wp_{21}(u)$, $z = \wp_{11}(u)$, and denote the above symmetrical determinant of four rows and columns by Δ, the equation $\Delta = 0$ represents a quartic surface having a node at $x = 0$, $y = 0$, $z = \infty$; the equation is in fact a quadratic in z. For any value of θ the plane $\theta^2 - \theta x - y = 0$ is a tangent plane of the nodal cone, whose equation is at once found to be $x^2 + 4y = 0$, and two such planes $\theta^2 - \theta x - y = 0$, $\phi^2 - \phi x - y = 0$ cut in the line $x = \theta + \phi$, $y = -\theta\phi$. The equation $\Delta = 0$ can be found easily to reduce, when $x = \theta + \phi$, $y = -\theta\phi$, to

$$[4(\theta - \phi)^2 z - F(\theta, \phi)]^2 = 4f(\theta)f(\phi),$$

where $f(x) = \lambda_0 + \lambda_1 x + \dots + \lambda_4 x^4 + 4x^5$. We have thus the parametric representation of the surface in terms of two arbitrary parameters θ, ϕ. The equation $\Delta = 0$ may be supposed to arise geometrically as follows. If ξ, η, ζ, τ be homogeneous coordinates, and

$$Q_1 = 4(\eta\tau - \zeta^2), \quad Q_2 = 4(\eta\zeta - \xi\tau), \quad Q_3 = 4(\zeta\xi - \eta^2),$$

$$P_4 = -\lambda_0\xi^2 + \lambda_1\xi\eta - \lambda_2\eta^2 + \lambda_3\eta\zeta - \lambda_4\zeta^2 + 4\zeta\tau,$$

the equation $$Q = xQ_1 + yQ_2 + zQ_3 + P_4 = 0,$$

for varying parameters x, y, z, represents a system of quadric surfaces having six common points, namely those where the cubic space curve

$$\xi/1 = -\eta/\theta = \zeta/\theta^2 = -\tau/\theta^3$$

is intersected by the quadric $P_4 = 0$; these are $(0, 0, 0, 1)$ and the five points θ of the cubic curve in which θ is one of the roots of $f(\theta) = 0$. The quadric Q will be a cone of vertex (ξ, η, ζ, τ) if the four equations $\partial Q/\partial\xi = 0$, $\partial Q/\partial\eta = 0$,

$\partial Q/\partial \zeta = 0$, $\partial Q/\partial \tau = 0$ be satisfied; eliminating ξ, η, ζ, τ from these equations we have the relation $\Delta = 0$. If we eliminate x, y, z we obtain also a homogeneous quartic relation for ξ, η, ζ, τ, say $\omega = 0$, given at length below; this is capable of being put into the form

$$3\left(\frac{\partial P_4}{\partial \xi}\frac{\partial F}{\partial \tau} - \frac{\partial P_4}{\partial \tau}\frac{\partial F}{\partial \xi}\right) = \frac{\partial P_4}{\partial \eta}\frac{\partial F}{\partial \zeta} - \frac{\partial P_4}{\partial \zeta}\frac{\partial F}{\partial \eta},$$

where
$$F = 6\xi\eta\zeta\tau - 4\zeta^3\xi - 4\eta^3\tau + 3\eta^2\zeta^2 - \xi^2\tau^2,$$

and represents a quartic surface having nodes at the common points of the quadrics $Q_1 = 0$, $Q_2 = 0$, $Q_3 = 0$, $P_4 = 0$. Any point of the chord (θ, ϕ) of the space cubic is represented by

$$\xi = 1 + m, \quad \eta = -(\theta + m\phi), \quad \zeta = \theta^2 + m\phi^2, \quad \tau = -(\theta^3 + m\phi^3);$$

by substitution of these in the equation $\omega = 0$ we find that this chord cuts the surface in

$$\xi = \Theta - \Phi, \quad \eta = -\Theta\phi + \Phi\theta, \quad \zeta = \Theta\phi^2 - \Phi\theta^2, \quad \tau = -\Theta\phi^3 + \Phi\theta^3,$$

and another point obtained from this by changing the sign of Φ, where

$$\Theta^2 = f(\theta), \quad \Phi^2 = f(\phi);$$

as a chord of the space cubic can be drawn through an arbitrary point of space, these formulae give a parametric representation of the surface $\omega = 0$ in terms of two arbitrary parameters θ, ϕ.

Further, it is not difficult to verify that the equation

$$Q_2(\xi')\,Q_1(\xi) - Q_1(\xi')\,Q_2(\xi) - P_4(\xi')\,Q_3(\xi) + Q_3(\xi')\,P_4(\xi) = 0,$$

when $(\xi', \eta', \zeta', \tau')$ is any point on $\omega = 0$, represents a cone whose vertex is the remaining intersection with $\omega = 0$ of the line joining the node $(0, 0, 0, 1)$ of $\omega = 0$ to the point $(\xi', \eta', \zeta', \tau')$; putting, as above,

$$\xi' = \Theta - \Phi, \quad \eta' = -\Theta\phi + \Phi\theta, \text{ etc.},$$

we find

$$Q_2(\xi') : Q_1(\xi') : P_4(\xi') : Q_3(\xi') = \theta + \phi : \theta\phi : -E_{\theta,\phi} : 1,$$

where
$$E_{\theta,\phi} = \tfrac{1}{4}[F(\theta, \phi) - 2\Theta\Phi]\,(\theta - \phi)^{-2};$$

the cone has therefore the form

$$(\theta + \phi)\,Q_1(\xi) - \theta\phi Q_2(\xi) + E_{\theta,\phi}Q_3(\xi) + P_4(\xi) = 0,$$

and this, compared with $xQ_1 + yQ_2 + zQ_3 + P_4 = 0$, gives the preceding parametric expression for $\Delta = 0$,

$$x = \theta + \phi, \quad y = -\theta\phi, \quad z = E_{\theta,\phi}.$$

It will be found that the surface $\omega = 0$ is also represented parametrically by means of

$$\xi = \wp_{222}(u), \quad \eta = \wp_{221}(u), \quad \zeta = \wp_{211}(u), \quad \tau = \wp_{111}(u).$$

CHAPTER II.

THE DIFFERENTIAL EQUATIONS FOR THE SIGMA FUNCTIONS.

12. SUPPOSE now that x, y, z, which we may regard as the coordinates of a point in three dimensions, satisfy the equation

$$\Delta = \begin{vmatrix} -\lambda_0 & \tfrac{1}{2}\lambda_1 & 2z & -2y \\ \tfrac{1}{2}\lambda_1 & -(\lambda_2+4z) & \tfrac{1}{2}\lambda_3+2y & 2x \\ 2z & \tfrac{1}{2}\lambda_3+2y & -(\lambda_4+4x) & 2 \\ -2y & 2x & 2 & 0 \end{vmatrix} = 0,$$

that is, lie upon a quartic surface, the properties of which will more particularly concern us later; let Δ_{ij} denote the minor, in this determinant, of the jth element of the ith row. We find on expansion

$$\tfrac{1}{4}\Delta_{11} = \lambda_2 + \lambda_3 x + \lambda_4 x^2 + 4xy + 4x^3 + 4z,$$

$$\tfrac{1}{4}\Delta_{22} = \lambda_0 + \lambda_4 y^2 + 4xy^2 - 4yz,$$

$$\tfrac{1}{4}\Delta_{33} = \lambda_0 x^2 - \lambda_1 xy + \lambda_2 y^2 + 4y^2 z,$$

$$\tfrac{1}{4}\Delta_{44} = \tfrac{1}{16}(\lambda_1^2\lambda_4 + \lambda_0\lambda_3^2 - 4\lambda_0\lambda_2\lambda_4) + (\tfrac{1}{4}\lambda_1^2 - \lambda_0\lambda_2)\,x$$
$$+ \tfrac{1}{2}\lambda_0\lambda_3 y + (\tfrac{1}{4}\lambda_1\lambda_3 - \lambda_0\lambda_4)\,z + \lambda_0 y^2 + \lambda_1 yz + \lambda_2 z^2 - 4\lambda_0 xz + 4z^3,$$

$$\tfrac{1}{4}\Delta_{12} = \tfrac{1}{2}\lambda_1 + \tfrac{1}{2}\lambda_3 y + \lambda_4 xy - 2xz + 2y^2 + 4x^2 y,$$

$$\tfrac{1}{4}\Delta_{13} = -\tfrac{1}{2}\lambda_1 x + \lambda_2 y + \tfrac{1}{2}\lambda_3 xy + 4yz + 2x^2 z + 2xy^2,$$

$$\tfrac{1}{4}\Delta_{14} = -\tfrac{1}{8}\lambda_1\lambda_3 - \tfrac{1}{4}\lambda_1\lambda_4 x + (\tfrac{1}{2}\lambda_2\lambda_4 - \tfrac{1}{2}\lambda_1 - \tfrac{1}{8}\lambda_3^2)\,y - \lambda_2 z$$
$$- \lambda_1 x^2 + 2\lambda_2 xy - \lambda_3 y^2 - \tfrac{1}{2}\lambda_3 xz + 2\lambda_4 yz - 2y^3 + 6xyz - 4z^2,$$

$$\tfrac{1}{4}\Delta_{23} = -\lambda_0 x + \tfrac{1}{2}\lambda_1 y + \tfrac{1}{2}\lambda_3 y^2 + 2y^3 + 2xyz,$$

$$\tfrac{1}{4}\Delta_{24} = -\tfrac{1}{4}\lambda_0\lambda_3 - \tfrac{1}{2}\lambda_0\lambda_4 x + (\tfrac{1}{4}\lambda_1\lambda_4 - \lambda_0)\,y - \tfrac{1}{2}\lambda_1 z - 2\lambda_0 x^2 + \lambda_1 xy + \tfrac{1}{2}\lambda_3 yz$$
$$+ 2y^2 z + 2xz^2,$$

$$\tfrac{1}{4}\Delta_{34} = \tfrac{1}{8}\lambda_1^2 - \tfrac{1}{2}\lambda_0\lambda_2 - \tfrac{1}{4}\lambda_0\lambda_3 x + \tfrac{1}{8}\lambda_1\lambda_3 y - 2\lambda_0 z - \lambda_0 xy + \tfrac{1}{2}\lambda_1 y^2 - \tfrac{1}{2}\lambda_1 xz$$
$$+ \lambda_2 yz + 4yz^2,$$

while Δ itself is given by

$$\tfrac{1}{16}\Delta = \tfrac{1}{16}\lambda_1^2 - \tfrac{1}{4}\lambda_0\lambda_2 - \tfrac{1}{4}\lambda_0\lambda_3 x + \tfrac{1}{8}\lambda_1\lambda_3 y - \lambda_0 z - \tfrac{1}{4}\lambda_0\lambda_4 x^2 + (\tfrac{1}{4}\lambda_1\lambda_4 - \lambda_0)\,xy$$
$$+ (\tfrac{1}{2}\lambda_1 - \tfrac{1}{4}\lambda_2\lambda_4 + \tfrac{1}{16}\lambda_3^2)\,y^2 - \tfrac{1}{2}\lambda_1 xz + \lambda_2 yz - \lambda_0 x^3 + \lambda_1 x^2 y - \lambda_2 xy^2$$
$$+ \tfrac{1}{2}\lambda_3(y^3 + xyz) - \lambda_4 y^2 z + 4yz^2 + (xz - y^2)^2.$$

Now let ξ, η, ζ, τ be four quantities determined by

$$\xi^2 = \tfrac{1}{4}\Delta_{11} = \lambda_2 + \lambda_3 x + \lambda_4 x^2 + 4xy + 4x^3 + 4z,$$

and

$$\frac{\xi}{\Delta_{11}} = \frac{\eta}{\Delta_{12}} = \frac{\zeta}{\Delta_{13}} = \frac{\tau}{\Delta_{14}},$$

wherein, it is understood that x, y, z are supposed subject to the relation $\Delta = 0$; then, as Δ is symmetrical,

$$\eta^2 = \left(\frac{\eta}{\xi}\right)^2 \xi^2 = \frac{1}{4}\left(\frac{\Delta_{12}}{\Delta_{11}}\right)^2 \Delta_{11} = \frac{1}{4}\frac{\Delta_{11}\Delta_{22}}{\Delta_{11}} = \tfrac{1}{4}\Delta_{22},$$

$$\xi\eta = \frac{\eta}{\xi}\xi^2 = \frac{1}{4}\cdot\frac{\Delta_{12}}{\Delta_{11}}\Delta_{11} = \tfrac{1}{4}\Delta_{12},$$

and so on.

If now

$$P = \xi\frac{\partial}{\partial x} + \eta\frac{\partial}{\partial y} + \zeta\frac{\partial}{\partial z}, \quad Q = \eta\frac{\partial}{\partial x} + \zeta\frac{\partial}{\partial y} + \tau\frac{\partial}{\partial z};$$

it can be easily verified that

$$P\eta = Q\xi, \quad P\zeta = Q\eta, \quad P\tau = Q\zeta.$$

For, of these, the first equation, multiplying by $\xi\eta$, is the same as

$$\left(\Delta_{11}\frac{\partial}{\partial x} + \Delta_{12}\frac{\partial}{\partial y} + \Delta_{13}\frac{\partial}{\partial z}\right)\Delta_{22} = \left(\Delta_{22}\frac{\partial}{\partial x} + \Delta_{23}\frac{\partial}{\partial y} + \Delta_{24}\frac{\partial}{\partial z}\right)\Delta_{11},$$

or

$$\Delta_{11}(4y^2) + \Delta_{12}(2\lambda_4 y + 8xy - 4z) + \Delta_{13}(-4y) = \Delta_{22}(\lambda_3 + 2\lambda_4 x + 4y + 12x^2) + \Delta_{23}(4x) + \Delta_{24}(4);$$

from the determinant we have

$$0 = 2y\left[-2y\Delta_{11} + 2x\Delta_{12} + 2\Delta_{13}\right],$$

$$0 = -2\left[2z\Delta_{21} + (2y + \tfrac{1}{2}\lambda_3)\Delta_{22} - (4x + \lambda_4)\Delta_{23} + 2\Delta_{24}\right] - (\lambda_4 + 6x)\left[-2y\Delta_{21} + 2x\Delta_{22} + 2\Delta_{23}\right];$$

adding these respectively to the two sides of the equation to be proved, it reduces to the identity

$$\Delta_{12}(2\lambda_4 y + 12xy - 4z) = \Delta_{21}(2\lambda_4 y + 12xy - 4z).$$

The second equation, multiplying by $\eta\zeta$, is the same as

$$\left(\Delta_{21}\frac{\partial}{\partial x} + \Delta_{22}\frac{\partial}{\partial y} + \Delta_{23}\frac{\partial}{\partial z}\right)\Delta_{33} = \left(\Delta_{32}\frac{\partial}{\partial x} + \Delta_{33}\frac{\partial}{\partial y} + \Delta_{34}\frac{\partial}{\partial z}\right)\Delta_{22},$$

or

$$\Delta_{21}(2\lambda_0 x - \lambda_1 y) + \Delta_{22}(-\lambda_1 x + 2\lambda_2 y + 8yz) + \Delta_{23}(4y^2) = \Delta_{32}(4y^2) + \Delta_{33}(2\lambda_4 y + 8xy - 4z) + \Delta_{34}(-4y);$$

the determinant gives

$$0 = 2x\,[-\lambda_0\Delta_{21} + \tfrac{1}{2}\lambda_1\Delta_{22} + 2z\Delta_{23} - 2y\Delta_{24}]$$
$$+ 2y\,[\tfrac{1}{2}\lambda_1\Delta_{21} - (4z+\lambda_2)\,\Delta_{22} + (2y+\tfrac{1}{2}\lambda_3)\,\Delta_{23} + 2x\Delta_{24}]\,;$$

$$0 = 2y\,[2z\Delta_{31} + (2y+\tfrac{1}{2}\lambda_3)\,\Delta_{32} - (4x+\lambda_4)\,\Delta_{33} + 2\Delta_{34}]$$
$$+ 2z\,[-2y\Delta_{31} + 2x\Delta_{32} + 2\Delta_{33}]\,;$$

adding these respectively to the two sides of the equation to be proved it reduces to the identity

$$\Delta_{23}\,(8y^2 + 4xz + \lambda_3 y) = \Delta_{32}\,(8y^2 + 4xz + \lambda_3 y).$$

Similarly with the equation $P\tau = Q\zeta$.

The relation connecting x, y, z, and the equations defining ξ, η, ζ, τ, enable us to express z rationally in x, y, ξ, namely

$$z = \tfrac{1}{4}\,[\xi^2 - \lambda_2 - \lambda_3 x - \lambda_4 x^2 - 4xy - 4x^3],$$

and so to replace $\Delta = 0$ by a rational integral equation $\Psi(x, y, \xi) = 0$, while η, ζ, τ are rationally expressible by x, y, ξ. The equation $\Psi(x, y, \xi) = 0$ may be interpreted as that of a surface of the eighth order, two points of which correspond to any one point of $\Delta = 0$, but one point of $\Delta = 0$ to any one point of this. We consider now two integrals of the form

$$w_2 = \int (A\,dx + B\,dy), \quad w_1 = \int (C\,dx + D\,dy),$$

where A, B, C, D are certain rational functions of x, y, ξ; namely we put

$$dw_2 = \frac{\zeta dx - \eta dy}{\zeta\xi - \eta^2}, \quad dw_1 = \frac{-\eta dx + \xi dy}{\zeta\xi - \eta^2}\,;$$

the conditions that these should be perfect differentials,

$$\frac{d}{dy}\left(\frac{\zeta}{\zeta\xi - \eta^2}\right) + \frac{d}{dx}\left(\frac{\eta}{\zeta\xi - \eta^2}\right) = 0, \quad \frac{d}{dx}\left(\frac{\xi}{\zeta\xi - \eta^2}\right) + \frac{d}{dy}\left(\frac{\eta}{\zeta\xi - \eta^2}\right) = 0,$$

wherein $\displaystyle \frac{d}{dx} = \frac{\partial}{\partial x} - \left(\frac{\partial\Delta}{\partial x}\Big/\frac{\partial\Delta}{\partial z}\right)\frac{\partial}{\partial z}; \quad \frac{d}{dy} = \frac{\partial}{\partial y} - \left(\frac{\partial\Delta}{\partial y}\Big/\frac{\partial\Delta}{\partial z}\right)\frac{\partial}{\partial z}$,

are at once verified; for, from the unexpanded determinant Δ we have

$$\frac{\partial\Delta}{\partial x} = 2\Delta_{24} - 4\Delta_{33} + 2\Delta_{42} = 4\,(\Delta_{24} - \Delta_{33}) = 16\,(\eta\tau - \zeta^2),$$

$$\frac{\partial\Delta}{\partial y} = -2\Delta_{14} + 2\Delta_{23} + 2\Delta_{32} - 2\Delta_{41} = 4\,(\Delta_{23} - \Delta_{14}) = 16\,(\eta\zeta - \xi\tau),$$

$$\frac{\partial\Delta}{\partial z} = 2\Delta_{13} - 4\Delta_{22} + 2\Delta_{31} = 4\,(\Delta_{13} - \Delta_{22}) = 16\,(\zeta\xi - \eta^2),$$

and hence

$$\xi\frac{d}{dx}+\eta\frac{d}{dy}=\xi\frac{\partial}{\partial x}+\eta\frac{\partial}{\partial y}-\frac{\xi(\eta\tau-\zeta^2)+\eta(\eta\zeta-\xi\tau)}{\zeta\xi-\eta^2}\frac{\partial}{\partial z}$$
$$=\xi\frac{\partial}{\partial x}+\eta\frac{\partial}{\partial y}+\zeta\frac{\partial}{\partial z}=P,$$
$$\eta\frac{d}{dx}+\zeta\frac{d}{dy}=\eta\frac{\partial}{\partial x}+\zeta\frac{\partial}{\partial y}-\frac{\eta(\eta\tau-\zeta^2)+\zeta(\eta\zeta-\xi\tau)}{\zeta\xi-\eta^2}\frac{\partial}{\partial z}$$
$$=\eta\frac{\partial}{\partial x}+\zeta\frac{\partial}{\partial y}+\tau\frac{\partial}{\partial z}=Q,$$

giving $$(\zeta\xi-\eta^2)\frac{d}{dx}=\zeta P-\eta Q,\quad (\zeta\xi-\eta^2)\frac{d}{dy}=\xi Q-\eta P;$$

the conditions are

$$(\zeta\xi-\eta^2)\left(\frac{d\xi}{dx}+\frac{d\eta}{dy}\right)-\left(\xi\frac{d}{dx}+\eta\frac{d}{dy}\right)(\zeta\xi-\eta^2)=0,$$
$$(\zeta\xi-\eta^2)\left(\frac{d\eta}{dx}+\frac{d\zeta}{dy}\right)-\left(\eta\frac{d}{dx}+\zeta\frac{d}{dy}\right)(\zeta\xi-\eta^2)=0,$$

or

$$\zeta P\xi-\eta Q\xi+\xi Q\eta-\eta P\eta=P(\zeta\xi-\eta^2),\quad \zeta P\eta-\eta Q\eta+\xi Q\zeta-\eta P\zeta=Q(\zeta\xi-\eta^2),$$

and in virtue of $P\eta=Q\xi$, $P\zeta=Q\eta$, these are the identities

$$\zeta P\xi-\eta P\eta+\xi P\zeta-\eta P\eta=P(\zeta\xi-\eta^2),\quad \zeta Q\xi-\eta Q\eta+\xi Q\zeta-\eta Q\eta=Q(\zeta\xi-\eta^2).$$

Putting $\frac{1}{16}\Delta=\Psi(x, y, \xi)$, we have $\zeta\xi-\eta^2=\frac{1}{16}\frac{\partial\Delta}{\partial z}=\frac{2}{\xi}\frac{\partial\Psi}{\partial\xi}$, and

$$w_2=\tfrac{1}{2}\int\frac{\zeta\xi dx-\xi\eta dy}{\partial\Psi/\partial\xi}=\tfrac{1}{8}\int(\Delta_{13}dx-\Delta_{12}dy)\Big/\frac{\partial\Psi}{\partial\xi},$$
$$w_1=\tfrac{1}{2}\int\frac{-\xi\eta dx+\xi^2 dy}{\partial\Psi/\partial\xi}=\tfrac{1}{8}\int(-\Delta_{12}dx+\Delta_{11}dy)\Big/\frac{\partial\Psi}{\partial\xi},$$

wherein Δ_{13}, Δ_{12}, Δ_{11}, $\partial\Psi/\partial\xi$ may be expressed as rational functions of ξ, x, y.

It may be verified directly that for all values of x, y, ξ, even infinite values, satisfying the equation $\Psi(x, y, \xi)=0$, these integrals are finite. For the sake of brevity however we shall follow the easier plan of shewing that they are reducible to familiar forms.

For this, define two quantities t_1, t_2 by means of the equations

$$t_1+t_2=x,\quad t_1t_2=-y,$$

and thence two quantities s_1, s_2 by means of the equations

$$s_1=t_1\xi+\eta,\quad s_2=t_2\xi+\eta,$$

wherein η is the rational function of x, y, ξ given by $\eta = \xi\Delta_{12}/\Delta_{11}$. Then from the explicit equations

$$\xi^2 = \tfrac{1}{4}\Delta_{11}, \quad \xi\eta = \tfrac{1}{4}\Delta_{12}, \quad \eta^2 = \tfrac{1}{4}\Delta_{22},$$

it is at once verified that

$$s_1^2 = \lambda_0 + \lambda_1 t_1 + \lambda_2 t_1^2 + \lambda_3 t_1^3 + \lambda_4 t_1^4 + 4t_1^5, = f(t_1), \text{ say},$$

and $\quad s_2^2 = f(t_2),$

and also that

$$s_1 s_2 = -y\xi^2 + x\xi\eta + \eta^2 = \tfrac{1}{4}(-y\Delta_{11} + x\Delta_{12} + \Delta_{22}),$$

which, from the equation $\Delta = 0$, is the same as

$$s_1 s_2 = \tfrac{1}{4}(\Delta_{22} - \Delta_{13}) = -(\zeta\xi - \eta^2);$$

thus
$$dw_2 = \frac{\zeta(dt_1 + dt_2) + \eta(t_2 dt_1 + t_1 dt_2)}{-s_1 s_2},$$

and since, from $\Delta = 0$, $-y\xi + x\eta + \zeta = 0$, or $\zeta = -(t_1 + t_2)\eta - t_1 t_2 \xi = -\eta t_2 - t_1 s_2$, this gives

$$dw_2 = \frac{t_1 dt_1}{s_1} + \frac{t_2 dt_2}{s_2};$$

while
$$dw_1 = \frac{-\eta(dt_1 + dt_2) - \xi(t_2 dt_1 + t_1 dt_2)}{-s_1 s_2} = \frac{dt_1}{s_1} + \frac{dt_2}{s_2}.$$

Now we have developed the theory of these integrals in the preceding chapter; and we know thence that w_1, w_2 are always finite, and that x, y are single-valued functions of w_1, w_2; from their values $x = t_1 + t_2$, $y = -t_1 t_2$, coupled with $\xi = (s_1 - s_2)/(t_1 - t_2)$, $\xi^2 = \tfrac{1}{4}\Delta_{11}$, it can be calculated that

$$z = [F(t_1, t_2) - 2s_1 s_2] / 4(t_1 - t_2)^2,$$

and hence z is also a single-valued function, where as before

$$F(t_1, t_2) = \sum_{m=0} (t_1 t_2)^m [2\lambda_{2m} + \lambda_{2m+1}(t_1 + t_2)].$$

It is therefore possible to prove these facts as to x, y, z directly from the expressions

$$w_2 = \tfrac{1}{8}\int (\Delta_{13} dx - \Delta_{12} dy) \Big/ \frac{\partial \Psi}{\partial \xi}, \quad w_1 = \tfrac{1}{8}\int (-\Delta_{12} dx + \Delta_{11} dy) \Big/ \frac{\partial \Psi}{\partial \xi},$$

and, as will appear, it is of considerable theoretical interest to do this. These integral expressions shew then that the functions x, y of w_1, w_2 are such that

$$\frac{\partial x}{\partial w_2} = \xi, \quad \frac{\partial x}{\partial w_1} = \eta, \quad \frac{\partial y}{\partial w_2} = \eta, \quad \frac{\partial y}{\partial w_1} = \zeta,$$

and so
$$\frac{\partial x}{\partial w_1} = \frac{\partial y}{\partial w_2},$$

while, in virtue of the easily verifiable identity

$$\xi \frac{\partial \Delta}{\partial x} + \eta \frac{\partial \Delta}{\partial y} + \zeta \frac{\partial \Delta}{\partial z} = 0,$$

we have

$$\zeta = \xi \frac{\partial z}{\partial x} + \eta \frac{\partial z}{\partial y},$$

so that

$$\frac{\partial y}{\partial w_1} = \frac{\partial z}{\partial w_2};$$

thus we may introduce two functions of w_2, w_1 by means of

$$Z_2 = -\int (x\,dw_2 + y\,dw_1), \qquad Z_1 = -\int (y\,dw_2 + z\,dw_1);$$

then

$$\frac{\partial Z_2}{\partial w_1} = -y = \frac{\partial Z_1}{\partial w_2},$$

and we may introduce a function $\Sigma(w_1, w_2)$ by means of

$$\log \Sigma = \int (Z_2 dw_2 + Z_1 dw_1),$$

and so have

$$Z_1 = \frac{1}{\Sigma}\frac{\partial \Sigma}{\partial w_1}, \quad Z_2 = \frac{1}{\Sigma}\frac{\partial \Sigma}{\partial w_2}.$$

$$x = -\frac{\partial Z_2}{\partial w_2} = -\frac{\partial^2}{\partial w_2^2}\log \Sigma, \quad y = -\frac{\partial^2}{\partial w_2 \partial w_1}\log \Sigma, \quad z = -\frac{\partial^2}{\partial w_1^2}\log \Sigma;$$

and if these last be respectively called, for a little, P_{22}, P_{21}, P_{11}, we have

$$\xi = \frac{\partial x}{\partial w_2}, = P_{222}, \text{ say}, \quad \eta = \frac{\partial x}{\partial w_1} = \frac{\partial y}{\partial w_2}, = P_{221}, \text{ say}, \quad \zeta = \frac{\partial y}{\partial w_1} = \frac{\partial z}{\partial w_2}, = P_{211}, \text{ say},$$

while from the easily verifiable identity

$$\eta \frac{\partial \Delta}{\partial x} + \zeta \frac{\partial \Delta}{\partial y} + \tau \frac{\partial \Delta}{\partial z} = 0,$$

we have

$$\tau = \eta \frac{\partial z}{\partial x} + \zeta \frac{\partial z}{\partial y} = \frac{\partial z}{\partial w_1}, = P_{111}, \text{ say}.$$

The integrals Z_2, Z_1 agree in form with integrals previously considered; in fact

$$-dZ_2 = (t_1 + t_2)\left(\frac{t_1 dt_1}{s_1} + \frac{t_2 dt_2}{s_2}\right) - t_1 t_2 \left(\frac{dt_1}{s_1} + \frac{dt_2}{s_2}\right) = \frac{t_1^2 dt_1}{s_1} + \frac{t_2^2 dt_2}{s_2},$$

while

$$-dZ_1 = -t_1 t_2 \left(\frac{t_1 dt_1}{s_1} + \frac{t_2 dt_2}{s_2}\right) + \frac{F(t_1, t_2) - 2s_1 s_2}{4(t_1 - t_2)^2}\left(\frac{dt_1}{s_1} + \frac{dt_2}{s_2}\right),$$

and we can verify that

$$\frac{1}{4s_1}\left[\frac{F(t_1, t_2) - 2s_1 s_2}{(t_1 - t_2)^2} - 4t_1^2 t_2\right] = \frac{\lambda_3 t_1 + 2\lambda_4 t_1^2 + 12 t_1^3}{4s_1} - \tfrac{1}{2}\frac{d}{dt_1}\left(\frac{s_1 - s_2}{t_1 - t_2}\right),$$

this being, after changing s_2 into $-s_2$ and multiplying throughout by $\frac{1}{s_2}$, the same as the identity remarked, Chapter I., p. 10, namely

$$\frac{1}{4s_1 s_2}\frac{F(t_1, t_2) + 2s_1 s_2}{(t_1 - t_2)^2} = \frac{t_2}{s_2}\cdot\frac{t_1^2}{s_1} + \frac{1}{s_2}\cdot\frac{\lambda_3 t_1 + 2\lambda_4 t_1 + 12t_1^3}{4s_1} + \frac{d}{dt_1}\left(\frac{s_2 + s_1}{2s_2(t_2 - t_1)}\right);$$

thus in the notation previously used (p. 10)

$$-dZ_2 = dL_2^{t_1} + dL_2^{t_2}, \qquad -dZ_1 = dL_1^{t_1} + dL_1^{t_2} - d\left(\tfrac{1}{2}\frac{s_1 - s_2}{t_1 - t_2}\right).$$

On the whole then the integrals w_2, w_1 differ only by additive constants from the integrals previously used

$$u_1^{t_1, a_1} + u_1^{t_2, a_2}, \quad u_2^{t_1, a_1} + u_2^{t_2, a_2},$$

while Z_2, Z_1 differ only by arbitrary additive constants from the functions previously denoted (pp. 36, 37) by $\zeta_2(w_1, w_2)$, $\zeta_1(w_1, w_2)$ and the general form of function Σ is

$$e^{A_1 w_1 + A_2 w_2 + B}\,\vartheta(w_1 + C_1,\ w_2 + C_2),$$

where A_1, A_2, B, C_1, C_2 are arbitrary constants. This is a single-valued function, and an integral function; and the integrals thus make x, y, z quadruply-periodic functions of w_1, w_2.

But another consequence follows from these integral forms. From

$$P^2_{222} = \xi^2 = \tfrac{1}{4}\Delta_{11} = \lambda_2 + \lambda_3 x + \lambda_4 x^2 + 4xy + 4x^3 + 4z,$$

we have
$$2P_{222}P_{2222} = \tfrac{1}{4}\frac{\partial \Delta_{11}}{\partial w_2} = \tfrac{1}{4}\left(\xi\frac{\partial}{\partial x} + \eta\frac{\partial}{\partial y} + \zeta\frac{\partial}{\partial z}\right)\Delta_{11},$$

or
$$2\xi P_{2222} = \xi(\lambda_3 + 2\lambda_4 x + 4y + 12x^2) + \eta(4x) + 4\zeta,$$

which, since the form of Δ gives

$$-2y\xi + 2x\eta + 2\zeta = 0,$$

leads to
$$2\xi P_{2222} = \xi(\lambda_3 + 2\lambda_4 x + 4y + 12x^2) + 4y\xi,$$

so that
$$P_{2222} - 6P_{22}^2 = \tfrac{1}{2}\lambda_3 + \lambda_4 P_{22} + 4P_{21},$$

where
$$P_{2222} = \frac{\partial^2}{\partial w_2^2}P_{22}, \qquad P_{22} = -\frac{\partial^2}{\partial w_2^2}\log\Sigma, \text{ etc.}$$

Putting, as before,

$$P = \xi\frac{\partial}{\partial x} + \eta\frac{\partial}{\partial y} + \zeta\frac{\partial}{\partial z}, \qquad Q = \eta\frac{\partial}{\partial x} + \zeta\frac{\partial}{\partial y} + \tau\frac{\partial}{\partial z},$$

it may be shewn that

$$P\xi = 6x^2 + \tfrac{1}{2}\lambda_3 + \lambda_4 x + 4y, \qquad P\eta = Q\xi = 6xy + \lambda_4 y - 2z,$$
$$P\zeta = Q\eta = 4y^2 + 2xz + \tfrac{1}{2}\lambda_3 y, \quad P\tau = Q\zeta = 6yz - \lambda_0 - \tfrac{1}{2}\lambda_1 x + \lambda_2 y,$$

and hence, from the equations

$$P^2_{222} = \tfrac{1}{4}\Delta_{11}, \quad P^2_{221} = \tfrac{1}{4}\Delta_{22}, \quad P^2_{211} = \tfrac{1}{4}\Delta_{33}, \quad P^2_{111} = \tfrac{1}{4}\Delta_{44},$$

if we now replace P_{22}, P_{222}, P_{2222} by $\wp_{22}$, $\wp_{222}$, $\wp_{2222}$, etc., that

$$\wp_{2222} - 6\wp_{22}^2 = \tfrac{1}{2}\lambda_3 + \lambda_4 x + 4y, \quad \wp_{1111} - 6\wp_{11}^2 = -\tfrac{1}{2}\lambda_0\lambda_4 + \tfrac{1}{8}\lambda_1\lambda_3 - 3\lambda_0 x + \lambda_1 y + \lambda_2 z,$$
$$\wp_{2221} - 6\wp_{22}\wp_{21} = \lambda_4 y - 2z, \quad \wp_{2111} - 6\wp_{21}\wp_{11} = -\lambda_0 - \tfrac{1}{2}\lambda_1 x + \lambda_2 y,$$
$$\wp_{2211} - 2\wp_{22}\wp_{11} - 4\wp_{21}^2 = \tfrac{1}{2}\lambda_3 y.$$

These equations are satisfied by $\vartheta(w_1, w_2)$, and, as their form alone shews, by $e^{A_1w_1 + A_2w_2 + B}\vartheta(w_1 + C_1, w_2 + C_2)$, where $A_1, A_2, \dots$ are five arbitrary constants. Their deduction given here, from the forms for w_2, w_1 as integrals of total differentials, shews that they are self-consistent; that their most general integral is of the form $e^{A_1w_1 + A_2w_2 + B}\vartheta(w_1 + C_1, w_2 + C_2)$ will be obvious when it is shewn conversely that they lead backwards to the forms for w_2 and w_1 as integrals of total differentials. It is sufficient to indicate how this may be done; and it may be remarked in passing that it was in carrying out this process that the forms $\wp^2_{222} = \frac{1}{4}\Delta_{11}$ were at first discovered; the preceding deduction of these forms, though artificial, has been adopted as requiring less numerical computation. If these five differential equations be all satisfied by a single function σ of w_1, w_2, with

$$\wp_{22} = -\frac{\partial^2}{\partial w_2^2}\log\sigma, \qquad \wp_{2222} = \frac{\partial^2}{\partial w_2^2}\wp_{22}, \text{ etc.},$$

then there are four identities such as

$$\frac{\partial}{\partial w_1}\wp_{2222} = \frac{\partial}{\partial w_2}\wp_{2221}, \qquad \frac{\partial}{\partial w_1}\wp_{2221} = \frac{\partial}{\partial w_2}\wp_{2211};$$

substituting herein the values of $\wp_{2222}, \wp_{2221}, \dots$ given by the differential equations we have four equations which are linear and homogeneous in the four functions $\wp_{222}, \wp_{221}, \wp_{211}, \wp_{111}$, and linear also in $\wp_{22}, \wp_{21}, \wp_{11}$. Eliminating the former functions we find that $x = \wp_{22}$, $y = \wp_{21}$, $z = \wp_{11}$ are connected by the determinantal equation $\Delta = 0$, while $\xi = \wp_{222}$, $\eta = \wp_{221}$, $\zeta = \wp_{211}$, $\tau = \wp_{111}$ have their ratios determined by

$$\frac{\xi}{\Delta_{11}} = \frac{\eta}{\Delta_{12}} = \frac{\zeta}{\Delta_{13}} = \frac{\tau}{\Delta_{14}},$$

where Δ_{ij} is the minor in Δ of the jth element of the ith row. Since Δ is symmetrical, and therefore $\Delta_{ij}\Delta_{ik} = \Delta_{ii}\Delta_{jk}$, this is the same as

$$\frac{\xi^2}{\Delta_{11}} = \frac{\eta^2}{\Delta_{22}} = \dots = \frac{\xi\eta}{\Delta_{12}} = \dots = \frac{\zeta\tau}{\Delta_{34}},$$

and it is required only to find these ratios. Putting $\wp_{222} = \mu\Delta_{11}$, $\wp_{221} = \mu\Delta_{12}$, etc., we have

$$\wp_{2222} = \frac{\partial\mu}{\partial u_2}\Delta_{11} + \mu^2\left(\Delta_{11}\frac{\partial\Delta_{11}}{\partial x} + \Delta_{12}\frac{\partial\Delta_{11}}{\partial y} + \Delta_{13}\frac{\partial\Delta_{11}}{\partial z}\right),$$
$$\wp_{2221} = \frac{\partial\mu}{\partial u_2}\Delta_{12} + \mu^2\left(\Delta_{11}\frac{\partial\Delta_{12}}{\partial x} + \Delta_{12}\frac{\partial\Delta_{12}}{\partial y} + \Delta_{13}\frac{\partial\Delta_{12}}{\partial z}\right),$$

from which, substituting for $\wp_{2222}$ and $\wp_{2221}$ from the differential equations, and eliminating $\partial\mu/\partial u_2$, we find μ^2 as a rational function of x, y, z, and in fact, as is seen on carrying out the work, $\mu^2 = \frac{1}{4\Delta_{11}}$. Then the equations $x = \wp_{22}$, $y = \wp_{21}$, give at once $dx = \xi dw_2 + \eta dw_1$, $dy = \eta dw_2 + \zeta dw_1$, from which the forms for w_2, w_1 as integrals of total differentials are obtained at once. By differentiating $\wp_{222} = \mu\Delta_{11}$, $\wp_{221} = \mu\Delta_{12}$ in regard to u_1, and eliminating $\partial\mu/\partial u_1$, we also obtain a form for μ^2 as a rational function of x, y, z; and similarly a form for μ^2 is obtained in two ways by taking such a pair as $\wp_{221} = \mu\Delta_{12}$, $\wp_{211} = \mu\Delta_{13}$, and so on; that these various ways lead to the same form for μ^2 is clear by the deduction we have made of the differential equations from the forms of w_2, w_1 as integrals of total differentials; but conversely we could start from the differential equations and verify this fact from them.

13. The differential equations are capable of a much more general form. This may be regarded as a consequence of the fact that if in the integrals $\int dt/s$, $\int t\,dt/s$, where $s^2 = \lambda_0 + \ldots + \lambda_6 t^6$, we replace t by a form $(At+B)/(Ct+D)$, they are changed into linear functions of themselves. It will however be more interesting to establish the transformation directly from the differential equations; and we begin with the general form of these and reduce it to the form obtained above. Let then u_1, u_2 be independent variables, σ, or $\sigma(u)$, a dependent function, and

$$x = -\frac{\partial^2}{\partial u_2^2}\log\sigma, \qquad y = -\frac{\partial^2}{\partial u_2 \partial u_1}\log\sigma, \qquad z = -\frac{\partial^2}{\partial u_1^2}\log\sigma,$$

these being also respectively denoted by $\wp_{22}(u)$, $\wp_{21}(u)$, $\wp_{11}(u)$, and $\partial^2\wp_{22}/\partial u_2^2$ by $\wp_{2222}$, etc.; let $a_0, a_1, \ldots, a_6$ be any constants and, for brevity,

$$Q_{2222} = \wp_{2222} - 6\wp_{22}^2, \quad Q_{2221} = \wp_{2221} - 6\wp_{22}\wp_{21}, \quad Q_{2211} = \wp_{2211} - 2\wp_{22}\wp_{11} - 4\wp_{21}^2;$$
$$Q_{1111} = \wp_{1111} - 6\wp_{11}^2, \quad Q_{2111} = \wp_{2111} - 6\wp_{21}\wp_{11},$$

consider the five equations

$$\begin{aligned}
-\tfrac{1}{3}Q_{2222} &= a_2a_6 - 4a_3a_5 + 3a_4^2 &&+ a_4x - 2a_5y + a_6z,\\
-\tfrac{1}{3}Q_{2221} &= \tfrac{1}{2}(a_1a_6 - 3a_2a_5 + 2a_3a_4) &&+ a_3x - 2a_4y + a_5z,\\
-\tfrac{1}{3}Q_{2211} &= \tfrac{1}{6}(a_0a_6 - 9a_2a_4 + 8a_3^2) &&+ a_2x - 2a_3y + a_4z,\\
-\tfrac{1}{3}Q_{2111} &= \tfrac{1}{2}(a_0a_5 - 3a_1a_4 + 2a_2a_3) &&+ a_1x - 2a_2y + a_3z,\\
-\tfrac{1}{3}Q_{1111} &= a_0a_4 - 4a_1a_3 + 3a_2^2 &&+ a_0x - 2a_1y + a_2z.
\end{aligned}$$

It is at once verified that if

$$\Delta_1 = \frac{\partial}{\partial u_1} - \frac{\partial}{\partial u_1'}, \qquad \Delta_2 = \frac{\partial}{\partial u_2} - \frac{\partial}{\partial u_2'},$$

we may write

$$\wp_{\mu\nu} = -\frac{1}{2\sigma^2(u)}\Delta_\mu\Delta_\nu\sigma(u)\sigma(u'), \qquad Q_{\lambda\mu\nu\rho} = -\frac{1}{2\sigma^2(u)}\Delta_\lambda\Delta_\mu\Delta_\nu\Delta_\rho\sigma(u)\sigma(u'),$$

where, after the differentiations have been performed, we are to replace u_1', u_2' by u_1 and u_2. Using the ordinary symbolical notation put further, in any expression in which $a_0, a_1, \ldots, a_6$ enter linearly,

$$a_0 = \alpha_1^6, \quad a_1 = \alpha_1^5\alpha_2, \quad a_2 = \alpha_1^4\alpha_2^2, \ldots, a_6 = \alpha_2^6,$$

confusion being prevented, in case squares and products of the second order enter, by the use of another set of symbolical quantities β_1, β_2, such that also $a_0 = \beta_1^6 \ldots a_6 = \beta_2^6$, and similarly for expressions of higher dimension in $a_0 \ldots a_6$; then, with $(\alpha\beta) = \alpha_1\beta_2 - \alpha_2\beta_1$, it is at once verified that

$$a_0a_4 - 4a_1a_3 + 3a_2^2 = \tfrac{1}{2}\alpha_1^2\beta_1^2(\alpha\beta)^4, \quad a_2a_6 - 4a_3a_5 + 3a_4^2 = \tfrac{1}{2}\alpha_2^2\beta_2^2(\alpha\beta)^4,$$

$$\tfrac{1}{2}(a_1a_6 - 3a_2a_5 + 2a_3a_4) = \tfrac{1}{4}\alpha_2\beta_2(\alpha_1\beta_2 + \alpha_2\beta_1)(\alpha\beta)^4,$$

$$\tfrac{1}{2}(a_0a_5 - 3a_1a_4 + 2a_2a_3) = \tfrac{1}{4}\alpha_1\beta_1(\alpha_1\beta_2 + \alpha_2\beta_1)(\alpha\beta)^4,$$

$$\tfrac{1}{6}(a_0a_6 - 9a_2a_4 + 8a_3^2) = \tfrac{1}{12}(\alpha_1^2\beta_2^2 + 4\alpha_1\alpha_2\beta_1\beta_2 + \alpha_2^2\beta_1^2)(\alpha\beta)^4;$$

hence if the differential equations written down, taken in the order of those involving Q_{2222}, Q_{2221}, Q_{2211}, Q_{2111}, Q_{1111}, be multiplied respectively by h_2^4, $4h_2^3h_1$, $6h_2^2h_1^2$, $4h_2h_1^3$, h_1^4, where h_2, h_1 are arbitrary quantities, and then added, it is at once seen that they give

$$\tfrac{1}{3}\Delta_h^4\sigma\sigma' = (\alpha\beta)^4\alpha_h^2\beta_h^2 . \sigma\sigma' - \alpha_h^4(\alpha\Delta)^2\sigma\sigma',$$

where $\quad \Delta_h = h_1\Delta_1 + h_2\Delta_2, \quad \alpha_h = \alpha_1h_1 + \alpha_2h_2, \quad (\alpha\Delta) = \alpha_1\Delta_2 - \alpha_2\Delta_1,$

and, as before, after differentiation u_1', u_2' are to be replaced by u_1, u_2.

Now let $\lambda_1, \mu_1, \lambda_2, \mu_2$ be arbitrary constants whose determinant $\lambda_1\mu_2 - \lambda_2\mu_1$ is supposed not to vanish, and will presently be taken equal to unity; put

$$u_1 = \lambda_1v_1 + \mu_1v_2, \quad u_1' = \lambda_1v_1' + \mu_1v_2', \quad h_1 = \lambda_1k_1 + \mu_1k_2,$$

$$u_2 = \lambda_2v_1 + \mu_2v_2, \quad u_2' = \lambda_2v_1' + \mu_2v_2', \quad h_2 = \lambda_2k_1 + \mu_2k_2;$$

further let A_1, A_2, B_1, B_2 be symbolical quantities defined by

$$A_1 = \alpha_1\lambda_1 + \alpha_2\lambda_2, \quad B_1 = \beta_1\lambda_1 + \beta_2\lambda_2,$$

$$A_2 = \alpha_1\mu_1 + \alpha_2\mu_2, \quad B_2 = \beta_1\mu_1 + \beta_2\mu_2,$$

so that, for instance,

$$A_1^6 = a_0\lambda_1^6 + 6a_1\lambda_1^5\lambda_2 + \ldots + a_6\lambda_2^6;$$

we denote A_1, A_2, B_1, B_2 respectively by α_λ, α_μ, β_λ, β_μ; we have then

$$\frac{\partial}{\partial v_1} = \lambda_1\frac{\partial}{\partial u_1} + \lambda_2\frac{\partial}{\partial u_2}, \qquad \frac{\partial}{\partial v_2} = \mu_1\frac{\partial}{\partial u_1} + \mu_2\frac{\partial}{\partial u_2},$$

and
$$\nabla_1 = \frac{\partial}{\partial v_1} - \frac{\partial}{\partial v_1'} = \lambda_1\Delta_1 + \lambda_2\Delta_2, = \Delta_\lambda, \text{ say},$$

$$\nabla_2 = \frac{\partial}{\partial v_2} - \frac{\partial}{\partial v_2'} = \mu_1\Delta_1 + \mu_2\Delta_2, = \Delta_\mu, \text{ say},$$

and hence
$$\Delta_h = h_1\Delta_1 + h_2\Delta_2 = k_1\nabla_1 + k_2\nabla_2 = \nabla_k,$$

with
$$(AB) = (\lambda\mu)(\alpha\beta), \quad (A\nabla) = (\lambda\mu)(\alpha\nabla).$$

Thus the differential equations are the same as

$$\tfrac{1}{3}\nabla_k{}^4\Sigma\Sigma' = (\lambda\mu)^{-4}(AB)^4 A_k{}^2 B_k{}^2 . \Sigma\Sigma' - (\lambda\mu)^{-2} A_k{}^2 (A\nabla)^2 \Sigma\Sigma',$$

where $\Sigma(v_1, v_2) = \sigma(u_1, u_2)$; herein k_1, k_2, being independent linear functions of the arbitrary quantities h_1, h_2, are themselves arbitrary, and the equation, save for the powers of $(\lambda\mu)$ which enter, is of precisely the same form as that from which it is derived; supposing $(\lambda\mu) = \lambda_1\mu_2 - \lambda_2\mu_1 = 1$, we may then equate coefficients of like powers of k_1, k_2, and shall so obtain five differential equations of precisely the original form, save that $a_0, a_1, \dots, a_6$ are respectively replaced by $A_0 = \alpha_\lambda{}^6 = a_0\lambda_1{}^6 + \dots + a_6\lambda_2{}^6$, $A_1 = \alpha_\lambda{}^5\alpha_\mu = a_0\lambda_1{}^5\mu_1 + \dots, \dots, A_6 = \alpha_\mu{}^6$; these are the coefficients of the powers and products of k_1, k_2 when we write

$$a_0h_1{}^6 + 6a_1h_1{}^5h_2 + \dots + a_6h_2{}^6 = A_0k_1{}^6 + 6A_1k_1{}^5k_2 + \dots + A_6k_2{}^6.$$

The functions

$$P_{22} = -\frac{\partial^2}{\partial v_2{}^2}\log\Sigma, \qquad P_{21} = -\frac{\partial^2}{\partial v_2\partial v_1}\log\Sigma, \qquad P_{11} = -\frac{\partial^2}{\partial v_1{}^2}\log\Sigma$$

are then given by

$$P_{22} = \mu_2{}^2\wp_{22} + 2\mu_2\mu_1\wp_{21} + \mu_1{}^2\wp_{11}, \quad P_{21} = \mu_2\lambda_2\wp_{22} + (\mu_2\lambda_1 + \mu_1\lambda_2)\wp_{21} + \mu_1\lambda_1\wp_{11},$$
$$P_{11} = \lambda_2{}^2\wp_{22} + 2\lambda_2\lambda_1\wp_{21} + \lambda_1{}^2\wp_{11},$$

and there are similar equations for the differential coefficients of the third and higher orders.

We can now choose the four constants $\lambda_1, \lambda_2, \mu_1, \mu_2$ to satisfy three conditions in addition to the one already imposed, $\lambda_1\mu_2 - \lambda_2\mu_1 = 1$. For instance we can take

$$A_0 = 0, \quad A_6 = 0, \quad 6A_1 + 15A_2 + 20A_3 + 15A_4 + 6A_5 = 0,$$

so that, for arbitrary x,

$$A_0 + 6A_1x + \dots + A_6x^6 = 6A_1x(1-x)(1-p_1x)(1-p_2x)(1-p_3x);$$

or we can take $A_6 = 0$, $6A_5 = 4$, in addition to another condition, which may be for instance $A_4 = 0$.

We shall limit ourselves to taking $A_6 = 0$, $6A_5 = 4$; for this it is necessary that $\mu_2 = \mu_1\theta$, where θ is a root of the equation

$$f(\theta) = a_0 + 6a_1\theta + \dots + a_6\theta^6 = 0;$$

taking $\lambda_2 = 0$, we have then $\lambda_1\mu_2 = 1$, and

$$\tfrac{2}{3} = A_5 = \alpha_\lambda\alpha_\mu{}^5 = a_0\lambda_1\mu_1{}^5 + 5a_1\lambda_1\mu_1{}^4\mu_2 + \dots + a_5\lambda_1\mu_2{}^5 = \lambda_1\mu_1{}^5(a_0 + 5a_1\theta + \dots + a_5\theta^5),$$

or

$$\tfrac{2}{3}\mu_2{}^{-4} = a_0\theta^{-5} + 5a_1\theta^{-4} + \dots + a_5;$$

then

$$P_{22} = \mu_2{}^2[\wp_{22} + 2\theta^{-1}\wp_{21} + \theta^{-2}\wp_{11}], \quad P_{21} = \wp_{21} + \theta^{-1}\wp_{11}, \quad P_{11} = \mu_2{}^{-2}\wp_{11}.$$

Now put

$$A_0 = \lambda_0, \quad 6A_1 = \lambda_1, \quad 15A_2 = \lambda_2, \quad 20A_3 = \lambda_3, \quad 15A_4 = \lambda_4,$$

and

$$X = P_{22} - \tfrac{1}{10}\lambda_4 = P_{22} - \tfrac{3}{2}A_4, \quad Y = P_{21} - \tfrac{1}{40}\lambda_3 = P_{21} - \tfrac{1}{2}A_3, \quad Z = P_{11} - \tfrac{1}{10}\lambda_2 = P_{11} - \tfrac{3}{2}A_2,$$

so that

$$X = -\frac{\partial^2}{\partial v_2^2}\log\Sigma_1, \qquad Y = -\frac{\partial^2}{\partial v_2 \partial v_1}\log\Sigma_1, \qquad Z = -\frac{\partial^2}{\partial v_1^2}\log\Sigma_1,$$

where $\Sigma_1 = e^H\Sigma, \quad H = \tfrac{3}{4}A_4 v_2^2 + \tfrac{1}{2}A_3 v_2 v_1 + \tfrac{3}{4}A_2 v_1^2,$

and put $P_{2222} = \dfrac{\partial^2 X}{\partial v_2^2}$, etc.

Then it can be verified that the differential equations take the forms previously obtained; for instance

$$-2P_{22}^2 + A_2A_6 - 4A_3A_5 + 3A_4^2 + A_4P_{22} - 2A_5P_{21} + A_6P_{11},$$

which is the value of $-\tfrac{1}{3}\dfrac{\partial^4}{\partial v_2^4}\log\Sigma(v)$, becomes equal to

$$-2(X + \tfrac{3}{2}A_4)^2 - \tfrac{8}{3}A_3 + 3A_4^2 + A_4(X + \tfrac{3}{2}A_4) - \tfrac{4}{3}(Y + \tfrac{1}{2}A_3),$$

or

$$-2X^2 - \tfrac{10}{3}A_3 - 5A_4X - \tfrac{4}{3}Y,$$

or

$$-\tfrac{1}{3}(6X^2 + \tfrac{1}{2}\lambda_3 + \lambda_4 X + 4Y),$$

as in the differential equation of p. 48.

We recall now (pp. 13, 25) that the dependent variable of the previous differential equations was a function

$$\Sigma\Sigma e^{Cv^2 + 2Hvn + i\pi\tau n^2},$$

where H is a matrix of non-vanishing determinant, such that if the periods for the integrals

$$V_1^{x,a} = \int_a^x y^{-1}dx, \qquad V_2^{x,a} = \int_a^x y^{-1}x\,dx$$

be given by

$\int y^{-1}dx$	$2\omega_{11}$	$2\omega_{12}$	$2\omega_{11}'$	$2\omega_{12}'$
$\int y^{-1}x\,dx$	$2\omega_{21}$	$2\omega_{22}$	$2\omega_{21}'$	$2\omega_{22}'$,

then $2H\omega = \pi i$, $2H\omega' = \pi i\tau$; while C was such that

$$\int_a^x\int_c^z \frac{F(x,z) + 2ys}{4(x-z)^2}\frac{dx}{y}\frac{dz}{s} = \Pi_{z,c}^{x,a} - 2\Sigma\Sigma C_{rs}V_r^{x,a}V_s^{z,c}$$

To obtain the dependent variable of the generalised form of the differential equations we are thus, as appears from the preceding work, to multiply by e^H, where $H = -\tfrac{1}{20}\lambda_4 v_2^2 - \tfrac{1}{40}\lambda_3 v_2 v_1 - \tfrac{1}{20}\lambda_2 v_1^2$, and afterwards to replace v_1, v_2 by u_1, u_2 determined from the equations

$$u_1 = \mu_2^{-1}v_1 + \mu_2\theta^{-1}v_2, \quad u_2 = \mu_2 v_2,$$

where $\qquad \frac{2}{3}\mu_2^{-4} = a_0\theta^{-5} + \ldots + a_5.$

Now let

$$c_{22} = C_{22} - \tfrac{1}{20}\lambda_4, \quad c_{21} = C_{21} - \tfrac{1}{80}\lambda_3, \quad c_{11} = C_{11} - \tfrac{1}{20}\lambda_2;$$

add, to the equation above which defines C, the quantity

$$2\left\{\tfrac{1}{20}\lambda_4 V_2^{x,a} V_2^{z,c} + \tfrac{1}{80}\lambda_3 (V_2^{x,a} V_1^{z,c} + V_2^{z,c} V_1^{x,a}) + \tfrac{1}{20}\lambda_2 V_1^{x,a} V_1^{z,c}\right\}$$

or $$2\int \left\{\tfrac{1}{20}\lambda_4 xz + \tfrac{1}{80}\lambda_3 (x+z) + \tfrac{1}{20}\lambda_2\right\} \frac{dx}{y}\frac{dz}{s};$$

it is at once found, with the values $A_0 = \lambda_0$, $6A_1 = \lambda_1$, etc., as given above, that the expression

$$2(A_0 + 3A_1 x + 3A_2 x^2 + A_3 x^3) + 6(A_1 + 3A_2 x + 3A_3 x^2 + A_4 x^3)\, z$$
$$+ 6(A_2 + 3A_3 x + 3A_4 x^2 + A_5 x^3)\, z^2 + 2(A_3 + 3A_4 x + 3A_5 x^2 + A_6 x^3)\, z^3$$

is equal to

$$F(x, z) + 8(x-z)^2 \left\{\tfrac{1}{20}\lambda_4 xz + \tfrac{1}{80}\lambda_3 (x+z) + \tfrac{1}{20}\lambda_2\right\},$$

the expression $F(x, z)$ being as before $\Sigma (xz)^i [2\lambda_{2i} + \lambda_{2i+1}(x+z)]$; and it will be seen that the former of these expressions can be written symbolically as $2(A_1 + A_2 x)^3 (A_1 + A_2 z)^3$; finally notice that if we put

$$x = (\lambda_2 + \mu_2 t)/(\lambda_1 + \mu_1 t),$$

we have

$$dx\,(a_0 + 6a_1 x + \ldots + a_6 x)^{-\frac{1}{2}} = \lambda_1 dt (A_0 + 6A_1 t + \ldots)^{-\frac{1}{2}} + \mu_1 t\, dt (A_0 + 6A_1 t + \ldots)^{-\frac{1}{2}},$$
$$x\,dx\,(a_0 + 6a_1 x + \ldots \qquad)^{-\frac{1}{2}} = \lambda_2 dt (A_0 + 6A_1 t + \ldots)^{-\frac{1}{2}} + \mu_2 t\, dt (A_0 + 6A_1 t + \ldots)^{-\frac{1}{2}};$$

we can then formulate the result of our transformation as follows:—

The differential equations of p. 49

$$-\tfrac{1}{3}\wp_{2222}(u) = a_2 a_6 - 4a_3 a_5 + 3a_4^2 + a_4 \wp_{22} - 2a_5 \wp_{21} + a_6 \wp_{11} - 2\wp_{22}^2,$$
etc., $\qquad$ etc.,

are satisfied by

$$\sigma(u) = \Sigma\Sigma e^{cu^2 + 2hun + i\pi\tau n^2},$$

where, if 2ω, $2\omega'$ be determined for the sextic $f(x) = a_0 + 6a_1 x + \ldots + a_6 x^6$, and a certain dissection of the surface representing $y^2 = f(x)$, as the periods of the integrals $\int_a^x y^{-1} dx$, $\int_a^x x y^{-1} dx$, then h is a matrix of non-vanishing determinant, τ a symmetrical matrix of non-vanishing determinant determined respectively by $2h\omega = \pi i$, $2h\omega' = \pi i \tau$; and c is a symmetrical matrix, determined, if $f(x)$ be symbolically written $\alpha_x^6 = (\alpha_1 + \alpha_2 x)^6$, and $s^2 = f(z)$, by the fact that

$$\int_a^x \int_c^z \frac{2\alpha_x^3 \alpha_z^3 + 2ys}{4(x-z)^2} \frac{dx}{y}\frac{dz}{s} + 2\int_a^x \int_c^z [c_{22} xz + c_{12}(x+z) + c_{11}] \frac{dx}{y}\frac{dz}{s}$$

is the normal elementary integral of the third kind $\Pi_{z,\,c}^{x,\,a}$.

The differential equations being thus shewn to have an invariantive character, various properties of the quartic surface which is represented by the relation connecting $\wp_{22}$, $\wp_{21}$, $\wp_{11}$ are at once deducible. This is explained below, in the chapter dealing with the geometry of this surface.

But the form obtained for the differential equations,

$$\tfrac{1}{3}\Delta_h{}^4\sigma\sigma' = (\alpha\beta)^4\alpha_h{}^2\beta_h{}^2 . \sigma\sigma' - \alpha_h{}^4(\alpha\Delta)^2\sigma\sigma',$$

is of importance also as shewing almost at a glance how the differential equations may be used to obtain the expansion of the integral function $\sigma(u)$. This is explained below, in the chapter on the expansions. And these expansions in their turn enable us to prove succinctly various relations involving the functions $\wp_{22}(u)$, $\wp_{21}(u)$, $\wp_{11}(u)$; the properties developed in the next chapter in regard to the geometry of the surface are for the most part restricted to those which interpret these analytical relations.

CHAPTER III.

ANALYTICAL RESULTS RELATING TO THE ASSOCIATED QUARTIC SURFACES.

14. Intimately related with the theory of the functions under consideration are two quartic surfaces. We give now certain elementary properties of these, deduced, for clearness, independently of preceding results.

To illustrate one step in the argument we presently employ, consider first a simple example. Let a quadratic form, of non-vanishing determinant,

$$a_{11}\xi_1^2 + a_{22}\xi_2^2 + a_{33}\xi_3^2 + 2a_{23}\xi_2\xi_3 + 2a_{31}\xi_3\xi_1 + 2a_{12}\xi_1\xi_2,$$

which we denote by $a\xi^2$, become, by a transformation written $\xi = \mu\xi'$, that is by

$$\xi_r = \mu_{r1}\xi_1' + \mu_{r2}\xi_2' + \mu_{r3}\xi_3', \qquad (r = 1, 2, 3),$$

changed to $a'\xi'^2$ or

$$a_{11}'\xi_1'^2 + a_{22}'\xi_2'^2 + a_{33}'\xi_3'^2 + 2a_{23}'\xi_2'\xi_3' + 2a_{31}'\xi_3'\xi_1' + 2a_{12}'\xi_1'\xi_2',$$

so that
$$a'\xi'^2 = a\xi^2 = a\mu\xi' . \mu\xi' = \bar{\mu}a\mu\xi'^2,$$

and therefore $a' = \bar{\mu}a\mu$, namely

$$\begin{pmatrix} a_{11}' & a_{12}' & a_{13}' \\ a_{21}' & a_{22}' & a_{23}' \\ a_{31}' & a_{32}' & a_{33}' \end{pmatrix} = \begin{pmatrix} \mu_{11} & \mu_{21} & \mu_{31} \\ \mu_{12} & \mu_{22} & \mu_{32} \\ \mu_{13} & \mu_{23} & \mu_{33} \end{pmatrix} \begin{pmatrix} a_{11} & a_{12} & a_{13} \\ a_{21} & a_{22} & a_{23} \\ a_{31} & a_{32} & a_{33} \end{pmatrix} \begin{pmatrix} \mu_{11} & \mu_{12} & \mu_{13} \\ \mu_{21} & \mu_{22} & \mu_{23} \\ \mu_{31} & \mu_{32} & \mu_{33} \end{pmatrix};$$

if Δ, Δ', M denote respectively the determinants of a, a' and μ, this gives $\Delta' = M^2\Delta$. Now the relation $a' = \bar{\mu}a\mu$ is the same as $a'^{-1} = \mu^{-1}a^{-1}\bar{\mu}^{-1}$, obtained by taking the inverse of both sides; if p_1, p_2, p_3 be three variables, and $(p_1', p_2', p_3') = \bar{\mu}(p_1, p_2, p_3)$, or $p = \bar{\mu}^{-1}p'$, we have therefore

$$a'^{-1}p'^2 = \mu^{-1}a^{-1}\bar{\mu}^{-1}p'^2 = a^{-1}\bar{\mu}^{-1}p' . \bar{\mu}^{-1}p' = a^{-1}p^2,$$

or, since

$$a^{-1} = \begin{pmatrix} \Delta^{-1}A_{11}, & \Delta^{-1}A_{21}, & \Delta^{-1}A_{31} \\ \Delta^{-1}A_{12}, & \Delta^{-1}A_{22}, & \Delta^{-1}A_{32} \\ \Delta^{-1}A_{13}, & \Delta^{-1}A_{23}, & \Delta^{-1}A_{33} \end{pmatrix},$$

we have

$$\begin{vmatrix} a_{11}' & a_{12}' & a_{13}' & p_1' \\ a_{21}' & a_{22}' & a_{23}' & p_2' \\ a_{31}' & a_{32}' & a_{33}' & p_3' \\ p_1' & p_2' & p_3' & 0 \end{vmatrix} = M^2 \begin{vmatrix} a_{11} & a_{12} & a_{13} & p_1 \\ a_{21} & a_{22} & a_{23} & p_2 \\ a_{31} & a_{32} & a_{33} & p_3 \\ p_1 & p_2 & p_3 & 0 \end{vmatrix},$$

the determinant on the right being the quadratic form $a^{-1}p^2$ multiplied by $-\Delta$. The transformation $p' = \bar{\mu}p$ gives $p'\xi'$, or $p_1'\xi_1' + p_2'\xi_2' + p_3'\xi_3'$, equal to $\bar{\mu}p\xi' = \mu\xi'p = \xi p = p\xi$; conversely $p'\xi' = p\xi$ defines the transformation of p from that of ξ.

Consider now the expression

$$2(\theta\phi)^2(\beta\theta)(\beta\phi) - \alpha_\theta{}^3\alpha_\phi{}^3,$$

where

$$\alpha_\theta = \alpha_1\theta_1 + \alpha_2\theta_2, \quad \alpha_\phi = \alpha_1\phi_1 + \alpha_2\phi_2, \quad (\theta\phi) = \theta_1\phi_2 - \theta_2\phi_1, \quad (\beta\theta) = \beta_1\theta_2 - \beta_2\theta_1,$$
$$(\beta\phi) = \beta_1\phi_2 - \beta_2\phi_1;$$

partially expanded this is

$$2\beta_1{}^2\theta_2\phi_2(\theta_1{}^2\phi_2{}^2 + \theta_2{}^2\phi_1{}^2 - 2\theta_1\theta_2\phi_1\phi_2) - 2\beta_1\beta_2(\theta_1\phi_2 + \theta_2\phi_1)(\theta_1\phi_2 - \theta_2\phi_1)^2$$
$$+ 2\beta_2{}^2\theta_1\phi_1(\theta\phi)^2 - \{\alpha_1{}^3\theta_1{}^3(\alpha_1{}^3\phi_1{}^3 + 3\alpha_1{}^2\alpha_2\phi_1{}^2\phi_2 + 3\alpha_1\alpha_2{}^2\phi_1\phi_2{}^2 + \alpha_2{}^3\phi_2{}^3)$$
$$+ 3\alpha_1{}^2\alpha_2\theta_1{}^2\theta_2\alpha_\phi{}^3 + 3\alpha_1\alpha_2{}^2\theta_1\theta_2{}^2\alpha_\phi{}^3 + \alpha_2{}^3\theta_2{}^3\alpha_\phi{}^3\};$$

suppose that, in the fully-expanded form, $\beta_1{}^2$, $\beta_1\beta_2$, $\beta_2{}^2$, which enter linearly, are replaced respectively by x, $-y$ and z; that $\theta_1{}^3$, $\theta_1{}^2\theta_2$, $\theta_1\theta_2{}^2$, $\theta_2{}^3$, which also enter linearly, are replaced respectively by ξ, $-\eta$, ζ and $-\tau$; that $\phi_1{}^3$, $\phi_1{}^2\phi_2$, $\phi_1\phi_2{}^2$, $\phi_2{}^3$ are also replaced respectively by ξ, $-\eta$, ζ, $-\tau$; and that $\alpha_1{}^6$, $\alpha_1{}^5\alpha_2$, $\alpha_1{}^4\alpha_2{}^2, \ldots, \alpha_2{}^6$ are replaced respectively by $a_0, a_1, a_2, \ldots, a_6$. The expression then becomes the quadratic form in ξ, η, ζ, τ,

$$4x(\eta\tau - \zeta^2) + 4y(\eta\zeta - \xi\tau) + 4z(\zeta\xi - \eta^2)$$
$$- \xi(a_0\xi - 3a_1\eta + 3a_2\zeta - a_3\tau) - \eta(-3a_1\xi + 9a_2\eta - 9a_3\zeta + 3a_4\tau)$$
$$- \zeta(3a_2\xi - 9a_3\eta + 9a_4\zeta - 3a_5\tau) - \tau(-a_3\xi + 3a_4\eta - 3a_5\zeta + a_6\tau),$$

whose coefficients form the matrix

$$K = \begin{pmatrix} -a_0, & 3a_1, & -3a_2 + 2z, & a_3 - 2y \\ 3a_1, & -9a_2 - 4z, & 9a_3 + 2y, & -3a_4 + 2x \\ -3a_2 + 2z, & 9a_3 + 2y, & -9a_4 - 4x, & 3a_5 \\ a_3 - 2y, & -3a_4 + 2x, & 3a_5, & -a_6 \end{pmatrix},$$

so that, using ξ to stand for the row (ξ, η, ζ, τ), the quadratic form may be written $K\xi^2$.

Now subject ξ, η, ζ, τ to a linear transformation, as in the illustration just considered, but not to the most general transformation in four variables, but to that, depending only on three parameters, which is defined thus: let

$\lambda_1,\ \lambda_2,\ \mu_1,\ \mu_2$ be four parameters subject to $\lambda_1\mu_2 - \lambda_2\mu_1 = 1$; put, in the symbolical expression we have used to define the quadratic form $K\xi^2$,

$$\theta_1 = \lambda_1\theta_1' + \mu_1\theta_2',\quad \phi_1 = \lambda_1\phi_1' + \mu_1\phi_2',\quad \beta_1 = \lambda_1\beta_1' + \mu_1\beta_2',\quad \alpha_1' = \alpha_1\lambda_1 + \alpha_2\lambda_2,\quad = \alpha_\lambda,$$
$$\theta_2 = \lambda_2\theta_1' + \mu_2\theta_2',\quad \phi_2 = \lambda_2\phi_1' + \mu_2\phi_2',\quad \beta_2 = \lambda_2\beta_1' + \mu_2\beta_2',\quad \alpha_2' = \alpha_1\mu_1 + \alpha_2\mu_2,\quad = \alpha_\mu;$$

since these give

$$\alpha_\theta = \alpha_\lambda\theta_1' + \alpha_\mu\theta_2' = \alpha_{\theta'},\quad \alpha_\phi = \alpha_{\phi'},\quad (\theta\phi) = (\theta'\phi'),\quad (\beta\theta) = (\beta'\theta'),\quad (\beta\phi) = (\beta'\phi'),$$

they leave the form quite unaltered; they give as the transformation for $\xi,\ \eta,\ \zeta,\ \tau$, if, of course, we take $\xi' = \theta_1'^3$, etc.,

$$(\xi, \eta, \zeta, \tau) = \begin{pmatrix} \lambda_1^3, & -3\lambda_1^2\mu_1, & 3\lambda_1\mu_1^2, & -\mu_1^3 \\ -\lambda_1^2\lambda_2, & 2\lambda_1\lambda_2\mu_1 + \lambda_1^2\mu_2, & -\lambda_2\mu_1^2 - 2\lambda_1\mu_1\mu_2, & \mu_1^2\mu_2 \\ \lambda_1\lambda_2^2, & -(2\lambda_1\lambda_2\mu_2 + \lambda_2^2\mu_1), & \lambda_1\mu_2^2 + 2\lambda_2\mu_1\mu_2, & -\mu_1\mu_2^2 \\ -\lambda_2^3, & 3\lambda_2^2\mu_2, & -3\lambda_2\mu_2^2, & \mu_2^3 \end{pmatrix} (\xi', \eta', \zeta', \tau'),$$

or its equivalent

$$(\xi', \eta', \zeta', \tau') = \begin{pmatrix} \mu_2^3, & 3\mu_2^2\mu_1, & 3\mu_2\mu_1^2, & \mu_1^3 \\ \mu_2^2\lambda_2, & 2\mu_2\mu_1\lambda_2 + \mu_2^2\lambda_1, & \lambda_2\mu_1^2 + 2\mu_2\mu_1\lambda_1, & \mu_1^2\lambda_1 \\ \mu_2\lambda_2^2, & 2\mu_2\lambda_2\lambda_1 + \mu_1\lambda_2^2, & \mu_2\lambda_1^2 + 2\mu_1\lambda_1\lambda_2, & \mu_1\lambda_1^2 \\ \lambda_2^3, & 3\lambda_2^2\lambda_1, & 3\lambda_2\lambda_1^2, & \lambda_1^3 \end{pmatrix} (\xi, \eta, \zeta, \tau);$$

at the same time $x = \theta_1^2,\ y = -\theta_1\theta_2,\ z = \theta_2^2$ are connected with $x' = \theta_1'^2$, $y' = -\theta_1'\theta_2',\ z' = \theta_2'^2$ by the linear transformation

$$(x, y, z, 1) = \begin{pmatrix} \lambda_1^2, & -2\lambda_1\mu_1, & \mu_1^2, & 0 \\ -\lambda_1\lambda_2, & \lambda_1\mu_2 + \lambda_2\mu_1, & -\mu_1\mu_2, & 0 \\ \lambda_2^2, & -2\lambda_2\mu_2, & \mu_2^2, & 0 \\ 0, & 0, & 0, & 1 \end{pmatrix} (x', y', z', 1),$$

which is afterwards denoted by $(x, y, z, 1) = m\,(x', y', z', 1)$, or its equivalent

$$(x', y', z', 1) = \begin{pmatrix} \mu_2^2, & 2\mu_2\mu_1, & \mu_1^2, & 0 \\ \mu_2\lambda_2, & \lambda_1\mu_2 + \lambda_2\mu_1, & \mu_1\lambda_1, & 0 \\ \lambda_2^2, & 2\lambda_2\lambda_1, & \lambda_1^2, & 0 \\ 0, & 0, & 0, & 0 \end{pmatrix} (x, y, z, 1);$$

while

$$a_0' = \alpha_\lambda^6 = a_0\lambda_1^6 + 6a_1\lambda_1^5\lambda_2 + \dots + a_6\lambda_2^6,\qquad a_1' = \alpha_\lambda^5\alpha_\mu,\ \dots,\ a_6' = \alpha_\mu^6.$$

With these changes we have

$$K\xi^2 = K'\xi'^2,$$

that is

$$4x(\eta\tau - \zeta^2) + \dots + (-a_0\xi^2 + \dots - a_6\tau^2)$$
$$= 4x'(\eta'\tau' - \zeta'^2) + \dots + (-a_0'\xi'^2 + \dots - a_0'\tau'^2).$$

Thus if we write the transformation for ξ, η, ζ, τ in the form $\xi = \mu\xi'$, we have

$$K' = \bar{\mu}K\mu;$$

and, since, as is easily verified, the determinant of μ is $(\lambda_1\mu_2 - \lambda_2\mu_1)^6$, or unity, we have, as in the illustrative example previously considered, the consequence that the determinant

$$\begin{vmatrix} -a_0, & 3a_1, & -3a_2+2z, & a_3-2y, & c_0 \\ 3a_1, & -9a_2-4z, & 9a_3+2y, & -3a_4+2x, & -3c_1 \\ -3a_2+2z, & 9a_3+2y, & -9a_4-4x, & 3a_5, & 3c_2 \\ a_3-2y, & -3a_4+2x, & 3a_5, & -a_6, & -c_3 \\ c_0, & -3c_1, & 3c_2, & -c_3, & 0 \end{vmatrix}$$

is unaltered by the transformation, provided the transformed quantities c_0', c_1', c_2', c_3' be defined by the identity

$$c_0\xi - 3c_1\eta + 3c_2\zeta - c_3\tau = c_0'\xi' - 3c_1'\eta' + 3c_2'\zeta' - c_3'\tau';$$

this identity gives, if we write, symbolically, $c_0 = \gamma_1^3$, $c_1 = \gamma_1^2\gamma_2$, $c_2 = \gamma_1\gamma_2^2$, $c_3 = \gamma_2^3$, and similarly $c_0' = \gamma_1'^3$, $c_1' = \gamma_1'^2\gamma_2'$, ..., the equation

$$\gamma_\theta^3 = \gamma_{\theta'}'^3;$$

thus the equations of transformation for c_0, c_1, c_2, c_3 are

$$c_0' = \gamma_\lambda^3 = c_0\lambda_1^3 + 3c_1\lambda_1^2\lambda_2 + 3c_2\lambda_1\lambda_2^2 + c_3\lambda_2^3, \quad c_1' = \gamma_\lambda^2\gamma_\mu, \quad c_2' = \gamma_\lambda\gamma_\mu^2, \quad c_3' = \gamma_\mu^3.$$

In explicit form the ten equations expressed by $K' = \bar{\mu}K\mu$ are

$$K_{ij}' = \sum_r \mu_{ri}(K\mu)_{rj} = \sum_r \sum_s K_{rs}\mu_{ri}\mu_{sj},$$

these giving every element of the matrix K' as a linear function of the elements of the matrix K.

Further, it will be remarked that the equations above which express x', y', z' in terms of x, y, z are the same as those occurring in the previous chapter (p. 51) to express P_{22}, P_{21}, P_{11} in terms of $\wp_{22}, \wp_{21}, \wp_{11}$; and if we there form the corresponding equations to express $P_{222}, P_{221}, \dots$ in terms of $\wp_{222}, \wp_{221}, \dots$, namely, by means of the equations there occurring

$$\frac{\partial}{\partial v_2} = \mu_2\frac{\partial}{\partial u_2} + \mu_1\frac{\partial}{\partial u_1}, \qquad \frac{\partial}{\partial v_1} = \lambda_2\frac{\partial}{\partial u_2} + \lambda_1\frac{\partial}{\partial u_1},$$

it is at once seen that these are the same as those whereby here $\xi', \eta', \zeta', \tau'$ are expressed in terms of ξ, η, ζ, τ.

Taking in particular $\lambda_1, \mu_1, \lambda_2, \mu_2$ so that

$$a_6' = \alpha_\mu^6 = 0, \quad 6a_5' = 6\alpha_\lambda\alpha_\mu^5 = 4,$$

putting then

$$a_0' = \lambda_0, \quad 6a_1' = \lambda_1, \quad 15a_2' = \lambda_2, \quad 20a_3' = \lambda_3, \quad 15a_4' = \lambda_4$$

and

$$X = x' - \tfrac{1}{10}\lambda_4 = x' - \tfrac{3}{2}a_4', \quad Y = y' - \tfrac{1}{40}\lambda_3 = y' - \tfrac{1}{2}a_3', \quad Z = z' - \tfrac{1}{10}\lambda_2 = z' - \tfrac{3}{2}a_2',$$

the matrix K' takes the form

$$\begin{pmatrix} -\lambda_0\,, & \tfrac{1}{2}\lambda_1 \,, & 2Z \,, & -2Y \\ \tfrac{1}{2}\lambda_1\,, & -(4Z+\lambda_2), & 2Y+\tfrac{1}{2}\lambda_3\,, & 2X \\ 2Z\,, & 2Y+\tfrac{1}{2}\lambda_3\,, & -(4X+\lambda_4), & 2 \\ -2Y, & 2X\,, & 2\,, & 0 \end{pmatrix},$$

of which the determinant has occurred already (pp. 38, 41), under the name Δ. Thus it appears that the functions $\wp_{22}, \wp_{21}, \wp_{11}$ which satisfy the generalised differential equations of p. 49 are connected by the determinantal equation $|K| = 0$, obtained by equating to zero the determinant of the matrix K, and that the corresponding functions $\wp_{222}, \wp_{221}, \ldots$ are given by

$$(l_0\wp_{222}+l_1\wp_{221}+l_2\wp_{211}+l_3\wp_{111})^2=-\tfrac{1}{4}\begin{vmatrix} -a_0\,, & 3a_1\,, & -3a_2+2z, & a_3-2y\,, & l_0 \\ 3a_1\,, & -9a_2-4z, & 9a_3+2y\,, & -3a_4+2x, & l_1 \\ -3a_2+2z, & 9a_3+2y, & -9a_4-4x, & 3a_5\,, & l_2 \\ a_3-2y\,, & -3a_4+2x, & 3a_5\,, & -a_6\,, & l_3 \\ l_0\,, & l_1\,, & l_2\,, & l_3\,, & 0 \end{vmatrix}$$

We denote the determinant of K by ∇; by differentiating the unexpanded equation $\nabla = 0$, we have, if ∇_{ij} denote the minor of the jth element of the ith row, and ξ, η, ζ, τ denote the general functions $\wp_{22}$, etc.,

$$\frac{\partial\nabla}{\partial x} = 2\nabla_{24} - 4\nabla_{33} + 2\nabla_{42} = 16\,(\eta\tau - \zeta^2),$$

$$\frac{\partial\nabla}{\partial y} = -2\nabla_{14} + 2\nabla_{23} + 2\nabla_{32} + 2\nabla_{41} = 16\,(\eta\zeta - \xi\tau),$$

$$\frac{\partial\nabla}{\partial z} = 2\nabla_{13} - 4\nabla_{22} + 2\nabla_{31} = 16\,(\zeta\xi - \eta^2),$$

while, if the variable $t\ (=1)$ be introduced to render ∇ homogeneous in x, y, z, t,

$$\begin{aligned} \frac{\partial\nabla}{\partial t} &= -a_0\nabla_{11} + 6a_1\nabla_{12} - 6a_2\nabla_{13} - 9a_2\nabla_{22} + 2a_3\nabla_{14} + 18a_3\nabla_{23} - 6a_4\nabla_{24} \\ &\qquad - 9a_4\nabla_{33} + 6a_5\nabla_{34} - a_6\nabla_{44}, \\ &= 4\,(-a_0\xi^2 + 6a_1\xi\eta - 6a_2\xi\zeta - 9a_2\eta^2 + 2a_3\xi\tau + 18a_3\eta\zeta - 6a_4\eta\tau \\ &\qquad - 9a_4\zeta^2 + 6a_5\zeta\tau - a_6\tau^2). \end{aligned}$$

If we write

$$Q_1 = 4\,(\eta\tau - \zeta^2), \quad Q_2 = 4\,(\eta\zeta - \xi\tau), \quad Q_3 = 4\,(\zeta\xi - \eta^2),$$
$$Q_4 = (-a_0\xi^2 + 6a_1\xi\eta - \ldots - a_6\tau^2),$$

the quadratic form in ξ, η, ζ, τ whose coefficient-system gives the matrix K has the form

$$xQ_1 + yQ_2 + zQ_3 + Q_4,$$

wherein, however, x, y, z do not necessarily satisfy the equation $\nabla = 0$; if we denote them therefore by x_1, y_1, z_1, and denote by x, y, z a point satisfying $\nabla = 0$, the quadratic form may be written

$$x_1 \frac{\partial \nabla}{\partial x} + y_1 \frac{\partial \nabla}{\partial y} + z_1 \frac{\partial \nabla}{\partial z} + \frac{\partial \nabla}{\partial t},$$

and its vanishing represents the tangent plane to $\nabla = 0$ at (x, y, z).

It may be remarked in passing that the determinant of five rows and columns occurring above, consisting of the determinant ∇ with the elements $c_0, -3c_1, 3c_2, -c_3, 0$ written to make a fifth row and a fifth column, if we change the sign of the first and third columns, then of the second, fourth and fifth rows, then divide the second and third columns, as also the second and third rows by 3, and write $\frac{2}{9}x = b_2$, $\frac{2}{9}y = b_1$, $\frac{2}{9}z = b_0$, becomes

$$\begin{vmatrix} a_0, & a_1, & a_2 - 3b_0, & a_3 - 9b_1, & c_0 \\ a_1, & a_2 + 2b_0, & a_3 + b_1, & a_4 - 3b_2, & c_1 \\ a_2 - 3b_0, & a_3 + b_1, & a_4 + 2b_2, & a_5, & c_2 \\ a_3 - 9b_1, & a_4 - 3b_2, & a_5, & a_6, & c_3 \\ c_0, & c_1, & c_2, & c_3, & 0 \end{vmatrix};$$

and it follows by what has been proved that this is unaltered in value by replacing a_r by $a_\lambda^{6-r} a_\mu^r$, b_r by $B_\lambda^{2-r} B_\mu^r$, where $B_1{}^2 = b_0$, $B_1 B_2 = b_1$, $B_2{}^2 = b_2$, and c_r by $\gamma_\lambda^{3-r} \gamma_\mu^r$, wherein $\lambda_1\mu_2 - \lambda_2\mu_1 = 1$; namely, for linear transformations of determinant unity it is an absolute invariant of the three binary forms, sextic, cubic and quadratic, denoted by $a_x{}^6$, $\gamma_x{}^3$, $B_x{}^2$. So the determinant of four rows and columns obtained by omitting the last row and column of this, is an invariant of the sextic and quadratic. And herein b_0, b_1, b_2 may be replaced by any the same constant multiples of themselves.

15. From the invariant character of the matrix K we can now obtain certain geometric properties of the surface $\nabla = |K| = 0$.

Firstly, as we have seen (pp. 57, 59), by means of equations of the form $X = \mu_2{}^2 x + 2\mu_2\mu_1 y + \mu_1{}^2 z - \frac{3}{2}\alpha_\lambda{}^2\alpha_\mu{}^4$, $Y = \mu_2\lambda_2 x + (\mu_2\lambda_1 + \mu_1\lambda_2) y + \mu_1\lambda_1 z - \frac{1}{2}\alpha_\lambda{}^3\alpha_\mu{}^3$, $Z = \lambda_2{}^2 x + 2\lambda_2\lambda_1 y + \lambda_1{}^2 z - \frac{3}{2}\alpha_\lambda{}^4\alpha_\mu{}^2$,

where $\lambda_1, \mu_1, \lambda_2, \mu_2$ are such that $\lambda_1\mu_2 - \lambda_2\mu_1 = 1$, $\alpha_\mu{}^6 = 0$, $\alpha_\lambda\alpha_\mu{}^5 = \frac{2}{3}$, it is reduced to the form $\Delta = 0$, in X, Y, Z, of which the expanded form has been given before (p. 41); supplying a multiplier $T\,(=1)$, to render the equation homogeneous, we have $\nabla = 16F$, where F is of the form

$$F = T^2 P - T[\lambda_0 X^3 - \lambda_1 X^2 Y + \lambda_2 X Y^2 - \tfrac{1}{2}\lambda_3 (Y^3 + XYZ) + \lambda_4 Y^2 Z - 4YZ^2] + (XZ - Y^2)^2;$$

thus $T = 0$ gives $F = (XZ - Y^2)^2$, so that the surface touches the plane at infinity along the conic $XZ - Y^2 = 0$; also, in form,

$$\frac{\partial F}{\partial X} = TL + 2Z(XZ - Y^2), \quad \frac{\partial F}{\partial Y} = TM - 4Y(XZ - Y^2),$$

$$\frac{\partial F}{\partial Z} = TN + 2X(XZ - Y^2),$$

$$\frac{\partial F}{\partial T} = 2TP - [\lambda_0 X^3 - \lambda_1 X^2 Y + \lambda_2 X Y^2 - \tfrac{1}{2}\lambda_3 (Y^3 + XYZ) + \lambda_4 Y^2 Z - 4YZ^2];$$

the surfaces $\partial F/\partial X=0$, $\partial F/\partial Y=0$, $\partial F/\partial Z=0$, $\partial F/\partial T=0$ thus meet $T=0$ respectively on the conic $XZ-Y^2=0$ and the line $Z=0$, the conic $XZ-Y^2=0$ and the line $Y=0$, the conic $XZ-Y^2=0$ and the line $X=0$, and on the cubic $\lambda_0X^3-\ldots-4YZ^2=0$; the six intersections at infinity of the conic and this cubic are given by $Y=-\theta X$, $Z=\theta^2X$ where, as we see at once on substituting in the cubic, θ is a root of the equation

$$\lambda_0+\lambda_1\theta+\lambda_2\theta^2+\lambda_3\theta^3+\lambda_4\theta^4+4\theta^5=0,$$

together with $X=0$, $Y=0$, $Z=1$, corresponding to $\theta=\infty$. Also when X, Y, Z are infinite we have

$$\begin{aligned}XZ-Y^2&=(\mu_2^2x+2\mu_2\mu_1y+\mu_1^2z)(\lambda_2^2x+2\lambda_2\lambda_1y+\lambda_1^2z)\\&\qquad-[\mu_2\lambda_2x+(\mu_2\lambda_1+\mu_1\lambda_2)y+\mu_1\lambda_1z]^2\\&=xz-y^2.\end{aligned}$$

Thus we infer that the surface $\nabla=0$ touches the plane at infinity along the conic $xz-y^2=0$, and has nodes on this conic at the six points

$$\frac{x}{1}=\frac{y}{-\theta}=\frac{z}{\theta^2}=\infty,$$

where θ is any one of the roots of the equation

$$a_0+6a_1\theta+15a_2\theta^2+\ldots+a_6\theta^6=0.$$

Further, by taking the coefficients of transformation λ_1, μ_1, λ_2, μ_2 to satisfy the equations

$$\lambda_1\mu_2-\lambda_2\mu_1=1,\quad \alpha_\lambda{}^6=0,\quad \alpha_\mu{}^6=0,$$

the transformed form of ∇ becomes of the shape

$$\begin{vmatrix}0, & \tfrac12\lambda_1, & 2Z, & -2Y\\ \tfrac12\lambda_1, & -(4Z+\lambda_2), & 2Y+\tfrac12\lambda_3, & 2X\\ 2Z, & 2Y+\tfrac12\lambda_3, & -(4X+\lambda_4), & \tfrac12\lambda_5\\ -2Y, & 2X, & \tfrac12\lambda_5, & 0\end{vmatrix},$$

differing from Δ in having $\lambda_0=0$ and λ_5 not necessarily equal to 4; when expanded this is

$$\begin{aligned}&(\tfrac14\lambda_1\lambda_5-4XZ)^2+4Y[\lambda_1X(4X+\lambda_4)+\lambda_5Z(4Z+\lambda_2)\\&\quad+(\tfrac14\lambda_1\lambda_5+4XZ)(2Y+\tfrac12\lambda_3)]+4Y^2[(2Y+\tfrac12\lambda_3)^2-(4X+\lambda_4)(4Z+\lambda_2)];\end{aligned}$$

thus the plane $Y=0$ touches the surface along a conic lying on $\frac14\lambda_1\lambda_5=4XZ$. Now the transformation to these coordinates is given by $\lambda_1\mu_2-\lambda_2\mu_1=1$, $\mu_2=\mu_1\theta$, $\lambda_2=\lambda_1\phi$, where θ, ϕ are any two different roots of the equation

$$a_0+6a_1\theta+15a_2\theta^2+\ldots+a_6\theta^6=0,$$

and

$$(X,Y,Z)=\begin{pmatrix}\mu_2^2, & 2\mu_2\mu_1, & \mu_1^2\\ \mu_2\lambda_2, & \mu_2\lambda_1+\mu_1\lambda_2, & \mu_1\lambda_1\\ \lambda_2^2, & 2\lambda_2\lambda_1, & \lambda_1^2\end{pmatrix}(x,y,z)-(\tfrac32\alpha_\lambda{}^2\alpha_\mu{}^4,\ \tfrac12\alpha_\lambda{}^3\alpha_\mu{}^3,\ \tfrac32\alpha_\lambda{}^4\alpha_\mu{}^2),$$

in particular

$$Y = \mu_2\lambda_2 x + (\mu_2\lambda_1 + \mu_1\lambda_2)\, y + \mu_1\lambda_1 z - \tfrac{1}{2}\frac{\alpha_\lambda{}^3\alpha_\mu{}^3}{(\lambda_1\mu_2 - \lambda_2\mu_1)^2}.$$

Dividing this by $\mu_1\lambda_1$, and denoting $\alpha_1 + \alpha_2\theta$ by α_θ, we infer that the plane $P_{\theta,\,\phi}$ or

$$\theta\phi x + (\theta + \phi)\, y + z - \frac{\alpha_\theta{}^3\,\alpha_\phi{}^3}{2\,(\theta - \phi)^2} = 0,$$

touches the surface $\nabla = 0$ along a conic lying on the quadric

$$\left[\theta^2 x + 2\theta y + z - \frac{3\alpha_\theta{}^4\alpha_\phi{}^2}{2\,(\theta - \phi)^2}\right]\left[\phi^2 x + 2\phi y + z - \frac{3\alpha_\theta{}^2\alpha_\phi{}^4}{2\,(\theta - \phi)^2}\right] = \tfrac{9}{4}\,\frac{\alpha_\theta\alpha_\phi{}^5\,.\,\alpha_\theta{}^5\alpha_\phi}{(\theta - \phi)^4}.$$

We have had the relation $K' = \bar{\mu} K \mu$ for the transformation of the matrix K (p. 58), equivalent to $K_{ij}' = \sum_r \sum_s K_{rs}\mu_{ri}\mu_{sj}$, and here $-2Y$ occurs as the fourth element K_{14}' in the first row of K'; the elements μ_{r1}, μ_{s4} in the matrix μ of the transformation $\xi = \mu\xi'$ are (p. 57)

$$(\lambda_1{}^3,\ -\lambda_1{}^2\lambda_2,\ \lambda_1\lambda_2{}^2,\ -\lambda_2{}^3) \quad \text{and} \quad (-\mu_1{}^3,\ \mu_1{}^2\mu_2,\ -\mu_1\mu_2{}^2,\ \mu_2{}^3);$$

thus, dividing by $\mu_1{}^3\lambda_1{}^3$, the plane $P_{\theta,\,\phi}$ can also be written

$$K(1,\ -\theta,\ \theta^2,\ -\theta^3)\,(1,\ -\phi,\ \phi^2,\ -\phi^3) = 0,$$

and this can be at once verified to be equivalent with the form above. There are thus fifteen such planes touching the surface $\nabla = 0$ along a conic, beside the plane at infinity.

If now $\theta_1, \theta_2, \ldots, \theta_6$ denote the roots of the equation

$$a_0 + 6a_1\theta + 15a_2\theta^2 + \ldots + a_6\theta^6 = 0,$$

we can prove that the point of concurrence of the three planes $P_{\theta_1,\,\theta_2}$, $P_{\theta_1,\,\theta_3}$, $P_{\theta_2,\,\theta_3}$ is on $\nabla = 0$, and is a node, and coincides with the point of concurrence of $P_{\theta_4,\,\theta_5}$, $P_{\theta_4,\,\theta_6}$, $P_{\theta_5,\,\theta_6}$; the surface has therefore ten nodes of this form, beside the six nodes proved to exist at infinity. To prove this, we first transform the ten equations $P_{\theta,\,\phi}$ into the forms which they take when the equation $\nabla = 0$ is transformed to $\Delta = 0$; these special forms will be of interest later in considering the expansion of the sigma functions in series.

It has been remarked that the plane $P_{\theta,\,\phi}$ is given by

$$K(1,\ -\theta,\ \theta^2,\ -\theta^3)\,(1,\ -\phi,\ \phi^2,\ -\phi^3);$$

further it is part of our definition of the transformation (p. 57), that the ratios of the quantities $(1,\ -\theta,\ \theta^2,\ -\theta^3)$ are transformed by the same law as the quantities $(\xi,\ \eta,\ \zeta,\ \tau)$, previously denoted by $\xi = \mu\xi'$; the equation of $P_{\theta,\,\phi}$,

$$\theta\phi x + (\theta + \phi)\, y + z = \frac{\alpha_\theta{}^3\alpha_\phi{}^3}{2\,(\theta - \phi)^2},$$

is therefore invariantive, and we may suppose, herein, x, y, z to be the variables denoted by x', y', z' on p. 57, and θ, ϕ to be the roots of the transformed sextic. In particular let

$$\alpha_x^6 = \lambda_0 + \lambda_1 x + \lambda_2 x^2 + \lambda_3 x^3 + \lambda_4 x^4 + 4x^5, = f(x), \text{ say},$$

and put, as before, p. 59, for x, y, z respectively,

$$X + \tfrac{1}{10}\lambda_4, \quad Y + \tfrac{1}{40}\lambda_3, \quad Z + \tfrac{1}{10}\lambda_2;$$

the equation is thus, on utilising the identity given, p. 53, which connects $2\alpha_\theta^3 \alpha_\phi^3$ with $F(\theta, \phi) = \sum_{i=0} (\theta\phi)^i [2\lambda_{2i} + \lambda_{2i+1}(\theta + \phi)]$, found to be

$$\theta\phi X + (\theta + \phi) Y + Z = \frac{F(\theta, \phi)}{4(\theta - \phi)^2},$$

where now θ, ϕ are any two roots of $f(x) = 0$, or consist of one of these roots together with the root ∞, which has not been expressed in our non-homogeneous method of writing the transformation; when ϕ is ∞, the transformed equation is

$$\theta X + Y = \{\tfrac{1}{4}\phi^{-1}(\theta - \phi)^{-2}[2\lambda_0 + \lambda_1(\theta + \phi) + \ldots + 2\theta^2\phi^2\lambda_4 + 4\theta^2\phi^2(\theta + \phi)]\},$$

where we are to take the limit of the right side for $\phi = \infty$, which is θ^2. There are thus ten singular planes, $P_{\theta, \phi}$, of the form

$$\theta\phi X + (\theta + \phi) Y + Z - \tfrac{1}{4}(\theta - \phi)^{-2} F(\theta, \phi) = 0,$$

where θ, ϕ are any two roots of $f(x) = 0$, and five, P_θ, of the form

$$\theta X + Y - \theta^2 = 0,$$

where θ is any root of $f(x) = 0$, beside the plane at infinity.

Denoting $\tfrac{1}{4}(\theta - \phi)^{-2} F(\theta, \phi)$ by $e_{\theta, \phi}$, it is at once evident that the planes P_θ, P_ϕ, $P_{\theta, \phi}$ intersect in the point $X = \theta + \phi$, $Y = -\theta\phi$, $Z = e_{\theta, \phi}$; let θ', ϕ', ψ' denote the roots of $f(x) = 0$ other than θ, ϕ; the plane $P_{\theta', \phi'}$ passes through the same point if

$$\theta'\phi'(\theta + \phi) - \theta\phi(\theta' + \phi') = e_{\theta', \phi'} - e_{\theta, \phi};$$

by writing $e_{\theta, \phi}$ in the form $\tfrac{1}{4}(\theta - \phi)^{-2}[F(\theta, \phi) - f(\theta) - f(\phi)]$ it is at once found to reduce to $\theta\phi(\theta' + \phi') + \psi'(\theta\phi + \theta'\phi')$, which establishes this identity; thus also the planes $P_{\phi', \psi'}$ and $P_{\theta', \psi'}$ pass through the same point. If in addition to the conditions $\alpha_\mu^6 = 0$, $\alpha_\lambda \alpha_\mu^5 = \tfrac{2}{3}$, $\lambda_1\mu_2 - \lambda_2\mu_1 = 1$, imposed on the four quantities λ_1, μ_1, λ_2, μ_2, in order to obtain the equation $\Delta = 0$, we make also $\alpha_\lambda^6 = 0$, the transformed sextic has also $\lambda_0 = 0$ and the ten points $(\theta + \phi, -\theta\phi, e_{\theta, \phi})$ break up into a set of six of this form, where θ, ϕ are any two roots of the equation $\lambda_1 + \lambda_2\theta + \lambda_3\theta^2 + \lambda_4\theta^3 + 4\theta^4 = 0$, together with four of coordinates of the form $(\theta, 0, \tfrac{1}{4}\lambda_1\theta^{-1})$; that this last point is a node appears at once from the transformed form of Δ, already given, p. 61,

$$(\lambda_1 - 4XZ)^2 + 4Y[4\lambda_1 X^2 + \lambda_1\lambda_4 X + \tfrac{1}{2}\lambda_3(\lambda_1 + 4XZ) + 4\lambda_2 Z + 16Z^2]$$
$$+ 4Y^2[(2Y + \tfrac{1}{2}\lambda_3)^2 - (4X + \lambda_4)(4Z + \lambda_2) + 2(\lambda_1 + 4XZ)] = 0,$$

wherein the coefficient of $4Y$ is reduced to zero by $X=\theta$, $Z=\frac{1}{4}\lambda_1\theta^{-1}$, provided

$$\lambda_1\theta^{-2}[4\theta^4+\lambda_4\theta^3+\lambda_3\theta^2+\lambda_2\theta+\lambda_1]=0;$$

thus it follows that $(\theta+\phi,\ -\theta\phi,\ e_{\theta,\phi})$ is a node of $\Delta=0$ and an intersection of six singular tangent planes. It is at once evident that the node of $\Delta=0$, corresponding to the infinite root of the transformed sextic, namely the point $X=0$, $Y=0$, $Z=\infty$, lies on each of the five planes $\theta X+Y-\theta^2=0$, as well as on the plane at infinity; that the node $X/1=-Y/\theta=Z/\theta^2=\infty$, lies on the six singular tangent planes constituted by, the plane at infinity, the plane $\theta X+Y-\theta^2=0$, and the four planes $\theta\phi X+(\theta+\phi)Y+Z-e_{\theta,\phi}=0$, where ϕ is one, other than θ, of the roots of the equation

$$\lambda_0+\lambda_1\theta+\ldots+4\theta^5=0;$$

and that conversely the plane $\theta X+Y-\theta^2=0$ contains, beside the node $X=0$, $Y=0$, $Z=\infty$, and the node $X/1=-Y/\theta=Z/\theta^2=\infty$, the four nodes $(\theta+\phi,\ -\theta\phi,\ e_{\theta,\phi})$, where ϕ is any one of the roots, other than θ, of the same quintic; while lastly the plane $\theta\phi X+(\theta+\phi)Y+Z-e_{\theta,\phi}=0$ contains, beside the two nodes $X/1=-Y/\theta=Z/\theta^2=\infty$, $X/1=-Y/\phi=Z/\phi^2=\infty$, the node $(\theta+\phi,\ -\theta\phi,\ e_{\theta,\phi})$, and the three nodes $(\theta'+\phi',\ -\theta'\phi',\ e_{\theta',\phi'})$, where θ', ϕ' are any two roots of the same quintic other than θ and ϕ.

The sixteen nodes of $\nabla=0$ thus lie in sixes upon sixteen planes each touching the surface along a conic, while through each node there pass six of these planes; in particular, as was stated above, if θ, ϕ, ψ, θ', ϕ', ψ', be the roots of the fundamental sextic, one node is the intersection of the six planes $P_{\theta,\phi}$, $P_{\theta,\psi}$, $P_{\phi,\psi}$, $P_{\theta',\phi'}$, $P_{\theta',\psi'}$, $P_{\phi',\psi'}$. If θ, ϕ, ψ be the roots of the cubic $p_0+3p_1x+3p_2x^2+p_3x^3=0$, and θ', ϕ', ψ' of $q_0+3q_1x+3q_2x^2+q_3x^3=0$, the fundamental sextic $a_0+6a_1x+\ldots+a_6x^6$ being written as a product of the cubics, or say, symbolically

$$\alpha_x^6=p_x^3q_x^3,$$

the node in question has coordinates x, y, z obtainable by equating powers of the arbitrary quantity λ in the equation

$$x\lambda^2+2y\lambda+z=-\tfrac{9}{20}(pq)^2p_\lambda q_\lambda,$$

or, what is the same thing, of the arbitrary quantities λ, μ in the equation

$$x\lambda\mu+y(\lambda+\mu)+z=-\tfrac{9}{40}(pq)^2(p_\lambda q_\mu+p_\mu q_\lambda).$$

To prove this result we may either proceed as before, first shewing this equation to be of invariantive character and then considering a particular system of coordinates for which the coordinates of the point (x, y, z) are known; or we may proceed directly as follows, with the notation of symbolical algebra. Writing $\alpha_x=\alpha_1x_1+\alpha_2x_2$, and differentiating the equation $\alpha_x^6=p_x^3q_x^3$ three times with the operator $z_1\partial/\partial x_1+z_2\partial/\partial x_2$, we find

$$20\,\alpha_x^3\alpha_z^3=p_x^3q_z^3+p_z^3q_x^3+9\,(p_x^2p_z\cdot q_xq_z^2+p_xp_z^2\cdot q_x^2q_z);$$

but

$$(xz)^2 (pq)^2 (p_x q_z + p_z q_x) = (p_x^2 q_z^2 + p_z^2 q_x^2 - 2p_x p_z q_x q_z)(p_x q_z + p_z q_x)$$
$$= p_x^3 q_z^3 + p_z^3 q_x^3 - (p_x^2 p_z \cdot q_x q_z^2 + p_x p_z^2 \cdot q_x^2 q_z);$$

write now $x_1 = 1$, $x_2 = \theta$, $z_1 = 1$, $z_2 = \phi$, with $p_\theta^3 = 0$, $p_\phi^3 = 0$; thus

$$20\, \alpha_\theta^3 \alpha_\phi^3 = -9\, (\theta\phi)^2 (pq)^2 (p_\theta q_\phi + p_\phi q_\theta),$$

and the result to be proved becomes, in the particular case when the arbitrary quantities λ, μ are replaced by θ, ϕ,

$$x\theta\phi + y(\theta + \phi) + z = \tfrac{1}{2}(\theta\phi)^{-2} \alpha_\theta^3 \alpha_\phi^3,$$

which is of the form of one of the six planes passing through the point whose coordinates are stated to be given by the formula. The result is then obvious.

One further remark must be made; the transformations of the surface ∇ so far employed have changed the nodes which are at infinity among themselves, and the finite nodes among themselves; there is, however, geometrically no such essential separation of the sixteen nodes into these two sets, any two of the sixteen being equipollent (gleichberechtigt). We do not stop now to prove this, as it is unnecessary for our purpose; it will appear incidentally below.

16. Associated with the surface $\nabla = 0$, which in future we may call Kummer's surface, is another surface, also of the fourth order, having a point to point correspondence with Kummer's surface, but in some respects simpler; to this surface, called Weddle's surface, we must, for the sake of the periodic functions by which it is expressed, devote some remarks.

If as before K denote the matrix whose determinant is ∇, each of the four expressions denoted by $K(\xi, \eta, \zeta, \tau)$, of which for instance the first is (p. 56)

$$-a_0\xi + 3a_1\eta + (-3a_2 + 2z)\zeta + (a_3 - 2y)\tau,$$

is linear in x, y, z. We can then write

$$K(\xi, \eta, \zeta, \tau) = W(x, y, z, 1),$$

where W is the matrix

$$W = \begin{pmatrix} 0, & -2\tau, & 2\zeta, & -a_0\xi + 3a_1\eta - 3a_2\zeta + a_3\tau \\ 2\tau, & 2\zeta, & -4\eta, & 3a_1\xi - 9a_2\eta + 9a_3\zeta - 3a_4\tau \\ -4\zeta, & 2\eta, & 2\xi, & -3a_2\xi + 9a_3\eta - 9a_4\zeta + 3a_5\tau \\ 2\eta, & -2\xi, & 0, & a_3\xi - 3a_4\eta + 3a_5\zeta - a_6\tau \end{pmatrix},$$

and the Weddle surface is that expressed in homogeneous coordinates ξ, η, ζ, τ by the vanishing of the determinant of this.

We have denoted by $\xi = \mu\xi'$ the general transformation of ξ, η, ζ, τ, considered here (p. 58); denote similarly the general transformation of x, y, z, by $(x, y, z, 1) = m(x', y', z', 1)$. We have seen that with

$$Q_1 = 4(\eta\tau - \zeta^2), \quad Q_2 = 4(\eta\zeta - \xi\tau), \quad Q_3 = 4(\zeta\xi - \eta^2)$$

and

$$Q_4 = -a_0\xi^2 + 6a_1\xi\eta - 6a_2\zeta\xi - 9a_2\eta^2 + 2a_3\xi\tau + 18a_3\eta\zeta - 6a_4\eta\tau - 9a_4\zeta^2 + 6a_5\zeta\tau - a_6\tau^2,$$

the expression $xQ_1 + yQ_2 + zQ_3 + Q_4$ is unaltered by this transformation; thus if Q_1', Q_2', Q_3', Q_4' be the transformed values of Q_1, Q_2, Q_3, Q_4, we have $(Q_1', Q_2', Q_3', Q_4') = \bar{m}(Q_1, Q_2, Q_3, Q_4)$. Also if W' denote the transformed form of W, namely the matrix whose first row consists of the elements $0, -2\tau'$, $2\zeta', -a_0'\xi' + 3a_1'\eta' - 3a_2'\zeta' + a_3'\tau'$, we have, as we have seen that $K' = \bar{\mu}K\mu$,

$$W'(x', y', z', 1) = K'(\xi', \eta', \zeta', \tau') = \bar{\mu}K\mu\xi' = \bar{\mu}K(\xi, \eta, \zeta, \tau) = \bar{\mu}W(x, y, z, 1)$$
$$= \bar{\mu}Wm(x', y', z', 1),$$

and hence $$W' = \bar{\mu}Wm,$$

whereby every element of W' is expressed as a linear function of the elements of W; and the determinants $|W'|$, $|W|$ are equal.

Considering the cubic curve in space expressed by

$$\frac{\xi}{1} = \frac{\eta}{-\theta} = \frac{\zeta}{\theta^2} = \frac{\tau}{-\theta^3},$$

and in particular the six points $\theta_1, \theta_2, \ldots, \theta_6$ upon this, where $\theta_1, \theta_2, \ldots, \theta_6$ are the roots of the equation

$$a_0 + 6a_1\theta + 15a_2\theta^2 + \ldots + a_6\theta^6 = 0,$$

the cones $Q_1 = 0$, $Q_2 = 0$, $Q_3 = 0$ contain the cubic curve, and the cone $Q_4 = 0$ passes through the six points, as is obvious at once on substitution. The quartic surface expressed by $|W| = 0$, or, as we shall write, $\Omega = 0$, may be regarded as arising by the elimination of $x, y, z, 1$ from the four equations

$$\partial Q/\partial\xi = 0, \quad \partial Q/\partial\eta = 0, \quad \partial Q/\partial\zeta = 0, \quad \partial Q/\partial\tau = 0,$$

where $Q = 0$, denoting

$$xQ_1 + yQ_2 + zQ_3 + Q_4 = 0,$$

is the most general quadric through the six points; it is thus the locus of the vertices of quadric cones containing these six points. The cone formed by joining any point of the cubic curve to all other points of the curve is a quadric cone; the surface Ω thus contains the cubic curve. A degenerate quadric cone containing the six points is formed by any pair of planes of which one contains three of the six points, and the other the other three; thus $\Omega = 0$ contains the ten lines of intersection of these pairs. And if any point be taken on the straight line joining two of the six points, a quadric cone can be constructed with this point as vertex to contain the six points; the surface Ω thus contains also the fifteen joining lines of the six points. Also each of the six points is a node on the surface, as may be seen directly by taking such a transformation as makes one of the roots θ of the fundamental sextic become infinite, and verifying that if $a_6 = 0$ the equation $\Omega = 0$ contains no term in τ^3.

These properties are derived by regarding $|W| = 0$ as arising from the assumption of the consistence of the four equations expressed by $W(x, y, z, 1) = 0$. We may however regard $|W| = 0$ as arising from assuming the consistence of the four equations expressed by $\overline{W}(\xi', \eta', \zeta', \tau') = 0$; these are the equations $\xi'\partial Q_r/\partial\xi + \eta'\partial Q_r/\partial\eta + \zeta'\partial Q_r/\partial\zeta + \tau'\partial Q_r/\partial\tau = 0$, for $r = 1, 2, 3, 4$; they express that the polar planes of (ξ, η, ζ, τ) in regard to the four quadrics $Q_1 = 0$, $Q_2 = 0$, $Q_3 = 0$, $Q_4 = 0$ are concurrent, or that the points (ξ, η, ζ, τ), $(\xi', \eta', \zeta', \tau')$ are conjugate to one another in regard to all the quadrics passing through the six base points, and as they are symmetrical in regard to these two points (ξ) and (ξ'), the surface Ω also contains $(\xi', \eta', \zeta', \tau')$. If we put

$$F = 6\xi\eta\zeta\tau - 4\zeta^3\xi - 4\eta^3\tau + 3\eta^2\zeta^2 - \xi^2\tau^2,$$

so that $F = 0$ is the developable surface generated by the tangent lines of the cubic curve $\xi/1 = -\eta/\theta = \zeta/\theta^2 = -\tau/\theta^3$, it is at once seen, by evaluating the minor determinants of the elements of the last column of the matrix W, that $\xi', \eta', \zeta', \tau'$ are expressible in terms of ξ, η, ζ, τ by means of

$$\frac{\xi'}{\dfrac{\partial F}{\partial \tau}} = \frac{\eta'}{-\dfrac{1}{3}\dfrac{\partial F}{\partial \zeta}} = \frac{\zeta'}{\dfrac{1}{3}\dfrac{\partial F}{\partial \eta}} = \frac{\tau'}{-\dfrac{\partial F}{\partial \xi}},$$

so that the equation $\Omega = 0$ can also be expressed by

$$\frac{\partial Q}{\partial \xi}\frac{\partial F}{\partial \tau} - \frac{1}{3}\frac{\partial Q}{\partial \eta}\frac{\partial F}{\partial \zeta} + \frac{1}{3}\frac{\partial Q}{\partial \zeta}\frac{\partial F}{\partial \eta} - \frac{\partial Q}{\partial \tau}\frac{\partial F}{\partial \xi} = 0,$$

wherein Q is the general quadric through the six base points; and as this relation is merely an identity when for Q are written either Q_1 or Q_2 or Q_3 it is sufficient, to represent Ω, to write Q_4 in place of Q. We may interpret this form geometrically by introducing the line coordinates, $l = bc' - b'c$, $m = ca' - c'a$, $n = ab' - a'b$, $l' = da' - d'a$, $m' = db' - d'b$, $n' = dc' - d'c$, of the line of intersection of two planes

$$a\xi + b\eta + c\zeta + d\tau = 0, \quad a'\xi + b'\eta + c'\zeta + d'\tau = 0;$$

then the equation expresses that the polar plane of (ξ, η, ζ, τ) in regard to the developable $F = 0$, is intersected by the polar planes of (ξ, η, ζ, τ) in regard to all the quadrics $Q = 0$, in lines belonging to the linear complex $l + 3l' = 0$; and $(\xi', \eta', \zeta', \tau')$ is the pole in this complex of the polar plane of (ξ, η, ζ, τ) in regard to $F = 0$. Putting

$$\frac{\xi'}{\dfrac{\partial F}{\partial \tau}} = \frac{\eta'}{-\dfrac{1}{3}\dfrac{\partial F}{\partial \zeta}} = \dots = \dots = \sigma,$$

it can be proved that

$$\frac{Q_1(\xi', \eta', \zeta', \tau')}{Q_1(\xi, \eta, \zeta, \tau)} = \frac{Q_2(\xi', \eta', \zeta', \tau')}{Q_2(\xi, \eta, \zeta, \tau)} = \frac{Q_3(\xi', \eta', \zeta', \tau')}{Q_3(\xi, \eta, \zeta, \tau)} = 4\sigma^2 F(\xi, \eta, \zeta, \tau);$$

hence it follows that the joining line of (ξ, η, ζ, τ) and $(\xi', \eta', \zeta', \tau')$ has for its intersections with $Q_1 = 0$ the same two points as with $Q_2 = 0$, and with $Q_3 = 0$, namely is a chord of the cubic curve $\xi/1 = -\eta/\theta = \zeta/\theta^2 = -\tau/\theta^3$; it is divided harmonically at (ξ, η, ζ, τ) and $(\xi', \eta', \zeta', \tau')$*.

If $Q_1 = 0$, $Q_2 = 0$, $Q_3 = 0$, $Q_4 = 0$ be any four quadric surfaces whatever, the conditions that the quadric $Q = xQ_1 + yQ_2 + zQ_3 + Q_4 = 0$ should be a cone with vertex at (ξ, η, ζ, τ) are expressed by the four equations such as

$$x\partial Q_1/\partial\xi + y\partial Q_2/\partial\xi + z\partial Q_3/\partial\xi + \partial Q_4/\partial\xi = 0,$$

which we may denote by $W_\xi(x, y, z, 1) = 0$, or $W_\xi(x) = 0$, where W_ξ denotes a certain matrix; if $\Omega = |W_\xi|$, the equation $\Omega = 0$ represents a quartic surface, the Jacobian of Q_1, Q_2, Q_3, Q_4. When this is satisfied the four equations expressed by $\overline{W}_\xi(\xi') = 0$, obtained by multiplying the rows of Ω respectively by $\xi', \eta', \zeta', \tau'$, can all be satisfied, and the points (ξ, η, ζ, τ), $(\xi', \eta', \zeta', \tau')$ are conjugate in regard to all the quadrics $Q_1 = 0$, $Q_2 = 0$, $Q_3 = 0$, $Q_4 = 0$. We can write $W_\xi(x)$ in the form $K_x(\xi)$, where K_x is a symmetrical matrix, and when $Q = 0$ is a cone, the parameters $(x, y, z, 1)$ are the coordinates of a point on the quartic surface $|K_x| = 0$. It can be shewn that, under this condition, the polar plane of $(\xi', \eta', \zeta', \tau')$, in regard to this cone, is the tangent plane of $\Omega = 0$ at $(\xi, \eta, \zeta, \tau) = 0$. For putting down the relation $\overline{W}_\xi(\xi') = 0$ for consecutive corresponding points $(\xi + d\xi)$, $(\xi' + d\xi')$, we have to the first approximation

$$\overline{W}_{d\xi}(\xi') + \overline{W}_\xi(d\xi') = 0,$$

leading, by $W_\xi(x) = 0$, if (x) denote $(x, y, z, 1)$, to

$$\overline{W}_{d\xi}(\xi')(x) = -\overline{W}_\xi(d\xi')(x) = -W_\xi(x)(d\xi') = 0;$$

thus the arbitrary increments $(d\xi)$ satisfy a linear equation

$$Ad\xi + Bd\eta + Cd\zeta + Dd\tau = 0,$$

in which A, B, C, D are definite functions of (ξ, η, ζ, τ); the tangent plane of $\Omega = 0$ at (ξ, η, ζ, τ), if (X, Y, Z, T), or (X), be current coordinates, is thus

$$\overline{W}_X(\xi')(x) = 0, = W_X(x)(\xi') = K_x(X)(\xi') = K_x(\xi')(X) = W_{\xi'}(x)(X);$$

or

$$X\left[x\frac{\partial Q_1(\xi')}{\partial\xi'} + y\frac{\partial Q_2(\xi')}{\partial\xi'} + z\frac{\partial Q_3(\xi')}{\partial\xi'} + \frac{\partial Q_4(\xi')}{\partial\xi'}\right] + \dots = 0,$$

which is the polar plane of (ξ') in regard to the cone $xQ_1 + yQ_2 + zQ_3 + Q_4 = 0$†.

* It is easy to see that the tangents of the cubic curve belong to the complex $l + 3l' = 0$, and that any point of this curve and its osculating plane are pole and polar plane in this complex. For this complex cf. Reye, *Géométrie de Position* (Chemin), Deuxme Partie (1882), p. 114.

† The quartic surfaces $\Omega = 0$, $|K_x| = 0$ are considered by Cayley, *Collected Papers*, vol. vii, p. 160. The above construction for the tangent plane of the Jacobian is proved geometrically for the case of four quadrics with six points common by H. Bateman, *Proc. Lond. Math. Soc.*, New Series, vol. iii (1905), p. 232.

Pass back now for a moment to the functional relations; the general differential equations of p. 49, if we differentiate that one involving $\wp_{2222}$ in regard to u_1, and that one involving $\wp_{2221}$, in regard to u_2, and then subtract, lead to an equation linear in $\wp_{22}, \wp_{21}, \wp_{11}$, and also linear in $\wp_{222}, \wp_{221}, \wp_{211}, \wp_{111}$; and there are four equations similarly obtainable; replacing $\wp_{22}, \ldots$ by $x, \ldots$ and $\wp_{222}, \ldots$ by $\xi, \ldots$, these are the four equations expressible either by $K(\xi, \eta, \zeta, \tau) = 0$, or $W(x, y, z, 1) = 0$; thus the surface $\nabla = |K| = 0$ is satisfied by writing $x = \wp_{22}(u)$, $y = \wp_{21}(u)$, $z = \wp_{11}(u)$, and the surface $\Omega = |W| = 0$ is satisfied by writing $\xi = \wp_{222}(u)$, $\eta = \wp_{221}(u)$, $\zeta = \wp_{211}(u)$, $\tau = \wp_{111}(u)$. Either of these two sets of functions can be expressed algebraically in terms of two parameters; see above p. 40, and below p. 77.

17. With a view to having ready to hand concrete geometrical interpretations of certain functional relations which will be subsequently obtained, we desire to give now the proof of a group of birational transformations of which the surfaces $\nabla = 0$, $\Omega = 0$ are each susceptible. The relations expressed by $W(x, y, z, 1) = K(\xi, \eta, \zeta, \tau) = 0$ establish a point to point correspondence between these surfaces; we shall prove the transformations for the surface $\Omega = 0$, and thence deduce the corresponding formulae for $\nabla = 0$.

Put, as before

$$Q_1 = 4(\eta\tau - \zeta^2), \quad Q_2 = 4(\eta\zeta - \xi\tau), \quad Q_3 = 4(\zeta\xi - \eta^2),$$
$$Q_4 = -a_0\xi^2 + 6a_1\xi\eta - 6a_2\xi\zeta - 9a_2\eta^2 + 2a_3\xi\tau + 18a_3\eta\zeta - 6a_4\eta\tau - 9a_4\zeta^2 + 6a_5\zeta\tau - a_6\tau^2$$

and
$$P_4 = Q_4 + \tfrac{3}{2}a_4Q_1 + \tfrac{1}{2}a_3Q_2 + \tfrac{3}{2}a_2Q_3$$
$$= -a_0\xi^2 + 6a_1\xi\eta - 15a_2\eta^2 + 20a_3\eta\zeta - 15a_4\zeta^2 + 6a_5\zeta\tau - a_6\tau^2$$

so that $P_4 = 0$ is, equally with $Q_4 = 0$, a quadric passing through the six base points, which becomes, for

$$a_0 = \lambda_0, \quad 6a_1 = \lambda_1, \quad 15a_2 = \lambda_2, \quad 20a_3 = \lambda_3, \quad 15a_4 = \lambda_4, \quad 6a_5 = 4, \quad a_6 = 0,$$

reduced to
$$P_4 = -\lambda_0\xi^2 + \lambda_1\xi\eta - \lambda_2\eta^2 + \lambda_3\eta\zeta - \lambda_4\zeta^2 + 4\zeta\tau;$$

while, correspondingly,

$$W\begin{pmatrix} 1 & 0 & 0 & \tfrac{3}{2}a_4 \\ 0 & 1 & 0 & \tfrac{1}{2}a_3 \\ 0 & 0 & 1 & \tfrac{3}{2}a_2 \\ 0 & 0 & 0 & 1 \end{pmatrix} = \begin{pmatrix} 0 & -2\tau & 2\zeta & -a_0\xi + 3a_1\eta \\ 2\tau & 2\zeta & -4\eta & 3a_1\xi - 15a_2\eta + 10a_3\zeta \\ -4\zeta & 2\eta & 2\xi & -10a_3\eta - 15a_4\zeta + 3a_5\tau \\ 2\eta & -2\xi & 0 & 3a_5\zeta - a_6\tau \end{pmatrix},$$

of which the left side will be denoted by WP, where P denotes the second matrix. When $a_6 = 0$, the surface $\Omega = 0$ has a node at $(0, 0, 0, 1)$, corresponding to the infinite root of the fundamental sextic; let $a_6 = 0$, $6a_5 = 4$, $15a_4 = \lambda_4$, etc., and let (ξ, η, ζ, τ), $(\xi_1, \eta_1, \zeta_1, \tau_1)$ be two points of $\Omega = 0$ collinear with this node; we first verify* directly that

* Geometrically, the equation

$$-Q_2(\xi_1)\,Q_1(\xi) + Q_1(\xi_1)\,Q_2(\xi) + P_4(\xi_1)\,Q_3(\xi) - Q_3(\xi_1)\,P_4(\xi) = 0$$

represents a cone with vertex at the remaining intersection of the Weddle surface with the line joining the node $(0, 0, 0, 1)$ to $(\xi_1, \eta_1, \zeta_1, \tau_1)$.

$$\begin{pmatrix} 0 & -2\tau_1 & 2\zeta_1 & -\lambda_0\xi_1 + \frac{1}{2}\lambda_1\eta_1 \\ 2\tau_1 & 2\zeta_1 & -4\eta_1 & \frac{1}{2}\lambda_1\xi_1 - \lambda_2\eta_1 + \frac{1}{2}\lambda_3\zeta_1 \\ -4\zeta_1 & 2\eta_1 & 2\xi_1 & \frac{1}{2}\lambda_3\eta_1 - \lambda_4\zeta_1 + 2\tau_1 \\ 2\eta_1 & -2\xi_1 & 0 & 2\zeta_1 \end{pmatrix} (-Q_2, Q_1, P_4, -Q_3) = 0,$$

where P_4 has the form given above. We have denoted the general matrix from which this is derived by W, and its determinant by Ω; we shall denote this matrix, with ξ, η, ζ, τ for variables, by w, and its determinant by ω, indicating the substitution of $(\xi_1, \eta_1, \zeta_1, \tau_1)$ for (ξ, η, ζ, τ) by writing w_1 instead of w; similarly $Q_1^{(1)}$, $Q_2^{(1)}$, etc. will denote the result of substituting $\xi_1, \ldots$ for $\xi, \ldots$. We may suppose $\xi_1 = \xi$, $\eta_1 = \eta$, $\zeta_1 = \zeta$. We are to prove

$$w_1(-Q_2, Q_1, P_4, -Q_3) = 0, = w(-Q_2^{(1)}, Q_1^{(1)}, P_4^{(1)}, -Q_3^{(1)}):$$

it is at once found, with $\xi_1 = \xi$, $\eta_1 = \eta$, $\zeta_1 = \zeta$, that

$$Q_1^{(1)} = Q_1 + 4\eta(\tau_1 - \tau),\quad Q_2^{(1)} = Q_2 - 4\xi(\tau_1 - \tau),\quad Q_3^{(1)} = Q_3,\quad P_4^{(1)} = P_4 + 4\zeta(\tau_1 - \tau),$$

or say

$$(-Q_2^{(1)}, Q_1^{(1)}, P_4^{(1)}, -Q_3^{(1)}) = (-Q_2, Q_1, P_4, -Q_3) + 4(\tau_1 - \tau)(\xi, \eta, \zeta, 0)$$

and that
$$w(\xi, \eta, \zeta, 0) = -\tfrac{1}{2}(Q_1, Q_2, Q_3, 0);$$

hence

$$w(-Q_2^{(1)}, Q_1^{(1)}, P_4^{(1)}, -Q_3^{(1)}) = w(-Q_2, Q_1, P_4, -Q_3) - 2(\tau_1 - \tau)(Q_1, Q_2, Q_3, 0);$$

now, since $\xi Q_1 + \eta Q_2 + \zeta Q_3 = 0$, we may put

$$w(-Q_2, Q_1, P_4, -Q_3) = (2N_1, 2N_2, 2N_3, 0),$$

where N_1, N_2, N_3 are certain cubic polynomials in ξ, η, ζ, τ; then since

$$\overline{w}(\xi, \eta, \zeta, \tau) = (Q_1, Q_2, Q_3, P_4),$$

we have

$$\begin{aligned} 2(N_1\xi + N_2\eta + N_3\zeta) &= w(-Q_2, Q_1, P_4, -Q_3)(\xi, \eta, \zeta, \tau) \\ &= \overline{w}(\xi, \eta, \zeta, \tau)(-Q_2, Q_1, P_4, -Q_3) \\ &= (Q_1, Q_2, Q_3, P_4)(-Q_2, Q_1, P_4, -Q_3) \\ &= -Q_1Q_2 + Q_2Q_1 + Q_3P_4 - P_4Q_3 \\ &= 0, \end{aligned}$$

as well as

$$Q_1\xi + Q_2\eta + Q_3\zeta = 0;$$

thus identically

$$\frac{N_2Q_3 - N_3Q_2}{\xi} = \frac{N_3Q_1 - N_1Q_3}{\eta} = \frac{N_1Q_2 - N_2Q_1}{\zeta},$$

and we find in fact on computation that these fractions are all equal to -4ω, where ω is the determinant of w. Thus, when ξ, η, ζ, τ satisfy the equation $\omega = 0$, we have

$$\frac{N_1}{Q_1} = \frac{N_2}{Q_2} = \frac{N_3}{Q_3}.$$

But when both (ξ, η, ζ, τ), and $(\xi, \eta, \zeta, \tau_1)$ satisfy the equation $\omega = 0$, or

$$-\lambda_0\xi(3\xi\eta\zeta - 2\eta^3 - \xi^2\tau) + \lambda_1(\xi\eta^2\zeta - \xi^2\eta\tau + \xi^2\zeta^2 - \eta^4) + \lambda_2\eta(\xi\eta\tau - 2\xi\zeta^2 + \eta^2\zeta)$$
$$+ \lambda_3(\xi\zeta^3 - \eta^3\tau) - \lambda_4\zeta(\xi\zeta\tau - 2\eta^2\tau + \eta\zeta^2) + 4(\xi\zeta\tau^2 - \eta\zeta^2\tau - \eta^2\tau^2 + \zeta^4) = 0,$$

we find, by an easy calculation,

$$\tau_1 - \tau = \frac{N_3}{Q_3}.$$

On the whole then we have

$$w(-Q_2^{(1)}, Q_1^{(1)}, P_4^{(1)}, -Q_3^{(1)}) = (2N_1, 2N_2, 2N_3, 0) - 2(\tau_1 - \tau)(Q_1, Q_2, Q_3, 0)$$
$$= 0,$$

as we desired to prove.

This result relates to the case when the fundamental sextic has the form $\lambda_0 + \lambda_1 x + \ldots + \lambda_4 x^4 + 4x^5$, and the points (ξ, η, ζ, τ), $(\xi_1, \eta_1, \zeta_1, \tau_1)$ are collinear with the node $(0, 0, 0, 1)$ of $\omega = 0$. By transformation we can obtain the corresponding result when the fundamental sextic has its general form and the two points considered are collinear with any node of $\Omega = 0$, and thence again the result for $\omega = 0$ when the two points considered are collinear with any node of this.

Attach dashes to the variables which have been used in the preceding verification, and so write the result obtained,

$$w_1' j (Q_1', Q_2', Q_3', P_4') = 0,$$

where

$$j = \begin{pmatrix} 0 & -1 & 0 & 0 \\ 1 & 0 & 0 & 0 \\ 0 & 0 & 0 & 1 \\ 0 & 0 & -1 & 0 \end{pmatrix}.$$

Now take (ξ, η, ζ, τ), $(\xi_1, \eta_1, \zeta_1, \tau_1)$ collinear with any node

$$\frac{\xi}{\psi^3} = \frac{\eta}{-\psi^2} = \frac{\zeta}{\psi} = \frac{\tau}{-1},$$

of $\Omega = 0$, where ψ is any root of the sextic

$$(\alpha_1\psi + \alpha_2)^6 = \alpha_\psi^6 = F(\psi)$$
$$= a_0\psi^6 + 6a_1\psi^5 + 15a_2\psi^4 + 20a_3\psi^3 + 15a_4\psi^2 + 6a_5\psi + a_6 = 0,$$

and take four coefficients of transformation $\lambda_1, \lambda_2, \mu_1, \mu_2$ defined by (p. 51)

$$\lambda_2 = 0,\ \ \mu_1 = \mu_2\psi,\ \ \lambda_1\mu_2 = 1,\ \ 4\mu_2^{-4} = 6a_0\psi^5 + \ldots = F'(\psi);$$

put also (pp. 57, 69)

$$\varpi = mP' = \begin{pmatrix} \lambda_1^2 & -2\lambda_1\mu_1 & \mu_1^2 & 0 \\ -\lambda_1\lambda_2 & \lambda_1\mu_2 + \lambda_2\mu_1 & -\mu_1\mu_2 & 0 \\ \lambda_2^2 & -2\lambda_2\mu_2 & \mu_2^2 & 0 \\ 0 & 0 & 0 & 1 \end{pmatrix}\begin{pmatrix} 1 & 0 & 0 & \frac{3}{2}\alpha_\lambda^2\alpha_\mu^4 \\ 0 & 1 & 0 & \frac{1}{2}\alpha_\lambda^3\alpha_\mu^3 \\ 0 & 0 & 1 & \frac{3}{2}\alpha_\lambda^4\alpha_\mu^2 \\ 0 & 0 & 0 & 1 \end{pmatrix},$$

and $\quad (\xi, \eta, \zeta, \tau) = \mu(\xi', \eta', \zeta', \tau'), \quad (\xi_1, \eta_1, \zeta_1, \tau_1) = \mu(\xi_1', \eta_1', \zeta_1', \tau_1'),$

the matrix μ being given explicitly in terms of $\lambda_1, \mu_1, \lambda_2, \mu_2$ on p. 57; then $\bar{\mu}Wm$ is of the same form as the matrix W but has coefficients $a_r' = \alpha_\lambda^{6-r}\alpha_\mu^r$ in place of a_r, and variables $(\xi', \eta', \zeta', \tau')$ in place of ξ, η, ζ, τ (p. 66), and $\bar{\mu}WmP'$ or $\bar{\mu}W\varpi$ is of the form w (p. 69) in variables $(\xi', \eta', \zeta', \tau')$ and coefficients

$$\lambda_0 = a_0' = \alpha_\lambda^6, \quad \lambda_1 = a_1', \ldots, \quad \lambda_4 = a_4', \quad \lambda_5 = 4, \quad \lambda_6 = 0;$$

thus we have

$$w_1' = \bar{\mu}W_1\varpi;$$

further Q_1, Q_2, Q_3, Q_4 being as on p. 66, $\bar{m}(Q_1, Q_2, Q_3, Q_4)$ is (Q_1', Q_2', Q_3', Q_4'), in the variables $(\xi', \eta', \zeta', \tau')$, as we have seen, so that $\bar{P}'\bar{m}(Q_1, Q_2, Q_3, Q_4)$ is (Q_1', Q_2', Q_3', P_4') as on p. 69; thus

$$(Q_1', Q_2', Q_3', P_4') = \bar{\varpi}(Q_1, Q_2, Q_3, Q_4).$$

Hence, the equation

$$w_1'j(Q_1', Q_2', Q_3', P_4') = 0,$$

is the same as

$$\bar{\mu}W_1\varpi j\bar{\varpi}(Q_1, Q_2, Q_3, Q_4) = 0.$$

In passing from the variables x, y, z to x', y', z', and thence to (X, Y, Z) (p. 60) we have put successively $(x, y, z, 1) = m(x', y', z', 1)$ and $(x', y', z', 1) = P'(X, Y, Z, 1)$, so that $(x, y, z, 1) = \varpi(X, Y, Z, 1)$; put

$$\gamma = ij = \begin{pmatrix} 0 & -i & 0 & 0 \\ i & 0 & 0 & 0 \\ 0 & 0 & 0 & i \\ 0 & 0 & -i & 0 \end{pmatrix},$$

so that, as we see easily, $\gamma^2 = 1$, and define a matrix Γ_θ by means of

$$\Gamma_\theta^{-1} = \varpi\gamma\bar{\varpi} = \varpi\gamma^{-1}\bar{\varpi}, \quad \text{or} \quad \gamma = \bar{\varpi}\Gamma_\theta\varpi,$$

so that Γ_θ^{-1} is a skew symmetrical matrix whose elements are functions of the quantity θ, where $\theta = \psi^{-1}$, and

$$a_0 + 6a_1\theta + 15a_2\theta^2 + \ldots + a_6\theta^6 = 0,$$

and, if

$$(x_1, y_1, z_1, 1) = \varpi(X_1, Y_1, Z_1, 1), \quad (x_2, y_2, z_2, 1) = \varpi(X_2, Y_2, Z_2, 1),$$

$$\begin{aligned}\Gamma_\theta(x_1, y_1, z_1, 1)(x_2, y_2, z_2, 1) &= \Gamma_\theta\varpi(X_1, Y_1, Z_1, 1) \,.\, \varpi(X_2, Y_2, Z_2, 1) \\ &= \bar{\varpi}\Gamma_\theta\varpi(X_1, Y_1, Z_1, 1)(X_2, Y_2, Z_2, 1) \\ &= \gamma(X_1, Y_1, Z_1, 1)(X_2, Y_2, Z_2, 1);\end{aligned}$$

thus finally the relation above becomes, if we omit the factor $\bar{\mu}$, whose determinant is not zero, and multiply throughout by i,

$$W_1\Gamma_\theta^{-1}(Q_1, Q_2, Q_3, Q_4) = 0,$$

and here, as we easily calculate,

$$\Gamma_\theta^{-1} = \begin{pmatrix} 0 & -r' & q' & p \\ r' & 0 & -p' & q \\ -q' & p' & 0 & r \\ -p & -q & -r & 0 \end{pmatrix},$$

where

$$\rho p = \psi^2, \quad \rho q = -\psi, \quad \rho r = 1, \quad \rho p' = \tfrac{1}{2}(a_0\psi^3 + 3a_1\psi^2 + 3a_2\psi + a_3),$$
$$\rho q' = -\tfrac{1}{2}(a_0\psi^4 + 6a_1\psi^3 + 12a_2\psi^2 + 10a_3\psi + 3a_4),$$
$$\rho r' = \tfrac{1}{2}(a_0\psi^5 + 6a_1\psi^4 + 15a_2\psi^3 + 19a_3\psi^2 + 12a_4\psi + 3a_5),$$
$$\rho = \sqrt{-\tfrac{1}{4}F'(\psi)} = \sqrt{-\tfrac{1}{4}(6a_0\psi^5 + \dots)},$$

so that
$$pp' + qq' + rr' = -1;$$

and this is the covariantive form corresponding to the case when (ξ, η, ζ, τ), $(\xi_1, \eta_1, \zeta_1, \tau_1)$ are collinear with any node $\xi = -\eta/\theta = \zeta/\theta^2 = -\tau/\theta^3$ of $\Omega = 0$, the fundamental sextic being $(\theta = \psi^{-1})$

$$\alpha_\psi^6 = F(\psi) = a_0\psi^6 + 6a_1\psi^5 + \dots + a_6 = 0.$$

The forms of p', q', r' are given by the statement, easily verified, that if σ be an arbitrary quantity

$$2\rho(p'\sigma^2 - q'\sigma + r') = (\alpha_\psi^3\alpha_\sigma^3 - \alpha_\psi^6)/(\sigma - \psi) = \alpha_\psi^3\alpha_\sigma^3/(\sigma - \psi),$$

where $\alpha_\psi = \alpha_1\psi + \alpha_2, \quad \alpha_\sigma = \alpha_1\sigma + \alpha_2, \quad \alpha_1^6 = a_0, \quad \alpha_1^5\alpha_2 = a_1$, etc.,

so that

$$\alpha_\psi^3\alpha_\sigma^3 = \sigma^3(a_0\psi^3 + 3a_1\psi^2 + 3a_2\psi + a_3) + 3\sigma^2(a_1\psi^3 + 3a_2\psi^2 + 3a_3\psi + a_4)$$
$$+ 3\sigma(a_2\psi^3 + 3a_3\psi^2 + 3a_4\psi + a_5) + a_3\psi^3 + 3a_4\psi^2 + 3a_5\psi + a_6,$$

and the whole matrix Γ_θ is determined by the statement that, for arbitrary σ,

$$2\rho\Gamma_\theta(\sigma^2, -\sigma, 1, 0), = 2\rho\begin{pmatrix} 0, & -r, & q, & p' \\ r, & 0, & -p, & q' \\ -q, & p, & 0, & r' \\ -p', & -q', & -r', & 0 \end{pmatrix}(\sigma^2, -\sigma, 1, 0),$$
$$= 2(\sigma - \psi)\left(1, \sigma + \psi, \sigma\psi, -\frac{\alpha_\sigma^3\alpha_\psi^3}{2(\sigma - \psi)^2}\right).$$

To modify the equation $W_1\Gamma_\theta^{-1}(Q_1, Q_2, Q_3, Q_4) = 0$ to the form suitable for the case when the Weddle surface is $\omega = 0$, we take *any four constants* $\lambda_1, \lambda_2, \mu_1, \mu_2$ such that $\lambda_1\mu_2 - \lambda_2\mu_1 = 1$, and put

$$\varpi^{-1} = P'^{-1}m^{-1} = \begin{pmatrix} \mu_2^2 & 2\mu_2\mu_1 & \mu_1^2 & -\tfrac{3}{2}\alpha_\lambda^2\alpha_\mu^4 \\ \mu_2\lambda_2 & \mu_2\lambda_1 + \mu_1\lambda_2 & \mu_1\lambda_1 & -\tfrac{1}{2}\alpha_\lambda^3\alpha_\mu^3 \\ \lambda_2^2 & 2\lambda_2\lambda_1 & \lambda_1^2 & -\tfrac{3}{2}\alpha_\lambda^4\alpha_\mu^2 \\ 0 & 0 & 0 & 1 \end{pmatrix},$$

and

$$F(\psi) = (\alpha_1\psi + \alpha_2)^6 = (\alpha_\lambda\psi' + \alpha_\mu)^6 . (\lambda_1 - \lambda_2\psi)^6 = F_1(\psi') . (\lambda_1 - \lambda_2\psi)^6,$$

where $\psi' = (\mu_2\psi - \mu_1)/(\lambda_1 - \lambda_2\psi)$;

then we find

$$\varpi^{-1}\Gamma_\theta^{-1}\bar{\varpi}^{-1} = \begin{pmatrix} 0 & -r' & q' & p \\ r' & 0 & -p' & q \\ -q' & p' & 0 & r \\ -p & -q & -r & 0 \end{pmatrix}, = \gamma_{\theta'}^{-1}, \text{ say, } (\theta' = \psi'^{-1}),$$

where, with

$$\lambda_0 = \alpha_\lambda^6,\ \lambda_1 = 6\alpha_\lambda^5\alpha_\mu,\ \lambda_2 = 15\alpha_\lambda^4\alpha_\mu^2, \ldots,\ \lambda_6 = \alpha_\mu^6,\ \rho_1 = [-\tfrac{1}{4}dF_1(\psi')/d\psi']^{\frac{1}{2}},$$

we have

$$\rho_1 p = \psi'^2,\ \rho_1 q = -\psi',\ \rho_1 r = 1,\ \rho_1 p' = \tfrac{1}{2}(\lambda_0\psi'^3 + \tfrac{1}{2}\lambda_1\psi'^2),$$

$$\rho_1 q' = -\tfrac{1}{2}(\lambda_0\psi'^4 + \lambda_1\psi'^3 + \lambda_2\psi'^2 + \tfrac{1}{2}\lambda_3\psi'),$$

$$\rho_1 r' = \tfrac{1}{2}(\lambda_0\psi'^5 + \lambda_1\psi'^4 + \lambda_2\psi'^3 + \lambda_3\psi'^2 + \lambda_4\psi' + \tfrac{1}{2}\lambda_5),$$

so that $pp' + qq' + rr' = -1,$

and the equation $\bar{\mu}W_1\Gamma_\theta^{-1}(Q_1, Q_2, Q_3, Q_4) = 0,$

written in the form

$$\bar{\mu}W_1\varpi . \varpi^{-1}\Gamma_\theta^{-1}\bar{\varpi}^{-1} . \bar{\varpi}(Q_1, Q_2, Q_3, Q_4) = 0,$$

becomes (p. 72), if we further suppose (p. 51)

$$\lambda_2 = 0,\ \mu_1 = \mu_2\psi_0,\ \lambda_1\mu_2 = 1,\ 4\mu_2^{-4} = 6a_0\psi_0^5 + \ldots = F'(\psi_0),$$

where ψ_0 is a particular root of $F(\psi) = 0$, the equation

$$w_1\gamma_{\theta'}^{-1}(Q_1, Q_2, Q_3, P_4) = 0,$$

where θ' is any root of the *sextic*,

$$\lambda_0 + \lambda_1\theta' + \lambda_2\theta'^2 + \ldots + \lambda_4\theta'^4 + 4\theta'^5 = 0,$$

and $P_4 = -\lambda_0\xi^2 + \lambda_1\xi\eta - \lambda_2\eta^2 + \lambda_3\eta\zeta - \lambda_4\zeta^2 + 4\zeta\tau,$

the form of w being given on p. 70. This form includes the case when $\psi' = 0$ or $\theta' = \infty$; then

$$\rho_1^2 = -\tfrac{1}{4}(6\lambda_0\psi'^5 + \ldots + 4) = -1,\ \rho_1 = -i, \text{ say},$$

$$p = 0,\ q = 0,\ r = i,\ p' = 0,\ q' = 0,\ r' = i,$$

and $\gamma_{\theta'}^{-1}$ reduces to γ^{-1}.

When ψ' is not zero we have $\rho_1 r' = -1$, and $\rho_1 p'$, $\rho_1 q'$ may be taken in the forms

$$\rho_1 p' = -\frac{1}{2}\left(\frac{1}{\psi'}\right)^2(\tfrac{1}{2}\lambda_1\psi'^4 + \lambda_2\psi'^3 + \lambda_3\psi'^2 + \lambda_4\psi' + 4),$$

$$\rho_1 q' = \frac{1}{2}\left(\frac{1}{\psi'}\right)(\tfrac{1}{2}\lambda_3\psi'^2 + \lambda_4\psi' + 4).$$

Also, if σ be an arbitrary quantity, $\tau = \frac{1}{\sigma}$, $\theta' = \frac{1}{\psi'}$, and $e_{\theta,\tau}$ be given as before by

$$4(\theta - \tau)^2 e_{\theta,\tau} = \sum_{r=0}^{2} (\theta\tau)^r [2\lambda_{2r} + \lambda_{2r+1}(\theta + \tau)],$$

we have $$\rho_1 (p'\sigma^2 - q'\sigma + r') = (\sigma - \psi')\sigma\psi' e_{\theta',\tau}.$$

And, if $$f(\theta') = \lambda_0 + \lambda_1\theta' + \lambda_2\theta'^2 + \lambda_3\theta'^3 + \lambda_4\theta'^4 + 4\theta'^5,$$

we have $$\rho_1^2 = -\tfrac{1}{4}F_1'(\psi') = \tfrac{1}{4}\psi'^4 f'(\theta')$$
$$= \tfrac{1}{4}\psi'^4 (\lambda_1 + 2\lambda_2\theta' + \ldots + 4\lambda_4\theta'^3 + 20\theta'^4),$$

or $$\kappa_1 = \rho_1\theta'^2 = \sqrt{\tfrac{1}{4}f'(\theta')},$$

so that

$$\kappa_1 p = 1,\ \kappa_1 q = -\theta',\ \kappa_1 r = \theta'^2,\ \kappa_1 p' = -\tfrac{1}{2}(\tfrac{1}{2}\lambda_1 + \lambda_2\theta' + \lambda_3\theta'^2 + \lambda_4\theta'^3 + 4\theta'^4),$$
$$\kappa_1 q' = \tfrac{1}{2}(\tfrac{1}{2}\lambda_3\theta' + \lambda_4\theta'^2 + 4\theta'^3), \qquad \kappa_1 r' = -\theta'^2.$$

If (x_1, y_1, z_1) be a point determined from (ξ, η, ξ, τ) by

$$(x_1, y_1, z_1, 1) = C\Gamma^{-1}(Q_1, Q_2, Q_3, Q_4)$$

where C is a number, so taken that the fourth quantity on the right, as on the left, is unity, the fundamental equation (p. 72)

$$W_1\Gamma^{-1}(Q_1, Q_2, Q_3, Q_4) = 0$$

gives $$W_1(x_1, y_1, z_1, 1) = 0,$$

so that (x_1, y_1, z_1) is on the surface $\nabla = 0$, and is the point previously (p. 65) associated with the point $(\xi_1, \eta_1, \zeta_1, \tau_1)$ of $\Omega = 0$. In the same way the point (x, y, z) determined by

$$(x, y, z, 1) = C_1\Gamma^{-1}(Q_1^{(1)}, Q_2^{(1)}, Q_3^{(1)}, Q_4^{(1)})$$

is on $\nabla = 0$, and is the point associated with (ξ, η, ζ, τ). The tangent plane of $\nabla = 0$ at (x, y, z) is (p. 59), if X, Y, Z be current coordinates,

$$XQ_1 + YQ_2 + ZQ_3 + Q_4 = 0,$$

and contains the point (x_1, y_1, z_1) if only

$$C\Gamma^{-1}(Q_1, Q_2, Q_3, Q_4)(Q_1, Q_2, Q_3, Q_4) = 0,$$

which is satisfied identically in virtue of the skew character of Γ^{-1}. Thus each of the points (x, y, z), (x_1, y_1, z_1) is on the tangent plane of the other, and their joining line is a bitangent of the surface $\nabla = 0$. We shall call (x_1, y_1, z_1) the satellite point of (x, y, z) associated with the root ψ of the fundamental sextic which occurs in Γ, there being six such satellite points, one for each root; they are the points of contact of the tangent lines to the plane quartic curve in which $\nabla = 0$ is intersected by the tangent plane of ∇ at (x, y, z), drawn from the double point, (x, y, z), of this curve; denoting the equation of $\nabla = 0$ in homogeneous coordinates x, y, z, t, when $\frac{x}{t}, \frac{y}{t}, \frac{z}{t}$ have been written for x, y, z, by $F(x, y, z, t) = t^4\nabla$, the satellite point is determined (see p. 59) by

$$(x_1, y_1, z_1, t_1) = \Gamma^{-1}\left(\frac{\partial F}{\partial x}, \frac{\partial F}{\partial y}, \frac{\partial F}{\partial z}, \frac{\partial F}{\partial t}\right).$$

In particular when the fundamental sextic equation has an infinite root, and f denotes what F becomes when we put $a_5 = \frac{2}{3}$, $a_6 = 0$, and at the same time put x, y, z, t for $x - \frac{3}{2}a_4 t$, $y - \frac{1}{2}a_3 t$, $z - \frac{3}{2}a_2 t$, t, the satellite point of (x, y, z) corresponding to the infinite root is (see p. 70)

$$(x_1, y_1, z_1, t_1) = 4\begin{pmatrix} 0 & -1 & 0 & 0 \\ 1 & 0 & 0 & 0 \\ 0 & 0 & 0 & 1 \\ 0 & 0 & -1 & 0 \end{pmatrix}(Q_1, Q_2, Q_3, P_4)$$

$$= 4(-Q_2, Q_1, P_4, -Q_3) = \left(-\frac{\partial f}{\partial y}, \frac{\partial f}{\partial x}, \frac{\partial f}{\partial t}, -\frac{\partial f}{\partial z}\right),$$

and the tangent plane* to $f = 0$, or say $\Delta = 0$, at (x, y, z) is

$$Xy_1 - Yx_1 - Z + z_1 = 0,$$

in terms of the satellite point (x_1, y_1, z_1); it can, as we have found the matrix $\gamma_{\theta'}$ (p. 74), be similarly expressed in terms of the other satellite points. This equation arises below from the functional relations obtained; geometrically it expresses that the tangent plane at (x, y, z) of $\Delta = 0$ is the focal plane of (x_1, y_1, z_1) in the linear complex expressed, in line coordinates (l, m, n, l', m', n'), by

$$n + n' = 0.$$

In general terms, the bitangents of $\nabla = 0$ are rays of six linear complexes expressed by

$$\Gamma(X, Y, Z, T)(x_1, y_1, z_1, t_1) = 0,$$

or, in line coordinates, by

$$pl' + qm' + rn' + p'l + q'm + r'n = 0,$$

where p, q, r, p', q', r' have the values given previously (p. 73).

Two further remarks should be added. Taking the case when in the fundamental sextic $\lambda_6 = 0$, $\lambda_5 = 4$, let $x = \wp_{22}(u)$, $y = \wp_{21}(u)$, $z = \wp_{11}(u)$, $\xi = \wp_{222}(u)$, $\eta = \wp_{221}(u)$, etc., so that $\Delta(\xi, \eta, \zeta, \tau) = 0$; let the satellite point of (x, y, z) be denoted by (x', y', z') and $(\xi', \eta', \zeta', \tau')$ be determined to correspond, so that $\Delta'(\xi', \eta', \zeta', \tau') = 0$, and $\xi'/\xi = \eta'/\eta = \zeta'/\zeta$. With $Q_1 = 4(\eta\tau - \zeta^2)$, $Q_2 = 4(\eta\zeta - \xi\tau)$, $Q_3 = 4(\zeta\xi - \eta^2)$, and P_4 as before, we have

$$\frac{x'}{Q_2} = \frac{y'}{-Q_1} = \frac{z'}{-P_4} = \frac{1}{Q_3},$$

* Any surface of which the tangent plane is $z = ax + by + f(a, b)$ satisfies a differential equation $z - px - qy = f(p, q)$. Comparing

$$Xp + Yq - Z + z - px - qy = 0 \text{ with } X\wp_{21}(u) - Y\wp_{22}(u) - Z + \wp_{11}(u) = 0,$$

we have for the Kummer surface $p = \wp_{21}(u) = y'$, $q = -\wp_{22}(u) = -x'$, $z - px - qy = \wp_{11}(u)$, and hence $\Delta(-q, p, z - px - qy) = 0$, where Δ is the symmetrical determinant of the text.

so that $$-y'\xi+x'\eta+\zeta=0, \quad -y'\eta+x'\zeta+\tau=0,$$
while we also have, from the form of Δ,
$$-y\xi+x\eta+\zeta=0, \quad -y'\xi'+x'\eta'+\zeta'=0,$$
and hence
$$\frac{\xi}{x-x'}=\frac{\eta}{y-y'}=\frac{\zeta}{z-z'}=\frac{\zeta}{xy'-x'y}=\frac{\tau}{y'(y-y')-x'(z-z')}.$$

If then
$$x=t_1+t_2, \quad y=-t_1t_2, \quad s_1=t_1\xi+\eta, \quad s_2=t_2\xi+\eta,$$
$$x'=t_1'+t_2', \quad y'=-t_1't_2', \quad s_1'=t_1'\xi'+\eta', \quad s_2'=t_2'\xi'+\eta',$$
we have
$$\frac{s_1'-s_2'}{t_1'-t_2'}=\xi', \quad \frac{s_1't_2'-s_2't_1'}{t_1'-t_2'}=-\eta',$$
$$\frac{s_1't_2'^2-s_2't_1'^2}{t_1'-t_2'}=-t_1't_2'\xi'-(t_1'+t_2')\eta'=y'\xi'-x'\eta'=\zeta',$$
and
$$\frac{s_1't_2'^3-s_2't_1'^3}{t_1'-t_2'}=-(t_1'+t_2')t_1't_2'\xi'-(t_1'^2+t_1't_2'+t_2'^2)\eta'$$
$$=y'x'\xi'-(x'^2+y')\eta'=x'\zeta'-y'\eta'=\frac{\zeta'}{\zeta}(x'\zeta-y'\eta)$$
$$=-\frac{\zeta'}{\zeta}\tau,$$
so that
$$\frac{s_1'-s_2'}{\xi}=\frac{s_1't_2'-s_2't_1'}{-\eta}=\frac{s_1't_2'^2-s_2't_1'^2}{\zeta}=\frac{s_1't_2'^3-s_2't_1'^3}{-\tau},$$
which are to be compared with the formulae (p. 38)
$$\frac{s_1-s_2}{\xi}=\frac{s_1t_2-s_2t_1}{-\eta}=\frac{s_1t_2^2-s_2t_1^2}{\zeta}=\frac{\frac{1}{4}[s_1\psi(t_2,t_1)-s_2\psi(t_1,t_2)](t_1-t_2)^{-2}}{-\tau}.$$

In other words (cf. p. 40) the chord of the cubic curve
$$\xi/1=-\eta/\theta=\zeta/\theta^2=-\tau/\theta^3,$$
which passes through the point (ξ, η, ζ, τ) of the Weddle surface, cuts the cubic in the points $\theta=t_1'$, $\theta=t_2'$, where (t_1', t_2') are the hyperelliptic parameters associated, not with (ξ, η, ζ, τ), but with its satellite point $(\xi', \eta', \zeta', \tau')$; so that, if u' be the hyperelliptic arguments associated with this latter point, we have
$$u_r^{t_1', a_1}+u_r^{t_2', a_2}=u_r'.$$

From the relations
$$-y'\xi+x'\eta+\zeta=0, \quad -y'\eta+x'\zeta+\tau=0$$
we have
$$\zeta dx'-\eta dy'=-(x'd\zeta-y'd\eta+d\tau), \quad \xi dy'-\eta dx'=x'd\eta-y'd\xi+d\zeta.$$
Also
$$s_1s_2=(t_1\xi+\eta)(t_2\xi+\eta)=-y\xi^2+x\xi\eta+\eta^2=-\zeta\xi+\eta^2=-\tfrac{1}{4}Q_3,$$
and
$$s_1^2s_2^2=16(a_1-t_1)(a_1-t_2)(a_2-t_1)(a_2-t_2)\ldots(c-t_1)(c-t_2),$$

where a_1, a_2, c_1, c_2, c are the finite roots of the fundamental sextic, so that, if

$$P_{a_1} = y + a_1 x - a_1^2, \text{ etc.}, \quad P_{a_1}' = y' + a_1 x' - a_1^2, \text{ etc.},$$

we have

$$s_1^2 s_2^2 = -16 P_{a_1} P_{a_2} \dots$$

and

$$\frac{\xi}{\xi'} = \frac{\eta}{\eta'} = \frac{\zeta}{\zeta'} = \frac{\sqrt{Q_3}}{\sqrt{Q_3'}} = \frac{Q_3^{\frac{1}{2}}}{\sqrt{-4s_1's_2'}} = \frac{Q_3^{\frac{1}{2}}}{4i(-P_{a_1}'P_{a_2}'\dots)^{\frac{1}{4}}};$$

further the cone containing the space cubic $\xi/1 = -\eta/\theta =$ etc., whose vertex is at the point θ of the curve, is $C_\theta = 0$, where

$$C_\theta = Q_1 - \theta Q_2 + \theta^2 Q_3 = -Q_3(y' + \theta x' - \theta^2),$$

so that

$$-P_{a_1}'P_{a_2}' \dots = Q_3^{-5} C_{a_1} C_{a_2} \dots = Q_3^{-6} Q_3 C_{a_1} C_{a_2} C_{c_1} C_{c_2} C_c,$$

and thus

$$\frac{\xi}{\xi'} = \dots = \frac{Q_3^2}{4i(Q_3 C_{a_1} C_{a_2} \dots)^{\frac{1}{4}}}.$$

Hence (cf. p. 43)

$$du_2' = \frac{\zeta' dx' - \eta' dy'}{\zeta'\xi' - \eta'^2} = \frac{\xi}{\xi'} \frac{\zeta dx' - \eta dy'}{\zeta\xi - \eta^2} = \frac{Q_3^2}{4i(Q_3 C_{a_1} \dots)^{\frac{1}{4}}} \frac{-x' d\zeta + y' d\eta - d\tau}{\frac{1}{4} Q_3}$$

$$= -\frac{Q_1 d\eta + Q_2 d\zeta + Q_3 d\tau}{i(Q_3 C_{a_1} \dots)^{\frac{1}{4}}},$$

and

$$du_1' = \frac{-\eta' dx' + \xi' dy'}{\zeta'\xi' - \eta'^2} = \frac{Q_3^2}{4i(Q_3 C_{a_1} \dots)^{\frac{1}{4}}} \frac{x' d\eta - y' d\xi + d\zeta}{\frac{1}{4} Q_3}$$

$$= \frac{Q_1 d\xi + Q_2 d\eta + Q_3 d\zeta}{i(Q_3 C_{a_1} \dots)^{\frac{1}{4}}}.$$

These are forms given by Schottky, *Crelle*, CV., 1889, p. 249.

Taking the expressions on p. 41 for ξ'^2, etc., it is found, for $\omega = 0$, that

$$\frac{\xi^2}{\xi'^2} = \frac{Q_3^3}{16\sigma}:$$

where

$$\sigma = Q_1[\lambda_1 \xi\eta - \lambda_2 \eta^2 + \lambda_3 \eta\zeta - \lambda_4(\eta\tau + \zeta^2) + 8\zeta\tau]$$
$$+ Q_2[\lambda_0 \xi\eta - \lambda_4 \zeta\tau + 4\tau^2]$$
$$+ Q_3[\lambda_0(\zeta\xi + \eta^2) - \lambda_1 \eta\zeta + \lambda_2 \zeta^2 - \lambda_3 \zeta\tau],$$

while

$$4\omega = Q_1[\lambda_2 \xi\eta - \lambda_3 \eta^2 + \lambda_4 \eta\zeta - 4\zeta^2]$$
$$+ Q_2[-\lambda_0 \xi^2 + \lambda_1 \xi\eta]$$
$$+ Q_3[-2\lambda_0 \xi\eta + \lambda_1(\zeta\xi + \eta^2) - \lambda_2 \eta\zeta + \lambda_3 \zeta^2 - \lambda_4 \zeta\tau + 4\tau^2];$$

hence

$$\frac{Q_3^4}{-16(Q_3 C_{a_1} \dots)^{\frac{1}{2}}} = \frac{1}{16} \frac{Q_3^3}{\sigma},$$

or

$$(Q_3 C_{a_1} \dots)^{\frac{1}{2}} = -\sigma Q_3,$$

so that Schottky's forms for the integrals of the first kind are expressed so as to contain only a square root.

18. Consider now two matrices Γ_1, Γ_2 corresponding to the roots ψ_1, ψ_2 of the sextic equation of p. 73; with the values for $p_1 \ldots p_1' \ldots$ and $p_2 \ldots p_2' \ldots$ there given, we have, identically,

$$\begin{aligned}\rho_1\rho_2\,(p_1p_2' + q_1q_2' + r_1r_2' + p_1'p_2 + q_1'q_2 + r_1'r_2) &\\ = \psi_1^2\,(a_0\psi_2^3 + 3a_1\psi_2^2 + 3a_2\psi_2 + a_3) + \ldots + (a_0\psi_1^5 + 6a_1\psi_1^4 + \ldots + 3a_5) &\\ = (\psi_1 - \psi_2)^{-1}\,[a_0\,(\psi_1^6 - \psi_2^6) + 6a_1\,(\psi_1^5 - \psi_2^5) + \ldots + 6a_5\,(\psi_1 - \psi_2)], &\end{aligned}$$

which is zero because ψ_1, ψ_2 are both roots of the sextic; hence

$$\Gamma_1\Gamma_2^{-1} = \begin{pmatrix} 0 & -r_1 & q_1 & p_1' \\ r_1 & 0 & -p_1 & q_1' \\ -q_1 & p_1 & 0 & r_1' \\ -p_1' & -q_1' & -r_1' & 0 \end{pmatrix}\begin{pmatrix} 0 & -r_2' & q_2' & p_2 \\ r_2' & 0 & -p_2' & q_2 \\ -q_2' & p_2' & 0 & r_2 \\ -p_2 & -q_2 & -r_2 & 0 \end{pmatrix}$$

$$\begin{matrix} -r_1r_2' - q_1q_2' - p_1'p_2 & q_1p_2' - p_1'q_2 & r_1p_2' - p_1'r_2 & -r_1q_2 + q_1r_2 \\ p_1q_2' - q_1'p_2 & -r_1r_2' - p_1p_2' - q_1'q_2 & r_1q_2' - q_1'r_2 & r_1p_2 - p_1r_2 \\ p_1r_2' - r_1'p_2 & q_1r_2' - r_1'q_2 & -q_1q_2' - p_1p_2' - r_1'r_2 & -q_1p_2 + p_1q_2 \\ -q_1'r_2' + r_1'q_2' & p_1'r_2' - r_1'p_2' & -p_1'q_2' + q_1'p_2' & -p_1'p_2 - q_1'q_2 - r_1' \end{matrix}$$

from this it follows that we have the equations

$$\Gamma_1\Gamma_2^{-1} + \Gamma_2\Gamma_1^{-1} = 0, \quad \Gamma_1^{-1}\Gamma_2 + \Gamma_2^{-1}\Gamma_1 = 0, \quad (\Gamma_1\Gamma_2^{-1})^2 = -1 = (\Gamma_1^{-1}\Gamma_2)^2,$$

of which the others are the same as the first, either being equivalent with what in geometrical phraseology is expressed by saying that the linear complexes associated with Γ_1 and Γ_2 are in involution, or are apolar.

Take then the correspondence (pp. 75, 76) of the surface ∇ expressed by

$$(x_1, y_1, z_1, t_1) \equiv \Gamma_1^{-1}\left(\frac{\partial F}{\partial x}, \frac{\partial F}{\partial y}, \frac{\partial F}{\partial z}, \frac{\partial F}{\partial t}\right), \ldots\ldots\ldots\ldots\ldots (A_1)$$

he sign $\equiv$ being used in place of $=$, to indicate that we disregard a common actor of x_1, y_1, z_1, t_1; the geometrical interpretation of this correspondence which has been given shews that, in virtue of

$$F(x, y, z, t) = 0, \quad F(x_1, y_1, z_1, t_1) = 0,$$

his is equivalent with

$$(x, y, z, t) \equiv \Gamma_1^{-1}\left(\frac{\partial F}{\partial x_1}, \frac{\partial F}{\partial y_1}, \frac{\partial F}{\partial z_1}, \frac{\partial F}{\partial t_1}\right);$$

then we take

$$(x_{12}, y_{12}, z_{12}, t_{12}) \equiv \Gamma_2^{-1}\left(\frac{\partial F}{\partial x_1}, \frac{\partial F}{\partial y_1}, \frac{\partial F}{\partial z_1}, \frac{\partial F}{\partial t_1}\right),$$

hat is $$(x_{12}, y_{12}, z_{12}, t_{12}) \equiv \Gamma_2^{-1}\Gamma_1\,(x, y, z, t), \ldots\ldots\ldots\ldots\ldots\ldots (A_{12})$$

ie equation $\Gamma_2^{-1}\Gamma_1 + \Gamma_1^{-1}\Gamma_2 = 0$ gives

$$(x_{12}, y_{12}, z_{12}, t_{12}) \equiv (x_{21}, y_{21}, z_{21}, t_{21}), \quad (x, y, z, t) \equiv \Gamma_2^{-1}\Gamma_1\,(x_{12}, y_{12}, z_{12}, t_{12}),$$

and the equation (A_{12}) determines an involutory linear transformation of the surface $\nabla = 0$ into itself.

If we further put

$$(x_{123}, y_{123}, z_{123}, t_{123}) \equiv \Gamma_3^{-1}\left(\frac{\partial F}{\partial x_{12}}, \frac{\partial F}{\partial y_{12}}, \frac{\partial F}{\partial z_{12}}, \frac{\partial F}{\partial t_{12}}\right),$$

and notice that any linear transformation

$$(x, y, z, t) = h(x_{12}, y_{12}, z_{12}, t_{12}),$$

or

$$x = h_{11}x_{12} + h_{12}y_{12} + h_{13}z_{12} + h_{14}t_{12},$$
$$y = h_{21}x_{12} + h_{22}y_{12} + h_{23}z_{12} + h_{24}t_{12},$$
$$\cdots\cdots\cdots\cdots\cdots\cdots$$

gives

$$\frac{\partial F}{\partial x_{12}} = h_{11}\frac{\partial F}{\partial x} + h_{21}\frac{\partial F}{\partial y} + h_{31}\frac{\partial F}{\partial z} + h_{41}\frac{\partial F}{\partial t}, \text{ etc.,}$$

namely,

$$\left(\frac{\partial F}{\partial x_{12}}, \frac{\partial F}{\partial y_{12}}, \frac{\partial F}{\partial z_{12}}, \frac{\partial F}{\partial t_{12}}\right) = \bar{h}\left(\frac{\partial F}{\partial x}, \frac{\partial F}{\partial y}, \frac{\partial F}{\partial z}, \frac{\partial F}{\partial t}\right),$$

we shall have, as the transposed of the matrix $\Gamma_1^{-1}\Gamma_2$ is $\Gamma_2\Gamma_1^{-1}$,

$$(x_{123}, y_{123}, z_{123}, t_{123}) \equiv \Gamma_3^{-1}\Gamma_2\Gamma_1^{-1}\left(\frac{\partial F}{\partial x}, \frac{\partial F}{\partial y}, \frac{\partial F}{\partial z}, \frac{\partial F}{\partial t}\right) \quad\ldots\ldots\ldots(A_{123})$$

It can be shewn that the matrix $\Gamma_3^{-1}\Gamma_2\Gamma_1^{-1}$ is a symmetrical matrix, independent, save for sign, of the order of the suffixes, and that the transformation A_{123} is also involutory. To prove it a symmetrical matrix, notice that its transposed matrix is

$$\overline{\Gamma_1^{-1}}\,\overline{\Gamma_2}\,\overline{\Gamma_3^{-1}} = (-\Gamma_1^{-1})(-\Gamma_2)(-\Gamma_3^{-1}) = -\Gamma_1^{-1}\Gamma_2\Gamma_3^{-1} = \Gamma_1^{-1}\Gamma_3\Gamma_2^{-1},$$

because $\Gamma_2\Gamma_3^{-1} = -\Gamma_3\Gamma_2^{-1}$, and this $= -\Gamma_3^{-1}\Gamma_1\Gamma_2^{-1} = \Gamma_3^{-1}\Gamma_2\Gamma_1^{-1}$, which is the original matrix; to prove it independent of the order of the suffixes 1, 2, 3, notice that

$$\Gamma_3^{-1}\Gamma_2\Gamma_1^{-1} = -\Gamma_3^{-1}\Gamma_1\Gamma_2^{-1} = -\Gamma_2^{-1}\Gamma_3\Gamma_1^{-1} = \Gamma_2^{-1}\Gamma_1\Gamma_3^{-1}$$
$$= -\Gamma_1^{-1}\Gamma_2\Gamma_3^{-1} = \Gamma_1^{-1}\Gamma_3\Gamma_2^{-1},$$

each of these equalities arising from the equations $\Gamma_r^{-1}\Gamma_s = -\Gamma_s^{-1}\Gamma_r$; to prove the transformation involutory, denote it by

$$(x', y', z', t') \equiv \Gamma_3^{-1}\Gamma_2\Gamma_1^{-1}\left(\frac{\partial F}{\partial x}, \frac{\partial F}{\partial y}, \frac{\partial F}{\partial z}, \frac{\partial F}{\partial t}\right) \equiv \Gamma_3^{-1}\Gamma_2(x_1, y_1, z_1, t_1),$$

so that

$$\left(\frac{\partial F}{\partial x_1}, \frac{\partial F}{\partial y_1}, \frac{\partial F}{\partial z_1}, \frac{\partial F}{\partial t_1}\right) \equiv \Gamma_2\Gamma_3^{-1}\left(\frac{\partial F}{\partial x'}, \frac{\partial F}{\partial y'}, \frac{\partial F}{\partial z'}, \frac{\partial F}{\partial t'}\right),$$

because $\Gamma_2\Gamma_3^{-1}$ is the transposed of $\Gamma_3^{-1}\Gamma_2$; then

$$(x, y, z, t) \equiv \Gamma_1^{-1}\left(\frac{\partial F}{\partial x_1}, \frac{\partial F}{\partial y_1}, \frac{\partial F}{\partial z_1}, \frac{\partial F}{\partial t_1}\right) \equiv \Gamma_1^{-1}\Gamma_2\Gamma_3^{-1}\left(\frac{\partial F}{\partial x'}, \frac{\partial F}{\partial y'}, \frac{\partial F}{\partial z'}, \frac{\partial F}{\partial t'}\right),$$

which, rearranging the suffixes, expresses x, y, z, t by the same functions of x', y', z', t' as does A_{123} express x', y', z', t' in terms of x, y, z, t.

If for an instant we write

$$(x_{123}, y_{123}, z_{123}, t_{123}) \equiv \begin{pmatrix} a & h & g & u \\ h & b & f & v \\ g & f & c & w \\ u & v & w & d \end{pmatrix}^{-1} \left(\frac{\partial F}{\partial x}, \frac{\partial F}{\partial y}, \frac{\partial F}{\partial z}, \frac{\partial F}{\partial t}\right),$$

the pole of the tangent plane

$$X\frac{\partial F}{\partial x} + Y\frac{\partial F}{\partial y} + Z\frac{\partial F}{\partial z} + \frac{\partial F}{\partial t} = 0,$$

in regard to the quadric

$$\Pi = aX^2 + bY^2 + cZ^2 + d + 2fYZ + 2gZX + 2hXY + 2uX + 2vY + 2wZ = 0,$$

is given by the three equations

$$(ax' + hy' + gz' + ut')\Big/\frac{\partial F}{\partial x} = \frac{1}{2}\frac{\partial \Pi}{\partial y'}\Big/\frac{\partial F}{\partial y} = . = .\,,$$

and thus coincides with $(x_{123}, y_{123}, z_{123}, t_{123})$.

As we have obtained a point $(x_{123}, \ldots)$ from $(x, \ldots)$, so we can obtain points $(x_{124}, \ldots)$ etc., there being twenty in all. It can however be shewn that $(x_{123}, \ldots)$ is the same as $(x_{456}, \ldots)$, namely that

$$\Gamma_3^{-1}\Gamma_2\Gamma_1^{-1} \equiv \Gamma_4^{-1}\Gamma_5\Gamma_6^{-1},$$

or

$$\Gamma_1\Gamma_2^{-1}\Gamma_3\Gamma_4^{-1}\Gamma_5\Gamma_6^{-1} \equiv 1.$$

Of this result a geometrical proof can be given, founded on the interpretation of the transformation $\Gamma_3^{-1}\Gamma_2\Gamma_1^{-1}$ as a reciprocation in regard to a quadric surface, which has just been noticed; we shall give an analytical proof, having, it would seem, an interest of its own; not to interrupt too far our present work, it is placed as a note below (Appendix to Part I., Note I.).

Assuming this result we have now shewn that, from any point (x, y, z, t) of the surface $\nabla = 0$, can be found 31 other points of the surface, whose coordinates are rational functions of (x, y, z, t); these are, first, the six

$$(x_i, y_i, z_i, t_i) \equiv \Gamma_i^{-1}\left(\frac{\partial F}{\partial x}, \frac{\partial F}{\partial y}, \frac{\partial F}{\partial z}, \frac{\partial F}{\partial t}\right),$$

whose geometrical determination from (x, y, z, t) has been described; then there are the fifteen points

$$(x_{ij}, y_{ij}, z_{ij}, t_{ij}) \equiv \Gamma_i^{-1}\Gamma_j(x, y, z, t),$$

obtained from (x, y, z, t) by a linear transformation; and, last, there are the ten points

$$(x_{ijk}, y_{ijk}, z_{ijk}, t_{ijk}) \equiv \Gamma_i^{-1}\Gamma_j\Gamma_k^{-1}\left(\frac{\partial F}{\partial x}, \frac{\partial F}{\partial y}, \frac{\partial F}{\partial z}, \frac{\partial F}{\partial t}\right),$$

which, as we have seen, are the poles of the tangent plane of $\nabla = 0$ at (x, y, z, t), taken in regard to ten particular quadric surfaces. Each of these correspondences is involutory, in the sense that they are respectively equivalent with

$$(x, y, z, t) \equiv \Gamma_i^{-1}\left(\frac{\partial F}{\partial x_i}, \frac{\partial F}{\partial y_i}, \frac{\partial F}{\partial z_i}, \frac{\partial F}{\partial t_i}\right),$$

$$(x, y, z, t) \equiv \Gamma_i^{-1}\Gamma_j(x_{ij}, y_{ij}, z_{ij}, t_{ij}),$$

$$(x, y, z, t) \equiv \Gamma_i^{-1}\Gamma_j\Gamma_k^{-1}\left(\frac{\partial F}{\partial x_{ijk}}, , ,\right).$$

If the writing of $\partial F/\partial x$, $\partial F/\partial y$, ... be denoted by T, the symbols of the 32 points are

$$1, \quad \Gamma_i^{-1}T, \quad \Gamma_i^{-1}\Gamma_j, \quad \Gamma_i^{-1}\Gamma_j\Gamma_k^{-1}T,$$

or, if $\Gamma_i^{-1}T = S_i$, are, in virtue of $T^2 = 1$ and $S_i^2 = 1$,

$$1, \quad S_i, \quad S_iS_j, \quad S_iS_jS_k,$$

which, because $S_iS_j = S_jS_i$ and $S_1S_2S_3S_4S_5S_6 = 1$, represent a group of 32 transformations, every one equal to its inverse, and every two commutable with one another. By application of all the operations of the group to any one of the 32 points, all the other points are obtainable. The sixteen operations $1, \Gamma_i^{-1}\Gamma_j$ form a group by themselves; the sixteen points arising from (x, y, z, t) by the operations of this subgroup, lie by sixes on sixteen planes, of which six pass through every one of the sixteen points; for consider the plane represented, when X, Y, Z, T are current coordinates, by

$$\Gamma_i(x, y, z, t)(X, Y, Z, T) = 0;$$

it contains x, y, z, t since Γ_i is a skew symmetrical matrix; it contains $(x_{ij}, y_{ij}, z_{ij}, t_{ij})$ provided

$$\Gamma_i(x, y, z, t)\,\Gamma_i^{-1}\Gamma_j(x, y, z, t) = 0,$$

which, since the transposed of the matrix Γ_i is $-\Gamma_i$, is the same as

$$\Gamma_i\Gamma_i^{-1}\Gamma_j(x, y, z, t)(x, y, z, t) = 0,$$

and is satisfied because Γ_j is a skew symmetrical matrix. The plane in question thus contains the six points (x, y, z, t), $(x_{ij}, \ldots)$ for $j \neq i$; next consider the plane

$$\Gamma_1\Gamma_2^{-1}\Gamma_3(x, y, z, t)(X, Y, Z, T) = 0;$$

since the transposed of the matrix $\Gamma_1^{-1}\Gamma_2$ is $\Gamma_2\Gamma_1^{-1}$, and

$$\Gamma_2\Gamma_1^{-1}\Gamma_1\Gamma_2^{-1}\Gamma_3(x, y, z, t)(x, y, z, t) = 0,$$

it follows that the plane contains the point $\Gamma_1^{-1}\Gamma_2(x, y, z, t)$; and thence, as $\Gamma_1\Gamma_2^{-1}\Gamma_3 = \Gamma_2\Gamma_3^{-1}\Gamma_1 = \Gamma_3\Gamma_1^{-1}\Gamma_2$, and $\Gamma_1\Gamma_2^{-1}\Gamma_3 \equiv \Gamma_4\Gamma_5^{-1}\Gamma_6$ the same plane contains the points

$$\Gamma_2^{-1}\Gamma_3(x, y, z, t), \quad \Gamma_3^{-1}\Gamma_1(x, y, z, t), \quad \Gamma_4^{-1}\Gamma_5(x, y, z, t), \quad \Gamma_5^{-1}\Gamma_6(x, y, z, t),$$
$$\Gamma_6^{-1}\Gamma_4(x, y, z, t);$$

there are six planes whose coefficients are the four quantities $\Gamma_i(x, y, z, t)$, and ten planes such as that whose coefficients are the four quantities $\Gamma_1\Gamma_2^{-1}\Gamma_3(x, y, z, t)$; the six planes $\Gamma_i(x, y, z, t)$ pass through (x, y, z, t), and the six planes $\Gamma_1\Gamma_2^{-1}\Gamma_i(x, y, z, t)$ pass through the point $\Gamma_1^{-1}\Gamma_2(x, y, z, t)$.

CHAPTER IV.

THE EXPANSION OF THE SIGMA FUNCTIONS.

19. THE differential equations denoted (p. 50) by

$$\tfrac{1}{3}\Delta_h^4\sigma\sigma' = (\alpha\beta)^4\alpha_h^2\beta_h^2 \,.\, \sigma\sigma' - \alpha_h^4(\alpha\Delta)^2\sigma\sigma'$$

have been seen (p. 48) to be satisfied by an integral function

$$e^{a_1u_1 + a_2u_2 + b}\,\vartheta(u_1 + c_1,\ u_2 + c_2),$$

where $\vartheta(u_1, u_2)$ is a power series in u_1, u_2 converging for all finite values of these, and a_1, a_2, c_1, c_2, b are arbitrary constants. By choosing these constants suitably we can introduce various simplifications into the form of the solution, and then, as we know, by the formula here put down, the general integral, we can obtain this by reintroducing the constants into the particular integral. We have seen in particular (p. 24) that the equations are satisfied both by odd and by even functions. Consider first an even function; we have for any values of u_1, u_2, if σ, σ_1, σ_{12} denote $\sigma(u)$, $\partial\sigma/\partial u_1$, $\partial^2\sigma/\partial u_1\partial u_2$, etc.,

$$\wp_{22} = -(\sigma\sigma_{22} - \sigma_2^2)/\sigma^2, \quad \wp_{21} = -(\sigma\sigma_{21} - \sigma_2\sigma_1)/\sigma^2, \quad \wp_{11} = -(\sigma\sigma_{11} - \sigma_1^2)/\sigma^2,$$

$$\wp_{222} = -(\sigma^2\sigma_{222} - 3\sigma\sigma_2\sigma_{22} + 2\sigma_2^3)/\sigma^3, \text{ etc.,}$$

so that, if $\sigma(0) = 1$, $\sigma_1(0) = 0$, $\sigma_2(0) = 0$,

$$\wp_{22}(0) = -\sigma_{22}(0), \quad \wp_{21}(0) = -\sigma_{21}(0), \quad \wp_{11}(0) = -\sigma_{11}(0),$$

$$\wp_{222}(0) = \wp_{221}(0) = \wp_{211}(0) = \wp_{111}(0) = 0\,;$$

the last equations shew that the values $u_1 = 0$, $u_2 = 0$ make vanish all the minors of the determinant ∇ (cf. p. 59), so that the point is a node of the surface $\nabla = 0$; it is however not at infinity since $\wp_{22}(0)$, etc., are finite; and denoting these last quantities, the coordinates of a finite node of the surface $\nabla = 0$, by x_0, y_0, z_0, the development has the form

$$\sigma(u) = 1 - \tfrac{1}{2}(x_0u_2^2 + 2y_0u_2u_1 + z_0u_1^2) + \text{terms of fourth and higher order}\,;$$

it will presently be seen that the terms of the fourth and higher order are determined, from those of the second, directly by the differential equations; the series then represents one of the ten even functions before met with (p. 24).

Consider next the case of an odd function; as then $\sigma(0)=0$, we have also $\wp_{22}(0)=\infty$, $\wp_{21}(0)=\infty$, $\wp_{11}(0)=\infty$, and the point $u_1=0$, $u_2=0$ is at infinity on the surface $\nabla=0$; as we approach this point, however, the ratios $\wp_{22}(u):\wp_{21}(u):\wp_{11}(u)$, being those of $\sigma\sigma_{22}-\sigma_2^2:\sigma\sigma_{21}-\sigma_2\sigma_1:\sigma\sigma_{11}-\sigma_1^2$, become the same as $\sigma_2^2:\sigma_2\sigma_1:\sigma_1^2$; now the terms of the fourth and third order in ∇ are easily seen to be

$$(xz-y^2)^2-a_0x^3+6a_1x^2y-3a_2(x^2z+4xy^2)+4a_3(3xyz+2y^3)-3a_4(xz^2+4y^2z)+6a_5yz^2-a_6z^3,$$

and, for $x=-(\sigma\sigma_{22}-\sigma_2^2)/\sigma^2$, etc., we find

$$xz-y^2=\{\sigma(\sigma_{22}\sigma_{11}-\sigma_{12}^2)-(\sigma_{22}\sigma_1^2+\sigma_{11}\sigma_2^2-2\sigma_{21}\sigma_2\sigma_1)\}/\sigma^3,\ =P\sigma^{-3},\text{ say,}$$

so that $\nabla=0$ is equivalent with

$$P^2+a_0(\sigma\sigma_{22}-\sigma_2^2)^3+\dots+a_6(\sigma\sigma_{11}-\sigma_1^2)^3+\sigma^2H=0,$$

where H is an integral function of u_1, u_2; for $\sigma=0$, $\sigma_{22}=0$, $\sigma_{21}=0$, $\sigma_{11}=0$ this reduces to

$$-a_0\sigma_2^6+6a_1\sigma_2^5\sigma_1-15a_2\sigma_2^4\sigma_1^2+20a_3\sigma_2^3\sigma_1^3-15a_4\sigma_2^2\sigma_1^4+6a_5\sigma_2\sigma_1^5-a_6\sigma_1^6=0,$$

and the ratio $\sigma_2(0)/\sigma_1(0)$ is the negative of a root ψ of the equation

$$F(\psi)=a_0\psi^6+6a_1\psi^5+15a_2\psi^4+\dots+6a_5\psi+a_6=0;$$

thus the terms of first order in the expansion of an odd function are, save for a constant multiplier, of the form $u_1-u_2\psi$, and the values $u_1=0$, $u_2=0$ are associated with one of the infinite nodes of the surface, there being, as we have also previously seen (p. 24), six odd functions. It will be seen below that the terms of third and higher orders are directly determined from those of the first by the differential equations.

We apply these results now, first to obtain some terms of any even function; we use for this the general form of the differential equations, as affording the most convenient way of explaining the general method of using the differential equations for the expansion of the functions: and then to obtain some terms of the expansion of a particular odd function, which, for several reasons, appears fit to be regarded as the fundamental sigma function.

20. An even function is of the form

$$1+\frac{U_2}{2!}+\frac{U_4}{4!}+\frac{U_6}{6!}+\dots,$$

where U_r denotes a homogeneous polynomial of dimension r in u_1 and u_2; we have expressed U_2 above in terms of the coordinates of a node of the surface $\nabla=0$, and we have previously found these coordinates (p. 64). It appears thus that

$$U_2=\tfrac{9}{20}(pq)^2p_uq_u,$$

where $p_u{}^3 q_u{}^3$, or $(p_1u_1+p_2u_2)^3(q_1u_1+q_2u_2)^3$, is one of the ten ways of writing

$$a_0u_1{}^6+6a_1u_1{}^5u_2+15a_2u_1{}^4u_2{}^2+\ldots+6a_5u_1u_2{}^5+a_6u_2{}^6$$

as a product of two cubic factors. If, now, in the differential equation

$$\tfrac{1}{6}\Delta_h{}^4\sigma\sigma'=\tfrac{1}{2}(\alpha\beta)^4\alpha_h{}^2\beta_h{}^2\,.\,\sigma\sigma'-\tfrac{1}{2}\alpha_h{}^4(\alpha\Delta)^2\sigma\sigma',$$

we equate the terms of aggregate dimension $2n$ in u_1, u_1', u_2, u_2' on the two sides, we obtain, if we put

$$d_1=\frac{\partial}{\partial u_1},\quad d_2=\frac{\partial}{\partial u_2},\quad d_1'=\frac{\partial}{\partial u_1'},\quad d_2'=\frac{\partial}{\partial u_2'},\quad \delta=h_1d_1+h_2d_2,\quad \delta'=h_1d_1'+h_2d_2',$$

the equation following, which we shall refer to as the determining equation,

$$\begin{aligned}\tfrac{1}{3}(\delta^4-4\delta^3\delta'+3\delta^2\delta'^2)&\left\{\frac{U_{2n+4}}{(2n+4)!}+\frac{U_{2n+2}U_2'}{(2n+2)!\,2!}+\frac{U_{2n}U_4'}{2n!\,4!}+\ldots\right.\\&\left.+\frac{U_2U'_{2n+2}}{2!\,(2n+2)!}+\frac{U'_{2n+4}}{(2n+4)!}\right\}\\&=\tfrac{1}{2}(\alpha\beta)^4\alpha_h{}^2\beta_h{}^2\left\{\frac{U_{2n}}{2n!}+\frac{U_{2n-2}U_2'}{(2n-2)!\,2!}+\frac{U_{2n-4}U_4'}{(2n-4)!\,4!}+\ldots\right.\\&\left.+\frac{U_2U'_{2n-2}}{2!\,(2n-2)!}+\frac{U'_{2n}}{(2n)!}\right\}\\&-\alpha_h{}^4\{\alpha_1{}^2(d_2{}^2-d_2d_2')-2\alpha_1\alpha_2(d_2d_1-d_2d_1')+\alpha_2{}^2(d_1{}^2-d_1d_1')\}\\&\times\left\{\frac{U_{2n+2}}{(2n+2)!}+\frac{U_{2n}U_2'}{2n!\,2!}+\ldots+\frac{U_2U'_{2n}}{2!\,2n!}+\frac{U'_{2n+2}}{(2n+2)!}\right\};\end{aligned}$$

but, if U_r be a homogeneous polynomial in u_1, u_2 of dimension r, which we may write symbolically $(p_1u_1+p_2u_2)^r$ or $p_u{}^r$, we have

$$\frac{\delta^sU_r}{r!}=\frac{p_u{}^{r-s}p_h{}^s}{(r-s)!},$$

and if in this we put u_1 for h_1 and u_2 for h_2, it becomes $p_u{}^r/(r-s)!$ or $U_r/(r-s)!$; as in our differential equations the h_1, h_2 are arbitrary and we are to put u_1, u_2 for u_1', u_2' after differentiation, the substitution $h_1=u_1$, $h_2=u_2$ after differentiation is allowable; thereby, from

$$(\delta^4-4\delta^3\delta'+3\delta^2\delta'^2)\,\frac{U_mU_k'+U_kU_m'}{m!\,k!}$$

if both m and k be greater than 4, we shall obtain

$$\begin{aligned}\frac{U_m}{(m-4)!}\frac{U_k}{k!}+\frac{U_k}{(k-4)!}\frac{U_m}{m!}&-4\left(\frac{U_m}{(m-3)!}\frac{U_k}{(k-1)!}+\frac{U_k}{(k-3)!}\frac{U_m}{(m-1)!}\right)\\&+3\left(\frac{U_m}{(m-2)!}\frac{U_k}{(k-2)!}+\frac{U_k}{(k-2)!}\frac{U_m}{(m-2)!}\right),\end{aligned}$$

or say
$$2C_{m,k}U_mU_k,$$

where

$$2C_{m,k}=\frac{1}{m!\,(k-4)!}-\frac{4}{(m-1)!\,(k-3)!}+\frac{6}{(m-2)!\,(k-2)!}-\frac{4}{(m-3)!\,(k-1)!}+\frac{1}{(m-4)!\,k!};$$

the same formula applies to cases where m, or k, is less than 4, provided it be understood that terms which would involve in their denominators factorials of negative numbers are to be omitted. In particular, if $m=2n+4$, $k=0$, or if $m=2n+2$, $k=2$, we have

$$2C_{2n+4,0}=\frac{1}{(2n)!},\quad 2C_{2n+2,2}=\frac{1}{(2n-2)!\,2!}-\frac{4}{(2n-1)!}+\frac{6}{(2n)!};$$

thus the left side of the determining equation has the form

$$\frac{1}{3}\frac{U_{2n+4}}{(2n)!}+\frac{1}{3}\sum_{k=1}^{n+1}C_{2n+4-2k,\,2k}U_{2n+4-2k}U_{2k},$$

where under the sign of summation no polynomial U_r occurs for which the suffix r is greater than $2n+2$; from the form of the determining equation it is thus clear that the differential equations determine U_{2n+4} in terms of polynomials U_r of less suffix; taking then, in turn, $n=0$, $n=1$, etc., all the terms of the expansion of the sigma function are seen to be determined when those of zero and of two dimensions are given. It may be worth while however to enter into more detail as to the form of the right side of the determining equation; if $U_m=p_u{}^m$, $U_k=q_u{}^k$, we have

$$\alpha_u{}^4(\alpha_1{}^2d_2{}^2-2\alpha_1\alpha_2d_1d_2+\alpha_2{}^2d_1{}^2)\frac{p_u{}^m}{m!}=\frac{1}{(m-2)!}(\alpha_1p_2-\alpha_2p_1)^2p_u{}^{m-2}\alpha_u{}^4,$$

this being a polynomial in u_1, u_2 of dimension $m+2$, whose coefficients are linear functions both of the coefficients in U_m and of those of the sextic $\alpha_u{}^6$ or f; denote this by $\frac{1}{(m-2)!}(f,U_m)_2$; further

$$\alpha_u{}^4[\alpha_1{}^2d_2d_2'-2\alpha_1\alpha_2d_2d_1'+\alpha_2{}^2d_1d_1']\frac{p_u{}^mq_{u'}{}^k+p_{u'}{}^mq_u{}^k}{m!\,k!}$$
$$=\frac{1}{(m-1)!\,(k-1)!}\alpha_u{}^4\{\alpha_1{}^2(p_u{}^{m-1}q_{u'}{}^{k-1}p_2q_2+p_{u'}{}^{m-1}q_u{}^{k-1}p_2q_2)-\dots\},$$

becomes, on putting u_1, u_2 for u_1', u_2',

$$\frac{2}{(m-1)!\,(k-1)!}\alpha_u{}^4(\alpha_1{}^2p_2q_2-\alpha_1\alpha_2p_2q_1-\alpha_1\alpha_2p_1q_2+\alpha_2{}^2p_1q_1)p_u{}^{m-1}q_u{}^{k-1}$$

or

$$\frac{2}{(m-1)!\,(k-1)!}(\alpha p)(\alpha q)\alpha_u{}^4p_u{}^{m-1}q_u{}^{k-1},$$

where (αp) denotes $\alpha_1p_2-\alpha_2p_1$; we may denote this by

$$\frac{2}{(m-1)!\,(k-1)!}(f;\,U_m,\,U_k)_{211};$$

then

$$\alpha_u^4 [\alpha_1^2 (d_2^2 - d_2 d_2') - 2\alpha_1\alpha_2 (d_2 d_1 - d_2 d_1') + \alpha_2^2 (d_1^2 - d_1 d_1')] \frac{U_m U_k' + U_m' U_k}{m\,!\,k\,!},$$

when u_1', u_2' are replaced by u_1, u_2, is equal to

$$\frac{U_k (f, U_m)_2}{k\,!\,(m-2)\,!} - 2\frac{(f;\, U_m, U_k)_{211}}{(k-1)\,!\,(m-1)\,!} + \frac{U_m (f, U_k)_2}{m\,!\,(k-2)\,!},$$

it being supposed that neither k nor m is less than 2. The value assumed by the other terms of the right side of the determining equation when u_1', u_2' are replaced by u_1, u_2, needs no explanation.

The terms of second degree in the expansion of the sigma function have been seen to be an integral covariant of the two cubics into which the fundamental sextic is split in order to define the particular even function under consideration; it is manifest from the previous work that the terms of any other degree are also an integral covariant of these cubics.

21. If we attempt to apply the preceding method to determine an odd function

$$U_1 + \frac{U_3}{3\,!} + \frac{U_5}{5\,!} + \dots,$$

the differential equations will similarly determine

$$(\delta^4 - 4\delta^3\delta' + 3\delta^2\delta'^2)(U_{2n+3}U_1' + U'_{2n+3}U_1)/(2n+3)\,!$$

in terms of $U_1, U_3, \dots, U_{2n+1}$; on putting, after differentiation, u_1, u_2 for u_1', u_2' and u_1, u_2 for h_1, h_2, this gives

$$U_1\, U_{2n+3} \left\{\frac{1}{(2n-1)\,!} - \frac{4}{(2n)\,!}\right\}, \; = \frac{(2n-4)\, U_1\, U_{2n+3}}{(2n)\,!};$$

thus the terms U_{2n+3} are determined in terms of preceding terms, except when $n = 2$; namely U_3 and U_5, in succession, are determined from U_1, which we have found to be of the form $c\,(u_1 - \psi u_2)$, and $U_9, U_{11}, \dots$, without exception, are determined from preceding terms; but U_7 is not so determined. It is necessary then, presumably, in order to use the differential equations to determine U_7, to keep them distinct, that is, to abstain from replacing the arbitrary quantities h_1, h_2 by u_1, u_2; it is to be remarked however that the five separate equations are in general more than is necessary: after four differentiations of a term $U_1U'_{2n+3} + U_1'U_{2n+3}$ there results, when u_1', u_2' are replaced by u_1, u_2, a binary polynomial of $2n$ dimensions in u_1, u_2; thus each differential equation gives $2n+1$ linear equations for the determination of the coefficients of U_{2n+3}, and the aggregate of the differential equations gives $5\,(2n+1)$ linear equations for the $2n+4$ coefficients in U_{2n+3}; these are known, by the theory preceding, to be consistent, and that they are sufficient, except when $2n+3 = 7$, is shewn above; but in general they are more than sufficient, and it will be shewn below that when U_3 and U_5 are found we can determine the terms U_7 and U_9 simultaneously, by equating terms of dimension six in the differential equations, and this without utilising all the linear equations given by the differential equations.

In order to justify this statement in detail, it is sufficient to take the differential equations in the forms to which they are reduced by such a linear transformation of the arguments u_1, u_2 as corresponds to a transformation of the associated sextic to the form

$$u_1(\lambda_0 u_1^5 + \lambda_1 u_1^4 u_2 + \lambda_2 u_1^3 u_2^2 + \lambda_3 u_1^2 u_2^3 + \lambda_4 u_1 u_2^4 + 4u_2^5),$$

this linear transformation of the arguments being accompanied by a multiplication of the sigma function by an exponential $e^{Au_1^2+Bu_1u_2+Cu_2^2}$ equivalent with the addition of certain constants to the second logarithmic derivatives $\wp_{22}, \wp_{21}, \wp_{11}$; this has been explained in detail in a previous section (pp. 49—52). The forms obtained, which we shall utilise, were, writing x, y, z for $\wp_{22}, \wp_{21}, \wp_{11}$,

$$\begin{aligned}
\wp_{2222} - 6\wp_{22}^2 &= \tfrac{1}{2}\lambda_3 + \lambda_4 x + 4y,\\
\wp_{2221} - 6\wp_{22}\wp_{21} &= \lambda_4 y - 2z,\\
\wp_{2211} - 2\wp_{22}\wp_{11} - 4\wp_{21}^2 &= \tfrac{1}{2}\lambda_3 y,\\
\wp_{2111} - 6\wp_{21}\wp_{11} &= -\lambda_0 - \tfrac{1}{2}\lambda_1 x + \lambda_2 y,\\
\wp_{1111} - 6\wp_{11}^2 &= -\tfrac{1}{2}\lambda_0\lambda_4 + \tfrac{1}{8}\lambda_1\lambda_3 - 3\lambda_0 x + \lambda_1 y + \lambda_2 z;
\end{aligned}$$

multiplying these by $h_2^4, 4h_2^3h_1, \dots, h_1^4$, and adding, we obtain

$$\begin{aligned}
&(\delta^4 - 4\delta^3\delta' + 3\delta^2\delta'^2)\,\sigma\sigma' \\
&= \tfrac{1}{2}P\sigma\sigma' + [A(d_2^2 - d_2 d_2') + B(d_2 d_1 - d_2 d_1') + C(d_1^2 - d_1 d_1')]\,\sigma\sigma',
\end{aligned}$$

where
$$\begin{aligned}
P &= -\lambda_3 h_2^4 + 8\lambda_0 h_2 h_1^3 + (\lambda_0\lambda_4 - \tfrac{1}{4}\lambda_1\lambda_3)\,h_1^4,\\
A &= \lambda_4 h_2^4 - 2\lambda_1 h_2 h_1^3 - 3\lambda_0 h_1^4,\\
B &= 4h_2^4 + 4\lambda_4 h_2^3 h_1 + 3\lambda_3 h_2^2 h_1^2 + 4\lambda_2 h_2 h_1^3 + \lambda_1 h_1^4,\\
C &= -8h_2^3 h_1 + \lambda_2 h_1^4.
\end{aligned}$$

With the general form of the fundamental sextic the linear terms in an odd function have been shewn (p. 84) to be a constant multiple of $u_1 - \psi u_2$ where ψ is a root of the equation $a_0\psi^6 + 6a_1\psi^5 + \dots + a_6 = 0$; with the transformed form now under consideration one of these roots is zero; we shall therefore consider that particular function for which the linear terms, in the notation now being employed, reduce to u_1; any other is conversely derivable from this by transformation. Putting

$$\sigma = U_1 + \frac{U_3}{3!} + \frac{U_5}{5!} + \dots,$$

where U_{2n-1} is a homogeneous polynomial in u_1, u_2 of dimension $(2n-1)$, with $U_1 = u_1$, and equating terms of dimension zero in the differential equation, we have

$$\tfrac{1}{6}(\delta^4 - 4\delta^3\delta' + 3\delta^2\delta'^2)(U_1U_3' + U_3U_1')$$
$$= [A(d_2^2 - d_2d_2') + B(d_2d_1 - d_2d_1') + C(d_1^2 - d_1d_1')]\,u_1u_1',$$

and hence
$$-\tfrac{2}{3}\delta^3U_3\,.\,\delta'U_1' = -Cd_1d_1'u_1u_1',$$

which, putting u_1, u_2 for u_1', u_2' after differentiation, and $h_1 = u_1$, $h_2 = u_2$, gives

$$4U_3u_1 = -8u_2^3u_1 + \lambda_2u_1^4,$$

or
$$U_3 = \tfrac{1}{4}\lambda_2u_1^3 - 2u_2^3.$$

Equating terms of aggregate dimension 2, in u_1, u_2, u_1', u_2', we have

$$(\delta^4 - 4\delta^3\delta' + 3\delta^2\delta'^2)\left(\frac{U_1U_5' + U_5U_1'}{5\,!} + \frac{U_3U_3'}{3\,!\,3\,!}\right)$$
$$= \tfrac{1}{2}Pu_1u_1' + [A(d_2^2 - d_2d_2') + \ldots]\,\frac{U_1U_3' + U_3U_1'}{3\,!},$$

and this gives, when we replace u_1', u_2' and h_1, h_2 by u_1, u_2,

$$u_1U_5 - 4\frac{u_1U_5}{2} - 4\frac{U_3^2}{2} + 3\frac{U_3^2}{1}$$
$$= \tfrac{1}{2}P_0u_1^2 + A_0(-2u_2u_1) + B_0(+u_2^2) + C_0(\tfrac{1}{4}\lambda_2u_1^2 - \tfrac{1}{8}\lambda_2u_1^2 - \tfrac{1}{8}\lambda_2u_1^2),$$

leading to

$$-U_5 = 2\lambda_4u_2^5 + \tfrac{5}{2}\lambda_3u_2^4u_1 + 5\lambda_2u_2^3u_1^2 + 5\lambda_1u_2^2u_1^3 + 10\lambda_0u_2u_1^4$$
$$+ (\tfrac{1}{2}\lambda_0\lambda_4 - \tfrac{1}{8}\lambda_1\lambda_3 - \tfrac{1}{16}\lambda_2^2)\,u_1^5.$$

For the determination of U_7, as has been explained, a more laborious process may be followed. Picking out the terms of aggregate dimension 6 in u_1, u_2, u_1', u_2' in the composite differential equation

$$(\delta^4 - 4\delta^3\delta' + 3\delta^2\delta'^2)\,\sigma\sigma' = \tfrac{1}{2}P\sigma\sigma' + \ldots,$$

we have, for the determination of the $8 + 10 = 18$ coefficients in U_7 and U_9, the 35 equations obtained by equating the coefficients of $h_2^{4-r}h_1^ru_2^{6-s}u_1^s$, for $r = 0 \ldots 4$, $s = 0 \ldots 6$; putting

$$U_7 = H_0u_2^7 + \frac{7\,!}{6\,!}H_1u_2^6u_1 + \frac{7\,!}{2\,!\,5\,!}H_2u_2^5u_1^2 + \ldots,$$

$$U_9 = K_0u_2^9 + 9K_1u_2^8u_1 + \frac{9\,!}{2\,!\,7\,!}K_2u_2^7u_1^2 + \ldots,$$

it is found that the 14 equations obtained, by taking the coefficients of $h_2^4u_2^{6-s}u_1^s$, $h_2^3h_1u_2^{6-s}u_1^s$, for $s = 0 \ldots 6$, that is, the first two of the five separate differential equations, determine

$$H_0,\ H_1, \ldots, H_6,\quad K_0, \ldots, K_5,$$

beside furnishing a single relation connecting H_7 and K_6; the remaining coefficient H_7, of U_7, together with K_6, may then be found by taking the coefficients of $h_2^2 h_1^2 u_2 u_1^5$ in the composite differential equation; and finally the remaining three coefficients of U_9, namely K_7, K_8, K_9, may be determined by taking the terms in $h_2^2 h_1^2 u_1^6$, $h_1^4 u_2 u_1^5$, $h_1^4 u_1^6$ respectively; and having thereby determined U_7 we may verify the form simultaneously obtained for U_9 by putting, in the composite differential equation, after differentiation, $h_1 = u_1$, $h_2 = u_2$. Except as, perhaps, the best practical method, and to secure accuracy, not all the work indicated is really necessary, since the covariantive character of the expansions enables us to determine all the coefficients in U_7 from one of them, and similarly for the terms of any other dimension, as will be exemplified in detail. Nor is it necessary to give here the actual computation; the results, found by the method, are

$$H_0 = -(\lambda_3 + 2\lambda_4^2),$$
$$H_1 = -(2\lambda_2 + \tfrac{1}{2}\lambda_3\lambda_4),$$
$$H_2 = -(2\lambda_1 + \tfrac{1}{2}\lambda_2\lambda_4),$$
$$H_3 = -(2\lambda_0 + \tfrac{1}{8}\lambda_2\lambda_3 + \tfrac{1}{2}\lambda_1\lambda_4),$$
$$H_4 = -(\tfrac{1}{4}\lambda_1\lambda_3 + \lambda_0\lambda_4 + \tfrac{1}{8}\lambda_2^2),$$
$$H_5 = -(\tfrac{3}{2}\lambda_0\lambda_3 + \tfrac{1}{4}\lambda_1\lambda_2),$$
$$H_6 = -(\tfrac{11}{2}\lambda_0\lambda_2 - \lambda_1^2),$$
$$H_7 = \tfrac{1}{64}\lambda_2^3 + \tfrac{3}{32}\lambda_1\lambda_2\lambda_3 - \tfrac{15}{8}\lambda_0\lambda_2\lambda_4 - \tfrac{1}{2}\lambda_0\lambda_1 + \tfrac{3}{8}\lambda_0\lambda_3^2 + \tfrac{3}{8}\lambda_1^2\lambda_4$$

for U_7; and for U_9 are

$$K_0 = 16\lambda_2 - 6\lambda_3\lambda_4 - 2\lambda_4^3,$$
$$K_1 = -\tfrac{1}{4}\lambda_3^2 - 8\lambda_1 - 4\lambda_2\lambda_4 - \tfrac{1}{2}\lambda_3\lambda_4^2,$$
$$K_2 = -\tfrac{1}{4}\lambda_2\lambda_3 - 4\lambda_1\lambda_4 - \tfrac{1}{2}\lambda_2\lambda_4^2 - 20\lambda_0,$$
$$K_3 = -6\lambda_0\lambda_4 - \tfrac{1}{8}\lambda_2\lambda_3\lambda_4 - \tfrac{1}{2}\lambda_1\lambda_4^2 - \tfrac{1}{2}\lambda_2^2 - \tfrac{1}{4}\lambda_1\lambda_3,$$
$$K_4 = -\lambda_0\lambda_3 - \lambda_1\lambda_2 - \lambda_0\lambda_4^2 - \tfrac{1}{4}\lambda_1\lambda_3\lambda_4 - \tfrac{1}{8}\lambda_2^2\lambda_4,$$
$$K_5 = -\tfrac{1}{2}\lambda_1^2 - \tfrac{1}{32}\lambda_2^2\lambda_3 - \tfrac{1}{16}\lambda_1\lambda_3^2 - \tfrac{5}{4}\lambda_0\lambda_3\lambda_4 - \tfrac{1}{4}\lambda_1\lambda_2\lambda_4 - \lambda_0\lambda_2,$$
$$K_6 = -\tfrac{1}{32}\lambda_2^3 - \tfrac{3}{16}\lambda_1\lambda_2\lambda_3 - \tfrac{7}{4}\lambda_0\lambda_2\lambda_4 - 2\lambda_0\lambda_1 - \tfrac{3}{4}\lambda_0\lambda_3^2 + \tfrac{1}{4}\lambda_1^2\lambda_4,$$
$$K_7 = -10\lambda_0^2 + \tfrac{1}{4}\lambda_0\lambda_1\lambda_4 - \tfrac{33}{8}\lambda_0\lambda_2\lambda_3 + \tfrac{9}{16}\lambda_1^2\lambda_3 - \tfrac{3}{32}\lambda_1\lambda_2^2,$$
$$K_8 = -\tfrac{51}{4}\lambda_0\lambda_2^2 + \tfrac{5}{2}\lambda_0\lambda_1\lambda_3 - 4\lambda_0^2\lambda_4 + 3\lambda_1^2\lambda_2,$$
$$K_9 = \tfrac{1}{256}\lambda_2^4 + \tfrac{5}{2}\lambda_1^3 + \tfrac{3}{64}\lambda_1\lambda_2^2\lambda_3 - \tfrac{75}{16}\lambda_0\lambda_2^2\lambda_4 - \tfrac{21}{2}\lambda_0\lambda_1\lambda_2 + \tfrac{9}{8}\lambda_0\lambda_2\lambda_3^2$$
$$+ \tfrac{9}{8}\lambda_1^2\lambda_2\lambda_4 + \tfrac{27}{2}\lambda_0^2\lambda_3 - \tfrac{9}{64}\lambda_1^2\lambda_3^2 + \tfrac{9}{8}\lambda_0\lambda_1\lambda_3\lambda_4 - \tfrac{9}{4}\lambda_0^2\lambda_4^2.$$

22. The simplicity of the forms of the differential equations which have just been used arose partly from the addition of certain constants to the functions $\wp_{22}$, $\wp_{21}$, $\wp_{11}$ (see p. 52); we introduce now the more general function

$$\sigma_K = e^H \sigma, \quad H = -\tfrac{1}{20}(\lambda_4 u_2^2 + \tfrac{1}{2}\lambda_3 u_2 u_1 + \lambda_2 u_1^2),$$

and write

$$u_1(\lambda_0 u_1^5 + \lambda_1 u_1^4 u_2 + \lambda_2 u_1^3 u_2^2 + \lambda_3 u_1^2 u_2^3 + \lambda_4 u_1 u_2^4 + 4u_2^5)$$
$$= 4(A_0 u_2^5 + 5A_1 u_2^4 u_1 + 10A_2 u_2^3 u_1^2 + 10A_3 u_2^2 u_1^3 + 5A_4 u_2 u_1^4 + A_5 u_1^5)\, u_1,$$

so that

$$A_0 = 1, \quad A_1 = \tfrac{1}{20}\lambda_4, \quad A_2 = \tfrac{1}{40}\lambda_3, \quad A_3 = \tfrac{1}{40}\lambda_2, \quad A_4 = \tfrac{1}{20}\lambda_1, \quad A_5 = \tfrac{1}{4}\lambda_0;$$

putting $\sigma_K = V_1 + V_3 + V_5 + \ldots, = e^H\left(U_1 + \frac{U_3}{3!} + \frac{U_5}{5!} + \ldots\right),$

where each V denotes a homogeneous polynomial of the dimension indicated by its suffix, we have

$$V_1 = U_1,$$
$$V_3 = \frac{U_3}{3!} + HU_1,$$
$$V_5 = \frac{U_5}{5!} + H\frac{U_3}{3!} + \frac{H^2}{2!}U_1,$$

and so on. The forms $V_1, V_3, V_5, \ldots$ are then unaltered by any transformation

$$u_2 = u_2' + hu_1', \quad u_1 = u_1',$$

provided the correspondingly changed values $A_0', A_1', A_2', \ldots$ are also introduced, those namely given by

$$A_0(u_2' + hu_1')^5 + 5A_1(u_2' + hu_1')^4 u_1' + \ldots = A_0' u_2'^5 + 5A_1' u_2'^4 u_1' + \ldots,$$

or $$A_r' = A_r + h\delta A_r + \frac{1}{2}h^2\delta^2 A_r + \ldots,$$

where

$$\delta = A_0\frac{\partial}{\partial A_1} + 2A_1\frac{\partial}{\partial A_2} + 3A_2\frac{\partial}{\partial A_3} + 4A_3\frac{\partial}{\partial A_4} + 5A_4\frac{\partial}{\partial A_5}.$$

Now if

$$V(A_0', A_1', \ldots, u_2', u_1', \ldots) = V(A_0, A_1, \ldots, u_2, u_1, \ldots),$$

then, as $u_2' = u_2 - hu_1$,

$$\left(\delta - u_1\frac{\partial}{\partial u_2}\right)V(A_0, A_1, \ldots, u_2, u_1, \ldots) = 0;$$

thus, if $V_m = P_0 u_2^m + mP_1 u_2^{m-1}u_1 + \tfrac{1}{2}m(m-1)P_2 u_2^{m-2}u_1^2 + \ldots,$

we have $\delta P_0 = 0, \quad \delta P_1 = P_0, \quad \delta P_2 = 2P_1, \ldots, \delta P_m = mP_{m-1},$

and so $$V_m = \left(1 + \frac{u_2}{u_1}\delta + \frac{1}{2!}\frac{u_2^2}{u_1^2}\delta^2 + \ldots\right)P_m u_1^m,$$

which we may denote by

$$V_m = e^{u_1^{-1}u_2\delta}P_m u_1^m.$$

When we carry out the changes of notation we find in fact

$$\sigma_K(u_1, u_2) = \left(1 + u_1^{-1}u_2\delta + \frac{1}{2!}u_1^{-2}u_2^2\delta^2 + \ldots\right)\sigma_K(u_1, 0),$$

where

$$\sigma_K(u, 0) = u - \tfrac{1}{3}A_3u^3 + \tfrac{1}{6}(5A_2A_4 - 3A_3^2 - 2A_1A_5)u^5$$
$$+ \tfrac{1}{126}(67A_3^3 + 60A_2^2A_5 + 75A_1A_4^2 - 66A_1A_3A_5 - 135A_2A_3A_4 - A_4A_5)u^7$$
$$+ \tfrac{1}{4536}\{250A_4^3 + 2910A_2A_3^2A_4 + 276A_1A_3^2A_5 + 108A_2A_5^2 + 900A_1A_2A_4A_5 - 1171A_3^4 - 348A_3A_4A_5 - 900A_1A_3A_4^2 - 1125A_2^2A_4^2 - 180A_1^2A_5^2 - 720A_2^2A_3A_5\}u^9$$
$$+ \text{etc.}$$

The full values for

$$\sigma_K(u_1, u_2) = V_1 + V_3 + V_5 + \ldots$$

are

$$V_1 = u_1, \quad V_3 = -\tfrac{1}{3}(u_2^3 + 3A_1u_2^2u_1 + 3A_2u_2u_1^2 + A_3u_1^3),$$
$$V_5 = \tfrac{1}{6}u_1\{3(A_1^2 - A_2)u_2^4 + 6(A_1A_2 - A_3)u_2^3u_1 + (3A_2^2 + 2A_1A_3 - 5A_4)u_2^2u_1^2 + 2(A_2A_3 - A_5)u_2u_1^3 + (-3A_3^3 + 5A_2A_4 - 2A_1A_5)u_1^4\},$$
$$V_7 = \tfrac{1}{126}(A_1^2 - A_2)u_2^7 + \tfrac{1}{18}(5A_1A_2 - 2A_3 - 3A_1^3)u_2^6u_1 + \tfrac{1}{6}(4A_2^2 - A_4 - 3A_1^2A_2)u_2^5u_1^2$$
$$+ \tfrac{1}{18}(23A_2A_3 - 10A_1A_4 - A_5 - 3A_1^2A_3 - 9A_1A_2^2)u_2^4u_1^3$$
$$+ \tfrac{1}{18}(23A_3^2 - 10A_2A_4 - 3A_2^3 - 4A_1A_5 - 6A_1A_2A_3)u_2^3u_1^4$$
$$+ \tfrac{1}{6}(5A_3A_4 + 2A_1^2A_5 + 3A_1A_3^2 - 4A_2A_5 - 5A_1A_2A_4 - A_2^2A_3)u_2^2u_1^5$$
$$+ \tfrac{1}{18}(10A_4^2 + 6A_1A_2A_5 + 9A_2A_3^2 - 10A_3A_5 - 15A_2^2A_4)u_2u_1^6$$
$$+ \tfrac{1}{126}(67A_3^3 + 60A_2^2A_5 + 75A_1A_4^2 - 66A_1A_3A_5 - 135A_2A_3A_4 - A_4A_5)u_1^7;$$

while

$$V_9 = \frac{u_2^9}{567}(A_3 - 3A_1A_2 + 2A_1^3)$$
$$+ \frac{u_2^8u_1}{504}(21A_1^4 + 16A_1A_3 - 34A_1^2A_2 - A_2^2 - 2A_4)$$
$$+ \frac{u_2^7u_1^2}{126}(-35A_1A_2^2 + 21A_1^3A_2 + 11A_2A_3 + 3A_1^2A_3 + A_1A_4 - A_5)$$
$$+ \frac{u_2^6u_1^3}{108}(-39A_2^3 + 27A_1^2A_2^2 - 10A_1A_2A_3 + 6A_1^3A_3 + 13A_2A_4 + 5A_1^2A_4 + 4A_3^2 - 6A_1A_5)$$
$$+ \frac{u_2^5u_1^4}{18}(3A_1A_2^3 - 14A_2^2A_3 + 3A_1^2A_2A_3 + 10A_1A_2A_4 + A_3A_4 - 3A_1^2A_5)$$
$$+ \frac{u_2^4u_1^5}{72}(3A_2^4 + 12A_1A_2^2A_3 + 30A_1^2A_2A_4 + 4A_3A_5 + 20A_2^2A_4 + 40A_1A_3A_4 - 5A_4^2 - 62A_2A_3^2 - 12A_1A_2A_5 - 12A_1^3A_5 - 18A_1^2A_3^2)$$
$$+ \frac{u_2^3u_1^6}{54}(-5A_1A_4^2 + 30A_2A_3A_4 + 20A_1A_3A_5 - 18A_1^2A_2A_5 + 45A_1A_2^2A_4 - 27A_1A_2A_3^2 + 3A_2^3A_3 - 2A_4A_5 - 31A_3^3 - 15A_2^2A_5)$$
$$+ \frac{u_2^2u_1^7}{252}(85A_2A_4^2 + 132A_1^2A_3A_5 + 270A_1A_2A_3A_4 + 105A_2^3A_4 + 12A_1A_4A_5 - 75A_3^2A_4 - 63A_2^2A_3^2 - 16A_2A_3A_5 - 162A_1A_2^2A_5 - 134A_1A_3^3 - 4A_5^2 - 150A_1^2A_4^2)$$

$$+\frac{u_2u_1^8}{126}(10A_3A_4^2+135A_2^2A_3A_4+66A_1A_2A_3A_5+26A_2A_4A_5$$
$$-67A_2A_3^3-31A_3^2A_5-4A_1A_5^2-75A_1A_2A_4^2-60A_2^3A_5)$$
$$+\frac{u_1^9}{4536}(250A_4^3+2910A_2A_3^2A_4+276A_1A_3^2A_5+108A_2A_5^2+900A_1A_2A_4A_5$$
$$-1171A_3^4-348A_3A_4A_5-900A_1A_3A_4^2-1125A_2^2A_4^2-180A_1^2A_5^2$$
$$-720A_2^2A_3A_5).$$

23. From the expansion which precedes we can obtain that of any odd function in terms of variables u_1', u_2' associated with the general form,

$$a_0u_1'^6+6a_1u_1'^5u_2'+\ldots+a_6u_2'^6,$$

of the fundamental sextic; for this we have only to write

$$u_1=m(u_1'-\psi u_2'),\quad u_2=nu_1'+pu_2',$$

where $m(p+n\psi)=1$, and change the notation for the constants by means of the identity

$$4m(u_1'-\psi u_2')[A_5m^5(u_1'-\psi u_2')^5+\ldots+A_0(nu_1'+pu_2')^5]=a_0u_1'^6+\ldots+a_6u_2'^6.$$

Instead of doing this we shall obtain, as far as the terms of the third degree, the expansion of any other odd function than that considered above, for the reduced case when the differential equations have the form given by

$$(\delta^4-4\delta^3\delta'+3\delta^2\delta'^2)\sigma\sigma'=\tfrac{1}{2}P\sigma\sigma'+[A(d_2^2-d_2d_2')+B(d_2d_1-d_2d_1')$$
$$+C(d_1^2-d_1d_1')]\sigma\sigma';$$

putting $$\sigma=u_1-\psi u_2+\frac{U_3}{3!}+\ldots,=U_1+\frac{U_3}{3!}+\ldots,$$

and equating terms of zero dimension in u_1, u_2, u_1', u_2' on the two sides of the equation, there results

$$(\delta^4-4\delta^3\delta'+3\delta^2\delta'^2)\frac{U_1U_3'+U_3U_1'}{3!}=[A(d_2^2-d_2d_2')+\ldots]U_1U_1',$$

leading, when u_1', u_2' and h_1, h_2 are replaced by u_1, u_2, to

$$4U_1U_3=A_0\psi^2-B_0\psi+C_0,$$

where A_0, B_0, C_0 are the values of A, B, C when h_1, h_2 are replaced by u_1, u_2; the right side is found to be of the form

$$(u_1-\psi u_2)H-3u_1u_2^3(\lambda_0\psi^5+\lambda_1\psi^4+\lambda_2\psi^3+\lambda_3\psi^2+\lambda_4\psi+4);$$

as ψ makes this last quintic function vanish, we therefore find

$$-4U_3=u_2^3(\lambda_4\psi-4)+3u_2^2u_1\psi(\lambda_0\psi^3+\lambda_1\psi^2+\lambda_2\psi+\lambda_3)$$
$$+3u_2u_1^2\psi(\lambda_0\psi^2+\lambda_1\psi+\lambda_2)+u_1^3(3\lambda_0\psi^2+\lambda_1\psi-\lambda_2).$$

24. As a last example we find the terms of the fourth order in an even function with the same reduced form of the sextic and differential equations.

As in the general case (p. 83), if the constant term be taken to be unity, the terms of the second order will be $-\frac{1}{2}(x_0u_2^2+2y_0u_2u_1+z_0u_1^2)$, where

$$x_0=\wp_{22}(0)=-\partial^2\log\sigma(0)/\partial u_2^2, \text{ etc.},$$

are the coordinates of one of the finite nodes of the surface $\Delta=0$; equating terms of zero dimension in the differential equations, we have, if

$$\sigma=1+\tfrac{1}{2}U_2+\tfrac{1}{24}U_4+\dots,$$

$$(\delta^4-4\delta^3\delta'+3\delta^2\delta'^2)\left(\frac{U_4+U_4'}{4!}+\frac{U_2U_2'}{2!2!}\right)=\tfrac{1}{2}P+\{A(d_2^2-d_2d_2')+\dots\}\frac{U_2+U_2'}{2!},$$

leading to

$$\begin{aligned}-U_4&=3U_2^2-\tfrac{1}{2}P_0+A_0x_0+B_0y_0+C_0z_0\\&=u_2^4(3x_0^2+\tfrac{1}{2}\lambda_3+\lambda_4x_0+4y_0)+4u_2^3u_1(3x_0y_0+\lambda_4y_0-2z_0)\\&+6u_2^2u_1^2(x_0z_0+2y_0^2+\tfrac{1}{2}\lambda_3y_0)+4u_2u_1^3(3y_0z_0-\lambda_0-\tfrac{1}{2}\lambda_1x_0+\lambda_2y_0)\\&+u_1^4(3z_0^2-\tfrac{1}{2}\lambda_0\lambda_4+\tfrac{1}{8}\lambda_1\lambda_3-3\lambda_0x_0+\lambda_1y_0+\lambda_2z_0).\end{aligned}$$

It will be noticed that in the coefficients of the powers of u_2, u_1 here, the linear and constant terms are the same as in the fundamental differential equations of p. 88. The reason for this will appear below.

25. In the preceding expansions the arguments have throughout been denoted by u_1, u_2; they are not the same in the various cases; in order to give clearness some remarks may be made. For the function

$$\vartheta(u)=\Sigma e^{au^2+2hun+i\pi\tau n^2},$$

the coefficients x_0, y_0, z_0 in the expansion

$$\frac{\vartheta(u)}{\vartheta(0)}=1-\tfrac{1}{2}(x_0u_2^2+2y_0u_2u_1+z_0u_1^2)+\dots$$

are the values of $\wp_{22}(0)$, $\wp_{21}(0)$, $\wp_{11}(0)$, where $\wp_{22}(u)=-\partial^2\log\vartheta(u)/\partial u_2^2$, etc. We have proved (p. 38) that if, with $s^2=\lambda_0+\lambda_1t+\dots+4t^5$, $=f(t)$,

$$u_1\equiv\int_{a_1}^{t_1}\frac{dt}{s}+\int_{a_2}^{t_2}\frac{dt}{s},\quad u_2\equiv\int_{a_1}^{t_1}\frac{tdt}{s}+\int_{a_2}^{t_2}\frac{tdt}{s},$$

where the sign $\equiv$ means that additive integral multiples of periods are disregarded, then

$$t_1+t_2=\wp_{22}(u),\quad t_1t_2=-\wp_{21}(u),\quad F(t_1,t_2)-2s_1s_2=4(t_1-t_2)^2\wp_{11}(u);$$

hence putting t_1, t_2 at a_1 and a_2,

$$x_0=a_1+a_2,\quad y_0=-a_1a_2,\quad z_0=\tfrac{1}{4}F(a_1,a_2)/(a_1-a_2)^2,$$

the branch-place values a_1, a_2 being those used (p. 31) in describing the dissection of the Riemann surface whereby the matrix τ, and the matrices h and a, are determined.

For any other even function we have a similar expansion; without entering into unnecessary detail, such a function has been shewn to be of the form

$$\Phi(u) = e^{p_1 u_1 + p_2 u_2 + b} \vartheta(u_1 - A_1, u_2 - A_2);$$

expressing u_1, u_2 in terms of t_1, t_2 as above, and putting (p. 29)

$$A_1 \equiv \int_{a_1}^{\theta} \frac{dt}{s} + \int_{a_2}^{\phi} \frac{dt}{s}, \quad A_2 \equiv \int_{a_1}^{\theta} \frac{tdt}{s} + \int_{a_2}^{\phi} \frac{tdt}{s},$$

the coefficients x_0, y_0, z_0 occurring in the expansion of $\Phi(u)/\Phi(0)$ are the values, for $u_1 = 0$, $u_2 = 0$, of the expressions

$$-\frac{\partial^2}{\partial u_r \partial u_s} \log \Phi(u) = -\frac{\partial^2}{\partial u_r \partial u_s} \log \vartheta(u_1 - A_1, u_2 - A_2),$$

namely, preserving the notation $\wp_{rs}(u) = -\partial^2 \log \vartheta(u)/\partial u_r \partial u_s$, are the values of $\wp_{rs}(A_1, A_2)$; thus $x_0 = \theta + \phi$, $y_0 = -\theta\phi$. As to z_0 the general form is simplified here in virtue of the fact that θ, ϕ are roots of the equation $f(t) = 0$; to make this perfectly evident we recall two facts: first, every one of the ten even functions Φ is obtained (p. 24) by taking A_1, A_2 so that

$$2A_1 = 2\omega_{11}m_1 + 2\omega_{12}m_2 + 2\omega_{11}'m_1' + 2\omega_{12}'m_2',$$

$$2A_2 = 2\omega_{21}m_1 + 2\omega_{22}m_2 + 2\omega_{21}'m_1' + 2\omega_{22}'m_2',$$

where m_1, m_2, m_1', m_2' are such integers that $m_1m_1' + m_2m_2'$ is even, with proper corresponding values of the constants p_1, p_2 in the outstanding exponential; every one of the six odd functions is also so obtainable provided $m_1m_1' + m_2m_2'$ be odd: second, if by the rule of p. 32 we calculate the values

$$A_1 = \int_{a_1}^{\theta} \frac{dt}{s} + \int_{a_2}^{\phi} \frac{dt}{s}, \quad A_2 = \int_{a_1}^{\theta} \frac{tdt}{s} + \int_{a_2}^{\phi} \frac{tdt}{s},$$

we find that they correspond to even functions when θ, ϕ are any two different roots of the quintic $f(t) = 0$, and correspond to odd functions when ϕ is the infinite place a, and θ is either one of the roots of $f(t) = 0$ or is also the infinite place. It follows then that in the function above $\wp_{11}(A_1, A_2)$ reduces from $\frac{1}{4}(\theta - \phi)^{-2}[F(\theta, \phi) - \theta'\phi']$, where $\theta'^2 = f(\theta)$, $\phi'^2 = f(\phi)$, to

$$e_{\theta,\phi} = \tfrac{1}{4}(\theta - \phi)^{-2} F(\theta, \phi);$$

and we have

$$\frac{\Phi}{\Phi_0} = 1 - \tfrac{1}{2}\{(\theta + \phi)u_2^2 - 2\theta\phi u_2 u_1 + e_{\theta,\phi} u_1^2\} + \dots .$$

26. For an odd function

$$\Phi(u) = e^{p_1 u_1 + p_2 u_2 + b} \vartheta(u_1 - A_1, u_2 - A_2),$$

we may consider two cases: first that when

$$A_1 \equiv \int_{a_1}^{\theta} \frac{dt}{s} + \int_{a_2}^{a} \frac{dt}{s}, \quad A_2 \equiv \int_{a_1}^{\theta} \frac{tdt}{s} + \int_{a_2}^{a} \frac{tdt}{s},$$

where θ is one of the roots of $f(t)=0$; then the quantities

$$-\partial^2 \log \Phi(0)/\partial u_r \partial u_s,$$

or $\wp_{rs}(A_1, A_2)$, are infinite, but have finite ratios obtainable by proceeding to a limit from the general formulae when t_1, t_2 are finite,

$$\wp_{22}(u^{t_1, a_1} + u^{t_2, a_2}) = t_1 + t_2, \quad \wp_{21}(u^{t_1, a_1} + u^{t_2, a_2}) = -t_1 t_2,$$

$$\wp_{11}(u^{t_1, a_1} + u^{t_2, a_2}) = \frac{F(t_1, t_2) - 2s_1 s_2}{4(t_1 - t_2)^2},$$

namely, $\wp_{22}(A) : \wp_{21}(A) : \wp_{11}(A) = 1 : -\theta : \theta^2$; these however are, as previously remarked (p. 84) the ratios $\Phi_2{}^2 : \Phi_2\Phi_1 : \Phi_1{}^2$, where $\Phi_r = \partial\Phi(A)/\partial u_r$. Thus the linear terms in the development of the function $\Phi(u)$, with the values of A_1, A_2 here taken, are, save for a constant multiplier, $u_1 - \theta^{-1}u_2$. Lastly, for the odd function $\Phi(u)$ in which

$$A_1 \equiv \int_{a_1}^{a} \frac{dt}{s} + \int_{a_2}^{a} \frac{dt}{s}, \quad A_2 \equiv \int_{a_1}^{a} \frac{tdt}{s} + \int_{a_2}^{a} \frac{tdt}{s},$$

the argument is similar to, but *not* a particular case of, that just given; both are particular cases of the argument for the case when the fundamental equation is a sextic, not a quintic. Either for that reason, or because we have exhausted all the other cases, there can be no doubt of the result: the odd function $\Phi(u)$ in this case is that given, save for a constant factor, by the expansion (p. 89)

$$\sigma(u) = u_1 + \tfrac{1}{6}(\tfrac{1}{4}\lambda_2 u_1{}^3 - 2u_2{}^3) + \dots .$$

It is interesting to verify that this is in accord with a result previously found (p. 34) as to the necessary and sufficient form of the expression of the arguments of the function $\vartheta(u)$ in terms of one arbitrary variable in order that the function may vanish identically. In accordance therewith, $\sigma(u)$ vanishes when

$$u_r - u_r^{a, a_1} - u_r^{a, a_2} \equiv u_r^{x, a} + u_r^{a_1, a_2}, \qquad r = 1, 2$$

where $$u_r^{x, z} = \int_z^x \frac{t^{r-1}dt}{s};$$

as (p. 32) $$-u_r^{a, a_2} \equiv u_r^{a, a_2},$$

this is the same as $$u_r \equiv u_r^{x, a},$$

which, by replacing (x) by its conjugate position, may equally be written

$$u_r \equiv u_r^{a, x};$$

herein (x) is any position on the Riemann surface $s^2 = f(t)$. Considering now the case when (x) is near to the infinite place a, putting $x = \xi^{-2}$ in the forms

$$u_1 = \int_x^a \frac{dt}{s}, \quad u_2 = \int_x^a \frac{tdt}{s},$$

we have, when ξ is small,

$$u_1 = \int d\xi \, . \, \xi^2 (1 + \tfrac{1}{4}\lambda_4\xi^2 + \tfrac{1}{4}\lambda_3\xi^4 - \dots)^{-\frac{1}{2}}$$

$$= \tfrac{1}{3}\xi^3 - \tfrac{1}{40}\lambda_4\xi^5 + (\tfrac{3}{896}\lambda_4^2 - \tfrac{1}{56}\lambda_3)\,\xi^7 + \dots,$$

$$u_2 = \xi - \tfrac{1}{24}\lambda_4\xi^3 + (\tfrac{3}{640}\lambda_4^2 - \tfrac{1}{40}\lambda_3)\,\xi^5 + \dots,$$

and the substitution of these series in the expansion for $\sigma(u)$ given above reduces it to zero identically.

27. *In what follows we shall regard the function $\sigma(u)$ of pp. 89, 90, which is of the form,*

$$\sigma(u) = e^{p_1u_1 + p_2u_2 + b}\, \vartheta(u - u^{a,\,a_1} - u^{a,\,a_2}),$$

as fundamental; and shall put

$$\wp_{rs}(u) = -\frac{\partial^2}{\partial u_r \partial u_s} \log \sigma(u).$$

From the equations such as (p. 38) $-\partial^2 \log \vartheta(u^{t_1,\,a_1} + u^{t_2,\,a_2})/\partial u_2^2 = t_1 + t_2$, *we shall then have such equations as*

$$-\partial^2 \log \sigma(u^{a,\,t_1} + u^{a,\,t_2})/\partial u_2^2 = t_1 + t_2,$$

where, in both integrals of the argument on the left, one of the limits is the infinite branch-place a; in other words, if we put

$$u_1 = \int_{t_1}^{\infty} \frac{dt}{s} + \int_{t_2}^{\infty} \frac{dt}{s}, \quad u_2 = \int_{t_1}^{\infty} \frac{t\,dt}{s} + \int_{t_2}^{\infty} \frac{t\,dt}{s},$$

we shall have

$$\wp_{22}(u) = t_1 + t_2, \quad \wp_{21}(u) = -t_1t_2, \quad \wp_{11}(u) = \frac{F(t_1, t_2) - 2s_1s_2}{4(t_1 - t_2)^2}.$$

Then the arguments $u_1 = 0$, $u_2 = 0$ are those associated with the node of the surface $\Delta = 0$ at the infinite end of the axis of z, and the arguments

$$u_1 = \int_t^{\infty} \frac{dt}{s}, \quad u_2 = \int_t^{\infty} \frac{t\,dt}{s},$$

are those associated with the points of $\Delta = 0$ lying on the singular conic at infinity. An even function then has an expansion

$$e^{p_1u_1 + p_2u_2} \frac{\sigma(u + \Omega_q)}{\sigma(\Omega_q)} = 1 - \tfrac{1}{2}(x_0u_2^2 + 2y_0u_2u_1 + z_0u_1^2) + \dots,$$

where $\qquad x_0 = \wp_{22}(\Omega_q) = \wp_{22}(u^{a,\,\theta} + u^{a,\,\phi}) = \theta + \phi$, etc.

CHAPTER V.

CERTAIN FUNCTIONAL RELATIONS AND THEIR GEOMETRICAL INTERPRETATION.

28. It follows by a preceding investigation (pp. 20, 21), that if τ be a symmetrical matrix of two rows and columns, such that the real part of the quadratic form $i\tau n^2$, which is the same as $i(\tau_{11}n_1^2 + 2\tau_{12}n_1n_2 + \tau_{22}n_2^2)$, is necessarily negative, an analytical integral function of two variables v_1, v_2 which satisfies the conditions

$$\phi(v_1 + 1, v_2) = \phi(v_1, v_2) = \phi(v_1, v_2 + 1),$$

$$\phi(v_1 + \tau_{11}, v_2 + \tau_{21}) = e^{H_1}\phi(v_1, v_2), \quad \phi(v_1 + \tau_{12}, v_2 + \tau_{22}) = e^{H_2}\phi(v_1, v_2),$$

where $\qquad H_1 = -4\pi i(v_1 + \tfrac{1}{2}\tau_{11}), \quad H_2 = -4\pi i(v_2 + \tfrac{1}{2}\tau_{22}),$

is expressible as a sum of four theta functions, in the form

$$\sum_h B_h \Theta\left(2v, 2\tau \,\middle|\, \begin{matrix}\tfrac{1}{2}h\\ 0\end{matrix}\right),$$

when h denotes in turn the pairs (0, 0), (0, 1), (1, 0), (1, 1). It follows thence that in terms of any four such functions ϕ, which are themselves linearly independent, any other such function ϕ can be linearly expressed.

The conditions for ϕ are included, as was shewn, in the single equation

$$\phi(v + m + \tau m') = e^{-4\pi i m'(v + \frac{1}{2}\tau m')}\phi(v);$$

if a be an arbitrary symmetrical matrix of two rows and columns, and $h, \omega, \omega', \eta, \eta'$ such matrices of two rows and columns that

$$\pi i = 2h\omega, \quad \pi i\tau = 2h\omega', \quad \eta = 2a\omega, \quad \eta' = 2a\omega' - \bar{h},$$

it was shewn (p. 25) that, for arbitrary p, p', each of which is a row of two elements,

$$a(u + \Omega_p)^2 - au^2 - 2\pi ip'(v + \tfrac{1}{2}\tau p') - 2\pi ipp' = H_p(u + \tfrac{1}{2}\Omega_p) - \pi ipp',$$
$$= \lambda_p(u), \text{ say,}$$

where $\qquad \Omega_p = 2\omega p + 2\omega' p', \quad H_p = 2\eta p + 2\eta' p', \quad hu = \pi iv;$

it follows therefore that an integral analytical function, $\psi(u)$, of two variables u_1, u_2, which for arbitrary integer pairs m, m', satisfies the equation

$$\psi(u + 2\omega m + 2\omega' m') = e^{2\lambda_m(u)}\psi(u),$$

is expressible linearly in terms of any four such functions ψ which are themselves linearly independent.

29. Now we proved the equation, when m, m' are pairs of integers,

$$\vartheta(u+\Omega_m, q) = e^{\lambda_m(u) + 2\pi i(mq'-m'q)}\vartheta(u, q);$$

therefore, as $$\lambda_m(u+w) + \lambda_m(u-w) = 2\lambda_m(u),$$

it follows that when q consists of half integers, the product

$$\vartheta(u+w, q)\,\vartheta(u-w, q)$$

is such a function $\psi(u)$.

Thus also $\sigma^2(u)$ and, because the functions $\wp_{22}(u)$, etc., are periodic, each of the following functions, which are known to be integral functions,

$$\sigma^2(u),\quad \sigma^2(u)\,\wp_{22}(u),\quad \sigma^2(u)\,\wp_{21}(u),\quad \sigma^2(u)\,\wp_{11}(u),\quad \sigma^2(u)\,[\wp_{2222}(u) - 6\wp_{22}{}^2(u)],$$

is such a function $\psi(u)$, and there is therefore a linear equation with constant coefficients connecting these five functions; this is one of the five differential equations previously discussed.

Or again, the five functions

$$\sigma^2(u)\,[\wp_{\lambda\mu\nu\rho}(u) - 2\wp_{\mu\nu}(u)\,\wp_{\lambda\rho}(u) - 2\wp_{\nu\lambda}(u)\,\wp_{\mu\rho}(u) - 2\wp_{\lambda\mu}(u)\,\wp_{\nu\rho}(u)],$$

which occur on the left sides of these differential equations, are themselves connected by a linear homogeneous equation, obtainable by eliminating the functions $\wp_{22}(u)$, $\wp_{21}(u)$, $\wp_{11}(u)$, and the constant term, from the differential equations.

30. Another illustration is furnished by the five integral functions of u

$$\sigma(u+v)\,\sigma(u-v),\quad \sigma^2(u)\,\sigma^2(v),\quad \sigma^2(u)\,\sigma^2(v)\,\wp_{22}(u),\quad \sigma^2(u)\,\sigma^2(v)\,\wp_{21}(u),$$
$$\sigma^2(u)\,\sigma^2(v)\,\wp_{11}(u);$$

thus the function $\sigma(u+v)\,\sigma(u-v)/\sigma^2(u)\,\sigma^2(v)$ is expressible as a linear function of $\wp_{22}(u)$, $\wp_{21}(u)$, $\wp_{11}(u)$, with coefficients independent of u; its form shews that it is equally a linear function of $\wp_{22}(v)$, $\wp_{21}(v)$, $\wp_{11}(v)$; and it is changed in sign when u, v are interchanged. Thus

$$\frac{\sigma(u+v)\,\sigma(u-v)}{\sigma^2(u)\,\sigma^2(v)} = A[\wp_{22}(u) - \wp_{22}(v)] + B[\wp_{21}(u) - \wp_{21}(v)] + C[\wp_{11}(u) - \wp_{11}(v)]$$
$$+ F[\wp_{21}(u)\,\wp_{11}(v) - \wp_{11}(u)\,\wp_{21}(v)] + G[\wp_{11}(u)\,\wp_{22}(v) - \wp_{11}(v)\,\wp_{22}(u)]$$
$$+ H[\wp_{22}(u)\,\wp_{21}(v) - \wp_{21}(u)\,\wp_{22}(v)],$$

where A, B, C, F, G, H are constants. Taking now the expansion (p. 89)

$$\sigma(u) = u_1 + \tfrac{1}{24}\lambda_2 u_1{}^3 - \tfrac{1}{3}u_2{}^3 + \dots,$$

and denoting by H_4, H_6 power series in u_1, u_2 beginning respectively with terms of the fourth and sixth dimension, we have, if σ, σ_{22}, ... denote $\sigma(u)$, $\sigma_{22}(u)$, ...

$$\sigma^2(u)\wp_{22}(u) = -\sigma\sigma_{22} + \sigma_2^2 \;= 2u_1u_2 + H_4,$$
$$\sigma^2(u)\wp_{21}(u) = -\sigma\sigma_{21} + \sigma_2\sigma_1 = -u_2^2 + H_4,$$
$$\sigma^2(u)\wp_{11}(u) = -\sigma\sigma_{11} + \sigma_1^2 \;= \;1 \;+ H_4,$$

and hence

$$\sigma^2(u)\sigma^2(v)[\wp_{22}(u) - \wp_{22}(v)] = 2u_1u_2v_1^2 - 2v_1v_2u_1^2 + H_6,$$
$$\sigma^2(u)\sigma^2(v)[\wp_{21}(u) - \wp_{21}(v)] = \quad u_1^2v_2^2 - \quad u_2^2v_1^2 + H_6,$$
$$\sigma^2(u)\sigma^2(v)[\wp_{11}(u) - \wp_{11}(v)] = v_1^2 - u_1^2 + \tfrac{1}{12}\lambda_2(v_1^4 - u_1^4) + \tfrac{2}{3}(u_1u_2^3 - v_1v_2^3) + H_6,$$
$$\sigma^2(u)\sigma^2(v)[\wp_{21}(u)\wp_{11}(v) - \wp_{11}(u)\wp_{21}(v)] = v_2^2 - u_2^2 + H_4,$$
$$\sigma^2(u)\sigma^2(v)[\wp_{11}(u)\wp_{22}(v) - \wp_{22}(u)\wp_{11}(v)] = 2v_1v_2 - 2u_1u_2 + H_4,$$
$$\sigma^2(u)\sigma^2(v)[\wp_{22}(u)\wp_{21}(v) - \wp_{21}(u)\wp_{22}(v)] = 2v_1v_2u_2^2 - 2u_1u_2v_2^2 + H_6.$$

On the other hand, up to terms of the fourth order,

$$\sigma(u+v)\,\sigma(u-v) = [u_1 + v_1 + \tfrac{1}{24}\lambda_2(u_1+v_1)^3 - \tfrac{1}{3}(u_2+v_2)^3]\,[u_1 - v_1 + \tfrac{1}{24}\lambda_2(u_1-v_1)^3 - \tfrac{1}{3}(u_2-v_2)^3]$$
$$= u_1^2 - v_1^2 + \tfrac{1}{12}\lambda_2(u_1^4 - v_1^4) - \tfrac{2}{3}(u_1u_2^3 - v_1v_2^3) - 2(u_1u_2v_2^2 - v_1v_2u_2^2);$$

in this last the only quadratic terms are those in $u_1^2 - v_1^2$; comparing with the quadratic terms in

$$\sigma^2(u)\sigma^2(v)[A\{\wp_{22}(u) - \wp_{22}(v)\} + \dots + H\{\wp_{22}(u)\wp_{21}(v) - \wp_{21}(u)\wp_{22}(v)\}],$$

we infer, therefore, that $C = -1$, $F = 0$, $G = 0$; and comparing the quartic terms we infer $A = 0$, $B = 0$, $H = 1$; on the whole therefore we have

$$\frac{\sigma(u+v)\,\sigma(u-v)}{\sigma^2(u)\,\sigma^2(v)} = \wp_{22}(u)\wp_{21}(v) - \wp_{21}(u)\wp_{22}(v) + \wp_{11}(v) - \wp_{11}(u).$$

We return to this formula later; it will be seen that the geometrical interpretation furnishes another proof of it; references to another analytical proof are given in the Bibliographical Notes, at the end of the Volume.

31. Next take any even theta function, so that

$$\sigma(u, q) = 1 - \tfrac{1}{2}(x_0u_2^2 + 2y_0u_2u_1 + z_0u_1^2) + H_4;$$

the square of this function is then expressible in the form

$$\sigma^2(u)\,[A\wp_{22}(u) + B\wp_{21}(u) + C\wp_{11}(u) + D],$$

so that

$$1 - (x_0u_2^2 + 2y_0u_2u_1 + z_0u_1^2) + H_4 = A(2u_1u_2 + H_4) + B(-u_2^2 + H_4) + C(1 + H_4) + D(u_1^2 + H_4),$$

and hence $\qquad A = -y_0, \quad B = x_0, \quad C = 1, \quad D = -z_0;$

thus $$\frac{\sigma^2(u,q)}{\sigma^2(u)} = -y_0\wp_{22}(u) + x_0\wp_{21}(u) + \wp_{11}(u) - z_0,$$

a result obtainable, as we can easily see, from the formula for

$$\sigma(u+v)\,\sigma(u-v) \div \sigma^2(u)\,\sigma^2(v),$$

by making v equal to the appropriate even half-period.

32. Similarly if $\sigma(u, q), = u_1 - \theta^{-1}u_2 +$ terms of third and higher dimension, be an odd theta function, multiplied by a proper constant, its square is expressible in the form

$$\sigma^2(u)\,[A\wp_{22}(u) + B\wp_{21}(u) + C\wp_{11}(u) + D],$$

so that

$$(u_1 - \theta^{-1}u_2)^2 = A\,(2u_1u_2) + B(-u_2^2) + C(1) + D(u_1^2),$$

and hence

$$\frac{\sigma^2(u, q)}{\sigma^2(u)} = -\theta^{-1}\wp_{22}(u) - \theta^{-2}\wp_{21}(u) + 1.$$

33. These formulae should be associated with others: writing

$$\wp_{rs}(u, q) = -\partial^2 \log \sigma(u, q)/\partial u_r \partial u_s,$$

we have equations

$$\sigma^2(u, q)\,\wp_{rs}(u, q) = \sigma^2(u)\,[A\wp_{22}(u) + B\wp_{21}(u) + C\wp_{11}(u) + D],$$

where A, B, C, D are different for different pairs r, s, and for different characteristics q. Writing

$$\sigma(u, q) = 1 - \tfrac{1}{2}(x_0u_2^2 + 2y_0u_2u_1 + z_0u_1^2)$$
$$+ \tfrac{1}{24}(Pu_2^4 + 4Qu_2^3u_1 + 6Ru_2^2u_1^2 + 4Su_2u_1^3 + Tu_1^4) + \dots,$$

the terms up to those of dimension 2, in

$$\sigma^2(u, q)\,\wp_{rs}(u, q) = -\sigma(u, q)\,\sigma_{rs}(u, q) + \sigma_r(u, q)\,\sigma_s(u, q),$$

for the respective cases $r = 2, s = 2$; $r = 2, s = 1$; $r = 1, s = 1$, are

$$x_0 + \tfrac{1}{2}(x_0^2 - P)\,u_2^2 \quad + (x_0y_0 - Q)\,u_2u_1 + \tfrac{1}{2}(2y_0^2 - x_0z_0 - R)\,u_1^2,$$
$$y_0 + \tfrac{1}{2}(x_0y_0 - Q)\,u_2^2 \quad + (x_0z_0 - R)\,u_2u_1 + \tfrac{1}{2}(y_0z_0 - S)\,u_1^2,$$
$$z_0 + \tfrac{1}{2}(2y_0^2 - x_0z_0 - R)\,u_2^2 + (y_0z_0 - S)\,u_2u_1 + \tfrac{1}{2}(z_0^2 - T)\,u_1^2;$$

comparing these with the terms up to those of dimension 2 in the expression by means of the functions $\sigma^2(u)\,\wp_{22}(u)$, etc., that is, with

$$A\,(2u_2u_1) + B(-u_2^2) + C + Du_1^2,$$

we find easily, in the respective cases, the values of A, B, C, D; now $\sigma(u, q)$ is of the form $e^H\sigma(u + \Omega_q)$, where H is linear in u_1 and u_2, and Ω_q is a half period; if α denote the half period by which we pass from $\vartheta(u)$ to $\sigma(u)$, and A that by which we pass from $\vartheta(u)$ to $\sigma(u, q)$, we have (pp. 95—97)

$$(\Omega_q)_1 \equiv A_1 - \alpha_1 \equiv \int_a^\theta \frac{dt}{s} + \int_a^\phi \frac{dt}{s}, \quad (\Omega_q)_2 \equiv \int_a^\theta \frac{t\,dt}{s} + \int_a^\phi \frac{t\,dt}{s},$$

and $\wp_{rs}(u, q)$ is $\wp_{rs}(u + \Omega_q)$; taking account of the formula previously found (§ 31) for $\sigma^2(u, q)$, we can thus express each of $\wp_{rs}(u + \Omega_q)$ as the quotient of two linear functions of $\wp_{22}(u)$, $\wp_{21}(u)$, $\wp_{11}(u)$; using a factor of proportionality ρ, in fact equal to $\sigma^2(u, q)/\sigma^2(u)$, the result may be written, if $u' = u + \Omega_q$,

$$[\rho\wp_{22}(u'),\ \rho\wp_{21}(u'),\ \rho\wp_{11}(u'),\ \rho] = M[\wp_{22}(u),\ \wp_{21}(u),\ \wp_{11}(u),\ 1]$$

where M, a matrix of four rows and columns, is found on computation to be such that, if

$$j = \begin{pmatrix} 0 & -1 & 0 & 0 \\ 1 & 0 & 0 & 0 \\ 0 & 0 & 0 & 1 \\ 0 & 0 & -1 & 0 \end{pmatrix},\quad j^{-1} = \begin{pmatrix} 0 & 1 & 0 & 0 \\ -1 & 0 & 0 & 0 \\ 0 & 0 & 0 & -1 \\ 0 & 0 & 1 & 0 \end{pmatrix} = -j,$$

then

$$Mj = \begin{pmatrix} \tfrac{1}{2}(P - x_0^2) & \tfrac{1}{2}(Q - x_0y_0) & \tfrac{1}{2}(R + x_0z_0 - 2y_0^2) & x_0 \\ \tfrac{1}{2}(Q - x_0y_0) & \tfrac{1}{2}(R - x_0z_0) & \tfrac{1}{2}(S - y_0z_0) & y_0 \\ \tfrac{1}{2}(R + x_0z_0 - 2y_0^2) & \tfrac{1}{2}(S - y_0z_0) & \tfrac{1}{2}(T - z_0^2) & z_0 \\ x_0 & y_0 & z_0 & 1 \end{pmatrix},$$

this being a symmetrical matrix. We have previously had the matrix j (p. 71), in a formula which is essentially connected with this, we have found previously the values of P, Q, R, S, T in terms of x_0, y_0, z_0, (p. 94), and we have found also (p. 95)

$$x_0 = \theta + \phi,\quad y_0 = -\theta\phi,\quad z_0 = e_{\theta,\phi};$$

thus the symmetrical matrix Mj, and therefore also M, can be expressed in terms of θ, ϕ and the coefficients in the fundamental quintic.

It can be verified that each of the four expressions given by

$$M(x_0, y_0, z_0, 1),\ \text{ or }\ Mj(y_0, -x_0, -1, z_0)$$

vanishes; of this the geometrical interpretation will appear.

34. Consider similarly an odd function

$$\sigma(u, q) = u_1 - \psi u_2 + \tfrac{1}{6}(pu_2^3 + 3qu_2^2u_1 + 3ru_2u_1^2 + su_1^3) + \dots;$$

up to quadratic terms the expressions

$$\sigma^2(u, q)\,\wp_{22}(u, q),\ \text{etc.},$$

or

$$\sigma_2^2 - \sigma\sigma_{22},\quad \sigma_1\sigma_2 - \sigma\sigma_{12},\quad \sigma_1^2 - \sigma\sigma_{11},$$

where

$$\sigma_2 = \partial\sigma(u, q)/\partial u_2,\ \text{etc.},$$

are respectively

$$\begin{array}{llll} \psi^2 & - (p + q\psi)\,u_2u_1 & - (q + r\psi)\,u_1^2, \\ -\psi + \tfrac{1}{2}(p + q\psi)\,u_2^2 & & - \tfrac{1}{2}(r + s\psi)\,u_1^2, \\ 1 + (q + r\psi)\,u_2^2 & + (r + s\psi)\,u_2u_1 & & ; \end{array}$$

comparing these with the terms up to those of dimension 2 in

$$\sigma^2(u)\,[A\wp_{22}(u)+B\wp_{21}(u)+C\wp_{11}(u)+D],$$

we obtain the expressions for

$$\frac{\sigma^2(u,q)}{\sigma^2(u)}\wp_{22}(u,q),\quad \frac{\sigma^2(u,q)}{\sigma^2(u)}\wp_{21}(u,q),\quad \frac{\sigma^2(u,q)}{\sigma^2(u)}\wp_{11}(u,q);$$

we have previously (§ 32) found the expression for $\sigma^2(u,q)/\sigma^2(u)$; hence as before if Ω_q be the half period given, with $\theta=\psi^{-1}$, by

$$(\Omega_q)_1=\int_a^\theta \frac{dt}{s},\quad (\Omega_q)_2=\int_a^\theta \frac{t\,dt}{s},$$

the functions $\wp_{22}(u+\Omega_q)$, etc., are expressible as fractional linear functions in $\wp_{22}(u)$, etc., by formulae given, if ρ be a factor of proportionality, in fact equal to $\sigma^2(u,q)/\sigma^2(u)$, by

$$[\rho\wp_{22}(u'),\ \rho\wp_{21}(u'),\ \rho\wp_{11}(u'),\ \rho]=N[\wp_{22}(u),\ \wp_{21}(u),\ \wp_{11}(u),\ 1],$$

where $u'=u+\Omega_q$, and N is a matrix of four rows and columns given by

$$Nj=\begin{pmatrix} 0 & \tfrac12(p+q\psi) & q+r\psi & \psi^2\\ -\tfrac12(p+q\psi) & 0 & \tfrac12(r+s\psi) & -\psi\\ -(q+r\psi) & -\tfrac12(r+s\psi) & 0 & 1\\ -\psi^2 & \psi & -1 & 0\end{pmatrix}$$

where the matrix on the right is skew symmetrical, and j is the matrix previously employed. We have previously found the values of $p,\ q,\ r,\ s$ (p. 93). It can be verified that the expressions given by $N(1,-\theta,\theta^2,0)$, where $\theta=\psi^{-1}$, are all zero.

If we substitute the values of $p,\ q,\ r,\ s$ we find

$$Nj=\begin{pmatrix} 0 & -r' & q' & \psi^2\\ r' & 0 & -p' & -\psi\\ -q' & p' & 0 & 1\\ -\psi^2 & \psi & -1 & 0\end{pmatrix},$$

where

$$p'=\tfrac12(\lambda_0\psi^3+\tfrac12\lambda_1\psi^2),\quad q'=-\tfrac12(\lambda_0\psi^4+\lambda_1\psi^3+\lambda_2\psi^2+\tfrac12\lambda_3\psi),\quad r'=-1;$$

compare this form now with that obtained on p. 74; putting, with a slight simplification of the notation there adopted, which will not lead to confusion because we do not further use the sextic there denoted by $F(\psi)$,

$$F(\psi)=\lambda_0\psi^6+\lambda_1\psi^5+\dots+4\psi,$$

and
$$\rho_\theta=[-\tfrac14F'(\psi)]^{\frac12},\quad \theta=\psi^{-1},$$

we have
$$Nj=\rho_\theta\gamma_\theta^{-1},\quad j=-i\gamma=-i\gamma^{-1},$$

and
$$N=i\rho_\theta\gamma_\theta^{-1}\gamma.$$

So that
$$\frac{\sigma^2(u,q)}{\sigma^2(u)}[\wp_{rs}(u+\Omega_q)] = i\rho_\theta\gamma_\theta^{-1}\gamma\,[\wp_{rs}(u)],$$
where $[\wp_{rs}(u)]$ denotes $[\wp_{22}(u),\ \wp_{21}(u),\ \wp_{11}(u),\ 1]$.

Thus the equations expressing the functions $\wp_{rs}(u+\Omega_q)$ in terms of $\wp_{rs}(u)$ are the same as those given by the transformation A_{1r} of p. 79, r having five values according to the root ψ, other than zero, of the sextic $F(\psi)$.

We have at once
$$N^2 = -\rho_\theta^2\gamma_\theta^{-1}\gamma\cdot\gamma_\theta^{-1}\gamma = \rho_\theta^2\gamma_\theta^{-1}\gamma\cdot\gamma^{-1}\gamma_\theta = \rho_\theta^2,$$
and hence
$$\frac{\sigma^2(u+\Omega_q,q)}{\sigma^2(u+\Omega_q)}[\wp_{rs}(u)] = N[\wp_{rs}(u+\Omega_q)] = \rho_\theta^2\frac{\sigma^2(u)}{\sigma^2(u,q)}[\wp_{rs}(u)],$$
or
$$\frac{\sigma^2(u+\Omega_q,q)}{\sigma^2(u+\Omega_q)} = \rho_\theta^2\frac{\sigma^2(u)}{\sigma^2(u,q)}.$$

Similarly for the symmetric matrix Mj of § 33, we can verify by actual computation, on the hypothesis that neither θ nor ϕ is infinite, that
$$\rho_\theta\rho_\phi\gamma_\theta^{-1}\gamma_\phi j = -(\theta-\phi)\,\theta^{-2}\phi^{-2}Mj\,;$$
the work is rather long, but is facilitated by using where convenient the alternative forms given p. 74 for p' and q', and the fact that the coordinates $x_0=\theta+\phi$, $y_0=-\theta\phi$, $z_0=e_{\theta\phi}$ make all the minors of the determinant Δ vanish; these minors are given at length on p. 41; making use of the identities $\gamma_\theta^{-1}\gamma_\phi=-\gamma_\phi^{-1}\gamma_\theta$, $\gamma_\theta^{-1}\gamma=-\gamma^{-1}\gamma_\theta$, etc. (p. 79), and putting
$$f(\theta)=\lambda_0+\lambda_1\theta+\ldots+\lambda_4\theta^4+4\theta^5,$$
and
$$\mu_\theta=\rho_\theta\theta^2=\sqrt{\tfrac{1}{4}f'(\theta)},$$
we thus have
$$M=-\frac{\mu_\theta\mu_\phi}{\theta-\phi}\gamma_\theta^{-1}\gamma_\phi,$$
$$Mj=i\frac{\mu_\theta\mu_\phi}{\theta-\phi}\gamma_\theta^{-1}\gamma_\phi\gamma^{-1},\quad jM=i\frac{\mu_\theta\mu_\phi}{\theta-\phi}\gamma_\theta\gamma_\phi^{-1}\gamma,\quad M^2=-\frac{\mu_\theta^2\mu_\phi^2}{(\theta-\phi)^2},$$
and therefore, when $\sigma(u,q)$ is an even function,
$$\frac{\sigma^2(u,q)}{\sigma^2(u)}[\wp_{rs}(u+\Omega_q)] = -\frac{\mu_\theta\mu_\phi}{\theta-\phi}\gamma_\theta^{-1}\gamma_\phi[\wp_{rs}(u)].$$
It thus appears that the fifteen transformations A_{rs} of p. 79 are all obtained by adding half periods to the argument u.

When $\sigma(u,q)$ is an odd function Ω_q is, save for multiples of periods, of the form $u^{a,\theta}$; when $\sigma(u,q)$ is an even function, Ω_q is the sum of two expressions of this form; thus the last result can be obtained by two successive applications of the formula just previously obtained for an odd function.

35. Consider now the formula (§ 30)

$$\frac{\sigma(u+v)\,\sigma(u-v)}{\sigma^2(u)\,\sigma^2(v)} = j\,[\wp_{rs}(u)]\,[\wp_{rs}(v)]\,;$$

we know, if Ω_q denote a half period, that

$$\sigma(u+\Omega_q) = e^{A_1u_1+A_2u_2+B}\,\sigma(u, q),$$

where A_1, A_2, B are independent of u, but depend on q; hence adding Ω_q to u in the formula, we have

$$\frac{\sigma(u+v, q)\,\sigma(u-v, q)}{\sigma^2(u)\,\sigma^2(v)} = \frac{\sigma^2(u, q)}{\sigma^2(u)}\,j\,[\wp_{rs}(u+\Omega_q)]\,[\wp_{rs}(v)]\,;$$

thus when $\sigma(u, q)$ is an *odd* function, putting in the value found for the matrix N, we have, with $\Omega_q \equiv u^{a,\theta}$,

$$\frac{\sigma(u+v, q)\,\sigma(u-v, q)}{\sigma^2(u)\,\sigma^2(v)} = \rho_\theta\gamma\gamma_\theta^{-1}\gamma\,[\wp_{rs}(u)]\,[\wp_{rs}(v)],$$

which, when θ is infinite, $\rho_\infty = -i$ (p. 74), gives, for the right side,

$$-i\gamma\,[\wp_{rs}(u)]\,[\wp_{rs}(v)] = j\,[\wp_{rs}(u)]\,[\wp_{rs}(v)],$$

and when θ is not infinite, replacing $\gamma\gamma_\theta^{-1}$ by $-\gamma_\theta\gamma^{-1}$, gives, for the right side,

$$-\rho_\theta\gamma_\theta\,[\wp_{rs}(u)]\,[\wp_{rs}(v)]\,;$$

and when $\sigma(u, q)$ is an *even* function, $\Omega_q \equiv u^{a,\theta} + u^{a,\phi}$,

$$\frac{\sigma(u+v, q)\,\sigma(u-v, q)}{\sigma^2(u)\,\sigma^2(v)} = i\,\frac{\mu_\theta\mu_\phi}{\theta-\phi}\,\gamma_\theta\gamma_\phi^{-1}\gamma\,[\wp_{rs}(u)]\,[\wp_{rs}(v)].$$

From these formulae we have, respectively,
for the case of an odd function,

$$\begin{aligned}\frac{\sigma(u+v, q)\,\sigma(u-v, q)}{\sigma^2(u, q)\,\sigma^2(v, q)} &= \frac{\sigma^2(u)}{\sigma^2(u, q)}\,\frac{\sigma^2(v)}{\sigma^2(v, q)}\,jN\,[\wp_{rs}(u)]\,[\wp_{rs}(v)]\\ &= jN\,.\,N^{-1}\,[\wp_{rs}(u+\Omega_q)]\,.\,N^{-1}\,[\wp_{rs}(v+\Omega_q)]\\ &= \bar{N}^{-1}j\,[\wp_{rs}(u+\Omega_q)]\,[\wp_{rs}(v+\Omega_q)]\\ &= -\frac{1}{\rho_\theta}\,\gamma_\theta\,[\wp_{rs}(u+\Omega_q)]\,[\wp_{rs}(v+\Omega_q)],\end{aligned}$$

and, when $\sigma(u, q)$ is an even function,

$$\frac{\sigma(u+v, q)\,\sigma(u-v, q)}{\sigma^2(u, q)\,\sigma^2(v, q)} = i\,\frac{\theta-\phi}{\mu_\theta\mu_\phi}\,\gamma_\theta\gamma_\phi^{-1}\gamma\,[\wp_{rs}(u+\Omega_q)]\,[\wp_{rs}(v+\Omega_q)].$$

Now since γ_c, γ_{c_1}, γ_{c_2}, γ, γ_{a_1}, γ_{a_2} are in involution, where c, c_1, c_2, a_1, a_2 denote the roots of $f(\theta)=0$, we know (Appendix to Part I., Note I.) that the matrix

$$\begin{pmatrix} \gamma_{a_2}\gamma_{a_1}^{-1}\gamma_c xx', & \gamma\gamma_{a_2}^{-1}\gamma_c xx', & \gamma_{a_1}\gamma^{-1}\gamma_c xx', & \gamma_c xx' \\ \gamma_{a_2}\gamma_{a_1}^{-1}\gamma_{c_1} xx', & \gamma\gamma_{a_2}^{-1}\gamma_{c_1} xx', & \gamma_{a_1}\gamma^{-1}\gamma_{c_1} xx', & \gamma_{c_1} xx' \\ \gamma_{a_2}\gamma_{a_1}^{-1}\gamma_{c_2} xx', & \gamma\gamma_{a_2}^{-1}\gamma_{c_2} xx', & \gamma_{a_1}\gamma^{-1}\gamma_{c_2} xx', & \gamma_{c_2} xx' \\ -i\gamma xx', & -i\gamma_{a_1} xx', & -i\gamma_{a_2} xx', & -i\gamma\gamma_{a_1}^{-1}\gamma_{a_2} xx' \end{pmatrix}$$

is orthogonal. Let us suppose the signs of the square roots denoted by $\mu_c, \mu_{c_1}, \ldots$ chosen so that (Appendix, *loc. cit.*)

$$\gamma_c^{-1}\gamma\gamma_{c_1}^{-1}\gamma_{a_1}\gamma_{c_2}^{-1}\gamma_{a_2} = i\,;$$

then this matrix can also be written in the form

$$\begin{pmatrix} i\gamma_{c_1}\gamma_{c_2}^{-1}\gamma xx', & \gamma_{a_2}\gamma_c^{-1}\gamma xx', & -\gamma_{a_1}\gamma_c^{-1}\gamma xx', & \gamma_c xx' \\ i\gamma_{c_2}\gamma_c^{-1}\gamma xx', & \gamma_{a_2}\gamma_{c_1}^{-1}\gamma xx', & -\gamma_{a_1}\gamma_{c_1}^{-1}\gamma xx', & \gamma_{c_1} xx' \\ i\gamma_c\gamma_{c_1}^{-1}\gamma xx', & \gamma_{a_2}\gamma_{c_2}^{-1}\gamma xx', & -\gamma_{a_1}\gamma_{c_2}^{-1}\gamma xx', & \gamma_{c_2} xx' \\ -i\gamma xx', & -i\gamma_{a_1} xx', & -i\gamma_{a_2} xx', & -i\gamma_{a_1}\gamma_{a_2}^{-1}\gamma xx' \end{pmatrix}$$

but we have seen, if

$$(x, y, z, t) = [\wp_{22}(u), \wp_{21}(u), \wp_{11}(u), 1],$$
$$(x', y', z', t') = [\wp_{22}(v), \wp_{21}(v), \wp_{11}(v), 1],$$

that

$$\frac{\sigma(u+v)\,\sigma(u-v)}{\sigma^2(u)\,\sigma^2(v)} = -\,i\gamma xx',$$

$$\frac{\sigma(u+v,\theta)\,\sigma(u-v,\theta)}{\sigma^2(u)\,\sigma^2(v)} = -\,\rho_\theta\gamma_\theta xx',$$

$$\frac{\sigma(u+v,\theta\phi)\,\sigma(u-v,\theta\phi)}{\sigma^2(u)\,\sigma^2(v)} = i\,\frac{\mu_\theta\mu_\phi}{\theta-\phi}\,\gamma_\theta\gamma_\phi^{-1}\gamma xx',$$

where $\mu_\theta = \theta^2\rho_\theta$; hence if

$$\sigma(u+v)\,\sigma(u-v) = [a],$$
$$\sigma(u+v,\theta)\,\sigma(u-v,\theta) = [\theta],$$
$$\sigma(u+v,\theta\phi)\,\sigma(u-v,\theta\phi) = [\theta, \phi],$$

by multiplying every element of the matrix by $\sigma^2(u)\,\sigma^2(v)$, we infer that the matrix

$$\Sigma = \begin{pmatrix} \frac{c_1-c_2}{\mu_{c_1}\mu_{c_2}}[c_1, c_2], & -i\frac{a_2-c}{\mu_{a_2}\mu_c}[a_2, c], & i\frac{a_1-c}{\mu_{a_1}\mu_c}[a_1, c], & -\frac{1}{\rho_c}[c] \\ \frac{c_2-c}{\mu_{c_2}\mu_c}[c_2, c], & -i\frac{a_2-c_1}{\mu_{a_2}\mu_{c_1}}[a_2, c_1], & i\frac{a_1-c_1}{\mu_{a_1}\mu_{c_1}}[a_1, c_1], & -\frac{1}{\rho_{c_1}}[c_1] \\ \frac{c-c_1}{\mu_c\mu_{c_1}}[c, c_1], & -i\frac{a_2-c_2}{\mu_{a_2}\mu_{c_2}}[a_2, c_2], & i\frac{a_1-c_2}{\mu_{a_1}\mu_{c_2}}[a_1, c_2], & -\frac{1}{\rho_{c_2}}[c_2] \\ [a], & \frac{i}{\rho_{a_1}}[a_1], & \frac{i}{\rho_{a_2}}[a_2], & -\frac{a_1-a_2}{\mu_{a_1}\mu_{a_2}}[a_1, a_2] \end{pmatrix}$$

is orthogonal. As will be seen (Appendix, *loc. cit.*), there can be formed 15 such orthogonal matrices; presumably they are obtainable from Σ by addition of half periods to the argument u.

A particular case of this result is obtained by dividing each element by $\sigma^2(u)$, and then putting $v = 0$; since we have (§§ 31, 32)

$$\frac{\sigma^2(u,\theta\phi)}{\sigma^2(u)} = P_{\theta,\phi}, \quad \frac{\sigma^2(u,\theta)}{\sigma^2(u)} = -\,\theta^{-2}P_\theta,$$

P_θ, $P_{\theta,\phi}$ being as on p. 63, we infer that

$$\Pi = \begin{pmatrix} \frac{c_1-c_2}{\mu_{c_1}\mu_{c_2}} P_{c_1c_2}, & -i\frac{a_2-c}{\mu_{a_2}\mu_c} P_{a_2c}, & i\frac{a_1-c}{\mu_{a_1}\mu_c} P_{a_1c}, & \frac{1}{\mu_c} P_c \\ \frac{c_2-c}{\mu_{c_2}\mu_c} P_{c_2c}, & -i\frac{a_2-c_1}{\mu_{a_2}\mu_{c_1}} P_{a_2c_1}, & i\frac{a_1-c_1}{\mu_{a_1}\mu_{c_1}} P_{a_1c_1}, & \frac{1}{\mu_{c_1}} P_{c_1} \\ \frac{c-c_1}{\mu_c\mu_{c_1}} P_{cc_1}, & -i\frac{a_2-c_2}{\mu_{a_2}\mu_{c_2}} P_{a_2c_2}, & i\frac{a_1-c_2}{\mu_{a_1}\mu_{c_2}} P_{a_1c_2}, & \frac{1}{\mu_{c_2}} P_{c_2} \\ 1 \quad , & -\frac{i}{\mu_{a_1}} P_{a_1} \quad , & -\frac{i}{\mu_{a_2}} P_{a_2} \quad , & -\frac{a_1-a_2}{\mu_{a_1}\mu_{a_2}} P_{a_1a_2} \end{pmatrix}$$

is also orthogonal. For instance, taking the first and last columns, we have

$$(c_1-c_2) P_c P_{c_1c_2} + (c_2-c) P_{c_1} P_{c_2c} + (c-c_1) P_{c_2} P_{cc_1} = (a_1-a_2) \frac{\mu_c\mu_{c_1}\mu_{c_2}}{\mu_{a_1}\mu_{a_2}} P_{a_1a_2},$$

while, since $\mu_\theta^2 = \frac{1}{4} f'(\theta)$, we have

$$\left(\frac{\mu_c\mu_{c_1}\mu_{c_2}}{\mu_{a_1}\mu_{a_2}}\right)^2$$
$$= \frac{(c-a_1)(c-a_2)(c_1-a_1)(c_1-a_2)(c_2-a_1)(c_2-a_2)(c_1-c_2)^2(c_2-c)^2(c-c_1)^2}{(a_1-a_2)^2(a_1-c)(a_1-c_1)(a_1-c_2)(a_2-c)(a_2-c_1)(a_2-c_2)}$$
$$= (c_1-c_2)^2 (c_2-c)^2 (c-c_1)^2/(a_1-a_2)^2,$$

so that

$$(c_1-c_2) P_c P_{c_1c_2} + (c_2-c) P_{c_1} P_{c_2c} + (c-c_1) P_{c_2} P_{cc_1}$$
$$= \pm (c_1-c_2)(c_2-c)(c-c_1) P_{a_1a_2},$$

an equation easy to verify directly, with the upper sign on the right side.

Again, if in the matrix Σ, we put $v = u$ and then replace $2u$ by u, we infer that the matrix

$$\Sigma_1 = \begin{pmatrix} \frac{c_1-c_2}{\mu_{c_1}\mu_{c_2}} \sigma(u, c_1c_2), & -i\frac{a_2-c}{\mu_{a_2}\mu_c} \sigma(u, a_2c), & i\frac{a_1-c}{\mu_{a_1}\mu_c} \sigma(u, a_1c), & 0 \\ \frac{c_2-c}{\mu_{c_2}\mu_c} \sigma(u, c_2c), & -i\frac{a_2-c_1}{\mu_{a_2}\mu_{c_1}} \sigma(u, a_2c_1), & i\frac{a_1-c_1}{\mu_{a_1}\mu_{c_1}} \sigma(u, a_1c_1), & 0 \\ \frac{c-c_1}{\mu_c\mu_{c_1}} \sigma(u, cc_1), & -i\frac{a_2-c_2}{\mu_{a_2}\mu_{c_2}} \sigma(u, a_2c_2), & i\frac{a_1-c_2}{\mu_{a_1}\mu_{c_2}} \sigma(u, a_1c_2), & 0 \\ 0 \quad , & 0 \quad , & 0 \quad , & -\frac{a_1-a_2}{\mu_{a_1}\mu_{a_2}} \sigma(u, a_1a_2) \end{pmatrix}$$

is orthogonal; thus for instance

$$\left(\frac{a_1-a_2}{\mu_{a_1}\mu_{a_2}}\right)^2 \sigma^2(u, a_1a_2) = \left(\frac{c_1-c_2}{\mu_{c_1}\mu_{c_2}}\right)^2 \sigma^2(u, c_1c_2)$$
$$+ \left(\frac{c_2-c}{\mu_{c_2}\mu_c}\right)^2 \sigma^2(u, c_2c) + \left(\frac{c-c_1}{\mu_c\mu_{c_1}}\right)^2 \sigma^2(u, cc_1),$$

and

$$0 = (c_1 - c_2)(a_2 - c)\,\sigma(u, c_1c_2)\,\sigma(u, a_2c) + (c_2 - c)(a_2 - c_1)\,\sigma(u, c_2c)\,\sigma(u, a_2c_1)$$
$$+ (c - c_1)(a_2 - c_2)\,\sigma(u, cc_1)\,\sigma(u, a_2c_2),$$

of which the first is equivalent to

$$\left(\frac{a_1 - a_2}{\mu_{a_1}\mu_{a_2}}\right)^2 P_{a_1a_2} = \left(\frac{c_1 - c_2}{\mu_{c_1}\mu_{c_2}}\right)^2 P_{c_1c_2} + \left(\frac{c_2 - c}{\mu_{c_2}\mu_c}\right)^2 P_{c_2c} + \left(\frac{c - c_1}{\mu_c\mu_{c_1}}\right)^2 P_{cc_1},$$

and the second to

$$(c_1 - c_2)(a_2 - c)\sqrt{P_{c_1c_2}P_{a_2c}} + (c_2 - c)(a_2 - c_1)\sqrt{P_{c_2c}P_{a_2c_1}}$$
$$+ (c - c_1)(a_2 - c_2)\sqrt{P_{cc_1}P_{a_2c_2}} = 0.$$

36. As an alternative method of obtaining results just obtained by consideration of the orthogonal matrix, and as an example of the application of a principle which appears at first sight slightly more general than that so far employed in this chapter, we give now a formula which, in virtue of those already proved, furnishes an irrational form for the relation $\Delta = 0$ connecting the functions $\wp_{22}(u)$, $\wp_{21}(u)$, $\wp_{11}(u)$.

As in preceding investigations it follows that an analytical integral function of u_1, u_2 which for any integers m, m', and a positive integer r, satisfies the equation

$$\phi(u + \Omega_m) = e^{r\lambda_m(u)}\,\phi(u),$$

the notation being as before, is expressed linearly by r^2 functions of the same kind. An analytical integral function may however be such that it satisfies an equation

$$\psi(u + \Omega_m) = e^{r\lambda_m(u) + cm + c'm'}\,\psi(u),$$

where $$cm + c'm' = c_1m_1 + c_2m_2 + c_1'm_1' + c_2'm_2',$$

and c_1, c_2, c_1', c_2' are any constants; it can then be shewn, just as before, that it is expressible also by at most r^2 such functions; we do not give the proof because it will appear that this is really included in the preceding case (Part II., below). But now, if $\psi(u)$ be an odd or an even function—and it can be proved that this cannot be so unless each of c_1, c_2, c_1', c_2' is an integral multiple of πi—it can be further shewn that there do not exist always as many as r^2 linearly independent functions $\psi(u)$. In fact when r is even, if $\psi(-u) = \epsilon\psi(u)$, so that ϵ is $+1$ or -1, the number of linearly independent functions $\psi(u)$ is at most $\frac{1}{2}r^2 + 2\epsilon$ when each of c_1, c_2, c_1', c_2' is zero or an even multiple of πi, and is otherwise $\frac{1}{2}r^2$ independently of ϵ; so that for $r = 2$ there is no odd function for which c_1, c_2, c_1', c_2' are even multiples of πi, and there are four even functions, while when c_1, c_2, c_1', c_2' are not even multiples of πi there are two such odd functions linearly independent and the same number of even functions; it is this result which we proceed to illustrate. When r is odd the number which are linearly independent is at most $\frac{1}{2}(r^2 + \epsilon e^{-\pi i\mu\mu'})$, where $(c, c') = \pi i(\mu, \mu')$.

We have discussed, beside the function $\sigma(u)$, five odd functions, each associated with one root of the quintic equation

$$\lambda_0 + \lambda_1\theta + \lambda_2\theta^2 + \lambda_3\theta^3 + \lambda_4\theta^4 + 4\theta^5 = 0,$$

these being those denoted above by $\sigma(u, q)$; one of them may be denoted by $\sigma(u, \theta_1)$. We have also discussed even functions, each associated with two roots of this quintic; one of these may be denoted by $\sigma(u, \theta_1\theta_2)$. Consider the three products

$$\sigma(u, \theta_1)\,\sigma(u, \theta_2\theta_3), \quad \sigma(u, \theta_2)\,\sigma(u, \theta_3\theta_1), \quad \sigma(u, \theta_3)\,\sigma(u, \theta_1\theta_2);$$

the function $\sigma(u, \theta_1)$ is, save for a constant multiplier, the same as $\vartheta(u, q)$ of p. 25, where the characteristic q is that associated with the half periods

$$(\Omega_q)_1 = \left(\int_{a_1}^{a} + \int_{a_2}^{a} + \int_{a}^{\theta_1}\right)\frac{dt}{s}, \quad (\Omega_q)_2 = \left(\int_{a_1}^{a} + \int_{a_2}^{a} + \int_{a}^{\theta_1}\right)\frac{tdt}{s},$$

while similarly the function $\sigma(u, \theta_1\theta_2)$ is associated with the half periods

$$(\Omega_q)_1 = \left(\int_{a_1}^{a} + \int_{a_2}^{a} + \int_{a}^{\theta_1} + \int_{a}^{\theta_2}\right)\frac{dt}{s}, \quad (\Omega_q)_2 = \left(\int_{a_1}^{a} + \int_{a_2}^{a} + \int_{a}^{\theta_1} + \int_{a}^{\theta_2}\right)\frac{tdt}{s},$$

as explained before (pp. 94—96). Thus each of the three products above is of the character assigned to the function ψ in the explanation above, being an odd function for which the quantities c_1, c_2, c_1', c_2' are not zero or even multiples of πi. Thus there exists an equation

$$A\sigma(u, \theta_1)\,\sigma(u, \theta_2\theta_3) + B\sigma(u, \theta_2)\,\sigma(u, \theta_3\theta_1) + C\sigma(u, \theta_3)\,\sigma(u, \theta_1\theta_2) = 0,$$

wherein A, B, C are constants.

And the preceding expansions enable us to determine the coefficients; for the terms of first order in the expansion of the left side are

$$A(u_1 - \theta_1^{-1}u_2) + B(u_1 - \theta_2^{-1}u_2) + C(u_1 - \theta_3^{-1}u_2),$$

shewing that $A = \theta_1(\theta_2 - \theta_3)$, $B = \theta_2(\theta_3 - \theta_1)$, $C = \theta_3(\theta_1 - \theta_2)$.

We have previously (§§ 31, 32) expressed each of the quotients

$$\frac{\sigma^2(u, \theta_1)}{\sigma^2(u)}, \quad \frac{\sigma^2(u, \theta_1\theta_2)}{\sigma^2(u)}$$

as a linear function of $\wp_{22}(u)$, $\wp_{21}(u)$, $\wp_{11}(u)$; if these forms be substituted in the equation above, an irrational form of the equation $\Delta = 0$ is obtained; if

$$x_1 = \theta_2 + \theta_3, \quad y_1 = -\theta_2\theta_3, \quad z_1 = e_{\theta_2, \theta_3}, \text{ etc.}$$

and x, y, z denote $\wp_{22}(u)$, $\wp_{21}(u)$, $\wp_{11}(u)$, this is

$$\Sigma(\theta_2 - \theta_3)(xy_1 - yx_1 + z_1 - z)^{\frac{1}{2}}(y + \theta_1 x - \theta_1^2)^{\frac{1}{2}} = 0.$$

If a_1, a_2 be the roots of the fundamental quintic other than θ_1, θ_2, θ_3; and

$$l = (\theta_1 - a_1)(\theta_1 - a_2), \quad m = (\theta_2 - a_1)(\theta_2 - a_2), \quad n = (\theta_3 - a_1)(\theta_3 - a_2),$$

we find $$(\theta_2 - \theta_3)P_{\theta_2, \theta_3} = (\theta_2 - \theta_3)P_{a_1, a_2} + mP_{\theta_3} - nP_{\theta_2};$$

thus, if $\xi = y + \theta_1 x - \theta_1^2, \quad \eta = y + \theta_2 x - \theta_2^2, \quad \zeta = y + \theta_3 x - \theta_3^2,$

$$\tau = x a_1 a_2 + y(a_1 + a_2) + z - e_{a_1, a_2},$$

and $\lambda = \theta_2 - \theta_3, \quad \mu = \theta_3 - \theta_1, \quad \nu = \theta_1 - \theta_2,$

we have

$$\{\lambda\xi(\lambda\tau + m\zeta - n\eta)\}^{\frac{1}{2}} + \{\mu\eta(\mu\tau + n\xi - l\zeta)\}^{\frac{1}{2}} + \{\nu\zeta(\nu\tau + l\eta - m\xi)\}^{\frac{1}{2}} = 0.$$

37. We can give an interpretation of the formula for the function

$$\frac{\sigma(u+v)\,\sigma(u-v)}{\sigma^2(u)\,\sigma^2(v)},$$

which places the form obtained for the right side in connexion with the results obtained above in considering the geometry (p. 76). Though entailing repetition it appears well to make the present account self-contained.

Regard v as fixed, and $\wp_{22}(u)$, $\wp_{21}(u)$, $\wp_{11}(u)$ as the coordinates of a variable point; the equation

$$\wp_{22}(u)\,\wp_{21}(v) - \wp_{21}(u)\,\wp_{22}(v) + \wp_{11}(v) - \wp_{11}(u) = 0,$$

which we may denote by

$$x y_1 - y x_1 + z_1 - z = 0,$$

is that of a plane passing through (x_1, y_1, z_1) (being in fact that of the polar plane of (x_1, y_1, z_1) in the linear complex denoted in the usual notation by $n + n' = 0$). The function $\sigma(u)$ has been seen previously (p. 96) to vanish for $u = u^{a, t}$, that is for

$$u_1 = \int_t^\infty \frac{dt}{s}, \quad u_2 = \int_t^\infty \frac{t\,dt}{s},$$

where $s^2 = \lambda_0 + \lambda_1 t + \ldots + \lambda_4 t^4 + 4t^5$, and, save for integral multiples of periods, only for values so expressible (the zero values $-u^{a,t}$ for example being obtainable by taking $u^{a,t'}$, where (t') is the place conjugate to (t)); hence the product $\sigma(u+v)\,\sigma(u-v)$ vanishes for

$$u \equiv v + u^{a,t}, \quad u \equiv -v + u^{a,t'},$$

where the sign $\equiv$ indicates the possible omission of multiples of the periods; of these, if (t') be conjugate to (t), the second is $u \equiv -(v + u^{a,t})$, and, as $\wp_{22}(-u) = \wp_{22}(u)$, etc., gives the same point of the surface $\Delta = 0$ as does the first. The curve of intersection of $\Delta = 0$ with the plane $xy_1 - yx_1 + z_1 - z = 0$ has therefore points each representable once by

$$x = \wp_{22}(v + u^{a,t}), \quad y = \wp_{21}(v + u^{a,t}), \quad z = \wp_{11}(v + u^{a,t}),$$

where (t) is variable. This curve will have a double point, and the plane touch $\Delta = 0$, if we can satisfy, by properly choosing (t) and (t_1), the three equations

$$\wp_{rs}(v + u^{a,t}) = \wp_{rs}(v + u^{a,t_1}).$$

Now first, the three equations $\wp_{rs}(u) = \wp_{rs}(u')$ require, as the differential equations of Chap. II. shew, that

$$\wp_{rstm}(u) = \wp_{rstm}(u'), \text{ while } \wp_{rst}(u) = \pm\, \wp_{rst}(u'),$$

the negative sign for the functions of three suffixes being capable of derivation from the positive sign by changing the sign of u'; similarly by the equations derivable by differentiation from the differential equations all derivatives of $\wp_{rs}(u)$ are equal to the corresponding derivatives of $\wp_{rs}(u')$, or of $\wp_{rs}(-u')$, so that, for arbitrarily small arguments w,

$$\wp_{rs}(u+w) = \wp_{rs}(u'+w), \qquad \wp_{rst}(u+w) = \wp_{rst}(u'+w),$$

or $$\wp_{rs}(u+w) = \wp_{rs}(-u'+w), \quad \wp_{rst}(u+w) = \wp_{rst}(-u'+w);$$

we can however express $u+w$ in terms of these functions in the form

$$u_1 + w_1 = \int A\,dx + B\,dy, \qquad u_2 + w_2 = \int B\,dx + C\,dy,$$

where A, B, C are rational in $x = \wp_{22}(u+w)$, $y = \wp_{21}(u+w)$, $\xi = \wp_{222}(u+w)$; thus we have

$$u + w = u' + w + \text{period}, \text{ or } u + w = -u' + w + \text{period},$$

and so $$u = \pm\, u' + \text{period}.$$

The only double point of the curve now under consideration is therefore to be obtained by considering the equations

$$v + u^{a,t} \equiv v + u^{a,t_1},$$

or the equations $$v + u^{a,t} \equiv -(v + u^{a,t_1}).$$

As to the former, equivalent to $u_1^{t_1,t} \equiv 0$, $u_2^{t_2,t} \equiv 0$, they are satisfied only by the obvious solution $(t_1) = (t)$ (p. 30); the latter, equivalent to

$$u^{a,t} + u^{a,t_1} \equiv -2v,$$

are, for general values of v, satisfied by one and only one pair of positions (t), (t_1) (p. 29), given (p. 97), by

$$\wp_{22}(2v) = t + t_1, \ \wp_{21}(2v) = -tt_1, \ s = t\wp_{222}(2v) + \wp_{221}(2v), \ s_1 = t_1\wp_{222}(2v) + \wp_{221}(2v),$$

where $s^2 = \lambda_0 + \lambda_1 t + \ldots + 4t^5$; thus, with $x_1 = \wp_{22}(v)$, etc., and general values of v, the equation

$$xy_1 - x_1 y + z_1 - z = 0$$

represents a tangent plane touching the surface $\Delta = 0$ at the point

$$w = v + u^{a,t},$$

where $$t^2 - t\wp_{22}(2v) - \wp_{21}(2v) = 0.$$

When $\sigma(u^{x,a} + 2v)$ vanishes identically for all positions of (x), the equations $u^{a,t} + u^{a,t_1} \equiv -2v$ have an infinite number of solutions; this is only when $2v$ is a period, and then we may take (t) arbitrarily and (t_1) the position conjugate to (t); in that case the plane touches the surface $\Delta = 0$ all along its intersection; namely the sixteen singular tangent planes previously found are given by the equations

$$\sigma(u + \Omega_q) = 0,$$

when Ω_q is any half period; we have already seen that $\sigma(u) = 0$ corresponds to the plane at infinity; the equation of the singular tangent plane is given by

$$x\wp_{21}(\Omega_q) - y\wp_{22}(\Omega_q) + \wp_{11}(\Omega_q) - z = 0,$$

which compared with (§§ 31, 32),

$$\theta x + y - \theta^2 = 0, \quad \text{or} \quad \theta\phi x + (\theta + \phi) y + z - e_{\theta,\phi} = 0,$$

gives either $\quad \wp_{22}(\Omega_q)/1 = -\wp_{21}(\Omega_q)/\theta = \wp_{11}(\Omega_q)/\theta^2 = \infty,$

or $\quad \wp_{22}(\Omega_q) = \theta + \phi, \quad \wp_{21}(\Omega_q) = -\theta\phi, \quad \wp_{11}(\Omega_q) = e_{\theta,\phi},$

shewing that the half periods are the values of u at the nodes.

Considering the case of an ordinary tangent plane, depending on a parameter v, with point of contact given by

$$w \equiv v + u^{a,t},$$

where $\quad u^{a,t} + u^{a,t_1} \equiv -2v,$

if we take two positions (k), (k_1) given by

$$u^{a,k} + u^{a,k_1} \equiv -2w,$$

we shall have $\quad u^{a,k} + u^{a,k_1} \equiv -2v - 2u^{a,t} \equiv u^{a,t_1} - u^{a,t},$

or $\quad u^{t',k} + u^{t_1,k_1} \equiv 0,$

where (t') is the position congruent to (t), and hence (p. 29) the positions (k), (k_1) are, taken in proper order, the same as (t') and (t_1), and

$$v \equiv w + u^{a,k},$$

so that the point $\wp_{22}(v)$, $\wp_{21}(v)$, $\wp_{11}(v)$ of the surface $\Delta = 0$ is derived from $\wp_{22}(w)$, $\wp_{21}(w)$, $\wp_{11}(w)$ just as this is derived from the former. Thus, if $x_1' = \wp_{22}(w)$, etc., the plane

$$xy_1' - yx_1' + z_1' - z = 0,$$

touches the surface at the point v. The former plane passing through v, since every point of its section of the surface is given by $u \equiv v + u^{a,t}$, and the latter through w, it follows that the straight line joining the points v and w is a bitangent of the surface $\Delta = 0$, and v is one of the six points of contact of tangents to the quartic plane section drawn from its double point w. Expressed in terms of the parameter w of the point of contact, the tangent plane is thus

$$x\wp_{21}(w - u^{a,t}) - y\wp_{22}(w - u^{a,t}) + \wp_{11}(w - u^{a,t}) - z = 0,$$

where (t) is a particular position given, in association with another position (t_1), by $u^{a,t} + u^{a,t_1} \equiv -2(w - u^{a,t})$, that is

$$u^{a,t_1} - u^{a,t} \equiv -2w.$$

Thus t_1, t are the roots of the equation

$$t^2 - t\wp_{22}(2w) - \wp_{21}(2w) = 0,$$

and the points of the tangent section are given indifferently by

$$u = w - u^{a,t} + u^{a,\theta}, \quad u = -w - u^{a,t_1} + u^{a,\theta},$$

where (θ) varies, being (t) or (t_1) at the point of contact according as this is approached along one or other of the inflexional branches; thus for these branches respectively we have at the point of contact w,

$$\frac{du_2}{du_1} = t \text{ or } t_1,$$

and the differential equation of the asymptotic curves of the surface is

$$\left(\frac{du_2}{du_1}\right)^2 - \frac{du_2}{du_1}\wp_{22}(2u) - \wp_{21}(2u) = 0.$$

If (t) be a fixed position, this differential equation is obviously satisfied by the curve given for variable (θ) by

$$2u \equiv u^{a,t} - u^{a,\theta};$$

thus the asymptotic lines are given by

$$t^2 - t\wp_{22}(2u) - \wp_{21}(2u) = 0,$$

where t is constant along any particular one.

Every point of the section of the tangent plane with the surface $\Delta = 0$ has a parameter of the form $w - u^{a,t} + u^{a,\lambda}$; take in particular (λ) at a branch-place, so that $u^{a,\lambda}$ is a half period Ω_q; the tangent plane at this point is then

$$x\wp_{21}(w - u^{a,t} + \Omega_q - u^{a,h}) - \text{etc.} = 0,$$

where (h) is a particular position given, in association with another position (h_1), by

$$u^{a,h_1} - u^{a,h} \equiv -2(w - u^{a,t} + \Omega_q),$$

or
$$u^{a,h_1} - u^{a,h} \equiv u^{a,t_1} + u^{a,t} - 2\Omega_q,$$

so that (h) is the conjugate position on the Riemann surface either of (t_1) or (t); in the former case the argument $w - u^{a,t} + \Omega_q - u^{a,h}$ would be $w + \Omega_q + u^{a,t_1} - u^{a,t}$ or $-(w - \Omega_q)$, save for multiples of the periods; in the latter case it would be $w + \Omega_q$; in either case the tangent plane is

$$x\wp_{21}(w + \Omega_q) - \ldots = 0,$$

and passes through w if $\sigma(2w + \Omega_q)\,\sigma(\Omega_q) = 0$, and therefore if $\sigma(\Omega_q) = 0$, or $\vartheta(\Omega_p + \Omega_q) = 0$, where p denotes the characteristic $\frac{1}{2}\begin{pmatrix}1\,1\\0\,1\end{pmatrix}$ (cf. p. 34), that is if $\Omega_p + \Omega_q$ be an odd half period. We thus have the result that the bitangents to $\Delta = 0$ drawn from the point w touch the surface in $v \equiv w - u^{a,t}$, where $u^{a,t_1} - u^{a,t} \equiv -2w$, and in the five points $v + \Omega_q$, where Ω_q denotes in turn the half periods $u^{a,\theta}$ in which θ is a root of $\lambda_0 + \lambda_1\theta + \ldots + 4\theta^5 = 0$; for it is easily seen that with these values $\Omega_p + \Omega_q$ is an odd half period (see p. 32). More symmetrically, with a slight change of notation, the points of contact of the bitangents from $\pm w$ are given by $v \equiv w + u^{\theta,t}$, where (θ) denotes in turn the six branch-places of the Riemann surface on which $u^{\theta,t}$ is computed, and (t) denotes either of the two places given by

$$t^2 - t\wp_{22}(2w) - \wp_{21}(2w) = 0, \quad \text{and} \quad s = t\wp_{222}(2w) + \wp_{221}(2w).$$

This result is also obtainable by considering the vanishing of the function $\sigma_\theta(u+v)\,\sigma_\theta(u-v)$.

38. The two points $\pm w$, $\pm v$, capable of representation in the forms

$$-2w \equiv u^{a,t_1} - u^{a,t}, \quad -2v \equiv u^{a,t_1} + u^{a,t},$$

which are the points of contact of a bitangent associated with the first linear complex, may be called *twin points*, or each may be called the *satellite* of the other; since t, t_1 are the roots of either of the quadratics

$$t^2 - t\wp_{22}(2w) - \wp_{21}(2w) = 0, \qquad t^2 - t\wp_{22}(2v) - \wp_{21}(2v) = 0,$$

these points are such that

$$\wp_{22}(2w) = \wp_{22}(2v), \qquad \wp_{21}(2w) = \wp_{21}(2v).$$

Two arguments u, u' capable of representation in the forms

$$u \equiv u^{a,t_1} + u^{a,t}, \qquad u' \equiv u^{a,t_1} - u^{a,t},$$

may be called *conjugate* arguments, and the associated points $\pm u$, $\pm u'$ may be called conjugate points; since $\wp_{22}(u) = \wp_{22}(u')$, $\wp_{21}(u) = \wp_{21}(u')$, it follows that conjugate points are the intersections of the Kummer surface with an arbitrary straight line through the node which lies at the infinite end of the axis of z, what we may call the primary node of the surface; putting

$$x = \wp_{22}(u), \quad y = \wp_{21}(u), \quad z = \wp_{11}(u), \quad z_0 = \wp_{11}(u')$$

it follows from the equation of the surface that

$$z + z_0 = \frac{2xy^2 - \frac{1}{2}\lambda_3 xy + \lambda_4 y^2 + \frac{1}{2}\lambda_1 x - \lambda_2 y + \lambda_0}{x^2 + 4y}.$$

Further

$$du_1' = \frac{dt_1}{s_1} - \frac{dt}{s} = \frac{1}{t_1 - t}\left\{-(t_1+t)\left(\frac{dt_1}{s_1} + \frac{dt}{s}\right) + 2\left(\frac{t_1 dt_1}{s_1} + \frac{t\,dt}{s}\right)\right\}$$

$$= \frac{-x\,du_1 + 2du_2}{\sqrt{x^2+4y}},$$

$$du_2' = \frac{t_1 dt_1}{s_1} - \frac{t\,dt}{s} = \frac{1}{t_1 - t}\left\{-2t_1 t\left(\frac{dt_1}{s_1} + \frac{dt}{s}\right) + (t_1+t)\left(\frac{t_1 dt_1}{s_1} + \frac{t\,dt}{s}\right)\right\}$$

$$= \frac{2y\,du_1 + x\,du_2}{\sqrt{x^2+4y}},$$

so that we have, as is easy to verify, with $x = \wp_{22}(u)$, $y = \wp_{21}(u)$,

$$\frac{\partial}{\partial u_2}\left[\frac{-x}{(x^2+4y)^{\frac{1}{2}}}\right] + \frac{\partial}{\partial u_1}\left[\frac{2}{(x^2+4y)^{\frac{1}{2}}}\right] = 0,$$

$$\frac{\partial}{\partial u_2}\left[\frac{2y}{(x^2+4y)^{\frac{1}{2}}}\right] - \frac{\partial}{\partial u_1}\left[\frac{x}{(x^2+4y)^{\frac{1}{2}}}\right] = 0,$$

and, also, the incidental consequence that with any point of the Kummer surface may be associated, not only the everywhere finite integrals u_1, u_2, but also the other everywhere finite integrals

$$u_1' = \int \frac{-x\,du_1 + 2du_2}{(x^2+4y)^{\frac{1}{2}}}, \qquad u_2' = \int \frac{2y\,du_1 + x\,du_2}{(x^2+4y)^{\frac{1}{2}}},$$

where $x = \wp_{22}(u)$, $y = \wp_{21}(u)$; the former pair, u_1, u_2, can each be expressed in the form $\int A\,dx + B\,dy$, where A, B are rational in x, y and ξ, $= \wp_{222}(u)$; the latter pair cannot be so expressed.

The line joining the two conjugate points $\pm u$, $\pm u'$, is the intersection of the tangent planes

$$t^2 - tx - y = 0, \quad t_1^2 - t_1 x - y = 0,$$

of the cone $x^2 + 4y = 0$; this is the tangent cone of the Kummer surface at the primary node, and its generators each cut the surface in one finite point, conjugate to the node $u' = 0$, lying upon the unicursal octavic curve expressed by

$$u = 2u^{a,t}, \quad \wp_{22}(u) = 2t, \quad \wp_{21}(u) = -t^2, \quad \wp_{11}(u) = (1, t)_8 / f(t),$$

where*, as the explicit equation $\Delta = 0$, p. 41, or the value $\dfrac{F(t', t) - 2T'T}{4(t'-t)^2}$, by making $t' = t$, shews

$$(1, t)_8 = \tfrac{1}{16}\lambda_1^2 - \tfrac{1}{4}\lambda_0\lambda_2 - \tfrac{1}{2}\lambda_0\lambda_3 t - (\tfrac{1}{8}\lambda_1\lambda_3 + \lambda_0\lambda_4)t^2 - (\tfrac{1}{2}\lambda_1\lambda_4 + 6\lambda_0)t^3$$
$$- (\tfrac{7}{2}\lambda_1 + \tfrac{1}{4}\lambda_2\lambda_4 - \tfrac{1}{16}\lambda_3^2)t^4 - 2\lambda_2 t^5 - \tfrac{1}{2}\lambda_3 t^6 + t^8,$$

while $$f(t) = \lambda_0 + \lambda_1 t + \lambda_2 t^2 + \ldots + 4t^5.$$

* It can be shewn that

$$(1, t)_8 = \frac{1}{16}\left[\frac{df(t)}{dt}\right]^2 - \frac{1}{4}f(t)\,[\lambda_2 + 2\lambda_3 t + 4\lambda_4 t^2 + 24t^3]$$
$$= \frac{1}{16}f'^2 + \frac{1}{8}f\left\{\left[\frac{\partial^2}{\partial t'^2}F(t', t)\right]_{t'=t} - f''\right\}.$$

In general, if $\xi = \wp_{222}(u)$, $\eta = \wp_{221}(u)$, $\zeta = \wp_{211}(u)$, $\tau = \wp_{111}(u)$ be the coordinates of a point of the Weddle surface, and $u \equiv u^{a,\theta} + u^{a,\phi}$, the points θ, ϕ of the cubic curve

$$\xi/1 = -\eta/\theta = \zeta/\theta^2 = -\tau/\theta^3,$$

may be geometrically obtained by projecting (ξ, η, ζ, τ), from the node $(0, 0, 0, 1)$, to the satellite point $(\xi', \eta', \zeta', \tau')$, and drawing the chord of the cubic curve through $(\xi', \eta', \zeta', \tau')$. The coordinates of $(\xi', \eta', \zeta', \tau')$ are then in the ratios

$$\frac{1}{\Theta} - \frac{1}{\Phi} : -\left(\frac{\theta}{\Theta} + \frac{\phi}{\Phi}\right) : \frac{\theta^2}{\Theta} - \frac{\phi^2}{\Phi} : -\left(\frac{\theta^3}{\Theta} + \frac{\phi^3}{\Phi}\right),$$

Each of the tangent planes $t^2 - tx - y = 0$, $t_1^2 - t_1 x - y = 0$ cuts the Kummer surface in a plane quartic curve, with a cusp at infinity whose tangent is the generator along which the plane touches the cone. Consider one of the points $\pm u$ where these quartics intersect; let x, y, z be its coordinates; for a consecutive point $u + du$ of the quartic on $t^2 - tx - y = 0$, and the conjugate point $u' + du'$, we have

$$du_1' = \frac{dt_1}{s_1} = du_1, \qquad du_2' = \frac{t_1 dt_1}{s_1} = du_2,$$

so that, for variable pairs of conjugate points on this quartic, $u - u'$ is constant, equal therefore to the corresponding difference $2u^{a, t}$ for the pair of points $u = 2u^{a, t}$, $u' = 0$, lying on the generator of contact of the plane $t^2 - tx - y = 0$, and cone $x^2 + 4y = 0$. Also, on the cuspidal quartic,

$$du_1 = \frac{-x\,du_1 + 2du_2}{(x^2+4y)^{\frac{1}{2}}}, \qquad du_2 = \frac{2y\,du_1 + x\,du_2}{(x^2+4y)^{\frac{1}{2}}},$$

both leading to
$$\left(\frac{du_2}{du_1}\right)^2 - x\frac{du_2}{du_1} - y = 0,$$

which is thus the differential equation of the pairs of cuspidal quartic curves on the Kummer surface obtained by drawing tangent planes to the cone

---

where $\Theta^2 = f(\theta)$, $\Phi^2 = f(\phi)$, the fourth intersection of this chord of the cubic with the Weddle surface having coordinates obtainable from these by changing the sign of Φ. For the case when $\theta = \phi = t$, the point $\xi = \wp_{222}(2u^{a, t})$, etc., is such that there is a tangent of the cubic curve passing through $(\xi', \eta', \zeta', \tau')$, namely the tangent at the point t of the cubic; this cuts the Weddle surface again in $\left(\frac{1}{T} : -\frac{t}{T} : \frac{t^2}{T} : -\frac{t^3}{T}\right)$, where $T^2 = f(t)$, namely meets the surface in three points at t, so that the cubic is an asymptotic curve on the Weddle surface; the point $(\xi', \eta', \zeta', \tau')$ has for coordinates the ratios of the limits, when $\theta = \phi = t$, of

$$\frac{\frac{1}{\Theta} - \frac{1}{\Phi}}{\theta - \phi}, \quad -\frac{\frac{\theta}{\Theta} - \frac{\phi}{\Phi}}{\theta - \phi}, \quad \frac{\frac{\theta^2}{\Theta} - \frac{\phi^2}{\Phi}}{\theta - \phi}, \quad -\frac{\frac{\theta^3}{\Theta} - \frac{\phi^3}{\Phi}}{\theta - \phi},$$

which are
$$\frac{d}{dt}(T^{-1}), \quad \frac{d}{dt}(-tT^{-1}), \quad \frac{d}{dt}(t^2T^{-1}), \quad \frac{d}{dt}(-t^3T^{-1}),$$

or
$$\xi' : \eta' \quad \zeta' \,.\, \tau' = f' \,.\, 2f - tf' \,.\, -4tf + t^2 f' \quad 6t^2 f - t^3 f',$$

and this is the tangential, on the Weddle surface, of the point t of the cubic curve. The locus of $(\xi', \eta', \zeta', \tau')$ on the Weddle surface is thus a unicursal curve of order 7. The quartic developable surface $F = 0$, of p. 67, is the locus of the tangents of the cubic curve; its complete intersection with the Weddle surface thus consists of the cubic curve counted three times, together with this unicursal septic curve, which meets the cubic at the six fundamental nodes. The locus of the point $\xi = \wp_{222}(2u^{a, t})$, etc., can be found, by using the values

$$x = 2t, \quad y = -t^2, \quad z = (1, t)_8 / f(t)$$

in the expressions of p. 41, to be a unicursal curve of order 16. The cone joining the node $(0, 0, 0, 1)$ to the unicursal septic curve, which contains this unicursal curve of order 16, is to be found by eliminating t from the two equations $t^2\xi' + 2t\eta' + \zeta' = 0$, $2f\xi' = f'(t\xi' + \eta')$, and is of order 7; its intersection, of order 28, contains, beside the two curves of orders 7 and 16, the five lines joining the node $(0, 0, 0, 1)$ to the other nodes.

$x^2+4y=0$ from a variable point $x=\wp_{22}(u)$, etc. of the surface. We have $x=t_1+t$, $y=-t_1t$; thus along the cuspidal quartic $t_1^2-t_1x-y=0$ we have $dx_1=dt$, $dy_1=-t_1dt$, and therefore, du_1, du_2 denoting as before increments along the quartic $t^2-tx-y=0$, we have

$$\frac{dy_1}{dx_1}=-\frac{du_2}{du_1};$$

the differential equation for the pairs of cuspidal quartics may thus be equally written

$$\left(\frac{dy}{dx}\right)^2+x\frac{dy}{dx}-y=0,$$

an ordinary Clairaut equation with $\lambda^2-\lambda x-y=0$ as its integral. To reduce this form directly to the former, it is necessary, after substituting

$$dx=\xi du_2+\eta du_1,\quad dy=\eta du_2+\zeta du_1,$$

to utilise the identities

$$\frac{\zeta^2+\eta\zeta x-\eta^2y}{-y}=\frac{-2\eta\zeta-(\eta^2+\zeta\xi)x+2\xi\eta y}{x}=\frac{\eta^2+\xi\eta x-\xi^2y}{1},$$

which follow at once on substituting $\zeta=\xi y-\eta x$. Furthermore the identity

$$du_1dy_1+du_2dx_1=0,$$

is equivalent, either with

$$du_2[\wp_{222}(u)du_2^{(1)}+\wp_{221}(u)du_1^{(1)}]+du_1[\wp_{221}(u)du_2^{(1)}+\wp_{211}(u)du_1^{(1)}]=0,$$

that is $\qquad \xi du_2du_2^{(1)}+\eta(du_2du_1^{(1)}+du_1du_2^{(1)})+\zeta du_1du_1^{(1)}=0,$

where $du_2^{(1)}$, $du_1^{(1)}$ are increments along the quartic $t_1^2-t_1x-y=0$, or with

$$\xi dy dy_1-\eta(dxdy_1+dydx_1)+\zeta dxdx_1=0,$$

which, dividing by $dxdx_1$, is the same as the identity

$$-\xi y+\eta x+\zeta=0.$$

Comparing this work with that previously given we see that the arguments v, w of two twin points are connected by

$$v_1=\int\frac{-\wp_{22}(2w)dw_1+2dw_2}{[\wp_{22}^2(2w)+4\wp_{21}(2w)]^{\frac{1}{2}}},\qquad v_2=\int\frac{2\wp_{21}(2w)dw_1+\wp_{22}(2w)dw_2}{[\wp_{22}^2(2w)+4\wp_{21}(2w)]^{\frac{1}{2}}},$$

equivalent to $\wp_{22}(2v)=\wp_{22}(2w)$, $\wp_{21}(2v)=\wp_{21}(2w)$; we have shewn that these are satisfied by rational expressions for $\wp_{22}(v)$, $\wp_{21}(v)$, $\wp_{11}(v)$ in terms of $\wp_{22}(w)$, $\wp_{21}(w)$, $\wp_{11}(w)$; it will be seen that $\wp_{22}(2u)$, $\wp_{21}(2u)$ are rational invariants, in x, y, z, of a group of birational transformations. Further, we see, if w be a variable point on an asymptotic curve of the Kummer surface, that the point $2w$ is a point of a cuspidal quartic $t^2-t\wp_{22}(u)-\wp_{21}(u)=0$; that the satellite point v of w also lies on the asymptotic curve, and $v-w$ is constant along the asymptotic curve, being equal to $2u^{a,t}$; also that all the 32 points $w+\frac{1}{2}\Omega$, $v+\frac{1}{2}\Omega$, where Ω is any period, also lie on the asymptotic curve and are common to the two asymptotic curves through w; and so on. And if (x, y, z) be the coordinates of w, and (x', y', z') those of v, we have, as follows from the equation $xy'-yx'+z'-z=0$ at w, or from the differential equation of the asymptotic curves*,

$$\frac{dx'}{dx}=\frac{dy'}{dy}=\frac{\wp_{222}(v)}{\wp_{222}(w)}=\frac{\wp_{221}(v)}{\wp_{221}(w)}=\frac{\wp_{211}(v)}{\wp_{211}(w)},$$

so that the tangent lines of the asymptotic curve, at the twin points v, w, project upon the plane $z=0$ into parallel lines. All the cuspidal quartics touch the unicursal octavic intersection of $x^2+4y=0$ given by $u=2u^{a,t}$; thus the asymptotic curves all touch the singular conics of the Kummer surface, which constitute the parabolic curve†.

39. A bitangent is a chord of the Kummer surface whose intersections coincide in two pairs. Consider now any chord. For this let the tangent plane $x\wp_{21}(\alpha)-y\wp_{22}(\alpha)+\wp_{11}(\alpha)-z=0$, be called the tangent plane α; let (t_1), (t_2), (t_3), (t_4) be four arbitrary positions on the Riemann surface, and let

$$\alpha=\tfrac{1}{2}(u^{a,t_1}+u^{a,t_2}+u^{a,t_3}+u^{a,t_4}),\quad \beta=\tfrac{1}{2}(-u^{a,t_1}-u^{a,t_2}+u^{a,t_3}+u^{a,t_4});$$

the four arguments

$$a=\alpha-u^{a,t_1},\quad b=\alpha-u^{a,t_2},\quad c=\alpha-u^{a,t_3},\quad d=-\alpha+u^{a,t_4},$$

are then such that $\sigma(a-\alpha)$, $\sigma(b-\alpha)$, $\sigma(c-\alpha)$, $\sigma(d+\alpha)$ are all zero, and are therefore upon the plane α; they are respectively equal to

$$a=\beta+u^{a,t_2},\quad b=\beta+u^{a,t_1},\quad c=-\beta+u^{a,t_4},\quad d=\beta-u^{a,t_3},$$

and are therefore, similarly, upon the plane β; thus they belong to four collinear points. Conversely let $\pm a$, $\pm b$, be any two points of the Kummer surface; take (t_1), (t_2), (t_3), (t_4) so that

$$u^{a,t_1}-u^{a,t_2}=b-a,\quad u^{a,t_3}+u^{a,t_4}=b+a,$$

or

$$a=\tfrac{1}{2}(-u^{a,t_1}+u^{a,t_2}+u^{a,t_3}+u^{a,t_4})=\alpha-u^{a,t_1},$$
$$b=\tfrac{1}{2}(\;\;u^{a,t_1}-u^{a,t_2}+u^{a,t_3}+u^{a,t_4})=\alpha-u^{a,t_2};$$

then, as before, the line joining these points cuts the surface again in $\pm c$, $\pm d$ where

$$c=\alpha-u^{a,t_3},\quad d=-\alpha+u^{a,t_4}.$$

* The differential equation of the asymptotic lines, for a surface whose tangent plane is $lx+my+nz=0$, is $dx\,dl+dy\,dm+dz\,dn=0$.

† See Klein u. Lie, *Berlin. Monatsber.* 1870; Reichardt, *Nova Acta Leopoldina*, L. 1887, p. 479; Hudson, *Kummer's quartic surface*, p. 195.

Put $u = u^{a,t_1} + u^{a,t_2}$, $u' = u^{a,t_1} - u^{a,t_2}$, $v = u^{a,t_3} + u^{a,t_4}$, $v' = u^{a,t_3} - u^{a,t_4}$;

then we have $a + b = v$, $c + d = -v'$; $a - b = -u'$, $c - d = u$,

as well as

$$a + c = u^{a,t_2} + u^{a,t_4}, \quad a - c = -u^{a,t_1} + u^{a,t_3},$$
$$b + d = -u^{a,t_2} + u^{a,t_4}, \quad b - d = u^{a,t_1} + u^{a,t_3},$$

and

$$b + c = u^{a,t_1} + u^{a,t_4}, \quad b - c = -u^{a,t_2} + u^{a,t_3},$$
$$a + d = -u^{a,t_1} + u^{a,t_4}, \quad a - d = u^{a,t_2} + u^{a,t_3}.$$

Introduce now the following phraseology; if $\pm u$, $\pm v$ be any two points of the Kummer surface, let the two points $\pm(u + v)$, $\pm(u - v)$ be called their forward derivatives; they are uniquely determined when $\pm u$, $\pm v$, are given. If $\frac{1}{2}\Omega$ denote any half period, $\pm u$, $\pm v$ are the forward derivatives of the two points $\pm\frac{1}{2}(u+v)+\frac{1}{2}\Omega$, $\pm\frac{1}{2}(u-v)+\frac{1}{2}\Omega$, so that $\pm\frac{1}{2}(u+v)+\frac{1}{2}\Omega$, $\pm\frac{1}{2}(u-v)+\frac{1}{2}\Omega$ may be called the backward derivatives of $\pm u$, $\pm v$; these consist of sixteen pairs of points. Then the results just obtained may be stated by saying that if four collinear points of the Kummer surface be divided into two pairs, either of the forward derivatives of one pair is conjugate to a forward derivative of the other pair; thus each mode of taking the two pairs gives rise to two straight lines through the primary node, and the four collinear points give rise to six straight lines through the primary node; in other words, including the whole result, if a, b, c, d be four collinear points in any order, we have

$$\wp_{22}(b + c) = \wp_{22}(a + \epsilon d), \quad \wp_{21}(b - c) = \wp_{21}(a - \epsilon d),$$

where the signs of a, b, c, d are arbitrary, but ϵ, $= \pm 1$, must be suitably taken. Further the sixteen pairs of backward derivatives $\pm\frac{1}{2}(a + b) + \frac{1}{2}\Omega$, $\pm\frac{1}{2}(c + d) + \frac{1}{2}\Omega$, consist of sixteen pairs of twin points, the points of contact of sixteen bitangents, and there are six such sets, each of sixteen bitangents, associated with the four collinear points, two such sets belonging to each mode of dividing the four collinear points into two sets of two.

It is easy to see the modification arising when the four collinear points consist of two couples of collinear points (v, v, w, w), lying on a bitangent. The forward derivatives consist then of $(0, 0)$, the primary node, of $(v + w, v + w)$, occurring twice, being the coincident intersections of the conic at infinity with a line through the primary node, of $(v - w, v - w)$, occurring twice, being also the coincident intersections of the conic at infinity with a line through the primary node, and of $(2v, 2w)$, which are then conjugate points, as we have already found (§ 38). In fact the set of tangent planes α, β, ..., in general four in number, which can be drawn to the Kummer surface through the four collinear points, contains in this case coincident planes.

40. The differential equation given above for the asymptotic lines of the Kummer surface

$$\left(\frac{du_2}{du_1}\right)^2 - \frac{du_2}{du_1}\wp_{22}(2u) - \wp_{21}(2u) = 0,$$

enables us at once to find rational expressions for $\wp_{22}(2u)$, $\wp_{21}(2u)$ in terms of $\wp_{22}(u)$, $\wp_{21}(u)$, $\wp_{11}(u)$. For the asymptotic lines of a surface in homogeneous coordinates x, y, z, t being*

$$\begin{vmatrix} x, & x_1, & x_2, & d^2x \\ y, & y_1, & y_2, & d^2y \\ z, & z_1, & z_2, & d^2z \\ t, & t_1, & t_2, & d^2t \end{vmatrix} = 0,$$

where x, y, z, t are supposed expressed in terms of two parameters u, v, and

$$x_1 = \frac{\partial x}{\partial u}, \qquad d^2x = \frac{\partial^2 x}{\partial u^2} du^2 + 2\frac{\partial^2 x}{\partial u \partial v} du dv + \frac{\partial^2 x}{\partial v^2} dv^2,$$

we have for $x = \wp_{22}(u)$, $y = \wp_{21}(u)$, $z = \wp_{11}(u)$, $t = 1$, as the differential equation,

$$\begin{vmatrix} \xi, & \eta, & \wp_{2222} du_2^2 + 2\wp_{2221} du_2 du_1 + \wp_{2211} du_1^2 \\ \eta, & \zeta, & \wp_{2221} du_2^2 + 2\wp_{2211} du_2 du_1 + \wp_{2111} du_1^2 \\ \zeta, & \tau, & \wp_{2211} du_2^2 + 2\wp_{2111} du_2 du_1 + \wp_{1111} du_1^2 \end{vmatrix} = 0,$$

where $\xi = \wp_{222}(u)$, etc. Comparing this with the form

$$\left(\frac{du_2}{du_1}\right)^2 - \frac{du_2}{du_1}\wp_{22}(2u) - \wp_{21}(2u) = 0,$$

we infer, if as usual $Q_1 = 4(\eta\tau - \zeta^2)$, $Q_2 = 4(\eta\zeta - \xi\tau)$, $Q_3 = 4(\zeta\xi - \eta^2)$, that

$$\wp_{22}(2u) = -2\frac{Q_1\wp_{2221}(u) + Q_2\wp_{2211}(u) + Q_3\wp_{2111}(u)}{Q_1\wp_{2222}(u) + Q_2\wp_{2221}(u) + Q_3\wp_{2211}(u)},$$

$$\wp_{21}(2u) = -\frac{Q_1\wp_{2211}(u) + Q_2\wp_{2111}(u) + Q_3\wp_{1111}(u)}{Q_1\wp_{2222}(u) + Q_2\wp_{2221}(u) + Q_3\wp_{2211}(u)},$$

and, for the equations of the asymptotic curves,

$$\begin{aligned} &Q_1[t^2\wp_{2222}(u) + 2t\wp_{2221}(u) + \wp_{2211}(u)] \\ &+ Q_2[t^2\wp_{2221}(u) + 2t\wp_{2211}(u) + \wp_{2111}(u)] \\ &+ Q_3[t^2\wp_{2211}(u) + 2t\wp_{2111}(u) + \wp_{1111}(u)] = 0. \end{aligned}$$

It is found (see pp. 41 and 48) that the quintic terms in this are

$$16(xz - y^2)^2[t^2x + 2ty + z];$$

as we can eliminate $(xz - y^2)^2$ by means of the equation $\Delta = 0$ (p. 41), the asymptotic curves lie on surfaces of order 4.

Another way of finding the expressions for $\wp_{22}(2u)$, $\wp_{21}(2u)$, is by the equations of p. 117, expressing the integrals at the satellite point in terms of those at the original point; these give, if $M = [\wp_{22}^2(2w) + 4\wp_{21}(2w)]^{\frac{1}{2}}$,

$$\frac{\partial v_2}{\partial w_2} = \frac{\wp_{22}(2w)}{M} = -\frac{\partial v_1}{\partial w_1},$$

$$\frac{\partial v_2}{\partial w_1} = \frac{2\wp_{21}(2w)}{M}, \quad \frac{\partial v_1}{\partial w_2} = \frac{2}{M}.$$

* Darboux, *Théorie des Surfaces*, Partie I. p. 138.

We have however found (p. 78)

$$dv_2 = + \frac{Q_1 d\eta + Q_2 d\zeta + Q_3 d\tau}{i\,(Q_3 C_{a_1} C_{a_2} C_c C_{c_1} C_{c_2})^{\frac{1}{4}}}, \qquad dv_1 = - \frac{Q_1 d\xi + Q_2 d\eta + Q_3 d\zeta}{i\,(Q_3 C_{a_1} C_{a_2} C_c C_{c_1} C_{c_2})^{\frac{1}{4}}},$$

where $Q_1 = 4(\eta\tau - \zeta^2)$, etc., $\xi = \wp_{222}(2w)$, etc., $C_\theta = Q_1 - \theta Q_2 + \theta^2 Q_3$; thus

$$\frac{2}{M} = - \frac{Q_1 \wp_{2222}(w) + Q_2 \wp_{2221}(w) + Q_3 \wp_{2211}(w)}{i\,(Q_3 C_{a_1} C_{a_2} C_c C_{c_1} C_{c_2})^{\frac{1}{4}}}$$

together with expressions for $\wp_{22}(2w)$ and $\wp_{21}(2w)$ identical with those above. The denominator which occurs here has been seen (p. 78) to be the square root of σQ_3, where σ is a certain quartic expression in ξ, η, ζ, τ; if $A = Q_1 \wp_{2222}(u) + \ldots$, $B = Q_1 \wp_{2221}(u) + \ldots$, $C = Q_1 \wp_{2211}(u) + \ldots$, we thus find $B^2 - AC = \sigma Q_3$.

41. Another way, depending on the use of Abel's theorem, or rather its converse, in which the functions $\wp_{22}(2u), \ldots$ may be obtained, is of geometrical interest.

To the points $\pm u$, $\pm 2u$, of the Weddle surface, associate pairs of places (θ), (ϕ), and (α), (β), of the Riemann surface, by means of the equations

$$u \equiv u^{\theta, a} + u^{\phi, a}, \quad 2u \equiv u^{\alpha, a} + u^{\alpha, \beta};$$

without alteration of the points of the Weddle surface both (θ) and (ϕ) may be together replaced by their conjugate places on the Riemann surface, as may the places (α), (β). We have then

$$u^{\alpha, a} + u^{\beta, a} + 2u^{\theta, a} + 2u^{\phi, a} \equiv 0,$$

shewing (Appendix to Part I., Note II.) that there exists a rational function on the Riemann surface, of the sixth order, with all its poles at infinity, vanishing twice in each of (θ), (ϕ) and once in each of (α), (β); this function must be of the form

$$t^3 - \nu t^2 + \mu t - \lambda + \rho s,$$

where $s^2 = f(t)$, and the coefficients λ, μ, ν, ρ are to be determined by means of

$$\theta^3 - \nu\theta^2 + \mu\theta - \lambda + \rho\Theta = 0, \qquad \phi^3 - \nu\phi^2 + \mu\phi - \lambda + \rho\Phi = 0,$$

$$3\theta^2 - 2\nu\theta + \mu + \tfrac{1}{2}\rho\,\frac{f'(\theta)}{\Theta} = 0, \qquad 3\phi^2 - 2\nu\phi + \mu + \tfrac{1}{2}\rho\,\frac{f'(\phi)}{\Phi} = 0,$$

where Θ, Φ are the values of s at (θ) and (ϕ). The function being so determined, the places (α), (β) are found as the remaining zeros, and thence $\wp_{22}(2u) = \alpha + \beta$, $\wp_{21}(2u) = -\alpha\beta$. The conditions are those found by expressing the identity

$$(t^3 - \nu t^2 + \mu t - \lambda)^2 - \rho^2 f(t) = (t-\theta)^2 (t-\phi)^2 (t-\alpha)(t-\beta),$$

or, if $x = \theta + \phi = \wp_{22}(u)$, $y = -\theta\phi = \wp_{21}(u)$, $X = \wp_{22}(2u)$, $Y = \wp_{21}(2u)$, by expressing that $(t^2 - tx - y)^2 (t^2 - tX - Y) + \rho^2 f(t)$

is the square of a cubic function of t; when x and y only are given this last form gives the two sets of corresponding values for X and Y. The four conditional equations give

$$\lambda\left(\frac{1}{\Phi}-\frac{1}{\Theta}\right)+\mu\left(\frac{\theta}{\Theta}-\frac{\phi}{\Phi}\right)-\nu\left(\frac{\theta^2}{\Theta}-\frac{\phi^2}{\Phi}\right)+\frac{\theta^3}{\Theta}-\frac{\phi^3}{\Phi}=0,$$

shewing that the plane $\lambda\xi+\mu\eta+\nu\zeta+\tau=0$ passes through the point $\Theta-\Phi$, $-(\Theta\phi-\Phi\theta)$, $\Theta\phi^2-\Phi\theta^2$, $-(\Theta\phi^3-\Phi\theta^3)$, which (pp. 40, 116) is the satellite point of u on the Weddle surface, obtained from $\pm u$ by projection from the node (0, 0, 0, 1), and lies upon the chord of the cubic curve joining the points $(1, -\theta, \theta^2, -\theta^3)$, $(1, -\phi, \phi^2, -\phi^3)$; the conditional equations give, however, also

$$\frac{\partial}{\partial\theta}\left(\frac{\lambda-\mu\theta+\nu\theta^2-\theta^3}{\Theta}\right)=0,\quad \frac{\partial}{\partial\phi}\left(\frac{\lambda-\mu\phi+\nu\phi^2-\phi^3}{\Phi}\right)=0,$$

shewing that the plane $\lambda\xi+\mu\eta+\nu\zeta+\tau=0$ contains every consecutive point of the Weddle surface; it is thus the tangent plane of the surface at the satellite point of $\pm u$.

The point $$\frac{\partial}{\partial\theta}\left(\frac{1}{\Theta}\right):\frac{\partial}{\partial\theta}\left(\frac{-\theta}{\Theta}\right):\frac{\partial}{\partial\theta}\left(\frac{\theta^2}{\Theta}\right):\frac{\partial}{\partial\theta}\left(\frac{-\theta^3}{\Theta}\right),$$

which clearly lies on the tangent plane, is the remaining intersection of the Weddle surface with the tangent line of the cubic curve at $(1, -\theta, \theta^2, -\theta^3)$, and is on the unicursal septic (p. 116) which is the tangential on the Weddle surface of the cubic space curve. The point having the same derivation from ϕ is also on the tangent plane. Further the equations

$$\alpha^3-\nu\alpha^2+\mu\alpha-\lambda+\rho A=0,\quad \beta^3-\nu\beta^2+\mu\beta-\lambda+\rho B=0,$$

where $A^2=f(\alpha)$, etc., shew that the point satellite to $\pm 2u$ is also on the tangent plane.

The tangent plane of the Weddle surface at the point P', satellite to $\pm u$, has been seen (p. 68) to be the polar plane, of the point reciprocal to P' on the Weddle surface, in regard to a cone $x'Q_1+y'Q_2+z'Q_3+P_4=0$ with vertex at P'; if then the tangent planes of this cone which contain the chord (θ, ϕ) of the cubic curve be momentarily written

$$A_1\xi+\ldots+D_1\tau=0,\quad A_2\xi+\ldots+D_2\tau=0,$$

there is an identity of the form

$$-\rho^2(x'Q_1+y'Q_2+z'Q_3+P_4)=(\lambda\xi+\mu\eta+\nu\zeta+\tau)^2 \\ -(A_1\xi+\ldots+D_1\tau)(A_2\xi+\ldots+D_2\tau);$$

take the particular case of this when $\xi:\eta:\zeta:\tau=1, -t, t^2, -t^3$; then the left side reduces to $\rho^2 f(t)$, and the first term of the right side to

$$(t^3-\nu t^2+\mu t-\lambda)^2;$$

as each of the planes $A_1\xi+\ldots+D_1\tau=0$, $A_2\xi+\ldots+D_2\tau=0$ passes through θ and ϕ, the second term of the right side contains the factor $(t-\theta)^2(t-\phi)^2$;

the remaining factor is $(t-\alpha)(t-\beta)$, where $(1, -\alpha, \alpha^2, -\alpha^3)$, $(1, -\beta, \beta^2, -\beta^3)$ are the remaining intersections with the cubic curve respectively of the plane $A_1\xi + \ldots + D_1\tau = 0$ and $A_2\xi + \ldots + D_2\tau = 0$ and the identity becomes that previously obtained. In other words, if the point $\pm u$ be joined to the node (0, 0, 0, 1), the join giving the satellite point P'; if the cone with P' as vertex to contain the six common points of the quadrics Q_1, Q_2, Q_3, P_4, be constructed; then the tangent planes of this cone which contain the chord of the cubic curve through P', cut the cubic curve again in points α, β, which are upon the chord of the cubic through the satellite point of the point $\pm 2u$.

The condition determining $\wp_{22}(2u)\ldots$ may thus also be expressed by saying, if $\bar{Q}_1$, $\bar{Q}_2$, $\bar{Q}_3$, $\bar{P}_4$, denote the values of $Q_1, \ldots$ for the point $\pm u$ (cf. p. 76 for the equations $x'/\bar{Q}_2 = \ldots$), that the quadric following, for a proper value of μ $(=\rho^2/\bar{Q}_3)$,

$$\{\theta\phi\alpha\xi + [\theta\phi + \alpha(\theta+\phi)]\eta + (\theta+\phi+\alpha)\zeta + \tau\}$$
$$\times\{\theta\phi\beta\xi + [\theta\phi + \beta(\theta+\phi)]\eta + (\theta+\phi+\beta)\zeta + \tau\}$$
$$-\mu\{\bar{Q}_2Q_1 - \bar{Q}_1Q_2 - \bar{P}_4Q_3 + \bar{Q}_3P_4\}$$

must be the square of a plane, namely of the tangent plane at $\pm u'$; the conditions for this are, that in the discriminantal matrix of this quadric, every minor of two rows and columns be zero.

If $\pm u'$ be the arguments associated with P', the satellite point of $\pm u$, we know that $\wp_{22}(2u') = \wp_{22}(2u)$, $\wp_{21}(2u') = \wp_{21}(2u)$; hence if the cone be drawn to contain the six common points of the quadrics Q_1, Q_2, Q_3, P_4, with

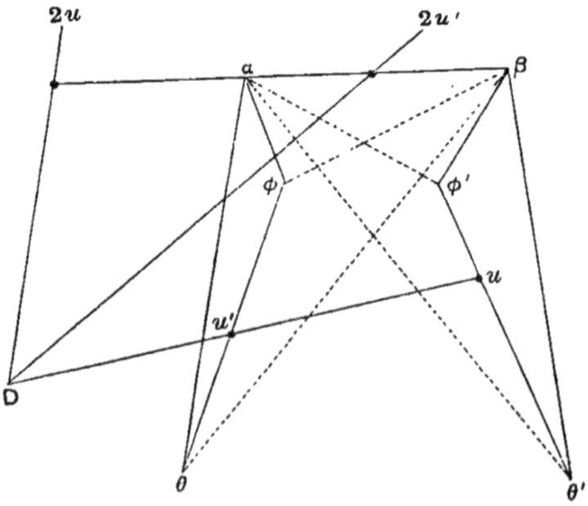

its vertex at $\pm u$, the tangent planes of the cone, passing through the chord of the cubic curve through $\pm u$, will also cut the cubic curve in the points α, β, and the satellite point of the point $\pm 2u'$ will lie on the chord α, β of the cubic, and on the tangent plane of the Weddle surface at $\pm u$. If θ', ϕ' be the two points of the cubic curve, on the chord of this drawn through $\pm u$, we may draw the diagram annexed, where D denotes the node $(0, 0, 0, 1)$, which may help to keep the relations in mind.

In order that $l_0\xi + l_1\eta + l_2\zeta + l_3\tau = 0$ should touch the cone

$$(a, b, c, d, f, g, h, u, v, w)(\xi, \eta, \zeta, \tau)^2 = 0$$

it is sufficient, beside the condition that the plane passes through the vertex of the cone, that

$$\begin{vmatrix} b & f & v & l_1 \\ f & c & w & l_2 \\ v & w & d & l_3 \\ l_1 & l_2 & l_3 & 0 \end{vmatrix} = 0;$$

applying this to the cone $x'Q_1 + y'Q_2 + z'Q_3 + P_4 = 0$, when $l_0 = \alpha\theta\phi$, $l_1 = \alpha(\theta + \phi) + \theta\phi$, $l_2 = \alpha + \theta + \phi$, $l_3 = 1$, we find the quadratic equation for α, β in terms of θ, ϕ; putting $x = \theta + \phi$, $y = -\theta\phi$, and using $xy' - x'y + z' - z = 0$, we thus find

$$2(x - x')^2 \wp_{22}(2u) = 2\lambda_2 + \lambda_3(x + x') + 2\lambda_4 xx' + 4xx'(x + x') + 4xy + 4x'y' + 4z + 4z',$$

$$2(x - x')^2 \wp_{21}(2u) = \tfrac{1}{2}\lambda_2\lambda_4 - \tfrac{1}{8}\lambda_3^2 + 2\lambda_2(x + x') + \lambda_3(xx' - y - y') + \lambda_4(z + z' - xy' - x'y) + 8(xz' + x'z) - 2(xx' + y + y')^2;$$

$f = 0$ being the equation of the Kummer surface we have (p. 76)

$$x' = \frac{\partial f}{\partial y} \Big/ \frac{\partial f}{\partial z}, \text{ and therefore } (x - x')\frac{\partial f}{\partial z} = x\frac{\partial f}{\partial z} - \frac{\partial f}{\partial y}.$$

The cone $x'Q_1 + y'Q_2 + z'Q_3 + P_4 = 0$, with vertex at $\pm u'$, intersects the Weddle surface near $\pm u'$ in a locus whose projection from the node D gives, near $\pm u$, the locus represented by $-x'\wp_{22}(U) + y'\wp_{21}(U) + z' - \wp_{11}(U) = 0$, for which then, as our previous investigation of the asymptotic lines of the Kummer surface shews,

$$\left(\frac{du_2}{du_1}\right)^2 - \wp_{22}(2u)\frac{du_2}{du_1} - \wp_{21}(2u) = 0;$$

putting here (see p. 117),

$$\frac{du_2}{du_1} = \left[X\frac{du_2'}{du_1'} + 2Y\right] \Big/ \left[2\frac{du_2'}{du_1'} - X\right],$$

where $X = \wp_{22}(2u) = \wp_{22}(2u')$, $Y = \wp_{21}(2u) = \wp_{21}(2u')$, it is at once found to reduce to

$$\left(\frac{du_2'}{du_1'}\right)^2 - \wp_{22}(2u')\frac{du_2'}{du_1'} - \wp_{21}(2u') = 0,$$

that is

$$\left(\frac{du_2'}{du_1'} - \alpha\right)\left(\frac{du_2'}{du_1'} - \beta\right) = 0.$$

And in fact if $\left(\frac{du_2}{du_1}\right)_1$ and $\left(\frac{du_2}{du_1}\right)_2$ give two directions through the point $\pm u$ which are harmonic in regard to the directions given by

$$\left(\frac{du_2}{du_1}\right)^2 - X\frac{du_2}{du_1} - Y = 0,$$

while $\left(\frac{du_2'}{du_1'}\right)_1$, $\left(\frac{du_2'}{du_1'}\right)_2$ are the directions at $\pm u'$ obtained from these respectively by projection from the node (0, 0, 0, 1), we have

$$\left(\frac{du_2'}{du_1'}\right)_1 = \left(\frac{du_2}{du_1}\right)_2, \quad \left(\frac{du_2'}{du_1'}\right)_2 = \left(\frac{du_2}{du_1}\right)_1.$$

42. Consider now the asymptotic lines of the Weddle surface; their directions at $\pm u$ are given by a determinantal equation

$$\begin{vmatrix} \wp_{222}(u), & \wp_{2222}(u), & \wp_{2221}(u), & d^2\wp_{222}(u) \\ \dots & \dots & \dots & \dots \\ \dots & \dots & \dots & \dots \\ \wp_{111}(u), & \wp_{2111}(u), & \wp_{1111}(u), & d^2\wp_{111}(u) \end{vmatrix} = 0,$$

but the algebraic work is simpler if we proceed as follows: expressing that the tangent plane $\lambda\xi + \mu\eta + \nu\zeta + \tau = 0$ contains the point whose coordinates are

$$\xi = \frac{1}{\Theta} - \frac{1}{\Phi} + d\theta\frac{\partial}{\partial\theta}\left(\frac{1}{\Theta}\right) + d\phi\frac{\partial}{\partial\phi}\left(\frac{-1}{\Phi}\right) + \tfrac{1}{2}d\theta^2\frac{\partial^2}{\partial\theta^2}\left(\frac{1}{\Theta}\right) + \tfrac{1}{2}d\phi^2\frac{\partial^2}{\partial\phi^2}\left(\frac{-1}{\Phi}\right),$$

$$\eta = \frac{-\theta}{\Theta} + \frac{\phi}{\Phi} + d\theta\frac{\partial}{\partial\theta}\left(\frac{-\theta}{\Theta}\right) + d\phi\frac{\partial}{\partial\phi}\left(\frac{\phi}{\Phi}\right) + \tfrac{1}{2}d\theta^2\frac{\partial^2}{\partial\theta^2}\left(\frac{-\theta}{\Theta}\right) + \tfrac{1}{2}d\phi^2\frac{\partial^2}{\partial\phi^2}\left(\frac{\phi}{\Phi}\right),$$

and similar expressions, we obtain, beside the three equations already found,

$$\frac{\lambda - \mu\theta + \nu\theta^2 - \theta^3}{\Theta} = \frac{\lambda - \mu\phi + \nu\phi^2 - \phi^3}{\Phi},$$

$$\frac{\partial}{\partial\theta}\left(\frac{\lambda - \mu\theta + \nu\theta^2 - \theta^3}{\Theta}\right) = 0, \quad \frac{\partial}{\partial\phi}\left(\frac{\lambda - \mu\phi + \nu\phi^2 - \phi^3}{\Phi}\right) = 0,$$

the further equation

$$d\theta^2\frac{\partial^2}{\partial\theta^2}\left(\frac{\lambda - \mu\theta + \nu\theta^2 - \theta^3}{\Theta}\right) = d\phi^2\frac{\partial^2}{\partial\phi^2}\left(\frac{\lambda - \mu\phi + \nu\phi^2 - \phi^3}{\Phi}\right),$$

for the asymptotic lines; putting $T^2 = f(t)$, differentiating twice the identity in t,

$$\left(\frac{\lambda - \mu t + \nu t^2 - t^3}{T}\right)^2 - \rho^2 = \frac{(t^2 - tx - y)(t^2 - tX - Y)}{f(t)},$$

and then putting $t = \theta$, we find

$$\frac{\lambda - \mu\theta + \nu\theta^2 - \theta^3}{\Theta}\frac{\partial^2}{\partial\theta^2}\left(\frac{\lambda - \mu\theta + \nu\theta^2 - \theta^3}{\Theta}\right) = (\theta - \phi)^2\frac{(\theta - \alpha)(\theta - \beta)}{\Theta^2},$$

so that the asymptotic lines are given by

$$\frac{(\theta-\alpha)(\theta-\beta)}{\Theta^2}\,d\theta^2=\frac{(\phi-\alpha)(\phi-\beta)}{\Phi^2}\,d\phi^2,$$

a result obtained in this way by Mr H. Bateman, *Proc. Lond. Math. Soc.* New Series, Vol. III. (1905), p. 235. Putting herein

$$du_1=\frac{d\theta}{\Theta}+\frac{d\phi}{\Phi},\quad du_2=\frac{\theta d\theta}{\Theta}+\frac{\phi d\phi}{\Phi},$$

and reducing, it becomes, replacing $\theta+\phi$, $\theta\phi$, $\alpha+\beta$, $\alpha\beta$ respectively by x, $-y$, X, $-Y$,

$$(x-X)\left(\frac{du_2}{du_1}\right)^2+2(y-Y)\frac{du_2}{du_1}+xY-yX=0;$$

this is the relation for $\dfrac{du_2}{du_1}$ when we move along an asymptotic line at the point $\pm u'$; putting (p. 117)

$$\frac{du_2}{du_1}=\left(X\frac{du_2'}{du_1'}+2Y\right)\Big/\left(2\frac{du_2'}{du_1'}-X\right),$$

we can verify algebraically, though the fact is obvious from the geometrical interpretation above given for this transformation, that the differential equation for $\dfrac{du_2'}{du_1'}$ is precisely the same, so that the asymptotic directions project from the node (0, 0, 0, 1) into asymptotic directions; putting then $X=X'$, $Y=Y'$, $x=Q_2'/Q_3'$, $y=-Q_1'/Q_3'$, we have the form for the differential equation of the asymptotic lines at $\pm u'$; finally dropping the dashes, the asymptotic lines at $\pm u$ are given by

$$(Q_2-XQ_3)\left(\frac{du_2}{du_1}\right)^2-2(Q_1+YQ_3)\frac{du_2}{du_1}+Q_1X+Q_2Y=0,$$

that is by

$$\begin{vmatrix} Q_1 & -Y & du_2^2 \\ Q_2 & X & 2du_2du_1 \\ Q_3 & 1 & du_1^2 \end{vmatrix}=0;$$

and are therefore harmonic in regard to the directions given by each of the two equations

$$\text{(i)}\qquad \left(\frac{du_2}{du_1}\right)^2-X\frac{du_2}{du_1}-Y=0,$$

$$\text{(ii)}\qquad Q_3\left(\frac{du_2}{du_1}\right)^2-Q_2\frac{du_2}{du_1}+Q_1=0.$$

It follows conversely that each of these two equations gives a pair of conjugate directions; that the latter (ii) does so can easily be seen geometrically; a geometrical proof that the former (i) also does so would enable us to write down the differential equation of the asymptotic lines at once;

the fact is equivalent with the statement that *the Weddle and the Kummer surfaces are such that the asymptotic directions on either correspond to conjugate directions on the other*, a relation projectively generalising that considered by Lie between two surfaces of which the asymptotic lines of one correspond to the lines of curvature of the other (*Geom. der Berührungs-transformationen** (1896), pp. 473, 636); it was by relating the Kummer surface in this particular way that the asymptotic lines of Kummer's surface were first determined, by Lie, *Compt. Rend.* LXXI. (1871), p. 579. In regard to these conjugate directions, (i), we have proved (p. 117) that they are given by

$$t^2 - tX - Y = 0,$$

that they are the tangents of the intersection of the cone

$$xQ_1 + yQ_2 + zQ_3 + P_4 = 0$$

with the Weddle surface at the vertex of the cone, that any element at $\pm u$ of a particular curve t is projected from the node (0, 0, 0, 1) into an element of the same curve at $\pm u'$, the arguments u', u being such that $u' - u \equiv u^{a, t}$, and that the curve t is given by $2u \equiv u^{a, t} + u^{a, \beta}$, for variable β. With regard to the directions (ii), consider first the cone joining the point θ of the cubic curve to all other points of the cubic curve, whose equation is given by

$$\theta^2 Q_3 - \theta Q_2 + Q_1 = 0\,;$$

it passes through the point $\pm u'$, or P', for which $\xi' = \frac{1}{\Phi} - \frac{1}{\Theta}$, $\eta' = -\frac{\phi}{\Phi} + \frac{\theta}{\Theta}$, etc., and, as we have seen, the tangent plane of the Weddle surface at this point passes through the point

$$\frac{\partial}{\partial\theta}\left(\frac{1}{\Theta}\right) : \frac{\partial}{\partial\theta}\left(\frac{-\theta}{\Theta}\right) : \frac{\partial}{\partial\theta}\left(\frac{\theta^2}{\Theta}\right) : \frac{\partial}{\partial\theta}\left(\frac{-\theta^3}{\Theta}\right),$$

or T, which (p. 116) is the tangential on the Weddle surface of the point θ of the cubic curve; in other words the quintic curve of intersection with the Weddle surface, other than the cubic curve, of the cone $\theta^2 Q_3 - \theta Q_2 + Q_1 = 0$, is the curve of contact of the tangent cone to the Weddle surface from the point T; let P_1' be the point of this curve of contact lying on the chord joining θ to $\phi + d\phi$; the tangent planes of the Weddle surface at P' and P_1' are tangent planes of the cone of contact, touching this along the generators TP' and TP_1'; thus they ultimately intersect in $P'T$, which is thus the conjugate direction on the Weddle surface to $P'P_1'$. Consider now the similar cone $\phi^2 Q_3 - \phi Q_2 + Q_1 = 0$, containing the cubic curve, with vertex at ϕ; its tangent line at P' joins the points

$$\frac{1}{\Phi} - \frac{1}{\Theta}, \quad \frac{-\phi}{\Phi} + \frac{\theta}{\Theta}, \ldots,$$

$$\frac{\partial}{\partial\theta}\left(\frac{1}{\Phi} - \frac{1}{\Theta}\right), \quad \frac{\partial}{\partial\theta}\left(\frac{-\phi}{\Phi} + \frac{\theta}{\Theta}\right), \ldots,$$

* Also, Lie, *Math. Annal.* v. (1871); Darboux, *Théorie*, Nos. 157, 164.

namely is the line $P'T$; thus the two cones

$$\theta^2 Q_3 - \theta Q_2 + Q_1 = 0, \quad \phi^2 Q_3 - \phi Q_2 + Q_1 = 0,$$

or the curves of contact of the tangent cones to the Weddle surface from the points

$$\frac{\partial}{\partial\theta}\left(\frac{1}{\Theta}\right) : \frac{\partial}{\partial\theta}\left(\frac{-\theta}{\Theta}\right) : \ldots, \quad \frac{\partial}{\partial\phi}\left(\frac{1}{\Phi}\right) : \frac{\partial}{\partial\phi}\left(\frac{-\phi}{\Phi}\right) : \ldots,$$

give conjugate directions on the surface at P'. We can find the differential equations for these curves: for consistence of notation consider the corresponding curve $\theta'^2 Q_3 - \theta' Q_2 + Q_1 = 0$, passing through $\pm u$, where θ', ϕ' are the extremities of the chord of the cubic curve through $\pm u$. This projects into a locus near $\pm u'$ represented by $\theta'^2 - \theta' x' - y' = 0$, which gives, as we have seen (p. 117)

$$\left(\frac{du_2'}{du_1'}\right)^2 - x'\frac{du_2'}{du_1'} - y' = 0;$$

herein put

$$\frac{du_2'}{du_1'} = (Xp + 2Y)/(2p - X),$$

where $p = \dfrac{du_2}{du_1}$; we thence have, for the differential equation of the curve

$$\theta'^2 Q_3 - \theta' Q_2 + Q_1 = 0,$$

the form

$$p^2(X^2 - 2Xx' - 4y') + p(4XY - 4Yx' + X^2x' + 4Xy') + 4Y^2 + 2YXx' - X^2y' = 0,$$

which can be shewn to be the same as

$$(X^2 + 4Y)(p^2 - x'p - y') - 2(Xx' + 2Y + 2y')(p^2 - pX - Y) = 0,$$

so that the curves $t^2Q_3 - tQ_2 + Q_1 = 0$ through $\pm u$, the curves $t^2 - tX - Y = 0$ through $\pm u$, and the curves given by the differential equation $p^2 - px' - y' = 0$, or

$$\text{(ii)} \quad Q_3\left(\frac{du_2}{du_1}\right)^2 - Q_2\left(\frac{du_2}{du_1}\right) + Q_1 = 0,$$

through $\pm u$, belong to the same involution; this is in accordance with what we have found, the asymptotic directions being the double rays for the involution, and the equations

$$\text{(i)} \quad t^2 - tX - Y = 0,$$

$$\text{(iii)} \quad t^2Q_3 - tQ_2 + Q_1 = 0,$$

$$\text{(ii)} \quad Q_3\left(\frac{du_2}{du_1}\right)^2 - Q_2\left(\frac{du_2}{du_1}\right) + Q_1 = 0,$$

defining three pairs of conjugate directions; the directions (ii) are the harmonic conjugates of the directions (iii) in regard to the directions (i).

For the space cubic

$$u = u^{t,\,a}, \quad 2u = 2u^{t,\,u}, \quad X = 2t, \quad Y = -t^2, \quad Q_1 = 0, \quad Q_2 = 0, \quad Q_3 = 0,$$

and the equation of the asymptotic lines is satisfied by the vanishing of its coefficients. For $u = 2u^{t, a}$, $\theta = \phi = t$, and the equation

$$(\theta - \alpha)(\theta - \beta)\frac{d\theta^2}{\Theta^2} = (\phi - \alpha)(\phi - \beta)\frac{d\phi^2}{\Phi^2}$$

is satisfied; thus the unicursal septic and its projection, a unicursal 16-thic (p. 116, note), are both asymptotic lines.

43. Another method of determining the functions $\wp_{22}(2u)$, etc., is as follows; if in the equation

$$\frac{\sigma(v+u)\,\sigma(v-u)}{\sigma^2(v)\,\sigma^2(u)} = \wp_{22}(v)\,\wp_{21}(u) - \wp_{21}(v)\,\wp_{22}(u) + \wp_{11}(u) - \wp_{11}(v)$$

we put $v_1 = u_1 + t_1$, $v_2 = u_2 + t_2$, where t_1, t_2 are small, and equate the coefficients of t_1 and t_2, we shall have, from the coefficient of t_2, the identity

$$y\xi - x\eta = \zeta,$$

where $x = \wp_{22}(u)$, $\xi = \wp_{222}(u)$, etc., and from the coefficient of t_1,

$$\frac{\sigma(2u)}{\sigma^4(u)} = y\eta - x\zeta - \tau, \;= M, \text{ say};$$

taking second logarithmic differential coefficients of this we infer

$$\wp_{22}(2u) = \frac{4xM^2 - MM_{22} + M_2^2}{4M^2}, \quad \wp_{21}(2u) = \frac{4yM^2 - MM_{21} + M_2M_1}{4M^2},$$

$$\wp_{11}(2u) = \frac{4zM^2 - MM_{11} + M_1^2}{4M^2}.$$

Now (pp. 39, 41)

$$M^2 = y^2\eta^2 + x^2\zeta^2 + \tau^2 - 2xy\eta\zeta - 2y\eta\tau + 2x\zeta\tau$$

$$= -\tfrac{1}{4}\begin{vmatrix} -\lambda_0 & \tfrac{1}{2}\lambda_1 & 2z & -2y & 0 \\ \tfrac{1}{2}\lambda_1 & -(\lambda_2 + 4z) & \tfrac{1}{2}\lambda_3 + 2y & 2x & -y \\ 2z & \tfrac{1}{2}\lambda_3 + 2y & -(\lambda_4 + 4x) & 2 & x \\ -2y & 2x & 2 & 0 & 1 \\ 0 & -y & x & 1 & 0 \end{vmatrix}$$

is an integral polynomial of degree 4, in fact equal to

$$\tfrac{1}{16}(\lambda_1^2\lambda_4 + \lambda_0\lambda_3^2 - 4\lambda_0\lambda_2\lambda_4) + (\tfrac{1}{2}\lambda_1^2 - 2\lambda_0\lambda_2)\,x + \lambda_0\lambda_3 y + (\tfrac{1}{4}\lambda_1\lambda_3 - \lambda_0\lambda_4)\,z$$
$$- \tfrac{1}{2}\lambda_0\lambda_3 x^2 + (\lambda_0\lambda_4 + \tfrac{1}{4}\lambda_1\lambda_3)\,xy + (4\lambda_0 - \tfrac{1}{2}\lambda_1\lambda_4)\,y^2 - 8\lambda_0 xz + 2\lambda_1 yz + \lambda_2 z^2$$
$$+ 4\lambda_0 x^2 y - 2\lambda_1 xy^2 - z(\lambda_1 x^2 - 2\lambda_2 xy + \lambda_3 y^2) + 4z^3 + \lambda_0 x^4 - \lambda_1 x^3 y + \lambda_2 x^2 y^2$$
$$- \lambda_3 xy^3 + \lambda_4 y^4 - 4y^3 z + 4yz(xz - y^2),$$

and it is found on computation that this is the same, identically, as

$$-\tfrac{1}{8}[Q_1\wp_{2222}(u) + Q_2\wp_{2221}(u) + Q_3\wp_{2211}(u)] + \tfrac{1}{16}\Delta(8x + \lambda_4),$$

where $\tfrac{1}{16}\Delta$ is the vanishing expression, given p. 41, wherein the highest terms are $(xz-y^2)^2$. Further, differentiating the identity $y\xi - x\eta - \zeta = 0$ in regard to u_1 we find

$$-y\wp_{2221} + x\wp_{2211} + \wp_{2111} = \zeta\xi - \eta^2,$$

and hence

$$M_2 = -2(\zeta\xi - \eta^2), \quad M_1 = y\wp_{2211} - x\wp_{2111} - \wp_{1111},$$

$$M_{22} = -2(\xi\wp_{2211} - 2\eta\wp_{2221} + \zeta\wp_{2222}), \quad M_{21} = -2(\xi\wp_{2111} - 2\eta\wp_{2211} + \zeta\wp_{2221}),$$

while

$$M_{11} = \zeta\wp_{2211} - \eta\wp_{2111} + y\wp_{22111} - x\wp_{21111} - \wp_{11111},$$

so that each of M_2, M_1 is a rational polynomial in x, y, z, and each of M_{22}, M_{21}, M_{11} is a linear function of ξ, η, ζ, τ with coefficients rational in x, y, z; as the squares and products of ξ, η, ζ, τ are rational in x, y, z, we can express each of $\wp_{22}(2u)$, $\wp_{21}(2u)$, $\wp_{11}(2u)$ rationally in x, y, z. We do not develop the expressions.

44. We have seen (p. 114) that if $\pm w$ be any point of the Kummer surface, and (t) be either of the places of the Riemann surface determined by

$$\left.\begin{aligned} t^2 - t\wp_{22}(2w) - \wp_{21}(2w) &= 0 \\ s = t\wp_{222}(2w) + \wp_{221}(2w) & \end{aligned}\right\}, \text{ or, say, by } 2w \equiv u^{t,\,a} + u^{t_1,\,a},$$

then the other points of contact of the bitangents through $\pm w$ have arguments $\pm(w + u^{\theta,\,t})$, where θ is in turn one of the roots of the fundamental sextic (including infinity or $\theta = a$). We have also seen that

$$\wp_{22}(2w) = \wp_{22}(2w + 2u^{a,\,t}), \quad \wp_{21}(2w) = \wp_{21}(2w + 2u^{a,\,t});$$

as $u^{\theta,\,t} = u^{a,\,t} + u^{\theta,\,a} = u^{a,\,t} +$ half period, the functions $\wp_{22}(2w)$, $\wp_{21}(2w)$ have the same value at w as at each of the six derived points. If $\pm v$ be one of these six points we have

$$2v \equiv 2w + 2u^{\theta,\,t} \equiv u^{t,\,\theta} + u^{t_1,\,\theta} - 2u^{t,\,\theta} = -u^{t,\,\theta} + u^{t_1,\,\theta} = u^{t',\,\theta} + u^{t_1,\,\theta},$$

where (t') is the conjugate place of the Riemann surface to (t). Thus the place of the Riemann surface associated with v as is (t) with w is the place (t'), and when we derive from v as we derived from w, we obtain places

$$v + u^{\phi,\,t'} \equiv w + u^{\theta,\,t} - u^{\phi,\,t} \equiv w + u^{\theta,\,\phi},$$

that is places (including w itself) whose arguments differ from that of w by half periods. The transformation from w to v is in fact that given by the transformation A_r (p. 79), and the next step gives places of the Kummer surface derived by the transformations $A_r^{-1}A_s$. We thus get on the whole 32 places, as on p. 81. For each of these 32 places the functions $\wp_{22}(2u)$, $\wp_{21}(2u)$ have the same value, and they are invariants of the group of 32 birational transformations.

For the Weddle surface the transformations are equivalent only to projections from the six nodes in turn. Putting

$$U_{\phi\psi} = \phi\psi\xi + (\phi + \psi)\eta + \zeta,$$

$$U_{\theta\phi\psi} = \theta\phi\psi\xi + (\phi\psi + \psi\theta + \theta\phi)\eta + (\theta + \phi + \psi)\eta + \zeta, \text{ etc.},$$

where the six nodes are

$(0, 0, 0, 1)$, $(1, -\theta, \theta^2, -\theta^3)$, $(1, -\phi, \ldots)$, $(1, -\psi, \ldots)$, $(1, -m, \ldots)$, $(1, -n, \ldots)$, and putting

$$X = \frac{(\theta - m)\, U_{\phi\psi}}{U_{\theta\phi\psi}}, \quad Y = \frac{(\phi - m)\, U_{\psi\theta}}{U_{\theta\phi\psi}}, \quad Z = \frac{(\psi - m)\, U_{\theta\phi}}{U_{\theta\phi\psi}},$$

with
$$a = \frac{\theta - m}{\theta - n}, \quad b = \frac{\phi - m}{\phi - n}, \quad c = \frac{\psi - m}{\psi - n},$$

the Weddle surface has nodes at $(0, 0, 0)$, at the infinite ends of the axes of X, Y, Z, at $(1, 1, 1)$ and at (a, b, c), its equation takes a simple form, and the coordinates of the transformed points can be explicitly expressed without much difficulty. Regarding X, Y, Z as rectangular Cartesian coordinates, the 32 points are the corners of four rectangular parallelepipeds; one of these is obtained from the original point (X, Y, Z) by projections from the three infinite nodes θ, ϕ, ψ, the others are obtained respectively from (X_0, Y_0, Z_0), (X_1, Y_1, Z_1), (X_a, Y_a, Z_a), also by projections from these infinite nodes, where (X_0, Y_0, Z_0) is the point obtained from (X, Y, Z) by projection from the node $(0, 0, 0)$, and similarly (X_1, Y_1, Z_1) and (X_a, Y_a, Z_a) are obtained from (X, Y, Z) by projection from the nodes $(1, 1, 1)$, (a, b, c). It is found that there are two rational functions H, K of the coordinates X, Y, Z which have the same value at all the corners of the first rectangular parallelepiped, have also the same values, respectively $\frac{1}{H}$, $\frac{1}{K}$, at the corners of the second rectangular parallelepiped, have also the same values, respectively K, H, at the third set of eight corners, and finally have the same values, respectively $\frac{1}{K}$, $\frac{1}{H}$, at the last set of eight corners. Thus any symmetric function of the four quantities H, $\frac{1}{H}$, K, $\frac{1}{K}$ has the same value at each of the 32 points, and it would be an interesting problem to express $\wp_{22}(2u)$, $\wp_{21}(2u)$ each in this way; if this is possible. The function H, in terms of our original coordinates, is

$$\frac{(\theta - m)(\phi - m)(\psi - m)}{(\theta - n)(\phi - n)(\psi - n)} \frac{U_{mn} U_{\phi\psi} U_{\psi\theta} U_{\theta\phi}}{(\zeta\xi - \eta^2)\, U^2_{\theta\phi\psi}},$$

which then has the same value for all the eight arguments

$$w, \quad w + u^{\theta, t}, \quad w + u^{\phi, t}, \quad w + u^{\psi, t},$$
$$w + u^{\theta, \phi}, \quad w + u^{\phi, \psi}, \quad w + u^{\theta, \psi}, \quad w + u^{\theta, \phi} + u^{\psi, t}.$$

We have, as remarked in an Example given below,

$$U^2_{\theta\phi} = 4 P_\theta P_\phi P_{\theta\phi}, \quad U^2_{\theta\phi\psi} = 4 P_{\phi\psi} P_{\psi\theta} P_{\theta\phi},$$

where
$$P_\theta = y + \theta x - \theta^2, \quad P_{\theta\phi} = \theta\phi x + (\theta + \phi) y + z - e_{\theta\phi},$$

so that H can be expressed (irrationally) in terms of x, y, z.

We do not pursue this matter. See *Proc. Lond. Math. Soc.* (1903–4), Ser. 2, Vol. I. p. 247, where the formulae are given at length.

45. The formula

$$\frac{\sigma(u+v)\,\sigma(u-v)}{\sigma^2(u)\,\sigma^2(v)} = \wp_{22}(u)\,\wp_{21}(v) - \wp_{21}(u)\,\wp_{22}(v) + \wp_{11}(v) - \wp_{11}(u)$$

can be used to obtain the expressions for the functions

$$\wp_{22}(u+v), \quad \wp_{21}(u+v), \quad \wp_{11}(u+v)$$

in terms of functions of u and v.

Let $\wp_{22}(u) = x$, etc., $\wp_{22}(v) = x_1$, etc., $\wp_{222}(u) = \xi$, etc., $\wp_{222}(v) = \xi_1$, etc.,

and
$$M = xy_1 - x_1 y + z_1 - z;$$

differentiating logarithmically in regard to u_2 and v_2, and adding the results, we have

$$\zeta_2(u+v) - \zeta_2(u) - \zeta_2(v) = \frac{1}{2}\left(\frac{\partial M}{\partial u_2} + \frac{\partial M}{\partial v_2}\right)\Big/ M;$$

differentiating this in regard to u_2 and v_2, and subtracting and adding the results, we get

$$M\left\{\frac{\partial^2 M}{\partial u_2^2} - \frac{\partial^2 M}{\partial v_2^2}\right\} - \left\{\left(\frac{\partial M}{\partial u_2}\right)^2 - \left(\frac{\partial M}{\partial v_2}\right)^2\right\} = 2M^2(x - x_1),$$

and
$$4M^2\{\wp_{22}(u+v) + \wp_{22}(u) + \wp_{22}(v)\} = P + Q,$$

where
$$P = \left(\frac{\partial M}{\partial u_2}\right)^2 + \left(\frac{\partial M}{\partial v_2}\right)^2 - M\left(\frac{\partial^2 M}{\partial u_2^2} + \frac{\partial^2 M}{\partial v_2^2}\right) + 6M^2(x + x_1),$$

$$Q = 2\left(\frac{\partial M}{\partial u_2}\frac{\partial M}{\partial v_2} - M\frac{\partial^2 M}{\partial u_2 \partial v_2}\right);$$

we have
$$\frac{\partial M}{\partial u_2} = y_1\xi - x_1\eta - \zeta = (y_1 - y)\,\xi - (x_1 - x)\,\eta,$$

$$\frac{\partial^2 M}{\partial u_2^2} = (y_1 - y)\,\wp_{2222}(u) - (x_1 - x)\,\wp_{2221}(u),$$

$$\frac{\partial^2 M}{\partial u_2 \partial v_2} = \xi\eta_1 - \xi_1\eta,$$

so that P is expressible rationally in x, y, z, x_1, y_1, z_1, and both P and Q can be expressed, of course, rationally in x, y, ξ and x_1, y_1, ξ_1. Similar formulae can be found for $\wp_{21}(u+v)$ and $\wp_{11}(u+v)$.

Or we may adopt another method. Let

$$u \equiv u^{\theta_1, a} + u^{\theta_2, a}, \quad v \equiv u^{\theta_3, a} + u^{\theta_4, a}, \quad w \equiv u^{\theta_5, a} + u^{\theta_6, a},$$

and
$$u + v + w \equiv 0;$$

there exists then on the Riemann surface a rational function of order six having its poles at infinity, and vanishing in (θ_1), (θ_2), (θ_3), (θ_4), (θ_5), (θ_6) (see Appendix to Part I., Note II.); say this is

$$t^3 - \nu t^2 + \mu t - \lambda + \rho s,$$

where $s^2 = f(t)$; the coefficients ν, μ, λ, ρ are then found from four equations such as

$$\theta_i^3 - \nu\theta_i^2 + \mu\theta_i - \lambda + \rho\Theta_i = 0, \qquad i = 1,\ 2,\ 3,\ 4,$$

where Θ_i is the value of s at the place (θ_i) of the Riemann surface; and when the function is found, the places (θ_5), (θ_6) are determined without ambiguity; there exists then the identity in t

$$(t^3 - \nu t^2 + \mu t - \lambda)^2 - \rho^2 f(t) = \phi(t),$$

where $\phi(t)$ is the product of the six factors $t - \theta_i$, and, since

$$\wp_{22}(u) = \theta_1 + \theta_2, \quad \wp_{22}(v) = \theta_3 + \theta_4, \quad \wp_{22}(w) = \theta_5 + \theta_6,$$

we have
$$\wp_{22}(u+v) + \wp_{22}(u) + \wp_{22}(v) = 2\nu + 4\rho^2,$$

where in ν, ρ, determined as above, we are to substitute

$$\theta_1 + \theta_2 = \wp_{22}(u), \quad \theta_1\theta_2 = -\wp_{21}(u), \quad \theta_3 + \theta_4 = \wp_{22}(v), \quad \theta_3\theta_4 = -\wp_{21}(v),$$
$$\Theta_1 = \theta_1\wp_{222}(u) + \wp_{221}(u), \quad \Theta_2 = \theta_2\wp_{222}(u) + \wp_{221}(u),$$
$$\Theta_3 = \theta_3\wp_{222}(v) + \wp_{221}(v), \quad \Theta_4 = \theta_4\wp_{222}(v) + \wp_{221}(v).$$

The functions $\wp_{21}(u+v)$, $\wp_{11}(u+v)$ can also be calculated, their values $-\theta_5\theta_6$, E_{θ_5,θ_6} or $\frac{1}{4}[F(\theta_5, \theta_6) - 2\Theta_5\Theta_6]/(\theta_5 - \theta_6)^2$, being determined by the knowledge of the remaining zeros of the rational function above.

The relations are capable of important geometrical interpretation. Consider the six points $(1, -\theta_i, \theta_i^2, -\theta_i^3)$ upon the cubic space curve, each being associated with its proper quantity Θ_i, definite in sign, as above. Denoting by $b_1, b_2, \ldots, b_5$ the roots of $f(t)$, the identity above gives

$$b_i^3 - \nu b_i^2 + \mu b_i - \lambda = \sqrt{\phi(b_i)};$$

the right side we may denote by Φ_i; it is definite when λ, μ, ν are determined. The plane

$$\lambda\xi + \mu\eta + \nu\zeta + \tau = 0$$

passes then through the fifteen points of the Weddle surface such as

$$\left(\frac{1}{\Theta_i} - \frac{1}{\Theta_j},\ \frac{-\theta_i}{\Theta_i} + \frac{\theta_j}{\Theta_j},\ \frac{\theta_i^2}{\Theta_i} - \frac{\theta_j^2}{\Theta_j},\ \frac{-\theta_i^3}{\Theta_i} + \frac{\theta_j^3}{\Theta_j}\right),$$

which we may call the point (θ_i, θ_j), and also through fifteen points

$$\left(\frac{1}{\Phi_i} - \frac{1}{\Phi_j},\ \frac{-b_i}{\Phi_i} + \frac{b_j}{\Phi_j},\ \frac{b_i^2}{\Phi_i} - \frac{b_j^2}{\Phi_j},\ \frac{-b_i^3}{\Phi_i} + \frac{b_j^3}{\Phi_j}\right),\ \left(\frac{1}{\Phi_i},\ \frac{-b_i}{\Phi_i},\ \frac{b_i^2}{\Phi_i},\ \frac{-b_i^3}{\Phi_i} + 1\right),$$

and is thus symmetrical in regard to the two sets of six points $(\theta_1, \ldots, \theta_6)$, $(b_1, \ldots, b_5, \infty)$, lying on the cubic curve. In particular it cuts the edges of the tetrahedron $(\theta_1, \theta_2, \theta_3, \theta_4)$ in six points lying on four straight lines, since the points (θ_1, θ_2), (θ_2, θ_3), (θ_3, θ_1) are manifestly collinear. It can now be proved that, to every quadric surface through one of the sets of six points, corresponds a quadric through the other set of six points, touching the former quadric along a conic lying on the plane $\lambda\xi + \mu\eta + \nu\zeta + \tau = 0$*.

To see this in the simplest way, put

$$\xi = X + Y + Z + T, \qquad \eta = -(\theta_1 X + \theta_2 Y + \theta_3 Z + \theta_4 T),$$
$$\zeta = \theta_1^2 X + \theta_2^2 Y + \theta_3^2 Z + \theta_4^2 T, \quad \tau = -(\theta_1^3 X + \theta_2^3 Y + \theta_3^3 Z + \theta_4^3 T),$$

giving

$$-(\theta_1 - \theta_2)(\theta_1 - \theta_3)(\theta_1 - \theta_4) X = \theta_2\theta_3\theta_4\xi + (\theta_2\theta_3 + \theta_2\theta_4 + \theta_3\theta_4)\eta + (\theta_2 + \theta_3 + \theta_4)\zeta + \tau,$$

and so on, so that $X = 0$, $Y = 0$, $Z = 0$, $T = 0$ are the faces of the tetrahedron $\theta_1, \theta_2, \theta_3, \theta_4$; substituting in

$$Q = 4x(\eta\tau - \zeta^2) + 4y(\eta\zeta - \xi\tau) + 4z(\zeta\xi - \eta^2)$$
$$- \lambda_0\xi^2 + \lambda_1\xi\eta - \lambda_2\eta^2 + \lambda_3\eta\zeta - \lambda_4\zeta^2 + 4\zeta\tau,$$

it is at once found that this reduces to

$$Q = -(\Theta_1 X + \Theta_2 Y + \Theta_3 Z + \Theta_4 T)^2 + 4\Sigma YZ(\theta_2 - \theta_3)^2 P_{\theta_2, \theta_3} \ldots\ldots (\text{I}),$$

where $$P_{\theta_2, \theta_3} = \theta_2\theta_3 x + (\theta_2 + \theta_3) y + z - \frac{F(\theta_2, \theta_3) - 2\Theta_2\Theta_3}{4(\theta_2 - \theta_3)^2};$$

now, for the point (θ_i, θ_j), if the difference $\theta_i - \theta_j$ be denoted by (ij), we have

$$(14)(24)(34)\, T = \frac{(1i)(2i)(3i)}{\Theta_i} - \frac{(1j)(2j)(3j)}{\Theta_j},$$

and so on; thus for the point (θ_1, θ_4) we have

$$(21)(31)(41)\, X = \frac{(21)(31)(41)}{\Theta_1}, \quad Y = 0, \quad Z = 0,$$
$$(14)(24)(34)\, T = -\frac{(14)(24)(34)}{\Theta_4},$$

so that this point, and similarly the other points (θ_2, θ_4), (θ_3, θ_4), and generally, all the points (θ_i, θ_j), lie upon the plane $\Theta_1 X + \Theta_2 Y + \Theta_3 Z + \Theta_4 T = 0$, which is therefore the same as $\lambda\xi + \mu\eta + \nu\zeta + \tau = 0$. Thus, considering the particular case of the identity (I) in which the current point is upon the cubic curve, namely putting $\xi, \eta, \zeta, \tau = 1, -t, t^2, -t^3$, we have the identity

$$f(t) = A(t^3 - \nu t^2 + \mu t - \lambda)^2 + B(t - \theta_1)(t - \theta_2)(t - \theta_3)(t - \theta_4)(t - \theta_5')(t - \theta_6'),$$

* The condition for a quadric surface to reduce to the square of a plane is the vanishing of all minors of two rows and columns in the discriminantal matrix of the quadric; and the conditions for a symmetrical matrix of n rows that all minors of $n - r$ rows and columns vanish are $\frac{1}{2}(r+1)(r+2)$ in number [Sylvester, *Coll. Papers*, Vol. I. p. 147]. Thus through four arbitrary points a determinate number, in fact 8, quadrics can be drawn to have plane contact with an arbitrary quadric.

where A, B are certain constants, and θ_5', θ_6' are the remaining intersections, other than $\theta_1, \theta_2, \theta_3, \theta_4$, of the quadric

$$R = \Sigma YZ(\theta_2 - \theta_3)^2 P_{\theta_2, \theta_3} = 0$$

with the cubic curve; as this identity is of the same form as that originally deduced from Abel's theorem, we infer that θ_5', θ_6' are the same as θ_5, θ_6, and have so proved the theorem. And this, to resume, is equivalent to the statement: *Let* $\pm u$, $\pm v$ *be two arbitrary points of the Weddle surface,* P', Q' *their projections from the node* (0, 0, 0, 1); *let* θ_1, θ_2 *be the extremities of the chord of the cubic through* P', *and* θ_3, θ_4 *the extremities of the chord through* Q'; *the arguments* $\pm u$, $\pm v$ *determine definite signs for the associated radicals* Θ_1, Θ_2, Θ_3, Θ_4, *and so determine a definite plane* ϖ *through the three points*

$$(\Theta_2 - \Theta_1, -\theta_1\Theta_2 + \theta_2\Theta_1, \ldots), \quad (\Theta_4 - \Theta_3, -\theta_3\Theta_4 + \theta_4\Theta_3, \ldots),$$
$$(\Theta_3 - \Theta_1, -\theta_1\Theta_3 + \theta_3\Theta_1, \ldots);$$

taking then any quadric Q *through the nodes of the Weddle surface, there is a definite quadric* R *through the four points* $(\theta_1, \theta_2, \theta_3, \theta_4)$ *having contact with* Q *along a conic lying on this plane* ϖ; *all these quadrics* R, *as* Q *varies, intersect the cubic curve again in the same two points* θ_5, θ_6; *with proper signs for* Θ_5, Θ_6, *the point* $\pm(u + v)$ *is the projection, from the node* (0, 0, 0, 1), *of the point* $(\Theta_6 - \Theta_5, -\theta_5\Theta_6 + \theta_6\Theta_5, \ldots)$. The complete geometrical figure, allowing all possibilities for the signs of Θ_1, Θ_2, Θ_3, Θ_4, will involve 8 planes; each quadric Q will have plane contact with 8 quadrics R through the four points $\theta_1, \theta_2, \theta_3, \theta_4$, and there will be 8 resulting pairs of points θ_5, θ_6; the 8 planes give two tetrahedra which with the tetrahedron $\theta_1, \theta_2, \theta_3, \theta_4$ are in fourfold perspective; but we refrain from further consideration of the general figure. The points θ_5, θ_6, by substituting

$$(21)(31)(41)X = (\theta_2 - t)(\theta_3 - t)(\theta_4 - t), \text{ etc.},$$

in the quadric R, are found from the quadratic equation

$$\Sigma(\theta_2 - \theta_3)(\theta_1 - \theta_4)[E_{\theta_2, \theta_3}(t - \theta_1)(t - \theta_4) + E_{\theta_1, \theta_4}(t - \theta_2)(t - \theta_3)] = 0,$$

where $$E_{\theta, \phi} = \tfrac{1}{4}[F(\theta, \phi) - 2\Theta\Phi]/(\theta - \phi)^2.$$

The quadric R is of the form

$$xR_1 + yR_2 + zR_3 + S = 0,$$

where

$$R_1 = 4\Sigma(\theta_2 - \theta_3)^2 \theta_2\theta_3 YZ, \quad R_2 = 4\Sigma(\theta_2 - \theta_3)^2(\theta_2 + \theta_3)YZ, \quad R_3 = 4\Sigma(\theta_2 - \theta_3)^2 YZ$$

are the same as Q_1, Q_2, Q_3, and pass through the cubic curve, while

$$S = -4\Sigma(\theta_2 - \theta_3)^2 E_{\theta_2\theta_3} YZ$$
$$= -\Sigma[F(\theta_2, \theta_3) - 2\Theta_2\Theta_3]YZ,$$

contains the six points $\theta_1, \ldots, \theta_6$. The quadric R, written momentarily in the form

$$fYZ + gZX + hXY + uXT + vYT + wZT = 0,$$

will be a cone if

$$\begin{vmatrix} 0 & h & g & u \\ h & 0 & f & v \\ g & f & 0 & w \\ u & v & w & 0 \end{vmatrix} = 0,$$

or

$$\sqrt{uf} + \sqrt{vg} + \sqrt{wh} = 0,$$

so that

$$\Sigma (\theta_1 - \theta_4)(\theta_2 - \theta_3) \sqrt{P_{\theta_1, \theta_4} P_{\theta_2, \theta_3}} = 0,$$

represents, with x, y, z as current coordinates, a Kummer surface.

Of this P_{θ_2, θ_3}, P_{θ_1, θ_4}, etc., are six tropes, and therefore as the quadric R is symmetrical in regard to the six points $\theta_1, \dots, \theta_6$, fifteen tropes are given by the fifteen tangent planes $P_{\theta_i, \theta_j} = 0$ of the original Kummer surface; the plane P_{θ_i, θ_j} touches the original Kummer surface at the point satellite to $(u^{a, \theta_i} + u^{a, \theta_j})$. The planes P_{θ_2, θ_3}, P_{θ_3, θ_1}, P_{θ_1, θ_2} meet the plane at infinity in the chords joining the points u^{a, θ_1}, u^{a, θ_2}, u^{a, θ_3}, and since

$$u^{a, \theta_1} + u^{a, \theta_2} + u^{a, \theta_3} - (u^{a, \theta_2} + u^{a, \theta_3}) = u^{a, \theta_1},$$

the point $u^{a, \theta_1} + u^{a, \theta_2} + u^{a, \theta_3}$ lies upon the plane P_{θ_2, θ_3}, and hence is the intersection of P_{θ_2, θ_3}, P_{θ_3, θ_1}, P_{θ_1, θ_2}, and therefore a node of the new Kummer surface: from the relation

$$u^{a, \theta_1} + u^{a, \theta_2} + u^{a, \theta_3} + u^{a, \theta_4} + u^{a, \theta_5} + u^{a, \theta_6} = 0,$$

connecting six points on the conic at infinity $zx - y^2 = 0$, the planes P_{θ_4, θ_5}, P_{θ_5, θ_6}, P_{θ_4, θ_6} also pass through this point; and thus ten nodes of the new Kummer surface are determined by dividing the six points $\theta_1, \dots, \theta_6$ into two sets of three in all possible ways. Further the point at infinity

$$x/1 = -y/\theta_1 = z/\theta_1^2 = \infty$$

reduces, save for the infinite factor, each of P_{θ_1, θ_4}, P_{θ_1, θ_2}, P_{θ_1, θ_3}, or say, reduces each of u, h, g in

$$u^2 f^2 + v^2 g^2 + w^2 h^2 - 2vwgh - 2wuhf - 2uvfg,$$

to zero, and is thus a node of the new Kummer surface; thus we have six other nodes, at infinity, and the remaining trope, the plane at infinity, of the new Kummer surface, which has thus a singular conic common with the original Kummer surface.

By eliminating x, y, z from the four equations such as

$$hY + gZ + uT = 0$$

we can form the equation of the corresponding Weddle surface, having $\theta_1, \dots, \theta_6$ as nodes, which thus appears as the locus of the poles of the plane $\lambda\xi + \mu\eta + \nu\zeta + \tau = 0$ in regard to a properly chosen ∞^2 of the quadrics $xQ_1 + yQ_2 + zQ_3 + P_4 = 0$, namely the coefficients x, y, z must satisfy the relation

$$\Sigma (\theta_1 - \theta_4)(\theta_2 - \theta_3) \sqrt{P_{\theta_1, \theta_4} P_{\theta_2, \theta_3}} = 0.$$

The equation of a Weddle surface referred to four of its nodes as tetrahedron of reference is well known, and the new surface will be of the form

$$A_1 \frac{U_{\theta_5\theta_6\theta_1}}{U_{\theta_2\theta_3\theta_4}} + A_2 \frac{U_{\theta_5\theta_6\theta_2}}{U_{\theta_3\theta_1\theta_4}} + A_3 \frac{U_{\theta_5\theta_6\theta_3}}{U_{\theta_1\theta_2\theta_4}} + A_4 \frac{U_{\theta_5\theta_6\theta_4}}{U_{\theta_1\theta_2\theta_3}} = 0.$$

Denoting the quadric S, in terms of ξ, η, ζ, τ, by

$$S = -x'Q_1 - y'Q_2 - z'Q_3 - \mu_0\xi^2 + \mu_1\xi\eta - \mu_2\eta^2 + \mu_3\eta\zeta - \mu_4\zeta^2 + \mu_5\zeta\tau - \mu_6\tau^2,$$

the identity

$$P_4 = -\frac{1}{\rho^2}(\lambda\xi + \mu\eta + \nu\zeta + \tau)^2 + S$$

shews that the polar planes of any point in regard to the quadrics P_4 and S meet on the plane $\lambda\xi + \mu\eta + \nu\zeta + \tau = 0$; if in

$$-2\lambda_0\xi\xi' + \lambda_1(\xi\eta' + \xi'\eta) - 2\lambda_2\eta\eta' + \ldots = -\frac{2}{\rho^2}(\lambda\xi + \ldots)(\lambda\xi' + \ldots)$$
$$-4x'(\eta\tau' + \eta'\tau - 2\zeta\zeta') - 4y'(\eta\zeta' + \eta'\zeta - \xi\tau' - \xi'\tau) - 4z'(\zeta\xi' + \zeta'\xi - 2\eta\eta')$$
$$-2\mu_0\xi\xi' + \ldots - 2\mu_6\tau\tau'$$

we put

$$\xi = 1,\ \eta = -\theta_1,\ \zeta = \theta_1^2,\ \tau = -\theta_1^3, \text{ and } \xi' = 1,\ \eta' = -\theta_2,\ \zeta' = \theta_2^2,\ \tau' = -\theta_2^3,$$

we obtain

$$-F(\theta_1, \theta_2) = -2\Theta_1\Theta_2 - 4(\theta_1 - \theta_2)^2[x'\theta_1\theta_2 + y'(\theta_1 + \theta_2) + z']$$
$$-\sum_{i=0}^{3}(\theta_1\theta_2)^i[2\mu_{2i} + \mu_{2i+1}(\theta_1 + \theta_2)],$$

whereby the tangent plane of the original Kummer surface,

$$\theta_1\theta_2 x + (\theta_1 + \theta_2)y + z - \frac{F(\theta_1, \theta_2) - 2\Theta_1\Theta_2}{4(\theta_1 - \theta_2)^2} = 0,$$

at once takes the form

$$\theta_1\theta_2(x - x') + (\theta_1 + \theta_2)(y - y') + z - z' - \frac{G(\theta_1, \theta_2)}{4(\theta_1 - \theta_2)^2} = 0,$$

proper for a singular tangent plane of the new Kummer surface; with this notation also, the equation of the new Weddle surface will differ only from that of the old in the substitution of $\mu_0, \mu_1, \ldots$ for $\lambda_0, \lambda_1, \ldots$; denoting them by Ω, Ω' we have then, since Ω is linear in $\lambda_0, \lambda_1, \lambda_2, \ldots$ (see pp. 78 and 67),

$$\Omega - \Omega' = \frac{\partial H}{\partial\xi}\frac{\partial F}{\partial\tau} - \frac{1}{3}\frac{\partial H}{\partial\eta}\frac{\partial F}{\partial\zeta} + \frac{1}{3}\frac{\partial H}{\partial\zeta}\frac{\partial F}{\partial\eta} - \frac{\partial H}{\partial\tau}\frac{\partial F}{\partial\xi},$$

where $$H = -\frac{1}{\rho^2}(\lambda\xi + \mu\eta + \nu\zeta + \tau)^2 - x'Q_1 - y'Q_2 - z'Q_3,$$

viz. $$\Omega - \Omega' = -\frac{2}{\rho^2}(\lambda\xi + \mu\eta + \nu\zeta + \tau)\left(\lambda\frac{\partial F}{\partial\tau} - \tfrac{1}{3}\mu\frac{\partial F}{\partial\zeta} + \tfrac{1}{3}\nu\frac{\partial F}{\partial\eta} - \frac{\partial F}{\partial\xi}\right);$$

thus the two Weddle surfaces cut (i) in the cubic curve, which is an asymptotic line upon each, so that the surfaces touch along this curve, (ii) in a plane quartic curve lying upon $\lambda\xi + \mu\eta + \nu\zeta + \tau = 0$, (iii) upon the first polar, in regard to the developable quartic surface $F = 0$, of the pole of the plane $\lambda\xi + \mu\eta + \nu\eta + \zeta = 0$ in the linear complex $l + 3l' = 0$, previously noticed (p. 67); beside the cubic, which is an asymptotic line on this first polar, this gives a sextic curve.

It would be interesting to follow out the relations between these Weddle surfaces corresponding to the relations between the associated Kummer surfaces; we refrain from this. But when $\theta_1 = \theta_3 = \theta$ and $\theta_2 = \theta_4 = \phi$, the arguments u, v become equal, the plane $\Theta_1 X + \ldots = 0$, passing through the points

$$\left[\frac{1}{\Theta} - \frac{1}{\Phi}, \frac{-\theta}{\Theta} + \frac{\phi}{\Phi}, \ldots\right], \quad \left[\frac{\partial}{\partial\theta}\left(\frac{1}{\Theta}\right), \frac{\partial}{\partial\theta}\left(\frac{-\theta}{\Theta}\right), \ldots\right],$$
$$\left[\frac{\partial}{\partial\phi}\left(\frac{1}{\Phi}\right), \frac{\partial}{\partial\phi}\left(\frac{-\phi}{\Phi}\right), \ldots\right],$$

becomes the tangent plane of the Weddle surface at the first point, and the figure becomes that previously considered in determining the functions $\wp_{22}(2u), \ldots$ (p. 123). For that case, with the notation previously used, the new Kummer and Weddle surfaces are to be determined from the quadric

$$R = (x - x')\,Q_1 + (y - y')\,Q_2 + (z - z')\,Q_3$$
$$+ \frac{1}{\rho^2}(A\xi + B\eta + C\zeta + \tau)(A'\xi + B'\eta + C'\zeta + \tau),$$

where the last term represents the product of the tangent planes of the cone $x'Q_1 + y'Q_2 + z'Q_3 + P_4 = 0$ which pass through the chord θ, ϕ of the cubic.

It is possible to determine a new Weddle surface with six arbitrary points of the cubic $\theta_1, \ldots, \theta_6$ as nodes; this intersects the original in a curve of the tenth degree, beside touching it along the cubic. See Darboux, *Bull. des Sc. Math.* I. (1870), p. 357; Bateman, *Proc. Lond. Math. Soc.* III. (1905), p. 237.

It is possible in another way to determine a new Kummer surface with nodes upon the old one, and tropes touching the old one, the two surfaces touching along an octavic curve (Klein, *Math. Annal.* XXVII. (1886), p. 136; Rohn, *Math. Annal.* XV. (1879), pp. 350—352; Reye, *Crelle*, XCVII. (1884), p. 248; Hudson, *Kummer's Quartic Surface*, p. 159); taking each of ϵ_1, ϵ_2, ϵ_3, ϵ_4 to be ± 1, and $\theta_1, \ldots, \theta_6$ arbitrarily, the nodes are the sixteen points

$$\tfrac{1}{2}\left(u^{a,\theta_1} + \epsilon_1 u^{a,\theta_2} + \epsilon_2 u^{a,\theta_3} + \epsilon_3 u^{a,\theta_4} + \epsilon_4 u^{a,\theta_5} - \epsilon_1\epsilon_2\epsilon_3\epsilon_4 u^{a,\theta_6}\right),$$

and the tropes are the tangent planes of the original Kummer surface touching at the points satellite to

$$\tfrac{1}{2}\left(u^{a,\theta_1} + \epsilon_1 u^{a,\theta_2} + \epsilon_2 u^{a,\theta_3} + \epsilon_3 u^{a,\theta_4} + \epsilon_4 u^{a,\theta_5} + \epsilon_1\epsilon_2\epsilon_3\epsilon_4 u^{a,\theta_6}\right).$$

After Reichardt, *Nova Acta Leopoldina*, L. 1887, p. 476, the octavic curves of contact of the ∞^6 Kummer surfaces so obtainable are given, in our notation, by

$$m + m_1 [\wp_{21}(2u) + b_1\wp_{22}(2u) - b_1^2]^{\frac{1}{2}} + \ldots + m_5 [\wp_{21}(2u) + b_5\wp_{22}(2u) - b_5^2]^{\frac{1}{2}} = 0,$$

where $m, m_1, \ldots, m_5$ are arbitrary, and $b_1, \ldots, b_5$ are the roots of the quintic $f(t) = 0$.

46. The equation expressing the functions $\wp_{222}(u)$, etc. in terms of the functions $\wp_{22}(u)$, etc., of pp. 39, 59, is in connexion with the theory of certain cubic surfaces with four nodes, which touch the Kummer surface along sextic curves represented by $l_0\wp_{222}(u) + \ldots = 0$; these correspond to plane sections of the Weddle surface. As the following brief account shews, the theory of these surfaces and their reciprocal, the Steiner quartic surface, is of considerable geometrical interest.

Consider the quadric

$$xQ_1 + yQ_2 + zQ_3 + P_4 = 0,$$

where $\quad Q_1 = 4(\eta\tau - \zeta^2), \quad Q_2 = 4(\eta\zeta - \xi\tau), \quad Q_3 = 4(\zeta\xi - \eta^2),$

and $\quad P_4 = -\lambda_0\xi^2 + \lambda_1\xi\eta - \lambda_2\eta^2 + \lambda_3\eta\zeta - \lambda_4\zeta^2 + 4\zeta\tau.$

Take also an arbitrary plane

$$l_0\xi + l_1\eta + l_2\zeta + l_3\tau = 0.$$

The conditions that the quadric should touch the plane in the point $(\xi_1, \eta_1, \zeta_1, \tau_1)$ are the equations

$$x\frac{\partial Q_1}{\partial \xi_1} + y\frac{\partial Q_2}{\partial \xi_1} + z\frac{\partial Q_3}{\partial \xi_1} + \frac{\partial P_4}{\partial \xi_1} + \varpi l_0 = 0,$$

$$x\frac{\partial Q_1}{\partial \eta_1} + y\frac{\partial Q_2}{\partial \eta_1} + z\frac{\partial Q_3}{\partial \eta_1} + \frac{\partial P_4}{\partial \eta_1} + \varpi l_1 = 0,$$

$$x\frac{\partial Q_1}{\partial \zeta_1} + y\frac{\partial Q_2}{\partial \zeta_1} + z\frac{\partial Q_3}{\partial \zeta_1} + \frac{\partial P_4}{\partial \zeta_1} + \varpi l_2 = 0,$$

$$x\frac{\partial Q_1}{\partial \tau_1} + y\frac{\partial Q_2}{\partial \tau_1} + z\frac{\partial Q_3}{\partial \tau_1} + \frac{\partial P_4}{\partial \tau_1} + \varpi l_3 = 0,$$

$$l_0\xi_1 + l_1\eta_1 + l_2\zeta_1 + l_3\tau_1 = 0,$$

leading, for (x, y, z), to the sole condition

$$C = \begin{vmatrix} -\lambda_0, & \tfrac{1}{2}\lambda_1, & 2z, & -2y, & l_0 \\ \tfrac{1}{2}\lambda_1, & -(4z+\lambda_2), & \tfrac{1}{2}\lambda_3 + 2y, & 2x, & l_1 \\ 2z, & \tfrac{1}{2}\lambda_3 + 2y, & -(\lambda_4 + 4x), & 2, & l_2 \\ -2y, & 2x, & 2, & 0, & l_3 \\ l_0, & l_1, & l_2, & l_3, & 0 \end{vmatrix} = 0,$$

and, for $(\xi_1, \eta_1, \zeta_1, \tau_1)$, to no other condition than $l_0\xi_1 + l_1\eta_1 + l_2\zeta_1 + l_3\tau_1 = 0$.

If $C_{r,s}$ denote the minor of the sth element of the rth row of C, we have, to express $(\xi_1, \eta_1, \zeta_1, \tau_1)$ in terms of (x, y, z),

$$\frac{\xi_1}{C_{11}} = \frac{\eta_1}{C_{12}} = \frac{\zeta_1}{C_{13}} = \frac{\tau_1}{C_{14}},$$

where the denominators are quadric functions, and, to express (x, y, z) in terms of $(\xi_1, \eta_1, \zeta_1, \tau_1)$,

$$\frac{x}{D_1} = \frac{y}{D_2} = \frac{z}{D_3} = \frac{1}{D_4},$$

where D_1, D_2, D_3, D_4 are the determinants, with proper signs, obtained by omitting the columns in order in the matrix

$$\begin{pmatrix} 0\ , & -2\tau_1, & 2\zeta_1\ , & -\lambda_0\xi_1 + \tfrac{1}{2}\lambda_1\eta_1\ , & l_0 \\ 2\tau_1\ , & 2\zeta_1\ , & -4\eta_1, & \tfrac{1}{2}\lambda_1\xi_1 - \lambda_2\eta_1 + \tfrac{1}{2}\lambda_3\zeta_1, & l_1 \\ -4\zeta_1, & 2\eta_1\ , & 2\xi_1\ , & \tfrac{1}{2}\lambda_3\eta_1 - \lambda_4\zeta_1 + 2\tau_1\ , & l_2 \\ 2\eta_1\ , & -2\xi_1, & 0\ , & 2\zeta_1\ , & l_3 \end{pmatrix},$$

and are cubic functions. This gives a representation of the cubic surface $C = 0$ upon the plane $l_0\xi + l_1\eta + l_2\zeta + l_3\tau = 0$.

By immediate differentiation of the determinant C we have, when (x, y, z) is upon $C = 0$,

$$\frac{\partial C}{\partial x} = 4(C_{24} - C_{33}),\quad \frac{\partial C}{\partial y} = 4(C_{23} - C_{14}),\quad \frac{\partial C}{\partial z} = 4(C_{13} - C_{22}),$$

and
$$\frac{\partial C}{\partial t} = -\lambda_0 C_{11} + \lambda_1 C_{12} - \lambda_2 C_{22} + \lambda_3 C_{23} - \lambda_4 C_{33} + 4C_{34} + 2(l_0 C_{15} + l_1 C_{25} + l_2 C_{35} + l_3 C_{45}),$$

where $t\ (= 1)$ is introduced, only for differentiation, to render C homogeneous in x, y, z, t; since $C_{11}C_{rs} = C_{1r}C_{1s}$ when $C = 0$, and

$$l_0 C_{15} + l_1 C_{25} + l_2 C_{35} + l_3 C_{45} = 0,$$

we have, if we multiply by C_{11} and replace the ratios $C_{11} : C_{12} : C_{13} : C_{14}$ by $\xi_1 : \eta_1 : \zeta_1 : \tau_1$,

$$\frac{\partial C}{\partial x} : \frac{\partial C}{\partial y} : \frac{\partial C}{\partial z} : \frac{\partial C}{\partial t} = Q_1 : Q_2 : Q_3 : P_4$$

and the surface reciprocal to $C = 0$ is therefore represented upon the plane by

$$x' = Q_1/P_4,\quad y' = Q_2/P_4,\quad z' = Q_3/P_4,$$

where $Q_1 = 4(\eta_1\tau_1 - \zeta_1^2)$, etc., and is thus a quartic surface; denote it by S. In terms of the coordinates (x, y, z) of the corresponding point of the surface C, the tangent plane at any point of S is

$$xX + yY + zZ + 1 = 0,$$

where X, Y, Z are current coordinates; it thus cuts S in a locus whose representative upon the plane $l_0\xi + l_1\eta + l_2\zeta + l_3\tau = 0$ is given by

$$xQ_1 + yQ_2 + zQ_3 + P_4 = 0,$$

that is by two straight lines, since, in virtue of $C=0$, this quadric touches the plane. The curve upon S which corresponds to a straight line in the plane $l_0\xi+l_1\eta+l_2\zeta+l_3\tau=0$ is cut by any plane $AX+BY+CZ+D=0$ in as many points as is the straight line by the conic $AQ_1+BQ_2+CQ_3+P_4=0$, and is thus a conic. The surface S has thus the property of being cut by any of its tangent planes in two conics, and the reciprocal surface C has the property that its tangent cone, drawn from any point of itself, breaks up into two quadric cones. These two conics upon S will coincide, and the surface be touched by a plane at all points of a conic, if the two straight lines

$$xQ_1+yQ_2+zQ_3+P_4=0, \quad l_0\xi+l_1\eta+l_2\zeta+l_3\tau=0$$

coincide; we investigate now the condition for this: the quadric $xQ_1+\ldots=0$ must be a cone touched by $l_0\xi+\ldots=0$. Now a quadric

$$U=(a,\, b,\, c,\, d,\, f,\, g,\, h,\, u,\, v,\, w \between \xi,\, \eta,\, \zeta,\, \tau)^2$$

will be a cone, with vertex at $(\xi_0, \eta_0, \zeta_0, \tau_0)$, if the four equations

$$a\xi_0+h\eta_0+g\zeta_0+u\tau_0=0, \quad \ldots, \quad \ldots, \quad \ldots,$$

are satisfied; it will touch $l_0\xi+\ldots=0$ at $(\xi', \eta', \zeta', \tau')$ if we have the five equations

$$a\xi'+h\eta'+g\zeta'+u\tau'+\varpi l_0=0, \quad \ldots, \quad \ldots, \quad \ldots, \quad l_0\xi'+\ldots=0;$$

let the minors in

$$\Gamma=\begin{pmatrix} a, & h, & g, & u, & l_0 \\ h, & b, & f, & v, & l_1 \\ g, & f, & c, & w, & l_2 \\ u, & v, & w, & d, & l_3 \\ l_0, & l_1, & l_2, & l_3, & 0 \end{pmatrix}$$

be denoted by the corresponding capital letters; thus the determinant $|\Gamma|$ is zero and

$$\frac{\xi'}{A}=\frac{\eta'}{H}=\frac{\zeta'}{G}=\frac{\tau'}{U}=\frac{\varpi}{L_0}; \quad \frac{\xi'}{H}=\ldots=\frac{\varpi}{L_1}; \ldots$$

but from the five equations

$$a\xi_0+h\eta_0+g\zeta_0+u\tau_0=0, \quad \ldots, \quad \ldots, \quad \ldots, \quad l_0\xi_0+l_1\eta_0+\ldots=0,$$

we have $L_0=0$, as well as $L_1=0$, $L_2=0$, $L_3=0$; we infer thus that the conditions that the surface $U=0$ should be a cone touched by $l_0\xi+\ldots=0$ are that all the first minors of Γ should vanish*. This requires, according to Sylvester, three algebraically independent relations among the elements of Γ (Sylvester, *Phil. Mag.* 1850, Vol. XXXVII pp. 363—370, or *Collected*

* In another phraseology the two first invariant factors of the matrix Γ for the root zero must be both of exponent unity, a result following from the two equation sets $\Gamma(\xi', \eta', \zeta', \tau', \varpi)=0$, $\Gamma(\zeta_0, \eta_0, \zeta_0, \tau_0, 0)=0$. Cf. the theorem quoted in Appendix to Part I., Note I.

Papers, Vol. I. p. 147). Returning then to the case now being considered, the two straight lines

$$xQ_1 + yQ_2 + zQ_3 + P_4 = 0, \quad l_0\xi + l_1\eta + l_2\zeta + l_3\tau = 0,$$

will coincide if x, y, z be such as to satisfy the three conditions necessary that all the first minors of the determinant C should vanish. This agrees with the consequence that then each of $\partial C/\partial x$, $\partial C/\partial y$, $\partial C/\partial z$, $\partial C/\partial t$, which as before remarked are linear functions of these first minors, would vanish; for a singular plane of S must correspond to a double point of the reciprocal surface* C. We can further use the representation upon the plane to determine these nodes of C. Let

$$(1, -\theta, \theta^2, -\theta^3), \quad (1, -\phi, \phi^2, -\phi^3), \quad (1, -\psi, \psi^2, -\psi^3)$$

be the intersections of the plane $l_0\xi + \ldots = 0$ with the common cubic curve of the quadrics Q_1, Q_2, Q_3, so that $l_0 : l_1 : l_2 : l_3 = \theta\phi\psi : \Sigma\theta\phi : \Sigma\theta : 1$; denote

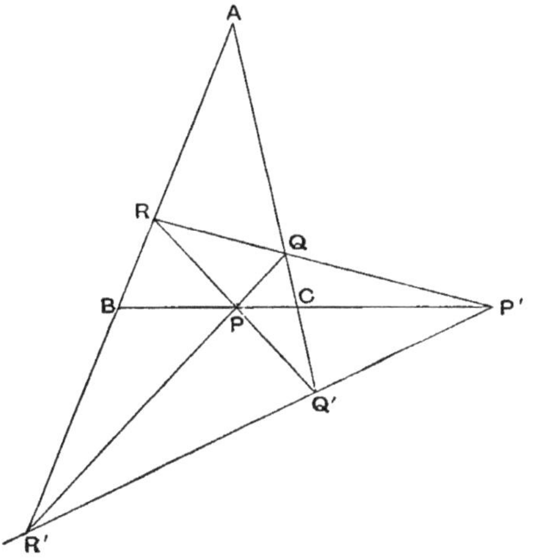

these points by A, B, C; it is found at once on computation that the Weddle surface cuts the side AB in two points P, P' of coordinates

$$(\Theta + \Phi, \ -(\Theta\phi + \Phi\theta), \ \Theta\phi^2 + \Phi\theta^2, \ -(\Theta\phi^3 + \Phi\theta^3))$$

and $$(\Theta - \Phi, \ -(\Theta\phi - \Phi\theta), \ \Theta\phi^2 - \Phi\theta^2, \ -(\Theta\phi^3 - \Phi\theta^3)),$$

where $$\Theta^2 = \lambda_0 + \lambda_1\theta + \lambda_2\theta^2 + \lambda_3\theta^3 + \lambda_4\theta^4 + 4\theta^5$$

and $$\Phi^2 = \lambda_0 + \lambda_1\phi + \lambda_2\phi^2 + \lambda_3\phi^3 + \lambda_4\phi^4 + 4\phi^5.$$

We thus have four straight lines $P'QR$, $Q'RP$, $R'PQ$, $P'Q'R'$, and the

* Incidentally we see that any symmetrical determinantal equation, whose elements are rational in three coordinates x, y, z, whatever be the order of the determinant, represents a surface whose nodes make all the first minors vanish.

diagram given. Or the points P, Q, P', Q', R, R', and hence the points A, B, C, may be defined thus: the quadrics Q_1, Q_2, Q_3, P_4 cut the plane $l_0\xi + \ldots = 0$ in four conics; the condition that a self-polar triangle of a conic

$$(a_1, b_1, c_1, f_1, g_1, h_1 \between y_1, y_2, y_3)^2 = 0$$

should be possible circumscribed about a conic whose tangential equation is

$$(A, B, C, F, G, H \between l, m, n)^2 = 0,$$

is known to be

$$Aa_1 + Bb_1 + Cc_1 + 2Ff_1 + 2Gg_1 + 2Hh_1 = 0,$$

namely linear in A, B, C, F, G, H; thus the general tangential conic so harmonically inscribed to each of four given conics involves linearly two arbitrary parameters and is one of a set of conics touching four straight lines; among these conics there are three point-pairs, say P, P'; Q, Q'; R, R', and these will be conjugate pairs of points in regard to the four given conics, and therefore conjugate pairs in regard to the four quadrics Q_1, Q_2, Q_3, P_4. It is a known property of conics that if three collinear points L, M, N be taken respectively on PP', QQ', RR' and then three other points L', M', N' respectively on PP', QQ', RR', and so that each of $LL'PP'$, $MM'QQ'$, $NN'RR'$ is a harmonic range, then L', M', N' are collinear. Consider the general quadric $xQ_1 + yQ_2 + zQ_3 + P_4 = 0$, where x, y, z is any point on the cubic surface $C = 0$; the two lines in which it intersects the plane $l_0\xi + \ldots = 0$ can be shewn to be two such lines as LMN, $L'M'N'$. For substituting in this quadric the coordinates

$$\Theta + \Phi + m(\Theta - \Phi), \quad -(\Theta\phi + \Phi\theta) - m(\Theta\phi - \Phi\theta),$$
$$\Theta\phi^2 + \Phi\theta^2 + m(\Theta\phi^2 - \Phi\theta^2), \quad -(\Theta\phi^3 + \Phi\theta^3) - m(\Theta\phi^3 - \Phi\theta^3),$$

putting

$$f(\theta, \phi) = 2\lambda_0 + \lambda_1(\theta + \phi) + \theta\phi[2\lambda_2 + \lambda_3(\theta + \phi)] + \theta^2\phi^2[2\lambda_4 + 4(\theta + \phi)],$$
$$E_{\theta,\phi} = \frac{f(\theta, \phi) - 2\Theta\Phi}{4(\theta - \phi)^2}, \quad E'_{\theta,\phi} = \frac{f(\theta, \phi) + 2\Theta\Phi}{4(\theta - \phi)^2},$$

we find

$$x\theta\phi + y(\theta + \phi) + z - E'_{\theta,\phi} = m^2[x\theta\phi + y(\theta + \phi) + z - E_{\theta,\phi}],$$

which gives two points harmonic in regard to R and R', coinciding with R or R' according as $m = 0$ or ∞. The two lines LMN, $L'M'N'$ correspond, as we have seen, to two conics lying on a tangent plane of the surface S; if they coincide with one another they must coincide with one of the four lines $P'QR$, $Q'RP$, $R'PQ$, $P'Q'R'$; for these cases respectively we have clearly

(i) $$x\phi\psi + y(\phi + \psi) + z - E_{\phi\psi} = 0, \quad x\theta\phi + y(\theta + \phi) + z - E'_{\theta\phi} = 0,$$
$$x\theta\psi + y(\theta + \psi) + z - E'_{\theta\psi} = 0,$$

. . . .

(iv) $$x\phi\psi + y(\phi + \psi) + z - E_{\phi\psi} = 0, \quad x\theta\phi + y(\theta + \phi) + z - E_{\theta\phi} = 0,$$
$$x\theta\psi + y(\theta + \psi) + z - E_{\theta\psi} = 0;$$

corresponding then, for example, to the equations (iv), we have the singular plane

$$\begin{vmatrix} X, & Y, & Z, & T \\ \phi\psi, & \phi+\psi, & 1, & -E_{\phi\psi} \\ \theta\phi, & \theta+\phi, & 1, & -E_{\theta\phi} \\ \theta\psi, & \theta+\psi, & 1, & -E_{\theta\psi} \end{vmatrix} = 0$$

of the surface S and the node (x, y, z) of the surface $C = 0$. The planes

$$x\phi\psi + y(\phi+\psi) + z - E_{\phi\psi} = 0, \quad x\phi\psi + y(\phi+\psi) + z - E'_{\phi\psi} = 0,$$

are tangent planes* of the Kummer surface

$$\Delta = \begin{vmatrix} -\lambda_0, & \tfrac{1}{2}\lambda_1, & 2z, & -2y \\ \tfrac{1}{2}\lambda_1, & -(4z+\lambda_2), & \tfrac{1}{2}\lambda_3 + 2y, & 2x \\ 2z, & \tfrac{1}{2}\lambda_3 + 2y, & -(4x+\lambda_4), & 2 \\ -2y, & 2x, & 2, & 0 \end{vmatrix} = 0,$$

both passing through the line at infinity joining the points

$$x/1 = -y/\phi = z/\phi^2 = \infty, \quad x/1 = -y/\psi = z/\psi^2 = \infty.$$

Further when $xQ_1 + yQ_2 + zQ_3 + P_4 = 0$ represents a cone, the point (x, y, z) is on the Kummer surface $\Delta = 0$. It appears then that the surface $C = 0$ has four nodes, these being, if $l_0 = \theta\phi\psi$, $l_1 = \Sigma\theta\phi$, $l_2 = \Sigma\theta$, $l_3 = 1$, four of the eight intersections, in threes, of the three pairs of tangent planes to the Kummer surface $\Delta = 0$ which can be drawn through the lines at infinity joining the three points $x/1 = -y/\theta = z/\theta^2 = \infty$, etc. of $\Delta = 0$; and these four nodes lie on $\Delta = 0$. Since every point of $\Delta = 0$ is capable of representation in the form

$$x = t_1 + t_2, \quad y = -t_1 t_2, \quad z = E_{t_1, t_2} \quad .$$

there appears incidentally the algebraic result†, that if θ, ϕ, ψ be arbitrary,

* In fact, if $u \equiv u^{a,\phi} + u^{a,\psi}$, the former has the form $x\wp_{21}(v) - y\wp_{22}(v) + \wp_{11}(v) - z = 0$, and touches $\Delta = 0$ at the first satellite point of v; the second depends similarly on the conjugate point $\bar{v} \equiv u^{a,\phi} - u^{a,\psi}$. See p. 112.

† If (θ), (ϕ), (ψ), be any three places of the Riemann surface, and we determine two places (t_1), (t_2), so that

$$u^{a,t_1} + u^{a,t_2} \equiv u^{a,\theta} + u^{a,\phi} + u^{a,\psi},$$

we have

$$u^{a,t_1} + u^{a,t_2} - (u^{a,\theta} + u^{a,\phi}) \equiv u^{a,\psi},$$

shewing that the point $\pm(u^{a,\theta} + u^{a,\phi})$ lies on the tangent plane of the Kummer surface touching the surface at the satellite point of $\pm(u^{a,t_1} + u^{a,t_2})$, and that therefore

$$t_1 t_2(\theta+\phi) - \theta\phi(t_1+t_2) = E_{t_1,t_2} - E_{\theta,\phi}.$$

The places (t_1), (t_2) are thus the zeros, other than $(\theta, -\Theta)$, $(\phi, -\Phi)$, $(\psi, -\Psi)$, of the rational function

$$\begin{vmatrix} t^2, & t, & 1, & -s \\ \theta^2, & \theta, & 1, & \Theta \\ \phi^2, & \phi, & 1, & \Phi \\ \psi^2, & \psi, & 1, & \Psi \end{vmatrix}.$$

two other quantities t_1, t_2 can be found so that

$$t_1t_2(\phi+\psi)-(t_1+t_2)\phi\psi = E_{t_1t_2}-E_{\phi\psi},$$
$$t_1t_2(\theta+\phi)-(t_1+t_2)\theta\phi = E_{t_1t_2}-E_{\theta\phi},$$
$$t_1t_2(\theta+\psi)-(t_1+t_2)\theta\psi = E_{t_1t_2}-E_{\theta\psi},$$

and one of the four singular tangent planes of the surface S is correspondingly

$$(t_1+t_2)X-t_1t_2Y+E_{t_1t_2}Z+1=0,$$

the others being derived from this by substituting for t_1, t_2 the couples similarly derived from θ, ϕ, ψ after change in the sign respectively of Θ, of Φ and of Ψ. Let the cone

$$(t_1+t_2)Q_1-t_1t_2Q_2+E_{t_1t_2}Q_3+P_4=0,$$

which touches the plane $l_0\xi+\ldots=0$ along the line $P'Q'R'$, be denoted by $V_4=0$, and the plane $l_0\xi+\ldots=0$ by $\varpi=0$; draw any plane σ_4 through $P'Q'R'$, and let the tangent plane of V_4 along the other generator lying on σ_4 be called ϖ_4; we have then an identity of the form

$$V_4=\varpi\varpi_4-\sigma_4^2;$$

now the points of the surface S are given by equations $X=Q_1'$, $Y=Q_2'$, $Z=Q_3'$, $T=P_4'$, where $Q_1', Q_2', \ldots$ are the homogeneous quadrics in ξ, η, ζ obtained by writing $\tau=-(\theta\phi\psi\xi+\Sigma\theta\phi\,.\,\eta+\Sigma\theta\,.\,\zeta)$ respectively in $Q_1, Q_2, \ldots$; take for σ_4 the plane joining $(0, 0, 0, 1)$ to $P'Q'R'$, namely

$$\begin{vmatrix} \xi, & \eta, & \zeta, & 0 \\ 1, & -\theta, & \theta^2, & \Theta \\ 1, & -\phi, & \phi^2, & \Phi \\ 1, & -\psi, & \psi^2, & \Psi \end{vmatrix}=0,$$

so that we may write

$$\sigma_4=\Theta[\phi\psi\xi+(\phi+\psi)\eta+\zeta]+\Phi[\psi\theta\xi+(\psi+\theta)\eta+\zeta]$$
$$+\Psi[\theta\phi\xi+(\theta+\phi)\eta+\zeta],$$

or say

$$\sigma_4=y_1+y_2+y_3;$$

we have then, if T_1 denote a constant multiple of the linear function

$$(t_1+t_2)X-t_1t_2Y+E_{t_1t_2}Z+T,$$

and similarly X_1, Y_1, Z_1 denote the linear functions associated with the lines $P'QR$, $Q'RP$, $R'PQ$, as a representation of the coordinates of the points of the surface S, the formulae

$$T_1=(y_1+y_2+y_3)^2,\quad X_1=(-y_1+y_2+y_3)^2,\quad Y_1=(y_1-y_2+y_3)^2,$$
$$Z_1=(y_1+y_2-y_3)^2,$$

which lead to

$$y_1(T_1+X_1-Y_1-Z_1)=y_2(T_1+Y_1-Z_1-X_1)=y_3(T_1+Z_1-X_1-Y_1),$$

and the surface S is given by

$$\sqrt{X_1} + \sqrt{Y_1} + \sqrt{Z_1} + \sqrt{T_1} = 0,$$

the reciprocal surface C being given similarly by

$$1/X_1 + 1/Y_1 + 1/Z_1 + 1/T_1 = 0.$$

47. Now let the determinant

$$\begin{vmatrix} -\lambda_0, & \tfrac{1}{2}\lambda_1, & 2z, & -2y, & l_0, & m_0 \\ \tfrac{1}{2}\lambda_1, & -(\lambda_2 + 4z), & \tfrac{1}{2}\lambda_3 + 2y, & 2x, & l_1, & m_1 \\ 2z, & \tfrac{1}{2}\lambda_3 + 2y, & -(\lambda_4 + 4x), & 2, & l_2, & m_2 \\ -2y, & 2x, & 2, & 0, & l_3, & m_3 \\ n_0, & n_1, & n_2, & n_3, & 0, & 0 \\ p_0, & p_1, & p_2, & p_3, & 0, & 0 \end{vmatrix},$$

obtained by bordering the determinant Δ, be denoted by $\binom{lm}{np}$; of such form we have then cubic surfaces $\binom{l}{l} = 0$, $\binom{l}{m} = 0$, when Δ is bordered by only one row and column, the same or different; we have quadric surfaces $\binom{lm}{lm} = 0$, $\binom{lm}{ln} = 0$, when Δ is bordered by two rows and columns, the same or partially different, and we have a plane $\binom{lmn}{lmn} = 0$, when Δ is bordered by the same three rows and columns. If (ξ, η, ζ, τ) satisfy the three equations

$$l_0\xi + l_1\eta + l_2\zeta + l_3\tau = 0, \quad m_0\xi + m_1\eta + m_2\zeta + m_3\tau = 0,$$
$$n_0\xi + n_1\eta + n_2\zeta + n_3\tau = 0,$$

the plane $\binom{lmn}{lmn} = 0$ is the same as

$$4x(\eta\tau - \zeta^2) + 4y(\eta\zeta - \xi\tau) + 4z(\zeta\xi - \eta^2)$$
$$+ (-\lambda_0\xi^2 + \lambda_1\xi\eta - \lambda_2\eta^2 + \lambda_3\eta\zeta - \lambda_4\zeta^2 + 4\zeta\tau) = 0;$$

and the cubic $\binom{l}{l}$, which has above been denoted by C, has been shewn to be a cubic surface with four nodes. Considering the determinant $\binom{lm}{lm}$, and the minors of the elements (5, 5), (6, 6) and (5, 6), we have an identity

$$\binom{l}{l}\binom{m}{m} - \binom{l}{m}^2 = \Delta \binom{lm}{lm},$$

and this shews that the cubic surface $\binom{l}{l}$ touches the Kummer surface Δ at all its intersections with it, and therefore along a sextic curve, as also does the cubic surface $\binom{m}{m}$, and these two sextics are the complete intersection of Δ with the cubic surface $\binom{l}{m}$. Returning for a moment to the expression of $\Delta = 0$ by the hyperelliptic functions, the identity of p. 39 shews that the sextic curve on $\binom{l}{l}$ is given by

$$l_0\wp_{222}(u) + l_1\wp_{221}(u) + l_2\wp_{211}(u) + l_3\wp_{111}(u) = 0,$$

and it is to place this identity in a clear light that we have entered so far upon the theory of the cubic surface $\binom{l}{l}$. Considering similarly in the determinant $\binom{lmn}{lmn}$ the minors of the elements (6, 6), (7, 7) and (6, 7), we have an identity of the form

$$\binom{lm}{lm}\binom{ln}{ln} - \binom{lm}{ln}^2 = \binom{l}{l}\binom{lmn}{lmn}.$$

Thus wherever the plane $\binom{lmn}{lmn}$ meets the quadric $\binom{lm}{lm}$ it touches it, and the line of contact is on the quadric $\binom{lm}{ln}$; thus $\binom{lm}{lm}$, $\binom{ln}{ln}$ are quadric cones with a common tangent plane $\binom{lmn}{lmn}$, the generators of contact being generators of the quadric surface $\binom{lm}{ln}$, which therefore is also touched by the plane $\binom{lmn}{lmn}$, and the quadric $\binom{lm}{ln}$ has with each of the cones $\binom{lm}{lm}$, $\binom{ln}{ln}$, besides a common generator, an intersection which is a cubic space curve; further the whole intersection of the cone $\binom{lm}{lm}$ and the quadric $\binom{lm}{ln}$ lies upon the aggregate of the cubic surface $\binom{l}{l}$ and the plane $\binom{lmn}{lmn}$, of which the latter can only contain points of $\binom{lm}{lm}$ lying upon its generator of contact, so that the cubic space curve common to $\binom{lm}{lm}$ and $\binom{lm}{ln}$ lies upon the cubic surface $\binom{l}{l}$; as, by the same identity, the only points common to the cubic surface $\binom{l}{l}$ and the cone $\binom{lm}{lm}$, are points of contact of these, lying upon the quadric $\binom{lm}{ln}$, it follows that the cone $\binom{lm}{lm}$ touches the cubic surface

$\binom{l}{l}$ along a cubic space curve, as likewise does the cone $\binom{ln}{ln}$, and these two cubic curves are the complete intersection with $\binom{l}{l}$ of the quadric surface $\binom{lm}{ln}$. Further as the cone $\binom{lm}{lm}$ has a generator upon the quadric $\binom{lm}{ln}$, its vertex is upon this quadric; if this vertex be taken for origin of Cartesian coordinates the lowest terms on the left side, in the identity under discussion, are of the second or higher order; thus from the form of the right side the lowest terms in $\binom{l}{l}$ are of the first or higher order, and the vertex of the cone $\binom{lm}{lm}$ is thus upon the cubic surface $\binom{l}{l}$; what is in general the quartic cone of contact to $\binom{l}{l}$ drawn from a point of itself here contains $\binom{lm}{lm}$ as part of itself, and so breaks up into two quadric cones. Further, taking the origin at the point of intersection of the generators of contact of the cones $\binom{lm}{lm}$, $\binom{ln}{ln}$ with the plane $\binom{lmn}{lmn}$, this being as we have seen also the tangent plane at this point of the quadric $\binom{lm}{ln}$, the lowest terms on the left side of the identity under discussion consist presumably of the square of the plane $\binom{lmn}{lmn}$, which therefore, as we see from the right side, is the tangent plane, at this point, of the surface $\binom{l}{l}$. We have already seen that, regarding $m_0, m_1, \ldots$ and $n_0, n_1, \ldots$ as arbitrary, the plane $\binom{lmn}{lmn}$ is the general tangent plane of the surface $\binom{l}{l}$; it is not difficult to see that the cone $\binom{lm}{lm}$ may, by taking $m_0, m_1, \ldots$ suitably, be made a cone of contact with vertex at any point of $\binom{l}{l}$: for the vertex of the cone $\binom{lm}{lm}$ makes vanish all the first derivatives of the expression $\binom{lm}{lm}$; these first derivatives are seen, by differentiating the determinant $\binom{lm}{lm}$, to be linear functions of the first minors of this determinant; as previously remarked we can make all these first minors vanish by satisfying three algebraically independent conditions; the vertex of the cone $\binom{lm}{lm}$ is thus to be found by equating to zero three suitably chosen first minors, and the first minors, of which two rows and columns are chosen from the last two rows and columns of $\binom{lm}{lm}$, are linear in x, y, z. Geometrically, the condition that all the first minors of $\binom{lm}{lm}$ vanish is that the quadric

$$Q = 4x(\eta\tau - \zeta^2) + \ldots + (-\lambda_0\xi^2 + \ldots + 4\zeta\tau) = 0$$

should cut the plane $l_0\xi + \ldots = 0$ in two lines of which one lies upon the plane $m_0\xi + \ldots = 0$; this may be seen either directly* or by remarking that if $l_0\xi + \ldots = 0$, $m_0\xi + \ldots = 0$, $n_0\xi + \ldots = 0$ intersect in (ξ, η, ζ, τ), we have

$$Q = 4x(\eta\tau - \zeta^2) + \ldots + (-\lambda_0\xi^2 + \ldots + 4\zeta\tau) = \binom{lmn}{lmn},$$

while $\binom{lmn}{lmn}$ is a linear function of ten of the first minors of $\binom{lm}{lm}$ with coefficients which are squares and products of n_0, n_1, n_2, n_3; thus when all the first minors of $\binom{lm}{lm}$ vanish, the quadric Q vanishes for every point upon the line $l_0\xi + \ldots = 0$, $m_0\xi + \ldots = 0$; that it touches the plane $l_0\xi + \ldots = 0$ is expressed by the vanishing of the minor (6, 6) of $\binom{lm}{lm}$. We have thus reached the results, that if (x, y, z) be any point of the cubic surface C, or $\binom{l}{l}$, and the quadric

$$Q = 4x(\eta\tau - \zeta^2) + \ldots + (-\lambda_0\xi^2 + \ldots + 4\zeta\tau) = 0$$

cut the plane $l_0\xi + \ldots = 0$ in the two lines $m_0\xi + \ldots = 0$, $m_0'\xi + \ldots = 0$, the cone of contact to C from (x, y, z) breaks up into the quadric cones $\binom{lm}{lm}$, $\binom{lm'}{lm'}$; and further that the cones of contact $\binom{lm}{lm}$, $\binom{ln}{ln}$ from two different points of C have a common tangent plane touching C at a point where their cubic curves of contact cross one another. These quadric cones of contact correspond to conics lying on two different tangent planes of the surface S reciprocal to C, and we remarked before that each of these conics corresponds to a straight line in the plane $l_0\xi + \ldots = 0$; the point of intersection of these lines corresponds to a common point of the two conics and to a common tangent plane of the two cones $\binom{lm}{lm}$, $\binom{ln}{ln}$; and this plane is one of the four tangent planes to C which can be drawn through the line joining the

* Or in virtue of the theorem quoted, p. 164. If $(\xi'\eta'\zeta'\tau')$, $(\xi''\eta''\zeta''\tau'')$ be any two points on $m_0\xi + \ldots = 0$, the tangent planes $\xi\frac{\partial Q}{\partial \xi'} + \ldots$, $\xi\frac{\partial Q}{\partial \xi''} + \ldots$ are both of the form $\varpi(l_0\xi + \ldots) + v(m_0\xi + \ldots)$, so that the matrix of six rows and columns

$$A = \begin{pmatrix} \Delta & l & m \\ l & 0 & 0 \\ m & 0 & 0 \end{pmatrix}$$

satisfies $$A(\xi'\eta'\zeta'\tau'\varpi v) = 0 \text{ and } A(\xi''\eta''\zeta''\tau''\varpi'v') = 0.$$

vertices of the cones $\binom{lm}{lm}$, $\binom{ln}{ln}$. Further results in regard to the geometry are given in the following examples; the matter is by no means novel, as may be seen by consulting the following authorities, in which are placed first those mainly used for the account given here. (i) Reye, *Geometrie der Lage*, a beautiful geometrical account; (ii) Clebsch, *Crelle*, LXVII. (1867), an interesting analytical theory; (iii) Humbert, *Liouville*, 4th Series, IX. (1893), p. 99 (Hudson, *Kummer's Quartic Surface*, in particular, pp. 157, 198); (iv) Kummer, Weierstrass and Schröter, *Berlin. Akad.* 1863, reproduced in *Crelle*, LXIV. (1865); (v) Cremona, *Crelle*, LXIII. (1864), a geometrical account; (vi) Cayley, *Proc. Lond. Math. Soc.* III. (1872), or *Collected Papers*, Vol. VII.; (vii) Laguerre, *Nouv. Annal.* XI. (1872); (viii) Loria, *Teor. Geom.* 1896, p. 110, where a very full bibliography is given. The surface S was discovered by Steiner in 1844, and is called Steiner's quartic.

48. *Examples.* 1. In the representation of the Steiner quartic surface S upon the plane $l_0\xi + \dots$, two points upon the line BC, of our diagram (p. 142), which are harmonic in regard to the points P, P', give rise to the same point of S; and such points of S are upon a double line lying on the surface; there are three such double lines meeting in a triple point of S. The representation being $X : Y : Z : T = Q_1 : Q_2 : Q_3 : P_4$, as before, the triple point is $X = 0$, $Y = 0$, $Z = 0$, and one of the double lines is

$$X : Y : Z = \theta\phi : \theta + \phi : 1.$$

The reciprocal cubic surface C meets the plane at infinity in the three chords joining the points $x/1 = -y/\theta = z/\theta^2 = \infty$, $x/1 = -y/\phi = z/\phi^2 = \infty$, etc.

Ex. 2. The sextic curve along which the cubic surface C touches the Kummer surface Δ corresponds to a plane section of the Weddle surface, and the set of surfaces C for different values of l_0, l_1, l_2, l_3 correspond to all the plane sections of the Weddle surfaces. Thus any two surfaces $\binom{l}{l}$, $\binom{m}{m}$ touch in four points, and the quadric cone $\binom{lm}{lm}$ is an enveloping cone of both. The joining line of any two nodes of $\binom{l}{l}$ lies entirely upon the surface, and touches the Kummer surface.

Ex. 3. The two lines, say OL, OL', in which the quadric

$$xQ_1 + yQ_2 + zQ_3 + P_4 = 0$$

cuts the plane $l_0\xi + \dots = 0$, when (x, y, z) is upon the cubic surface $\binom{l}{l}$, are the double rays of the pencil in involution formed by tangents from O to the conics touching the four lines PQ', PQ, $P'Q'$, $P'Q$; they are therefore the tangents at O of the two conics which can be drawn to touch this quadrilateral and pass through O. The lines OL, OL' correspond on the surface S to the two conics in which a tangent plane of S cuts the surface. Thus the asymptotic lines of S, each defined as being tangent at any point K of S to one of the two conics in which the surface is cut by the tangent plane at K, correspond to the system of conics in the plane $l_0\xi + \ldots = 0$ which touch the quadrilateral $PQ'P'Q$; they are thus unicursal quartic curves in space, all touching the parabolic curve, which here breaks up into the four singular conics.

Ex. 4. The tangent lines of the space cubic along which the cubic surface C, or $\binom{l}{l}$, is touched by the cone $\binom{lm}{lm}$ intersect the surface C again in the points of an asymptotic line passing through the vertex of $\binom{lm}{lm}$.

This result is given by Laguerre, *Nouv. Annal.* XI. (1872), p. 342, who defines the surface C as obtained by equating to zero the cubinvariant

$$\begin{vmatrix} a_0 & a_1 & a_2 \\ a_1 & a_2 & a_3 \\ a_2 & a_3 & a_4 \end{vmatrix}$$

of the quartic $a_0t^4 + 4a_1t^3 + 6a_2t^2 + 4a_3t + a_4$, wherein a_0, a_1, a_2, a_3, a_4, are any linear functions of the coordinates. He shews that one asymptotic line is given by the vanishing of the quadrinvariant $a_0a_4 - 4a_1a_3 + 3a_2^2$.

The equations of the asymptotic lines of the surface $x^m + y^m + z^m = 1$, and of its reciprocal, are obtained by integration by Darboux, *La Théorie des Surfaces*, Partie I. p. 143. This includes the case here, by putting $m = \frac{1}{2}$. The method consists in writing

$$x^m = A\,(u-a)(v-a), \quad y^m = B\,(u-b)(v-b), \quad z^m = C\,(u-c)(v-c).$$

For the theory of the Steiner quartic surface and its reciprocal, and their asymptotic lines, and for the asymptotic lines of the Kummer surface from the point of view of line-geometry, see the following, and the references there given. Lie, *Geometrie der Berührungstransformationen* (Leipzig, 1896), pp. 352, 341, 475; Darboux, *La Théorie des Surfaces*, Note viii. Partie IV. p. 466; Jessop, *Line Complex* (1903), p. 225; Segre, *Crelle*, XCVIII. (1885), p. 302; Klein u. Lie, *Berlin. Monatsb.* 1870, p. 891; Reichardt, *Nova Acta Leopoldina*, L. 1887, p. 353; Hudson, *Kummer's Quartic Surface*, pp. 60, 111.

Ex. 5. We have defined the surfaces S, C by means of quadric functions Q_1, Q_2, Q_3, P_4 having six points in common. It is not difficult to see that the intersections of these quadrics with an arbitrary plane $l_0\xi + \ldots = 0$, which does not pass through any of the six intersections of the quadrics, may be taken to be the intersections with this plane of *any* four quadric surfaces U_1, U_2, U_3, U_4; and the surface S is equally capable of being represented by

$$X : Y : Z : T = U_1 : U_2 : U_3 : U_4.$$

The condition that $xU_1 + yU_2 + zU_3 + U_4 = 0$ should be a cone gives for x, y, z a locus, represented by the vanishing of a symmetric determinant, which is a quartic surface with, in general, 10 nodes.

Ex. 6. When in the preceding theory the plane $l_0\xi + \ldots = 0$ passes through one of the six common points of the quadrics Q_1, Q_2, Q_3, P_4 the cubic surface C becomes a ruled surface.

If $A^2 = \frac{1}{4}\Delta_{11}$, $AB = \frac{1}{4}\Delta_{12}$, etc., where $\Delta_{12}, \ldots$ are the minors (p. 41) of the determinant Δ, we find that

$$[\theta\phi A + (\theta + \phi) B + C]^2 = 4P_\theta P_\phi P_{\theta\phi} + (\theta - \phi)^{-2} (\Theta P_\theta - \Phi P_\phi)^2,$$

where θ, ϕ are any quantities,

$$\Theta^2 = \lambda_0 + \lambda_1\theta + \ldots + 4\theta^5, \quad \Phi^2 = \lambda_0 + \lambda_1\phi + \ldots + 4\phi^5,$$
$$P_\theta = y + \theta x - \theta^2, \quad P_{\theta\phi} = \theta\phi x + (\theta + \phi) y + z - E_{\theta\phi},$$
$$E_{\theta\phi} = \tfrac{1}{4} (\theta - \phi)^{-2} [F(\theta, \phi) - 2\Theta\Phi].$$

Thus when the plane $l_0\xi + \ldots = 0$ contains the common point $(0, 0, 0, 1)$ of the quadrics Q_1, Q_2, Q_3, P_4 the surface C is generated by the pairs of straight lines given, for different values of m, by

$$P_{\theta\phi} = m, \quad 4mP_\theta P_\phi + (\theta - \phi)^{-2} (\Theta P_\theta - \Phi P_\phi)^2 = 0.$$

Ex. 7. When the plane contains three of these intersections, the cubic surface C becomes a product of three planes. Namely if Θ^2 or $f(\theta) = 0$, $f(\phi) = 0$, $f(\psi) = 0$ we have

$$\begin{vmatrix} -\lambda_0, & \frac{1}{2}\lambda_1, & 2z, & -2y, & \theta\phi\psi \\ \frac{1}{2}\lambda_1, & -(\lambda_2 + 4z), & \frac{1}{2}\lambda_3 + 2y, & 2x, & \Sigma\theta\phi \\ 2z, & \frac{1}{2}\lambda_3 + 2y, & -(\lambda_4 + 4x), & 2, & \Sigma\theta \\ -2y, & 2x, & 2, & 0, & 1 \\ \theta\phi\psi, & \Sigma\theta\phi, & \Sigma\theta, & 1, & 0 \end{vmatrix}$$

$$= -16 [\phi\psi x + (\phi + \psi) y + z - e_{\phi\psi}] [\theta\phi x + (\theta + \phi) y + z - e_{\theta\phi}]$$
$$\times [\theta\psi x + (\theta + \psi) y + z - e_{\theta\psi}].$$

Ex. 8. The Kummer and Weddle surfaces being given by $\Delta = 0$, $\omega = 0$, where Δ, ω are certain determinants defined, pp. 41, 70, 78, prove that

$$Q_3^4 \Delta \left(\frac{Q_2}{Q_3}, -\frac{Q_1}{Q_3}, -\frac{P_4}{Q_3}\right) = 256\,\omega^2,$$

where $Q_1 = 4(\eta\tau - \zeta^2)$, etc., as before (Schottky, *Crelle*, CV. (1889), p. 241).

Ex. 9. Let $\quad f(t) = \lambda_0 + \lambda_1 t + \ldots + 4t^5 = 4P(t)\,Q(t)$,

where $\quad P(t) = (t - \theta)(t - \phi), \quad Q(t) = t^3 + At^2 + Bt + C.$

Prove that the result of eliminating t_1, t_2 between the equations

$$[(\phi-\theta)\,Q(\theta)]^{\frac{1}{2}}X=\theta^2-\theta(t_1+t_2)+t_1t_2,$$
$$[-(\phi-\theta)\,Q(\phi)]^{\frac{1}{2}}Y=\phi^2-\phi(t_1+t_2)+t_1t_2,$$
$$[-Q(\theta)\,Q(\phi)]^{\frac{1}{2}}Z=\left[\frac{\sqrt{P(t_1)\,Q(t_2)}-\sqrt{P(t_2)\,Q(t_1)}}{t_1-t_2}\right]^2,$$

is

$$a^2X^2+b^2Y^2+c^2Z^2-2bcYZ-2caZX-2abXY$$
$$-2\,[bcX(Y^2-Z^2)+caY(Z^2-X^2)+abZ(X^2-Y^2)+eXYZ]$$
$$+(aYZ+bZX+cXY)^2=0,$$

where

$$e=-\frac{Q(\theta)\,Q(\phi)}{\phi-\theta}[(\theta+\phi)(2\theta^2-5\theta\phi+2\phi^2)$$
$$+A(\theta^2-4\theta\phi+\phi^2)-B(\theta+\phi)-2C],$$

$$a=Q(\phi)\left(\frac{Q(\theta)}{\phi-\theta}\right)^{\frac{1}{2}},\quad b=Q(\theta)\left(\frac{-Q(\phi)}{\phi-\theta}\right)^{\frac{1}{2}},\quad c=-(\phi-\theta)[-Q(\theta)\,Q(\phi)]^{\frac{1}{2}}.$$

If

$$x=t_1+t_2,\quad y=-t_1t_2,\quad z=\frac{F(t_1,t_2)-2s_1s_2}{4(t_1-t_2)^2},$$

where $s_1^2=f(t_1)$, $s_2^2=f(t_2)$, and, as before,

$$P_\theta=y+\theta x-\theta^2,\quad P_{\theta\phi}=\theta\phi x+(\theta+\phi)\,y+z-e_{\theta\phi},$$

we have

$$[(\phi-\theta)\,Q(\theta)]^{\frac{1}{2}}X=-P_\theta,\quad [-(\phi-\theta)\,Q(\phi)]^{\frac{1}{2}}Y=-P_\phi,$$
$$[-Q(\theta)\,Q(\phi)]^{\frac{1}{2}}Z=P_{\theta\phi},$$

and the equation above is that of Kummer's surface referred to a so-called Rosenhain tetrahedron. The value of e is capable of the form

$$e=-\frac{Q(\theta)\,Q(\phi)}{\phi-\theta}\{(\phi-\theta)^2[2A+3(\theta+\phi)]-Q(\theta)-Q(\phi)\}.$$

Ex. 10. A Göpel tetrad of nodes is a set of four nodes of the Kummer surface of which the joining planes are not tropes. If the roots of $f(t)$ be denoted by a_1, a_2, c, c_1, c_2, such a set of nodes is

$$A(\infty,\,-\infty c,\,\infty c^2),\quad D(0,\,0,\,\infty),$$
$$B(c_1+c_2,\,-c_1c_2,\,e_{c_1c_2}),\quad C(a_1+a_2,\,-a_1a_2,\,e_{a_1a_2});$$

putting

$$a_1-c=\alpha_1,\quad a_2-c=\alpha_2,\quad c_1-c=\gamma_1,\quad c_2-c=\gamma_2,$$
$$P_\theta=y+\theta x-\theta^2,\quad P_{\theta\phi}=\theta\phi x+(\theta+\phi)\,y+z-e_{\theta\phi},$$

where θ, ϕ are any two roots of $f(t)$, we find, utilising the identity

$$a_1a_2(c_1+c_2)-c_1c_2(a_1+a_2)=e_{a_1a_2}-e_{c_1c_2},$$

that the planes DCA, DAB, BCD, BAC are respectively

$$P_c+\alpha_1\alpha_2=0,\quad P_c+\gamma_1\gamma_2=0,\quad P_{a_1a_2}-P_{c_1c_2}=0,\quad \gamma_1\gamma_2P_{a_1a_2}-\alpha_1\alpha_2P_{c_1c_2}=0;$$

using then $(\alpha_1\gamma_2)$ to denote $\alpha_1-\gamma_2=a_1-c_2$, etc., and σ as a factor of proportionality, and putting

$$\sigma\eta = (\alpha_1\gamma_2)(\alpha_2\gamma_1)[P_c + \alpha_1\alpha_2], \quad \sigma\zeta = (\alpha_1\gamma_2)(\alpha_2\gamma_1)[P_c + \gamma_1\gamma_2],$$
$$\sigma\xi = P_{a_1a_2} - P_{c_1c_2}, \quad \sigma\tau = \gamma_1\gamma_2 P_{a_1a_2} - \alpha_1\alpha_2 P_{c_1c_2},$$

we find
$$CP_{a_1a_2} = \sigma(\alpha_1\alpha_2\xi - \tau), \quad CP_{c_1c_2} = \sigma(\gamma_1\gamma_2\xi - \tau),$$
$$CP_{a_1c_1} = \sigma(\alpha_1\gamma_1\xi - \gamma_1\eta + \alpha_1\zeta - \tau), \qquad C(\alpha_1\gamma_2)(\alpha_2\gamma_1) = \sigma(\eta - \zeta),$$
$$CP_{a_2c_2} = \sigma(\alpha_2\gamma_2\xi - \gamma_2\eta + \alpha_2\zeta - \tau), \quad C(\alpha_1\gamma_2)(\alpha_2\gamma_1)P_c = \sigma(\alpha_1\alpha_2\zeta - \gamma_1\gamma_2\eta),$$

where
$$C = \alpha_1\alpha_2 - \gamma_1\gamma_2;$$

we have however the identity
$$(P_{a_1a_2}P_{c_1c_2})^{\frac{1}{2}} - (P_{a_1c_1}P_{a_2c_2})^{\frac{1}{2}} + (\alpha_1\gamma_2)(\alpha_2\gamma_1)(-P_c)^{\frac{1}{2}} = 0.$$

Rationalising this we find

$$(\alpha_1\gamma_1)^2(\alpha_2\gamma_2)^2[\lambda^2\xi^2\tau^2 + \eta^2\zeta^2] + (\gamma_1 - \gamma_2)^2[\alpha_1^2\alpha_2^2\zeta^2\xi^2 + \eta^2\tau^2] + (\alpha_1 - \alpha_2)^2[\gamma_1^2\gamma_2^2\xi^2\eta^2 + \zeta^2\tau^2]$$
$$- 2\delta(\eta\tau + \alpha_1\alpha_2\zeta\xi)(\zeta\tau + \gamma_1\gamma_2\xi\eta) - 2(\alpha_1 + \alpha_2)(\alpha_1\gamma_1)(\alpha_2\gamma_2)(\zeta\tau + \gamma_1\gamma_2\xi\eta)(\eta\zeta + \lambda\xi\tau)$$
$$+ 2\mu\xi\eta\zeta\tau \quad + 2(\gamma_1 + \gamma_2)(\alpha_1\gamma_1)(\alpha_2\gamma_2)(\lambda\xi\tau + \eta\zeta)(\alpha_1\alpha_2\zeta\xi + \eta\tau) = 0,$$

where
$$\lambda = \frac{(\alpha_1\gamma_2)(\alpha_2\gamma_1)}{(\alpha_1\gamma_1)(\alpha_2\gamma_2)}, \quad \delta = (\alpha_1 + \alpha_2)(\gamma_1 + \gamma_2) - 2(\alpha_1\alpha_2 + \gamma_1\gamma_2),$$
$$\mu = (\alpha_1\gamma_1)(\alpha_2\gamma_2)(\alpha_1\gamma_2)(\alpha_2\gamma_1) + \alpha_1\alpha_2(\gamma_1 + \gamma_2)^2 + \gamma_1\gamma_2(\alpha_1 + \alpha_2)^2 - 2(\alpha_1\alpha_2 + \gamma_1\gamma_2)^2.$$

The object of forming this equation was to make the remark that it allows the birational transformation
$$\xi = \frac{1}{\xi'}, \quad \eta = \frac{\lambda\alpha_1\alpha_2}{\eta'}, \quad \zeta = \frac{\lambda\gamma_1\gamma_2}{\zeta'}, \quad \tau = \frac{\alpha_1\alpha_2\gamma_1\gamma_2}{\tau'}.$$
It would be interesting to know* what transformation of the hyperelliptic arguments u_1, u_2 this corresponds to.

It is to be remarked that the tetrahedron of reference here taken is nugatory for the particular surface called the tetrahedroid, considered below.

Ex. 11. The surface (cf. Ex. 9, above)
$$X^2Y^2Z^2(a^2X^2 + b^2Y^2 + c^2Z^2 - 2bcYZ - 2caZX - 2abXY)$$
$$- 2XYZ[bcX(Y^2 - Z^2) + caY(Z^2 - X^2) + abZ(X^2 - Y^2) + eXYZ]$$
$$+ (aYZ + bZX + cXY)^2 = 0,$$
is a hyperelliptic surface, only one value of the parameters u_1, u_2 belonging to any point; prove that its hyperelliptic expression, when a, b, c, e have the values of Example 9 above, is
$$X = 2[-Q(\phi)]^{\frac{1}{2}} \frac{\theta^2 - \theta\wp_{22} - \wp_{21}}{\theta\phi\wp_{222} + (\theta + \phi)\wp_{221} + \wp_{211}},$$
$$Y = \quad 2[Q(\theta)]^{\frac{1}{2}} \frac{\phi^2 - \phi\wp_{22} - \wp_{21}}{\theta\phi\wp_{222} + (\theta + \phi)\wp_{221} + \wp_{211}},$$
$$Z = \quad 2(\phi - \theta)^{\frac{1}{2}} \frac{\theta\phi\wp_{22} + (\theta + \phi)\wp_{21} + \wp_{11} - e_{\theta\phi}}{\theta\phi\wp_{222} + (\theta + \phi)\wp_{221} + \wp_{211}}.$$

* A transformation of similar algebraic form for a Weddle surface is obtained by repeated projection from two nodes of the surface, and belongs, we have seen, to a finite group of 32 self-inverse transformations. *Proc. Lond. Math. Soc.* Ser. 2, Vol. I. (1903), p. 257.

Shew also that the section of the surface by a plane $Ax+By+Cz=1$ is a curve of deficiency 9; and that for the curve, in homogeneous coordinates X, Y, Z,

$$X^2Y^2Z^2[a^2X^2+\dots]-2XYZ[bcX(Y^2-Z^2)+\dots](AX+BY+CZ)^2 + (aYZ+bZX+cXY)^2(AX+BY+CZ)^4=0,$$

the adjoint quintic is

$$\begin{aligned} 0 &= XYZ[uX^2+vY^2+wZ^2+2u'YZ+2v'ZX+2w'XY] \\ &+[\lambda YZ(Y-Z)+\mu ZX(Z-X)+\nu XY(X-Y)](AX+BY+CZ)^2 \\ &+(PYZ+QZX+RXY)(AX+BY+CZ)^3, \end{aligned}$$

where $u, v, w, u', v', w', P, Q, R$ are arbitrary, but

$$\lambda = -a\frac{vC^2+wB^2-2u'BC}{(B+C)(Bc+Cb)},$$

while μ, ν have similar linear expressions in terms of u, v, w, u', v', w'. Cf. Humbert, *Liouville*, IX. (1893), p. 439.

These results have been worked out in view of an application in the second part of this volume.

Another hyperelliptic surface $\Psi(x, y, \xi)=0$ we have met with in the text (p. 43); it would be interesting to have the form of the integrals of the first kind for any plane section of this surface also.

Ex. 12. It has been remarked that the cubic surface $\binom{l}{l}$ of p. 146, becomes a ruled surface when the plane $l_0\xi+l_1\eta+l_2\zeta+l_3\tau=0$ passes through one common point of the quadrics Q_1, Q_2, Q_3, P_4, and breaks into three planes when the plane $l_0\xi+\dots=0$ contains three of these common points; when the plane contains two of these common points the intersection of the surface with the Kummer surface also degenerates; in fact, from the formula (p. 102)

$$\frac{\sigma^2(u;\theta\phi)}{\sigma^2(u)}[\wp_{rs}(u;\theta\phi)] = \begin{pmatrix} -h & a & u & -g \\ -b & h & v & -f \\ -f & g & w & -c \\ -v & u & d & -w \end{pmatrix}[\wp_{rs}(u)] = M[\wp_{rs}(u)],$$

where $u=\theta+\phi$, $v=-\theta\phi$, $w=e_{\theta\phi}$, $d=1$, comparing the result of twice differentiating logarithmically the last of the four equations represented by it, with the other equations it represents, we shall obtain each of the following expressions (wherein $P_{\theta\phi}=\theta\phi\wp_{22}(u)+(\theta+\phi)\wp_{21}(u)+\wp_{11}(u)-e_{\theta\phi}$)

$$[\theta\phi\wp_{222}(u)+(\theta+\phi)\wp_{221}(u)+\wp_{211}(u)]^2/P_{\theta\phi},$$

$$[\theta\phi\wp_{222}(u)+(\theta+\phi)\wp_{221}(u)+\wp_{211}(u)][\theta\phi\wp_{221}(u)+(\theta+\phi)\wp_{211}(u)+\wp_{111}(u)]/P_{\theta\phi},$$

$$[\theta\phi\wp_{221}(u)+(\theta+\phi)\wp_{211}(u)+\wp_{111}(u)]^2/P_{\theta\phi},$$

expressed as an integral polynomial in $\wp_{22}(u)$, $\wp_{21}(u)$, $\wp_{11}(u)$, their respective values being

$$\theta\phi\wp_{2222}(u)+(\theta+\phi)\wp_{2221}(u)+\wp_{2211}(u)$$
$$+2[-h\wp_{22}(u)+a\wp_{21}(u)+u\wp_{11}(u)-g]-2\wp_{22}(u).P_{\theta\phi},$$
$$\theta\phi\wp_{2221}(u)+(\theta+\phi)\wp_{2211}(u)+\wp_{2111}(u)$$
$$+2[-b\wp_{22}(u)+h\wp_{21}(u)+v\wp_{11}(u)-f]-2\wp_{21}(u).P_{\theta\phi},$$
$$\theta\phi\wp_{2211}(u)+(\theta+\phi)\wp_{2111}(u)+\wp_{1111}(u)$$
$$+2[-f\wp_{22}(u)+g\wp_{21}(u)+w\wp_{11}(u)-c]-2\wp_{11}(u).P_{\theta\phi}.$$

Thus, with λ arbitrary, the cubic surface

$$[\lambda\theta\phi\wp_{222}(u)+(\lambda\theta+\lambda\phi+\theta\phi)\wp_{221}(u)+(\lambda+\theta+\phi)\wp_{211}(u)+\wp_{111}(u)]^2=0,$$

contains the singular conic upon $P_{\theta\phi}=0$.

Notice also, from this formula, if $x=\wp_{22}(u)$, $y=\wp_{21}(u)$, $z=\wp_{11}(u)$, $x'=\wp_{22}(u;\ \theta\phi)$, $y'=\wp_{21}(u;\ \theta\phi)$, $z'=\wp_{11}(u;\ \theta\phi)$, that

$$[-vx'+uy'+dz'-w][-vx+uy+dz-w]$$
$$=M_{41}[M(xyz1)]_1+M_{42}[M(xyz1)]_2+M_{43}[M(xyz1)]_3+M_{44}[M(xyz1)]_4$$
$$=(M_{41}M_{11}+M_{42}M_{21}+M_{43}M_{31}+M_{44}M_{41})x+\dots$$
$$=(M^2)_{41}x+(M^2)_{42}y+(M^2)_{43}z+(M^2)_{44}.$$

Now $M^2=-\dfrac{\mu_\theta^2\mu_\phi^2}{(\theta-\phi)^2}$; thus the product is equal to the constant $\left(\dfrac{i\mu_\theta\mu_\phi}{\theta-\phi}\right)^2$.

This formula is analogous to the formula of the theory of elliptic functions

$$[\wp(u)-e][\wp(u+\omega)-e]=(e-e')(e-e'').$$

Ex. 13. *The tetrahedroid.* When the roots of the fundamental sextic are in involution, so that ∞, c; a_1, a_2; c_1, c_2 are conjugate pairs, and therefore

$$(c-c_1)(c-c_2)=(c-a_1)(c-a_2),$$

or say $\alpha_1\alpha_2=\gamma_1\gamma_2$, where $\alpha_1=a_1-c$, $\alpha_2=a_2-c$, $\gamma_1=c_1-c$, $\gamma_2=c_2-c$, write

$$\mathrm{a}=\left(\frac{\sqrt{\gamma_1}-\sqrt{\gamma_2}}{\sqrt{\gamma_1}+\sqrt{\gamma_2}}\right)^2,\qquad \mathrm{b}=\left(\frac{\sqrt{\alpha_1}-\sqrt{\alpha_2}}{\sqrt{\alpha_1}+\sqrt{\alpha_2}}\right)^2,\qquad p=\sqrt{\alpha_1\alpha_2}=\sqrt{\gamma_1\gamma_2};$$

then, with $\tau=t-c$, $x=\left(\dfrac{\tau-p}{\tau+p}\right)^2$, we find that

$$u_2-(p+c)u_1,\quad=\int\frac{(\tau-p)\,d\tau}{2[\tau(\tau-\alpha_1)(\tau-\alpha_2)(\tau-\gamma_1)(\tau-\gamma_2)]^{\frac{1}{2}}},$$

is equal to

$$\frac{1}{4}\sqrt{\frac{(1-\mathrm{a})(1-\mathrm{b})}{p}}\int\frac{dx}{\sqrt{(1-x)(\mathrm{a}-x)(\mathrm{b}-x)}},$$

and, with
$$y=\left(\frac{\tau+p}{\tau-p}\right)^2=\frac{1}{x},$$

$$u_2+(p-c)\,u_1, \quad =\int\frac{(\tau+p)\,d\tau}{2\,[\tau\,(\tau-\alpha_1)\,(\tau-\alpha_2)\,(\tau-\gamma_1)\,(\tau-\gamma_2)]^{\frac{1}{2}}},$$
$$=-\frac{1}{4}\sqrt{\frac{(\mathrm{a}^{-1}-1)\,(\mathrm{b}^{-1}-1)}{p}}\int\frac{dy}{\sqrt{(y-1)\,(y-\mathrm{a}^{-1})\,(y-\mathrm{b}^{-1})}}.$$

There are, thus, two everywhere finite integrals (of ambiguous sign) each of which is elliptic and possesses only two linearly independent periods.

If we put $H=\alpha_1+\alpha_2-\gamma_1-\gamma_2$ and

$$\xi=\frac{\alpha_2P_{a_1}-\alpha_1P_{a_2}}{\alpha_2-\alpha_1},\quad \eta=P_{a_1a_2}-\alpha_1\alpha_2H,\quad \zeta=P_{a_1a_2}+\alpha_1\alpha_2H-H\,\frac{\alpha_2P_{a_1}-\alpha_1P_{a_2}}{\alpha_2-\alpha_1},$$
$$\tau=P_{a_1a_2}-\alpha_1\alpha_2H-(\alpha_2P_{a_1}+\alpha_1P_{a_2}),$$

where, θ, ϕ being roots of the fundamental quintic,

$$P_\theta=y+\theta x-\theta^2,\quad P_{\theta\phi}=\theta\phi x+(\theta+\phi)\,y+z-e_{\theta\phi},$$

it is easy to verify that each of the planes $\xi=0$, $\eta=0$, $\zeta=0$, $\tau=0$ contains four of the sixteen nodes, the three summits of the quadrangle formed by the four nodes in any plane being the angular points in that plane of the tetrahedron $\xi\eta\zeta\tau$; namely

$\xi=0$	contains the nodes	(∞),	(c),	$(a_1,\ a_2)$,	$(c_1,\ c_2)$,
$\eta=0$	,, ,, ,,	(a_1),	(a_2),	$(c,\ a_1)$,	$(c,\ a_2)$,
$\zeta=0$	,, ,, ,,	(c_1),	(c_2),	$(c,\ c_1)$,	$(c,\ c_2)$,
$\tau=0$	,, ,, ,,	$(c_1,\ a_1)$,	$(c_1,\ a_2)$,	$(c_2,\ a_1)$,	$(c_2,\ a_2)$,

where (∞) denotes the node $(0, 0, \infty)$, (θ) denotes the node

$$x/1=-y/\theta=z/\theta^2=\infty,$$

and (θ, ϕ) denotes the node $(\theta+\phi,\ -\theta\phi,\ e_{\theta\phi})$; through each corner of the tetrahedron $\xi\eta\zeta\tau$ pass four tropes. We have previously (Ex. 9, p. 153) given the relation connecting the quantities P_{a_1}, P_{a_2}, $P_{a_1a_2}$, under the form of the equation referred to a Rosenhain tetrahedron. From this the equation referred to the tetrahedron $\xi\eta\zeta\tau$ can be calculated. But in fact this equation can be solved in terms of two arbitrary parameters x, y in the form

$$(\mathrm{a}-x)\,(y-\mathrm{a}^{-1})=M\frac{\eta^2}{\xi^2},\quad (\mathrm{b}-x)\,(y-\mathrm{b}^{-1})=M\frac{\zeta^2}{\xi^2},\quad (1-x)\,(y-1)=M\frac{\tau^2}{\xi^2},$$

where
$$M=16\alpha_1\alpha_2/(\alpha_1-\alpha_2)^2\,(\gamma_1-\gamma_2)^2;$$

thus the curves $x=$ constant, $y=$ constant lie on quadrics; in particular each of the planes $\xi=0$, $\eta=0$, $\zeta=0$, $\tau=0$ cuts the surface in two conics, intersecting in four nodes of the surface. This expression in terms of two parameters should be capable of derivation from the expression of the

Kummer surface in general, by use of the elliptic forms* of the integrals of the first kind. At full length the equation is

$$DB^2H^2\xi^4 + B^2\zeta^4 + H^2\tau^4 + D\eta^4 + 2(AH - B^2)(\eta^2\zeta^2 + H^2\xi^2\tau^2)$$
$$+ 2H(A - H)(\eta^2\tau^2 + B^2\xi^2\zeta^2) - 2HA(\zeta^2\tau^2 + D\xi^2\eta^2) = 0,$$

where $A = \alpha_1 + \alpha_2$, $B = \alpha_1 - \alpha_2$, $H = \alpha_1 + \alpha_2 - \gamma_1 - \gamma_2$, $D = H^2 + B^2 - 2AH$; and the surface is a form of the wave surface. We may put

$$\frac{1-x}{1-\text{a}} = \text{sn}^2(v, h), \quad \frac{\text{a}-x}{1-\text{a}} = -\text{cn}^2(v, h), \quad \frac{\text{b}-x}{1-\text{b}} = -\text{dn}^2(v, h), \quad h^2 = \frac{1-\text{a}}{1-\text{b}},$$

$$\frac{y-1}{\text{a}^{-1}-1} = \text{sn}^2(w, k), \quad \frac{y-\text{a}^{-1}}{\text{a}^{-1}-1} = -\text{cn}^2(w, k), \quad \frac{y-\text{b}^{-1}}{\text{b}^{-1}-1} = -\text{dn}^2(w, k), \quad k^2 = \frac{\text{a}^{-1}-1}{\text{b}^{-1}-1},$$

and so have

$$\frac{\eta}{\xi} = (\alpha_1 - \alpha_2)\,\text{cn}\, v\, \text{cn}\, w, \quad \frac{\zeta}{\xi} = (\gamma_1 - \gamma_2)\,\text{dn}\, v\, \text{dn}\, w, \quad \frac{\tau}{\xi} = (\alpha_1 - \alpha_2)\,\text{sn}\, v\, \text{sn}\, w.$$

The asymptotic lines, which are capable of derivation as a particular case of those previously obtained for the general Kummer surface, and the lines of curvature, are considered by Hudson, *Kummer's Quartic Surface*, Chapter X. and by Darboux, *Théor. Gén. des Surf.* Note VIII. Partie IV. p. 466.

Ex. 14. Consider the degenerescence of the Kummer surface when two of the six roots of the fundamental sextic become equal; as has been explained, we may, making a linear transformation, suppose, without loss of generality, that they both become infinite. For this, taking the equation for $\frac{1}{16}\Delta$ on p. 41, we may render it isobarically of weight 12, when x, y, z are reckoned of weights 4, 3, 2 and λ_i of weight i, by supplying in each term a proper power of $\frac{1}{4}\lambda_5$; the equation will then correspond to the form

$$\lambda_0 + \lambda_1 t + \ldots + \lambda_5 t^5,$$

of the fundamental sextic; putting then $\lambda_5 = 0$ the equation reduces to

$$\left(z - \frac{y^2}{x} + \tfrac{1}{4}\lambda_3\frac{y}{x} - \tfrac{1}{2}\lambda_4\frac{y^2}{x^2}\right)^2 = \left(x + \tfrac{1}{4}\lambda_4\right)\left(\lambda_0 - \lambda_1\frac{y}{x} + \lambda_2\frac{y^2}{x^2} - \lambda_3\frac{y^3}{x^3} + \lambda_4\frac{y^4}{x^4}\right),$$

a surface having $x = 0$, $y = 0$ as a double line, which, putting

$$\frac{y}{x} = -u, \quad \lambda_0 + \lambda_1 u + \lambda_2 u^2 + \lambda_3 u^3 + \lambda_4 u^4 = f(u),$$

$$z - \frac{y^2}{x} + \tfrac{1}{4}\lambda_3\frac{y}{x} - \tfrac{1}{2}\lambda_4\frac{y^2}{x^2} = v,$$

is satisfied by

$$x = -\tfrac{1}{4}\lambda_4 + \frac{v^2}{f(u)}, \quad y = \tfrac{1}{4}\lambda_4 u - \frac{uv^2}{f(u)}, \quad z = v + \tfrac{1}{4}(\lambda_3 u + \lambda_4 u^2) + \frac{u^2v^2}{f(u)}.$$

* By drawing variable planes through 2 nodes, any Kummer surface is expressible by elliptic functions of *variable* modulus. This modulus, I believe, is not constant so long as the six roots are distinct.

Now if in the equation

$$\frac{\lambda_0}{\alpha^4}+\frac{\lambda_1}{\alpha^3}+\frac{\lambda_2}{\alpha^2}+\frac{\lambda_3}{\alpha}+\lambda_4+\lambda_5\alpha=0,$$

we make $\alpha=\infty$, $\lambda_5=0$, we have $\lambda_5\alpha=-\lambda_4$; hence, with

$$F(\theta_i,\theta_j)=2\lambda_0+\lambda_1(\theta_i+\theta_j)+2\lambda_2\theta_i\theta_j+\lambda_3\theta_i\theta_j(\theta_i+\theta_j)+2\lambda_4\theta_i^2\theta_j^2+\lambda_5\theta_i^2\theta_j^2(\theta_i+\theta_j)$$
$$=-(\theta_i-\theta_j)^2[\lambda_2+\lambda_3(\theta_i+\theta_j)+\lambda_4(\theta_i+\theta_j)^2+\lambda_5(\theta_i+\theta_j)(\theta_i^2+\theta_i\theta_j+\theta_j^2)],$$

we have the following correspondences:

KUMMER SURFACE.	NEW SURFACE ($a=\infty$).
Nodes: $(0, 0, \infty)$, $\frac{x}{1}=\frac{y}{-a}=\frac{z}{a^2}=\infty$, $\frac{x}{1}=\frac{y}{-\theta_i}=\frac{z}{\theta_i^2}=\infty$.	Nodes: $(0, 0, \infty)$ twice; four given by $\frac{x}{1}=\frac{y}{-\theta_i}=\frac{z}{\theta_i^2}=\infty$.
Six nodes: $\frac{1}{4}\lambda_5(\theta_i+\theta_j)$, $-\frac{1}{4}\lambda_5\theta_i\theta_j$, $\frac{F(\theta_i,\theta_j)}{4(\theta_i-\theta_j)^2}$.	Nodes: three on axis of z, each of the form $0, 0, -\frac{1}{4}[\lambda_2+\lambda_3(\theta_i+\theta_j)+\lambda_4(\theta_i+\theta_j)^2]$, the third coordinate being $-\frac{1}{4}\lambda_4(\theta_i\theta_j+\theta_k\theta_l)$; at each of these the two tangent planes of the surface coincide.
Four nodes: $\frac{1}{4}\lambda_5(a+\theta_i)$, $-\frac{1}{4}\lambda_5 a\theta_i$, $\frac{F(a,\theta_i)}{4(a-\theta_i)^2}$.	Four nodes: $-\frac{1}{4}\lambda_4$, $\frac{1}{4}\lambda_4\theta_i$, $\frac{1}{4}(\lambda_3\theta_i+\lambda_4\theta_i^2)$.
Four tropes: $y+\theta_i x=\frac{1}{4}\lambda_5\theta_i^2$, beside $y+ax=\frac{1}{4}\lambda_5 a^2$, and plane at infinity.	Four tropes: $y+\theta_i x=0$, beside $x=-\frac{1}{4}\lambda_4$ and plane at infinity. Along $y+\theta_i x=0$ section of surface is two coincident straight lines, constituting a so-called torsal line.
Four tropes: $xa\theta_i+y(a+\theta_i)+z=\frac{F(a,\theta_i)}{4(a-\theta_i)^2}$.	Four tropes: $y+\theta_i x=0$. Thus as 8 nodes of original surface coincide in pairs in 4 new points, so 8 tropes coincide in pairs in 4 new planes.
Six tropes: $x\theta_i\theta_j+y(\theta_i+\theta_j)+z=\frac{F(\theta_i,\theta_j)}{4(\theta_i-\theta_j)^2}$.	Six tropes: $x\theta_i\theta_j+y(\theta_i+\theta_j)+z+\frac{1}{4}\lambda_4(\theta_i\theta_j+\theta_k\theta_l)$. These intersect in pairs on planes $x(\theta_i\theta_j-\theta_k\theta_l)+y(\theta_i+\theta_j-\theta_k-\theta_l)=0$, which is the single tangent plane at the singular point $0, 0, -\frac{1}{4}\lambda_4(\theta_i\theta_j+\theta_k\theta_l)$.

Thus the double line $x=0$, $y=0$, contains four singular points; through the double line pass four singular planes $y+\theta_i x=0$, each touching the surface along a torsal line; and each of these torsal lines contains two singular points, one being at infinity, the four finite ones lying on the plane $x+\frac{1}{4}\lambda_4=0$.

Substituting in terms of the parameters u, v we find

$$X \equiv x\theta_2\theta_3 + y(\theta_2+\theta_3) + z + \tfrac{1}{4}[\lambda_2 + \lambda_3(\theta_2+\theta_3) + \lambda_4(\theta_2+\theta_3)^2]$$

$$= v + \frac{v^2}{f(u)}(u-\theta_2)(u-\theta_3) + \tfrac{1}{4}\frac{(\theta_2-\theta_3)f(u)+(\theta_3-u)f(\theta_2)+(u-\theta_2)f(\theta_3)}{(\theta_2-\theta_3)(u-\theta_2)(u-\theta_3)}$$

$$= \frac{[v(u-\theta_2)(v-\theta_3)+\tfrac{1}{2}f(u)]^2}{(u-\theta_2)(u-\theta_3)f(u)};$$

putting similarly $Y \equiv x\theta_3\theta_1 + \text{etc.}$, $Z \equiv x\theta_1\theta_2 + \text{etc.}$,

so that $X=0$, $Y=0$, $Z=0$ is the singular point

$$-\tfrac{1}{4}\lambda_4,\quad \tfrac{1}{4}\lambda_4\theta_4,\quad \tfrac{1}{4}(\lambda_3\theta_4+\lambda_4\theta_4^2),$$

we thus find

$$(\theta_2-\theta_3)\sqrt{X(y+\theta_1 x)} + (\theta_3-\theta_1)\sqrt{Y(y+\theta_2 x)} + (\theta_1-\theta_2)\sqrt{Z(y+\theta_3 x)} = 0,$$

which is the same as

$$\Sigma\sqrt{(\theta_2-\theta_3)X(l'+mZ-nY)},$$

where l, m, n, l', m', n' are respectively 1, 1, 1, $\tfrac{1}{4}\lambda_4(\theta_4-\theta_1)(\theta_2-\theta_3)$, $\tfrac{1}{4}\lambda_4(\theta_4-\theta_2)(\theta_3-\theta_1)$, $\tfrac{1}{4}\lambda_4(\theta_4-\theta_3)(\theta_1-\theta_2)$, and are the coordinates of a line (the axis $x=0$, $y=0$); thus the surface is Plücker's complex surface. See Hudson, *Kummer's Quartic Surface*, Chapter VI. The irrational equation is the degenerescence of such forms as those on pp. 108, 110 here.

Now it can be shewn by actual substitution that the doubly-periodic function

$$\phi(u) = \rho[\zeta(u-\alpha_1) - \zeta(u-\alpha_2)],$$

satisfies the equation

$$\left(\frac{d\phi}{du}\right)^2 = \lambda_0 + \lambda_1\phi + \lambda_2\phi^2 + \lambda_3\phi^3 + \lambda_4\phi^4,$$

provided the invariants of the elliptic functions be

$$g_2 = \lambda_0\lambda_4 - \tfrac{1}{4}\lambda_1\lambda_3 + \tfrac{1}{12}\lambda_2^2,\quad g_3 = \tfrac{1}{6}\lambda_0\lambda_2\lambda_4 + \tfrac{1}{48}\lambda_1\lambda_2\lambda_3 - \tfrac{1}{16}\lambda_0\lambda_3^2 - \tfrac{1}{216}\lambda_2^3,$$

and $$\rho^2\lambda_4 = 1,\quad \wp(\alpha_1-\alpha_2) = (3\lambda_3^2 - 8\lambda_2\lambda_4)/48\lambda_4;$$

and that these give

$$\zeta(\alpha_1-\alpha_2) = \tfrac{1}{4}\rho\lambda_3,\quad \wp'(\alpha_1-\alpha_2) = (\tfrac{1}{2}\lambda_2\lambda_3\lambda_4 - \lambda_1\lambda_4^2 - \tfrac{1}{8}\lambda_3^3)/4\rho\lambda_4^2,$$

and also

$$\frac{\lambda_2}{12} + \tfrac{1}{4}\lambda_3\rho[\zeta(u-\alpha_1)-\zeta(u-\alpha_2)] + \tfrac{1}{2}[\zeta(u-\alpha_1)-\zeta(u-\alpha_2)]^2 = \tfrac{1}{2}[\wp(u-\alpha_1)+\wp(u-\alpha_2)].$$

Further the differential equations $\wp_{2222} - 6\wp_{22}^2 = \text{etc.}$, of p. 48, when we render them isobaric (reckoning $\wp_{22}$, $\wp_{21}$, $\wp_{11}$, λ_i as of weight 4, 3, 2, i) by supplying proper powers of $\tfrac{1}{4}\lambda_5$, and then put $\lambda_5 = 0$, can be integrated (as in *Camb. Phil. Proc.* XII. (1903), p. 230), and give for the corresponding σ-function, essentially,

$$[e^{mu_2}\sigma(u_1-\alpha_2) + e^{-mu_2}\sigma(u_1-\alpha_1)]\,e^{\frac{\lambda_2}{24}u_1^2},$$

where $m = \frac{1}{2}\sqrt{\lambda_4} = \frac{1}{2}\rho$, say; putting

$$\sigma(u_1 - a_2) = \sigma_2, \quad \sigma(u_1 - a_1) = \sigma_1, \quad \zeta(u_1 - a_2) = \zeta_2, \text{ etc.},$$

and $\Delta = e^{mu_2}\sigma_2 + e^{-mu_2}\sigma_1$, this leads to

$$x = \wp_{22} = -\frac{4m^2\sigma_1\sigma_2}{\Delta^2}, \qquad y = \wp_{21} = \frac{2m\sigma_1\sigma_2(\zeta_1 - \zeta_2)}{\Delta^2},$$

$$z = \wp_{11} = -\frac{\lambda_2}{12} + \frac{e^{mu_2}\sigma_2\wp_2 + e^{-mu_2}\sigma_1\wp_1}{\Delta} - \frac{\sigma_1\sigma_2(\zeta_1 - \zeta_2)^2}{\Delta^2},$$

and hence, with the relations above,

$$x + \tfrac{1}{4}\lambda_4 = \frac{1}{4\rho^2\Delta^2}[e^{mu_2}\sigma_2 - e^{-mu_2}\sigma_1]^2, \quad \frac{y}{x} = -\rho(\zeta_1 - \zeta_2) = -\phi(u_1),$$

$$z - \frac{y^2}{x} + \tfrac{1}{4}\lambda_3\frac{y}{x} - \tfrac{1}{2}\lambda_4\frac{y^2}{x^2} = -\tfrac{1}{2}(\wp_1 - \wp_2)\frac{e^{mu_2}\sigma_2 - e^{-mu_2}\sigma_1}{e^{mu_2}\sigma_2 + e^{-mu_2}\sigma_1},$$

while
$$\rho^2(\wp_1 - \wp_2)^2 = \left(\frac{d\phi}{du_1}\right)^2 = f(\phi) = f\left(-\frac{y}{x}\right),$$

so that we have the same relation connecting x, y, z as before.

The functions x, y, z are rationally expressible by the three*

$$e^{2mu_2}\frac{\sigma(u_1 - a_2)}{\sigma(u_1 - a_1)}, \quad \wp(u_1), \quad \wp'(u_1),$$

which are a set of three functions with three pairs of periods

$$\begin{array}{c|ccc} u_1 & 0, & 2\omega, & 2\omega', \\ u_2 & \dfrac{\pi i}{m}, & -\dfrac{\eta(a_1 - a_2)}{m}, & -\dfrac{\eta'(a_1 - a_2)}{m}, \end{array}$$

but the reverse expression is not rational.

Other particular cases when the roots of the fundamental sextic become equal can be similarly dealt with.

Ex. 15. The relations

$$u_2' = \int_0^{(u_1, u_2)} \frac{\wp_{22}(u)\,du_2 + 2\wp_{21}(u)\,du_1}{\sqrt{\wp_{22}^2(u) + 4\wp_{21}(u)}}, \qquad u_1' = \int_0^{(u_1, u_2)} \frac{2du_2 - \wp_{22}(u)\,du_1}{\sqrt{\wp_{22}^2(u) + 4\wp_{21}(u)}},$$

have been shewn (p. 117) to give $\wp_{22}(u') = \wp_{22}(u)$; $\wp_{21}(u') = \wp_{21}(u)$. It is found that for small values of u_1, u_2, the function $\sigma^4(u)[\wp_{22}^2(u) + 4\wp_{21}(u)]$, on expansion, has for its lowest terms

$$f(u_2, u_1) = 4u_2^5u_1 + \lambda_4u_2^4u_1^2 + \lambda_3u_2^3u_1^3 + \lambda_2u_2^2u_1^4 + \lambda_1u_2u_1^5 + \lambda_0u_1^6,$$

so that, to the first approximation, the relations are, if $v = u_2/u_1$,

$$u_2' = 2\int_\infty^v \frac{t\,dt}{\sqrt{f(t, 1)}}, \quad u_1' = 2\int_\infty^v \frac{dt}{\sqrt{f(t, 1)}}.$$

* These functions occur in a paper of Painlevé's, *Acta Math.* XXVII. (1903), p. 40, as a case of the degenerescence of Abelian functions of two variables.

Ex. 16. The most general linear homogeneous transformation which gives $xz - y^2 = x_0 z_0 - y_0^2$ is that used in the text,

$$(x, y, z) = \begin{pmatrix} \mu_2^2, & 2\mu_2\mu_1, & \mu_1^2 \\ \mu_2\lambda_2, & \mu_2\lambda_1 + \mu_1\lambda_2, & \mu_1\lambda_1 \\ \lambda_2^2, & 2\lambda_2\lambda_1, & \lambda_1^2 \end{pmatrix} (x_0, y_0, z_0),$$

where $\lambda_1, \mu_1, \lambda_2, \mu_2$ are arbitrary quantities for which $\lambda_1\mu_2 - \lambda_2\mu_1 = 1$.

Ex. 17. If in the equation

$$\sigma(u+v)\,\sigma(u-v) = \sigma^2(u)\,\sigma^2(v)\,[\wp_{22}(u)\,\wp_{21}(v) - \wp_{22}(v)\,\wp_{21}(u) + \wp_{11}(v) - \wp_{11}(u)],$$

we expand both sides in powers of v_1 and v_2, and put

$$\delta = v_1 \frac{\partial}{\partial u_1} + v_2 \frac{\partial}{\partial u_2}, \quad \delta' = v_1 \frac{\partial}{\partial u_1'} + v_2 \frac{\partial}{\partial u_2'},$$

we infer that the coefficients of the various powers of v_1, v_2 in the expression

$$(\delta - \delta')^{2n}\,\sigma(u)\,\sigma(u'),$$

where, after differentiation, u_1', u_2' are to be replaced by u_1, u_2, are all linear functions of the four quantities

$$\sigma^2(u)\,\wp_{22}(u), \quad \sigma^2(u)\,\wp_{21}(u), \quad \sigma^2(u)\,\wp_{11}(u), \quad \sigma^2(u).$$

Ex. 18. If $BP'P$ be a chord of the Weddle surface through the node B, and $RP'S$ the chord of the space cubic through P', the plane RBS touches the quadric cone whose vertex is P which contains the six nodes.

Ex. 19. If b be a root of the fundamental quintic $f(x)$, the so-called principal asymptotic curve of the Kummer surface expressed by

$$b^2 - b\wp_{22}(2u) - \wp_{21}(2u) = 0$$

is such (§ 37, p. 114) that the satellite points, for all the roots, of any point (w) of it, are obtained by the addition of half-periods $u^{\theta, b}$, one of these being zero. Thus the corresponding curve of the Weddle surface is the curve of contact of the enveloping cone from the node (b); and (cf. Ex. 12, p. 156) the curve on the Kummer surface $\Delta = 0$ lies upon

$$[y + bx - b^2]\left[\frac{\partial\Delta}{\partial x} - b\frac{\partial\Delta}{\partial y} + b^2\frac{\partial\Delta}{\partial z}\right] + \frac{1}{4}f'(b)\frac{\partial\Delta}{\partial z} = 0,$$

(cf. Ex. 18, and p. 123), and is an octavic curve. Applied to any point of this, the usual birational group of 32 transformations reduces to 16, all linear.

Ex. 20. Prove (see §§ 32, 35, 43) that the square root of

$$b^2 - b\wp_{22}(2u) - \wp_{21}(2u)$$

is expressible in a form

$$\frac{1}{M}\{\xi(p' + qz - ry) + \eta(q' + rx - pz) + \zeta(r' + py - qx)\},$$

where $M = y\eta - x\zeta - \tau$; and hence as the quotient of two polynomials rational in x, y, z, where $x = \wp_{22}(u)$, $\xi = \wp_{222}(u)$, etc.

APPENDIX TO PART I.

NOTE I.

SOME ALGEBRAICAL RESULTS IN CONNEXION WITH THE THEORY OF LINEAR COMPLEXES.

1. If (x, y, z, t), (x', y', z', t') be the coordinates of two points upon a straight line, the quantities

$$l = tx' - t'x, \quad m = ty' - t'y, \quad n = tz' - t'z,$$
$$l' = yz' - y'z, \quad m' = zx' - z'x, \quad n' = xy' - x'y,$$

which satisfy the identity

$$ll' + mm' + nn' = 0,$$

have ratios independent of the position upon the line of the two points, these being, if

$$aX + bY + cZ + dT = 0, \quad a'X + b'Y + c'Z + d'T = 0$$

be any two planes through the line, the same as the ratios of the quantities

$$bc' - b'c, \quad ca' - c'a, \quad ab' - a'b, \quad da' - d'a, \quad db' - d'b, \quad dc' - d'c.$$

The condition that any point $(XYZT)$ should be upon the line consists of any two of the four equations

$$\text{(i)} \quad l'T + mZ - nY = 0, \quad m'T + nX - lZ = 0, \quad n'T + lY - mX = 0,$$
$$l'X + m'Y + n'Z = 0,$$

and the condition that any plane

$$AX + BY + CZ + DT = 0$$

should pass through the line consists of any two of the four equations

$$\text{(ii)} \quad lD + m'C - n'B = 0, \quad mD + n'A - l'C = 0, \quad nD + l'B - m'A = 0,$$
$$lA + mB + nC = 0.$$

If l, m, n, l', m', n' be any quantities satisfying the identity

$$ll' + mm' + nn' = 0,$$

then two points (x, y, z, t), (x', y', z', t') can be found such that the quantities

$$tx' - t'x, \ldots, \quad yz' - y'z, \ldots,$$

have the ratios of l, m, n, l', m', n'; namely these are any two points on the line whose equations are given by (i).

2. Denote by ω_1, v_1 respectively the two matrices

$$\omega_1 = \begin{pmatrix} 0, & -n_1, & m_1, & l_1' \\ n_1, & 0, & -l_1, & m_1' \\ -m_1, & l_1, & 0, & n_1' \\ -l_1', & -m_1', & -n_1', & 0 \end{pmatrix}, \quad v_1 = \begin{pmatrix} 0, & -n_1', & m_1', & l_1 \\ n_1', & 0, & -l_1', & m_1 \\ -m_1', & l_1', & 0, & n_1 \\ -l_1, & -m_1, & -n_1, & 0 \end{pmatrix},$$

where $l_1, m_1, n_1, l_1', m_1', n_1'$ are any quantities satisfying the identity

$$\Delta_1 = l_1 l_1' + m_1 m_1' + n_1 n_1' = 0;$$

then the determinant of ω_1, and of every first minor of ω_1, is zero, and the matrix satisfies the equation

$$\omega_1 (\omega_1^2 + l^2 + m^2 + n^2 + l'^2 + m'^2 + n'^2) = 0,$$

and a similar statement holds for v_1; while also

$$\omega_1 v_1 = 0 = v_1 \omega_1.$$

Denote similar matrices by ω_2, v_2, supposing likewise that $\Delta_2 = 0$; assume also that

$$\Delta_{12} = l_1 l_2' + m_1 m_2' + n_1 n_2' + l_1' l_2 + m_1' m_2 + n_1' n_2 = 0;$$

we have at once by multiplication

$$\omega_1 v_2 = \begin{pmatrix} -n_1 n_2' - m_1 m_2' - l_1' l_2, & m_1 l_2' - m_2 l_1', & n_1 l_2' - n_2 l_1', & m_1 n_2 - m_2 n_1 \\ l_1 m_2' - l_2 m_1', & -n_1 n_2' - l_1 l_2' - m_1' m_2, & n_1 m_2' - m_2 n_1', & n_1 l_2 - n_2 l_1 \\ l_1 n_2' - l_2 n_1', & m_1 n_2' - m_2 n_1', & -m_1 m_2' - l_1 l_2' - n_1' n_2, & l_1 m_2 - l_2 m_1 \\ -m_1' n_2' + m_2' n_1', & -n_1' l_2' + n_2' l_1', & -l_1' m_2' + l_2' m_1', & -l_1' l_2 - m_1' m_2 - n_1' n_2 \end{pmatrix},$$

and hence, in virtue of $\Delta_{12} = 0$,

$$\omega_1 v_2 + \omega_2 v_1 = 0;$$

similarly

$$v_1 \omega_2 + v_2 \omega_1 = 0,$$

and thus

$$(\omega_1 v_2)^2 = 0, \quad (v_1 \omega_2)^2 = 0.$$

3. It is difficult to avoid references to the following algebraical theorem*, part of which we utilise below: let a be any square matrix, say of n rows and columns; let θ be any root of the determinantal equation $|a - \rho| = 0$, of multiplicity l; let the highest common factor in regard to ρ, of the first minors of the determinant $|a - \rho|$, divide by $(\rho - \theta)^{l_1}$, the highest common factor of the minors of $(n - 2)$ rows and columns divide by $(\rho - \theta)^{l_2}$, and so on, the minors of $(n - r)$ rows and columns not vanishing for $\rho = \theta$, so that $l_r = 0$; put $\epsilon_1 = l - l_1$, $\epsilon_2 = l_1 - l_2$, ..., $\epsilon_r = l_{r-1}$, so that

$$(\rho - \theta)^l = (\rho - \theta)^{\epsilon_1} (\rho - \theta)^{\epsilon_2} \dots (\rho - \theta)^{\epsilon_r};$$

the factors $(\rho - \theta)^{\epsilon_1}$, $(\rho - \theta)^{\epsilon_2}$, ... are called the first, second, ... invariant factors of the matrix $a - \rho$, or of the matrix a, for the root θ; the exponents

* See, for one proof, Jordan, *Cours d'Analyse*, III. (1896), p. 173; another is given *Proc. Camb. Phil. Soc.* XII. (1903), p. 65.

$\epsilon_1, \epsilon_2, \ldots, \epsilon_r$ are known to satisfy the inequalities $\epsilon_1 \geqq \epsilon_2 \geqq \epsilon_3 \geqq \ldots \epsilon_r > 0$. Let $\epsilon_1', \epsilon_2', \ldots, \epsilon_1'', \epsilon_2'', \ldots$ be these series for the other roots $\theta', \theta'', \ldots$ of $|a - \rho| = 0$, then the matrix a satisfies an equation

$$(a-\theta)^{\epsilon_1}(a-\theta')^{\epsilon_1'}(a-\theta'')^{\epsilon_1''}\ldots = 0,$$

and no other equation of the same or lower order. Further, denoting a set of n numbers by a single letter, such as x_1, or $x_2, \ldots$ or $y_1, \ldots$ or z_1, or $z_2, \ldots$, l sets, linearly independent of one another, can be found to satisfy the equations

$$(a-\theta)\,x_1 = 0, \quad (a-\theta)\,x_2 = x_1, \quad \ldots, \quad (a-\theta)\,x_{\epsilon_1} = x_{\epsilon_1 - 1},$$
$$(a-\theta)\,y_1 = 0, \quad (a-\theta)\,y_2 = y_1, \quad \ldots, \quad (a-\theta)\,y_{\epsilon_2} = y_{\epsilon_2 - 1},$$
$$\ldots\ldots\ldots\ldots\ldots\ldots\ldots\ldots\ldots\ldots\ldots\ldots\ldots\ldots\ldots\ldots$$
$$(a-\theta)\,z_1 = 0, \quad (a-\theta)\,z_2 = z_1, \quad \ldots, \quad (a-\theta)\,z_{\epsilon_r} = z_{\epsilon_r - 1},$$

where $(a-\theta)\,x_1$ denotes n equations for the n elements of x_1, and similarly $(a-\theta)\,x_2 = x_1$ denotes n equations for the n elements of x_2, and so on; and then the most general solution of the n linear equations for the n elements of x which are represented by $(a-\theta)\,x = 0$ is a linear function of the sets $x_1, y_1, \ldots, z_1$, the most general solution of the equations $(a-\theta)^2 x = 0$ is a linear function of the sets $x_1, y_1, \ldots, z_1, x_2, y_2, \ldots, z_2$, and so on. Further, if l' be the multiplicity of the root θ', similar l' sets of n quantities can be chosen to satisfy the corresponding sets of linear equations for the root θ', and similar sets for the remaining roots $\theta'', \ldots$, and the whole number $n = l + l' + l'' + \ldots$ such sets can be chosen to be linearly independent of one another. Conversely, when we have independent knowledge of the equations

$$(a-\theta)\,x_1 = 0, \ldots (a-\theta)\,x_{\epsilon_1} = x_{\epsilon_1 - 1},$$
$$\ldots\ldots\ldots\ldots\ldots\ldots\ldots\ldots\ldots\ldots,$$
$$(a-\theta)\,z_1 = 0, \ldots (a-\theta)\,z_{\epsilon_r} = z_{\epsilon_r - 1},$$

for all the roots, the sets $x_1, x_2, \ldots$ being linearly independent, we can infer the values of the exponents of the various invariant factors.

4. Thus the equation $(\omega_1 v_2)^2 = 0$ of § 2 shews that the equation $|\omega_1 v_2 - \rho| = 0$ has no root but $\rho = 0$, occurring therefore with multiplicity 4, and with multiplicity 2 in the minors of $|\omega_1 v_2 - \rho|$ of three rows and columns, the exponent of the first invariant factor being 2; it can be verified, in virtue of $\Delta_1 = 0$, $\Delta_2 = 0$, $\Delta_{12} = 0$, that every minor of $\omega_1 v_2$ of two rows and columns also vanishes, so that the second and third invariant factors of $\omega_1 v_2 - \rho$ are both linear, and there exist linearly independent sets

$$(u_1, v_1, w_1, p_1), \quad (u_2, v_2, w_2, p_2), \quad (u_3, v_3, w_3, p_3), \quad (u_4, v_4, w_4, p_4),$$

such that

$$\omega_1 v_2 (u_1, v_1, w_1, p_1) = 0, \quad \omega_1 v_2 (u_4, v_4, w_4, p_4) = (u_1, v_1, w_1, p_1),$$
$$\omega_1 v_2 (u_2, v_2, w_2, p_2) = 0, \quad \omega_1 v_2 (u_3, v_3, w_3, p_3) = 0;$$

now we have $\omega_1 v_2 \omega_2 = 0$, $\omega_1 v_2 \omega_1 = -\omega_2 v_1 \omega_1 = 0$; the equations $\omega_1 v_2 \omega_2 = 0$

express that the elements of any row of $\omega_1 v_2$ are proportional to the homogeneous coordinates of a point lying on the line $(l_2, m_2, n_2, l_2', m_2', n_2')$, or ω_2; similarly $\omega_1 v_2 \omega_1 = 0$ express that the line ω_1 contains the point whose coordinates are the elements of any row of $\omega_1 v_2$; in virtue of $\Delta_{12} = 0$ the lines ω_1, ω_2 have one point in common; this is then given by the elements of every row of $\omega_1 v_2$, the ratios of these elements being the same whatever the row; since $\overline{\omega_1 v_2} = \bar{v}_2 \bar{\omega}_1 = v_2 \omega_1 = -v_1 \omega_2$, it follows similarly from the equations $v_1 \omega_2 v_1 = 0$, $v_1 \omega_2 v_2 = 0$, that the coefficients in the plane containing ω_1, ω_2 are proportional to the elements of any column of $\omega_1 v_2$; the equations $\omega_1 v_2 (u, v, w, p) = 0$ express that the plane (u, v, w, p) contains the point whose coordinates are proportional to the elements of any row of $\omega_1 v_2$; thus (u_1, v_1, w_1, p_1), (u_2, v_2, w_2, p_2), (u_3, v_3, w_3, p_3) above are any three independent planes drawn through the point (ω_1, ω_2); and, denoting the plane and point (ω_1, ω_2) respectively by (a, b, c, d) and (x, y, z, t), we may write

$$\omega_1 v_2 = \begin{pmatrix} ax, & ay, & az, & at \\ bx, & by, & bz, & bt \\ cx, & cy, & cz, & ct \\ dx, & dy, & dz, & dt \end{pmatrix},$$

where if t be assigned, d must have an appropriate value; putting

$$\alpha = \begin{pmatrix} a & 0 & 0 & 0 \\ 0 & b & 0 & 0 \\ 0 & 0 & c & 0 \\ 0 & 0 & 0 & d \end{pmatrix}, \quad H = \begin{pmatrix} 1 & 1 & 1 & 1 \\ 1 & 1 & 1 & 1 \\ 1 & 1 & 1 & 1 \\ 1 & 1 & 1 & 1 \end{pmatrix}, \quad \xi = \begin{pmatrix} x & 0 & 0 & 0 \\ 0 & y & 0 & 0 \\ 0 & 0 & z & 0 \\ 0 & 0 & 0 & t \end{pmatrix},$$

this is the same as $$\omega_1 v_2 = \alpha H \xi.$$

5. If now we have three matrices ω_1, ω_2, ω_3 such that $\Delta_1 = 0$, $\Delta_2 = 0$, $\Delta_3 = 0$, and $\Delta_{23} = 0$, $\Delta_{31} = 0$, $\Delta_{12} = 0$, the associated lines have either a common point or a common plane, but, in the absence of further conditions, not both. When they have a common point we may write

$$\omega_1 v_2 = \alpha_3 H \xi, \quad \omega_2 v_3 = \alpha_1 H \xi, \quad \omega_3 v_1 = \alpha_2 H \xi,$$

and thence, if we denote by M, momentarily, the matrix

$$M = \alpha_1 \omega_1 + \alpha_2 \omega_2 + \alpha_3 \omega_3,$$

we have $$M v_1 = \alpha_1 (0) + \alpha_2 (-\alpha_3 H \xi) + \alpha_3 (\alpha_2 H \xi),$$

or, since the diagonal matrices α_2, α_3 are commutable, $M v_1 = 0$; similarly $M v_2 = 0$ and $M v_3 = 0$; thus the elements of any row of M are the coefficients of a plane containing all the lines ω_1, ω_2, ω_3; as they have no plane in common we infer that

$$\alpha_1 \omega_1 + \alpha_2 \omega_2 + \alpha_3 \omega_3 = 0,$$

which is equivalent to $$\omega_1 \alpha_1 + \omega_2 \alpha_2 + \omega_3 \alpha_3 = 0.$$

Similarly when $\omega_1, \omega_2, \omega_3$ have a plane, but not a point, in common,

$$\xi_1 v_1 + \xi_2 v_2 + \xi_3 v_3 = 0,$$

or

$$v_1 \xi_1 + v_2 \xi_2 + v_3 \xi_3 = 0.$$

Also, when $\omega_1, \omega_2, \omega_3$ meet in a point,

$$\omega_1 v_2 \omega_3 = \alpha_3 H \xi \omega_3 = \alpha_3 \alpha_1^{-1} \omega_2 v_3 \omega_3 = 0,$$

and this is the same as

$$\omega_1 v_2 \omega_3 = 0 = -\omega_2 v_1 \omega_3 = +\omega_2 v_3 \omega_1 = -\omega_3 v_2 \omega_1 = \omega_3 v_1 \omega_2 = -\omega_1 v_3 \omega_2;$$

and when $\omega_1, \omega_2, \omega_3$ lie in a plane, we have similarly

$$v_1 \omega_2 v_3 = 0,$$

wherein again the suffixes may be taken in any order.

6. Now consider

$$\Gamma_1 = \begin{pmatrix} 0, & -r_1, & q_1, & p_1' \\ r_1, & 0, & -p_1, & q_1' \\ -q_1, & p_1, & 0, & r_1' \\ -p_1', & -q_1', & -r_1', & 0 \end{pmatrix},$$

where $\Delta_1 = p_1 p_1' + q_1 q_1' + r_1 r_1' = -1$, so that the determinant $|\Gamma_1| = 1$ and

$$\Gamma_1^{-1} = \begin{pmatrix} 0, & -r_1', & q_1', & p_1 \\ r_1', & 0, & -p_1', & q_1 \\ -q_1', & p_1', & 0, & r_1 \\ -p_1, & -q_1, & -r_1, & 0 \end{pmatrix}.$$

Take two such matrices Γ_1, Γ_2, and suppose that

$$\Delta_{12} = p_1 p_2' + q_1 q_2' + r_1 r_2' + p_1' p_2 + q_1' q_2 + r_1' r_2 = 0;$$

it is then at once verified, as in the case of the matrices ω_1, ω_2, that

$$\Gamma_1 \Gamma_2^{-1} + \Gamma_2 \Gamma_1^{-1} = 0, \quad \Gamma_1^{-1} \Gamma_2 + \Gamma_2^{-1} \Gamma_1 = 0,$$

and hence that $\quad (\Gamma_1 \Gamma_2^{-1})^2 = -1, \quad (\Gamma_1^{-1} \Gamma_2)^2 = -1.$

Consider the determinantal equation $|\Gamma_1 \Gamma_2^{-1} - \rho| = 0$; it follows (§ 3) from $(\Gamma_1 \Gamma_2^{-1})^2 = -1$ that its roots are i and $-i$, and that each occurs in the first minors of $\Gamma_1 \Gamma_2^{-1} - \rho$ with a multiplicity one less than in $\Gamma_1 \Gamma_2^{-1} - \rho$; hence each is a double root of $|\Gamma_1 \Gamma_2^{-1} - \rho| = 0$, and the exponents of the invariant factors are 1, 1 for each root; we can therefore find four linearly independent sets (x_1, y_1, z_1, t_1), (x_2, y_2, z_2, t_2), etc., such that

$$(\Gamma_1 \Gamma_2^{-1} - i)(x_1, y_1, z_1, t_1) = 0, \quad (\Gamma_1 \Gamma_2^{-1} + i)(x_2, y_2, z_2, t_2) = 0,$$
$$(\Gamma_1 \Gamma_2^{-1} + i)(x_3, y_3, z_3, t_3) = 0, \quad (\Gamma_1 \Gamma_2^{-1} - i)(x_4, y_4, z_4, t_4) = 0.$$

Further $|\Gamma_1 - i\Gamma_2| = |\Gamma_1 \Gamma_2^{-1} - i|\,|\Gamma_2| = 0$, and so on; thus the matrices

$$\omega_1 = \Gamma_1 - i\Gamma_2, \quad \omega_1' = \Gamma_1 + i\Gamma_2, \quad v_1 = \Gamma_1^{-1} - i\Gamma_2^{-1}, \quad v_1' = \Gamma_1^{-1} + i\Gamma_2^{-1},$$

have each a vanishing determinant; the pair ω_1, v_1 are related to one another as are the two previously (§ 4) discussed with the same notation, and belong to a straight line; the pair ω_1', v_1' belong to another straight line; but, as

$$\omega_1 v_1' + \omega_1' v_1 = 2 + i(\Gamma_1\Gamma_2^{-1} - \Gamma_2\Gamma_1^{-1}) + 2 + i(\Gamma_2\Gamma_1^{-1} - \Gamma_1\Gamma_2^{-1}) = 4,$$

these two straight lines do not intersect.

7. Suppose now we have six matrices, of the form considered here,

$$\Gamma_1, \Gamma_2, \Gamma_3, \Gamma_4, \Gamma_5, \Gamma_6,$$

for which $\Delta_r = -1, \quad \Delta_{rs} = 0, \qquad r, s = 1, 2, \ldots, 6.$

Take any three of the six, Γ_1, Γ_3, Γ_5; take the remaining three in any order, say Γ_2, Γ_4, Γ_6; we have then six straight lines

$$\omega_1 = \Gamma_1 - i\Gamma_2, \quad \omega_2 = \Gamma_3 - i\Gamma_4, \quad \omega_3 = \Gamma_5 - i\Gamma_6,$$
$$\omega_1' = \Gamma_1 + i\Gamma_2, \quad \omega_2' = \Gamma_3 + i\Gamma_4, \quad \omega_3' = \Gamma_5 + i\Gamma_6;$$

now, if $\epsilon = i$ or $-i$,

$$(\Gamma_1 + i\Gamma_2)(\Gamma_3^{-1} + \epsilon\Gamma_4^{-1}) + (\Gamma_3 + \epsilon\Gamma_4)(\Gamma_1^{-1} + i\Gamma_2^{-1})$$
$$= \Gamma_1\Gamma_3^{-1} + \Gamma_3\Gamma_1^{-1} + i(\Gamma_2\Gamma_3^{-1} + \Gamma_3\Gamma_2^{-1}) + \epsilon(\Gamma_1\Gamma_4^{-1} + \Gamma_4\Gamma_1^{-1}) + i\epsilon(\Gamma_2\Gamma_4^{-1} + \Gamma_4\Gamma_2^{-1})$$
$$= 0;$$

thus, while the straight lines ω_1, ω_1' do not themselves intersect, each of them intersects the other four; similarly for the other couples ω_2, ω_2' and ω_3, ω_3'.

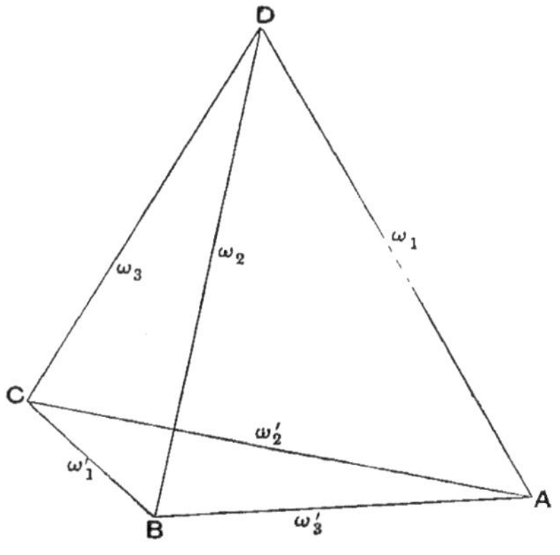

Take the point of intersection of ω_1 and ω_2; call it D; the line ω_3 intersects both ω_1 and ω_2 and so lies in their plane or passes through their intersection; the same is true of ω_3', which however does not intersect ω_3; thus either ω_3 passes through D, while ω_3' does not, or the converse; if we suppose the sign of every element in Γ_6 changed, if necessary—which still leaves all preceding conventions and results unaltered—we can then suppose

ω_3 to pass through D, and ω_3' to intersect ω_1 and ω_2, say in A and B; then ω_1' intersects ω_2 and ω_3', but not ω_1, and so passes through B, and it intersects ω_3, say in C; while ω_2' intersects ω_1, ω_3' and ω_3 and so passes through C and A, so that we have the figure annexed.

Let the points A, B, C, D be (x_1, y_1, z_1, t_1), (x_2, y_2, z_2, t_2), ..., each, for clearness sake, being associated with four definite numbers, not with three ratios; let the opposite planes be $a_1x + b_1y + c_1z + d_1t = 0$, etc., with the conventions $a_1x_1 + b_1y_1 + c_1z_1 + d_1t_1 = 1$, etc.; if α_r denote the diagonal matrix whose elements are a_r, b_r, c_r, d_r, and ξ_r the diagonal matrix whose elements are x_r, y_r, z_r, t_r, the sign of Γ_6 being settled by (see § 5)

$$(\Gamma_1 - i\Gamma_2)(\Gamma_3^{-1} - i\Gamma_4^{-1})(\Gamma_5 - i\Gamma_6) = 0, \quad (\Gamma_1^{-1} + i\Gamma_2^{-1})(\Gamma_3 + i\Gamma_4)(\Gamma_5^{-1} + i\Gamma_6^{-1}) = 0,$$

the tetrahedron is determined without ambiguity by the equations following, in which a constant factor is omitted in the right side of each,

$$\begin{array}{lll} \omega_1 v_2 = \alpha_3 H\xi_4, & \omega_2 v_3 = \alpha_1 H\xi_4, & \omega_3 v_1 = \alpha_2 H\xi_4; \\ \omega_1 v_2' = \alpha_2 H\xi_1, & \omega_2' v_3' = \alpha_4 H\xi_1, & \omega_3' v_1 = \alpha_3 H\xi_1; \\ \omega_2 v_3' = \alpha_3 H\xi_2, & \omega_3' v_1' = \alpha_4 H\xi_2, & \omega_1' v_2 = \alpha_1 H\xi_2; \\ \omega_3 v_1' = \alpha_1 H\xi_3, & \omega_1' v_2' = \alpha_4 H\xi_3, & \omega_2' v_3 = \alpha_2 H\xi_3. \end{array}$$

There are manifestly 15 such tetrahedra, according to the pairs (1, 2), (3, 4), (5, 6) into which the original matrices $\Gamma_1, \Gamma_2, \Gamma_3, \ldots, \Gamma_6$ are divided. Corresponding to the triplets of intersecting lines

$$(\omega_1, \omega_2, \omega_3), \quad (\omega_1', \omega_2', \omega_3), \quad (\omega_2', \omega_3', \omega_1), \quad (\omega_3', \omega_1', \omega_2),$$

we have now

$$\omega_1 v_2 \omega_3 = 0, \quad \omega_1' v_2' \omega_3 = 0, \quad \omega_1 v_2' \omega_3' = 0, \quad \omega_1' v_2 \omega_3' = 0,$$

and hence $$(\omega_1 v_2 + \omega_1' v_2')\,\omega_3 = 0, \quad (\omega_1 v_2' + \omega_1' v_2)\,\omega_3' = 0;$$

but

$$\omega_1 v_2 + \omega_1' v_2' = (\Gamma_1 - i\Gamma_2)(\Gamma_3^{-1} - i\Gamma_4^{-1}) + (\Gamma_1 + i\Gamma_2)(\Gamma_3^{-1} + i\Gamma_4^{-1})$$
$$= 2(\Gamma_1\Gamma_3^{-1} - \Gamma_2\Gamma_4^{-1}),$$
$$\omega_1 v_2' + \omega_1' v_2 = (\Gamma_1 - i\Gamma_2)(\Gamma_3^{-1} + i\Gamma_4^{-1}) + (\Gamma_1 + i\Gamma_2)(\Gamma_3^{-1} - i\Gamma_4^{-1})$$
$$= 2(\Gamma_1\Gamma_3^{-1} + \Gamma_2\Gamma_4^{-1}),$$

so that $$0 = \tfrac{1}{2}(\omega_1 v_2 + \omega_1' v_2')\,\omega_3 + \tfrac{1}{2}(\omega_1 v_2' + \omega_1' v_2)\,\omega_3'$$
$$= \Gamma_1\Gamma_3^{-1}(\omega_3 + \omega_3') - \Gamma_2\Gamma_4^{-1}(\omega_3 - \omega_3')$$
$$= 2\Gamma_1\Gamma_3^{-1}\Gamma_5 + 2i\Gamma_2\Gamma_4^{-1}\Gamma_6,$$

or $$\Gamma_1\Gamma_3^{-1}\Gamma_5 = -i\Gamma_2\Gamma_4^{-1}\Gamma_6,$$

giving $\Gamma_2^{-1}\Gamma_1\Gamma_3^{-1}\Gamma_5\Gamma_6^{-1}\Gamma_4 = -i$, or, as $\Gamma_2^{-1}\Gamma_1 = -\Gamma_1^{-1}\Gamma_2$, etc.,

$$\Gamma_1^{-1}\Gamma_2\Gamma_3^{-1}\Gamma_4\Gamma_5^{-1}\Gamma_6 = i.$$

Similarly by considering the triplets of coplanar lines, changing the sign of i throughout and replacing Γ_r by Γ_r^{-1}, we have

$$\Gamma_1\Gamma_2^{-1}\Gamma_3\Gamma_4^{-1}\Gamma_5\Gamma_6^{-1} = -i.$$

8. Assign now definite directions, DA, DB, DC, BC, CA, AB to the edges of the tetrahedron, and let the coordinates of a line directed from (x_1, y_1, z_1, t_1) to (x_2, y_2, z_2, t_2) be defined by

$$l = t_1 x_2 - t_2 x_1, \quad m = t_1 y_2 - t_2 y_1, \quad n = t_1 z_2 - t_2 z_1,$$
$$p = y_1 z_2 - y_2 z_1, \quad q = z_1 x_2 - z_2 x_1, \quad r = x_1 y_2 - x_2 y_1;$$

there will then be six such sets $(l_1, \ldots, r_1)$, $(l_3', \ldots, r_3')$ for the edges of the tetrahedron, the coordinates occurring in them being those of the corners; put further

$$\Omega_1 = \begin{pmatrix} 0, & -n_1, & m_1, & p_1 \\ n_1, & 0, & -l_1, & q_1 \\ -m_1, & l_1, & 0, & r_1 \\ -p_1, & -q_1, & -r_1, & 0 \end{pmatrix}, \quad V_1 = \begin{pmatrix} 0, & -r_1, & q_1, & l_1 \\ r_1, & 0, & -p_1, & m_1 \\ -q_1, & p_1, & 0, & n_1 \\ -l_1, & -m_1, & -n_1, & 0 \end{pmatrix},$$

and so on; we shall have then

$$\omega_1 = e\Omega_1, \quad \omega_1' = e'\Omega_1', \quad \omega_2 = f\Omega_2, \quad \omega_2' = f'\Omega_2', \quad \omega_3 = g\Omega_3, \quad \omega_3' = g'\Omega_3',$$

where e, e', f, f', g, g' are certain constants; and as $v_1 = \Gamma_1^{-1} - i\Gamma_2^{-1}$ is obtained by the same rearrangement of the elements in Γ_1^{-1}, Γ_2^{-1} as is $\omega_1 = \Gamma_1 - i\Gamma_2$ of the elements in Γ_1, Γ_2, we shall also have

$$v_1 = eV_1, \quad v_1' = e'V_1', \quad v_2 = fV_2, \quad v_2' = f'V_2', \quad v_3 = gV_3, \quad v_3' = g'V_3';$$

and the equations

$$\Gamma_1 = \tfrac{1}{2}(e\Omega_1 + e'\Omega_1'), \quad \Gamma_1^{-1} = \tfrac{1}{2}(eV_1 + e'V_1'),$$

give, in virtue of $\Omega_1 V_1 = 0$,

$$1 = \tfrac{1}{4}ee'(\Omega_1 V_1' + \Omega_1' V_1),$$

which, as before, is the same as

$$1 = -\tfrac{1}{4}ee'(p_1 l_1' + q_1 m_1' + r_1 n_1' + p_1' l_1 + q_1' m_1 + r_1' n_1)$$
$$= \tfrac{1}{4}ee' \begin{vmatrix} x_4 & y_4 & z_4 & t_4 \\ x_1 & y_1 & z_1 & t_1 \\ x_2 & y_2 & z_2 & t_2 \\ x_3 & y_3 & z_3 & t_3 \end{vmatrix}$$
$$= \tfrac{1}{4}ee'(4123), \text{ say;}$$

so we find
$$1 = \tfrac{1}{4}ff'(4231), \quad 1 = \tfrac{1}{4}gg'(4312),$$

or, if $(1234) = \Delta$,

$$ee' = -4\Delta^{-1}, \quad ff' = -4\Delta^{-1}, \quad gg' = -4\Delta^{-1}.$$

Take now

$$P = \begin{pmatrix} x_1, & x_2, & x_3, & x_4 \\ y_1, & y_2, & y_3, & y_4 \\ z_1, & z_2, & z_3, & z_4 \\ t_1, & t_2, & t_3, & t_4 \end{pmatrix}, \quad Q = \begin{pmatrix} a_1, & b_1, & c_1, & d_1 \\ a_2, & b_2, & c_2, & d_2 \\ a_3, & b_3, & c_3, & d_3 \\ a_4, & b_4, & c_4, & d_4 \end{pmatrix},$$

so that
$$QP = 1;$$

if Ω be a matrix formed, as are here $\Omega_1, \ldots$, in association with a straight line, which we suppose drawn from (ξ, η, ζ, τ) to $(\xi', \eta', \zeta', \tau')$, the sth element of the rth row of the matrix $\bar{P}\Omega P$ is given by

$$(\bar{P}\Omega P)_{rs} = \sum_i \sum_j \bar{P}_{ri}\Omega_{ij}P_{js} = \sum_{i,j} \Omega_{ij}(\bar{P}_{ri}\bar{P}_{sj} - \bar{P}_{rj}\bar{P}_{si})$$

$$= \Omega_{14}(x_r t_s - x_s t_r) + \ldots + \Omega_{23}(y_r z_s - y_s z_r) + \ldots$$

$$= \begin{vmatrix} \xi & \eta & \zeta & \tau \\ \xi' & \eta' & \zeta' & \tau' \\ x_r & y_r & z_r & t_r \\ x_s & y_s & z_s & t_s \end{vmatrix};$$

we therefore find $(\bar{P}\Omega_1 P)_{rs} = 0$, unless $r = 2$, $s = 3$ or $r = 3$, $s = 2$, while $(\bar{P}\Omega_1 P)_{rs} = -(\bar{P}\Omega_1 P)_{sr}$, and so for the others, and then

$$(\bar{P}\Omega_1 P)_{23} = (4123) = -\Delta, \quad (\bar{P}\Omega_1' P)_{14} = (2314) = \Delta, \quad (\bar{P}\Omega_2 P)_{31} = (4231) = -\Delta,$$

$$(\bar{P}\Omega_2' P)_{24} = (3124) = \Delta, \quad (\bar{P}\Omega_3 P)_{12} = -\Delta, \quad (\bar{P}\Omega_3' P)_{34} = \Delta.$$

Now take

$$m = \begin{pmatrix} \lambda & 0 & 0 & 0 \\ 0 & \mu & 0 & 0 \\ 0 & 0 & \nu & 0 \\ 0 & 0 & 0 & \rho \end{pmatrix}, \quad Pm = \varpi,$$

where λ, μ, ν, ρ are to be determined; thus

$$\varpi\Gamma_1\varpi = \tfrac{1}{2} m\bar{P}(\omega_1 + \omega_1')Pm = \tfrac{1}{2} m(e\bar{P}\Omega_1 P + e'\bar{P}\Omega_1' P)m$$

$$= \tfrac{1}{2} m \begin{pmatrix} 0 & 0 & 0 & e' \\ 0 & 0 & -e & 0 \\ 0 & e & 0 & 0 \\ -e' & 0 & 0 & 0 \end{pmatrix} m$$

$$= \tfrac{1}{2}\Delta \begin{pmatrix} 0, & 0, & 0, & \lambda\rho e' \\ 0, & 0, & -\mu\nu e, & 0 \\ 0, & \mu\nu e, & 0, & 0 \\ -\lambda\rho e', & 0, & 0, & 0 \end{pmatrix},$$

$$\varpi\Gamma_2\varpi = \frac{i}{2} mP(\omega_1 - \omega_1')Pm = \frac{i\Delta}{2} \begin{pmatrix} 0, & 0, & 0, & -\lambda\rho e' \\ 0, & 0, & -\mu\nu e, & 0 \\ 0, & \mu\nu e, & 0, & 0 \\ \lambda\rho e', & 0, & 0, & 0 \end{pmatrix};$$

similarly

$$\varpi\Gamma_3\varpi = \tfrac{1}{2}\Delta\begin{pmatrix} 0, & 0, & \lambda\nu f, & 0 \\ 0, & 0, & 0, & \mu\rho f' \\ -\lambda\nu f, & 0, & 0, & 0 \\ 0, & -\mu\rho f', & 0, & 0 \end{pmatrix},$$

$$\varpi\Gamma_4\varpi = \frac{i\Delta}{2}\begin{pmatrix} 0, & 0, & \lambda\nu f, & 0 \\ 0, & 0, & 0, & -\mu\rho f' \\ -\lambda\nu f, & 0, & 0, & 0 \\ 0, & \mu\rho f', & 0, & 0 \end{pmatrix},$$

$$\varpi\Gamma_5\varpi = \tfrac{1}{2}\Delta\begin{pmatrix} 0, & -\lambda\mu g, & 0, & 0 \\ \lambda\mu g, & 0, & 0, & 0 \\ 0, & 0, & 0, & \nu\rho g' \\ 0, & 0, & -\nu\rho g', & 0 \end{pmatrix},$$

$$\varpi\Gamma_6\varpi = \frac{i\Delta}{2}\begin{pmatrix} 0, & -\lambda\mu g, & 0, & 0 \\ \lambda\mu g, & 0, & 0, & 0 \\ 0, & 0, & 0, & -\nu\rho g' \\ 0, & 0, & \nu\rho g', & 0 \end{pmatrix};$$

herein take ρ equal to either of the two quantities given by $\rho^2 = \frac{1}{8}\Delta efg$, and $\lambda = \frac{1}{2}e/\rho$, $\mu = \frac{1}{2}f/\rho$, $\nu = \frac{1}{2}g/\rho$; then, as $ee' = ff' = gg' = -\dfrac{4}{\Delta}$, we have $\frac{1}{2}\Delta\lambda\rho e' = -1$, $\frac{1}{2}\Delta\mu\nu e = 1$, $\frac{1}{2}\Delta\mu\rho f' = -1$, $\frac{1}{2}\Delta\nu\lambda f = 1$, $\frac{1}{2}\Delta\nu\rho g' = -1$, $\frac{1}{2}\Delta\lambda\mu g = 1$, and so

$$\gamma_1 = \varpi\Gamma_1\varpi = \begin{pmatrix} 0, & 0, & 0, & -1 \\ 0, & 0, & -1, & 0 \\ 0, & 1, & 0, & 0 \\ 1, & 0, & 0, & 0 \end{pmatrix}, \quad \gamma_3 = \varpi\Gamma_3\varpi = \begin{pmatrix} 0, & 0, & 1, & 0 \\ 0, & 0, & 0, & -1 \\ -1, & 0, & 0, & 0 \\ 0, & 1, & 0, & 0 \end{pmatrix},$$

$$\gamma_5 = \varpi\Gamma_5\varpi = \begin{pmatrix} 0, & -1, & 0, & 0 \\ 1, & 0, & 0, & 0 \\ 0, & 0, & 0, & -1 \\ 0, & 0, & 1, & 0 \end{pmatrix},$$

$$\gamma_2 = \varpi\Gamma_2\varpi = \begin{pmatrix} 0, & 0, & 0, & i \\ 0, & 0, & -i, & 0 \\ 0, & i, & 0, & 0 \\ -i, & 0, & 0, & 0 \end{pmatrix}, \quad \gamma_4 = \varpi\Gamma_4\varpi = \begin{pmatrix} 0, & 0, & i, & 0 \\ 0, & 0, & 0, & i \\ -i, & 0, & 0, & 0 \\ 0, & -i, & 0, & 0 \end{pmatrix},$$

$$\gamma_6 = \varpi\Gamma_6\varpi = \begin{pmatrix} 0, & -i, & 0, & 0 \\ i, & 0, & 0, & 0 \\ 0, & 0, & 0, & i \\ 0, & 0, & -i, & 0 \end{pmatrix},$$

for each of which the invariant $(pp' + qq' + rr')$ is -1; and if we take

$$\varpi(X, Y, Z, T) = (x, y, z, t), \quad \varpi(X', Y', Z', T') = (x', y', z', t'),$$

namely

$$X = \frac{1}{\lambda}(a_1x + b_1y + c_1z + d_1t), \quad Y = \frac{1}{\mu}(a_2x + b_2y + c_2z + d_2t), \text{ etc.},$$

and put $$L = TX' - T'X, \quad P = YZ' - Y'Z, \text{ etc.},$$

we shall have, if $\Gamma_1(x, y, z, t)(x', y', z', t')$ and $\gamma_1(X, Y, Z, T)(X', Y', Z', T')$ be respectively denoted by $\Gamma_1 xx'$ and $\gamma_1 XX'$,

$$\Gamma_1 xx' = \gamma_1 XX' = -L + P, \quad \Gamma_3 xx' = \gamma_3 XX' = -M + Q,$$
$$\Gamma_5 xx' = \gamma_5 XX' = -N + R,$$
$$\Gamma_2 xx' = \gamma_2 XX' = i(L + P), \quad \Gamma_4 xx' = \gamma_4 XX' = i(M + Q),$$
$$\Gamma_6 xx' = \gamma_6 XX' = i(N + R).$$

9. These forms have various properties. Firstly by putting in $-L + P$,

$$X = -i\xi, \quad Y = i^{\frac{1}{2}}\eta, \quad Z = i^{\frac{1}{2}}\zeta, \quad T = \tau,$$
$$X' = -i\xi', \quad Y' = i^{\frac{1}{2}}\eta', \quad Z' = i^{\frac{1}{2}}\zeta', \quad T' = \tau',$$

$TX' - T'X$ changes to $-i(\tau\xi' - \tau'\xi)$, $YZ' - Y'Z$ changes to $i(\eta\zeta' - \eta'\zeta)$, and so, if L', P' denote the same functions of $\xi, \eta, \zeta, \tau, \xi', \eta', \zeta', \tau'$ that L, P are of $X, Y, Z, T, X', Y', Z', T'$, we have

$$-L + P = i(L' + P');$$

in other words

$$\begin{pmatrix} -i & 0 & 0 & 0 \\ 0 & i^{\frac{1}{2}} & 0 & 0 \\ 0 & 0 & i^{\frac{1}{2}} & 0 \\ 0 & 0 & 0 & 1 \end{pmatrix} \gamma_1 \begin{pmatrix} -i & 0 & 0 & 0 \\ 0 & i^{\frac{1}{2}} & 0 & 0 \\ 0 & 0 & i^{\frac{1}{2}} & 0 \\ 0 & 0 & 0 & 1 \end{pmatrix} = \gamma_2.$$

Similarly by $X = \eta$, $Y = \zeta$, $Z = \xi$, $T = \tau$, we find $\bar{\sigma}\gamma_1\sigma = \gamma_3$ where

$$\sigma = \begin{pmatrix} 0 & 1 & 0 & 0 \\ 0 & 0 & 1 & 0 \\ 1 & 0 & 0 & 0 \\ 0 & 0 & 0 & 1 \end{pmatrix};$$

it appears thus that all the six forms $\gamma_1, \gamma_2, \ldots, \gamma_6$ are capable of being written $\bar{\mu}\gamma_1\mu$, where μ is suitably chosen in each case. Nextly we find

$$\gamma_1^2 = -1, \quad \gamma_3^2 = -1, \quad \gamma_5^2 = -1,$$
$$\gamma_1\gamma_3 = -\gamma_3\gamma_1 = \gamma_5, \quad \gamma_3\gamma_5 = -\gamma_5\gamma_3 = \gamma_1, \quad \gamma_5\gamma_1 = -\gamma_1\gamma_5 = \gamma_3,$$
$$\gamma_2^2 = 1, \quad \gamma_4^2 = 1, \quad \gamma_6^2 = 1,$$
$$\gamma_2\gamma_4 = -\gamma_4\gamma_2 = i\gamma_6, \quad \gamma_4\gamma_6 = -\gamma_6\gamma_4 = i\gamma_2, \quad \gamma_6\gamma_2 = -\gamma_2\gamma_6 = i\gamma_4,$$

while $$\gamma_{2n-1}\gamma_{2n} = \gamma_{2n}\gamma_{2n-1}.$$

Further we have

$$\Sigma\{[L-P]^2+[i(L+P)]^2\}=-4\Sigma LP=0,$$

and hence

$$(\Gamma_1 xx')^2+(\Gamma_2 xx')^2+(\Gamma_3 xx')^2+(\Gamma_4 xx')^2+(\Gamma_5 xx')^2+(\Gamma_6 xx')^2=0.$$

And lastly, to come to a set of relations of particular importance to us, we have, as follows from the identity,

$$\begin{pmatrix} X+iY, & Z+iT \\ -Z+iT, & X-iY \end{pmatrix}\begin{pmatrix} X'-iY', & -Z'-iT' \\ Z'-iT', & X'+iY' \end{pmatrix}$$
$$=\begin{pmatrix} E-i(-N+R) & , -M+Q-i(-L+P) \\ -(-M+Q)-i(-L+P), & E+i(-N+R) \end{pmatrix},$$

where E denotes $XX'+YY'+ZZ'+TT'$, the equation

$$E^2+(-L+P)^2+(-M+Q)^2+(-N+R)^2$$
$$=(X^2+Y^2+Z^2+T^2)(X'^2+Y'^2+Z'^2+T'^2);$$

now $\gamma_1\gamma_3^{-1}\gamma_5=-\gamma_1\gamma_3\gamma_5=-\gamma_5^2=1,$

so that

$$\gamma_1\gamma_3^{-1}\gamma_5(X, Y, Z, T)(X', Y', Z', T'), \text{ or } \gamma_1\gamma_3^{-1}\gamma_5 XX', =E;$$

thus

$$(\gamma_1 XX')^2+(\gamma_3 XX')^2+(\gamma_5 XX')^2+(\gamma_1\gamma_3^{-1}\gamma_5 XX')^2$$
$$=(X^2+Y^2+Z^2+T^2)(X'^2+Y'^2+Z'^2+T'^2);$$

let, momentarily, a denote the matrix

$$a=\begin{pmatrix} (\gamma_1X)_1, & (\gamma_1X)_2, & (\gamma_1X)_3, & (\gamma_1X)_4 \\ (\gamma_3X)_1, & (\gamma_3X)_2, & (\gamma_3X)_3, & (\gamma_3X)_4 \\ (\gamma_5X)_1, & (\gamma_5X)_2, & (\gamma_5X)_3, & (\gamma_5X)_4 \\ (\gamma_1\gamma_3^{-1}\gamma_5X)_1, & (\gamma_1\gamma_3^{-1}\gamma_5X)_2, & (\gamma_1\gamma_3^{-1}\gamma_5X)_3, & (\gamma_1\gamma_3^{-1}\gamma_5X)_4 \end{pmatrix},$$

where $(\gamma_1X)_r$ denotes the rth of the four quantities $\gamma_1(X, Y, Z, T)$; then if

$$(\xi', \eta', \zeta', \tau')=a(X', Y', Z', T')$$

we have $\xi'=\gamma_1XX'$, $\eta'=\gamma_3XX'$, etc., and so

$$\xi'^2+\eta'^2+\zeta'^2+\tau'^2=(X^2+Y^2+Z^2+T^2)(X'^2+Y'^2+Z'^2+T'^2),$$

of which the left side is $aX'.aX'$ or $\bar{a}aX'^2$; we thus have

$$a\bar{a}=\bar{a}a=X^2+Y^2+Z^2+T^2,$$

and the matrix a is orthogonal, in the sense that the sum of the four products of corresponding elements in any two rows, or in any two columns, is zero, while the sum of the squares of the elements in any row, or in any column, is the same for each, being equal to $X^2+Y^2+Z^2+T^2$. Again we have $\gamma_2\gamma_4^{-1}\gamma_6=\gamma_2\gamma_4\gamma_6=i\gamma_6^2=i$, and, as before,

$$E^2+(L+P)^2+(M+Q)^2+(N+R)^2$$
$$=(X^2+Y^2+Z^2+T^2)(X'^2+Y'^2+Z'^2+T'^2),$$

so that, if b denote the matrix,

$$b = \begin{pmatrix} i(\gamma_2 X')_1 & i(\gamma_4 X')_1 & i(\gamma_6 X')_1 & X' \\ i(\gamma_2 X')_2 & i(\gamma_4 X')_2 & i(\gamma_6 X')_2 & Y' \\ i(\gamma_2 X')_3 & i(\gamma_4 X')_3 & i(\gamma_6 X')_3 & Z' \\ i(\gamma_2 X')_4 & i(\gamma_4 X')_4 & i(\gamma_6 X')_4 & T' \end{pmatrix},$$

we have as before

$$b\bar{b} = \bar{b}b = X'^2 + Y'^2 + Z'^2 + T'^2.$$

Now, with $x = \varpi X$, that is $(x, y, z, t) = \varpi (X, Y, Z, T)$, as in § 8, we have

$$\gamma_1 X = \bar{\varpi}\Gamma_1 \varpi X = \bar{\varpi}\Gamma_1 x,$$

and

$$\gamma_3 X = \bar{\varpi}\Gamma_3 x, \quad \gamma_5 X = \bar{\varpi}\Gamma_5 x,$$

$$\gamma_1\gamma_3^{-1}\gamma_5 X = \bar{\varpi}\Gamma_1\varpi \,.\, \varpi^{-1}\Gamma_3^{-1}\bar{\varpi}^{-1} \,.\, \bar{\varpi}\Gamma_5\varpi X = \bar{\varpi}\Gamma_1\Gamma_3^{-1}\Gamma_5 x;$$

while

$$i\gamma_2 X' = \gamma_4^{-1}\gamma_6 X' = \varpi^{-1}\Gamma_4^{-1}\bar{\varpi}^{-1} \,.\, \bar{\varpi}\Gamma_6\varpi X' = \varpi^{-1}\Gamma_4^{-1}\Gamma_6 x',$$

where $x' = \varpi X'$, and similarly $i\gamma_4 X' = \varpi^{-1}\Gamma_6^{-1}\Gamma_2 x'$ and $i\gamma_6 X' = \varpi^{-1}\Gamma_2^{-1}\Gamma_4 x'$: thus we have

$$ab = \begin{pmatrix} (\bar{\varpi}\Gamma_1 x)_1, & (\bar{\varpi}\Gamma_1 x)_2, & (\bar{\varpi}\Gamma_1 x)_3, & (\bar{\varpi}\Gamma_1 x)_4 \\ (\bar{\varpi}\Gamma_3 x)_1, & (\bar{\varpi}\Gamma_3 x)_2, & (\bar{\varpi}\Gamma_3 x)_3, & (\bar{\varpi}\Gamma_3 x)_4 \\ (\bar{\varpi}\Gamma_5 x)_1, & (\bar{\varpi}\Gamma_5 x)_2, & (\bar{\varpi}\Gamma_5 x)_3, & (\bar{\varpi}\Gamma_5 x)_4 \\ (\bar{\varpi}\Gamma_1\Gamma_3^{-1}\Gamma_5 x)_1, & (\bar{\varpi}\Gamma_1\Gamma_3^{-1}\Gamma_5 x)_2, & (\bar{\varpi}\Gamma_1\Gamma_3^{-1}\Gamma_5 x)_3, & (\bar{\varpi}\Gamma_1\Gamma_3^{-1}\Gamma_5 x)_4 \end{pmatrix}$$

$$\times \begin{pmatrix} (\varpi^{-1}\Gamma_4^{-1}\Gamma_6 x')_1, & (\varpi^{-1}\Gamma_6^{-1}\Gamma_2 x')_1, & (\varpi^{-1}\Gamma_2^{-1}\Gamma_4 x')_1, & (\varpi^{-1}x')_1 \\ (\varpi^{-1}\Gamma_4^{-1}\Gamma_6 x')_2, & (\varpi^{-1}\Gamma_6^{-1}\Gamma_2 x')_2, & (\varpi^{-1}\Gamma_2^{-1}\Gamma_4 x')_2, & (\varpi^{-1}x')_2 \\ (\varpi^{-1}\Gamma_4^{-1}\Gamma_6 x')_3, & (\varpi^{-1}\Gamma_6^{-1}\Gamma_2 x')_3, & (\varpi^{-1}\Gamma_2^{-1}\Gamma_4 x')_3, & (\varpi^{-1}x')_3 \\ (\varpi^{-1}\Gamma_4^{-1}\Gamma_6 x')_4, & (\varpi^{-1}\Gamma_6^{-1}\Gamma_2 x')_4, & (\varpi^{-1}\Gamma_2^{-1}\Gamma_4 x')_4, & (\varpi^{-1}x')_4 \end{pmatrix},$$

while

$$ab \,.\, \overline{ab} = ab\bar{b}\bar{a} = (X^2 + Y^2 + Z^2 + T^2)(X'^2 + Y'^2 + Z'^2 + T'^2);$$

now

$$\sum_{r=1}^{4} (\bar{\varpi}\Gamma_1 x)_r (\varpi^{-1}\Gamma_4^{-1}\Gamma_6 x')_r = \bar{\varpi}\Gamma_1 x \quad \varpi^{-1}\Gamma_4^{-1}\Gamma_6 x'$$

$$= \Gamma_6\Gamma_4^{-1}\bar{\varpi}^{-1} \,.\, \bar{\varpi}\Gamma_1 xx' = \Gamma_6\Gamma_4^{-1}\Gamma_1 xx',$$

and, since (§ 7),

$$\Gamma_1\Gamma_3^{-1}\Gamma_5 = -i\Gamma_2\Gamma_4^{-1}\Gamma_6 = -i\Gamma_4\Gamma_6^{-1}\Gamma_2,$$

$$\sum_{r=1}^{4} (\bar{\varpi}\Gamma_1\Gamma_3^{-1}\Gamma_5 x)_r (\varpi^{-1}\Gamma_4^{-1}\Gamma_6 x')_r = \Gamma_6\Gamma_4^{-1}\Gamma_1\Gamma_3^{-1}\Gamma_5 xx' = -i\Gamma_2 xx';$$

thus the matrix

$$c = ab = \begin{pmatrix} \Gamma_6\Gamma_4^{-1}\Gamma_1 xx', & \Gamma_2\Gamma_6^{-1}\Gamma_1 xx', & \Gamma_4\Gamma_2^{-1}\Gamma_1 xx', & \Gamma_1 xx' \\ \Gamma_6\Gamma_4^{-1}\Gamma_3 xx', & \Gamma_2\Gamma_6^{-1}\Gamma_3 xx', & \Gamma_4\Gamma_2^{-1}\Gamma_3 xx', & \Gamma_3 xx' \\ \Gamma_6\Gamma_4^{-1}\Gamma_5 xx', & \Gamma_2\Gamma_6^{-1}\Gamma_5 xx', & \Gamma_4\Gamma_2^{-1}\Gamma_5 xx', & \Gamma_5 xx' \\ -i\Gamma_2 xx', & -i\Gamma_4 xx', & -i\Gamma_6 xx', & -i\Gamma_2\Gamma_4^{-1}\Gamma_6 xx' \end{pmatrix},$$

where (x, y, z, t), (x', y', z', t') are arbitrary quantities, is shewn to be such that $c\bar{c} = \bar{c}c =$ a number, which in fact is

$$[(\varpi^{-1}x)_1^2 + (\varpi^{-1}x)_2^2 + (\varpi^{-1}x)_3^2 + (\varpi^{-1}x)_4^2] \times [(\varpi^{-1}x')_1^2 + (\varpi^{-1}x')_2^2 + (\varpi^{-1}x')_3^2 + (\varpi^{-1}x')_4^2],$$

namely, the matrix c is an orthogonal matrix.

Herein, as will be recalled (§ 7), Γ_1, Γ_3, Γ_5 are any three of the original six matrices, and Γ_2, Γ_4, Γ_6 are the remaining three in any order, but of these there is one, Γ_6, of which it may be necessary to change the sign of every element. It is at once seen, however, the matrix being written as here, that in expressing that the sum of the products of corresponding elements in any two rows, or any two columns, is zero, or in expressing that the sum of the squares of the elements in any row or column is the same for each, both signs for Γ_6 lead to the same result, and indeed any one of the six matrices $\Gamma_1, \Gamma_2, \ldots, \Gamma_6$ in the orthogonal matrix may be changed in sign without affecting the result. This caution is therefore unnecessary, and the result that the matrix above is orthogonal holds for any decomposition of the six matrices into two sets of three, independently of the order of those in a set, and independently of a factor -1 attached, or not attached, to any one or more matrix $\Gamma_1, \ldots, \Gamma_6$ throughout the matrix c.

NOTE II.

INTRODUCTORY PROOF OF ABEL'S THEOREM, AND ITS CONVERSE.

If

$$H(x) = \text{integral polynomial in } x + \frac{A}{x-a} + \ldots + \frac{A_\lambda}{(x-a)^{\lambda+1}} + \frac{B}{x-b} + \ldots + \frac{B_\mu}{(x-b)^{\mu+1}} + \ldots$$

be any rational function of x, it is obvious that the coefficient of x^{-1} in the expansion of $H(x)$ in descending powers of x, which is $A + B + \ldots$, is equal to the sum of the coefficients, of $(x-a)^{-1}$ in the expansion of $H(x)$ in ascending powers of $x - a$, of $(x-b)^{-1}$ in the expansion of $H(x)$ in ascending powers of $x - b, \ldots$, all the values $a, b, \ldots$ which are roots of the denominator of $H(x)$ being taken.

If
$$A(x) y^n + A_1(x) y^{n-1} + \ldots + A_n(x) = 0$$

be an irreducible equation in y, the coefficients $A(x), A_1(x), \ldots, A_n(x)$ being integral polynomials in x, and a be a finite value of x which is not a root of $A(x) = 0$, we assume that the values of y which satisfy this equation for values of x near to a, break up into a certain number of cycles, the constituents of a cycle which consists of m roots being expressible by power-series such as

$$y = b + b_1 t + b_2 t^2 + b_3 t^3 + \dots$$

wherein t is to be replaced in turn by the m roots of $t^m = x - a$; thus when the phase of $x - a$ increases by 2π, the phase of t increases by $2\pi/m$, and one of the roots of the cycle changes into another; for $x = a$ all the roots of the cycle give $y = b$, and the point $x = a$, $y = b$, regarded as the centre of the m expansions is said to constitute *one place*; if there be k cycles, consisting respectively of $m_1, \dots, m_k$ roots, we have $m_1 + \dots + m_k = n$; the ordinary case is when $k = n$ and $m_1 = m_2 = \dots = m_k = 1$, and it is only for a finite number of values of a that any other case arises; but we may have $k = 1$ and $m_1 = n$. The case of a finite value of a for which $A(x) = 0$ may be dealt with by putting $yA(x) = \eta$; for any one of the places which arise the appropriate expression for y is thus of the form $t^{-\lambda}\wp(t)$, where λ is a positive integer and $\wp(t)$ a power-series in t; the case of an infinite value of x may be dealt with by putting $x = \xi^{-1}$; the appropriate expressions for any one of the places are then of the form $x = t^{-m}$, $y = t^{-\lambda}\wp(t)$, where m is a positive integer, λ is an integer and $\wp(t)$ a power-series. This general statement has been sufficiently illustrated for the hyperelliptic case in the first chapter of this volume; the quantity t, which always vanishes at the place under consideration, *and is to be chosen so that no point in the immediate neighbourhood of the place arises twice over for different values of* t, is called the *parameter* for the place. A formal proof of the assumption as to the existence of such cycles is given below, in the first chapter of Part II. (p. 190).

The value of any rational function of x and y in the neighbourhood of any particular place can clearly then be expressed in a form $t^\mu \wp(t)$, where $\wp(t)$ is a power-series in t not vanishing for $t = 0$, and μ is an integer. If μ is positive, the function is said to vanish μ times at the place, or to the μth order; if μ is negative, the function is said to be infinite $(-\mu)$ times, or to have a pole of the $(-\mu)$th order at the place; and it can be proved that any function of x and y which has about every place a definite expression $t^\mu \wp(t)$ in which μ is a finite integer, is a rational function of x and y. The sum of the orders of zero of any rational function, for all the places where the function vanishes, is clearly finite, these places being obtainable by algebraic combination of the fundamental equation and of the condition obtained by equating the function to zero; we proceed to prove a theorem which, as will be seen, has as one corollary the theorem that the sum of the orders of the existing poles of the rational function is equal to the sum of the orders of its zeros; if for any place the (finite) value of the rational function $R(x, y)$ be A, and, in the neighbourhood of the place, $R(x, y) - A$ be of the form $t^m \wp(t)$ where $\wp(t)$ is a power-series not vanishing for $t = 0$, we say that the function is m times equal to A at the place—the general statement is that the total sum of the number of times that the function is equal to A at the various places is independent of A, and this number is called the order of the rational function.

The theorem in question, for a rational function $R(x, y)$, is expressed by

$$\left[R(x, y)\frac{dx}{dt}\right]_{t^{-1}} = 0,$$

the meaning being that in the neighbourhood of every one of the (necessarily finite number of) places where either $R(x, y)$ or x is infinite, each of $R(x, y)$ and dx/dt is to be expressed by the parameter t, the coefficient of t^{-1} in the product $R(x, y)\,dx/dt$ is to be taken, and the sum of all such coefficients is zero. The result is obvious if the elements of the theory of a Riemann surface be assumed, since the vanishing contour integral $\int R(x, y)\,dx$ round the period-loops is equal to the sum of the values of the integral round the logarithmic infinities of the integral; cf. p. 4 above; we can, however, give an elementary proof, which has also been previously given for the hyperelliptic case (p. 4). Consider a finite place $x = a$, which is the centre of a cycle of m roots $y_1, \ldots, y_m$, and having substituted, in $R(x, y)$, the value $x = a + t^m$ and the appropriate series for each of $y_1, \ldots, y_m$ in terms of t, form the sum

$$R(x, y_1) + \ldots + R(x, y_m);$$

each constituent of this sum is a series of integral powers of t with only a finite number of negative powers, and if $\omega = e^{2\pi i/m}$, the series are the same in the quantities $t, \omega t, \omega^2 t, \ldots$; thus the sum is a series of integral powers of t^m or $x - a$; and the coefficient of $(x-a)^{-1}$, or t^{-m}, in this series in $x - a$ is equal to the coefficient of t^{-1} in

$$R(x, y)\,mt^{m-1}, \quad \text{or} \quad R(x, y)\frac{dx}{dt}.$$

Consider next a place arising for an infinite value of x; putting $x = t^{-k}$ and the appropriate series for $y_1, \ldots, y_k$ in terms of t, and forming the sum

$$R(x, y_1) + \ldots + R(x, y_k),$$

we similarly obtain a series of integral powers of x^{-1}, in which the coefficient of x^{-1}, or t^k, is equal to the coefficient of t^{-1} in

$$R(x, y)\,kt^{-k-1}, \quad \text{or} \quad -R(x, y)\frac{dx}{dt}.$$

Now consider, for any value of x, the sum

$$H(x) = R(x, y_1) + \ldots + R(x, y_n),$$

where $y_1, \ldots, y_n$ are all the roots of the fundamental equation; this is a rational function of x only; for a finite value $x = a$, the coefficient of $(x-a)^{-1}$ in $H(x)$ is, as we have seen, equal to the sum of the coefficients of t^{-1} in $R(x, y)\,dx/dt$ at the various places arising for $x = a$; while for infinite x, the negative coefficient of x^{-1} in $H(x)$ is equal to the sum of the coefficients of t^{-1} in $R(x, y)\, dx/dt$ at the various places arising for $x = \infty$. It follows, therefore, by the remark at starting that, in the sense previously explained,

$$\left[R(x, y)\frac{dx}{dt}\right]_{t^{-1}} = 0,$$

and this is the theorem.

Remark. If $K(x, y)$ be any rational function, such that, near any place, $K(x, y) - A$ is of the form $t^m \wp(t)$, we see at once that, near this place,

$$\{K(x, y) - A\}^{-1} \cdot \frac{d}{dx}\{K(x, y) - A\} \cdot \frac{dx}{dt}$$

has, for coefficient of t^{-1}, the integer m. The number of times that $K(x, y)$ takes any value A is thus equal to the total number of its poles, as was remarked.

To apply this result to prove Abel's Theorem, let Z denote any rational function of x, y, these being connected by the fundamental algebraic equation $f(x, y) = 0$; the rational function $Z - \mu$, where μ is a constant, will then have a definite number, Q, of zeros, this number being independent of μ; and as μ varies these zeros will vary; for simplicity of statement we shall regard each of the zeros as of the first order, for all the values of μ which we consider, though, as will be seen, the result we obtain is unaffected by supposing two or more of them to coalesce into a multiple zero. Also let $R(x, y)$ be any rational function of (x, y) and $I = \int R(x, y)\, dx$. Now apply the equation

$$\left[\frac{1}{Z - \mu}\frac{dI}{dx} \cdot \frac{dx}{dt}\right]_{t^{-1}} = 0,$$

written in the form

$$\left[\left(\frac{1}{Z - \mu}\right)\frac{dI}{dt}\right]_{t^{-1}} = -\left[\left(\frac{dI}{dt}\right)\frac{1}{Z - \mu}\right]_{t^{-1}},$$

where on the left only those places are considered where $Z = \mu$ and dI/dt is finite, and on the right those where dI/dt is infinite (and possibly also $Z = \mu$). Let (x_i, y_i) be one of the places for which $Z = \mu$, and t the parameter for the neighbourhood of this place, so that, for a near position $(x_i + dx_i, y_i + dy_i)$, the value $\mu + d\mu$ of Z is given by $\mu + tA + \dots$; the corresponding contribution to the sum on the left is then given by

$$\frac{1}{A}\frac{dI}{dx_i}\frac{dx_i}{dt}, = \frac{dI}{dx_i} \cdot \frac{dx_i}{d\mu},$$

and the equation leads to

$$\sum_{i=1}^{Q} \frac{dI}{dx_i}\, dx_i = \left[\left(\frac{dI}{dt}\right) d \log(Z - \mu)\right]_{t^{-1}};$$

thus if $(x_1), \dots, (x_Q)$ be the places where Z vanishes, and $(a_1), \dots, (a_Q)$ the places where Z is infinite, we have

$$\sum_{i=1}^{Q} \int_{(a_i)}^{(x_i)} R(x, y)\, dx = \left[\left(\frac{dI}{dt}\right) \log Z\right]_{t^{-1}} - \lim_{\mu=\infty} \left[\left(\frac{dI}{dt}\right) \log (Z - \mu)\right]_{t^{-1}};$$

if we assume that no one of the places where Z is infinite coincides with a place at which the integral I is infinite, we can write, for large values of μ,

$$\log (Z - \mu) = \log (-\mu) - \frac{Z}{\mu} - \tfrac{1}{2}\frac{Z^2}{\mu^2} - \dots,$$

and hence, in virtue of $$\left[\frac{dI}{dt}\right]_{t^{-1}} = 0,$$
infer the result

$$\sum_{i=1}^{Q} \int_{(a_i)}^{(x_i)} R(x, y)\, dx = \left[\left(\frac{dI}{dt}\right) \log Z\right]_{t^{-1}},$$

which we may regard as a statement of Abel's Theorem.

Some particular cases may be referred to.

(i) When $I = \int R(x, y)\, dx$ is an integral of the first kind, the right side vanishes, and we have the result that if $u^{x,a}$ be any integral of the first kind, and $(x_1), \dots, (x_Q)$ be the zeros, and $(a_1), \dots, (a_Q)$ the poles of any rational function of (x, y), then

$$u^{x_1, a_1} + \dots + u^{x_Q, a_Q} = 0,$$

it being understood that, in the absence of a convention as to the paths of integration on the left, there must be added on the right a sum of integral multiples of the periods of the integral $u^{x,a}$.

(ii) When I is an elementary integral of the third kind, that is, is infinite at one place (α) like $\log t_\alpha$, where t_α is the parameter for this place, and infinite at another place (β) like $-\log t_\beta$, but not elsewhere, we have, whatever Z may be

$$\sum_{i=1}^{Q} \int_{(a_i)}^{(x_i)} R(x, y)\, dx = \log \frac{Z(\alpha)}{Z(\beta)},$$

where $Z(\alpha)$, $Z(\beta)$ denote the values of Z at these places.

(iii) If the fundamental algebraic equation be

$$y^2 - (4x^3 - g_2 x - g_3) = 0,$$

and $R(x, y) = x/y$, while Z is taken to be $(y - mx - c)/(y - m_0 x - c_0)$, we have $Q = 3$, and dI/dt is infinite only for $x = \infty$; putting, for the single place there occurring,

$$x = t^{-2}, \quad y = -2t^{-3}(1 - \tfrac{1}{8} g_2 t^4 - \dots),$$

we have $$\frac{dI}{dt} = \frac{1}{t^2}(1 - \tfrac{1}{8} g_2 t^4 - \dots),$$

$$\log \frac{y - mx - c}{y - m_0 x - c_0} = \log \frac{1 + \frac{1}{2}mt + \frac{1}{2}ct^3 - \dots}{1 + \frac{1}{2}m_0 t + \frac{1}{2}c_0 t^3 - \dots} = \tfrac{1}{2}(m - m_0)\, t + \dots,$$

and $$\left[\left(\frac{dI}{dt}\right)\log Z\right]_{t=1} = \tfrac{1}{2}(m - m_0);$$

if then (x_1, y_1), (x_2, y_2) and (x_3, y_3) be the three intersections of the straight line $y = mx + c$ with the cubic curve $y^2 = 4x^3 - g_2 x - g_3$, and (c_1), (c_2), (c_3) be arbitrary places, we have

$$\int_{(c_1)}^{(x_1)} \frac{xdx}{y} + \int_{(c_2)}^{(x_2)} \frac{xdx}{y} + \int_{(c_3)}^{(x_3)} \frac{xdx}{y} - \tfrac{1}{2}\frac{y_1 - y_2}{x_1 - x_2} = C,$$

where C is a quantity unaltered by replacing the straight line $y = mx + c$ by any other; putting, as usual

$$u = \int_x^\infty \frac{dx}{y}, \quad x = \wp(u), \quad \zeta(u) = \frac{1}{u} + \int_0^u \left[\frac{1}{u^2} - \wp(u)\right] du,$$

this is equivalent with

$$\zeta(u) + \zeta(v) - \zeta(u + v) + \tfrac{1}{2}\frac{\wp' u - \wp' v}{\wp u - \wp v} = \text{constant},$$

for arbitrary values of u and v; by expansion in powers of u for small values of u we at once find the constant to be zero.

Converse of Abel's Theorem.

If p denote the number of existing linearly independent integrals of the first kind, and two sets, each of Q places, $(x_1), \ldots, (x_Q)$ and $(a_1), \ldots, (a_Q)$, be such that

$$u_i^{x_1, a_1} + \ldots + u_i^{x_Q, a_Q} = 2M_1\omega_{i,1} + \ldots 2M_p\omega_{i,p} + 2M_1'\omega'_{i,1} + \ldots 2M_p'\omega'_{i,p},$$
$$(i = 1, \ldots, p),$$

there being one such equation for each of the integrals, $M_1, \ldots, M_p'$ being $2p$ integers independent of i, and $2\omega_{i,1}, \ldots, 2\omega'_{i,p}$ being the periods belonging to the integral $u_i^{x,a}$, then there exists a rational function of (x, y) having $(x_1), \ldots, (x_Q)$ for zeros and $(a_1), \ldots, (a_Q)$ for poles, of the first order. The paths of integration on the left are supposed to be the same in all the p equations, but are arbitrary; a modification of these paths will generally entail a modification in the integers $M_1, \ldots, M_p'$.

The proof of this result is similar for all cases, and may be explained in the hyperelliptic case, $p = 2$, for which we have given the necessary preliminary theorems in the text. The equations then lead, for paths on the dissected Riemann surface upon which the normal integrals $v_1^{x,a}$, $v_2^{x,a}$ are single-valued, to the equations

$$v_1^{x_1, a_1} + \ldots + v_1^{x_Q, a_Q} = M_1 + M_1'\tau_{11} + M_2'\tau_{21},$$

$$v_2^{x_1, a_1} + \ldots + v_2^{x_Q, a_Q} = M_2 + M_1'\tau_{21} + M_2'\tau_{22};$$

consider then the function e^H where

$$H = \Pi_{x_1, a_1}^{x, a} + \ldots + \Pi_{x_Q, a_Q}^{x, a} - 2\pi i\,(M_1'v_1^{x, a} + M_2'v_2^{x, a}),$$

the function $\Pi_{z, c}^{x, a}$ being the normal elementary integral of the third kind; in virtue of the period properties for the integrals the function e^H is at once seen to be unaltered across any period-loop, and it is expressible near any place by a series of integral powers of the parameter for that place, having zeros of the first order at $(x_1), \ldots, (x_Q)$ and poles of the first order at $(a_1), \ldots, (a_Q)$. It is thus such a rational function as is required. (Cf. pp. 7, 29.)

PART II.

THE REDUCTION OF THE THEORY OF MULTIPLY-PERIODIC FUNCTIONS TO THE THEORY OF ALGEBRAIC FUNCTIONS.

CHAPTER VI.

GENERAL INTRODUCTORY THEOREMS.

49. If a power-series, in the independent variables x, y,

$$a_{00} + a_{10}x + a_{01}y + \dots + a_{mn}x^m y^n + \dots,$$

converge for $x = x_0$, $y = y_0$, then it converges uniformly and absolutely for $|x| < |x_0|$, $|y| < |y_0|$.

For, convergence for x_0, y_0 requires that any batch of terms taken sufficiently far from the beginning of the series, and in particular any single term, shall be of arbitrary smallness; we can thus suppose $a_{mn}x_0^m y_0^n$ less in absolute value than an assigned finite real positive quantity M, for every value of m and n; then if $\xi = x/x_0$, $\eta = y/y_0$ we have $a_{mn}x^m y^n = \xi^m \eta^n a_{mn} x_0^m y_0^n$, and thus, for $|\xi| < 1$, $|\eta| < 1$, the absolute values of the terms of the series are less than those of the series

$$M(1 + \xi + \eta + \xi^2 + \xi\eta + \eta^2 + \dots),$$

which is convergent, having $M(1-\xi)^{-1}(1-\eta)^{-1}$ for sum. This enables us at once to prove the proposition as stated.

The given series thus represents a continuous function in the open region $|x| < |x_0|$, $|y| < |y_0|$; it can easily be shewn that this is true also of the series formed by differentiating the given series in regard to x or y, so that the given series is differentiable in the same region.

If $r < |x_0|$ and $|x_1| = r$, the series can be rewritten as a power-series in $x - x_1$ and y converging certainly for $|y| < |y_0|$, $|x - x_1| < |x_0| - r$. If for every x_1 such that $|x_1| = r$, the rewritten series converge for $|x - x_1| < |x_0| + D - r$, then the original series really converges* in the open region $|x| < |x_0| + D$, $|y| < |y_0|$. It may be, however, that there is a point (x', y') upon the boundary of the region of convergence of the original series, such that if

* A formal proof is given *Proc. Lond. Math. Soc.* Vol. xxxiv. (1902), p. 296.

(x_1', y_1') be taken anywhere in its neighbourhood, the rewritten series in $x - x_1', y - y_1'$ converges only for $|x - x_1'| < |x' - x_1'|$, $|y - y_1'| < |y' - y_1'|$; such a point is called a *singular point* of the function represented by the original series. With this definition it is clear, in view of the proposition just stated, that the region of convergence of the original series can be taken to be given by $|x| < R$, $|y| < S$, with a singular point (x', y') where $|x'| = R$, $|y'| \gtreqless S$ or $|x'| \gtreqless R$, $|y'| = S$.

Thus the value adopted for one of the two quantities R, S modifies the values possible for the other; in particular it may happen that R can be increased without limit if S be suitably diminished. As this is a point of difference between the cases of series of one variable and series of more than one variable, it may be desirable to give an example. Consider the power-series

$$1 + x + x^2 - xy + x^3 - 2x^2y + \tfrac{1}{2}xy^2 + \dots \qquad \dots\dots\dots\dots\dots(A)$$

obtained by writing the series

$$1 + xe^{-y} + x^2e^{-2y} + \dots \qquad \dots\dots\dots\dots\dots\dots\dots(B)$$

as a power-series in x and y. If the series (A) converge for $x = x_0$, $y = y_0$, it will as we have seen converge absolutely, and therefore written in any order, for $|x| < |x_0|$, $|y| < |y_0|$; it will therefore converge when written as the series (B); if however $x = re^{i\theta}$, $y = se^{i\phi} = \zeta + i\tau$, the series (B) converges only for $|x| < |e^y|$ or $\zeta > \log r$. Thus, near the origin, the series (A) converges only if $r < 1$, and taking a particular $r_0 < 1$, a region of convergence about the origin, circular for both x and y, can only be of the form $|x| < r_0$, $|y| < \log \dfrac{1}{r_0}$. Conversely $s < \log \dfrac{1}{r}$, or $re^s < 1$, ensures the convergence of

$$1 + r\left(1 + s + \frac{s^2}{2\,!} + \dots\right) + r^2\left(1 + 2s + \frac{4s^2}{2\,!} + \dots\right) + \dots \qquad \dots\dots(B')$$

and so the absolute convergence of the series (B) written in the form

$$1 + x\left(1 - y + \frac{y^2}{2\,!} + \dots\right) + x^2\left(1 - 2y + \frac{4y^2}{2\,!} + \dots\right) + \dots,$$

which can then be rearranged as the series (A). On the whole then a region of convergence about the origin for the series (A) is given by $|x| < r$, $|y| < s$, $r < e^{-s}$; thus r is less than unity but can be made as near thereto as we wish by taking s small enough; but on the other hand s may be made indefinitely great by taking r small enough.

50. Suppose that the original series converges uniformly in regard to the phases of x and y upon the two circumferences $|x| = r$, $|y| = s$; and that, for these values of x and y, the sum of the series is, in absolute value, less than the real positive quantity M. It can then be shewn that, for these values of x and y, every term of the series is also less than M, in absolute value; so that

$$|a_{mn}| < \frac{M}{r^m s^n}.$$

Denote the sum of the series by $f(x, y)$; put $\epsilon = e^{\frac{2\pi i}{h}}$, $\omega = e^{\frac{2\pi i}{k}}$, where h, k are positive integers; we have then, for $x = r\epsilon^{\mu}$, $y = s\omega^{\nu}$,

$$(r\epsilon^{\mu})^{-m}(s\omega^{\nu})^{-n} f(r\epsilon^{\mu}, s\omega^{\nu}) = a_{0,0}(r\epsilon^{\mu})^{-m}(s\omega^{\nu})^{-n} + \ldots + a_{m,n} + \ldots$$
$$+ a_{m',n'}(r\epsilon^{\mu})^{m'-m}(s\omega^{\nu})^{n'-n} + \ldots + H,$$

where H represents the remainder of the series beginning with terms of dimension $p - m - n + 1$ in x and y, after division by $x^m y^n$. Taking σ arbitrarily small we suppose p so large that $|H| < \sigma$. In this equation give to μ in turn the values $0, 1, \ldots, \mu' - 1$, and to ν the values $0, 1, \ldots, \nu' - 1$, add the results, and divide by the number of these, namely $\mu'\nu'$; we thus have

$$\frac{1}{\mu'\nu'} \sum_{\mu=0}^{\mu'-1} \sum_{\nu=0}^{\nu'-1} (r\epsilon^{\mu})^{-m}(s\omega^{\nu})^{-n} f(r\epsilon^{\mu}, s\omega^{\nu})$$

equal to

$$\frac{1}{\mu'\nu'} a_{0,0} r^{-m} s^{-n} \frac{1-(\epsilon^{-m})^{\mu'}}{1-\epsilon^{-m}} \cdot \frac{1-(\omega^{-n})^{\nu'}}{1-\omega^{-n}} + \ldots + a_{m,n} + \ldots$$
$$+ \frac{1}{\mu'\nu'} a_{m',n'} r^{m'-m} s^{n'-n} \frac{1-\epsilon^{(m'-m)\mu'}}{1-\epsilon^{m'-m}} \cdot \frac{1-\omega^{(n'-n)\nu'}}{1-\omega^{n'-n}} + \ldots + \frac{1}{\mu'\nu'} \Sigma H,$$

it being understood that h, k are taken so great that no one of the denominators

$$(1-\epsilon^{-m})(1-\omega^{-n}), \ldots, (1-\epsilon^{m'-m})(1-\omega^{n'-n}), \ldots,$$

is zero, as can be supposed by choosing h, k after σ and p are fixed. If M_1 be taken less than M to exceed the greatest modulus of $f(x, y)$ for $|x| = r$, $|y| = s$, the left side of this equation is in absolute value less than $r^{-m}s^{-n}M_1$; on the right side the term $\frac{1}{\mu'\nu'}\Sigma H$ is in absolute value less than σ, and the other terms, except $a_{m,n}$, diminish indefinitely when the arbitrary positive integers μ', ν' are indefinitely increased; thus we have

$$|a_{m,n}| < \frac{M_1}{r^m s^n} + \zeta,$$

where ζ is arbitrarily small, and hence, as desired,

$$|a_{m,n}| < \frac{M}{r^m s^n}.$$

Corollary. We have

$$|f(x, y)| \geqq |a_{0,0}| - \left| \sum_{m=1, n=1}^{\infty} a_{m,n} x^m y^n \right|,$$

and, if $|x| = \rho$, $|y| = \sigma$,

$$\left|\sum_{m=1, n=1}^{\infty} a_{m,n} x^m y^n\right| < M\Sigma\left(\frac{\rho}{r}\right)^m\left(\frac{\sigma}{s}\right)^n < M\left[\frac{1}{\left(1-\frac{\rho}{r}\right)\left(1-\frac{\sigma}{s}\right)} - 1\right],$$

so that

$$|f(x, y)| > |a_{0,0}| - M\left[\left(1-\frac{\rho}{r}\right)^{-1}\left(1-\frac{\sigma}{s}\right)^{-1} - 1\right],$$

which does not vanish so long as

$$\left(1-\frac{\rho}{r}\right)\left(1-\frac{\sigma}{s}\right) < \frac{M}{M + |a_{0,0}|}.$$

Herein r, s are arbitrary values such that the series converges for $|x| = r$, $|y| = s$, and M is any real positive quantity greater, absolutely, than $f(x, y)$, when $|x| = r$, $|y| = s$; so long as $|a_{0,0}| > 0$, we can always take ρ, σ so small that the inequality is satisfied. Thus if the origin is not a zero of the series it is an interior point of an assignable finite region within which no zeros are found.

51. Consider now the case when the origin is a vanishing point of the series. Arranged in powers of y let the series be

$$A_0 + A_1 y + A_2 y^2 + \dots,$$

where $A_0, A_1, A_2, \dots$ are power-series in x; of these A_0 vanishes for $x = 0$; we assume in the first instance that not all of $A_1, A_2, \dots$ vanish for $x = 0$; let A_n be the first that does not, so that the series is of the form

$$f(x, y) = x(B_0 + B_1 y + \dots + B_{n-1} y^{n-1}) + (C + xB_n) y^n + A_{n+1} y^{n+1} + \dots,$$

where $B_0, B_1, \dots, B_{n-1}, B_n, A_{n+1}, \dots$ are power-series in x, and C is a non-vanishing constant.

We shew now that a real positive quantity r can be assigned such that for any value of x less than r in absolute value, there are n values of y satisfying the equation

$$f(x, y) = 0,$$

all diminishing to zero with x, and that these are the roots of an equation

$$y^n + p_1 y^{n-1} + \dots + p_n = 0,$$

where $p_1, p_2, \dots, p_n$ are power-series in x, vanishing for $x = 0$, and converging for $|x| < r$.

Let

$$f_0 = f(0, y) = Cy^n + Dy^{n+1} + \dots,$$

and

$$f_1 = f_0 - f(x, y),$$

so that f_1 vanishes when x vanishes, identically in regard to y. Choosing σ so that f_0 does not vanish for $0 < |y| \leqq \sigma$, and so that $f(x, y)$ converges for $|y| < \sigma$ and sufficiently small x, and choosing σ_1 so that $0 < \sigma_1 < \sigma$, we may choose ρ so that $|f_1| < |f_0|$ for $|x| < \rho$ and $\sigma_1 < |y| < \sigma$. Then for a definite x, such that $|x| < \rho$, since $f = f_0\left(1 - \frac{f_1}{f_0}\right)$, we have

$$\frac{1}{f}\frac{\partial f}{\partial y} = \frac{1}{f_0}\frac{\partial f_0}{\partial y} - \frac{\partial}{\partial y}\sum_{\lambda=1}^{\infty}\frac{1}{\lambda}\left(\frac{f_1}{f_0}\right)^\lambda = \frac{1}{f_0}\frac{\partial f_0}{\partial y} - \frac{\partial}{\partial y}\sum_{\mu=-\infty}^{\infty} G_\mu(x)\, y^\mu,$$

where $G_\mu(x)$ is a power-series in x vanishing for $x = 0$,

$$= \frac{n}{y} - \frac{\partial}{\partial y}\sum_{\mu=-\infty}^{-1} G_\mu(x)\, y^\mu + G(y) - \frac{\partial}{\partial y}\sum_{\mu=0}^{\infty} G_\mu(x)\, y^\mu,$$

where $G(y)$ is a power-series in y; let the number of values of y, less than σ in absolute value, which satisfy $f(x, y) = 0$, for the definite value of x, be m, and denote these by $y_1, \ldots, y_m$, multiplicity being allowed for by repetition of these; then the difference

$$\frac{1}{f}\frac{\partial f}{\partial y} - \frac{1}{y - y_1} - \ldots - \frac{1}{y - y_m}$$

is expressible, for $|y| < \sigma$, as a power-series in y, say $K(y)$, and so, for y less than σ but greater in absolute value than the greatest of $y_1, \ldots, y_m$ and greater than σ_1, we have

$$\frac{1}{f}\frac{\partial f}{\partial y} = \frac{m}{y} + \sum_{\nu=1}^{\infty} y^{-\nu-1}(y_1^\nu + \ldots + y_m^\nu) + K(y);$$

as this must agree with the preceding expression we can infer

$$m = n, \quad y_1^\nu + \ldots + y_m^\nu = \nu G_{-\nu}(x);$$

putting then

$$(y - y_1)\ldots(y - y_n) = y^n + p_1 y^{n-1} + \ldots + p_n = \varpi,$$

we have

$$p_1 + G_{-1}(x) = 0, \quad 2p_2 + p_1 G_{-1}(x) + 2G_{-2}(x) = 0,$$

$$3p_3 + p_2 G_{-1}(x) + 2p_1 G_{-2}(x) + 3G_{-3}(x) = 0,$$

and so on, whereby it follows that $p_1, p_2, \ldots$ are power-series in x, vanishing for $x = 0$; also

$$\frac{1}{f}\frac{\partial f}{\partial y} = \frac{1}{\varpi}\frac{\partial \varpi}{\partial y} + K(y) = \frac{1}{\varpi}\frac{\partial \varpi}{\partial y} + G(y) - \frac{\partial}{\partial y}\sum_{\mu=0}^{\infty} G_\mu(x)\, y^\mu,$$

so that

$$f = \varpi U,$$

where U is of the form

$$Ae^{\int_0^y G(y)\,dy - \sum_{\mu=0}^{\infty} G_\mu(x)\, y^\mu} = A(\lambda_0 + \lambda_1 y + \lambda_2 y^2 + \ldots),$$

and $\lambda_0, \lambda_1, \lambda_2, \ldots$ are power-series in x, of which λ_0 reduces to unity for $x = 0$, while A, independent of y, is obtainable by comparing coefficients of y^n in

$$A_0 + A_1 y + A_2 y^2 + \ldots = A(p_n + p_1 y + \ldots + p_1 y^{n-1} + y^n)(\lambda_0 + \lambda_1 y + \lambda_2 y^2 + \ldots),$$

and is given by

$$A = A_n(\lambda_0 + \lambda_1 p_1 + \ldots + \lambda_n p_n)^{-1},$$

so that it is a power-series in x reducing for $x = 0$ to the constant term in the power-series A_n. For the values of x and y for which the series $G(y)$, $\sum_{\mu=0}^{\infty} G_\mu(x) y^\mu$ converge, the factor U does not vanish, as its exponential form shews; these series converge however for all sufficiently small values of x and y; thus all the roots of the equation $f(x, y) = 0$, for any sufficiently small x, which vanish with x, are those of the equation $\varpi = 0$.

If, still supposing $f(0, y)$ not to be identically zero, the terms of lowest order in $f(x, y)$ are of the nth order, so that A_0 vanishes to the nth order, A_1 to the $(n-1)$th order, ..., A_{n-1} to the first order, when $x = 0$, then the lowest terms in f_1 are of aggregate order n in x and y, as are the lowest terms in f_0; thus the lowest terms in $G_\mu(x) y^\mu$ are of order zero at least and $G_{-\nu}(x)$ is a power-series whose lowest terms are of order ν; the same is then the case for p_ν, which vanishes to the νth order when $x = 0$. We can if we wish, by a substitution, $x + \mu y$ for x, in $f(x, y)$, where μ is indeterminate, always suppose the case to be as here.

The case when $f(0, y)$ is identically zero has been excluded from the preceding; putting then $x = \lambda\xi + \mu\eta$, $y = \lambda'\xi + \mu'\eta$, the value of $f(x, y)$ when $\xi = 0$ is $f(\mu\eta, \mu'\eta)$, which is not identically zero in regard to η if μ and μ' be chosen with sufficient generality. Thus $f(x, y)$ can be written in the form

$$f(x, y) = (\eta^m + q_1\eta^{m-1} + \ldots + q_m) U,$$

where $q_1, \ldots, q_m$ are power-series in ξ vanishing for $\xi = 0$, and U is a power-series in ξ, η not vanishing for $\xi = 0$, $\eta = 0$. Supposing $\lambda\mu' - \lambda'\mu$ not zero, this decomposition replaces that of the preceding case.

A theorem, and demonstration, exactly analogous to the foregoing applies to the case of an equation $f(x_1, x_2, \ldots, x_m, y) = 0$, in which the number of independent variables is m.

Corollary. If $\phi_1, \ldots, \phi_n$ are n convergent power-series in the $n + m$ variables $x_1, \ldots, x_{n+m}$, all vanishing when these $n + m$ variables vanish, the linear terms in the series $\phi_1, \ldots, \phi_n$, say

$$\begin{array}{c} a_{1,1}x_1 + \ldots + a_{1,n+m}x_{n+m} \\ \cdots\cdots\cdots\cdots\cdots\cdots \\ a_{n,1}x_1 + \ldots + a_{n,n+m}x_{n+m}, \end{array}$$

being such that the determinant formed by the coefficients of $x_1, \ldots, x_n$, namely

$$\begin{vmatrix} a_{1,1} & \cdots & a_{1,n} \\ \cdots & \cdots & \cdots \\ a_{n,1} & \cdots & a_{n,n} \end{vmatrix},$$

is not zero, then the equations

$$\phi_1 = 0, \ \ldots, \ \phi_n = 0,$$

regarded as equations for $x_1, \ldots, x_n$, are satisfied by convergent power-series in $x_{n+1}, \ldots, x_{n+m}$, these being the only solutions of these equations for $x_1, \ldots, x_n$, within a certain neighbourhood of the origin.

For put

$$\xi_1 = a_{1,1}x_1 + \ldots + a_{1,n}x_n, \ \ldots, \ \xi_n = a_{n,1}x_1 + \ldots + a_{n,n}x_n,$$

so that the equations $\phi_1 = 0, \ldots, \phi_n = 0$, are

$$\xi_1 + a_{1,n+1}x_{n+1} + \ldots + a_{1,n+m}x_{n+m} + u_{1,2} + u_{1,3} + \ldots = 0,$$

....

$$\xi_n + a_{n,n+1}x_{n+1} + \ldots + a_{n,n+m}x_{n+m} + u_{n,2} + u_{n,3} + \ldots = 0,$$

where $u_{r,s}$ is a polynomial of dimension s in the $n+m$ variables

$$\xi_1, \ldots, \xi_n, x_{n+1}, \ldots, x_{n+m}.$$

If in the first equation we put $\xi_2 = 0, \ldots, \xi_n = 0, x_{n+1} = 0, \ldots, x_{n+m} = 0$ it reduces to a power-series in ξ_1 whose first term is ξ_1. It follows then, by the foregoing, that the only sets of values of $\xi_1, \ldots, \xi_n, x_{n+1}, \ldots, x_{n+m}$, in the immediate neighbourhood of the origin, which satisfy the equation $\phi_1 = 0$, are given by $\xi_1 + P = 0$, where P is a convergent power-series in

$$\xi_2, \ldots, \xi_n, x_{n+1}, \ldots, x_{n+m},$$

vanishing when these $n+m-1$ variables are all zero. If the resulting value of ξ_1 be substituted in the remaining equations $\phi_2 = 0, \ldots, \phi_n = 0$, they reduce to convergent power-series in $\xi_2, \ldots, \xi_n, x_{n+1}, \ldots, x_{n+m}$ of the form

$$\xi_r + a_{r,n+1}x_{n+1} + \ldots + a_{r,n+m}x_{n+m} + v_{r,2} + v_{r,3} + \ldots = 0, \qquad (r = 2, \ldots, n),$$

where $v_{r,s}$ is a polynomial of dimension s in the $n+m-1$ variables. Solving the first of these equations similarly for ξ_2, and substituting, and proceeding in this manner, we eventually obtain ξ_n as a power-series in $x_{n+1}, \ldots, x_{n+m}$, only, from which, by retracing the steps, we obtain in turn $\xi_{n-1}, \ldots, \xi_1$, and so eventually $x_1, \ldots, x_n$, all as power-series in $x_{n+1}, \ldots, x_{n+m}$.

52. Consider now what is represented, for sufficiently small values of x and y, by the equation

$$\varpi(x, y) \equiv y^n + p_1 y^{n-1} + \ldots + p_n = 0,$$

where $p_1, p_2, \ldots$ are converging power-series in x vanishing with x.

If the left side be capable of being written as a product of factors of the form

$$y^{n'} + p_1' y^{n'-1} + \ldots + p_{n'}',$$

wherein $p_1', \ldots, p_{n'}'$ are analytical functions single-valued about the origin, then p_r' is of the form $x^{-h_r}q_r$, where q_r is a converging power-series in x, and then, as all the roots of any factor are roots of $\varpi(x, y)$ and therefore vanish at the origin, we must have $h_r = 0$ and q_r must vanish for $x = 0$; every factor must thus be of the same form as $\varpi(x, y)$. As we could then deal similarly with each factor in turn, there is no loss of generality in assuming that $\varpi(x, y)$ is incapable of such decomposition.

This being assumed it can be shewn that the n roots of $\varpi(x, y)$ are expressible in the form

$$y = a_1 t + a_2 t^2 + \ldots,$$

where the right side represents a converging power-series in which t is to be replaced in turn by the n values of $x^{\frac{1}{n}}$; thus the n roots constitute one cycle, and belong to a single monogenic function, each root changing into another when x makes a circuit about the origin, and so on throughout the cycle, till after n circuits the original root reappears.

We have

$$\varpi_y'(x, y), = \partial\varpi(x, y)/\partial y, = ny^{n-1} + (n-1)p_1 y^{n-2} + \ldots + p_{n-1};$$

form the Sylvester y-resultant of $\varpi(x, y)$ and $\varpi_y'(x, y)$, which, being a rational integral polynomial in $p_1, \ldots, p_n$, is a power-series; this power-series cannot vanish identically, or $\varpi(x, y)$, $\varpi_y'(x, y)$ would have a common factor

$$y^{n'} + p_1' y^{n'-1} + \ldots + p_{n'}',$$

obtainable by the rational method of greatest common divisor; thus $p_1', \ldots, p_{n'}'$ would be rational in $p_1, \ldots, p_n$, and therefore each of the form $x^{-h_r} q_r$; we have excluded this by hypothesis. The Sylvester y-resultant vanishes for $x = 0$, since both $\varpi(x, y)$ and $\varpi_y'(x, y)$ vanish for $x = 0$, $y = 0$; but a region can be put about $x = 0$ within which no other zeros of this resultant are found; this region, taken circular, we call, momentarily, the domain of the origin. Let x_0 be a point of this domain other than the origin, and y_0 any one of the corresponding roots of $\varpi(x_0, y) = 0$, so that $\varpi_y'(x_0, y_0)$ is not zero; put $x = x_0 + \xi$, $y = y_0 + \eta$ in $\varpi(x, y)$, so obtaining

$$\frac{\partial\varpi(x_0, y_0)}{\partial x_0}\xi + \frac{\partial\varpi(x_0, y_0)}{\partial y_0}\eta + \ldots = 0;$$

by a particular case of the theorem in the Corollary of the preceding article this leads to a series

$$y = y_0 + A_1(x - x_0) + A_2(x - x_0)^2 + \ldots,$$

expressing, about x_0, the only root of $\varpi(x, y) = 0$ which reduces to y_0 when $x = x_0$. A precisely similar form, as power-series in $x - x_0$, is possible for the other roots of $\varpi(x, y) = 0$ in the neighbourhood of x_0. Let r be the least of the n radii of convergence of these n series belonging to x_0. Putting a small circle about the origin, and another circle just within the outer circumference of the domain of the origin, and considering the closed annulus so determined, and the value of r for each point x_0 of this annulus, we desire to shew that a number greater than zero exists such that r is everywhere greater than this; in other words that the lower limit of r for the points x_0 of the annulus is greater than zero.

To prove this we may proceed as follows: let x_0' be a point within the circle centre x_0 of radius r; to this point belong n expansions of y in powers of $x - x_0'$, directly derivable from $\varpi(x, y) = 0$, as before; let r' be the least of the radii of convergence of these; on the other hand, any one of the expansions in $x - x_0$ may be rewritten as a power-series in $x - x_0'$, converging at least as far as the circle centre x_0 of radius r, and in this form must agree with one of the series directly derived from $\varpi(x, y) = 0$ for the neighbourhood of x_0'; we see thus, that $r' \geqq r - |x_0' - x_0|$; but we similarly provè, beginning with the expansions about x_0', and supposing $|x_0 - x_0'| < r'$, that $r \geqq r' - |x_0' - x_0|$, and so have, for sufficiently small $|x_0 - x_0'|$,

$$r - |x_0 - x_0'| \leqq r' \leqq r + |x_0 - x_0'|$$

which shews that r varies continuously as x_0 varies; a continuous quantity over a finite region is known however to reach its lower limit, while r is never zero over the annulus considered; thus its lower limit is not zero.

Denote this lower limit by ρ; let x_1 be a point within the closed annulus and within the circumference of convergence of the series

$$y = y_0 + A_1(x - x_0) + A_2(x - x_0)^2 + \dots,$$

but at less than ρ from this circumference; let y_1 be the value represented by this series at x_1; there exists then, when x is near to x_1, one root of $\varpi(x, y) = 0$, reducing to y_1 when $x = x_1$, expressible by a power-series in $x - x_1$ converging for $|x - x_1| < \rho$, and therefore forming a continuation of the series above, *beyond its circle of convergence.*

It is thus clear that any root (y_0) of $\varpi(x, y) = 0$ can be continued completely round the closed annulus back to the neighbourhood of x_0; it may not however, after one circuit, resumè its value; it may change into another root. Let it resume its value after μ circuits; put then $x = t^\mu$, so that the phase of t increases by 2π when the phase of x increases by $2\pi\mu$; now, as we have considered the equation $\varpi(x, y) = 0$, consider the equation $\varpi(t^\mu, y)$, and the root of this reducing to y_0 for $t = t_0$, where $t_0^\mu = x_0$; by the reasoning given, this root is a single-valued function of t within the annulus, and developable, as a power-series in $t - t_0$, about any point t_0; thus, by Laurent's theorem, it is capable of a representation $\sum_{m=-\infty}^{\infty} a_m t^m$, valid for the whole of the annulus; if however M be greater than the modulus of this series for $|t| = R$, we have $|a_{-m}| < MR^m$; as all the roots of $\varpi(x, y) = 0$ vanish for $x = 0$, it follows that the negative powers of t, and the zero power, are absent from the series. Consider now the μ roots of $\varpi(x, y) = 0$, given by the series $\sum_1^\infty a_m t^m$ for $t = t \exp(2\pi i s/\mu)$, where $s = 0, 1, \ldots, \mu - 1$; denote them by $y_1, y_2, \ldots, y_\mu$; if h be a positive integer the sum $y_1^h + y_2^h + \ldots + y_\mu^h$ arises as a convergent power-series in t which is in fact a single-valued function of x and is thus a power-series in x, manifestly vanishing for $x = 0$; we infer then that $y_1, \ldots, y_\mu$ are the roots of an equation

$$y^\mu + q_1 y^{\mu-1} + \ldots + q_\mu = 0,$$

wherein $q_1, q_2, \ldots$ are power-series in x vanishing for $x = 0$; the factor of $\varpi(x, y)$ given by the left side must then, by our initial hypothesis, be identical with $\varpi(x, y)$ and $\mu = n$. And the proposition above stated is so proved, namely all the roots of $\varpi(x, y)$ are given by a power-series in t, and constitute a single monogenic function.

53. Consider now what is represented in the immediate neighbourhood of the origin by a simultaneous set of equations

$$G_1(x_1, x_2, \ldots, x_n) = 0, \ \ldots, \ G_m(x_1, x_2, \ldots, x_n) = 0,$$

wherein each of $G_1, G_2, \ldots$ denotes a power-series in the n variables vanishing for $x_1 = 0, x_2 = 0, \ldots, x_n = 0$, the number of equations being less than, equal to, or greater than n. We suppose $x_1, \ldots, x_n$ replaced by independent linear functions of new variables, $y_1, \ldots, y_n$, with unspecified coefficients, which coefficients we regard as implicit constants; then we may suppose that in the new equations in $y_1, \ldots, y_n$ there is no specialty of form which gives a distinction to any variable above the rest. We now introduce explicit constants, replacing $y_2, \ldots, y_n$ by $\eta_2, \ldots, \eta_n$ by means of the equations

$$\eta_2 = \lambda_{21} y_1 + y_2, \ \eta_3 = \lambda_{31} y_1 + \lambda_{32} y_2 + y_3, \ \ldots, \ \eta_n = \lambda_{n1} y_1 + \ldots + \lambda_{n, n-1} y_{n-1} + y_n;$$

the power-series then take forms

$$K_1(y_1, \eta_2, \ldots, \eta_n) = 0, \ \ldots, \ K_m(y_1, \eta_2, \ldots, \eta_n) = 0,$$

wherein the constants $\lambda_{21}, \lambda_{31}, \lambda_{32}, \ldots$ occur explicitly. We require the solutions $(y_1, \ldots, y_n)$ independent of these constants.

It is possible, as is shewn by an argument precisely like that previously given for the case of two variables, to deduce from $K_r(y_1, \eta_2, \ldots, \eta_n) = 0$ an equation

$$k_r \equiv y_1^{\mu_r} + k_{r,1} y_1^{\mu_r - 1} + \ldots + k_{r, \mu_r} = 0, \qquad (r = 1, 2, \ldots, m),$$

wherein $k_{r,1}, \ldots, k_{r,\mu_r}$ are power-series in $\eta_2, \ldots, \eta_n$ vanishing for $\eta_2 = 0, \ldots, \eta_n = 0$, this equation giving all the solutions of the y_1-equation $K_r = 0$ which vanish for $\eta_2 = 0, \ldots, \eta_n = 0$; as we are considering the equations $G_1 = 0, \ldots, G_m = 0$ for the neighbourhood of the origin it is thus sufficient for our purpose to consider only the equations $k_1 = 0, \ldots, k_m = 0$. Any one of the m polynomials in y_1 denoted by $k_1, \ldots, k_m$ may be capable of being written as a product of factors of the form

$$y_1^\mu + h_1 y_1^{\mu-1} + \ldots + h_\mu$$

where $h_1, \ldots, h_\mu$ are convergent power series vanishing for $\eta_2 = 0, \ldots, \eta_n = 0$, and any such factor may occur in any polynomial to higher than the first power; suppose the decompositions of this form carried out as far as possible, and let k_r' denote the product of the *different* factors of this form which enter into the polynomial k_r; every set of values of $y_1, \eta_2, \ldots, \eta_n$ which satisfy the simultaneous equations $k_1 = 0, \ldots, k_m = 0$ will satisfy the set of equations $k_1' = 0, \ldots, k_m' = 0$, and conversely; we therefore consider the system $k_1' = 0, \ldots, k_m' = 0$, instead of the system $k_1 = 0, \ldots, k_m = 0$. If $k_1', \ldots, k_m'$ have a common factor, a product of irreducible factors of the form which has been referred to, denote it by $p^{(n)}$, the exponent denoting the number of variables which (presumably, or possibly) enter into it, and let $k_1'', \ldots, k_m''$ be the results of dividing $k_1', \ldots, k_m'$ respectively by $p^{(n)}$. Then any point $y_1, \eta_2, \ldots, \eta_n$, in a certain near neighbourhood of the origin, which satisfies the original system of equations $G_1 = 0, \ldots, G_m = 0$, satisfies either $p^{(n)} = 0$, or all the equations $k_1'' = 0, \ldots, k_m'' = 0$; and any point of this neighbourhood satisfying either $p^{(n)} = 0$, or all the equations $k_1'' = 0, \ldots, k_m'' = 0$, satisfies the original system of equations.

Consider first of all the single equation $p^{(n)} = 0$, and, of this, any factor of the same form

$$q^{(n)} \equiv y_1^\lambda + r_1 y_1^{\lambda-1} + \ldots + r_\lambda,$$

wherein $r_1, \ldots, r_\lambda$ are converging power series vanishing for $\eta_2 = 0, \ldots, \eta_n = 0$, the factor being chosen so as to be incapable of further decomposition into factors of the same form; the points $y_1, y_2, \ldots, y_n$, in the neighbourhood of the origin, satisfying the equation $q^{(n)} = 0$, are first to be divided into two categories: those which do not, and those which do, also satisfy the derived equation $\partial q^{(n)}/\partial y_1 = 0$; the points of the latter category satisfy an equation $R = 0$, where R is the Sylvester resultant in regard to y_1 of $q^{(n)}$ and $\partial q^{(n)}/\partial y_1$, which, being a rational integral polynomial in the coefficients $r_1, \ldots, r_\lambda$ in $q^{(n)}$, is a power series in $\eta_2, \ldots, \eta_n$, manifestly vanishing at the origin; thus the points satisfying $q^{(n)} = 0$ are divided into the two categories

$$\left.\begin{array}{r} q^{(n)} = 0 \\ \partial q^{(n)}/\partial y_1 \neq 0 \end{array}\right| \begin{array}{l} q^{(n)} = 0 \\ R = 0; \end{array}$$

consider the solutions of $R = 0$ in the immediate neighbourhood of the origin; these are given by the vanishing of a certain number of irreducible factors of the form

$$q^{(n-1)} \equiv \eta_2^\mu + s_1 \eta_2^{\mu-1} + \ldots + s_\mu,$$

where $s_1, \ldots, s_\mu$ are power series in $\eta_3, \ldots, \eta_n$ vanishing at the origin; these in turn can be divided into two sets: those for which $\partial q^{(n-1)}/\partial \eta_2$ does not also vanish, and those for which it does; consider a point of the former set; the arbitrary coefficient λ_{21}, which, it will be remembered, was introduced in the substitution

$$\eta_2 = \lambda_{21} y_1 + y_2,$$

enters explicitly in the series $s_1, \ldots, s_\mu$; it enters also implicitly in η_2: differentiating the identity in λ_{21},

$$(\lambda_{21} y_1 + y_2)^\mu + s_1 (\lambda_{21} y_1 + y_2)^{\mu-1} + \ldots + s_\mu = 0,$$

in regard to λ_{21}, we thus have

$$y_1 \frac{\partial q^{(n-1)}}{\partial \eta_2} + \frac{\partial q^{(n-1)}}{\partial \lambda_{21}} = 0;$$

thereby the solutions of $q^{(n)} = 0$ are divided into three kinds

$$\begin{array}{c|c|c} q^{(n)} = 0 & q^{(n-1)} = 0 & q^{(n-1)} = 0 \\ \dfrac{\partial q^{(n)}}{\partial y_1} \neq 0 & y_1 \dfrac{\partial q^{(n-1)}}{\partial \eta_2} + \dfrac{\partial q^{(n-1)}}{\partial \lambda_{21}} = 0 & \dfrac{\partial q^{(n-1)}}{\partial \eta_2} = 0 \\ & \dfrac{\partial q^{(n-1)}}{\partial \eta_2} \neq 0 & \end{array}$$

where it must be understood that there are as many sets of equations of the second and third kinds as there are irreducible factors of R. We may now proceed similarly with the points of the third kind. By combining the two equations $q^{(n-1)} = 0$, $\partial q^{(n-1)}/\partial \eta_2 = 0$, we derive a power series in $\eta_3, \ldots, \eta_n$, vanishing at the origin, and hence a certain number of irreducible factors such as

$$q^{(n-2)} \equiv \eta_3^\nu + t_1 \eta_3^{\nu-1} + \ldots + t_\nu,$$

where $t_1, \ldots, t_\nu$ are power series in $\eta_4, \ldots, \eta_n$, vanishing at the origin; in $q^{(n-2)}$ there enter explicitly the arbitrary coefficients introduced by writing

$$\eta_3 = \lambda_{31} y_1 + \lambda_{32} y_2 + y_3;$$

considering first the points satisfying $q^{(n-2)} = 0$ for which $\partial q^{(n-2)}/\partial \eta_3$ is not zero, we obtain, differentiating in regard to λ_{31} and λ_{32},

$$y_1 \frac{\partial q^{(n-2)}}{\partial \eta_3} + \frac{\partial q^{(n-2)}}{\partial \lambda_{31}} = 0, \quad y_2 \frac{\partial q^{(n-2)}}{\partial \eta_3} + \frac{\partial q^{(n-2)}}{\partial \lambda_{32}} = 0, \quad \frac{\partial q^{(n-2)}}{\partial \eta_3} \neq 0$$

while the points for which $\partial q^{(n-2)}/\partial \eta_3 = 0$ lead similarly to equations not containing η_3. The points, in the neighbourhood of the origin, satisfying $p^{(n)} = 0$ are thus finally distributed into kinds, those of any kind being given by a certain (finite) number of sets of equations of the form

$$q^{(n-r)} = 0, \quad y_1 \frac{\partial q^{(n-r)}}{\partial \eta_{r+1}} + H_1 = 0, \quad \ldots, \quad y_r \frac{\partial q^{(n-r)}}{\partial \eta_{r+1}} + H_r = 0, \quad \frac{\partial q^{(n-r)}}{\partial \eta_{r+1}} \neq 0$$

wherein $q^{(n-r)}$ is of the form

$$q^{(n-r)} \equiv \eta_{r+1}^{\sigma} + u_1 \eta_{r+1}^{\sigma-1} + \ldots + u_\sigma,$$

$u_1, \ldots, u_\sigma$ denoting power series in $\eta_{r+2}, \ldots, \eta_n$ vanishing at the origin, and is incapable of being written as a product of other factors of the same form, while $H_1, \dots, H_r$ are each of the form

$$v_1 \eta_{r+1}^{\sigma-1} + \dots + v_\sigma,$$

$v_1, \dots, v_\sigma$ denoting power series in $\eta_{r+2}, \dots, \eta_n$. The points represented by such a set of equations do not form a closed aggregate; the aggregate is closed by the points satisfying $q^{(n-r)} = 0$, $\partial q^{(n-r)}/\partial \eta_{r+1} = 0$.

We saw that the points satisfying $G_1 = 0, \dots, G_m = 0$ were given either by $p^{(n)} = 0$ or by the simultaneous equations

$$k_1'' = 0, \ \dots, \ k_m'' = 0;$$

consider now the points satisfying these simultaneous equations. As the y_1-polynomials $k_1'', \dots, k_m''$ have no common factor of the same form, they cannot all be satisfied for arbitrary values of $\eta_2, \dots, \eta_n$; our first problem is to find all the relations connecting $\eta_2, \dots, \eta_n$ which follow from the hypothesis that $k_1'' = 0, \dots, k_m'' = 0$ have a common solution. Let $u_1, \dots, u_m$ and $v_1, \dots, v_m$ be arbitrary unassigned quantities; from the two equations

$$U \equiv u_1 k_1'' + \dots + u_m k_m'' = 0, \quad V \equiv v_1 k_1'' + \dots + v_m k_m'' = 0,$$

we can eliminate y_1, so obtaining an integral polynomial in $u_1, \dots, u_m$, $v_1, \dots, v_m$ with coefficients which are integral polynomials in the coefficients of the various powers of y_1 in $k_1'', \dots, k_m''$, say

$$\Sigma A u_1^{\lambda_1}, \ \dots, \ v_m^{\mu_m} = 0;$$

every one of the coefficients A must then be zero, and we so obtain a system of equations

$$H_1(\eta_2, \dots, \eta_n) = 0, \ \dots\dots, \ H_s(\eta_2, \dots, \eta_n) = 0$$

wherein each function H is a power series in $\eta_2, \dots, \eta_n$; these are all satisfied by the common solutions of the equations $k_1'' = 0, \dots, k_m'' = 0$, and in particular by the origin $\eta_2 = 0, \dots, \eta_n = 0$. Conversely, to any set of values of $\eta_2, \dots, \eta_n$ satisfying all the equations $H_1 = 0, \dots, H_s = 0$, corresponds at least one value of y_1 satisfying both $U = 0$ and $V = 0$, and this whatever values are given to $u_1, \dots, u_m, v_1, \dots, v_m$; such value, or values, of y_1 will therefore be independent of $u_1, \dots, u_m, v_1, \dots, v_m$, as appears also from the equations given below for determining them. Now let the equations $H_1 = 0, \dots, H_s = 0$ be replaced, for the neighbourhood of the origin, as before, by a set of equations

$$h_\sigma \equiv \eta_2^f + P_1 \eta_2^{f-1} + \dots + P_f = 0, \qquad (\sigma = 1, 2, \dots, s),$$

wherein $P_1, \dots, P_f$ are power series in $\eta_3, \dots, \eta_n$, vanishing at the origin; further let h_σ be written as a product of irreducible factors of the same form, and let h_σ' be the product of the different factors; the equations $h_1' = 0, \dots, h_s' = 0$ then give all the points in the neighbourhood of the origin which satisfy the equations $h_1, \dots, h_s = 0$; of the η_2-polynomials $h_1', \dots, h_s'$ let $p^{(n-1)}$ be the common factor of the same form, and the results of dividing these polynomials by this factor be respectively h_1'', ..., h_s''; then all the solutions of $H_1=0$, ..., $H_s=0$ in the neighbourhood of the origin satisfy either the equation $p^{(n-1)}=0$ or else they satisfy the system of equations $h_1''=0$, ..., $h_s''=0$; and conversely. Consider now first the equation $p^{(n-1)}=0$, in the variables $\eta_2, \eta_3, \ldots, \eta_n$; let $q^{(n-1)}$ be an irreducible factor of the same form; it contains the arbitrary parameter λ_{21} explicitly, and, since $\eta_2=\lambda_{21}y_1+y_2$, it contains it also implicitly; separating the solutions of $q^{(n-1)}=0$ into those for which $\partial q^{(n-1)}/\partial\eta_2$ does not vanish, and their limiting points for which $\partial q^{(n-1)}/\partial\eta_2=0$, we have, in the case of the solutions of the former kind, by differentiating the identity in λ_{21} expressed by $q^{(n-1)}=0$ when $\eta_2=\lambda_{21}y_1+y_2$, the equations

$$q^{(n-1)}=0, \qquad y_1\frac{\partial q^{(n-1)}}{\partial\eta_2}+\frac{\partial q^{(n-1)}}{\partial\lambda_{21}}=0, \qquad \frac{\partial q^{(n-1)}}{\partial\eta_2}\neq 0.$$

This is precisely the mode in which we previously dealt with the equation $q^{(n)}=0$; we can now proceed in the same way as before with the equations $q^{(n-1)}=0$, $\partial q^{(n-1)}/\partial\eta_2=0$. Considering then the equations $h_1''=0$, ..., $h_s''=0$, we can proceed as before, beginning by the elimination of η_2. And this mode of procedure can be continued until all the possibilities are exhausted: if at any stage we are considering an irreducible factor

$$\varpi\equiv\eta_\mu{}^\rho+\varpi_1\eta_\mu{}^{\rho-1}+\ldots+\varpi_\rho,$$

wherein $\varpi_1, \ldots, \varpi_\rho$ are power series in $\eta_{\mu+1}, \ldots, \eta_n$, vanishing at the origin, we first consider the solutions for which $\partial\varpi/\partial\eta_\mu$ is not zero; we have then an identity in arbitrary coefficients $\lambda_{\mu,1}, \ldots, \lambda_{\mu,\mu-1}$ obtained by replacing η_μ in ϖ by

$$\eta_\mu=\lambda_{\mu,1}y_1+\lambda_{\mu,2}y_2+\ldots+\lambda_{\mu,\mu-1}y_{\mu-1}+y_\mu,$$

the coefficients $\lambda_{\mu,1}, \ldots, \lambda_{\mu,\mu-1}$ entering explicitly in $\varpi_1, \ldots, \varpi_\mu$; thus by differentiating this identity $\varpi=0$ we have solutions given by $\varpi=0$, $\partial\varpi/\partial\eta_\mu\neq 0$, $y_1\dfrac{\partial\varpi}{\partial\eta_\mu}+\dfrac{\partial\varpi}{\partial\lambda_{\mu,1}}=0, \ldots, y_{\mu-1}\dfrac{\partial\varpi}{\partial\eta_\lambda}+\dfrac{\partial\varpi}{\partial\lambda_{\mu,\mu-1}}=0$, from which, if desired, $\eta_2, \ldots, \eta_{\mu-1}$ can be expressed in terms of $\eta_\mu, \eta_{\mu+1}, \ldots, \eta_n$ by means of

$$\eta_2=\lambda_{21}y_1+y_2, \qquad \eta_3=\lambda_{31}y_1+\lambda_{32}y_2+y_3, \ \ldots\ldots\ldots$$

The outcome of the whole investigation is thus as follows: If $G_1(x_1, \ldots, x_n), \ldots, G_m(x_1, \ldots, x_n)$ be any m power series in $x_1, \ldots, x_n$, vanishing at the origin, a neighbourhood of the origin, defined by such equations as $|x_1|<\delta_1, \ldots, |x_n|<\delta_n$, can be found such that all the solutions of the equations $G_1=0$, ..., $G_m=0$ lying in this neighbourhood are given by a finite number of sets of equations of the form

$$\left.\begin{aligned}\varpi=\eta_s{}^\mu+u_1\eta_s{}^{\mu-1}+\ldots+u_\mu=0\\ \eta_{s-1}=\frac{U_{s-1}}{\varpi'}, \quad \ldots\ldots\ldots\ldots\ldots, \quad \eta_1=\frac{U_1}{\varpi'}\end{aligned}\right\}$$

where $\eta_1, \ldots, \eta_n$ are independent linear functions of $x_1, \ldots, x_n$, the number s is one of the numbers $1, 2, \ldots, (n-1)$, the coefficients $u_1, \ldots, u_\mu$ are power series in $\eta_{s+1}, \eta_{s+2}, \ldots, \eta_n$ vanishing when these are all zero, the function ϖ is incapable of being written as a product of other factors of the same form, the denominator ϖ' denotes $\partial\varpi/\partial\eta_s$, the numerators $U_1, \ldots, U_{s-1}$ are each of the form

$$v_0\eta_s^{\mu-1} + v_1\eta_s^{\mu-2} + \ldots + v_{\mu-1},$$

where $v_0, \ldots, v_{\mu-1}$ are power series in $\eta_{s+1}, \eta_{s+2}, \ldots, \eta_n$ vanishing when these are all zero, and only such values of $\eta_{s+1}, \ldots, \eta_n$ are to be considered that ϖ' does not vanish simultaneously with ϖ; subject to this condition every solution of any one of these sets of equations within the prescribed neighbourhood of the origin gives rise to a solution of the original system. Herein each of the functions $U_1, \ldots, U_{s-1}$ is such that each of $\eta_1, \ldots, \eta_{s-1}$ vanishes when $\eta_{s+1}, \ldots, \eta_n$ all vanish, and every one of the functions $\eta_1, \ldots, \eta_{s-1}$ satisfies an equation of the same form as that, $\varpi = 0$, satisfied by η_s, with coefficients depending upon $\eta_{s+1}, \ldots, \eta_n$.

The points satisfying such a set of s equations may be said to constitute an irreducible construct of rank $n-s$ or of $2(n-s)$ dimensions, or an irreducible $2(n-s)$-fold; it is an open aggregate whose limiting points are those for which both $\varpi = 0$ and $\partial\varpi/\partial\eta_s = 0$; about any point $(\eta^0_{s+1}, \ldots, \eta^0_n)$ of it, other than the origin, each of $\eta_s, \eta_{s-1}, \ldots, \eta_1$ is representable as a power series in $\eta_{s+1} - \eta^0_{s+1}, \ldots, \eta_n - \eta^0_n$, as may be proved by an argument already applied for the case $n-s=1$; that all such power series are capable of analytical derivation from one of them is a proposition presumably true and presumably capable of a proof analogous to that which has been given for the case when $n-s=1$; when this is proved the construct may be described as monogenic, it being remembered that we consider its points only for the immediate neighbourhood of the origin.

Two such irreducible constructs, of the same or different dimensions, may have points, even in infinite number, in common with one another: but in every neighbourhood of such common point there are points not common to the two constructs.

Let $\quad \varpi \equiv y^m + (x_1, \ldots, x_n)_1 y^{m-1} + \ldots + (x_1, \ldots, x_n)_m = 0,$

be such an equation as has been considered, the coefficients $(x_1, \ldots, x_n)_1, \ldots, (x_1, \ldots, x_n)_m$ being power series vanishing at the origin, and the left side being incapable of being written as a product of factors of the same form; the points in the neighbourhood of the origin which satisfy $\varpi = 0$ are upon a certain $2n$-fold; of these the points which also satisfy $\partial\varpi/\partial y = 0$ are upon a certain $(2n-2)$-fold passing through the origin; in fact by elimination of y between $\varpi = 0$ and $\partial\varpi/\partial y = 0$ we obtain a certain necessary relation connecting $x_1, \ldots, x_n$. For the neighbourhood of any point $(a_1, \ldots, a_n)$, near the origin, which does not satisfy this relation connecting $x_1, \ldots, x_n$, every root y of $\varpi = 0$ can be expressed as a power series in $x_1 - a_1, \ldots, x_n - a_n$; this is obvious as in the case $n = 1$. Now let

$$v \equiv y^\mu + [x_1, \ldots, x_n]_1 y^{\mu-1} + \ldots + [x_1, \ldots, x_n]_\mu = 0$$

be another irreducible $2n$-fold; consider the quotient ϖ/v. We may eliminate y between the equations $\varpi = 0$, $v = 0$, and so obtain a relation connecting $x_1, \ldots, x_n$ defining, for the neighbourhood of the origin, a $(2n-2)$-fold, passing through the origin, upon which both ϖ and v vanish; the hypothesis that this relation vanishes identically is impossible since we have assumed that ϖ and v are irreducible. For any values $a_1, \ldots, a_n$ not satisfying this relation, and not satisfying the relation obtained by eliminating y between $\varpi = 0$ and $\partial\varpi/\partial y = 0$, we can determine m power series in $x_1 - a_1, \ldots, x_n - a_n$ making $\varpi = 0$ but not making $v = 0$; there are thus points in every neighbourhood of the origin at which the quotient ϖ/v vanishes; there are similarly points at which this quotient is infinite.

Suppose $x_1 = a_1, \ldots, x_n = a_n, y = b$ to be values for which both $\varpi = 0$ and $v = 0$, in a near neighbourhood of the origin; let $H(x_1, \ldots, x_n) = 0$ be the condition that $\varpi = 0$, $v = 0$ should have a common root, and $a_1, \ldots, a_n$ be taken within the region of convergence of $H(x_1, \ldots, x_n)$; putting $x_1 = a_1 + \xi_1$, $\ldots$, $x_n = a_n + \xi_n$, $y = b + \eta$, and expanding $\varpi = 0$, $v = 0$ in powers of $\xi_1, \ldots, \xi_n, \eta$, it is conceivable that the resulting power series may divide by a power series in $\xi_1, \ldots, \xi_n, \eta$ vanishing when these variables all vanish; in such case, for arbitrary values of $x_1, \ldots, x_n$ in the immediate neighbourhood of $a_1, \ldots, a_n$, the equations $\varpi = 0$, $v = 0$ will be satisfied by the same value of y; the equation $H(x_1, \ldots, x_n) = 0$ will therefore be satisfied for all arbitrary values of $x_1, \ldots, x_n$ in the immediate neighbourhood of $a_1, \ldots, a_n$; this however would involve that in $H(x_1, \ldots, x_n)$ all the coefficients were zero, and therefore that $\varpi = 0$, $v = 0$ had a common root for all arbitrarily small values of $x_1, \ldots, x_n$, contrary to hypothesis.

There exists then about the origin a region within which there is no point $(a_1, \ldots, a_n, b)$ such that the series $\varpi = 0$, $v = 0$ are divisible by the same power series in $x_1 - a_1, \ldots, x_n - a_n, y - b$ vanishing for $x_1 = a_1, \ldots, x_n = a_n, y = b$. See Weierstrass, *Ges. Werke*, II. (1895), p. 154.

Note. In the case of a simultaneous set of *rational* equations in several variables a similar theorem, but with a simpler proof, can be given. This is postponed to Chapter IX. below, where various propositions for rational functions are considered. In both cases it is necessary to bear in mind that we are considering only the solutions in the original variables (here denoted by $y_1, \ldots, y_n$) which are independent of the parameters $(\lambda_{21}, \lambda_{31}, \ldots)$ introduced; the indeterminateness of these is essential to the process as we have described it.

CHAPTER VII.

ON THE REDUCTION OF THE THEORY OF A MULTIPLY-PERIODIC FUNCTION TO THE THEORY OF ALGEBRAIC FUNCTIONS.

54. SUPPOSE that a function, $\phi(u)$, of n independent variables, $u_1, \dots, u_n$, is known to exist, its value about any finite point $(a_1, \dots, a_n)$ being unique and expressible by a quotient U/V, wherein U and V are power series in $u_1 - a_1, \dots, u_n - a_n$ converging in a certain neighbourhood, expressed say by $|u_1 - a_1| < \delta, \dots, |u_n - a_n| < \delta$, where δ is not zero. It is understood that two expressions U/V and U'/V' for the function which belong to the neighbourhoods of two points $(a_1, \dots, a_n)$ and $(a_1', \dots, a_n')$ agree with one another at all points common to their respective regions of validity; and it can be shewn that the existence of a definite number δ for every point $(a_1, \dots, a_n)$ involves that the lower limit of δ for every finite region is other than zero. If V do not vanish at $(a_1, \dots, a_n)$, then $1/V$ is expressible, and so therefore is the function, by a power series in $u_1 - a_1, \dots, u_n - a_n$, converging for a certain neighbourhood of $(a_1, \dots, a_n)$; then $(a_1, \dots, a_n)$ may be called an ordinary point of the function. If V vanish at $(a_1, \dots, a_n)$, but U do not vanish, then in whatever way we approach the point $(a_1, \dots, a_n)$ the value of the function increases indefinitely; such a point may be called a *pole* of the function—it is an ordinary point, and a vanishing point, for the inverse of the function. If U and V both vanish at $(a_1, \dots, a_n)$, let each be written, as previously explained, as a product $\varpi_1 \varpi_2 \dots \Phi$, where, $y, x_1, \dots, x_{n-1}$ being independent linear functions of $u_1 - a_1, \dots, u_n - a_n$, each factor $\varpi_1, \varpi_2, \dots$ is of the form

$$\varpi = y^\mu + (x_1, x_2, \dots)_1 y^{\mu-1} + \dots$$

in which $(x_1, x_2, \dots)_1$, etc., denote power series vanishing for $x_1 = 0, x_2 = 0, \dots$, and is incapable of being resolved into other factors of the same form, while Φ is a power series in $u_1 - a_1, \dots, u_n - a_n$ not vanishing at $(a_1, \dots, a_n)$ or for a certain neighbourhood of this point; then, either, every one of the factors ϖ occurring in V occurs also in U, and may be removed, in which case $(a_1, \dots, a_n)$ is again an ordinary point of the function, or this may not be the case; when this is not the case there are points of arbitrary nearness to $(a_1, \dots, a_n)$ at which V vanishes but U does not vanish, these lying on $(2n-2)$-folds given by the vanishing of one of the factors ϖ of V—these are poles of the function $\phi(u)$—and there are points of arbitrary nearness to $(a_1, \ldots, a_n)$ at which both U and V vanish, these lying on $(2n-4)$-folds given by the simultaneous vanishing of one of the factors ϖ of V and one of the factors ϖ of U—for such points the function assumes the form 0/0, the point $(a_1, \ldots, a_n)$ being the only such point in the neighbourhood considered when $n=2$: it can be shewn that in this case the function $\phi(u)$ has no definite value at $(a_1, \ldots, a_n)$; for let A be an arbitrary quantity; as U and V both vanish at $(a_1, \ldots, a_n)$ it can be shewn that there are points in every neighbourhood of $(a_1, \ldots, a_n)$ at which $U - AV$ vanishes, while V does not vanish; by approaching $(a_1, \ldots, a_n)$ by a suitable succession of points the function $\phi(u)$ can thus be made to take the value A at $(a_1, \ldots, a_n)$; we thus call $(a_1, \ldots, a_n)$ in this case a point of indeterminate value, or sometimes, an unessential singularity of the second kind, the name unessential singularity of the first kind being applied to poles. When $n=2$ the points of indetermination are discrete, that is about every one can be put a region containing no other such point; when $n=1$ they are absent; and this difference constitutes one of the special difficulties of the theory of functions of more than one independent variable.

55. At the risk of interrupting the general description now being given, it may be worth while to examine the preceding in more detail. Assuming that in the expression of the function $\phi(u)$ about the point $(a_1, \ldots, a_n)$ any power series in $u_1 - a_1, \ldots, u_n - a_n$ vanishing at $(a_1, \ldots, a_n)$ which divides both U and V has been divided out, there is a region about $(a_1, \ldots, a_n)$, which we may take to be given by an inequality of the form

$$|u_1 - a_1|^2 + \ldots + |u_n - a_n|^2 < r^2,$$

such that if U, V be rearranged as power series in $u_1 - u_1', \ldots, u_n - u_n'$ about any point $(u_1', \ldots, u_n')$ of this region, there is (p. 198), no common factor, a power series in $u_1 - u_1', \ldots, u_n - u_n'$, vanishing at $u_1', \ldots, u_n'$; let this region be momentarily called the *proper region* of $(a_1, \ldots, a_n)$; further, let any region be momentarily called a *suitable region* when it is wholly contained in the proper region of some point within or upon the boundary of itself. Putting $u_r = \xi_{2r-1} + i\xi_{2r}$, where $\xi_1, \ldots, \xi_{2n}$ are real, we may speak of $(u_1, \ldots, u_n)$ as represented by a point of real space of $2n$ dimensions; taking then any portion of this space, bounded suppose, for definiteness, by $4n$ planar $(2n-1)$-folds expressed by equations $\xi_r = b_r$, $\xi_r = c_r$, this may be already a suitable region according to the definition given above; if not, let it be divided by planar $(2n-1)$-folds expressed by equations of the form $\xi_r = d_r$ into a certain number, say m, of cells equal in all respects; among these cells fix upon any one, if any exist, which is not suitable in the sense explained, and let it be again divided into m cells, equal in all respects; and so on indefinitely; we say that by a finite number of steps the original region can be divided into subregions every one of which is suitable according to the definition. For an indefinitely continued sequence of cells, each continued in the preceding one of the sequence, and a definite fraction thereof in linear dimensions, must have a limiting point contained within or upon the boundary of the cells of the sequence; to this limiting point however belongs a proper region of assignable radius r, as above, and this proper region will contain all the cells of the sequence after a certain stage of the subdivision, and all these contained cells are thus suitable regions according to the definition. It follows thus that any finite portion of space can be divided into a finite number of suitable regions. Denote such a set of suitable regions say by $K_1, K_2, \ldots$, and let $(u_1^{(r)}, \ldots, u_n^{(r)})$ be a point whose proper region contains K_r; suppose K_r, K_s to be two suitable regions with a common $(2n-1)$-fold interface; the expressions for the function $\phi(u)$, say $\frac{U_r}{V_r}$ and $\frac{U_s}{V_s}$, which are valid over the proper regions of $(u_1^{(r)}, \ldots, u_n^{(r)})$ and $(u_1^{(s)}, \ldots, u_n^{(s)})$, will both be valid on this interface, and if $(u_1', \ldots, u_n')$ be any point of this interface, and we suppose each of U_r, V_r, U_s, V_s rearranged as power series in $u_1 - u_1', \ldots, u_n - u_n'$, and in this form denoted by U_r', V_r', U_s', V_s', we shall have for the immediate neighbourhood of $u_1', \ldots, u_n'$ the equality

$$\frac{U_r'}{V_r'} = \frac{U_s'}{V_s'}$$

wherein U_r', V_r' are not both divisible by any power series in $u_1 - u_1', \ldots, u_n - u_n'$ vanishing at $u_1', \ldots, u_n'$, nor U_s', V_s' similarly divisible. If now V_s' vanish at $(u_1', \ldots, u_n')$, which may or may not be the case, then any point in the immediate neighbourhood of $(u_1', \ldots, u_n')$ at which V_s' vanishes but U_s' does not vanish, must be a vanishing point for V_r', since otherwise $U_r' = V_r' U_s'/V_s'$ would not be finite, and any point in the immediate neighbourhood of $(u_1', \ldots, u_n')$ at which V_s' vanishes and U_s' also vanishes, being a point of indetermination for the quotient U_s'/V_s', must be a point of indetermination also for U_r'/V_r', so that V_r' must also vanish (as also U_r'). We see then how the points within K_r at which $\phi(u)$ is infinite (or indeterminate), if any exist, are continued into K_s; there is what we may call an infinity $(2n-2)$-fold for the function $\phi(u)$, expressed in any region K_r which contains points of it by the equation $V_r = 0$, and then in a contiguous region K_s containing points of it by the equation $V_s = 0$; and there is similarly a zero $(2n-2)$-fold expressed in any region which contains points of it by the vanishing of the associated numerator U: over the zero $(2n-2)$-fold the function $\phi(u)$ vanishes, over the infinity $(2n-2)$-fold it has poles, except for points common to both these $(2n-2)$-folds; these constitute a $(2n-4)$-fold over which the function is indeterminate.

56. Functions with the character which has been explained for $\phi(u)$ are the nearest analogue, among functions of more than one independent variable, of the single-valued functions of one variable having for finite values of the variable no singularities other than poles, and, as those functions, they may be described as behaving like rational functions for all finite values of the arguments, or as being meromorphic. Such a function of one variable which has no essential singularity at infinity is in fact a rational function; and similarly, for the case of n variables, if such a function is expressible, for all sufficiently large values of $u_1, \ldots, u_n$, as the quotient of power series in $u_1^{-1}, \ldots, u_n^{-1}$, and for all values of which $u_{r+1}, \ldots, u_n$ are sufficiently large while $u_1 - b_1, \ldots, u_r - b_r$ are sufficiently small, as a quotient of power series in $u_1 - b_1, \ldots, u_r - b_r, u^{-1}_{r+1}, \ldots, u_n^{-1}$, and this for all positions of $b_1, \ldots, b_r$, and for all values $r = 1, 2, \ldots, (n-1)$, then the function is actually a rational function (Hurwitz, *Crelle*, XCV. (1883), p. 201). In the case of functions of one variable, a single-valued function of meromorphic character can be expressed as the quotient of two integral functions; the same is true of functions of any number of variables, and the integral functions can be taken so that they vanish respectively only for the zero construct, and the infinity construct of the function, and the quotient assumes the form 0/0 only for the points common to these where the function is indeterminate. But the proof of this result is more difficult than in the case of functions of one variable. (See the Bibliographical Notes, at the end of the Volume.)

57. Leaving these general considerations we introduce now a further limitation for the function $\phi(u)$, by assuming it to be periodic, in the sense that there exist sets of n constants $P_1, \ldots, P_n$ which added simultaneously and respectively to $u_1, \ldots, u_n$, leave the value of the function unaltered, so that we have the equation, holding for every set of values of $u_1, \ldots, u_n$ for which $\phi(u)$ is definite,

$$\phi(u_1 + P_1, \ldots, u_n + P_n) = \phi(u_1, \ldots, u_n);$$

if there be more than $2n$ such sets, or columns, say $(P_1^{(k)}, \ldots, P_n^{(k)})$ for $k = 1, \ldots, (2n), (2n+1), \ldots$, it is manifest that among every $2n+1$ such columns there exists a linear relation expressed by n equations

$$c_1 P_h^{(1)} + c_2 P_h^{(2)} + \ldots + c_{2n+1} P_h^{(2n+1)} = 0, \qquad (h = 1, \ldots, n),$$

in which $c_1, \ldots, c_{2n+1}$ are real quantities (independent of h); there must then be a positive integer r lying between 1 and $(2n+1)$, such that every existing column of periods can be expressed, in terms of r appropriately chosen columns, in the form

$$Q_h = \lambda_1 P_h^{(1)} + \ldots + \lambda_r P_h^{(r)} \qquad (h = 1, \ldots, n),$$

wherein $\lambda_1, \ldots, \lambda_r$ are real constants, independent of h. We assume now that $\phi(u)$ is not capable of being regarded as a function of less than n linear functions of $u_1, \ldots, u_n$—which, clearly enough, would be a special case; it can then be proved that the constants $\lambda_1, \ldots, \lambda_r$, are necessarily rational numerical fractions, and that r columns of periods can be chosen, in place of

$P^{(1)}, \ldots, P^{(r)}$, in terms of which every other column of periods Q can be linearly expressed as above *but with rational integers for the coefficients* $\lambda_1, \ldots, \lambda_r$; further we assume that r has its greatest possible value, namely $2n$. Thus we assume that there exist $2n$ columns each of n quantities, $\omega_1^{(s)}, \ldots, \omega_n^{(s)}$, for $s = 1, 2, \ldots, (2n)$, such that, for every set of values of $u_1, \ldots, u_n$ for which $\phi(u)$ is definite, we have

$$\phi(u_1 + \omega_1^{(s)}, \ldots, u_n + \omega_n^{(s)}) = \phi(u_1, \ldots, u_n),$$

while every column of constants $Q_1, \ldots, Q_n$ which, for all such values of $u_1, \ldots, u_n$, give the equation

$$\phi(u_1 + Q_1, \ldots, u_n + Q_n) = \phi(u_1, \ldots, u_n),$$

is expressible in terms of the $2n$ columns $\omega^{(1)}, \ldots, \omega^{(2n)}$ linearly with integral coefficients in the form

$$Q_h = \omega_h^{(1)} M_1 + \ldots + \omega_h^{(2n)} M_{2n}, \qquad (h = 1, \ldots, n),$$

wherein $M_1, \ldots, M_{2n}$ are integers independent of h. The assumption then that $\phi(u)$ is not a function of less than n linear functions of $u_1, \ldots, u_n$, can be shewn* to involve that there exists no column of wholly infinitesimal periods;

* For the results assumed the reader may consult Weierstrass, *Ges. Werke*, II. (1895), p. 55 (reproduced in abstract in the writer's *Abel's Theorem*, p. 572); Riemann, *Werke* (1876), p. 276; Kronecker, *Werke*, III. i. (1899), p. 31. The argument of Weierstrass is for analytic functions; the following argument, suggested by Kronecker's paper, affords an easy and suggestive view of the connexion between the existence of infinitesimal periods and the reduction to less than n linear functions of the variables. Put $u_h = \xi_{2h-1} + i\xi_{2h}$ and regard $\phi(u)$ as a function of the $2n$ real variables $\xi_1, \ldots, \xi_{2n}$; in the space of these take a finite region throughout which $\phi(u)$ is continuous; then if ϵ be of foreagreed smallness, a number r other than zero can be assigned such that if (ξ) be any point within this region, we have $|\phi(\xi') - \phi(\xi)| < \epsilon$ for every neighbouring point (ξ') for which $\Sigma(\xi'_k - \xi_k)^2 < r^2$. Suppose now if possible that $\phi(u)$ has infinitesimal periods; then a set of real constants $\gamma_1, \ldots, \gamma_{2n}$, each in absolute value less than $r/(2n)^{\frac{1}{2}}$, can be found such that $\phi(\xi_1 + \gamma_1, \ldots, \xi_{2n} + \gamma_{2n}) = \phi(\xi_1, \ldots, \xi_{2n})$; taking points $\xi_1, \ldots, \xi_{2n}$, such that

$$\frac{\xi_1 - \xi_1^{(0)}}{\gamma_1} = \frac{\xi_2 - \xi_2^{(0)}}{\gamma_2} = \ldots = \frac{\xi_{2n} - \xi_{2n}^{(0)}}{\gamma_{2n}}, \ = \lambda, \text{ say},$$

where $(\xi_1^{(0)}, \ldots, \xi_{2n}^{(0)})$ is an arbitrary point within the region considered, and allowing λ to increase from zero, so long as λ is less than unity we have $\Sigma(\xi_k - \xi_k^{(0)})^2 < r^2$ and therefore $|\phi(\xi) - \phi(\xi^0)| < \epsilon$, while, when λ is unity, $\phi(\xi) = \phi(\xi^0)$; putting $\xi_k^{(0)} + \gamma_k = \xi_k^{(1)}$, as λ varies from unity to 2, we have $\Sigma(\xi_k - \xi_k^{(1)})^2 < r^2$, and therefore $|\phi(\xi) - \phi(\xi^1)| < \epsilon$, that is $|\phi(\xi) - \phi(\xi^{(0)})| < \epsilon$, while when $\lambda = 2$ we again have $\phi(\xi) = \phi(\xi^0)$. It appears then that for all points $\xi_k = \xi_k^{(0)} + \lambda\gamma_k$, we have $|\phi(\xi) - \phi(\xi^0)| < \epsilon$; now ϵ is an arbitrary quantity; this can only mean then that for all these points, lying within the region considered, we have $\phi(\xi) = \phi(\xi^0)$. But, if $\gamma_{2m-1} + i\gamma_{2m} = \Omega_m$ these points satisfy $u_h = u_h^{(0)} + \lambda\Omega_h$, $(h = 1, \ldots, n)$; not every one of $\Omega_1, \ldots, \Omega_n$ can be zero, say Ω_1 is not zero: put then

$$v_2 = \frac{\Omega_2}{\Omega_1} u_1 - u_2, \quad v_3 = \frac{\Omega_3}{\Omega_1} u_1 - u_3, \ \ldots, \quad v_n = \frac{\Omega_n}{\Omega_1} u_1 - u_n,$$

so that when $u_h = u_h^{(0)} + \lambda\Omega_h$ we have $v_2 = \frac{\Omega_2}{\Omega_1} u_1^{(0)} - u_2^{(0)} = v_2^{(0)}$, etc., and $\phi(u)$ has in general the form

$$\psi(u_1, v_2, \ldots, v_n) = \phi\left(u_1, \frac{\Omega_2}{\Omega_1} u_1 - v_2, \ldots, \frac{\Omega_n}{\Omega_1} u_1 - v_n\right);$$

what we have proved is that, so long as $v_2, \ldots, v_n$ are unchanged, $\psi(u_1, v_2, \ldots, v_n)$ is unchanged, namely, it is not possible to assign a set of n real quantities $\epsilon_1, \ldots, \epsilon_n$ each of arbitrary smallness and then to find a column of periods $Q_1, \ldots, Q_n$ for which all the inequalities $|Q_1| < \epsilon_1, \ldots, |Q_n| < \epsilon_n$ hold; thus the lower limit, for all possible integer values of $M_1, \ldots, M_{2n}$, of the sum

$$\sum_{h=1}^{n} |\omega_h^{(1)} M_1 + \ldots + \omega_h^{(2n)} M_{2n}|,$$

is greater than zero. From this it follows, if $\omega_h^{(k)} = \alpha_{h,k} + i\alpha_{n+h,k}$, for $h = 1, \ldots, n$ and $k = 1, \ldots, (2n)$, where $\alpha_{h,k}$ and $\alpha_{n+h,k}$ are real, that the determinant of $2n$ rows and columns $|\alpha_{r,s}|$, for $r, s = 1, \ldots, (2n)$, is other than zero; for the vanishing of this determinant would imply the existence of $2n$ equations

$$\sum_{r=1}^{2n} \lambda_r \alpha_{r,s} = 0, \qquad (s = 1, \ldots, 2n),$$

in which $\lambda_1, \ldots, \lambda_{2n}$ are real, and hence, if, with integer values of $M_1, \ldots, M_{2n}$, we put

$$\sum_{s=1}^{2n} \alpha_{r,s} M_s = A_r,$$

would imply the existence of the single equation

$$\sum_{r=1}^{2n} \lambda_r A_r = 0;$$

in this suppose λ_{2n} is a coefficient which is not zero; we know* that it is possible to choose the integers $M_1, \ldots, M_{2n}$ so that $A_1, \ldots, A_{2n-1}$ shall be respectively less in absolute value than any arbitrarily small quantities $\epsilon_1, \ldots, \epsilon_{2n-1}$ previously assigned; this single equation would then make it possible at the same time to take A_{2n} arbitrarily small; we have however proved that the function has not infinitesimal periods.

With such a system of periods $\omega_h^{(k)}$, we can then, if $u_1, \ldots, u_n$ be any complex values, find real quantities $E_1, \ldots, E_{2n}$ such that

$$u_h = E_1 \omega_h^{(1)} + \ldots + E_{2n} \omega_h^{(2n)}, \qquad (h = 1, \ldots, n),$$

or, putting $E_k = M_k + e_k$, where M_k is an integer and $0 \leqq e_k < 1$,

$$u_h - M_1 \omega_h^{(1)} - \ldots - M_{2n} \omega_h^{(2n)} = e_1 \omega_h^{(1)} + \ldots + e_{2n} \omega_h^{(2n)} \qquad (h = 1, \ldots, n);$$

the points given by the right side with the limitation $0 < e_k < 1$ are said to be interior to a *period cell* whose initial point is the origin; we speak of it as

even when u_1 changes. For the region under consideration, it is thus possible to write $\phi(u)$ so as to be a function only of the $(n-1)$ linear functions $v_2, \ldots, v_n$ of $u_1, u_2, \ldots, u_n$. It appears then that no single-valued function of n variables which is continuous over a limited continuum, and not a function of fewer than n variables, can have infinitesimal periods.

* For this proposition see Jacobi, *Ges. Werke*, t. II. p. 27, or *Crelle*, XIII. (1835), p. 55; Hermite, *Crelle*, XL. (1850), p. 310, *Crelle*, LXXXVIII. (1880), p. 10; Clebsch u. Gordan, *Abelsche Functionen* (1866), p. 130, and particularly Kronecker, *Werke*, III. i. (1899), pp. 49–109. Also Riemann, *Werke* (1876), p. 276; Appell, *Liouville*, VII. (1891), p. 207.

constructed in the real space of $2n$ dimensions wherein the co-ordinates are $\xi_1, \ldots, \xi_{2n}$ given by $u_h = \xi_{2h-1} + i\xi_{2h}$; it is bounded by $2n$ pairs of opposite $(2n-1)$-folds given by $e_k = 0$, $e_k = 1$. The whole of the $2n$-fold space may be supposed divided into such cells, and any point of this space is *congruent* to one point of the primary cell, the congruence being expressed by the equation above.

It should be remarked at once, however, that not any set of $2n^2$ quantities $\omega_h^{(k)}$, satisfying the conditions so far imposed, can constitute the $2n$ period columns of a function of n variables; one main result of the enquiry upon which we are now entering is that it is further necessary that, between the $2n$ periods associated with any one of the arguments $u_1, \ldots, u_n$ and those associated with any other of these arguments, there should exist an identical relation linear in the periods associated with each of these arguments; and that also, between the real parts of the periods associated with any one of the arguments $u_1, \ldots, u_n$ and the imaginary parts of these same periods, there should exist a relation expressed by saying that a certain expression linear in these real parts and also linear in these imaginary parts must be positive.

58. Take now n sets of constants $(a_1^{(r)}, \ldots, a_n^{(r)})$, for $r = 1, \ldots, n$, such that $u_1 = a_1^{(r)}, \ldots, u_n = a_n^{(r)}$ is a *regular* point for the function $\phi(u)$, namely, a point about which $\phi(u)$ can be expressed by an ordinary power series in $u_1 - a_1^{(r)}, \ldots, u_n - a_n^{(r)}$, and define n functions $\phi_r(u)$ by means of the equations

$$\phi_r(u) = \phi(u_1 + a_1^{(r)}, \ldots, u_n + a_n^{(r)}) - \phi(a_1^{(r)}, \ldots, a_n^{(r)}), \qquad (r = 1, \ldots, n),$$

so that

$$\phi_r(0) = 0,$$

while the Jacobian

$$\left|\begin{matrix} \dfrac{\partial \phi_1}{\partial u_1}, & \ldots, & \dfrac{\partial \phi_1}{\partial u_n} \\ \cdots & \cdots & \cdots \\ \dfrac{\partial \phi_n}{\partial u_1}, & \ldots, & \dfrac{\partial \phi_n}{\partial u_n} \end{matrix}\right|$$

reduces for $u_1 = 0, \ldots, u_n = 0$ to

$$\left|\begin{matrix} \dfrac{\partial \phi(a^{(1)})}{\partial a_1^{(1)}}, & \ldots, & \dfrac{\partial \phi(a^{(1)})}{\partial a_n^{(1)}} \\ \cdots & \cdots & \cdots \\ \dfrac{\partial \phi(a^{(n)})}{\partial a_1^{(n)}}, & \ldots, & \dfrac{\partial \phi(a^{(n)})}{\partial a_n^{(n)}} \end{matrix}\right|;$$

this determinant is not zero for all positions of the n points $(a^{(1)}), \ldots, (a^{(n)})$ since otherwise there would exist an equation

$$A_1 \frac{\partial \phi(a^{(1)})}{\partial a_1^{(1)}} + \ldots + A_n \frac{\partial \phi(a^{(1)})}{\partial a_n^{(1)}} = 0$$

holding for all positions of $(a^{(1)})$, wherein $A_1, \dots, A_n$ are independent of $(a^{(1)})$, and hence $\phi(u)$ would be expressible, over a $2n$-fold, by less than n linear functions of $u_1, \dots, u_n$.

We can thus suppose $(a^{(1)}), \dots, (a^{(n)})$ chosen so that the origin is an ordinary point for each of the functions $\phi_1(u), \dots, \phi_n(u)$, and a zero point for each, but not a zero point for their Jacobian; there is thus about the origin a finite region not containing any pole or singular point of $\phi_1(u), \dots, \phi_n(u)$, or of their Jacobian, or any point whereat this Jacobian vanishes, and the functions are expressible, for the neighbourhood of the origin, by power series

$$\phi_h = a_{h,1} u_1 + \dots + a_{h,n} u_n + \dots \qquad (h = 1, \dots, r),$$

such that the determinant $|a_{h,s}|$, for $h, s = 1, 2, \dots, n$, is not zero.

Instead now of considering all possible values of $u_1, \dots, u_n$, we apply $(n-1)$ restrictive conditions, and so obtain a construct of two (real) dimensions—as follows. Suppose $\phi_1(u), \dots, \phi_n(u)$ to be expressed in terms of the n independent functions

$$v_h = a_{h,1} u_1 + \dots + a_{h,n} u_n;$$

let

$$c_{h,1} x + c_{h,2} x^2 + \dots, \qquad (h = 1, \dots, n),$$

be n convergent power series in a single complex variable x, all vanishing for $x = 0$; consider the values of $v_1, \dots, v_n$ obtained by equating the functions $\phi_1, \dots, \phi_n$ to these power series, each to each. These conditions are expressed by

$$v_r = c_{r,1} x + c_{r,2} x^2 + \dots + \Phi_r, \qquad (r = 1, \dots, n),$$

where Φ_r represents the terms of second and higher orders in ϕ_r, with their sign changed, and these equations enable us, as we have shewn (p. 189), to express each of $v_1, \dots, v_n$ as a convergent power series in x, for sufficiently small values of x, these being the only values of $v_1, \dots, v_n$ satisfying these equations when x is sufficiently small. Let these series be represented by

$$v_r = k_{r,1} x + k_{r,2} x^2 + \dots; \qquad (r = 1, 2, \dots, n);$$

we desire to shew first, that even if the original power series to which the functions $\phi_1, \dots, \phi_n$ are equated reduce to polynomials of order n, so that for $s > n$, and every value of r, $(= 1, \dots, n)$ we have $c_{r,s} = 0$, we may still, by proper choice of the remaining n^2 coefficients $c_{r,s}$, $(r, s = 1, \dots, n)$, suppose that neither of the determinants of order n denoted by $|c_{r,s}|$, $|k_{r,s}|$ vanishes. Denoting the terms of order m in $v_1, \dots, v_n$ in the series Φ_r by $\{\dots, v_s, \dots\}_{r,m}$, we have in fact the identities,

$$k_{r,1} x + k_{r,2} x^2 + \dots = c_{r,1} x + c_{r,2} x^2 + \dots + \sum_{m=2}^{\infty} \{\dots, (k_{s,1} x + k_{s,2} x^2 + \dots), \dots\}_{r,m},$$

for $r = 1, \dots, n$, and hence, for $r = 1, \dots, n$ and $t = 2, 3, \dots, \infty$,

$$k_{r,1} = c_{r,1},$$

$$k_{r,t} = c_{r,t} + \text{coeff.}\, x^t \text{ in } \sum_{m=2}^{\infty} \{\dots, (k_{s,1} x + \dots + k_{s,t-1} x^{t-1}), \dots\}_{r,m},$$

where it will be noticed that on the right the second suffixes of the coefficients $k_{s,\sigma}$ that enter are less than t; the elements of the first column of the determinant $|c_{r,s}|$ are thus equal to the corresponding elements of the determinant $|k_{r,s}|$, and the elements of any other column of the determinant $|c_{r,s}|$ are each equal to the corresponding element of the determinant $|k_{r,s}|$ augmented by a polynomial in the quantities $k_{r,s}$ occurring in preceding columns of $|k_{r,s}|$, the lowest terms in this polynomial being of the second order; suppose then that arbitrary values for which the determinant $|k_{r,s}|$ is not zero are given to the n^2 quantities $k_{r,s}$ for $r, s = 1, 2, \ldots, n$, and the n^2 quantities $c_{r,s}$ are determined accordingly; it seems certain that the values of $k_{r,s}$ can be taken so that also the determinant $|c_{r,s}|$ is not zero; this being so, let all the quantities $c_{r,s}$ for $r = 1, \ldots, n$ but $s > n$, be taken zero; and then the quantities $k_{r,s}$ for $s > n$ be determined by the equation written above. Thus the equations

$$\phi_r(u) = c_{r,1}x + \ldots + c_{r,n}x^n, \qquad (r = 1, \ldots, n),$$

are such that they do not imply any linear equation

$$A_1\phi_1 + \ldots + A_n\phi_n = 0,$$

wherein $A_1, \ldots, A_n$ are independent of x, and they lead to converging series

$$v_r = \sum_{s=1}^{\infty} k_{r,s}\, x^s,$$

not satisfying any equation

$$B_1 v_1 + \ldots + B_n v_n = 0,$$

in which $B_1, \ldots, B_n$ are independent of x, and hence to converging series

$$u_r = \sum_{s=1}^{\infty} h_{r,s}\, x^s$$

wherein also $u_1, \ldots, u_n$ are connected by no linear homogeneous equation with coefficients independent of x.

For every sufficiently small value of x these equations define a set of values for $u_1, \ldots, u_n$, which, putting, as before, $u_r = \xi_{2r-1} + i\xi_{2r}$, we may represent as a real point in space of $2n$ dimensions; the series are presumably capable of analytic continuation beyond the neighbourhood of the origin; the whole aggregate of points so obtainable forms a $(2n-2)$-fold, and it is this which we now proceed to study in more detail.

Since the determinant $|c_{r,s}|$ does not vanish, the equations

$$\phi_r = c_{r,1}x + c_{r,2}x^2 + \ldots + c_{r,n}x^n$$

may be replaced by equations

$$f_1 = x, f_2 = x^2, \ldots, f_n = x^n,$$

where $f_1, f_2, \ldots, f_n$ are certain independent linear functions of $\phi_1, \ldots, \phi_n$; putting then

$$F_2 = f_2 - f_1^2, \ldots, F_n = f_n - f_1^n,$$

they may be replaced by

$$f_1 = x,\ F_2 = 0,\ \ldots,\ F_n = 0,$$

and it is at once seen that the Jacobians

$$\frac{\partial (f_1, F_2, \ldots, F_n)}{\partial (u_1, u_2, \ldots, u_n)},\ \frac{\partial (f_1, f_2, \ldots, f_n)}{\partial (u_1, u_2, \ldots, u_n)}$$

are equal; as the functions $f_1, \ldots, f_n$ are independent linear functions of $\phi_1, \ldots, \phi_n$ with constant coefficients, the latter Jacobian is a constant multiple of the Jacobian of $\phi_1, \ldots, \phi_n$, and does not vanish at or in the immediate neighbourhood of the origin $u_1 = 0, \ldots, u_n = 0$; nor therefore does the former; and thus the determinant

$$\left| \begin{array}{cccc} c_1, & c_2, & \ldots, & c_n \\ \frac{\partial F_2}{\partial u_1}, & \frac{\partial F_2}{\partial u_2}, & \ldots, & \frac{\partial F_2}{\partial u_n} \\ \ldots & \ldots & \ldots & \ldots \\ \frac{\partial F_n}{\partial u_1}, & \frac{\partial F_n}{\partial u_2}, & \ldots, & \frac{\partial F_n}{\partial u_n} \end{array} \right|$$

does not vanish for $u_2 = 0, \ldots, u_n = 0$ for all values of the constants $c_1, \ldots, c_n$.

59. Consider now the aggregate, O, of points $(u_1, \ldots, u_n)$ determined as follows; first exclude all points at which any one of the functions $\phi_1(u), \ldots, \phi_n(u)$, or, what is the same thing, any one of the functions $f_1, F_2, \ldots, F_n$, has a pole or a point of indetermination; from those remaining exclude further all points where the Jacobian $\partial(\phi_1, \ldots, \phi_n)/\partial(u_1, \ldots, u_n)$ vanishes; of non-excluded points take then only those for which the $(n-1)$ equations $F_2 = 0, \ldots, F_n = 0$ are satisfied. To this aggregate O adjoin now all its limiting points, namely all points infinitely near to which are found points of O; denote the resulting closed aggregate by C. That there are points belonging to the aggregate O has been shewn in what precedes; the origin is an ordinary point for the functions $\phi_1, \ldots, \phi_n$, and their Jacobian has at the origin a value not zero; there is thus about the origin a finite region every point of which is an ordinary point for the functions $\phi_1, \ldots, \phi_n$ and a non-vanishing point for their Jacobian; by supposing x sufficiently small, we can suppose that the values of $u_1, \ldots, u_n$ which satisfy the equations $\phi_r = c_{r,1}x + \ldots + c_{r,n}x^n$ are within this region—and these values satisfy the equations $F_2 = 0, \ldots, F_n = 0$.

Consider a point $(a_1, \ldots, a_n)$ of the aggregate O; in its neighbourhood the functions $F_2, \ldots, F_n$ are expressible by power series in $u_1 - a_1, \ldots, u_n - a_n$, and, since the Jacobian of $f_1, F_2, \ldots, F_n$ does not vanish at $(a_1, \ldots, a_n)$, we can choose constants $c_1, \ldots, c_n$ so that the Jacobian of $F_2, \ldots, F_n$ and the linear function $c_1(u_1 - a_1) + \ldots + c_n(u_n - a_n)$ does not vanish at $(a_1, \ldots, a_n)$. Taking then a parameter t, and restricting ourselves to sufficiently small values of this, we can (p. 189), from the n equations

$$F_2 = 0, \ldots, F_n = 0, \quad c_1(u_1 - a_1) + \ldots + c_n(u_n - a_n) = t,$$

obtain converging power series in t for the n quantities $u_1 - a_1, \ldots, u_n - a_n$, expressing all the points of the aggregate O which lie in a suitably limited neighbourhood of $(a_1, \ldots, a_n)$, and only points of this aggregate.

Consider next a point $(\alpha_1, \ldots, \alpha_n)$ which is a limiting point of the aggregate O. For points in its immediate neighbourhood each of the functions $F_2, \ldots, F_n$ is expressible in a form $F_r = N_r/D_r$ where N_r, D_r are converging power series in $u_1 - \alpha_1, \ldots, u_n - \alpha_n$, not both divisible by a power series in $u_1 - \alpha_1, \ldots, u_n - \alpha_n$ vanishing at $(\alpha_1, \ldots, \alpha_n)$; of these we may without loss of generality suppose that D_r vanishes at $\alpha_1, \ldots, \alpha_n$, or else is equal to unity. Suppose first that D_r vanishes at $(\alpha_1, \ldots, \alpha_n)$; there are then also points infinitely near to $(\alpha_1, \ldots, \alpha_n)$ at which D_r vanishes, these constituting a certain $(2n-2)$-fold continuum. These points do not belong to the aggregate O: for, taking such a point, $(\alpha_1', \ldots, \alpha_n')$, let D_r, N_r be written as power series in $u_1 - \alpha_1', \ldots, u_n - \alpha_n'$, becoming D_r', N_r'; then, when $(\alpha_1', \ldots, \alpha_n')$ is sufficiently near to $(\alpha_1, \ldots, \alpha_n)$, the series D_r', N_r' are not both divisible by a power series in $u_1 - \alpha_1', \ldots, u_n - \alpha_n'$, vanishing at $(\alpha_1', \ldots, \alpha_n')$, (p. 198), and therefore the fraction N_r'/D_r' is either infinite at $(\alpha_1', \ldots, \alpha_n')$ or assumes a form $0/0$; in either case $(\alpha_1', \ldots, \alpha_n')$ does not belong to the aggregate O. Thus the points of this aggregate, which, by hypothesis, exist, in infinite number, in the immediate neighbourhood of the limiting point $(\alpha_1, \ldots, \alpha_n)$, and satisfy the equation $F_r = 0$ (as well as the other equations $F_2 = 0, \ldots, F_n = 0$), do not satisfy $D_r = 0$, and must satisfy $N_r = 0$; the power series N_r must therefore vanish at $(\alpha_1, \ldots, \alpha_n)$. This is proved when D_r vanishes at $(\alpha_1, \ldots, \alpha_n)$; when $D_r = 1$, the equation $F_r = 0$ involves $N_r = 0$, and this, holding for points in the immediate neighbourhood of $(\alpha_1, \ldots, \alpha_n)$, must also be true at $(\alpha_1, \ldots, \alpha_n)$. The points of the aggregate O in the immediate neighbourhood of $(\alpha_1, \ldots, \alpha_n)$ are thus to be found among the solutions of the equations

$$N_2 = 0, \ldots, N_n = 0,$$

in each of which the left side is a power series in $u_1 - \alpha_1, \ldots, u_n - \alpha_n$ vanishing at $(\alpha_1, \ldots, \alpha_n)$; though conversely not all common solutions of these equations can be assumed to be points of the aggregate O.

All solutions of such a set of equations in which $u_1 - \alpha_1, \ldots, u_n - \alpha_n$ are sufficiently small are, however, as has been shewn (p. 196), points of a finite number of irreducible constructs each represented by a set of equations of the form

$$\varpi(w_n) \equiv w_n^{\mu} + (w_1, \ldots, w_m)_1 w_n^{\mu-1} + \ldots + (w_1, \ldots, w_m)_{\mu} = 0,$$

$$w_{m+1} = \varpi_{m+1}(w_n)/\varpi'(w_n), \ldots, w_{n-1} = \varpi_{n-1}(w_n)/\varpi'(w_n),$$

wherein $w_1, \ldots, w_n$ are independent homogeneous linear functions of $u_1 - \alpha_1, \ldots, u_n - \alpha_n$, the coefficients $(w_1, \ldots, w_m)_1, \ldots, (w_1, \ldots, w_m)_\mu$ are convergent power series vanishing when $w_1, w_2, \ldots, w_m$ all vanish, the symbol $\varpi'(w_n)$ represents $\partial\varpi(w_n)/\partial w_n$, the numerators $\varpi_{m+1}(w_n), \ldots, \varpi_{n-1}(w_n)$ are polynomials in w_n of dimension $\mu - 1$ whose coefficients are converging power series in $w_1, \ldots, w_m$, and only those values of $w_1, \ldots, w_m$ are to be considered for which $\varpi(w_n)$ and $\varpi'(w_n)$ do not simultaneously vanish; conversely all solutions of any such set of equations in which $w_1, \ldots, w_n$ are sufficiently small are solutions of the original equations $N_2 = 0, \ldots, N_n = 0$.

Such a set of equations, $n - m$ in number, represents a construct of $2m$ dimensions, there being m independent variables $w_1, \ldots, w_m$. If $(w_1^{(0)}, \ldots, w_n^{(0)})$ be a point of this construct, in the immediate neighbourhood of

$$w_1 = 0, \ldots, w_n = 0,$$

and we substitute $w_1^{(0)} + \lambda_1, \ldots, w_n^{(0)} + \lambda_n$ in place of $w_1, \ldots, w_n$, we obtain $(n - m)$ equations $H_r(\lambda_1, \ldots, \lambda_n) = 0$, wherein $H_r(\lambda_1, \ldots, \lambda_n)$ are power series in $\lambda_1, \ldots, \lambda_n$ vanishing when these are zero. If $m > 1$, so that $n - m + 1 < n$, we can therefore always find small values of $\lambda_1, \ldots, \lambda_n$, not all zero, to satisfy these equations and at the same time an equation $\gamma_1\lambda_1 + \ldots + \gamma_n\lambda_n = 0$, wherein $\gamma_1, \ldots, \gamma_n$ are arbitrary, and this without satisfying $\varpi'(w_n^{(0)} + \lambda_n) = 0$, since $\varpi'(w^{(0)}) \neq 0$; thus if $(u_1^{(0)}, \ldots, u_n^{(0)})$ and $(u_1^{(0)} + l_1, \ldots, u_n^{(0)} + l_n)$ be the values of $u_1, \ldots, u_n$ corresponding to $(w_1^{(0)}, \ldots, w_n^{(0)})$ and $(w_1^{(0)} + \lambda_1, \ldots, w_n^{(0)} + \lambda_n)$, since the points of the construct satisfy $N_2 = 0, \ldots, N_n = 0$, we can simultaneously satisfy the n equations

$$\left[\frac{\partial N_h}{\partial u_1}\right] l_1 + \ldots + \left[\frac{\partial N_h}{\partial u_n}\right] l_n = 0, \qquad c_1 l_1 + \ldots + c_n l_n = 0, \qquad (h = 2, \ldots, n),$$

where $\left[\frac{\partial N_h}{\partial u_s}\right]$ denotes a series reducing to $\frac{\partial N_h}{\partial u_s^{(0)}}$ when $l_1 = 0, \ldots, l_n = 0$, and $c_1, \ldots, c_n$ are arbitrary; from this it follows that, for all values of $c_1, \ldots, c_n$, the determinant

$$N = \begin{vmatrix} c_1, & c_2, & \ldots, & c_n \\ \frac{\partial N_2}{\partial u_1}, & \frac{\partial N_2}{\partial u_2}, & \ldots, & \frac{\partial N_2}{\partial u_n} \\ \ldots & \ldots & \ldots & \ldots \\ \frac{\partial N_n}{\partial u_1}, & \frac{\partial N_n}{\partial u_2}, & \ldots, & \frac{\partial N_n}{\partial u_n} \end{vmatrix}$$

vanishes at $(u_1^{(0)}, \ldots, u_n^{(0)})$; thus, when $m > 1$, the point $(u_1^{(0)}, \ldots, u_n^{(0)})$ does not belong to the construct O; for, for points of O we have $N_h = 0$, but $D_h \neq 0$, and thus

$$\frac{\partial F_h}{\partial u_s} = \frac{1}{D_h}\frac{\partial N_h}{\partial u_s} - \frac{N_h}{D_h^2}\frac{\partial D_h}{\partial u_s} = \frac{1}{D_h}\frac{\partial N_h}{\partial u_s},$$

so that the determinant N is equal to

$$D_2 D_3 \ldots D_n \begin{vmatrix} c_1, & c_2, & \ldots, & c_n \\ \frac{\partial F_2}{\partial u_1}, & \frac{\partial F_2}{\partial u_2}, & \ldots, & \frac{\partial F_2}{\partial u_n} \\ \ldots & \ldots & \ldots & \ldots \\ \frac{\partial F_n}{\partial u_1}, & \frac{\partial F_n}{\partial u_2}, & \ldots, & \frac{\partial F_n}{\partial u_n} \end{vmatrix},$$

which by hypothesis is not zero for points of O. The points of the construct O, which by definition do actually exist in any arbitrarily near neighbourhood of $(\alpha_1, \ldots, \alpha_n)$, are therefore among those solutions of the equations

$$N_2 = 0, \ldots, N_n = 0$$

which satisfy one or more sets of equations of the form

$$\varpi(w_n) \equiv w_n^{\mu} + (w_1)_1 w_n^{\mu-1} + \ldots + (w_1)_{\mu} = 0, \quad w_2 = \frac{\varpi_2(w_n)}{\varpi'(w_n)}, \ldots, w_{n-1} = \frac{\varpi_{n-1}(w_n)}{\varpi'(w_n)},$$

in which $m = 1$. Consider one such set of equations: we have proved (p. 190) that, when w_1, w_n are sufficiently small, all solutions of the equation $\varpi(w_n) = 0$ are obtainable by a finite number of pairs of equations of the form $w_1 = t^{\lambda}$, $w_n = \wp_n(t)$, where t is an arbitrary parameter, of sufficient smallness, and $\wp_n(t)$ a power series in t, vanishing for $t = 0$, its differential coefficient not vanishing for $t = 0$; from the symmetrical choice of the variables $w_1, \ldots, w_n$, the substitution of these values for w_1 and w_n in the expressions for $w_2, \ldots, w_{n-1}$ will lead to associated power series $w_2 = \wp_2(t), \ldots, w_{n-1} = \wp_{n-1}(t)$ also vanishing for $t = 0$. Thus all the points of the construct O, in a sufficiently near neighbourhood of the point $(\alpha_1, \ldots, \alpha_n)$, are among the values represented by a finite number of sets of equations of the form

$$u_1 = \alpha_1 + Q_1(t), \quad \ldots, \quad u_n = \alpha_n + Q_n(t),$$

wherein $Q_1(t), \ldots, Q_n(t)$ are power series, vanishing for $t = 0$, of such character as give, for sufficiently small values of the differences $u_1 - \alpha_1, \ldots, u_n - \alpha_n$, a unique value for t. Consider one of these sets of series which gives points of the construct O arbitrarily near to $(\alpha_1, \ldots, \alpha_n)$; then when these expressions for $u_1, \ldots, u_n$ are substituted in the power series $D_2, \ldots, D_n$, no one of the resulting power series in t can vanish identically, for we have seen that points, in the immediate neighbourhood of $(\alpha_1, \ldots, \alpha_n)$, for which one of $D_2, \ldots, D_n$ vanishes, do not belong to O; the power series in t obtained from $N_2, \ldots, N_n$ by the same substitution for $u_1, \ldots, u_n$, vanish for $t = 0$, but, elsewhere, in a sufficiently near neighbourhood of $t = 0$, they do not vanish, unless they vanish identically—which must then be the case, since points of O lie arbitrarily near to $(\alpha_1, \ldots, \alpha_n)$. Consider now the Jacobian

$$\partial(\phi_1, \ldots, \phi_n)/\partial(u_1, \ldots, u_n);$$

in the neighbourhood of $(\alpha_1, \ldots, \alpha_n)$ it is expressible as the quotient of two power series in $u_1-\alpha_1, \ldots, u_n-\alpha_n$; substituting $Q_1(t), \ldots, Q_n(t)$ for these differences the resulting *denominator* power series in t cannot vanish identically or the set of series $u_h=\alpha_h+Q_h(t)$ would not furnish any points of the construct O in the immediate neighbourhood of $(\alpha_1, \ldots, \alpha_n)$; the resulting *numerator* power series in t may vanish for $t=0$ but there exists a region about $t=0$ wherein no other zeros are found. It appears thus that if the series $u_1=\alpha_1+Q_1(t), \ldots, u_n=\alpha_n+Q_n(t)$ furnish points of the construct O in every arbitrarily near neighbourhood of $(\alpha_1, \ldots, \alpha_n)$, they represent points of this construct for all values of t of sufficient smallness. Taking this result, and the simpler result previously found for the neighbourhood of an ordinary point $(\alpha_1, \ldots, \alpha_n)$ of the construct O, we have the theorem:

Let $(c_1, \ldots, c_n)$ be any point of the construct C defined as above from the equations $F_2=0, \ldots, F_n=0$, that is either an ordinary point of the construct O, or a limiting point of this: there exists then a finite number of sets of series

$$u_1=c_1+Q_1(t), \ \ldots, \ u_n=c_n+Q_n(t),$$

each of which, for all values of t in absolute value less than an assignable number, represents points of the construct C in the neighbourhood of $(c_1, \ldots, c_n)$, and for $t=0$ represents the point $(c_1, \ldots, c_n)$; in particular when $(c_1, \ldots, c_n)$ is an ordinary point of C, that is a point of the construct O, there is only one such set of series; the series being such that all points of the construct O which lie in the neighbourhood of $c_1, \ldots, c_n$, given, say, by $|u_1-c_1|<\delta, \ldots, |u_n-c_n|<\delta$, are obtained, if only δ be supposed sufficiently small; while, under the same limitation, no point is obtained for two different values of t.

The construct C thus appears to be, in its smallest parts, similar to a construct defined by algebraic equations; this similarity is carried further by the three following properties:

(*a*) The limiting points of O are isolated—about any such point can be put a finite neighbourhood containing no other limiting point. For let $(c_1, \ldots, c_n)$ be any point of C, and let r be a real quantity as great as possible but such that, for $|t|<r, |t'|<r, \ldots$, all points of O which lie in a sufficiently near neighbourhood of $(c_1, \ldots, c_n)$ are given by one of the sets of series

$$u_1=c_1+Q_1(t), \ldots, u_n=c_n+Q_n(t); \ u_1=c_1+Q_1'(t'), \ldots, u_n=c_n+Q_n'(t'); \ \ldots\ldots$$

while every point represented by one of these sets of series is a point of O. Take $(b_1, \ldots, b_n)$ any point in this near neighbourhood of $(c_1, \ldots, c_n)$, and form the sum of the squares of the moduli of the differences

$$c_1+Q_1(t)-b_1, \ \ldots, \ c_n+Q_n(t)-b_n,$$

there being as many such sums as there are sets of series involved. Putting $t=\xi+i\eta$, and considering one of these sums for all values of ξ, η such that $\xi^2+\eta^2 \gtreqless r^2$, we have a continuous function of the real variables ξ, η, and there is a particular value of t for which the function is equal to the lower limit of its values for the limited range; if this lower limit is zero the point

$(b_1, \ldots, b_n)$ belongs to the construct O; if it is greater than zero there is a region about $(b_1, \ldots, b_n)$ which contains no point of O, and in that case $(b_1, \ldots, b_n)$ is not a limiting point of O. In other words, a region can be put about $(c_1, \ldots, c_n)$ such that every point of this other than $(c_1, \ldots, c_n)$ is either a point of O, or is not a limiting point of O; and this proves the result stated.

It follows from this that there cannot be more than a finite number of limiting points of O in any finite range of values of $u_1, \ldots, u_n$; for otherwise there would be a point (the limiting point or point of condensation of these limiting points) having in its immediate neighbourhood an infinite number of limiting points of O, and itself also a limiting point of O.

(*b*) For all not-zero values of t, up to a certain range, a set of series $u_1 = c_1 + Q_1(t), \ldots, u_n = c_n + Q_n(t)$ represents points of O; the series may converge for larger values of t; they then represent points of C for these larger values, which are not however necessarily points of O. For suppose the series converge for $t = t_0$; consider the points represented by

$$u_1 = c_1 + Q_1(\sigma t_0), \ldots, u_n = c_n + Q_n(\sigma t_0)$$

in which σ is real and less than unity: for sufficiently small values of σ greater than zero, say for $0 < \sigma < \sigma_1$ these series represent points of O; for $\sigma = \sigma_1$ they will then represent a limiting point of O—and not a point of O, since otherwise they would also represent points of O for values greater than σ_1, as follows at once by reconsidering the preceding conditions; if $\sigma_1 < 1$ put $\sigma = \sigma_1 + \rho$ and consider the series

$$u_1 = c_1 + Q_1(\sigma_1 t_0 + \rho t_0), \ldots, u_n = c_n + Q_n(\sigma_1 t_0 + \rho t_0)$$

supposed rewritten as power series in ρ: then for all sufficiently small *negative* values of ρ these rewritten series represent points of O; they represent therefore points of O for all positive and negative values of ρ less than a certain value; the original series thus represent points of O for $0 < \sigma < \sigma_1$, $\sigma_1 < \sigma < \sigma_1 + \sigma_2$, say, while for $\sigma = \sigma_1$, $\sigma = \sigma_1 + \sigma_2$ they represent limiting points of O; if $\sigma_1 + \sigma_2 < 1$ we can proceed similarly, and so on. Now there cannot be more than a finite number of limiting points of O in any finite range of values for $u_1, \ldots, u_n$, and therefore the process must after a finite number of steps lead to $\sigma = \sigma_1 + \sigma_2 + \ldots = 1$; the series

$$u_1 = c_1 + Q_1(\sigma t_0), \ldots, u_n = c_n + Q_n(\sigma t_0)$$

thus represent points of C for all values of σ up to and including $\sigma = 1$; and thus the series $u_1 = c_1 + Q_1(t), \ldots, u_n = c_n + Q_n(t)$ represent points of C for all values of t for which they converge.

(*c*) Hence, having obtained one set of series $u_r = c_r + Q_r(t)$ representing points of C, we can unreservedly use the ordinary method of analytical continuation to obtain other points. In order somewhat to emphasize this fact, which is of importance for our purpose, we examine it in further detail. Consider a region containing points of O, but no limiting points of O. About an included point $(u_1^{(0)}, \ldots, u_n^{(0)})$ of O we have expressions for the points of O of the form $u_r = u_r^{(0)} + P_r(t)$ in terms of a parameter

$$t = \lambda_1 (u_1 - u_1^{(0)}) + \ldots + \lambda_n (u_n - u_n^{(0)}),$$

where $\lambda_1, \ldots, \lambda_n$ are to be chosen so that the determinant

$$L = \begin{vmatrix} \lambda_1, & \ldots, & \lambda_n \\ \frac{\partial F_2}{\partial u_1}, & \ldots, & \frac{\partial F_2}{\partial u_n} \\ \ldots & \ldots & \ldots \\ \frac{\partial F_n}{\partial u_1}, & \ldots, & \frac{\partial F_n}{\partial u_n} \end{vmatrix}$$

does not vanish at $(u_1^{(0)}, \ldots, u_n^{(0)})$; about a neighbouring point $(u_1^{(1)}, \ldots, u_n^{(1)})$ we have similar expressions; if $\lambda_1, \ldots, \lambda_n$ be chosen so that the determinant L is other than zero also at $(u_1^{(1)}, \ldots, u_n^{(1)})$, the parameter about $(u_1^{(1)}, \ldots, u_n^{(1)})$ may be taken to be $s = \lambda_1 (u_1 - u_1^{(1)}) + \ldots + \lambda_n (u_n - u_n^{(1)}) = t - t_1$, where $t_1, = \lambda_1 (u_1^{(1)} - u_1^{(0)}) + \ldots + \lambda_n (u_n^{(1)} - u_n^{(0)})$, is the value of t at $(u_1^{(1)}, \ldots, u_n^{(1)})$; this point being supposed within the region of convergence of the series $u_r = u_r^{(0)} + P_r(t)$, it follows that the series about it may be obtained by rewriting $u_r = u_r^{(0)} + P_r(t_1 + s)$ in the form $u_r = u_r^{(1)} + Q_r(s)$. If $\mu_1, \ldots, \mu_n$, be any quantities, such that the determinant formed from L by replacing $\lambda_1, \ldots, \lambda_n$ by $\mu_1, \ldots, \mu_n$ does not vanish at $(u_1^{(1)}, \ldots, u_n^{(1)})$, the quantity $\sigma = \mu_1 (u_1 - u_1^{(1)}) + \ldots + \mu_n (u_n - u_n^{(1)})$ may be taken as parameter of a set of series about $(u_1^{(1)}, \ldots, u_n^{(1)})$; we have then $\sigma = H(s)$ and $s = K(\sigma)$, where $H(s)$, $K(\sigma)$ are converging power series each wanting the constant term but having the term with the first power of the variable, and $t = t_1 + K(\sigma)$ is the general form of the substitution for the parameter, by which we pass from the series in t about $(u_1^{(0)}, \ldots, u_n^{(0)})$, to the series in σ about $(u_1^{(1)}, \ldots, u_n^{(1)})$; in virtue of the form of $K(\sigma)$ this substitution is equivalent to an expression $\sigma = H(t - t_1)$, wherein $H(t - t_1)$ is a power series vanishing but having a non-vanishing differential coefficient for $t = t_1$. So long as we confine ourselves to a region containing no limiting points of the construct O we can continually pass from point to point in this way; suppose, however, now that $(u_1^{(1)}, \ldots, u_n^{(1)})$ is an ordinary point of the construct O which is not within the region of convergence of the series about $(u_1^{(0)}, \ldots, u_n^{(0)})$ represented by $u_r = u_r^{(0)} + P_r(t)$, but that, nevertheless, the series about $(u_1^{(1)}, \ldots, u_n^{(1)})$, given by the general theorem, which we may write in the form $u_r = u_r^{(1)} + R_r(\sigma)$, converge in a region partly overlapping the region of convergence of the series $u_r = u_r^{(0)} + P_r(t)$, so that by a substitution of the form

$$t - t' = k_1 (\sigma - \sigma') + k_2 (\sigma - \sigma')^2 + k_3 (\sigma - \sigma')^3 + \ldots,$$

in which k_1 is not zero, the two sets of series give the same values of

$u_1, \ldots, u_n$ for all values of t sufficiently near to t'; the series in σ are then also an analytical continuation of the series in t. This derived view of the process of continuation may be employed when we consider an extended portion of the construct C containing in addition to ordinary points of O also a limiting point $(\alpha_1, \ldots, \alpha_n)$, or several such points: we cannot then assume that the parameter of any one of the existing sets of series giving points of O in the immediate neighbourhood of the limiting point $(\alpha_1, \ldots, \alpha_n)$, is capable of expression in a form $\lambda_1(u_1 - \alpha_1) + \ldots + \lambda_n(u_n - \alpha_n)$; and if we take a sequence of ordinary points of O, say $(u_1^{(0)}, \ldots, u_n^{(0)})$, $(u_1^{(1)}, \ldots, u_n^{(1)})$, ..., converging to $(\alpha_1, \ldots, \alpha_n)$, it may happen that the radii of convergence of the sequence of sets of series, about these points in turn, tend to zero: consider the matter however in a converse order: we have proved that the limiting points of the construct O are isolated points: let $u_r = \alpha_r + P_r(t)$ be a set of series representing points of O in the immediate neighbourhood of the limiting point $(\alpha_1, \ldots, \alpha_n)$; if $\lambda_1, \ldots, \lambda_n$ be constants, the quantity

$$v = \lambda_1 u_1 + \ldots + \lambda_n u_n$$

is then expressible in the form $\alpha + P(t)$, and $dv/dt, = P'(t)$, is zero, in the immediate neighbourhood of $(\alpha_1, \ldots, \alpha_n)$, other than at this point itself, only for particular values of t; if $\lambda_1, \ldots, \lambda_n$ be so chosen that for the value $t = t_0$ this differential coefficient is not zero, and we put $t = t_0 + \rho$, and rearrange the series $v = \alpha + P(t_0 + \rho)$ in the form $v = v^{(0)} + Q(\rho)$, the series $Q(\rho)$ will contain the first power of ρ—so that, if we put

$$\tau = v - v^{(0)} = \lambda_1(u_1 - u_1^{(0)}) + \ldots + \lambda_n(u_n - u_n^{(0)}),$$

we have ρ equal to a power series in τ, beginning with the first power, and we have n equations $u_r = u_r^{(0)} + Q_r(\rho)$, equivalent to equations of the form $u_r = u_r^{(0)} + R_r(\tau)$. In this way then the set of series about the ordinary point $(u_1^{(0)}, \ldots, u_n^{(0)})$ of the construct O is an analytical continuation of one of the sets of series about the limiting point $(\alpha_1, \ldots, \alpha_n)$, and conversely.

The points obtainable, starting from a particular set of series, by the process of analytical continuation above explained, are said, after Weierstrass, to constitute a *monogenic* construct; we see that the construct C breaks up into a certain number of monogenic portions, each having the property that it is possible to pass from the neighbourhood of any point of it to the neighbourhood of any other point by a succession of analytical continuations in which the parameter is changed by a formula $t' = k_0 + k_1 t + k_2 t^2 + \ldots$, in which k_1 does not vanish, while it is impossible to pass from one monogenic portion to any other by such continuation. As to the number of such monogenic portions constituting the whole construct C no statement can be made at the present stage, though as we shall shew immediately, the number of such having points in any assigned finite portion of space is necessarily finite; but in regard to any one portion it can be proved that, if we consider a finite region of space, and the part of the monogenic portion under consideration which is included in this finite region, a number r can be assigned such that if $(a_1, \ldots, a_n)$ be any point of this portion other than a limiting point, the series $u_r = a_r + P_r(t)$, giving points about $(a_1, \ldots, a_n)$, converges certainly for $|t| \overline{\gtrless} r$. As regards the former statement, that there cannot be an infinite number of monogenic portions of the construct C having points in any assigned finite portion of space, we reason as follows: associate with every such portion a point of itself; if the number of monogenic portions within the region be infinite, these points can be chosen so as to be infinite in number; they will therefore have a point of condensation or limiting point, within or upon the boundary of the region, in the infinitely near neighbourhood of which will be found points lying upon an infinite number of monogenic portions of C; this however is contrary to the result arrived at above that all the points of C, in the immediate neighbourhood of any point, lie upon a *finite* number of constructs expressed by equations of the form

$$w_n^{\mu} + (w_1)_1 w_n^{\mu-1} + \ldots + (w_1)_{\mu} = 0, \quad w_2 = \ldots, \quad \ldots\ldots\ldots, \quad w_{n-1} = \ldots.$$

The second statement may be founded upon the fact that the radius of convergence of the series $u_r = u_r' + Q_r(t)$, which express the points of the construct O about any ordinary point $(u_1', \ldots, u_n')$, is a continuous function of the position of $(u_1', \ldots, u_n')$ upon O; and this follows from the possibility of continuation sketched above.

60. In what follows we shall be primarily concerned with the consideration of a particular one, arbitrarily chosen, of the monogenic portions of the construct C; to save constant repetition of words we shall call this *the Construct* Γ. Recalling the assumed periodic character of the function ϕ, and the consequent periodicity of the functions $F_2, \ldots, F_n$, imagine the whole of finite space divided, as explained before (p. 204), into congruent period cells. Save for exceptional constructs, the construct C consists of the whole locus represented by the equations $F_2 = 0, \ldots, F_n = 0$, and must therefore be periodic; it does not follow however that any one of the monogenic portions of C is periodic with the same periods. Fix attention upon one of the period cells, calling it the primary cell; to the part of the monogenic construct Γ which lies in any cell other than the primary cell, there will be a congruent part of C lying in the primary cell; this may or may not itself be part of Γ; since however, as we have shewn, only a finite number of different monogenic portions of C can have points in the primary cell, it follows that the parts of Γ lying in the various period cells must be congruent to only a finite number of parts; thus Γ consists of the repetition, by addition of periods, of only a finite number of parts; it is therefore also periodic, but its periods are, possibly, certain sums of integral multiples of the fundamental periods.

Consider now the values which the function f_1 (p. 207) takes upon Γ; it is to be shewn that f_1 takes every assignable complex value; and, points which are congruent to one another in regard to the original periods being counted as equivalent, that it takes each value the same finite number of times. For convenience we shall for a time denote f_1 simply by f.

The first point is to prove that f actually assumes every value. In the neighbourhood of an ordinary point $(a_1, \ldots, a_n)$ of Γ, the function f is expressible as a power series in $u_1 - a_1, \ldots, u_n - a_n$; it is hence expressible by a power series in t—and this does not vanish identically, since otherwise the Jacobian $\partial(f_1, f_2, \ldots, f_n)/\partial(u_1, \ldots, u_n)$ would vanish for all points of Γ in a certain neighbourhood of $(a_1, \ldots, a_n)$, contrary to the fact that this Jacobian vanishes only at the limiting points. In the neighbourhood of a singular point $(\alpha_1, \ldots, \alpha_n)$, the function f is expressible as a quotient of power series in $u_1 - \alpha_1, \ldots, u_n - \alpha_n$, and hence as a quotient of power series in t; we have seen (p. 209) that at near points of the construct Γ the denominator power series in

$$u_1 - \alpha_1, \ \ldots, \ u_n - \alpha_n$$

does not vanish, and hence the denominator power series in t does not vanish identically; thus also the numerator power series in t does not vanish identically, since otherwise the point would be a limiting point of points at which the Jacobian $\partial(f_1, f_2, \ldots, f_n)/\partial(u_1, \ldots, u_n)$ was zero; thus about a limiting point of Γ the function f is expressible in the form $t^{-\lambda}(A_0 + A_1 t + \ldots)$, wherein λ is an integer which may be zero or negative. The poles of the function f upon Γ are thus among the limiting points of Γ. If a small region of Γ be put about such a pole, the values of f at all points of this region are large, and the region can be chosen so small that at all interior points the value of f is in absolute value greater than an assigned real positive quantity M; there cannot be an infinite number of such poles in any finite portion of space $(u_1, \ldots, u_n)$; we can thus suppose every pole enclosed in such a circumpolar region, corresponding to the assigned number M; then for points of Γ within a finite portion of space $(u_1, \ldots, u_n)$, not included in any circumpolar region, the function f is everywhere finite, and therefore has an upper limit which is finite and assignable. For, to say that there were points of Γ at which f had a value greater than *any* assignable number would be to say that there was an infinite number of points of Γ at which f had a value greater than an assigned number; these would have a limiting point; this limiting point would be either an ordinary or limiting point of Γ, and thus a point of Γ; by hypothesis it would not be a pole of f, and hence about it f would be expressible by a power series in t involving no negative powers, and would thus be incapable of values beyond every limit. As now we have previously seen that Γ is a repetition of a finite number of portions, the repetition being effected by addition of periods, and f is periodic, all the values of which f is capable occur for points in the finite part of the space $(u_1, \ldots, u_n)$. We can thus assume, taking the circumpolar regions suitably, that M is the upper limit of the absolute value of f outside the polar regions, while for all points in circumpolar regions $|f| > M$; we do not thereby mean to assume the existence of any poles. Consider the points of Γ outside the circumpolar regions; let $(u^{(0)})$ be such a point and $f^{(0)}$ the corresponding value of f; for surrounding points we have $f - f^{(0)} = c_1 t + c_2 t^2 + \dots$, and points can be found in the neighbourhood of $u^{(0)}$ for which $f - f^{(0)}$ has any arbitrary value which is sufficiently small; mark the value $f^{(0)}$ upon a plane and the contiguous values of f obtainable for the neighbourhood of $u^{(0)}$, taking no account of the possibility that the same value of $f - f^{(0)}$ may arise for two or more points near to $u^{(0)}$; these points near $f^{(0)}$ will lie within a circle upon the f-plane, with centre at $f^{(0)}$, and every point within this circle will be mentally associable with one or more points $(u_1, \dots, u_n)$ near to $(u_1^{(0)}, \dots, u_n^{(0)})$. Let $(u_1', \dots, u_n')$ be a point of Γ near to $(u_1, \dots, u_n)$ associated with the value f' of f represented by a point within this circle; for all values of f sufficiently near to f' points near to $(u_1', \dots, u_n')$ can be found; we can thus, on the f-plane, put about f' another circle giving values of f actually arising on Γ. Let this process be carried out for all points $(u_1', \dots, u_n')$ near to $(u^{(0)})$, and then repeated; and let r_0 be the largest radius about $f^{(0)}$ so obtainable such that all values $f = f_0 + \rho e^{i\theta}$, for any value of $\rho < r_0$, and any value of θ, actually arise; it is understood that, if necessary, r_0 is limited by the condition that $|f_0 + \rho e^{i\theta}| < M$. This value of r_0 will be called the variability of f about $(u^{(0)})$. Similarly every other point $(u^{(1)})$ will have a variability, say $r^{(1)}$. It is now to be proved that this variability has, for all positions of (u) upon Γ outside the circumpolar regions, a lower limit greater than zero. When $(u^{(1)})$ is sufficiently near to $(u^{(0)})$, the variability circle of $(u^{(1)})$ upon the plane of f has its centre $f^{(1)}$ within the variability circle of $(u^{(0)})$, and extends at least as far as the circumference of this, so that $r^{(1)} \gtreqless r^{(0)} - |f^{(1)} - f^{(0)}|$; also, in the same case, the centre of the circle for $f^{(0)}$ is within that for $f^{(1)}$ and

$$r^{(0)} \gtreqless r^{(1)} - |f^{(1)} - f^{(0)}|;$$

thus

$$r^{(0)} - |f^{(1)} - f^{(0)}| \lesseqgtr r^{(1)} \lesseqgtr r^{(0)} + |f^{(1)} - f^{(0)}|;$$

by taking $(u^{(1)})$ sufficiently near to $(u^{(0)})$ we can however make $|f^{(1)} - f^{(0)}|$ as small as we may desire; it follows then that the variability is a continuous function of $(u_1, \dots, u_n)$ for points lying on Γ outside the circumpolar regions; as it is never zero it follows that its lower limit is not zero for points $(u_1, \dots, u_n)$ on Γ lying in any finite part of space, and therefore, in virtue of the periodicity of Γ, that its lower limit is not zero for points $(u_1, \dots, u_n)$ anywhere on Γ, outside the circumpolar regions. Let this lower limit be r. If then $f^{(0)}$ be the value of f at any point $(u^{(0)})$ of Γ, there exist points, outside the circumpolar regions, at which f takes any of the values $f^{(0)} + \rho e^{i\theta}$, where $\rho < r$ and θ is arbitrary. This however does not at once preclude the possibility that as f is made to pass through any range of values from $f^{(0)}$ to $f^{(0)} + \rho e^{i\theta}$, the corresponding point (u) may pass to infinity on Γ. This possibility may be illustrated by attempting to prove in a similar way, on the plane of a variable u, that the function $f = e^u$ takes the value zero; over any finite part of the plane the variability of the function $f = e^u$ has a lower limit other than zero; starting from the value $f^{(0)}$ for $u^{(0)}$, the point $u^{(1)}$ for any other value $f^{(1)}$ is given by $u^{(1)} - u^{(0)} = \log(f^{(1)}/f^{(0)})$; if $f^{(1)} = \frac{1}{2}f^{(0)}$ we have then $u^{(1)} = u^{(0)} - \log 2$; if next $f^{(2)} = \frac{1}{2}f^{(1)}$ we have again $u^{(2)} = u^{(1)} - \log 2 = u^{(0)} - 2\log 2$; and as we thus approach to the value 0 for f, while at every stage there is a definite position for u, yet these positions pass to infinity. Suppose then, returning to the case now under discussion, that the positions of (u) corresponding to values of f of the form $f^{(0)} + \rho' e^{i\theta}$, where ρ' denotes a series of values having ρ as their limit, are a series passing off to infinity; choose a set of portions such that Γ is made up of repetitions of these, by additions of periods; these portions lie entirely in a finite number of period cells; denote the aggregate of these cells as the fundamental volume; a series of points (u) upon Γ passing off to infinity may then be represented, so far as the values of f are concerned, by an indefinitely continued sequence of points in the fundamental volume; and, in the case supposed, there will then be an infinite number of such points, in the fundamental volume, and upon Γ, at which f takes values $f^{(0)} + \rho' e^{i\theta}$ for which ρ' is arbitrarily near to ρ. There is then a point, which will be upon Γ, in any arbitrarily near neighbourhood of which are found points for which f has values $f^{(0)} + \rho' e^{i\theta}$ in which ρ' is arbitrarily near to ρ; in virtue of the continuity of f, it follows that at this point f takes actually the value $f^{(0)} + \rho e^{i\theta}$. It appears thus that the neighbourhood of a point $(u^{(0)})$ at which f takes a value $f^{(0)} + \rho e^{i\theta}$, with $\rho < r$, may always be supposed to lie entirely in the finite region of space. Take now any point $(u^{(0)})$ of Γ and let $\xi^{(0)}$ be the value of f there; take any other value ξ for which $|\xi| < M$. The finite series of intermediate points $\xi^{(1)}, \xi^{(2)}, \ldots$, for which the differences

$$\xi^{(1)} - \xi^{(0)},\ \xi^{(2)} - \xi^{(1)},\ \ldots$$

are all of the same phase and all of absolute value $< r$, determines a finite series of points $(u^{(1)})$, $(u^{(2)})$, ... upon Γ at which f has in turn the values $\xi^{(1)}, \xi^{(2)}, \ldots$; and these lead then in a finite number of steps to a definite finite point at which $f = \xi$.

It appears thus, as M is arbitrarily great, that f takes every assignable value, and becomes infinite at a pole, somewhere upon Γ.

61. Having proved that the function f assumes upon Γ every complex value, we can prove that it takes any definite value only at a finite number of points, points for which the arguments $(u_1, \ldots, u_n)$ differ by a column of periods being counted as equivalent, and that it takes every complex value the same number of times.

For consider an irreducible set of portions of Γ, lying in a finite number of period cells, so chosen that any other point of Γ is reducible to a point included in this set, by additions of periods. The aggregate of these portions may be spoken of as the fundamental region of Γ. If f were capable of the same value for an infinite number of incongruent points, it would be capable of the same value for an infinite number of points of the fundamental region; and there would then, as this region is entirely contained in a finite portion of space, be a limiting point, itself therefore a point of Γ, in any neighbourhood of which, however small, f would take this value an infinite number of times. All the values of f in the neighbourhood of any point of Γ are however given by a finite number of expressions of the form

$$t^{-\lambda}(A + A_1 t + \dots),$$

and an equation of the form $\xi = t^{-\lambda}(A + A_1 t + \dots)$ is not satisfied by an infinite number of small values of t; thus f cannot have the value ξ at an infinite number of points arbitrarily near to any point of Γ.

Next, an equation $f = t^{-\lambda}(A + A_1 t + \dots)$, where λ is positive and greater than zero, means that the point about which it holds is a pole, and we may say that f there becomes infinite λ times: similarly an equation

$$f - f_0 = t^{\lambda}(A + A_1 t + \dots),$$

wherein λ is positive and greater than zero, may be expressed by saying that at the point about which it holds f takes λ times the value f_0; consider such a point as this last, the pole being included by the convention that for a pole $f - f_0$ shall be replaced by $1/f$. For values of f near to f_0, the equation

$$f - f_0 = t^{\lambda}(A + A_1 t + \dots)$$

gives λ small values of t, and hence λ places on Γ near to the point, at which f has any assigned value near to f_0; in other words the number of places where f has this near value is equal to the number of those where $f = f_0$; this identity in the number of places where f has its various values continues therefore for large variations of value. Considering then all the points of the fundamental region of Γ at which f takes any particular value, and supposing f to change continuously, each of these points is the beginning of a path upon Γ, and every one of these paths may be supposed to persist even through a point where one or more of them intersect; if one of these paths pass over the boundary of the fundamental region, then, since f has the periods which are fundamental for Γ, there enters at the same instant, at another point of the boundary, a path which may be taken as continuing, upon the fundamental region, the path which has passed out. The total number of times f takes any value within the fundamental region is thus the same whatever the value*. This number is the sum of the numbers for a certain finite

* We have already spoken of the $(2n-2)$-fold, in the real space of $2n$ dimensions, upon which the function f vanishes, and of the infinity $(2n-2)$-fold upon which $1/f$ vanishes. There exists similarly a $(2n-2)$-fold upon which f is equal to any assigned complex quantity ξ. What we have proved is that the number of its intersections with the 2-fold Γ, incongruent to one another in

number of period cells, chosen so that the portions of Γ which they contain are incongruent, and is thus the total number of incongruent positions for which f has the value.

62. Now denote by x the value of f upon the construct Γ, and, taking unassigned constants $\lambda_1, \ldots, \lambda_n$, put

$$u = \lambda_1 u_1 + \ldots + \lambda_n u_n,$$

and consider the function du/dx, regarded as depending upon x. We have shewn that upon the fundamental region of Γ every value of x arises the same finite number of times; with every complex value of x, not excluding the infinite value, may thus be associated a definite number of values of du/dx, the same for each value of x; it is easy to shew also that about every value x_0 of x the associated values of du/dx are expressible by series of integral powers of a root of $x - x_0$, the number of negative powers, if any, being finite, there being only a finite number of values x_0 for which negative powers enter; it being understood that for x_0 infinite the quantity $x - x_0$ means x^{-1}. When this is shewn it will follow that du/dx satisfies an algebraic equation whose coefficients are rational in x, the order of the equation being the number of values of du/dx associated with any value of x. To shew this, we remark that, first, about any ordinary point $(u^{(0)})$ of Γ, for which $x = x_0$, we have $u - u^{(0)}$ and $x - x_0$ each expressible by a single power series in a parameter t, and hence du/dx expressible by power series in a certain root of $x - x_0$, while, second, about a limiting point $(u^{(0)})$ of Γ, for which $x = x_0$ (including x_0 infinite), we have $u - u^{(0)}$ expressible by a finite number of power series in a parameter, and, corresponding to each of these, $x - x_0$ expressible by a single power series in the same parameter. If

$$(du/dx)_1, (du/dx)_2, \ldots$$

be the values of du/dx corresponding to any value of x, the algebraic equation is $F(y, x, \lambda_1, \ldots, \lambda_n) = 0$ where, with unassigned σ, the function

$$F(\sigma, x, \lambda_1, \ldots, \lambda_n)$$

is the product

$$\left[\sigma - \left(\frac{du}{dx}\right)_1\right]\left[\sigma - \left(\frac{du}{dx}\right)_2\right]\ldots\ldots,$$

and is a rational polynomial in $\lambda_1, \ldots, \lambda_n$.

If now $F(y, x, \lambda_1, \ldots, \lambda_n)$ is capable of being written as a product of factors each rational in x and y, let $f(y, x, \lambda_1, \ldots, \lambda_n)$ be such a factor, itself irreducible in this sense. The equation $f(y, x, \lambda_1, \ldots, \lambda_n) = 0$ thus defines a

regard to the periods, is finite and independent of ξ. It appears that a closed one-fold (or curve) can be put about the $(2n-2)$-fold $f=\xi$, and that the increment of $\log(f-\xi)$ along this closed one-fold is independent of ξ; but this requires explanations into which we cannot now enter.

monogenic algebraic construct; to each value of x this construct associates values of $u_1, \ldots, u_n$, expressed, since differentiation in regard to λ_s gives

$$\frac{du_s}{dx}\frac{\partial f}{\partial y}+\frac{\partial f}{\partial \lambda_s}=0,$$

by the equations

$$u_s=-\int\frac{\partial f/\partial\lambda_s}{\partial f/\partial y}\,dx;$$

these are therefore integrals of the first kind upon the algebraic construct; each is expressible for the neighbourhood of any value of x by a power series in a parameter t, and this parameter may be taken to be that employed upon the construct Γ; all the power series expressing u_s upon the algebraic construct may be regarded as analytic continuations of one of them, this being a known property for a monogenic algebraic construct. The construct Γ is however monogenic, all the power series for u_s upon Γ being similarly analytic continuations of one of them; it follows therefore that the values of u_s arising for the algebraic construct are the same as those arising for Γ, and hence that the algebraic function $F(y, x, \lambda_1, \ldots, \lambda_n)$, if not irreducible, is a power of the irreducible function $f(y, x, \lambda_1, \ldots, \lambda_n)$. In the latter case, if $F(y, x, \lambda_1, \ldots, \lambda_n)$ be the kth power of $f(y, x, \lambda_1, \ldots, \lambda_n)$, there would correspond to every point of the fundamental region of Γ one point of the algebraic construct, but to every point of the algebraic construct would correspond k places of the fundamental region of Γ, the values of y or du/dx being the same at these k places.

This however, holding for an arbitrary value of x and undetermined values of $\lambda_1, \ldots, \lambda_n$, would involve the existence of k sets of n constants, $\alpha_{1,h}, \ldots, \alpha_{n,h}$, for $h=1, 2, \ldots, k$, not necessarily different sets, such that if $(u_1, \ldots, u_n)$ be a point of the fundamental region of Γ, so also is

$$(u_1+\alpha_{1,h}, \ldots, u_n+\alpha_{n,h}),$$

while as x is the same at the k places, also

$$f(u_1+\alpha_{1,h}, \ldots, u_n+\alpha_{n,h})=f(u_1, \ldots, u_n);$$

the original n functions $\phi_1, \ldots, \phi_n$ (p. 205) would therefore have the periods $\alpha_{1,h}, \ldots, \alpha_{n,h}$, and therefore so would the original function $\phi(u_1, \ldots, u_n)$. We have however assumed at the outset that in speaking of the periods we were speaking of primitive periods of this function (p. 203). Thus $\alpha_{1,h}, \ldots, \alpha_{n,h}$ would be sums of integral multiples of the original periods; this however is contrary to the definition of the fundamental region of Γ, which is so constructed that no portion of it is a repetition, obtained by addition of the periods, of any other portion. It follows then that the function

$$F(y, x, \lambda_1, \ldots, \lambda_n)$$

is irreducible, and there is a definite one to one correspondence of the points of the algebraic construct with the points of the fundamental region of Γ.

63. To investigate this correspondence in more detail, we proceed as follows. Let the class of the algebraic construct $f(y, x, \lambda_1, \ldots, \lambda_n) = 0$ be p; we have seen (p. 207) that upon Γ the integrals $u_1, \ldots, u_n$ are not connected by any equation $c_1 u_1 + \ldots + c_n u_n = 0$, in which $c_1, \ldots, c_n$ are constants; they are therefore linearly independent upon the algebraic construct, and $p \geqq n$. Denoting normal integrals of the first kind upon the algebraic construct $f(y, x, \lambda_1, \ldots, \lambda_n) = 0$ by $V_1, \ldots, V_p$, we thus have equations

$$u_r = c_{r,1} V_1 + \ldots + c_{r,p} V_p, \qquad (r = 1, \ldots, n);$$

now without alteration of x and y we can assign to $V_1, \ldots, V_p$ values obtained by adding to them the respective elements of any one of $2p$ systems of constants, namely the periods; for V_α these constants belonging to the $2p$ systems are

$$(1)_{\alpha 1}, (1)_{\alpha 2}, \ldots, (1)_{\alpha p}, \quad \tau_{\alpha 1}, \ldots, \tau_{\alpha p}, \qquad (\alpha = 1, \ldots, p),$$

where $(1)_{\alpha\beta} = 0$ unless $\alpha = \beta$, while $(1)_{\alpha\alpha} = 1$; let $\Omega_{r,\alpha}$, $\Omega'_{r,\alpha}$ be the corresponding system of increments for u_r, so that

$$\Omega_{r,\alpha} = c_{r,\alpha}, \quad \Omega'_{r,\alpha} = c_{r,1}\tau_{1,\alpha} + \ldots + c_{r,p}\tau_{p,\alpha}, \qquad (r = 1, \ldots, n;\ \alpha = 1, \ldots, p),$$

and we have

$$u_r = \Omega_{r,1} V_1 + \ldots + \Omega_{r,p} V_p, \quad \Omega'_{r,\alpha} = \Omega_{r,1}\tau_{1,\alpha} + \ldots + \Omega_{r,p}\tau_{p,\alpha};$$

these equations we shall denote by

$$u = \Omega V, \quad \Omega' = \Omega\tau,$$

where Ω, Ω' denote matrices of type (n, p), and τ the symmetrical matrix, of type (p, p), belonging to the periods of the normal integrals $V_1, \ldots, V_p$ on the algebraic construct $f(y, x, \lambda_1, \ldots, \lambda_n)$. (Cf. p. 12 preceding.) If then Ω_0, τ_0, Ω_0' denote the matrices whose elements are the conjugate complexes of those of Ω, τ, Ω', and, as before, $\bar{\Omega}$ denotes the matrix obtained from Ω by transposing rows and columns, etc., we have

$$\bar{\Omega}' = \tau\bar{\Omega}, \quad \Omega\bar{\Omega}' = \Omega\tau\bar{\Omega} = \Omega'\bar{\Omega}, \quad \Omega'\bar{\Omega}_0 - \Omega\bar{\Omega}_0' = \Omega(\tau - \tau_0)\bar{\Omega}_0;$$

thus $\Omega\bar{\Omega}'$ is a symmetrical matrix, or

$$0 = \Omega'\bar{\Omega} - \Omega\bar{\Omega}' = (\Omega, \Omega')\begin{pmatrix} 0, & -1 \\ 1, & 0 \end{pmatrix}\begin{pmatrix} \bar{\Omega} \\ \bar{\Omega}' \end{pmatrix} = \Pi\epsilon_{2p}\bar{\Pi},$$

where Π denotes the matrix of type $(n, 2p)$ represented by (Ω, Ω'), and ϵ_{2p} is a matrix of type $(2p, 2p)$ whose elements are all zero except the elements of position $(\alpha, \alpha + p)$, for $\alpha = 1, 2, \ldots, p$, each of which is -1, and the elements $(\alpha + p, \alpha)$, each of which is $+1$. Also, if x, or $(x^{(1)}, \ldots, x^{(n)})$, be a row of n arbitrary quantities, and x_0 the row of n conjugate complex quantities, and $z = \bar{\Omega}x$, so that, as $\bar{\Omega}$ is of type (p, n), the row z is of p quantities, such as

$$z_\alpha = \Omega_{1,\alpha}x_1 + \Omega_{2,\alpha}x_2 + \ldots + \Omega_{n,\alpha}x_n, \qquad (\alpha = 1, \ldots, p),$$

and z_α is a period for $x_1u_1 + \ldots + x_nu_n$, and if we put $\tau = \rho + i\sigma$, $\tau_0 = \rho - i\sigma$, then

$$-i\Pi\epsilon_{2p}\bar{\Pi}_0x_0x = -i(\Omega'\bar{\Omega}_0 - \Omega\bar{\Omega}_0')x_0x = -i\Omega(\tau - \bar{\tau}_0)\bar{\Omega}_0x_0x$$
$$= -i(\tau - \tau_0)z_0z = -i(2i\sigma)z_0z = 2\sigma z_0z;$$

we know however (p. 7) that if $n_1, \ldots, n_p$ be any real quantities the real part of $i\tau n^2$, namely $-\sigma n^2$, is necessarily negative and greater than zero. Hence, for an arbitrary row x of n quantities, not all zero, we have, beside the identity $\Pi\epsilon_{2p}\bar{\Pi} = 0$, obtained above, the inequality

$$-i\Pi\epsilon\bar{\Pi}_{2p\,0}x_0x > 0.$$

Since the acquisition by $u_1, \ldots, u_n$ respectively of the increments

$$\Omega_{1\alpha}, \ldots, \Omega_{n,\alpha}$$

corresponds to a circuit by (x, y) on the algebraic construct, it will correspond to a path on Γ of a kind that leads again to the same values of x and y as at the starting point, and this for values of x which are arbitrary. We have shewn above that the end point of such a path is obtained from the initial point by addition of a set of periods to the arguments $u_1, \ldots, u_n$. If then the original periods associated with u_r (p. 204) be denoted by $\varpi_{r,s}$, for $r = 1, \ldots, n$ and $s = 1, \ldots, (2n)$, we have equations of the form

$$\Pi_{r,\alpha} = h_{1,\alpha}\varpi_{r,1} + \ldots + h_{2n,\alpha}\varpi_{r,2n}, \qquad r = 1, \ldots, n;\ \alpha = 1, \ldots, (2p)$$

wherein $h_{s,\alpha}$ is an integer, the general element of a matrix of type $(2n, 2p)$ which we shall denote by h; the equation may then be written in the form

$$\Pi = \varpi h.$$

We then have

$$0 = \Pi\epsilon_{2p}\bar{\Pi} = \varpi h\epsilon_{2p}\bar{h}\bar{\varpi} = \varpi M\bar{\varpi},$$

where $M, = h\epsilon_{2p}\bar{h}$, is a skew symmetrical matrix of integers of type $(2n, 2n)$; and

$$0 < -i\Pi\epsilon_{2p}\bar{\Pi}x_0x = -i\varpi h\epsilon_{2p}\bar{h}\bar{\varpi}x_0x = -i\varpi M\bar{\varpi}_0x_0x.$$

If each of the $2n$ quantities $\bar{\varpi}x$ be written in the form $\eta_s + i\zeta_s$, where η_s, ζ_s are real, so that we may write $\bar{\varpi}x = \eta + i\zeta$, the last inequality is

$$0 < -iM(\eta - i\zeta)(\eta + i\zeta) = -iM(\eta\eta + \zeta\zeta - i\zeta\eta + i\eta\zeta),$$

where, since M is skew symmetrical, $M\eta\eta = 0 = M\zeta\zeta$, and $M\zeta\eta = -M\eta\zeta$; thus we have

$$0 < M\eta\zeta,$$

and it is impossible to choose the n arbitrary quantities x so that the $2n$ quantities $M\eta$ are all zero, except of course by taking $x = 0$; if $\varpi = \alpha + i\beta$, so that α is the matrix whose elements are the real parts of the elements of the matrix ϖ, and β the matrix constituted by the imaginary parts, while $x = y + iz$, so that y is the set formed by the n real parts of the elements x, and z that formed by the imaginary parts, we have

$$\eta + i\zeta = \bar{\varpi}x = (\bar{\alpha} + i\bar{\beta})(y + iz), \quad \eta = \bar{\alpha}y - \bar{\beta}z = (\bar{\alpha}, \bar{\beta})(y, -z);$$

it is thus impossible to choose the $2n$ quantities y, z so that

$$M(\bar{\alpha}, \bar{\beta})(y, -z) = 0;$$

hence the matrices M and $(\bar{\alpha}, \bar{\beta})$ have each a determinant which does not vanish. The latter determinant is that of the matrix $\begin{pmatrix}\alpha\\ \beta\end{pmatrix}$ and, therefore, that of the determinant $\begin{pmatrix}\varpi\\ \beta\end{pmatrix}$; thus in ϖ not every determinant of n rows and columns can be zero (cf. p. 204 above); the matrix M is $h\epsilon_{2p}\bar{h}$, where h is of type $(2n, 2p)$, and $n \leqq p$; the determinant of M is thus expressible as a sum of products of determinants of type $(2n, 2n)$ formed from h; we thus infer that in h not every determinant of type $(2n, 2n)$ can be zero.

Now take matrices of integers, g of type $(2n, 2n)$ and m of type $(2p, 2p)$, each of determinant unity (see Appendix to Part II. Note I.), such that the matrix, of type $(2n, 2p)$, ghm, has the form

$$ghm = \begin{pmatrix} c_1, & 0, & 0, & . & . \\ 0, & c_2, & 0, & . & . \\ 0, & 0, & c_3, & . & . \\ . & . & . & . & . \end{pmatrix}, = c, \text{ say};$$

this equation enables us to express any determinant of type $(2n, 2n)$ from the matrix h as a sum of products of determinants from g^{-1}, c and m^{-1}; if any one of $c_1, c_2, c_3, \ldots, c_{2n}$ were zero, every determinant of c of type $(2n, 2n)$ would be zero and hence every determinant of h of this type, contrary to what is proved above. Now define the matrix ϖ' of type $(n, 2n)$ by means of $\varpi = \varpi' g$, so that Π, which is equal to ϖh, is equal to $\varpi' c m^{-1}$; as the last $2p - 2n$ columns of c consist of zeros, so also do the last $2p - 2n$ columns of $\varpi' c$, and therefore the last $2p - 2n$ rows of the square matrix m^{-1} do not come into consideration here; let ϖ_1' denote the first $2n$ columns of $\varpi' c$; thus ϖ_1' is of type $(n, 2n)$ and consists of the columns of ϖ' multiplied respectively by $c_1, c_2, c_3, \ldots, c_{2n}$; further let the matrix of type $(2n, 2p)$ constituted by the first $2n$ rows of m^{-1} be called k; it is unitary in the sense that its determinants of type $(2n, 2n)$ have unity for their highest common factor; then we have

$$\Pi = \varpi' c m^{-1} = (\varpi_1', 0)\begin{pmatrix}k\\ ..\end{pmatrix} = \varpi_1' k.$$

When h is itself unitary we have $ghm = (1, 0)$ and $gh = k$, $g = 1$, $k = h$.

Also, if f be any matrix of type $(2n, 2n)$, we have

$$\Pi m = (\varpi_1', 0), \quad km = (1_{2n}, 0), \quad fkm = (f, 0),$$

where 1_{2n} denotes a matrix of type $(2n, 2n)$ having unities in the diagonal, the other elements being zero, and 0, in the first equation denotes a matrix of type $(n, 2p-2n)$ with zero elements, in the last two equations denotes a matrix of type $(2n, 2p-2n)$ with zero elements. Thus fk cannot consist of integers unless f do so.

Now consider more particularly the correspondence between the construct Γ and the algebraic construct defined by the equation $f(y, x, \lambda_1, \ldots, \lambda_n) = 0$. Any two points (u), (u') of Γ for which

$$u_r' - u_r = \varpi_{r,1} N_1 + \ldots + \varpi_{r,2n} N_{2n}, \qquad (r = 1, \ldots, n),$$

wherein $N_1, \ldots, N_{2n}$ are integers independent of r, correspond, in virtue of the equations $x = f(u)$, $y = \lambda_1 du_1/dx + \ldots + \lambda_n du_n/dx$, to the same point of the algebraic construct; a path on Γ from (u) to (u') corresponds to a closed circuit on the Riemann surface representing the algebraic construct; thus

$$u_r' - u_r = \Omega_{r,1} t_1 + \ldots + \Omega_{r,p} t_p + \Omega'_{r,1} t_{p+1} + \ldots + \Omega'_{r,p} t_{2p},$$

where $t_1, \ldots, t_{2p}$ is a row of integers independent of r; denoting this by

$$u' - u = \Pi t$$

we have, in virtue of $\Pi = \varpi_1' k$, the equation $u' - u = \varpi_1' kt$ or say $u' - u = \varpi_1' \sigma$, where $\sigma = kt$ is a row of $2n$ integers; this is the same as

$$(A) \qquad u_r' - u_r = c_1 \varpi'_{r,1} \sigma_1 + \ldots + c_{2n} \varpi'_{r,2n} \sigma_{2n}, \qquad (r = 1, \ldots, n).$$

The periods ϖ', equal to ϖg^{-1}, where $|g| = 1$, are equivalent with the periods ϖ, the angular points of the period cells associated with them as on p. 204 being the same, save for order, as the angular points of the cells associated with the periods ϖ; the period cells associated with the periods ϖ_1' have not the same angular points, but only some of them, the first column of these periods being c_1 times the first column of the periods ϖ', and so on. If (u_r) be a point of the construct Γ, and we consider the points of space

$$(u_r), \quad (u_r + \varpi'_{r,1}), \quad (u_r + 2\varpi'_{r,1}), \quad (u_r + 3\varpi'_{r,1}), \ldots,$$

the formula (A) above shews that the first of these after (u_r) which can lie on Γ is $(u_r + c_1 \varpi'_{r,1})$, and similarly for the periods $\varpi'_{r,2}, \varpi'_{r,3}, \ldots, \varpi'_{r,2n}$; conversely, as is shewn by the formula $\Pi m = (\varpi_1', 0)$, obtained above, the periods ϖ_1' necessarily correspond to circuits on the Riemann surface. In other words the construct Γ is not periodic with the periods ϖ or ϖ', but only with the periods ϖ_1', of which the s-th column is obtained by multiplying the s-th column of ϖ' by c_s; and the algebraic construct given by $f(y, x, \lambda_1, \ldots, \lambda_n) = 0$ corresponds to a part of the construct Γ extending within $c_1 c_2 \ldots c_{2n}$ of the period cells associated with the periods ϖ'. The extent of Γ may thus be divided into regions, each lying within as many of these cells, each region having a one to one correspondence with the algebraic construct: if (x) be a place of the algebraic construct, there is no place (x') of it for which the equations

$$u_r^{x',x} = N_1 \varpi'_{r,1} + \ldots + N_{2n} \varpi'_{r,2n}, \qquad (r = 1, \ldots, n),$$

are all satisfied, $u_r^{x',x}$ denoting the difference of the values of u_r at (x) and (x'), and $N_1, \ldots, N_{2n}$ denoting integers independent of r, unless these integers are respectively integer multiples of the integers $c_1, c_2, \ldots, c_{2n}$.

Now (as in Appendix to Part II. Note II.) let a matrix of integers f, of type $(2n, 2n)$, be taken so that

$$fk\epsilon_{2p}\bar{k}\bar{f} = r\epsilon_{2n},$$

where, if $(1)_m$ denote the unit matrix of order m,

$$\epsilon_{2p} = \begin{pmatrix} 0 , & -(1)_p \\ (1)_p, & 0 \end{pmatrix}, \qquad \epsilon_{2n} = \begin{pmatrix} 0 , & -(1)_n \\ (1)_n, & 0 \end{pmatrix},$$

k is the matrix of integers previously used, of type $(2n, 2p)$, and r is a positive integer, taken as small as possible; then, defining two matrices (μ, μ'), each of type (n, n), by the equation $\varpi_1' = (\mu, \mu')f$, we have (p. 224)

$$0 = \Pi\epsilon_{2p}\bar{\Pi} = \varpi_1'k\epsilon_{2p}\bar{k}\bar{\varpi}_1' = (\mu, \mu')fk\epsilon_{2p}\bar{k}\bar{f}\begin{pmatrix}\bar{\mu} \\ \bar{\mu}'\end{pmatrix} = r(\mu, \mu')\,\epsilon_{2n}\begin{pmatrix}\bar{\mu} \\ \bar{\mu}'\end{pmatrix}$$

$$= r(\mu', -\mu)\begin{pmatrix}\bar{\mu} \\ \bar{\mu}'\end{pmatrix} = r(\mu'\bar{\mu} - \mu\bar{\mu}'),$$

and similarly, x being a row of n arbitrary quantities,

$$0 < -i\Pi\epsilon_{2p}\bar{\Pi}_0 x_0 x = -ir(\mu'\bar{\mu}_0 - \mu\bar{\mu}_0')x_0 x = -ir(\bar{\mu}'x\,.\,\bar{\mu}_0 x_0 - \bar{\mu}x\,.\,\bar{\mu}_0' x_0).$$

An incidental consequence of the last inequality is that the determinant of the matrix μ is not zero, since otherwise we could choose x to make both $\bar{\mu}x$ and $\bar{\mu}_0 x_0$ vanish*.

We can then put

$$\sigma = \mu^{-1}\mu',$$

and obtain, if $y = \bar{\mu}x, = \eta + i\zeta$, say, and $\sigma = \sigma_1 + i\sigma_2$,

$$0 = r\mu(\sigma - \bar{\sigma})\bar{\mu}, \text{ giving } \sigma = \bar{\sigma},$$

so that the matrix σ, of type (n, n), is symmetrical, together with

$$0 < -ir(\sigma y y_0 - \sigma_0 y_0 y) = 2r\sigma_2(\eta^2 + \zeta^2),$$

* More generally if J, of the form $\begin{pmatrix} \alpha & \beta \\ \alpha' & \beta' \end{pmatrix}^{-1}$, be any matrix of integers of type $(2n, 2n)$, such that $J\epsilon_{2n}\bar{J} = \epsilon_{2n}$, namely the matrix of a so-called linear transformation of order n, and we put $J_1 = J\begin{pmatrix} c & 0 \\ 0 & 1 \end{pmatrix}$, where c is any constant, the equation

$$fk\epsilon_{2p}\bar{k}\bar{f} = r\epsilon_{2n}$$

involves
$$J_1 fk\epsilon_{2p}\bar{k}\bar{f}\bar{J}_1 = cr\epsilon_{2n},$$

and we can, in the text, use $J_1 f$ instead of f; putting then $\varpi_1' = (\nu, \nu')J_1 f$, or $(\mu, \mu') = (\nu, \nu')J_1$, where ν, ν' are each matrices of type (n, n), it follows that $|\nu|$ is not zero; this is the same as that $|\mu\alpha + c\mu'\alpha'|$ is not zero. In particular, by $J^{-1} = \epsilon_{2n}$, the determinant of μ' is not zero.

which shews that if $q_1, \ldots, q_n$ be any n real quantities, the real part of the quadratic form $i\sigma q^2$ is necessarily negative. We can hence define a theta function

$$\Theta(v, \sigma) = \sum_{n=-\infty}^{\infty} \exp.(2\pi i v n + i\pi\sigma n^2).$$

Consider the change of the function $\Theta(\mu^{-1}u, \sigma)$ when the arguments $u_1, \ldots, u_n$ are respectively increased by the n quantities expressed by Πt, where t denotes a row of $2p$ integers: these are the increments corresponding to any closed circuit on the Riemann surface associated with the equation

$$f(y, x, \lambda_1, \ldots, \lambda_n) = 0.$$

Since $\Pi = \varpi_1' k = (\mu, \mu') f k$, the arguments $\mu^{-1}u$ will be increased respectively by the elements expressed by

$$\mu^{-1}(\mu, \mu') fkt = (1, \sigma) fkt = (1, \sigma)(l, l') = l + \sigma l',$$

where (l, l'), $= fkt$, is a set of $2n$ integers; the function $\Theta(\mu^{-1}u, \sigma)$ will thus be multiplied by

$$\exp.[-2\pi i l'(\mu^{-1}u + \tfrac{1}{2}\sigma l')].$$

It is thus possible, with this theta function, to form single valued functions of $u_1, \ldots, u_n$, of meromorphic character, which are unaltered by any circuit on the Riemann surface associated with the equation $f(y, x, \lambda_1, \ldots, \lambda_n) = 0$, and are therefore, since $u_1, \ldots, u_n$ are integrals of the first kind on this surface, expressible as rational functions of x and y. These functions, which we may denote by $\psi(u, \Pi)$, have not the periods ϖ'; but then, neither has the construct Γ: to a point $(u_1, \ldots, u_r)$ of Γ correspond $c_1 c_2 \ldots c_{2n}$ points of space congruent thereto in regard to the periods ϖ', namely those for which u_r is replaced by

$$u_r + \gamma_1 \varpi'_{r,1} + \ldots + \gamma_{2n} \varpi'_{r,2n},$$

where $\gamma_1 = 0, 1, \ldots, c_1 - 1$; $\gamma_2 = 0, 1, \ldots, c_2 - 1$; $\ldots$; $\gamma_{2n} = 0, 1, \ldots, c_{2n} - 1$, and of these, as we have shewn, only one, namely $(u_1, \ldots, u_n)$, lies on the construct Γ; since the complete construct C has the periods ϖ' these $c_1 c_2 \ldots c_{2n}$ places are upon as many monogenic portions of C. The functions $\psi(u, \Pi)$ have the periods properly belonging to the construct Γ: it is our aim in what follows clearly to establish that the function $\phi(u)$, and in general all single valued functions of meromorphic character with the periods ϖ, can be rationally expressed in terms of a finite number of functions $\psi(u, \Pi)$.

CHAPTER VIII.

DEFECTIVE INTEGRALS.

64. In the preceding chapter it has been shewn that the most general periodic function, of meromorphic character, leads to the consideration of a Riemann surface upon which, among the existing p linearly independent integrals of the first kind, are found n integrals, with n less than p or equal to p, whose $2p$ periods are expressible linearly in terms of only $2n$ quantities. With a view to throwing some light on the general question we consider in this chapter some general theorems for such a case, and some particular examples; it will be found that the result arrived at in the last chapter offers some peculiarities.

Suppose then $u_1, \dots, u_n$ to be linearly independent integrals of the first kind upon a Riemann surface, upon which there are in all p such integrals, and $n \leqq p$; let the $2p$ periods, or additive constants of indeterminateness, for u_r, upon the Riemann surface, be denoted by $\Pi_{r,\alpha}$, for $r = 1, \dots, n$ and $\alpha = 1, \dots, (2p)$, and the matrix of type $(n, 2p)$ formed by these quantities be called Π; suppose that we have equations

$$\Pi_{r,\alpha} = \varpi_{r,1} h_{1,\alpha} + \dots + \varpi_{r,2n} h_{2n,\alpha}$$

wherein $h_{s,\alpha}$ are integers, and $\varpi_{r,s}$ are other constants; so that if ϖ denote the matrix of type $(n, 2n)$ formed by the quantities $\varpi_{r,s}$ and h denote the matrix of integers of type $(2n, 2p)$ whose elements are $h_{s,\alpha}$, we may write

$$\Pi = \varpi h.$$

It can then be proved, just as in the last chapter (p. 224), that $\varpi M \overline{\varpi} = 0$ and $-i\varpi M \overline{\varpi}_0 x_0 x > 0$, where x is any set of n quantities not all zero, and $M, = h\epsilon_{2p}\overline{h}$, is a skew symmetrical matrix of integers of type $(2n, 2n)$. And thence as before that not every determinant of type $(2n, 2n)$ in h is zero.

We may then, also as before, find two square matrices of integers g, m, each of determinant unity, the former of type $(2n, 2n)$, the latter of type $(2p, 2p)$, such that ghm, of type $(2n, 2p)$, consists of zeros save in the places $(1, 1)$ $(2, 2), \dots, (2n, 2n)$ where are found positive integers $c_1, c_2, \dots, c_{2n}$, no one of which is zero; putting then $\varpi' = \varpi g^{-1}$, so that ϖ' is a set of quantities equivalent with ϖ, in the sense that either is linearly expressible by the other with integer coefficients, we have $\Pi m = \varpi' c = (a, 0)$, where a is a matrix of type $(n, 2n)$—replacing what was denoted in the last chapter by ϖ_1'—and 0 denotes a matrix of type $(n, 2p-2n)$ of which each element is zero; thence we have

$$\Pi = ak,$$

where k is a matrix of integers of type $(2n, 2p)$, in which the common divisor of determinants of type $(2n, 2n)$ is unity, this being obtained in fact from m^{-1} by omitting the last $(2p-2n)$ rows. Thus, in terms of the periods a, not only are the periods Π expressible with integer coefficients, but conversely, the formulae being $\Pi = ak$, $(a, 0) = \Pi m$. We can then find a matrix of integers k, of type $(2n, 2n)$ such that

$$fk\epsilon_{2p}\bar{k}\bar{f} = r\epsilon_{2n}$$

where r is a positive integer, which we take as small as possible; then defining the matrix (μ, μ') of type $(n, 2n)$ by means of $(\mu, \mu') = af^{-1}$ we can form a theta function of n variables $\Theta(\mu^{-1}u, \sigma)$, where $\sigma = \mu^{-1}\mu'$, it being a consequence of preceding formulae that the determinant of μ is not zero; and when $u_1, \ldots, u_n$ are increased by increments expressed by Πt, where t is a row of $2n$ integers, the arguments $\mu^{-1}u$ of the theta function are increased by the n quantities $l + \sigma l'$, where the integers l, l' are defined by $(l, l') = fkt$. We can thus construct single valued meromorphic functions of n variables $w_1, \ldots, w_n$ which have the periods a, or, what is the same thing, the periods Π; denote such a function in general by $\psi(w, a)$. Replacing $w_1, \ldots, w_n$ by the integrals $u_1, \ldots, u_n$, regarded as functions of a place (x) on the Riemann surface, such a function, being single valued on the undissected Riemann surface, is a rational function of (x); but we may more generally substitute

$$w_r = u_r^{x_1, z_1} + \ldots + u_r^{x_m, z_m}, \qquad (r = 1, \ldots, n),$$

m being arbitrary, and the function $\psi(w, a)$ is then a rational function of the $2m$ places $(x_1), \ldots, (x_m), (z_1), \ldots, (z_m)$.

In the case arrived at in the last chapter the equation $f(x, y, \lambda_1, \ldots, \lambda_n) = 0$, associated with the Riemann surface, is satisfied by $x = f(w)$, $y = \chi(w)$ where $f(w)$, $\chi(w)$ are single valued meromorphic functions of n variables $w_1, \ldots, w_n$, these variables being connected by $(n-1)$ relations of the form $F_k(w) = 0$, where $F_k(w)$ are also single valued meromorphic functions. All these meromorphic functions have $2n$ sets of simultaneous periods, namely those denoted above by ϖ', the periods of any one of these sets, say the s-th, being $\left(\frac{1}{c_s}\right)$th of the elements of the s-th set of periods a. Such a function may be denoted by $\psi(w, \varpi')$; it manifestly has the periods Π, or the periods a, and if $w_1, \ldots, w_n$ be replaced by the values at the point (x) of the Riemann surface of the integrals of the first kind $u_1, \ldots, u_n$, the function becomes a rational function on the Riemann surface; and we saw that if $u_1, \dots, u_n$ be the values at a point (x) of the integrals of the first kind, the arguments

$$w_1 = u_1 + \frac{N}{c_s} a_{1,s}, \quad w_2 = u_2 + \frac{N}{c_s} a_{2,s}, \quad \dots, \quad w_n = u_n + \frac{N}{c_s} a_{n,s},$$

wherein N is an integer, for which the function $\psi(w, \varpi')$ has the same value as for $w_1 = u_1, \dots, w_n = u_n$, do not arise on the Riemann surface unless N is an integral multiple of c_s.

In general for a Riemann surface having p integrals of the first kind, of which n integrals form a defective system, if, with the notation explained above, $\psi(w, a)$ be a single valued meromorphic function, and $u_1, \dots, u_n$ be the defective integrals regarded as functions of the place (x) of the surface, the function $\psi(u, a)$ is a rational function, as remarked. Taking two such rational functions $\xi = \psi_1(u, a)$, $\eta = \psi_2(u, a)$, it may be possible to choose these so that at the places where ξ has some one value, the corresponding values of η are all different: in that case x and y are expressible as rational functions of ξ and η, which are themselves connected by a rational equation; the values $u_1, \dots, u_n$, being functions of one place (x), are connected by $(n-1)$ relations, and, subject to these, the equation associated with the Riemann surface can be solved by single valued meromorphic functions of n variables. Or it may be that ψ_1, ψ_2 cannot be so chosen: then the values of η corresponding to a given value of ξ are each repeated a certain number say λ times, and the rational algebraic equation giving all the values of η corresponding to any value of ξ reduces to the λ-th power of an irreducible equation; then each of x and y satisfies an algebraic equation of order λ, the coefficients of which are rational in ξ and η and are thus single valued meromorphic functions. This latter case always arises when $n = 1$, $p > 1$, that is when there is a single integral of the first kind whose periods are expressible by only two quantities; for every algebraic equation connecting single valued meromorphic doubly periodic functions has $p = 1$: thus, if for an algebraic equation $f(x, y) = 0$ there be an integral of the first kind whose periods reduce to two, both x and y are roots of algebraic equations whose coefficients are rational in two quantities ξ, η connected by an equation of the form $\eta^2 = 4\xi^3 - g_2\xi - g_3$; the defective integral can then be algebraically transformed to have the form, $\int d\xi/\eta$, of an elliptic integral. In the general case of $n > 1$ and $p > n$, it is not to be assumed that the defective integrals $u_1, \dots, u_n$ are algebraically transformable to the forms appropriate for integrals of the first kind upon any single Riemann surface of class (deficiency) n: when x and y are rationally expressible by $\xi = \psi_1(u)$, $\eta = \psi_2(u)$, the rational relation connecting ξ and η has, it is well known, the same number of linearly independent integrals of the first kind as the original algebraic relation connecting x and y, and when x and y are merely algebraic functions of ξ and η, it is by no means obvious that the algebraic relation connecting ξ and η is capable of only n integrals of the first kind.

65. In the general case of n defective integrals of the first kind upon a Riemann surface possessing p integrals of the first kind we shall define two numbers, which arise in stating following general theorems:

(*a*) The *Index* r, which has already occurred in the formula

$$fk\epsilon_{2p}\bar{k}\bar{f} = r\epsilon_{2n},$$

this number being given its smallest positive value. As follows from Appendix to Part II., Note II., below, r is the first invariant factor of the skew symmetrical matrix N of type $(2n, 2n)$ defined by $N = k\epsilon_{2p}\bar{k}$, namely is the determinant of N divided by the highest common factor of all determinants of N of type $(2n-1, 2n-1)$. It is easy to prove that if the matrix Π be reduced in any way to the form $a'k'$, where k' is a matrix of integers of type $(2n, 2p)$ whose determinants of type $(2n, 2n)$ have unity for their highest common factor, then the corresponding value of the index r', namely the first invariant factor of the matrix $N' = k'\epsilon_{2p}\bar{k}'$, is equal to r. For first, we have, as on p. 224, not only $aN\bar{a} = 0$, but also $-iaN\bar{a}_0x_0x > 0$; from the latter we can infer as before that the determinant $|N|$ is not zero and that the determinant of type $(2n, 2n)$ formed by the real and imaginary parts of a is not zero. Similarly for N' and a'. It is a well known fact (proved in the Appendix, as above) that k, k' may be regarded as the first $2n$ rows of unitary matrices of integers of type $(2p, 2p)$; thence the equation $\Pi = ak = a'k'$ gives $(a, 0)\,H = (a', 0)\,H'$, where 0 denotes a matrix of zeros of type $(2n, 2p-2n)$, and H, H' are such unitary matrices. Thus we have $(a, 0) = (a', 0)H'H^{-1}$, and thus $a = a'G$, where G is a matrix of integers of type $(2n, 2n)$; similarly $a' = aG'$; thus $a = aG'G$; hence if A be the matrix of type $(2n, 2n)$ formed by the real and imaginary parts of a, we have $A\,(G'G-1) = 0$, and therefore, as $|A|$ is not zero, $G'G = 1$. This shews that each of G, G' is a unitary matrix. Then $ak = a'k' = aG'k'$ similarly gives $k = G'k'$ and therefore $N = G'N'\bar{G}'$; the invariant factors of $G'N'\bar{G}'$ are however the same as those of N'.

(*b*) If for every n places $(x_1), \ldots, (x_n)$ upon the Riemann surface there be $\sigma - 1$ other sets each of n places, $(x_1'), \ldots, (x_n')$, not entirely coinciding with the set $(x_1), \ldots, (x_n)$, such that the n equations

$$u_r^{x_1', x_1} + u_r^{x_2', x_2} + \ldots + u_r^{x_n', x_n} \equiv 0, \text{ (mod. } \Pi) \qquad (r = 1, \ldots, n)$$

are all satisfied, we call σ the *Multiplicity*. It is understood that permutation of the places of a set among themselves is not counted as altering the set.

66. Consider now the theta function $\Theta(\mu^{-1}w, \sigma)$, where $\Pi = ak$, the matrix k of type $(2n, 2p)$ being unitary in the sense that its minor determinants of type $(2n, 2n)$ are coprime, $fk\epsilon_{2p}\bar{k}\bar{f} = r\epsilon_{2n}$, we put $a = (\mu, \mu')f$ and

$\sigma = \mu^{-1}\mu'$, and w_i denotes $u_i - e_i$, the integrals $u_1, \ldots, u_n$ being regarded as functions of the place (x) of the Riemann surface and $e_1, \ldots, e_n$ being constants. We proceed to prove that this function has nr zeros upon the Riemann surface. When the arguments u are increased by Πt, where t denotes a set of $2p$ integers, the arguments $v = \mu^{-1}u$ are increased by $l + \sigma l'$ where l, l' each denotes a set of n integers given by $(l, l') = fkt$, and the function $\log \Theta$ is increased by $-2\pi i l'(v + \frac{1}{2}\sigma l')$. Upon the Riemann surface dissected along the $2p$ canonical period loops (a_β), (a'_β) the function Θ is single valued and capable of expansion about every point as a power series in the parameter for this point; the number of its zeros is thus given by the integral

$$\frac{1}{2\pi i}\int d \log \Theta$$

taken once positively round the edges of the period loops. In passing from the right to the left side of the period loop (a_β), the increments Πt of the functions u are given by taking every element of t zero except $t_\beta = 1$; similarly for the passage over (a'_β) we have every element of t zero save $t_{p+\beta} = 1$; we put

$$fk = \begin{pmatrix} H & K \\ H' & K' \end{pmatrix}$$

wherein each of H, K, H', K' is a matrix of integers of type (n, p); then for the passage across (a_β) the increments of the arguments $\mu^{-1}w$ are $l + \sigma l'$ where

$$l_i = H_{i,\beta}, \qquad l'_i = H'_{i,\beta}, \qquad \begin{pmatrix} i = 1, 2, \ldots, p \\ \beta = 1, 2, \ldots, n \end{pmatrix},$$

and the corresponding values for the period loop (a'_β) are

$$l_i = K_{i,\beta}, \qquad l'_i = K'_{i,\beta};$$

the contribution to the integral above arising from the two sides of the loop (a_β) is thus

$$-\sum_i \int H'_{i,\beta}\,(\mu^{-1}_{i,1}du_1 + \ldots + \mu^{-1}_{i,n}du_n)$$

taken once along the positive side of (a_β), namely is

$$-\sum_i H'_{i,\beta}\,(\mu^{-1}_{i,1}\Pi_{1,p+\beta} + \ldots + \mu^{-1}_{i,n}\Pi_{n,p+\beta}),$$

which, as $\mu^{-1}\Pi = (1, \sigma) fk = (H + \sigma H'. K + \sigma K')$, is the same as

$$-\sum_i H'_{i,\beta}\,(K + \sigma K')_{i,\beta},$$

or

$$-[\bar{H}'(K + \sigma K')]_{\beta,\beta};$$

the contribution from the two sides of the loop (a'_β) will similarly be

$$+\sum_i K'_{i,\beta}\,(\mu^{-1}_{i,1}\Pi_{i,\beta} + \ldots + \mu^{-1}_{i,n}\Pi_{n,\beta}),$$

or

$$[\bar{K}'(H + \sigma H')]_{\beta,\beta};$$

thus, as $(\bar{H}'\sigma K')_{\beta,\beta} = (\bar{K}'\bar{\sigma}H')_{\beta,\beta} = (\bar{K}'\sigma H')_{\beta,\beta}$, the whole integral is

$$\sum_{\beta=1}^{p} (\bar{K}'H - \bar{H}'K)_{\beta,\beta},$$

which is

$$\sum_{\beta=1}^{p}\sum_{i=1}^{n} (K'_{i,\beta}H_{i,\beta} - H'_{i,\beta}K_{i,\beta}),$$

or

$$\sum_{i=1}^{n} (K'\bar{H} - H'\bar{K})_{i,i};$$

we have however

$$\begin{pmatrix} H & K \\ H' & K' \end{pmatrix} \epsilon_{2p} \begin{pmatrix} \bar{H} & \bar{H}' \\ \bar{K} & \bar{K}' \end{pmatrix} = r\epsilon_{2n},$$

or

$$\begin{pmatrix} K\bar{H} - H\bar{K} & K\bar{H}' - H\bar{K}' \\ K'\bar{H} - H'\bar{K} & K'\bar{H}' - H'\bar{K}' \end{pmatrix} = r\begin{pmatrix} 0 & -1 \\ 1 & 0 \end{pmatrix},$$

so that

$$K'\bar{H} - \bar{K}H = r.$$

Hence the number of places (x) *on the Riemann surface for which the function* $\Theta[\mu^{-1}(u-e), \sigma]$ *vanishes, is* nr.

In case $n = p$ we have $k = 1$, $f = 1$, $r = 1$ and the number of zeros is p; the above is a very obvious generalisation of the method, due to Riemann, whereby this number p is found in the ordinary case. We proceed to employ Riemann's method further to find a relation connecting the values of the integrals u at the rn zeros, which generalises the corresponding ordinary relation.

Use the same notation as before, $w_i = u_i - e_i$, $v_i = (\mu^{-1}w)_i$, let $(x_1), \ldots, (x_{rn})$ be the rn zeros of $\Theta(v, \sigma)$, and let U be any integral of the first kind. Suppose the function $\log \Theta$ rendered single valued by means of a series of loops round the zeros, these being connected with the period loops. Round the zero-loops the integral

$$\frac{1}{2\pi i}\int \log \Theta \,.\, dU$$

is equal to

$$-\sum_{j=1}^{rn} U^{x_j, c},$$

where (c) is the initial point of all these loops—which we suppose* to be also upon all the period loops; this value is equal to the value of the integral taken round all the period loops. For the period loop (a_β) the increment of $\frac{1}{2\pi i}\log\Theta$ is

$$M_\beta - vl' - \tfrac{1}{2}\sigma l'^2,$$

where M_β is a certain integer and

$$l'_i = H'_{i,\beta},$$

and the contribution to the integral arising from the two sides of (a_β) is

$$\int (M_\beta - vl' - \tfrac{1}{2}\sigma l'^2)\, dU,$$

* A diagram of such a dissection is given for example in the author's *Abel's Theorem*, p. 395.

taken once along the positive side of (a_β); this may be regarded as the sum of three parts

$$\int M_\beta dU, \qquad \int \epsilon l' dU, \qquad -\int (\mu^{-1}u \,.\, l' + \tfrac{1}{2}\sigma l'^2)\, dU,$$

where $\epsilon = \mu^{-1}e$; if Ω_β, Ω'_β are the periods of U for the period loops (a_β), (a'_β), the second part, containing $e_1, \ldots, e_n$ explicitly, is equal to

$$\sum_{i=1}^{n} \epsilon_i H'_{i,\beta} \Omega'_\beta\,;$$

similarly for the loop (a'_β) we have a part containing $e_1, \ldots, e_n$ explicitly, which is equal to

$$-\sum_{i=1}^{n} \epsilon_i K'_{i,\beta} \Omega_\beta.$$

If in particular U is the integral u_q, then (Ω, Ω') consists of the q-th row of Π, or $ak, = (\mu, \mu') fk, = (\mu H + \mu' H', \mu K + \mu' K')$; then the part containing $e_1, \ldots, e_n$ explicitly, from the whole integral round the $2p$-period loops, is

$$\sum_{i=1}^{n} \epsilon_i \sum_{\beta=1}^{p} [H'_{i,\beta} (\mu K + \mu' K')_{q,\beta} - K'_{i,\beta} (\mu H + \mu' H')_{q,\beta}],$$

or

$$\sum_{i=1}^{n} \epsilon_i [(\mu K + \mu' K') \overline{H}' - (\mu H + \mu' H') \overline{K}']_{q,i},$$

or

$$\{[\mu (K\overline{H}' - H\overline{K}') + \mu' (K'\overline{H}' - H'\overline{K}')] \epsilon\}_q\,;$$

we have however

$$K\overline{H}' - H\overline{K}' = -r, \quad K'\overline{H}' - H'\overline{K}' = 0,$$

so that this reduces to

$$-r (\mu\epsilon)_q, = -r e_q.$$

The parts such as $\int M_\beta dU$ give altogether

$$\sum_\beta (M_\beta \Pi'_{q,\beta} - M'_\beta \Pi_{q,\beta}).$$

If we take another set of values for $e_1, \ldots, e_n$, the remaining parts of the whole integral, built up from contributions of the form

$$-\int (\mu^{-1}u \,.\, l' + \tfrac{1}{2}\sigma l'^2)\, dU,$$

will be unaffected. *On the whole then we can infer that if* (m_j), *for* $j = 1, \ldots, (rn)$, *be the zeros of the function*

$$\Theta\, (\mu^{-1} u^{x,\, m}, \sigma)$$

where (m) *is an arbitrary place of the Riemann surface, and* (x_j) *the zeros of the function*

$$\Theta\, [\mu^{-1} (u^{x,\, m} - e), \sigma],$$

then

$$\sum_{j=1}^{rn} u_q^{x_j,\, m_j} \equiv r e_q, \qquad (q = 1, 2, \ldots, n),$$

where the sign $\equiv$ indicates the omission of a linear aggregate of periods of the function $u_q^{x,m}$ with integral coefficients which are the same for all values of q.

For the case $n = p$, giving $r = 1$, this becomes a well known equation; in that case the congruences

$$\sum_{j=1}^{p} u_q^{x_j, m_j} \equiv e_q$$

suffice to determine the set (x_j) without ambiguity, and we can infer that the function

$$\Theta\{\mu^{-1}(u^{x,m} - u^{x_1,m_1} - \dots - u^{x_p,m_p}), \sigma\}$$

has the places $(x_1), \dots, (x_p)$ for zeros. But when $n < p$ we may have n equations of the form

$$u_q^{x'_1, x_1} + u_q^{x'_2, x_2} + \dots + u_q^{x'_n, x_n} \equiv 0,$$

as will be seen. Thus, though the rn zeros are, of course, determined by $e_1, \dots, e_n$, the n equations

$$\sum_{j=1}^{rn} u_q^{x_j, m_j} \equiv re_q$$

are not, by themselves, sufficient to determine these zeros.

67. The question naturally arises of the relation of the theta function of n variables just discussed to the theta function, $\Theta(V, \tau)$, of p variables, associated with the Riemann surface. We proceed to shew that there is a theta function of p variables, obtained by a transformation of order r, which contains as a factor the theta function of n variables.

The most general set of periods for a normal integral V_λ being of the form

$$\alpha_{\lambda,\mu} + \tau_{\lambda,1}\alpha'_{1,\mu} + \tau_{\lambda,2}\alpha'_{2,\mu} + \dots + \tau_{\lambda,p}\alpha'_{p,\mu}, \quad (\mu = 1, 2, \dots, (2p)),$$

wherein $\alpha_{\lambda,\mu}$, $\alpha'_{\nu,\mu}$ are integers, consider a matrix of periods for the normal integrals $V_1, \dots, V_p$, of type $(p, 2p)$, given by

$$(\alpha + \tau\alpha', \quad \beta + \tau\beta'),$$

or say

$$(1, \tau)\Delta,$$

where

$$\Delta = \begin{pmatrix} \alpha, & \beta \\ \alpha', & \beta' \end{pmatrix}$$

is a matrix of integers; take, correspondingly, such a set of linear functions $W_1, \dots, W_p$ of $V_1, \dots, V_p$ that for $W_1, \dots, W_p$, which are also integrals of the first kind, the period scheme reduces to the form $(1, \tau')$; that is, take

$$W = (\alpha + \tau\alpha')^{-1} V, \quad (\alpha + \tau\alpha')\tau' = \beta + \tau\beta';$$

in taking these it is provisionally assumed that the matrix $\alpha + \tau\alpha'$ is of non-vanishing determinant. The matrix τ is symmetrical, so that we have

$$(1, \tau)\epsilon_{2p}\begin{pmatrix} 1 \\ \overline{\tau} \end{pmatrix} = 0;$$

in order that τ' may be symmetrical we must similarly have

$$(1, \tau')\epsilon_{2p}\begin{pmatrix}1\\ \bar{\tau}'\end{pmatrix} = 0;$$

now if $P = \alpha + \tau\alpha'$, $Q = \beta + \tau\beta'$, we have $(1, \tau') = P^{-1}(1, \tau)\Delta$; thus we require

$$(1, \tau)\Delta\epsilon_{2p}\bar{\Delta}\begin{pmatrix}1\\ \bar{\tau}\end{pmatrix} = 0.$$

We assume then that the matrix Δ satisfies the equation

$$\Delta\epsilon_{2p}\bar{\Delta} = r\epsilon_{2p},$$

where r is a positive integer; we can then at once prove that the determinant of $\alpha + \tau\alpha'$ is not zero, that τ' is symmetrical and not of zero determinant, and that the real part of the quadratic form $i\tau'k^2$, where k is a row of p real quantities not all zero, is necessarily negative. The relation $\Delta\epsilon_{2p}\Delta = r\epsilon_{2p}$ is equivalent with $\bar{\Delta}^{-1}\epsilon_{2p}\Delta^{-1} = \frac{1}{r}\epsilon_{2n}$ and therefore with $\bar{\Delta}\epsilon_{2p}\Delta = r\epsilon_{2p}$.

For let y be a row of p quantities, not all zero, y_0 the row of conjugate complex quantities,

$$P = \alpha + \tau\alpha', \quad Q = \beta + \tau\beta' \text{ and } z = \begin{pmatrix}\bar{P}\\ \bar{Q}\end{pmatrix} y = (\bar{P}y, \bar{Q}y),$$

a set of $2p$ quantities; we have, since r is positive, (cf. p. 224)

$$\begin{aligned} 0 &< -ir(\tau - \tau_0)y_0y \\ &= -ir(1, \tau)\epsilon_{2p}\begin{pmatrix}1\\ \tau_0\end{pmatrix} y_0y = -i(1, \tau)\Delta\epsilon_{2p}\bar{\Delta}\begin{pmatrix}1\\ \tau_0\end{pmatrix} y_0y \\ &= -i(P, Q)\epsilon_{2p}\begin{pmatrix}\bar{P}_0\\ \bar{Q}_0\end{pmatrix} y_0y = -i\epsilon_{2p}z_0z = -i\epsilon_{2p}(\bar{P}_0y_0, \bar{Q}_0y_0)(\bar{P}y, \bar{Q}y) \\ &= -i(\bar{P}_0y_0 \,.\, \bar{Q}y - \bar{P}y \,.\, \bar{Q}_0y_0); \end{aligned}$$

this shews that the set y cannot be chosen, other than all zero, to make $\bar{P}y = 0$, $\bar{P}_0y_0$; thus the determinant of P is not zero; nor, similarly, is the determinant of Q, and the equation $P\tau' = Q$ determines τ', and $|\tau'| \neq 0$.

Further

$$(1, \tau)\epsilon_{2p}\begin{pmatrix}1\\ \bar{\tau}\end{pmatrix} = 0$$

gives at once, since $(1, \tau') = P^{-1}(1, \tau)\Delta$,

$$(1, \tau')\epsilon_{2p}\begin{pmatrix}1\\ \bar{\tau}'\end{pmatrix} = 0,$$

so that τ' is symmetrical; and similarly from

$$-i(1, \tau)\epsilon_{2p}\begin{pmatrix}1\\ \tau_0\end{pmatrix} y_0y > 0,$$

since

$$-i(1, \tau')\epsilon_{2p}\begin{pmatrix}1\\ \tau_0'\end{pmatrix} y_0y = -iP^{-1}(1, \tau)\Delta\epsilon_{2p}\bar{\Delta}\begin{pmatrix}1\\ \tau_0\end{pmatrix}\bar{P}_0^{-1}y_0y = -ir(1, \tau)\epsilon_{2p}\begin{pmatrix}1\\ \tau_0\end{pmatrix} t_0t,$$

where $t = \bar{P}^{-1}y$, we see that the real part of $i\tau' k^2$ is negative, and not zero, for all real values of $k_1, \ldots, k_p$ for which these are not all zero.

Now it is a known property that a matrix of integers Δ satisfying the relation $\Delta \epsilon_{2p} \bar{\Delta} = r\epsilon_{2p}$ can be constructed when the first n columns, and the $(p+1)$th to the $(p+n)$th columns only are given, provided that, of the relations expressed by $\Delta \epsilon_{2p} \bar{\Delta} = r\epsilon_{2p}$, all which contain only the elements of the given $2n$ columns are satisfied. (Frobenius, *Crelle*, LXXXIX. (1880), p. 40, or the author's *Abel's Theorem*, p. 676.)

Consider then a matrix in which the first n columns and the $(p+1)$th to the $(p+n)$th columns are given respectively by

$$\begin{pmatrix} \bar{K}' \\ -\bar{H}' \end{pmatrix} \text{ and } \begin{pmatrix} -\bar{K} \\ \bar{H} \end{pmatrix},$$

where H, K etc. are the matrices of integers occurring in the previous article (p. 233), and

$$\Pi = (\Omega, \Omega') = (\mu, \mu') \begin{pmatrix} H, & K \\ H', & K' \end{pmatrix},$$

so that we may write

$$\begin{pmatrix} \alpha, & \beta \\ \alpha', & \beta' \end{pmatrix} = \begin{pmatrix} \bar{K}', & \ldots, & -\bar{K}, & \ldots \\ -\bar{H}', & \ldots, & \bar{H}, & \ldots \end{pmatrix};$$

the equation $\bar{\Delta}\epsilon_{2p}\Delta = r\epsilon_{2p}$ is equivalent with

$$\bar{\alpha}\alpha' - \bar{\alpha}'\alpha = 0, \quad \bar{\beta}\beta' - \bar{\beta}'\beta = 0, \quad \bar{\alpha}\beta' - \bar{\alpha}'\beta = \bar{\beta}'\alpha - \bar{\beta}\alpha' = r,$$

and of these, the relations containing only the elements of the first n and the $(p+1)$th to $(p+n)$th columns of Δ are

$$K'\bar{H}' - H'\bar{K}' = 0, \quad K\bar{H} - H\bar{K} = 0, \quad K'\bar{H} - H'\bar{K} = H\bar{K}' - KH' = r,$$

which we know to be satisfied (p. 234); the matrix Δ can then be constructed as prescribed.

If $V_1, \ldots, V_p$ be the normal integrals on the Riemann surface, we have, as before, (p. 223)

$$u = \Omega V = (\mu H + \mu' H')V, \quad \Omega' = \Omega\tau = \mu K + \mu' K',$$

and hence, with $\sigma = \mu^{-1}\mu'$,

$$K + \sigma K' = (H + \sigma H')\tau,$$

or

$$(\bar{K}' - \tau\bar{H}')\sigma = -\bar{K} + \tau\bar{H};$$

now the first n columns of the matrix $\alpha + \tau\alpha'$ form the matrix $\bar{K}' - \tau\bar{H}'$, and the first n columns of the matrix $\beta + \tau\beta'$ form the matrix $-\bar{K} + \tau\bar{H}$; thus if we write

$$\alpha + \tau\alpha' = (\bar{K}' - \tau\bar{H}', R), \quad \beta + \tau\beta' = (-\bar{K} + \tau\bar{H}, S), \quad \tau' = \begin{pmatrix} \tau_1', & \bar{\tau}_2' \\ \tau_2', & \tau_3' \end{pmatrix},$$

where R, S are of type $(p, p-n)$ and τ_1' of type (n, n), the comparison of the first n columns of the matrices on the two sides of the equation

$$(\alpha + \tau\alpha')\tau' = \beta + \tau\beta',$$

leads to
$$(\bar{K}' - \tau\bar{H}')\tau_1' + R\tau_2' = -\bar{K} + \tau\bar{H};$$

thus, as $(\bar{K}' - \tau\bar{H}')\sigma = -\bar{K} + \tau\bar{H}$, we infer $\tau_1' = \sigma$, $\tau_2' = 0$, and the matrix τ' has the form
$$\tau' = \begin{pmatrix} \sigma & 0 \\ 0 & \rho \end{pmatrix}.$$

Therefore, if k denote a row of p integers, the quadratic form $\tau'k^2$ is a sum of two quadratic forms respectively in $k_1, \ldots, k_n$ and $k_{n+1}, \ldots, k_p$, say

$$\tau'k^2 = \sigma t^2 + \rho t'^2,$$

and the theta function associated with the Riemann surface,

$$\Theta(U, \tau') = \sum_{k=-\infty}^{\infty} \exp.\, 2\pi i\,(kU + \tfrac{1}{2}\tau'k^2),$$

is a product of two theta functions respectively of n variables and $p-n$ variables, namely

$$\sum_{t=-\infty}^{\infty} \exp.\, 2\pi i\,(tU^{(1)} + \tfrac{1}{2}\sigma t^2), \qquad \sum_{t'=-\infty}^{\infty} \exp.\, 2\pi i\,(t'U^{(2)} + \tfrac{1}{2}\rho t'^2),$$

where $U^{(1)}$ denotes the set $U_1, \ldots, U_n$ and $U^{(2)}$ the set $U_{n+1}, \ldots, U_p$.

And if $V_1, \ldots, V_p$ be the normal integrals of the first kind, and $u_1, \ldots, u_n$ the defective integrals, we have

$$\mu^{-1}u = (H + \sigma H')V;$$

now the p integrals $(\alpha + \tau\alpha')^{-1}V$ are the same as $\frac{1}{r}(\bar{\beta}' - \tau\bar{\alpha}')V$; the first n rows of $\bar{\beta}'$ constitute the matrix H, the first n rows of $\bar{\alpha}'$ constitute the matrix $-H'$; thus, as the first n rows of τ' are $(\sigma, 0)$, the first n rows of $\bar{\beta}' - \tau'\bar{\alpha}'$ form the matrix $H + \sigma H'$; therefore, putting

$$W = (\alpha + \tau\alpha')^{-1}V = \frac{1}{r}(\bar{\beta}' - \tau'\bar{\alpha}')V,$$

the arguments $\mu^{-1}u$ are $rW_1, rW_2, \ldots, rW_n$. *Thus the function of n variables*

$$\Theta(\mu^{-1}u, \sigma)$$

previously considered, is a factor of the function of p variables

$$\Theta(rW, \tau');$$

herein W denotes a set of linearly independent integrals of the first kind, having a period matrix $(1, \tau')$; this period matrix does not correspond however to a canonical dissection of the Riemann surface, but to such a set of $2p$ loops as gives for the normal integrals V a period matrix $(\alpha + \tau\alpha', \beta + \tau\beta')$; it is only when $r = 1$ that a new system of canonical loops can be drawn for which the period matrix, for the integrals V, is $(\alpha + \tau\alpha', \beta + \tau\beta')$. (See for example the author's *Abel's Theorem*, Chaps. XVIII. and XX.) The theorem that

$$\Theta\,[(\bar{\beta}' - \tau'\bar{\alpha}')\,V, \tau']/\Theta[(H + \sigma H')V, \sigma]$$

is an integral function of $V_1, \ldots, V_p$, is manifestly proved when $V_1, \ldots, V_p$ are p arbitrary arguments.

It follows at once from the preceding equations that beside the system of n defective integrals of the first kind, there is upon the Riemann surface, another system of $p - n$ defective integrals.

For introduce names for the remaining columns of the matrix Δ, writing

$$\begin{pmatrix} \alpha, & \beta \\ \alpha', & \beta' \end{pmatrix} = \begin{pmatrix} (\bar{K}', & \bar{Q}'), & -(\bar{K}, & \bar{Q}) \\ -(\bar{H}', & \bar{P}'), & (\bar{H}, & \bar{P}) \end{pmatrix},$$

leading to

$$r\begin{pmatrix} \alpha, & \beta \\ \alpha', & \beta' \end{pmatrix}^{-1} = \begin{pmatrix} \bar{\beta}', & -\bar{\beta} \\ -\bar{\alpha}', & \bar{\alpha} \end{pmatrix} = \begin{pmatrix} \begin{pmatrix} H \\ P \end{pmatrix}, & \begin{pmatrix} K \\ Q \end{pmatrix} \\ \begin{pmatrix} H' \\ P' \end{pmatrix}, & \begin{pmatrix} K' \\ Q' \end{pmatrix} \end{pmatrix},$$

each of the matrices P, Q, P', Q' being of type $(p-n, p)$. Then the p integrals rW, given by

$$rW = (\bar{\beta}' - \tau'\bar{\alpha}')\,V,$$

are

$$\left\{\begin{pmatrix} H \\ P \end{pmatrix} + \begin{pmatrix} \sigma & 0 \\ 0 & \rho \end{pmatrix}\begin{pmatrix} H' \\ P' \end{pmatrix}\right\}V, \quad = \begin{pmatrix} H + \sigma H' \\ P + \rho P' \end{pmatrix}V,$$

and consist of the n integrals $(H + \sigma H')V$ and the $(p-n)$ integrals $(P + \rho P')V$. The period scheme of the integrals rW is thus

$$\begin{pmatrix} H + \sigma H', & (H + \sigma H')\tau \\ P + \rho P', & (P + \rho P')\tau \end{pmatrix};$$

we have however
$$\tau'(\bar{\alpha} + \bar{\alpha}'\tau) = \bar{\beta} + \bar{\beta}'\tau,$$

or
$$\begin{pmatrix} \sigma & 0 \\ 0 & \rho \end{pmatrix}\left\{\begin{pmatrix} K' \\ Q' \end{pmatrix} - \begin{pmatrix} H' \\ P' \end{pmatrix}\tau\right\} = -\begin{pmatrix} K \\ Q \end{pmatrix} + \begin{pmatrix} H \\ P \end{pmatrix}\tau,$$

that is
$$\sigma(K' - H'\tau) = -K + H\tau, \quad \rho(Q' - P'\tau) = -Q + P\tau,$$

or
$$(H + \sigma H')\tau = K + \sigma K', \qquad (P + \rho P')\tau = Q + \rho Q',$$

and the period scheme of the integrals rW is thus

$$\begin{pmatrix} H + \sigma H', & K + \sigma K' \\ P + \rho P', & Q + \rho Q' \end{pmatrix},$$

shewing that the period scheme of the integrals $(P + \rho P')V$ is

$$(P + \rho P', \quad Q + \rho Q'),$$

namely that the periods of these integrals are sums of integral multiples of the $2(p-n)$ quantities $(1, \rho)$. The integrals $(P + \rho P')V$ thus form a second defective system; this we may fairly speak of as complementary to the former.

We have further

$$\begin{pmatrix} \begin{pmatrix} H \\ P \end{pmatrix}, & \begin{pmatrix} K \\ Q \end{pmatrix} \\ \begin{pmatrix} H' \\ P' \end{pmatrix}, & \begin{pmatrix} K' \\ Q' \end{pmatrix} \end{pmatrix} \epsilon_{2p} \begin{pmatrix} (\bar{H}, \bar{P}), & (\bar{H}', \bar{P}') \\ (\bar{K}, \bar{Q}), & (\bar{K}', \bar{Q}') \end{pmatrix} = r\epsilon_{2p};$$

the left side is found to be

$$\begin{pmatrix} \begin{pmatrix} K\bar{H} - H\bar{K}, & K\bar{P} - H\bar{Q} \\ Q\bar{H} - P\bar{K}, & Q\bar{P} - P\bar{Q} \end{pmatrix}, & \begin{pmatrix} K\bar{H}' - H\bar{K}', & K\bar{P}' - H\bar{Q}' \\ Q\bar{H}' - P\bar{K}', & Q\bar{P}' - P\bar{Q}' \end{pmatrix}, \\ \begin{pmatrix} K'\bar{H} - H'\bar{K}, & K'\bar{P} - H'\bar{Q} \\ Q'\bar{H} - P'\bar{K}, & Q'\bar{P} - P'\bar{Q} \end{pmatrix}, & \begin{pmatrix} K'\bar{H}' - H'\bar{K}', & K'\bar{P}' - H'\bar{Q}' \\ Q'\bar{H}' - P'\bar{K}', & Q'\bar{P}' - P'\bar{Q}' \end{pmatrix} \end{pmatrix}$$

and we can thus infer, beside

$$\begin{pmatrix} H & K \\ H' & K' \end{pmatrix} \epsilon_{2p} \begin{pmatrix} \bar{H} & \bar{H}' \\ \bar{K} & \bar{K}' \end{pmatrix} = r\epsilon_{2n},$$

that also

$$\begin{pmatrix} P & Q \\ P' & Q' \end{pmatrix} \epsilon_{2p} \begin{pmatrix} \bar{P} & \bar{P}' \\ \bar{Q} & \bar{Q}' \end{pmatrix} = r\epsilon_{2p-2n},$$

and

$$\begin{pmatrix} H & K \\ H' & K' \end{pmatrix} \epsilon_{2p} \begin{pmatrix} \bar{P} & \bar{P}' \\ \bar{Q} & \bar{Q}' \end{pmatrix} = 0.$$

The complementary system of defective integrals is thus, like the original system, of index r*.

68. We can prove that the function of p variables

$$\Theta(rW, \tau'), = \Theta[(\bar{\beta}' - \tau'\bar{\alpha}')V, \tau'],$$

regarded as a function of the place (x) of the Riemann surface, has rp zeros.

We have from $(\alpha + \tau\alpha')\tau' = \beta + \tau\beta'$ the equation

$$(\bar{\beta}' - \tau'\bar{\alpha}')\tau = -\bar{\beta} + \tau'\bar{\alpha},$$

---

* It is shewn in the Appendix to Part II., Note I., that we can write the matrix $\begin{pmatrix} P & Q \\ P' & Q' \end{pmatrix}$ in the form

$$\begin{pmatrix} P & Q \\ P' & Q' \end{pmatrix} = f'k',$$

where f' is of type $(2p-2n, 2p-2n)$, and k' is of type $(2p-2n, 2p)$ and has unity for the greatest common divisor of its determinants of order $2p-2n$, and that the most general forms of f', k' are $f'a$, $a^{-1}k'$, where a is a unitary matrix of type $(2p-2n, 2p-2n)$. And, in Note II., that a matrix f'' can be found such that

$$f''k'\epsilon_{2p}\bar{k}'\bar{f}'' = s\epsilon_{2p-2n},$$

where s is the first invariant factor of $k'\epsilon_{2p}\bar{k}'$. It follows from Appendix, Note II., that s divides r, and it appears probable that $s = r$, but this is not proved here. In the case of the matrix $\begin{pmatrix} H & K \\ H' & K' \end{pmatrix}$ the number r was introduced as the first invariant factor; but in the applications that have been given of the index it was the equation

$$\begin{pmatrix} H & K \\ H' & K' \end{pmatrix} \epsilon_{2p} \begin{pmatrix} \bar{H} & \bar{H}' \\ \bar{K} & \bar{K}' \end{pmatrix} = r\epsilon_{2n}$$

that was utilised.

and hence when the normal integrals V increase by $l+\tau l'$ the arguments $(\bar\beta'-\tau\bar\alpha')V$ increase by

$$(\bar\beta'-\tau'\bar\alpha')\,l+(-\bar\beta+\tau'\bar\alpha)\,l',$$

or

$$\bar\beta' l-\bar\beta l'+\tau'(-\bar\alpha' l+\bar\alpha l'),$$

or, say

$$k+\tau' k',$$

where $(k,k')=\begin{pmatrix}\bar\beta' & -\bar\beta\\ -\bar\alpha' & \bar\alpha\end{pmatrix}(l,l')=r\Delta^{-1}(l,l'),=\begin{pmatrix}M & N\\ M' & N'\end{pmatrix}(l,l')$, say,

and the function is multiplied by

$$\exp\left[-2\pi i\,(rWk'+\tfrac{1}{2}\tau' k'^2)\right].$$

Thus, considering the integral

$$\frac{1}{2\pi i}\int d\log\Theta\,(rW,\tau')$$

round the sides of the $2p$ canonical period loops for the integrals V, the contribution from the two sides of the loop (a_β) is

$$-\int d\,(rWk'),$$

taken once along the positive side of the loop, namely is the value, for $l_\beta=1$ and (l,l') otherwise zero, of

$$-\sum_{\gamma=1}^{p}k_\gamma'\,[(\bar\beta'-\tau'\bar\alpha')\,\tau]_{\gamma,\beta},$$

or

$$-\sum_{\gamma=1}^{p}M'_{\gamma\beta}\,(N+\tau' N')_{\gamma,\beta},$$

or

$$-[\bar M'(N+\tau' N')]_{\beta,\beta},$$

and the contribution from the two sides of the loop (a_β') is

$$-\int d\,(rWk'),$$

taken once positively along (a_β'), namely is the value, for $l'_\beta=1$, and (l,l') otherwise zero, of

$$\sum_{\gamma=1}^{p}k_\gamma'(\bar\beta'-\tau'\bar\alpha')_{\gamma,\beta}=\sum_{\gamma=1}^{p}N'_{\gamma,\beta}(M+\tau' M')_{\gamma,\beta}=[\bar N'(M+\tau' M')]_{\beta,\beta}=[(\bar M+\bar M'\tau')N']_{\beta,\beta}.$$

The number of zeros is thus

$$\sum_{\beta=1}^{p}(\bar M N'-\bar M' N)_{\beta,\beta}=\sum_{\beta=1}^{p}(\beta'\bar\alpha-\alpha'\bar\beta)_{\beta,\beta},$$

which is rp. Of these rp zeros we have shewn that rn belong to the factor $\Theta\,(\mu^{-1}u,\sigma)$.

The preceding result becomes easy to understand from another point of view. We proceed to prove that the function of p variables $\Theta\,(rW,\tau')$ is, save for an exponential factor, a polynomial of order r in 2^p functions $\Theta(V, \tau \mid q)$.

Let A denote the matrix

$$A = (\beta' - \alpha'\tau')\bar{\alpha}';$$

the relation $\Delta\epsilon_{2p}\bar{\Delta} = r\epsilon_{2p}$ is the same as

$$\begin{pmatrix} \beta\bar{\alpha} - \alpha\bar{\beta} & \beta\bar{\alpha}' - \alpha\bar{\beta}' \\ \beta'\bar{\alpha} - \alpha'\bar{\beta} & \beta'\bar{\alpha}' - \alpha'\bar{\beta}' \end{pmatrix} = r\begin{pmatrix} 0 & -1 \\ 1 & 0 \end{pmatrix},$$

so that A is a symmetrical matrix; let γ denote the p integers forming the diagonal of the matrix $\beta\bar{\alpha}$, and γ' the p integers forming the diagonal of $\beta'\bar{\alpha}'$; let V denote any p arguments; put

$$\phi(V, \tau) = e^{-\pi i A V^2}\,\Theta[(\bar{\beta}' - \tau'\bar{\alpha}')V, \tau'].$$

We have then, if l, l' be rows of p arbitrary integers,

$$\phi(V + l + \tau l', \tau)/\phi(V, \tau) = \exp[-2\pi i H],$$

where $$H = (\bar{\beta}' - \tau'\bar{\alpha}')Vk' + \tfrac{1}{2}\tau'k'^2 + \tfrac{1}{2}A[(V + l + \tau l')^2 - V^2],$$

the integers k, k' being, as before, given by

$$(k, k') = \begin{pmatrix} \bar{\beta}', & -\bar{\beta} \\ -\bar{\alpha}', & \bar{\alpha} \end{pmatrix}(l, l');$$

we proceed to shew that save for integers, the addition of which will not affect the value of $e^{-2\pi i H}$, we have

$$H = r(Vl' + \tfrac{1}{2}\tau l'^2) + \tfrac{1}{2}\gamma l' - \tfrac{1}{2}\gamma' l;$$

for in H the terms containing V are

$$(\bar{\beta}' - \tau'\bar{\alpha}')Vk' + A(l + \tau l')V,$$

or $$[(\beta' - \alpha'\tau')(-\bar{\alpha}'l + \bar{\alpha}l') + (\beta' - \alpha'\tau')\bar{\alpha}'(l + \tau l')]V,$$

or $$(\beta' - \alpha'\tau')(\bar{\alpha} + \bar{\alpha}'\tau)l'V,$$

or, since $$(\alpha + \tau\alpha')\tau' = \beta + \tau\beta', \quad \tau'(\bar{\alpha} + \bar{\alpha}'\tau) = \bar{\beta} + \bar{\beta}'\tau,$$

they are $$[\beta'(\bar{\alpha} + \bar{\alpha}'\tau) - \alpha'(\bar{\beta} + \bar{\beta}'\tau)]\,l'V,$$

or $$rl'V;$$

and the terms in H, of dimension 2 in l, l', are

$$\tfrac{1}{2}\tau'k'^2 + \tfrac{1}{2}A(l + \tau l')^2,$$

or $$\tfrac{1}{2}\tau'(-\bar{\alpha}'l + \bar{\alpha}l')(-\bar{\alpha}'l + \bar{\alpha}l') + \tfrac{1}{2}(\beta' - \alpha'\tau')\bar{\alpha}'(l + \tau l')^2,$$

or $$-\tfrac{1}{2}\alpha'\tau'(-\bar{\alpha}'l + \bar{\alpha}l')\,l + \tfrac{1}{2}\alpha\tau'(-\bar{\alpha}'l + \bar{\alpha}l')\,l'$$
$$+ \tfrac{1}{2}(\beta' - \alpha'\tau')\bar{\alpha}'l^2 + \tau(\beta' - \alpha'\tau')\bar{\alpha}'ll' + \tfrac{1}{2}\tau(\beta' - \alpha'\tau')\bar{\alpha}'\tau l'^2,$$

or $$\tfrac{1}{2}\beta'\bar{\alpha}'l^2 + [\tfrac{1}{2}\alpha\tau'\bar{\alpha} + \tfrac{1}{2}(-\beta + \alpha\tau')\bar{\alpha}'\tau]\,l'^2$$
$$+ [-\tfrac{1}{2}\alpha\tau'\bar{\alpha}' - \tfrac{1}{2}\alpha\tau'\bar{\alpha}' + (-\beta + \alpha\tau')\bar{\alpha}']\,ll',$$

that is $\frac{1}{2}\beta'\bar{a}'l^2 - \beta\bar{a}'ll' + [\frac{1}{2}\alpha\tau'(\bar{a} + \bar{a}'\tau) - \frac{1}{2}\beta(\bar{a}'\tau + \bar{a}) + \frac{1}{2}\beta\bar{a}]\, l'^2$

or, omitting integers, $\frac{1}{2}\beta'\bar{a}'l^2 + (\frac{1}{2}r\tau + \frac{1}{2}\beta\bar{a})\, l'^2$,

which, since $l_i^2 \equiv l_i$ (mod. 2), is equivalent, save for integers, with

$$\tfrac{1}{2}r\tau l'^2 + \tfrac{1}{2}\gamma l' - \tfrac{1}{2}\gamma' l.$$

On the whole then, as stated,

$$\phi(V + l + \tau l', \tau) = \exp[-2\pi i\, r(Vl' + \tfrac{1}{2}\tau l'^2) - \pi i\, \gamma l' + \pi i\, \gamma' l]\, \phi(V, \tau).$$

If for a moment we put

$$U = V + \frac{1}{2r}(\gamma + \tau\gamma'),$$

$$\psi(U, \tau) = e^{-\pi i\gamma' V}\phi(V, \tau),$$

we have

$$\frac{\psi(U + l + \tau l', \tau)}{\psi(U)} = e^{-\pi i\gamma'(l+\tau l') - 2\pi i r(Vl' + \frac{1}{2}\tau l'^2) - \pi i\gamma l' + \pi i\gamma' l}$$

$$= e^{-2\pi i r(Ul' + \frac{1}{2}\tau l'^2)},$$

and the function $\psi(U)$ is a particular case of that discussed p. 20 of Part I.; we thus have

$$\phi(V, \tau) = \sum_h B_h e^{\pi i\gamma' V}\Theta\left[rV + \tfrac{1}{2}(\gamma + \tau\gamma'),\, r\tau \left| \begin{matrix} h/r \\ 0 \end{matrix} \right.\right],$$

which, in virtue of the formula (p. 23, Part I.)

$$\Theta\left(v + q + \tau q', \tau \left| \begin{matrix} p' \\ p \end{matrix} \right.\right) = e^{-2\pi i q'(v + \frac{1}{2}\tau q') - 2\pi i q q' - 2\pi i p q'}\,\Theta\left(v, \tau \left| \begin{matrix} p' + q' \\ p + q \end{matrix} \right.\right),$$

is the same as

$$\phi(V, \tau) = \sum_h C_h\,\Theta\left[rV, r\tau \left| \begin{matrix} (h + \frac{1}{2}\gamma')/r \\ \frac{1}{2}\gamma \end{matrix} \right.\right],$$

where C_h is independent of V, and the summation extends to r^p terms, the symbol h denoting a row of p integers, each one of the set $0, 1, 2, \ldots, r-1$.

The function $\phi(V, \tau)$ is manifestly an even function of V; this is not the case for the single term $\Theta\left[rV, r\tau \left| \begin{matrix} (h + \frac{1}{2}\gamma')/r \\ \frac{1}{2}\gamma \end{matrix} \right.\right]$ occurring on the right; there arises then another term on the right corresponding with this one, and the expression on the right can be expressed in terms of less than r^p functions (*Abel's Theorem*, § 287). It can thence be shewn (*ibid.*, Chap. XX.) that $\phi(V, \tau)$ is expressible as a polynomial of the rth degree in 2^p theta functions of the form

$$\Theta\left(V, \tau \left| \begin{matrix} \frac{1}{2}\mu' \\ \frac{1}{2}\mu \end{matrix} \right.\right)$$

differing from one another only in their half-integer characteristics $\frac{1}{2}\begin{pmatrix} \mu' \\ \mu \end{pmatrix}$.

The function of n variables $\Theta(\mu^{-1}u, \sigma)$, whose arguments are linear functions of the p variables $V_1, \ldots, V_p$, is then a factor of this polynomial in the functions $\Theta\left[V, \tau \,\middle|\, \tfrac{1}{2}\binom{\mu'}{\mu}\right]$, in the sense that the quotient of these functions is an integral function of $V_1, \ldots, V_p$, for arbitrary values of these.

When V is regarded as the set of normal integrals of the first kind on the Riemann surface, each of these last theta functions, $\Theta\left[V, \tau;\, \tfrac{1}{2}\binom{\mu'}{\mu}\right]$, regarded as depending upon the place (x), is known to have p zeros; it is then to be expected that the polynomial of r-th degree in these functions, to which $\phi(V, \tau)$ is equal, should have rp zeros—as was previously proved.

69. If m denote the diagonal matrix of type (p, p) having all elements zero save those in the diagonal, the first n of which are each -1, the last $p-n$ of which are each $+1$, it is at once seen that the matrix, of type $(2p, 2p)$,

$$\begin{pmatrix} m & 0 \\ 0 & m \end{pmatrix},$$

belongs to a linear transformation; and that this transformation, applied to the period matrix

$$\tau' = \begin{pmatrix} \sigma & 0 \\ 0 & \rho \end{pmatrix},$$

leaves this unaltered. And hence that, when

$$\Delta = \begin{pmatrix} \alpha & \beta \\ \alpha' & \beta' \end{pmatrix}$$

is the matrix, belonging to a transformation of order r, of p. 238, the matrix

$$\Delta \begin{pmatrix} m & 0 \\ 0 & m \end{pmatrix} r\Delta^{-1}, = \begin{pmatrix} \alpha & \beta \\ \alpha' & \beta' \end{pmatrix} \begin{pmatrix} m & 0 \\ 0 & m \end{pmatrix} \begin{pmatrix} \bar{\beta}' & -\bar{\beta} \\ -\bar{\alpha}' & \bar{\alpha} \end{pmatrix},$$

is that of a transformation of order r^2, which, applied to the original period matrix τ, leaves this unaltered. The Riemann surface is therefore such that there is a complex multiplication, or principal transformation, of order r^2. If the compound matrix belonging to this be written

$$\begin{pmatrix} f & g \\ f' & g' \end{pmatrix}, = \Delta \begin{pmatrix} m & 0 \\ 0 & m \end{pmatrix} r\Delta^{-1},$$

we at once find

$$f + \tau f' = r(\alpha + \tau\alpha)\, m\, (\alpha + \tau\alpha')^{-1};$$

the general inference, that $\Theta\left[(f + \tau f')V, \tau\right]$ is expressible as an integral polynomial of order r^2 in 2^p functions $\Theta(V, \tau \mid q)$, is easily seen to be contained in the results already given.

70. The preceding investigations have sufficiently shewn the importance of the number r, the Index. Consider now* the equations

$$u_r^{x_1, c_1} + \ldots + u_r^{x_n, c_n} = U_r, \qquad (r = 1, \ldots, n),$$

* Wirtinger, *Untersuchungen über Thetafunctionen* (Leipzig, Teubner, 1895), p. 61; Wirtinger, "Zur Theorie der $2n$-fach periodischen Functionen," *Monatsh. f. Mathematik u. Physik*, VII. Jahrg. (1896).

where $(c_1),\dots,(c_n)$ are arbitrary places upon the Riemann surface, $U_1,\dots,U_n$ are arbitrary values, and we enquire as to the existence of places $(x_1),\dots,(x_n)$ to satisfy these equations.

With the function $\Theta(\mu^{-1}U, \sigma)$ we can form, as has been remarked, single valued functions of $U_1,\dots,U_n$, with no singularities for finite values of $U_1,\dots,U_n$ other than poles, having $2n$ systems of simultaneous periods, whose matrix is (μ, μ'). Let $\psi(U)$ denote such a function. We can then take n systems of constants $(a_1^{(r)},\dots,a_n^{(r)})$, for $r=1,\dots,n$, such that the Jacobian of the n functions $\psi_r(U)=\psi(U+a^{(r)})$ does not vanish for all values of $U_1,\dots,U_n$. The function

$$\psi_r(u_1^{x_1, c_1}+\dots+u_1^{x_n, c_n},\dots\dots, u_n^{x_1, c_1}+\dots+u_n^{x_n, c_n})$$

is then a rational function of the places $(x_1),\dots,(x_n)$ upon the Riemann surface. For when one place, say (x_1), makes a circuit upon the Riemann surface, the arguments are increased by quantities Πt, where t is a row of $2p$ integers, while

$$\Pi = ak = (\mu, \mu')fk = (\mu, \mu')\begin{pmatrix} H & K \\ H' & K' \end{pmatrix} = (\mu H + \mu' H', \mu K + \mu' K'),$$

where H, H', K, K' are matrices of integers; the function is thus single valued upon the Riemann surface in regard to each of $(x_1),\dots,(x_n)$; and for undetermined positions of $(x_2),\dots,(x_n)$ it is, as a function of (x_1), capable of expression about any place as a series of integral powers of the parameter involving only a finite number of negative powers. Put then

$$\psi_r(u_1^{x_1, c_1}+\dots+u_1^{x_n, c_n},\dots\dots) = H_r(x_1,\dots,x_n);$$

the Jacobian of the n functions $u_r^{x_1, c_1}+\dots+u_r^{x_n, c_n}$ in regard to $x_1,\dots,x_n$ is not in general zero; in fact, if $du_r^{x_s, c_s}/dx_s = \chi_r(x_s)$, this is only so when a linear function $A_1\chi_1(x)+\dots+A_n\chi_n(x)$, chosen so as to vanish at $(x_1),\dots,(x_{n-1})$, also of itself vanishes at (x_n). The n rational functions $H_1,\dots,H_n$ are thus in general independent, and a certain definite limited number of positions of $(x_1),\dots,(x_n)$, depending upon the form of these rational functions, can be chosen so that the equations

$$H_1(x_1,\dots,x_n)=C_1,\dots\dots, H_n(x_1,\dots,x_n)=C_n$$

are satisfied, for arbitrary assigned values of $C_1,\dots,C_n$. This number is independent of $C_1,\dots,C_n$. There are positions of $(x_1),\dots,(x_n)$ for which one or more of the rational functions $H_1,\dots,H_n$ become indeterminate; for positions of $(x_1),\dots,(x_n)$ in the immediate neighbourhood of but not constituting such a set of positions the functions have definite values. Now when $U_1,\dots,U_n$ have definite values the functions $\psi_r(U)$ have definite values in general. We infer therefore that the equations

$$u_r^{x_1, c_1}+\dots+u_r^{x_n, c_n} \equiv U_r \pmod{\Pi}, \qquad (r=1,\dots,n),$$

have, for assigned arbitrary finite values of $U_1,\dots,U_n$, a definite finite number of sets of solutions $(x_1), \dots, (x_n)$, this number being independent of $U_1, \dots, U_n$—there being exception to this result for values of $U_1, \dots, U_n$ belonging to certain continua of less than n (complex) dimensions, upon which the functions $\psi_1(U), \dots, \psi_n(U)$ become indeterminate.

The preceding reasoning is given only as provisional, the cases of exception not being examined completely; it may suffice for the present chapter, which is confessedly incomplete and only illustrative in its purpose.

With the assumption of the definiteness of the number of sets of solutions of the equations we can now determine this number.

Put

$$x_r = \xi_{2r-1} + i\xi_{2r}, \quad U_r = V_{2r-1} + iV_{2r}, \quad u_r^{x_s} = v^{(s)}_{2r-1} + iv^{(s)}_{2r}, \qquad (r, s = 1, 2, \dots, n),$$

so that each of $v^{(s)}_{2r-1}$, $v^{(s)}_{2r}$ is a function of the two real variables ξ_{2s-1}, ξ_{2s} for all values of r; we then have $2n$ equations

$$v_j^{(1)} + v_j^{(2)} + \dots\dots + v_j^{(n)} = V_j, \qquad (j = 1, 2, \dots, (2n));$$

we now allow each of $(x_1), \dots, (x_n)$ to take, independently of the others, all possible positions on the Riemann surface, and interpreting $V_1, \dots, V_{2n}$ as coordinates in a real space of $2n$ dimensions, we evaluate the volume described in this space by the corresponding point $(V_1, \dots, V_{2n})$, this volume being expressed by

$$\iint \dots \int dV_1\, dV_2 \dots dV_{2n},$$

or

$$\iint \dots \int \frac{\partial(V_1, \dots, V_{2n})}{\partial(\xi_1, \dots, \xi_{2n})}\, d\xi_1\, d\xi_2 \dots d\xi_{2n}.$$

Since

$$\partial V_{2r-1}/\partial \xi_{2s-1} = \partial v^{(s)}_{2r-1}/\partial \xi_{2s-1}, \quad \partial V_{2r-1}/\partial \xi_{2s} = \partial v^{(s)}_{2r-1}/\partial \xi_{2s}, \text{ etc.,}$$

the Jacobian herein contained is

$$\left| \begin{matrix} \dfrac{\partial v_1^{(1)}}{\partial \xi_1}, & \dfrac{\partial v_1^{(1)}}{\partial \xi_2}, & \dfrac{\partial v_1^{(2)}}{\partial \xi_3}, & \dfrac{\partial v_1^{(2)}}{\partial \xi_4}, & \dots & \dfrac{\partial v_1^{(n)}}{\partial \xi_{2n-1}}, & \dfrac{\partial v_1^{(n)}}{\partial \xi_{2n}} \\ \dfrac{\partial v_2^{(1)}}{\partial \xi_1}, & \dfrac{\partial v_2^{(1)}}{\partial \xi_2}, & \dfrac{\partial v_2^{(2)}}{\partial \xi_3}, & \dfrac{\partial v_2^{(2)}}{\partial \xi_4}, & \dots & \dfrac{\partial v_2^{(n)}}{\partial \xi_{2n-1}}, & \dfrac{\partial v_2^{(n)}}{\partial \xi_{2n}} \\ \dots & \dots & \dots & \dots & \dots & \dots & \dots \\ \dfrac{\partial v_{2n}^{(1)}}{\partial \xi_1}, & \dfrac{\partial v_{2n}^{(1)}}{\partial \xi_2}, & \dfrac{\partial v_{2n}^{(2)}}{\partial \xi_3}, & \dfrac{\partial v_{2n}^{(2)}}{\partial \xi_4}, & \dots & \dfrac{\partial v_{2n}^{(n)}}{\partial \xi_{2n-1}}, & \dfrac{\partial v_{2n}^{(n)}}{\partial \xi_{2n}} \end{matrix} \right|,$$

which, expanded as a sum of products of n binary determinants (see Appendix to Part II. Note III.) chosen respectively from the first and second, the third and fourth, ..., the $(2n-1)$th and $2n$-th columns, is equal to

$$\Sigma \pm \left(\frac{\partial v_{k_1}^{(1)}}{\partial \xi_1} \frac{\partial v_{k_2}^{(1)}}{\partial \xi_2} - \frac{\partial v_{k_2}^{(1)}}{\partial \xi_1} \frac{\partial v_{k_1}^{(1)}}{\partial \xi_2} \right) \left(\frac{\partial v_{k_3}^{(2)}}{\partial \xi_3} \frac{\partial v_{k_4}^{(2)}}{\partial \xi_4} - \frac{\partial v_{k_4}^{(2)}}{\partial \xi_3} \frac{\partial v_{k_3}^{(2)}}{\partial \xi_4} \right) \dots\dots,$$

wherein k_1, k_2, with $k_1 < k_2$, are any two of the numbers $1, 2, \dots, (2n)$, and

k_3, k_4, with $k_3 < k_4$, are also any two of these numbers other than k_1, k_2, and so on, and the sign $\pm$ is upper or lower according to the parity of the order $k_1, k_2, \ldots, k_{2n}$; if we write

$$\frac{\partial v^{(r)}_{k_{2r-1}}}{\partial \xi_{2r-1}} \frac{\partial v^{(r)}_{k_{2r}}}{\partial \xi_{2r}} - \frac{\partial v^{(r)}_{k_{2r-1}}}{\partial \xi_{2r}} \frac{\partial v^{(r)}_{k_{2r}}}{\partial \xi_{2r-1}} = [k_{2r-1}, k_{2r}],$$

the expansion is

$$\Sigma \pm [k_1, k_2][k_3, k_4] \ldots [k_{2n-1}, k_{2n}],$$

and in any term the only factor involving the two variables ξ_{2r-1}, ξ_{2r} is $[k_{2r-1}, k_{2r}]$.

Now when (x_r) describes the whole Riemann surface, the double integral $\int [k_{2r-1}, k_{2r}] d\xi_{2r-1} d\xi_{2r}$ is equal to the single integral $\int v_{k_{2r-1}} dv_{k_{2r}}$ extended along the edges of the $2p$ period loops; if we put $\Pi_{r,\alpha} = H_{2r-1,\alpha} + iH_{2r,\alpha}$, for $r = 1, \ldots, n$ and $\alpha = 1, \ldots, 2p$, the period increments of the function v_λ for passage of the loops are $H_{\lambda,\alpha}$, and we have

$$\int v_\lambda dv_\mu = \sum_{\beta=1}^{p} (H_{\lambda,\beta} H_{\mu,p+\beta} - H_{\lambda,p+\beta} H_{\mu,\beta}), \quad (\lambda, \mu = 1, 2, \ldots, 2n),$$

a quantity formed by a familiar rule from the λth and μth rows

$$\begin{array}{ll} H_{\lambda,1}, \ldots, H_{\lambda,p}, & H_{\lambda,p+1}, \ldots, H_{\lambda,2p} \\ H_{\mu,1}, \ldots, H_{\mu,p}, & H_{\mu,p+1}, \ldots, H_{\mu,2p} \end{array}$$

of the matrix $(H_{\lambda,\alpha})$, which we may call the combinant or the splice of these rows, and denote by $(\lambda, \mu)_H$. We have then

$$\int v_{k_{2r-1}} dv_{k_{2r}} = (k_{2r-1}, k_{2r})_H$$

where, if $\Pi = M + iN$, both M and N being matrices of type $(n, 2p)$ of real elements, we have

$$H = \begin{pmatrix} M \\ N \end{pmatrix},$$

a matrix of type $(2n, 2p)$, consisting of real quantities. The original integral thus becomes

$$\Sigma \pm (k_1, k_2)_H (k_3, k_4)_H \ldots (k_{2n-1}, k_{2n})_H;$$

here the number of terms is the same as in the expansion of a determinant of type $(2n, 2n)$ by binary determinants, namely

$$\binom{2n}{2}\binom{2n-2}{2} \ldots \binom{4}{2} = (n!)\, 1 \,.\, 3 \,.\, 5 \ldots (2n-1),$$

two terms, for instance, differing from one another only in the order of the first two of the n factors of a term, occurring separately; in fact however

$$(k_1, k_2)_H (k_3, k_4)_H = (k_3, k_4)_H (k_1, k_2)_H,$$

and so on; the value of the determinant is thus

$$(n!)\,\Sigma \pm (k_1, k_2)_H (k_3, k_4)_H \dots (k_{2n-1}, k_{2n})_H,$$

where the order of the n factors of any term is indifferent, and this is only the expansion in the form of a Pfaffian (see Appendix to Part II., Note III.), of the value

$$(n!)\,(\,|\,H\epsilon_{2p}\bar{H}\,|\,)^{\frac{1}{2}}.$$

Precisely the same deduction may be applied to any number of integrals of the first kind, independently of the existence of defective integrals; for instance, $u^{x,c}$ being any integral of the first kind, if we put

$$u^{x,c} = V_1 + iV_2, \quad x = \xi_1 + i\xi_2,$$

and denote the periods of $u^{x,c}$ for passage of the $2p$ period loops by

$$H_1 + iK_1, \ \dots, \ H_p + iK_p, \ H_1' + iK_1', \ \dots, \ H_p' + iK_p',$$

we have, as (x) traverses the Riemann surface,

$$\iint dV_1 dV_2 = H_1K_1' - H_1'K_1 + \dots + H_pK_p' - H_p'K_p,$$

the right side denoting the sum of the parallelograms whose perimeters are described by $U = u^{x,c}$, upon a plane of U, as (x) describes the sides of the period loops upon the Riemann surface.

If now $\Pi = \varpi h$, where ϖ is any matrix of type $(n, 2n)$, and h a matrix of type $(2n, 2p)$ consisting of integers, and $\Pi = M + iN$, $\varpi = \mu + i\nu$, we have $M = \mu h$, $N = \nu h$,

and
$$H = \begin{pmatrix}\mu\\ \nu\end{pmatrix} h,$$

so that
$$H\epsilon_{2p}\bar{H} = \begin{pmatrix}\mu\\ \nu\end{pmatrix} h\epsilon_{2p}\bar{h}\,(\bar{\mu}, \bar{\nu}),$$

and hence
$$\iint \dots \int dV_1 dV_2 \dots dV_n = (n!) \begin{vmatrix}\mu\\ \nu\end{vmatrix} (\,|\,h\epsilon_{2p}\bar{h}\,|\,)^{\frac{1}{2}},$$

wherein $\begin{vmatrix}\mu\\ \nu\end{vmatrix}$ denotes the volume of the period cell defined in the real space of $2n$ dimensions by the periods ϖ, and the other factor $(n!)\,(\,|\,h\epsilon_{2p}\bar{h}\,|\,)^{\frac{1}{2}}$ is a positive integer.

This is true when ϖ represents any set of periods in terms of integral multiples of which the periods Π can be expressed; if in particular we take $\Pi = ak$, where k is the unitary matrix of type $(2n, 2p)$ described earlier in this chapter (p. 230), and $(a, 0) = \Pi m$, then increments of $U_1, \dots, U_n$ which arise by closed circuits of any one of $(x_1), \dots, (x_n)$ on the Riemann surface, correspond to a change from a point (U) to a point which is congruent thereto in regard to the period cells associated with the periods a, and conversely; hence, assuming (p. 246) that, as $(x_1), \dots, (x_n)$ traverse the Riemann surface, the point (U) takes up every position the same number of times, we infer the result: *The number of different sets of solutions of the congruences*

$$u_r^{x_1, c_1} + \ldots + u_r^{x_n, c_n} \equiv U_r \,(\text{mod. } \Pi), \qquad (r = 1, 2, \ldots, n),$$

*before called the multiplicity, is**

$$(\,|\,k\epsilon_{2p}\bar{k}\,|\,)^{\frac{1}{2}},$$

the factor $n!$ being removed because a set of solutions is not affected by permutation of its constituents.

If (r, s) denote the splice of the rth and sth rows of the matrix k, this number of solutions of the congruences is the Pfaffian

$$\Sigma \pm (12)(34)(56)\ldots,$$

formed with $2n$ numbers. If the period loops be differently drawn on the Riemann surface, which comes to using periods $\Pi' = \Pi J$, in place of Π, where $J\epsilon_{2p}\bar{J} = \epsilon_{2p}$, the number, becoming $(\,|\,kJ\epsilon_{2p}\bar{J}\bar{k}\,|\,)^{\frac{1}{2}}$, is unaltered, as should be the case. If (Appendix to Part II., Note II.) g be a unitary matrix of integers of type $(2n, 2n)$ such that

$$gk\epsilon_{2p}\bar{k}\bar{g} = \begin{pmatrix} 0 & -d \\ d & 0 \end{pmatrix},$$

where d denotes a diagonal matrix of positive elements $d_1, d_2, \ldots, d_n$, wherein $d_2/d_1, d_3/d_2, \ldots d_n/d_{n-1}$ are integers, the multiplicity σ is also given by

$$\sigma = d_1 d_2 \ldots d_n.$$

We have seen that the index r is equal to the first invariant factor d_n; the two numbers are thus equal when $n = 1$. When $n = p$ we have $k = 1$, and the multiplicity is unity, as is known.

71. Consider the case when $n = 1$. We have shewn that we can write

$$\Pi = ak,$$

where k is a matrix of integers of type $(2, 2p)$, which is unitary, in the sense that its determinants of order 2 have unity for their greatest common divisor. We have then

$$k\epsilon_{2p}\bar{k} = \begin{pmatrix} 0 & -R \\ R & 0 \end{pmatrix},$$

where
$$R = \sum_{\sigma=1}^{p} (k_{1,\sigma}\, k_{2,\sigma+p} - k_{2,\sigma}\, k_{1,\sigma+p}),$$

is the splice of the two rows of k; according as R is positive or negative take now

$$f = \begin{pmatrix} 1 & 0 \\ 0 & 1 \end{pmatrix}, \text{ or } f = \begin{pmatrix} -1 & 0 \\ 0 & 1 \end{pmatrix},$$

and obtain
$$fk\epsilon_{2p}\bar{k}\bar{f} = r\epsilon_2 = r\begin{pmatrix} 0 & -1 \\ 1 & 0 \end{pmatrix},$$

where r is a positive integer (R or $-R$), as in the general case.

* It follows from preceding work that this is not zero (p. 225).

Put as before
$$fk = \begin{pmatrix} H, & K \\ H', & K' \end{pmatrix},$$
so that, if
$$k = \begin{pmatrix} k_1, & k_2 \\ k_1', & k_2' \end{pmatrix},$$
we have
$$fk = \begin{pmatrix} k_1, & k_2 \\ k_1', & k_2' \end{pmatrix}, \text{ or } \begin{pmatrix} -k_1, & -k_2 \\ k_1', & k_2' \end{pmatrix},$$
and the determinants of order 2 from this have unity for their greatest common divisor*.

It can now be shewn that a matrix J of integers can be chosen, of type $(2p, 2p)$, satisfying
$$J\epsilon_{2p}\bar{J} = \epsilon_{2p},$$
so that
$$\begin{pmatrix} H, & K \\ H', & K' \end{pmatrix} J = \begin{pmatrix} r, & 0, & 0, & \dots & 0; & 0, & 1, & 0, & \dots & 0 \\ 0, & 0, & 0, & \dots & 0; & 1, & 0, & 0, & \dots & 0 \end{pmatrix},$$
where the elements not written are zeros.

To make this clear consider the character of a matrix J. A linear transformation, expressed by a matrix of integers J of type $(2p, 2p)$ which satisfies the equivalent equations
$$J\epsilon_{2p}\bar{J} = \epsilon_{2p}, \quad \bar{J}\epsilon_{2p}J = \epsilon_{2p},$$
may also be defined by the fact that if, denoting rows of p quantities by x and x', and also by ξ, ξ', y, y', η, η', we put
$$(x, x') = J(\xi, \xi'), \quad (y, y') = J(\eta, \eta'),$$
the splice (1, 2), $= \sum_{i=1}^{p} (x_i y_i' - x_i' y_i)$, of the two rows
$$\begin{pmatrix} x & x' \\ y & y' \end{pmatrix},$$
is equal to the splice of the two rows
$$\begin{pmatrix} \xi & \xi' \\ \eta & \eta' \end{pmatrix};$$
for we have
$$\begin{pmatrix} x, & x' \\ y, & y' \end{pmatrix} = \begin{pmatrix} \xi, & \xi' \\ \eta, & \eta' \end{pmatrix} \bar{J},$$
and
$$\begin{pmatrix} 0, & -(1, 2) \\ (1, 2), & 0 \end{pmatrix} = \begin{pmatrix} x, & x' \\ y, & y' \end{pmatrix} \epsilon_{2p} \overline{\begin{pmatrix} x, & x' \\ y, & y' \end{pmatrix}} = \begin{pmatrix} \xi, & \xi' \\ \eta, & \eta' \end{pmatrix} \bar{J}\epsilon_{2p}J \overline{\begin{pmatrix} \xi, & \xi' \\ \eta, & \eta' \end{pmatrix}}.$$

If
$$\begin{pmatrix} a, & a' \\ b, & b' \end{pmatrix}$$
be a unitary matrix of type $(2n, 2p)$, that is a matrix of integers in which the determinants of order n have unity for their common divisor, and
$$\begin{pmatrix} a, & a' \\ b, & b' \end{pmatrix} J = \begin{pmatrix} A, & A' \\ B, & B' \end{pmatrix},$$

* In general the determinants of fk of order $2n$ have $d_n{}^n/d_1 d_2 \dots d_n$ as their common divisor.

we have $$\begin{pmatrix} a, & a' \\ b, & b' \end{pmatrix}(x, x') = \begin{pmatrix} A, & A' \\ B, & B' \end{pmatrix}(\xi, \xi');$$

also from $$\begin{pmatrix} a, & a' \\ b, & b' \end{pmatrix} = \begin{pmatrix} A, & A' \\ B, & B' \end{pmatrix} J^{-1},$$

since J is unitary and any determinant of $\begin{pmatrix} a, & a' \\ b, & b' \end{pmatrix}$ of order $2n$ is a sum of products of determinants from $\begin{pmatrix} A, & A' \\ B, & B' \end{pmatrix}$ and J^{-1}, each of order $2n$, it follows that $\begin{pmatrix} A, & A' \\ B, & B' \end{pmatrix}$ is unitary. Also, as

$$\begin{pmatrix} a, & a' \\ b, & b' \end{pmatrix} \epsilon_{2p} \begin{pmatrix} \bar{a} & \bar{b} \\ \bar{a}' & \bar{b}' \end{pmatrix} = \begin{pmatrix} A & A' \\ B & B' \end{pmatrix} \epsilon_{2p} \begin{pmatrix} \bar{A} & \bar{B} \\ \bar{A}' & \bar{B}' \end{pmatrix},$$

the splice of any two rows of $\begin{pmatrix} a, & a' \\ b, & b' \end{pmatrix}$ is equal to the splice of the two corresponding rows of $\begin{pmatrix} A, & A' \\ B, & B' \end{pmatrix}$.

Now particular linear transformations are:

I. That in which x_r and x_r' are replaced by linear functions of ξ_r and ξ_r' with numerical coefficients of determinant unity, the other $2p-2$ quantities x, x' being unaltered; for this evidently replaces $x_r y_r' - x_r' y_r$ by $\xi_r \eta_r' - \xi_r' \eta_r$, and leaves the other binary determinants $x_s y_s' - x_s' y_s$ unaltered. It corresponds to replacing the rth and $(p+r)$th columns of $\begin{pmatrix} a, & a' \\ b, & b' \end{pmatrix}$, which we may denote by c_r and c_r', by two columns C_r, C_r' given by

$$C_r = \lambda c_r + \mu c_r', \quad C_r' = \rho c_r + \sigma c_r', \quad \lambda\sigma - \mu\rho = 1.$$

A particular case is $$C_r = -c_r, \quad C_r' = -c_r'.$$

II. That in which

$$x_r = \xi_r, \quad x_s = \xi_s - \lambda\xi_r, \quad x_r' = \xi_r' + \lambda\xi_s', \quad x_s' = \xi_s',$$

for which $x_r y_r' - x_r' y_r + x_s y_s' - x_s' y_s$

$$= \xi_r(\eta_r' + \lambda\eta_s') - (\xi_r' + \lambda\xi_s')\eta_r + (\xi_s - \lambda\xi_r)\eta_s' - \xi_s'(\eta_s - \lambda\eta_r)$$
$$= \xi_r\eta_r' - \xi_r'\eta_r + \xi_s\eta_s' - \xi_s'\eta_s,$$

the variables other than x_r, x_s, x_r', x_s' being unaltered. It corresponds to a change of the columns of $\begin{pmatrix} a, & a' \\ b, & b' \end{pmatrix}$ expressed by

$$C_r = c_r - \lambda c_s, \quad C_s = c_s, \quad C_r' = c_r', \quad C_s' = c_s' + \lambda c_r'.$$

III. That in which

$$x_r = \xi_r, \quad x_s = \xi_s - \lambda\xi_r, \quad x_r' = \xi_r' + \lambda\xi_s' + \mu\xi_r, \quad x_s' = \xi_s',$$

which includes (II.), for $\mu = 0$, and is equivalent to an interchange of columns expressed by

$$C_r = c_r - \lambda c_s + \mu c_r', \quad C_s = c_s, \quad C_r' = c_r', \quad C_s' = c_s' + \lambda c_r'.$$

Suppose now $\begin{pmatrix} a, & a' \\ b, & b' \end{pmatrix}$ is of two rows only, or $n=1$. By transformations (I) we can first reduce all the first p elements of the second row to zero; then by transformations (II) we can reduce all the second p elements of the second row to zero except one of these, which cannot be zero since the determinants of $\begin{pmatrix} a, & a' \\ b, & b' \end{pmatrix}$ are not all zero; if this element be denoted by B_r', and $r \neq 1$, we can, first, by transformations (II), add the $(p+r)$th column to the $(p+1)$th, and then subtract the $(p+1)$th from the $(p+r)$th; we may thus suppose $r=1$; and the second row of the transformed matrix now has zero in every place except the $(p+1)$th. After this, leaving the first and $(p+1)$th columns untouched, we can similarly, by transformations (I) and (II) in turn, make the 2nd, 3rd, ... pth elements of the first row all zero, and the $(p+3)$th, $(p+4)$th, ..., $(2p)$th elements also all zero. The transformed form of the matrix $\begin{pmatrix} a, & a' \\ b, & b' \end{pmatrix}$ is now

$$\begin{pmatrix} Q & 0 & 0 & 0 & .. & R & S & 0 & 0 & .. \\ 0 & 0 & 0 & 0 & .. & P & 0 & 0 & 0 & .. \end{pmatrix};$$

since this is unitary we have $PS=1$; if $P=-1$ we can change the signs of the first and $(p+1)$th columns; we may thus take $P=1$, $S=1$; if further the splice of the two rows of $\begin{pmatrix} a, & a' \\ b, & b' \end{pmatrix}$ is r, we can then infer $Q=r$. The transformed matrix is thus

$$\begin{pmatrix} r & 0 & 0 & 0 & .. & R & 1 & 0 & 0 & .. \\ 0 & 0 & 0 & 0 & .. & 1 & 0 & 0 & 0 & .. \end{pmatrix}.$$

Lastly apply the transformation (III) in the form

$$C_2 = c_2 + Rc_1 - rRc_2', \quad C_1 = c_1, \quad C_2' = c_2', \quad C_1' = c_1' - Rc_2';$$

this replaces R by zero in the matrix, but effects no other change.

The transformation indicated is thus effected, and we have

$$\Pi J = (\mu, \mu')fkJ = (\mu, \mu')\begin{pmatrix} r & 0 & 0 & .. & 0 & 1 & 0 & .. \\ 0 & 0 & 0 & .. & 1 & 0 & 0 & .. \end{pmatrix}.$$

Now put $J = \begin{pmatrix} \gamma & \delta \\ \gamma' & \delta' \end{pmatrix}$ and take τ_1, a matrix of type (p, p), so that

$$(\gamma + \tau\gamma')\,\tau_1 = \delta + \tau\delta';$$

it can then be proved as in the earlier part of this chapter (p. 237) that, (i) the matrix $(\gamma + \tau\gamma')$ is of non-vanishing determinant, (ii) τ_1 is symmetrical, (iii), if $n_1, \dots, n_p$ be any p real quantities, the real part of $i\tau_1 n^2$ is necessarily negative and not zero; take also a system of p integrals $V_1', \dots, V_p'$ given in terms of the original normal integrals $V_1, \dots, V_p$ by

$$(\gamma + \tau\gamma')^{-1} V = V', \quad = (\bar{\delta}' - \tau_1\bar{\gamma}')\,V,$$

there will be* a new system of canonical period loops on the Riemann surface, for which V' are the normal integrals, having a period matrix $(1, \tau_1)$. And in particular, u being as before the defective integral under consideration, the integral $\frac{1}{r}\mu^{-1}u$, which from the equation above has† the period system following (where $\sigma = \mu^{-1}\mu'$),

$$\frac{1}{r}\mu^{-1}\Pi J = \left(1,\ 0,\ 0, \ldots;\ \frac{\sigma}{r},\ \frac{1}{r},\ 0, \ldots\right),$$

is equal to V_1', for there is only one integral having at the new period loops (a_β) the periods $1, 0, 0, \ldots$. It follows then that in τ_1 the first row reduces to its first two elements, these being σ/r and $1/r$. From the symmetrical form of the matrix τ_1 it is clear that $V_2', \ldots, V_p'$ form a defective system of $(p-1)$ integrals, the second period of V_2' being r times the $(p+1)$th, the $(p+1)$th periods of $V_3', \ldots, V_p'$ being all zero (cf. p. 240).

We have already reached the conclusion that when $n = 1$, the multiplicity is equal to the index r (p. 250); and from the equations

$$|f| = \pm 1, \quad fkJ = \begin{pmatrix} r & 0 & . & . & 0 & 1 & . & . \\ 0 & 0 & . & . & 1 & 0 & . & . \end{pmatrix},$$

which we have used, we have $(|k\epsilon_{2p}\bar{k}|)^{\frac{1}{2}} = r$. This involves the consequence that the equation

$$u^{x,c} \equiv U \pmod{\Pi}$$

is satisfied by r positions upon the Riemann surface.

We can give another proof of this, independent of the preceding investigation of the multiplicity. The periods Π are sums of integral multipliers of the periods ΠJ for the new period loops, and the congruence is equivalent with

$$V_1' = \frac{1}{r}\mu^{-1}u^{x,c} \equiv V\left(\text{mod. } \frac{1}{r}\mu^{-1}\Pi J\right), \quad \equiv V\left(\text{mod. } \frac{1}{r}, \frac{\sigma}{r}\right)$$

where V is an arbitrary constant, and V_1' is considered as a function of the position (x) on the Riemann surface. Now the elliptic theta function

$$\Theta(\mu^{-1}u^{x,c}, \sigma) = \Theta(rV_1', \sigma)$$

vanishes, as we know, for

$$rV_1' = M + M'\sigma + \frac{1+\sigma}{2},$$

* See the author's *Abel's Theorem*, p. 559.

† Another proof of the theorem is given in the author's *Abel's Theorem*, p. 658. It can be shewn in fact that a matrix J such as is required can be constructed with the first, second and $(p+1)$th columns of the form

$$\begin{pmatrix} \bar{K}' & r\bar{x}+\bar{K} & .. & \bar{x} & .. \\ -\bar{H}' & r\bar{y}-\bar{H} & .. & \bar{y} & .. \end{pmatrix},$$

where x, y are such columns of p integers that $r\bar{x}+\bar{K}$, $r\bar{y}-\bar{H}$ are $2p$ integers with unity as common factor. (In the proof referred to, p. 659, line 26 and p. 660, line 9 *for* 'constituents of the first' *read* 'constituents of the second.')

where M, M' are integers; the corresponding positions (x) are therefore such that the values of V_r' are congruent for modulus $\left(\frac{1}{r}, \frac{\sigma}{r}\right)$, and it is such positions that we wish above to enumerate. It has however been previously shewn (p. 234) that the function $\Theta(\mu^{-1}u^{x,c}, \sigma)$ has r vanishing points on the Riemann surface, and the proof was independent of the investigation of the multiplicity. The theorem is therefore proved.

To determine the solutions of the equation

$$u^{x,c} \equiv U \text{ (mod. } \Pi)$$

when U is given, we may form the two functions

$$\xi = \wp\,(\mu^{-1}u^{x,c};\ 1, \sigma) = \wp\,(\mu^{-1}U;\ 1, \sigma),$$
$$\eta = \wp'(\mu^{-1}u^{x,c};\ 1, \sigma) = \wp'(\mu^{-1}U;\ 1, \sigma),$$

which, since $\mu^{-1}\Pi = (H + \sigma H',\ K + \sigma K')$, are rational functions of the place (x). To each value of ξ belong the $2r$ solutions of the two congruences

$$u^{x,c} \equiv U, \quad u^{x,c} \equiv -U \text{ (mod. } \Pi),$$

of which however only the first r correspond to a given value of η. We infer therefore that, if $(x_1, y_1), \ldots, (x_r, y_r)$ be the solutions of the first congruence, there exists an equation

$$x^r + H_1 x^{r-1} + \ldots + H_r = 0,$$

whose roots are $x_1, \ldots, x_r$, wherein the coefficients $H_1, \ldots, H_r$ are single valued functions* of U, rational in ξ and η.

The existence of an equation

$$\mu^{-1}u^{x',c} = \mu^{-1}u^{x,c}$$

implies that x', y' are single valued doubly periodic functions of $\mu^{-1}u^{x,c}$, with periods 1, σ, and therefore rational in x, y. There is thus a $(1, 1)$ birational transformation of the Riemann surface into itself corresponding to every such equation; such a transformation is necessarily periodic, and if k be the index of periodicity, the equation can be birationally changed to a form $(s^k, t) = 0$ (Hurwitz, *Math. Annal.* XXXII. (1888), p. 291).

72. Pass now to some examples.

For the equation † (Kowalevski, *Acta Math.* IV. (1884), p. 393)

$$[x(ax+by)]^{\frac{1}{2}} + [y(cx+dy)]^{\frac{1}{2}} + [1+ex+fy]^{\frac{1}{2}} = 0,$$

or $F = [x(ax+by) + y(cx+dy) - (1+ex+fy)]^2 - 4xy(ax+by)(cx+dy) = 0,$

* Extensions of the reduction of the matrix $\begin{pmatrix} H & K \\ H' & K' \end{pmatrix}$ here given for $n=1$ are investigated by Poincaré, *American Journal*, Vol. VIII. (1886), p. 301, who gives various other results not referred to in the text.

† See Note, p. 272.

the general integral of the first kind,

$$\int \frac{(x\,dy - y\,dx)(Px + Qy + R)}{\partial F/\partial z},$$

where $\tfrac{1}{2}\dfrac{\partial F}{\partial z} = -[x(ax+by) + y(cx+dy) - (1+ex+fy)][2+ex+fy]$,

reduces for $P = 1$, $Q = 1$, $R = 2$ to a constant multiple of

$$\int \frac{x\,dy - y\,dx}{2[xy(ax+by)(cx+dy)]^{\frac{1}{2}}}, \quad = \int \frac{d\xi}{[4\xi(a+b\xi)(c+d\xi)]^{\frac{1}{2}}},$$

if $\xi = y/x$; putting also $\eta^2 = 4\xi(a+b\xi)(c+d\xi)$ we have

$$\frac{1}{x^2} + \frac{e+f\xi}{x} + \eta - (a+b\xi) - \xi(c+d\xi) = 0,$$

from which it appears that the index r is 2. And we find at once that if we take the self-inverse transformation

$$x' = -x(1+ex+fy)^{-1}, \quad y' = -y(1+ex+fy)^{-1}, \quad \text{and } ex_0 + fy_0 + 2 = 0,$$

then $$u^{x,\,x_0} = \int_{(x_0,\,y_0)}^{(x,\,y)} \frac{(ex+fy+2)\,dx}{\partial F/\partial y} = \int_{(x_0,\,y_0)}^{(x',\,y')} \frac{(ex+fy+2)\,dx}{\partial F/\partial y},$$

so that the two solutions of the congruence

$$u^{x,\,c} \equiv U$$

are (x, y) and (x', y').

According to the theory given in the text the remaining integrals are also defective; it would be interesting to verify this directly.

73. Another class of surfaces for which defective integrals arise are those represented by an equation

$$y^2 = (x^2 - c_1^2)(x^2 - c_2^2)\dots(x^2 - c^2_{2m+1}).$$

The first case of importance, where $m = 1$, was remarked by Legendre and Jacobi*; there are then two defective integrals each reducing to an elliptic integral. As sufficiently representing the general case we shall take $m = 2$, so that the equation, of deficiency 4, is

$$y^2 = (x^2 - c_1^2)(x^2 - c_2^2)(x^2 - c_3^2)(x^2 - c_4^2)(x^2 - c_5^2);$$

by $x^2 = \xi$ each of the integrals

$$\int \frac{x\,dx}{y}, \quad \int \frac{x^3\,dx}{y}$$

reduces to a hyperelliptic integral of deficiency 2, and, as will appear, these two form one system; the same is true of

$$\int \frac{dx}{y}, \quad \int \frac{x^2\,dx}{y},$$

as is seen by putting $x = x_1^{-1}$.

* Legendre, *Fonctions Elliptiques*; Jacobi, *Crelle*, VIII. (1832), p. 416.

Suppose, for definiteness, each of $c_1, \ldots, c_5$ to be real and positive, and $c_1 > c_2 > c_3 > c_4 > c_5$, and take the period loops in a usual manner, as in the figure :—

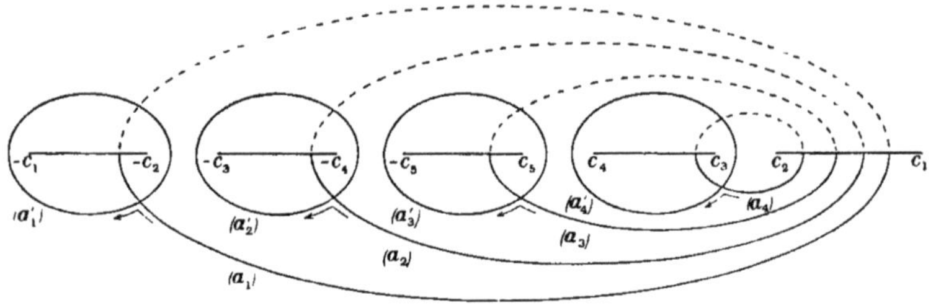

The value of y for a real $x > c_1$, in the lower sheet of the Riemann surface, being taken to be real and positive, and using A in general for a real positive quantity, the values of y in the lower sheet in the various segments of the real axis are indicated by the diagram :—

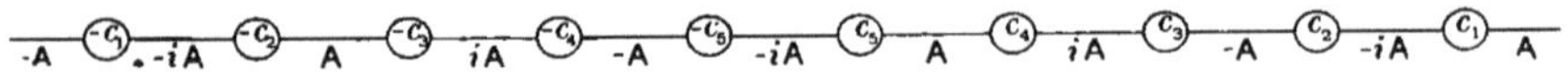

Thus, considering one of the two integrals

$$\int \frac{x\,dx}{y}, \quad \int \frac{x^3\,dx}{y},$$

which we may call u, and denoting by Ω_r, Ω_r' its period increments, for passage from the right to the left sides, respectively of the period loops (a_r), (a_r'), we have, by a well-known rule (p. 32 of this volume),

$$\Omega_1 = -2\int_{-c_1}^{-c_2} du = 2\int_{c_2}^{c_1} du = \Omega_4 + \Omega_3 + \Omega_2 + \Omega_1 = iH,$$

$$\Omega_1' - \Omega_2' = 2\int_{-c_2}^{-c_3} du = 2\int_{c_3}^{c_2} du = \Omega_4' = -K,$$

$$-\Omega_2 = 2\int_{-c_3}^{-c_4} du = -2\int_{c_4}^{c_3} du = \Omega_4 = iM,$$

$$\Omega_2' - \Omega_3' = 2\int_{-c_4}^{-c_5} du = 2\int_{c_5}^{c_4} du = \Omega_3' - \Omega_4' = N,$$

$$-\Omega_3 = 2\int_{-c_5}^{c_5} du = 0,$$

where each of H, K, M, N denotes a real positive quantity;

these equations give

$$\Omega_1 = iH,\quad \Omega_2 = -iM,\quad \Omega_3 = 0,\quad \Omega_4 = iM,$$
$$\Omega_1' = -2K + 2N,\qquad \Omega_2' = -K + 2N,$$
$$\Omega_3' = -K + N,\qquad \Omega_4' = -K.$$

For the two integrals under consideration let the respective quantities H, K, M, N be distinguished as H_1, K_1, M_1, N_1 and H_2, K_2, M_2, N_2; put, as in general,

$$\Pi = \begin{pmatrix} \Omega_{11} \dots \Omega_{14}, & \Omega_{11}' \dots \Omega_{14}' \\ \Omega_{21} \dots \Omega_{24}, & \Omega_{21}' \dots \Omega_{24}' \end{pmatrix};$$

we then have

$$\Pi = \begin{pmatrix} iH_1, & iM_1, & -K_1, & N_1 \\ iH_2, & iM_2, & -K_2, & N_2 \end{pmatrix} \begin{pmatrix} 1 & 0 & 0 & 0, & 0 & 0 & 0 & 0 \\ 0 & -1 & 0 & 1, & 0 & 0 & 0 & 0 \\ 0 & 0 & 0 & 0, & 2 & 1 & 1 & 1 \\ 0 & 0 & 0 & 0, & 2 & 2 & 1 & 0 \end{pmatrix},$$

of which the second matrix, having as one of its determinants

$$\begin{vmatrix} 1 & 0 & 0 & 0 \\ 0 & -1 & 0 & 0 \\ 0 & 0 & 1 & 1 \\ 0 & 0 & 1 & 0 \end{vmatrix},$$

is itself unitary, and may be denoted by k as before (p. 230), being of type $(2n, 2p)$ with $n = 2, p = 4$; the first matrix may then be denoted by a; the splice of the rth and sth rows of k being denoted by (r, s), we find

$$(1, 2) = 0,\quad (1, 3) = 2,\quad (1, 4) = 2,\quad (2, 3) = 0,\quad (2, 4) = -2,\quad (3, 4) = 0,$$

and hence
$$k\epsilon_{2p}\bar{k} = \begin{pmatrix} 0 & 0 & -2 & -2 \\ 0 & 0 & 0 & 2 \\ 2 & 0 & 0 & 0 \\ 2 & -2 & 0 & 0 \end{pmatrix},\quad |k\epsilon_{2p}\bar{k}| = 2^4;$$

also if
$$f = \begin{pmatrix} 1 & 0 & 0 & 0 \\ 0 & -1 & 0 & 0 \\ 0 & 0 & 1 & 0 \\ 0 & 0 & -1 & 1 \end{pmatrix},$$

we find
$$fk\epsilon_{2p}\bar{k}\bar{f} = 2\begin{pmatrix} 0 & 0 & -1 & 0 \\ 0 & 0 & 0 & -1 \\ 1 & 0 & 0 & 0 \\ 0 & 1 & 0 & 0 \end{pmatrix} = 2\epsilon_{2n}.$$

It appears thus that

$$u_1 = \int \frac{x\,dx}{y},\quad u_2 = \int \frac{x^3\,dx}{y},$$

form a defective system of integrals, with index 2 and multiplicity 4; the four sets of solutions of

$$\int_0^{(x_1)} \frac{x\,dx}{y} + \int_0^{(x_2)} \frac{x\,dx}{y} \equiv U_1, \quad \int_0^{(x_1)} \frac{x^3 dx}{y} + \int_0^{(x_2)} \frac{x^3 dx}{y} \equiv U_2,$$

are in fact obviously of the form

$$\{(x_1, y_1), (x_2, y_2)\}, \ \{(-x_1, y_1), (x_2, y_2)\}, \ \{(x_1, y_1), (-x_2, y_2)\}, \ \{(-x_1, y_1), (-x_2, y_2)\}.$$

To construct the theta function $\Theta(\mu^{-1}u, \sigma)$ we should put $a = (\mu, \mu')f$; we find then

$$\mu = i \begin{pmatrix} H_1, & -M_1 \\ H_2, & -M_2 \end{pmatrix},$$

$$\sigma = \mu^{-1}\mu' = i(H_1M_2 - H_2M_1)^{-1} \begin{pmatrix} M_1N_2 - M_2N_1 - M_1K_2 + M_2K_1, & M_1N_2 - M_2N_1 \\ H_1N_2 - H_2N_1 - H_1K_2 + H_2K_1, & H_1N_2 - H_2N_1 \end{pmatrix}.$$

74. As another example consider the surface associated with the equation $x^4 + y^4 = 1$.

Drawing cross-lines joining $x = 1$ to $x = i$, $x = -1$ to $x = i$ and $x = i$ to $x = -i$, the latter passing through $x = \infty$, and agreeing that on passing the first from right to left the sheets 1234 change respectively to 2341, on passing the second from right to left the sheets 1234 change respectively to 2341, while on passing the last from left to right the sheets 1234 change respectively to 2341, as indicated in the figure, and denoting the paths in the various sheets by the various kinds of line indicated, we may draw a system of canonical period loops as in the figure. The surface is of deficiency 3, and three integrals of the first kind are $\int \frac{y\,dx}{y^4}$, $\int \frac{xy\,dx}{y^4}$ and $\int \frac{y^2 dx}{y^4}$. Let the increments of any one of these for the left sides respectively of the loops (a_1), (a_2), (a_3), (b_1), (b_2), (b_3) be called Ω_1, Ω_2, Ω_3, Ω_1', Ω_2', Ω_3'; the first is obtained by a negative circuit of (b_1), and the fourth by a positive circuit of (a_1), and so on. Calling the branch places $x = 1$, $x = -1$, $x = i$ respectively by the numbers 1, 2, 3, and a single positive circuit about either of these by the same number, the circuits for the six periods are then respectively

Ω_1 ,	Ω_2 ,	Ω_3 ,	Ω_1' ,	Ω_2' ,	Ω_3'
31^{-1},	$3^{-1}1^{-1}2^{-2}$,	1312,	$2^{-1}1$,	$23^{-1}1^{-1}2$,	$13^2 2$,

where the symbol 31^{-1} means a circuit resolvable into a positive circuit about 3 followed by a negative circuit about 1, etc.

Now let $\epsilon = i^m$, where m is 1, 1 or 2 according as we are considering the first, second, or third of the integrals $\int \frac{y\,dx}{y^4}$, $\int \frac{xy\,dx}{y^4}$, $\int \frac{y^2 dx}{y^4}$, and let P, Q, R

17—2

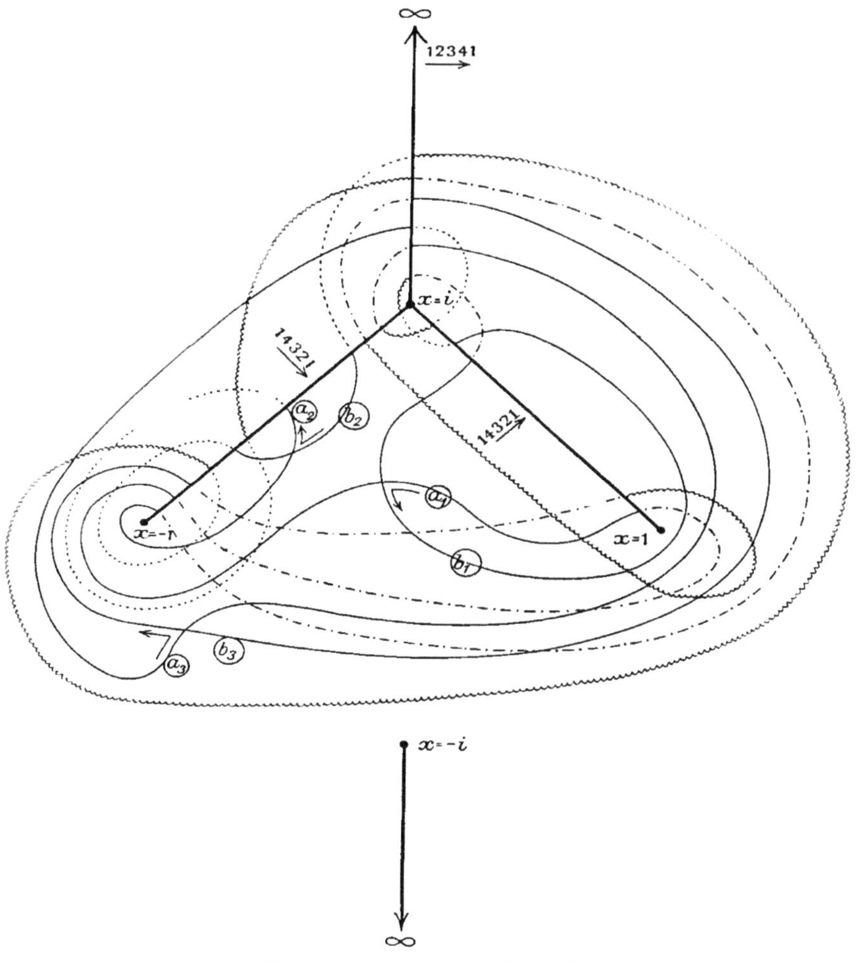

Canonical dissection for $x^4+y^4=1$.

First or lowest sheet, ——— ; second sheet, ... ; third sheet, ∿∿∿∿∿ ; fourth sheet, —·—·—·— ; the passages at the cross-lines are given by the rules marked in the diagram $\overrightarrow{12341}$, $\overrightarrow{14321}$.

denote the values of any one of these integrals taken in the first sheet from a point in the first sheet respectively to the branch places 1, 2 or 3; then the values obtained by the circuits put down above are respectively, if $\mu_i = 1 - \epsilon^i$,

$$\Omega_1 = R(1-\epsilon) + \epsilon(P - \epsilon^{-1}P) = -\mu_1(P-R),$$

$$\Omega_2 = R(1-\epsilon^{-1}) + \epsilon^{-1}P(1-\epsilon^{-1}) + \epsilon^{-2}Q(1-\epsilon^{-2}),$$

$$= \mu_2(P-Q) - \mu_3(P-R),$$

$$\Omega_3 = P(1-\epsilon) + \epsilon R(1-\epsilon) + \epsilon^2 P(1-\epsilon) + \epsilon^3 Q(1-\epsilon),$$
$$= \mu_3(P-Q) + (\mu_1 - \mu_2)(P-R),$$
$$\Omega_1' = Q(1-\epsilon^{-1}) + \epsilon^{-1}P(1-\epsilon) = -\mu_3(P-Q),$$
$$\Omega_2' = Q(1-\epsilon) + \epsilon R(1-\epsilon^{-1}) + P(1-\epsilon^{-1}) + \epsilon^{-1}Q(1-\epsilon),$$
$$= (\mu_3 - \mu_1)(P-Q) + \mu_1(P-R),$$
$$\Omega_3' = P(1-\epsilon) + \epsilon R(1-\epsilon^2) + \epsilon^3 Q(1-\epsilon),$$
$$= \mu_3(P-Q) + (\mu_1 - \mu_3)(P-R).$$

Put

$$A = \int_0^1 \frac{y\,dx}{y^4} = \frac{1}{4}\int_0^1 \frac{dt}{t^{\frac{3}{4}}(1-t)^{\frac{3}{4}}} = \frac{\Gamma^2(\frac{1}{4})}{4\sqrt{\pi}},$$

$$B = \int_0^1 \frac{x\,dx}{(1-x^4)^{\frac{3}{4}}} = \frac{A}{\sqrt{2}}; \qquad C = \int_0^1 \frac{dx}{(1-x^4)^{\frac{1}{2}}} = \frac{A}{\sqrt{2}},$$

so that

$$\int_0^{-1} \frac{y\,dx}{y^4} = -A, \quad \int_0^i \frac{y\,dx}{y^4} = iA, \quad \int_0^1 - \int_0^{-1} = 2A, \quad \int_0^1 - \int_0^i = (1-i)A,$$

$$\int_0^{-1} \frac{xy\,dx}{y^4} = B, \quad \int_0^i \frac{xy\,dx}{y^4} = -B, \quad \int_0^1 - \int_0^{-1} = 0, \quad \int_0^1 - \int_0^i = 2B,$$

$$\int_0^{-1} \frac{y^2dx}{y^4} = -C, \quad \int_0^i \frac{y^2dx}{y^4} = iC, \quad \int_0^1 - \int_0^{-1} = 2C, \quad \int_0^1 - \int_0^i = (1-i)C;$$

then with

$$u_1 = \frac{1}{2A}\int_0^x \frac{y\,dx}{y^4}, \quad u_2 = \frac{1}{2B}\int_0^x \frac{xy\,dx}{y^4}, \quad u_3 = \frac{1}{2C}\int_0^x \frac{y^2dx}{y^4},$$

the lower limit being $x = 0$, $y = 1$, taken to be in the first sheet, we have

for u_1, $\frac{P-Q}{2A} = 1$, $\frac{P-R}{2A} = \frac{1}{2}(1-i)$, $\mu_1 = 1-i$, $\mu_2 = 2$, $\mu_3 = 1+i$,

for u_2, $\frac{P-Q}{2B} = 0$, $\frac{P-R}{2B} = 1$, $\mu_1 = 1-i$, $\mu_2 = 2$, $\mu_3 = 1+i$,

for u_3, $\frac{P-Q}{2C} = 1$, $\frac{P-R}{2C} = \frac{1}{2}(1-i)$, $\mu_1 = 2$, $\mu_2 = 0$, $\mu_3 = 2$,

and the period scheme for u_1, u_2, u_3 is accordingly, from the results above,

u_1	i,	1,	i;	$-(1+i)$,	i,	0,
u_2	$-(1-i)$,	$-(1+i)$,	$-(1+i)$;	0,	$1-i$,	$-2i$,
u_3	$-(1-i)$,	$-(1-i)$,	$3-i$;	-2,	$1-i$,	2.

Put $$v_1 = u_1 = \frac{1}{2A}\int_0^x \frac{dx}{y^3}, \quad v_2 = iu_2/(1-i) = \frac{ie^{i\frac{\pi}{4}}}{2A}\int_0^x \frac{x\,dx}{y^3},$$

$$v_3 = u_3/(1-i) = \frac{e^{i\frac{\pi}{4}}}{2A}\int_0^x \frac{dx}{y^2};$$

then the periods can be respectively written,

$$v_1;\ (1, i)\begin{pmatrix} 0, & 1, & 0, & -1, & 0, & 0 \\ 1, & 0, & 1, & -1, & 1, & 0 \end{pmatrix},$$

$$v_2;\ (1, i)\begin{pmatrix} 0, & 1, & 1, & 0, & 0, & 1 \\ -1, & 0, & 0, & 0, & 1, & 1 \end{pmatrix},$$

$$v_3;\ (1, i)\begin{pmatrix} -1, & -1, & 2, & -1, & 1, & 1 \\ 0, & 0, & 1, & -1, & 0, & 1 \end{pmatrix},$$

and, for each integral, are sums of integral multiples of 1 and i, so that each integral is an elliptic integral; in each case 1 and i are actually periods, and so the multiplicity, calculated as $(|k\epsilon_6\bar{k}|)^{\frac{1}{2}}$, where k denotes in turn the matrices here written of two rows and six columns, is in each case 2, and each integral takes any value twice over on the Riemann surface; in each case $k\epsilon_6\bar{k} = 2\begin{pmatrix}0 & -1\\ 1 & 0\end{pmatrix}$, and the index, as in all cases of a single integral reducing to an elliptic integral (or $n = 1$), is equal to the multiplicity.

If we put
$$x = -e^{i\frac{\pi}{4}}\frac{\mu}{\lambda}, \quad y = e^{-i\frac{\pi}{4}}\frac{\nu}{\lambda}$$
the equation $x^4 + y^4 = 1$ reduces to $\lambda^4 + \mu^4 + \nu^4 = 0$, and is unaltered by 96 linear transformations; namely we may permute λ, μ, ν arbitrarily, and may multiply any two of λ, μ, ν each by a fourth root of unity, giving $6 \times 4 \times 4$ transformations. With these changes the integrals v_1, v_2, v_3 become respectively

$$v_1 = \frac{1}{2A}\int \lambda d\omega, \quad v_2 = \frac{1}{2A}\int \mu d\omega, \quad v_3 = \frac{1}{2A}\int \nu d\omega,$$

where
$$d\omega = \frac{\mu d\nu - \nu d\mu}{\lambda^3} = \frac{\nu d\lambda - \lambda d\nu}{\mu^3} = \frac{\lambda d\mu - \mu d\lambda}{\nu^3};$$

taking the first form of $d\omega$ it is manifest that dv_1 is unaltered by taking $\lambda' : \mu' : \nu' = -\lambda : \mu : \nu$, a transformation changing into itself any one of the four points for which $\lambda = 0$; thus if L denote one of these points we have

$$\int_{(L)}^{(\lambda, \mu, \nu)} \lambda d\omega = \int_{(L)}^{(-\lambda, \mu, \nu)} \lambda d\omega,$$

and the two points for which the integral v_1, integrated from any lower limit, takes the same value, are (λ, μ, ν) and $(-\lambda, \mu, \nu)$. Similarly for v_2 and v_3. If we put

$$\lambda^2 = -e^{-\frac{\pi i}{4}}[8\xi(\xi^2 - 1)]^{\frac{1}{2}}, \quad \mu = \xi + i, \quad \nu = -e^{-\frac{\pi i}{4}}(\xi - i),$$

which give $\lambda^4 + \mu^4 + \nu^4 = 0$, we at once have

$$\int \lambda d\omega = \int \frac{\mu d\nu - \nu d\mu}{\lambda^2} = i\sqrt{2}\int \frac{d\xi}{\sqrt{4\xi(\xi^2 - 1)}},$$

an elliptic integral of which the periods are $2A$ and $2Ai$; both $\xi = i(e^{-\frac{\pi i}{4}}\mu - \nu)/(e^{-\frac{\pi i}{4}}\mu + \nu)$, and $\eta = 2\xi^{\frac{1}{2}}(\xi^2 - 1)^{\frac{1}{2}} = 2\sqrt{2}e^{-\frac{\pi i}{4}}\lambda^2/(e^{-\frac{\pi i}{4}}\mu + \nu)^2$, are rational functions of the point (x, y) of the original surface $x^4 + y^4 = 1$, while conversely, x^2 and y^2, equal respectively to $e^{-\frac{\pi i}{4}}(\xi + i)^2/\eta\sqrt{2}$ and $e^{\frac{\pi i}{4}}(\xi - i)^2/\eta\sqrt{2}$, are rational in (ξ, η). A similar transformation to the same elliptic integral is possible for v_2 and v_3. This integral allows complex multiplication, for instance* by $\zeta = (\xi^2 - 1)/2i\xi$, and there are thus other transformations of the original integrals to the same elliptic integral.

The equation $x^4 + y^4 = 1$ can be solved by single valued functions of a single parameter in the form

$$x = e^{\frac{\pi i}{12}}\eta^2\left(\frac{\tau}{2}\right)\Big/\eta^2\left(\frac{1+\tau}{2}\right), \quad y = 2e^{\frac{\pi i}{12}}\eta^2(2\tau)/\eta^2\left(\frac{1+\tau}{2}\right),$$

where, with $q = e^{i\pi\tau}$,

$$\eta(\tau) = q^{\frac{1}{12}}\sum_{n=-\infty}^{\infty}(-1)^n q^{3n^2+n}.$$

See Weber, *Elliptische Functionen* (1891), p. 86. See also Dyck, *Math. Annal.*, XVII. (1880), p. 510.

Example. This case furnishes an interesting example of the distinction to be made between the algebraic definition of a normal system of periods, such namely as satisfies the equations expressed by $\Omega\epsilon\overline{\Omega} = 0$, and the geometrical definition by means of a canonical system of period loops forming a complete boundary of the Riemann surface. As is illustrated by a case below, it may sometimes be easier to determine algebraically a set of normal periods than to make a canonical dissection; but it is only for a system of periods determined by such a dissection that the formula obtained above for the multiplicity is proved to have the interpretation attached to it.

Take the integrals

$$(u_1', u_2', u_3') = \begin{pmatrix} \frac{1}{2}(1-i), & \frac{1}{2}(1-i), & 1-i \\ 0, & -\frac{1}{2}(1+i), & -\frac{1}{2}(1-i) \\ i, & i, & 1+2i \end{pmatrix}(v_1, v_2, v_3);$$

it is easily seen that their periods, calculated from the above scheme, are

$$\begin{array}{c|cccccc} u_1' & -(1-i), & 0, & 4-i; & -3, & 2, & 3 \\ u_2' & 0, & -i, & -2; & 1, & 0, & -(1+i) \\ u_3' & -(1+2i), & -1, & -1+6i; & 2-4i, & -1+2i, & -2+4i \end{array}$$

Denoting this scheme by Ω, we find at once that $\Omega\epsilon_6\overline{\Omega} = 0$, namely that the

* Cf. the author's *Abel's Theorem*, p. 637. It is necessary to take $r = \alpha^2 + \beta^2$ and to solve the congruences $\alpha k + \beta k' \equiv 0$, $-\beta k + \alpha k' \equiv 0$ (mod. r); the case $r = 2$ is that mentioned in the text. For this elliptic integral the complex multiplication is considered by Abel, *Œuvres*, I. (1881), p. 352, etc.

splice of any two rows is zero, and the periods obey the algebraic conditions for a set of normal periods. Putting now

$$H = \begin{pmatrix} 1 & -1 & 0 & 0 & 0 & -2 \\ 0 & 0 & -1 & -2 & 0 & -1 \\ 1 & -1 & 0 & -1 & 0 & -2 \\ 2 & -1 & 1 & 0 & -1 & -3 \\ 2 & 0 & 0 & -1 & 0 & -3 \\ 0 & 0 & 1 & 2 & -1 & 1 \end{pmatrix},$$

a matrix whose determinant is easily seen to be unity, the periods given by

$$\Omega' = \Omega H$$

are a set in terms of which the periods Ω may conversely be expressed with integral coefficients, and they are found to be

$$\Omega' = \begin{pmatrix} 1 & 0 & 0 & i & 0 & 0 \\ 0 & 1 & 0 & 0 & i & 0 \\ 0 & 0 & 1 & 0 & 0 & 2i \end{pmatrix};$$

we have then also $\Omega'\epsilon_6\overline{\Omega}' = 0$, that is $\Omega H\epsilon_6\overline{H}\overline{\Omega} = 0$, but not $H\epsilon_6\overline{H} = \epsilon_6$, and the periods Ω' are not a set arising from a canonical dissection of the Riemann surface; in fact we find

$$H\epsilon_6\overline{H} = \begin{pmatrix} 0 & 4 & 1 & -3 & 1 & -5 \\ -4 & 0 & -4 & -8 & -7 & 0 \\ -1 & 4 & 0 & -5 & -1 & -5 \\ 3 & 8 & 5 & 0 & 5 & -9 \\ -1 & 7 & 1 & -5 & 0 & -7 \\ 5 & 0 & 5 & 9 & 7 & 0 \end{pmatrix}.$$

The periods of u_1' being written, from the scheme Ω, in the form

$$(1, i)\begin{pmatrix} -1 & 0 & 4 & -3 & 2 & 3 \\ 1 & 0 & -1 & 0 & 0 & 0 \end{pmatrix},$$

since the determinants from k have unity as greatest common divisor, the multiplicity $(|k\epsilon_6\bar{k}|)^{\frac{1}{2}}$ is $3 + 3 = 6$; for u_2' we may similarly write the periods

$$(1, i)\begin{pmatrix} 0 & 0 & -2 & 1 & 0 & -1 \\ 0 & -1 & 0 & 0 & 0 & -1 \end{pmatrix},$$

and obtain the multiplicity 2; and for u_3', with the periods

$$(1, 2i)\begin{pmatrix} -1 & -1 & -1 & 2 & -1 & -2 \\ -1 & 0 & 3 & -2 & 1 & 2 \end{pmatrix},$$

the multiplicity is $2 + 2 - 1 - 2 + 6 = 7$. Thus the integral u_1' takes each value *six* times on the Riemann surface, the integral u_2' takes each value *twice*, and the integral u_3' takes each value *seven* times. We have

$$u_1' = \frac{1-i}{4A}\int (\lambda + \mu + 2\nu)\, d\omega,$$

$$u_2' = -\frac{1-i}{4A}\int (i\mu + \nu)\, d\omega,$$

$$u_3' = \frac{i}{2A}\int (\lambda + \mu + 2\nu - i\nu)\, d\omega\,;$$

the two places where u_2' has the same value are obtainable from the remark that the integral is unchanged by putting $\lambda = -i\lambda'$, $\mu = \nu'$, $\nu = -\mu'$, a self-corresponding point of this transformation being $\lambda = 0$, $\nu + i\mu = 0$. It is not obvious what are the six places where u_1' has the same value, or the seven places where u_3' has the same value. More generally we can find an infinite number of integrals of the form $Pu_1 + Qu_2 + Ru_3$, of which the periods are all expressible in the form $M + Ni$, where M and N are integers.

75. For another example we take the equation

$$y^3x + y + x^3 = 0.$$

If we put $s = -x$, $t = -y^2x$, which give $x = -s$, $y = s^3/(1-t)$, we have

$$s^7 = t(1-t)^2;$$

the two equations, so birationally related, are of deficiency 3, the integrals of the first kind being

$$\int \frac{s\,dt}{t(1-t)},\quad \int \frac{s^2dt}{t(1-t)},\quad \int \frac{s^4dt}{t(1-t)^2}.$$

We do not attempt to dissect the Riemann surface associated with the equation $s^7 = t(1-t)^2$, but consider the integrals on the plane of t. The values of s represented by the equation $s^7 = t(1-t)^2$ have cycles at $t = 0$, $t = 1$, $t = \infty$, at each of which all seven values change into one another; a closed circuit on the t-plane is equivalent, so far as giving rise to additive increments for the integrals, to a certain number of positive circuits of the points $t = 0$, $t = 1$; a closed circuit equivalent to f circuits positively round $t = 0$ and g circuits positively round $t = 1$ will lead back to the same value of s if $f + 2g \equiv 0$ (mod. 7), or $g \equiv 3f$. If $\epsilon = e^{\frac{2\pi i m}{7}}$, where $m = 1$, 2 or 4 according as we are considering the first, second or third of the integrals of the first kind written above, it is at once seen that the additive increment for the integral, by any closed path which leads back to the same value for s, is, save for a constant multiplier appropriate to the integral under consideration, a sum of integral multiples of the six quantities $\mu_1, \mu_2, \ldots, \mu_6$, where $\mu_h = 1 - \epsilon^h$. For consider a path consisting of f_1 positive circuits of $t = 0$, followed by

g_1 circuits of $t=1$, followed by f_2 circuits of $t=0$, followed by g_2 circuits of $t=1$, and so on; we may denote this by

$$(0)^{f_1}(1)^{g_1}(0)^{f_2}(1)^{g_2}\dots(0)^{f_r}(1)^{g_r},$$

where, for instance, f_1 or g_r, or both, may be zero; if the values of the integral under consideration, from the initial point of integration with a definite one of the seven determinations for s belonging to this value of t, straight to $t=0$, be called A, and straight to $t=1$, be called B, the closed circuit indicated above gives, for the integral, the value

$$A-\epsilon^{f_1}A+\epsilon^{f_1}(B-\epsilon^{2g_1}B)+\epsilon^{f_1+2g_1}(A-\epsilon^{f_2}A)$$
$$+\dots+\epsilon^{f_1+\dots+f_r+2(g_1+\dots+g_{r-1})}(B-\epsilon^{2g_r}B),$$

wherein, by hypothesis,

$$f_1+\dots+f_r+2(g_1+\dots+g_r)\equiv 0 \pmod{7};$$

it gives then

$$(A-B)\left[1-\epsilon^{f_1}+\epsilon^{f_1+2g_1}-\epsilon^{f_1+f_2+2g_1}+\dots-\epsilon^{f_1+\dots+f_r+2(g_1+\dots+g_{r-1})}\right],$$

or

$$(A-B)\left[\mu_{f_1}-\mu_{f_1+2g_1}+\mu_{f_1+f_2+2g_1}-\dots+\mu_{f_1+\dots+f_r+2(g_1+\dots+g_{r-1})}\right];$$

if then the integral under consideration be divided by $A-B$, and the quantities μ reduced by the rule $\mu_{h'}=\mu_h$ when $h'\equiv h \pmod{7}$, $\mu_0=1$, the additive indeterminatenesses of the integral will be expressible by sums of integral multiples, with multipliers the same for all the integrals, of the six quantities $\mu_1, \dots, \mu_6$. Thus, if

$$P=-\int_0^1\frac{s\,dt}{t(1-t)},\quad Q=-\int_0^1\frac{s^2dt}{t(1-t)},\quad R=-\int_0^1\frac{s^4dt}{t(1-t)^2},$$

so that, Γ_λ denoting the gamma function $\Gamma\left(\frac{\lambda}{7}\right)$, we have

$$P=-\frac{1}{\pi}\sin\frac{3\pi}{7}\Gamma_1\Gamma_2\Gamma_4,\quad Q=-\frac{1}{\pi}\sin\frac{\pi}{7}\Gamma_1\Gamma_2\Gamma_4,\quad R=-\frac{1}{\pi}\sin\frac{2\pi}{7}\Gamma_1\Gamma_2\Gamma_4,$$

a scheme of periods for the integrals

$$u_1=\frac{1}{P}\int_0^x\frac{s\,dt}{t(1-t)},\quad u_2=\frac{1}{Q}\int_0^x\frac{s^2dt}{t(1-t)},\quad u_3=\frac{1}{R}\int_0^x\frac{s^4dt}{t(1-t)^2}$$

is given by

u_1	μ_6,	μ_5,	μ_3;	μ_1,	μ_2,	μ_4
u_2	μ_5,	μ_3,	μ_6;	μ_2,	μ_4,	μ_1
u_3	μ_3,	μ_6,	μ_5;	μ_4,	μ_1,	μ_2

where $\mu_h=1-e^{\frac{2\pi ih}{7}}$, these being the values of the integrals for contours respectively Ω_6, Ω_5, Ω_3, Ω_1, Ω_2, Ω_4, where Ω_h denotes a contour passing h times positively round $t=0$ and $3h$ times positively round $t=1$.

We proceed to shew how, by taking suitable linear functions of the integrals and suitable combinations of the contours, subject to the condition that all period contours shall be integrally expressible by those adopted, the period scheme may be reduced* to

$$\begin{array}{c|cccccc} w_1 & 1, & 0, & 0, & \tau, & 0\,, & 0 \\ w_2 & 0, & 1, & 0, & 0, & 2\tau, & 0 \\ w_3 & 0, & 0, & 1, & 0, & 0\,, & 2\tau \end{array}$$

where $$\tau^2 = \frac{1}{2}(\tau - 1), \quad \tau = \frac{1 + i\sqrt{7}}{4}.$$

It follows that each of the integrals w_1, w_2, w_3 is an elliptic integral.

Putting

$$G = \begin{pmatrix} \mu_1, & \mu_2, & \mu_4 \\ \mu_2, & \mu_4, & \mu_1 \\ \mu_4, & \mu_1, & \mu_2 \end{pmatrix}, \qquad H = \begin{pmatrix} \mu_6, & \mu_5, & \mu_3 \\ \mu_5, & \mu_3, & \mu_6 \\ \mu_3, & \mu_6, & \mu_5 \end{pmatrix},$$

and $$A = \begin{pmatrix} 0, & 1, & 0 \\ 0, & 0, & 1 \\ 1, & 0, & 0 \end{pmatrix}, \qquad B = \begin{pmatrix} 1, & -1, & -1 \\ -1, & 1, & -1 \\ -1, & -1, & 1 \end{pmatrix},$$

so that $$A + B\tau = \begin{pmatrix} \tau, & 1-\tau, & -\tau \\ -\tau, & \tau, & 1-\tau \\ 1-\tau, & -\tau, & \tau \end{pmatrix},$$

it can be shewn that

$$G = (A + B\tau) H;$$

this can be established by direct calculation; since 1, 2 and 4 are the quadratic residues of 7, being the residues of 3^0, 3^2, and 3^4, we have, if $\epsilon = e^{\frac{2\pi i}{7}}$ (Gauss, *Werke*, Bd. II.; Kronecker, *Crelle*, CV. (1889), p. 267)

$$\epsilon + \epsilon^2 + \epsilon^4 = \tfrac{1}{2}(-1 + i\sqrt{7}) = 2\tau - 1, \quad \epsilon^3 + \epsilon^5 + \epsilon^6 = \tfrac{1}{2}(-1 - i\sqrt{7}) = -2\tau;$$

but perhaps the simplest mode of verification consists in proving that

$$GH = \begin{pmatrix} 7\;, & 4 - 2\tau, & 3 + 2\tau \\ 3 + 2\tau, & 7\;, & 4 - 2\tau \\ 4 - 2\tau, & 3 + 2\tau, & 7 \end{pmatrix}, \quad H^2 = \begin{pmatrix} 3 + 2\tau, & 2 + 6\tau, & 2 + 6\tau \\ 2 + 6\tau, & 3 + 2\tau, & 2 + 6\tau \\ 2 + 6\tau, & 2 + 6\tau, & 3 + 2\tau \end{pmatrix},$$

* No proof is given in the text that this scheme belongs to a canonical dissection of the corresponding Riemann Surface. In the period scheme given by Hurwitz, *Math. Annalen*, XXVI. (1886), p. 123, the quadratic form corresponding to the matrix of the last three columns

$$\begin{pmatrix} \tau\;, & \tau - 1, & -\tau \\ \tau - 1, & -\tau\;, & \tau \\ -\tau\;, & \tau\;, & \tau - 1 \end{pmatrix}$$

is not a definite form, the diagonal elements not being of the same sign. For Hurwitz's form, save for an interchange of the last two columns, see also Klein-Fricke, *Modulfunctionen*, II. (1892), p. 595.

and then that $$GH = (A + B\tau)H^2,$$
the steps being all very easy, the three matrices involved in the last equation being symmetrical about the cross-diagonal. The determinant of the matrix H is easily found to be $7(2\tau - 1)$, which is not zero.

Having proved that $G = (A + B\tau)H$, consider the integrals $w = Pu$, or

$$(w_1, w_2, w_3) = \begin{pmatrix} P_{11}, & P_{12}, & P_{13} \\ P_{21}, & P_{22}, & P_{23} \\ P_{31}, & P_{32}, & P_{33} \end{pmatrix} (u_1, u_2, u_3);$$

their scheme of periods is, for w_i,

$$P_{i1}H_{11} + P_{i2}H_{21} + P_{i3}H_{31}, \ \ldots, \ P_{i1}G_{13} + P_{i2}G_{23} + P_{i3}G_{33},$$

namely consists of the two matrices

$$PH, \ PG;$$

take $$P = \begin{pmatrix} -1, & 0, & 0 \\ 1, & 1, & 0 \\ 1, & 0, & 1 \end{pmatrix} H^{-1};$$

the six lines constituting the scheme of periods for w_1, w_2, w_3 are then formed by the juxtaposition of the two matrices

$$\begin{pmatrix} -1, & 0, & 0 \\ 1, & 1, & 0 \\ 1, & 0, & 1 \end{pmatrix}, \qquad \begin{pmatrix} -1, & 0, & 0 \\ 1, & 1, & 0 \\ 1, & 0, & 1 \end{pmatrix} H^{-1}G;$$

now we have remarked above that $GH^{-1} = A + B\tau$, or

$$GH^{-1} = \begin{pmatrix} \tau, & 1-\tau, & -\tau \\ -\tau, & \tau, & 1-\tau \\ 1-\tau, & -\tau, & \tau \end{pmatrix},$$

so that, from $H = \bar{H}$, $G = \bar{G}$,

$$H^{-1}G = \bar{H}^{-1}\bar{G} = \overline{GH^{-1}} = \begin{pmatrix} \tau, & -\tau, & 1-\tau \\ 1-\tau, & \tau, & -\tau \\ -\tau, & 1-\tau, & \tau \end{pmatrix};$$

hence the scheme of periods for w_1, w_2, w_3, is

w_1	-1,	0,	0,	$-\tau$,	τ,	$-1+\tau$
w_2	1,	1,	0,	1,	0 ,	$1-2\tau$
w_3	1,	0,	1,	0,	$1-2\tau$,	1

Now take other loops; the period columns in the scheme just obtained correspond respectively to Ω_6, Ω_5, Ω_3, Ω_1, Ω_2, Ω_4, where Ω_h denotes a loop going h times positively round $t = 0$ and $3h$ times positively round $t = 1$, this being a path which brings back s, and the subject of integration in each integral, to its initial value; we take the following loops

$$\Omega_6' = -\Omega_6 + \Omega_5 + \Omega_3, \quad \Omega_5' = \Omega_5, \quad \Omega_3' = \Omega_3,$$
$$\Omega_1' = \Omega_5 - \Omega_1, \quad \Omega_2' = \Omega_6 + \Omega_5 - \Omega_1 - \Omega_4, \quad \Omega_4' = \Omega_5 + \Omega_3 - \Omega_1 - \Omega_2,$$

in terms of which conversely the original loops are expressible, namely by

$$\Omega_6 = -\Omega_6' + \Omega_5' + \Omega_3', \quad \Omega_5 = \Omega_5', \quad \Omega_3 = \Omega_3',$$
$$\Omega_1 = \Omega_5' - \Omega_1', \quad \Omega_2 = \Omega_3' + \Omega_1' - \Omega_4', \quad \Omega_4 = -\Omega_6' + \Omega_5' + \Omega_3' + \Omega_1' - \Omega_2';$$

then the period scheme for w_1, w_2, w_3 becomes

$$\begin{pmatrix} -1, & 0, & 0, & -\tau, & \tau, & -1+\tau \\ 1, & 1, & 0, & 1, & 0, & 1-2\tau \\ 1, & 0, & 1, & 0, & 1-2\tau, & 1 \end{pmatrix} \begin{pmatrix} -1, & 0, & 0, & 0, & 1, & 0 \\ 1, & 1, & 0, & 1, & 1, & 1 \\ 1, & 0, & 1, & 0, & 0, & 1 \\ 0, & 0, & 0, & -1, & -1, & -1 \\ 0, & 0, & 0, & 0, & 0, & -1 \\ 0, & 0, & 0, & 0, & -1, & 0 \end{pmatrix}$$

which is the same as

$$\begin{array}{c|cccccc} w_1 & 1, & 0, & 0, & \tau, & 0, & 0 \\ w_2 & 0, & 1, & 0, & 0, & 2\tau, & 0 \\ w_3 & 0, & 0, & 1, & 0, & 0, & 2\tau \end{array}$$

where, u_1, u_2, u_3 being certain numerical multiples, previously specified, respectively of the integrals

$$\int_0^x \frac{s\,dt}{t(1-t)}, \quad \int_0^x \frac{s^2dt}{t(1-t)}, \quad \int_0^x \frac{s^4dt}{t(1-t)^2},$$

and μ_h denoting $1 - e^{\frac{2\pi ih}{7}}$, we have

$$(w_1, w_2, w_3) = \begin{pmatrix} -1 & 0 & 0 \\ 1 & 1 & 0 \\ 1 & 0 & 1 \end{pmatrix} \begin{pmatrix} \mu_6 & \mu_5 & \mu_3 \\ \mu_5 & \mu_3 & \mu_6 \\ \mu_3 & \mu_6 & \mu_5 \end{pmatrix}^{-1} (u_1, u_2, u_3).$$

It is thus clear that each of the integrals w_1, w_2, w_3 is reducible to an elliptic integral. The equation $y^3x + y + x^3 = 0$ has been much discussed. In the homogeneous form $xy^3 + yz^3 + zx^3 = 0$ it is transformed into itself by a linear group of 168 transformations; see for instance Klein-Fricke, *Modulfunctionen*, I. (1890), p. 692 ff.; Weber, *Algebra*, II. (1896), pp. 282, 433 ff., and the references there given to original authorities; also Burnside, *Theory of Groups* (1897), p. 302, and Poincaré, *Liouville*, Series 5, IX. (1903), p. 167. The number 168 is the greatest number of (1, 1) correspondences possible for a Riemann surface of deficiency $p = 3$ (Hurwitz, *Math. Annal.* XLI. (1893), p. 424). A rational function t of x, y, z can be given which is unaltered by the 168 transformations, and only by these; if this be taken as independent variable the functions du_1/dt, du_2/dt, du_3/dt satisfy a linear differential equation of the third order with coefficients rational in t whose monodromy group is then that of the 168 transformations (Hurwitz, *Math. Annal.* XXVI. (1886), p. 120). The independent variable being chosen so that the critical points are at $t=0$, $t=1$, $t=\infty$, denoting the dependent variable of the differential equation by y, and putting

$$x_1 = y, \quad x_2 = \frac{dy}{dt}, \quad x_3 = t(t-1)\frac{d^2y}{dt^2},$$

the differential equation may be replaced by the three

$$\left(\frac{dx_1}{dt}, \frac{dx_2}{dt}, \frac{dx_3}{dt}\right)$$
$$= \left[\begin{pmatrix} 0, & 1, & 0 \\ 0, & 0, & 0 \\ 0, & -\frac{72}{7}, & 0 \end{pmatrix} + \frac{1}{t}\begin{pmatrix} 0, & 0, & 0 \\ 0, & 0, & -1 \\ M, & \frac{20}{9}, & -3 \end{pmatrix} + \frac{1}{t-1}\begin{pmatrix} 0, & 0, & 0 \\ 0, & 0, & 1 \\ -N, & -\frac{3}{4}, & -2 \end{pmatrix}\right](x_1, x_2, x_3),$$

where $N = \frac{5}{8} + \frac{2}{63}$, $M = N - \frac{72.11}{7^3}$. It is at once seen that the matrices here multiplying $\frac{1}{t}$ and $\frac{1}{t-1}$ have both linear invariant factors, and that if $\theta_1, \theta_2, \theta_3$ and ϕ_1, ϕ_2, ϕ_3 be respectively their roots, we have

$$(e^{2\pi i\theta_1}, e^{2\pi i\theta_2}, e^{2\pi i\theta_3}) = (1, \omega, \omega^2),$$

where $\omega^3 = 1$, and

$$(e^{2\pi i\phi_1}, e^{2\pi i\phi_2}, e^{2\pi i\phi_3}) = (1, -1, -1).$$

Cf. the author's paper, *Proc. Lond. Math. Soc.*, XXXV. (1902), p. 371, and p. 347.

Note I. It may be enquired how far the preceding is capable of generalisation to the case of an equation

$$s^p = t^a(1-t)^b,$$

where p is a prime number, and a, b are positive integers less than p. The integral

$$\int \frac{s^\lambda dt}{t^\mu (1-t)^\nu}$$

will be of the first kind if μ be an integer just greater than $\lambda a/p$, which, if $\lambda < p$, is necessarily fractional, say if $\mu = E(\lambda a/p) + 1$, where $E(x)$ denotes the greatest integer contained in x; similarly $\nu = E(\lambda b/p) + 1$; and also $\mu + \nu - \frac{\lambda}{p}(a+b) - 1 > 0$, or

$$\frac{\lambda a}{p} - E\left(\frac{\lambda a}{p}\right) + \frac{\lambda b}{p} - E\left(\frac{\lambda b}{p}\right) < 1;$$

using Riemann's formula $\frac{1}{2}w - n + 1$ for the deficiency, we have, for $s^p = t^a(1-t)^b$, $1 + \frac{1}{2}(3p - 3 - 2p) = \frac{1}{2}(p-1)$, which then, for any positive prime p and $a < p$, $b < p$, is the number of integers λ less than p satisfying the last written inequality; in fact, if $\lambda' + \lambda = p$, since $\lambda a/p$ is not an integer, we have

$$E\left(\frac{\lambda a}{p}\right) + E\left(\frac{\lambda' a}{p}\right) = a - 1,$$

and

$$\frac{\lambda(a+b)}{p} - E\left(\frac{\lambda a}{p}\right) - E\left(\frac{\lambda b}{p}\right) + \frac{\lambda'(a+b)}{p} - E\left(\frac{\lambda' a}{p}\right) - E\left(\frac{\lambda' b}{p}\right) = 2.$$

If we put $\lambda a = [\lambda a] + Mp, \quad \lambda b = [\lambda b] + Np,$

where $[\lambda a]$, $[\lambda b]$ are the least positive residues, mod. p, the condition is the same as

$$[\lambda a] + [\lambda b] < p.$$

Denoting by g a proper (primitive) root of p, and putting $a \equiv g^{2h}$, $b \equiv g^{2k}$ (mod. p), if the inequality is to be satisfied by $\lambda \equiv g^{2\mu}$, whatever μ may be, so that the $\frac{1}{2}(p-1)$ values of λ are to be the quadratic residues of p as in the case $s^7 = t(1-t)^2$, the condition will be

$$[g^{2(h+\mu)}] + [g^{2(k+\mu)}] < p,$$

and will be satisfied only by those primes p of which every two quadratic residues have a sum less than p. It can be shewn that if p is of the form $4n+3$, the only possibility is $p = 7$. And no prime of the form $4n+3$ exists such that every two quadratic non-residues have a sum less than p.

Note II. We may consider more generally the case

$$y^n = (x - c_1)^{h_1} \dots (x - c_m)^{h_m},$$

where $n, h_1, \dots, h_m$ are positive integers, and each of $h_1, h_2, \dots, h_m$ and $h_1 + \dots + h_m$ is prime to n. The deficiency is then given by

$$(m+1)(n-1) - 2n = 2p - 2,$$

or

$$p = \tfrac{1}{2}(m-1)(n-1).$$

A positive circuit r times round c_1 and s times round c_2 will lead back to the same value of y if $h_1 r + h_2 s \equiv 0$ (mod. n); as h_2 is prime to n, this gives a value for s corresponding to an arbitrary value of r; we thus obtain, taking circuits round the $(m-1)$ pairs, (c_1, c_2), (c_1, c_3), ..., (c_1, c_m), with, in each case, r equal in turn to $1, 2, \dots, (n-1)$, in all

$$2p = (m-1)(n-1)$$

periods, of the form

$$(P_1 - P_2)\mu_1, \dots, (P_1 - P_2)\mu_{n-1};\ (P_1 - P_3)\mu_1, \dots, (P_1 - P_3)\mu_{n-1};\ \dots;$$
$$(P_1 - P_m)\mu_1, \dots, (P_1 - P_m)\mu_{n-1},$$

where $\mu_k = 1 - e^{\frac{2\pi i k}{n}}$ and P_k is the value of the integral taken from the initial point to the point $x = c_k$. There remain the problems of determining whether every period is an aggregate of these, and of determining $2p$ canonical loops on the corresponding Riemann surface; and of extending the results to the case where $n, h_1, \ldots, h_m$ are any integers. The forms of the integrals of the first kind are determined by Weierstrass, *Werke*, IV. (1902), pp. 135—145.

76. Another example of the occurrence of defective integrals of the first kind is furnished by the curve of order 8 given in Example 11, at the top of p. 155 of this volume. This curve has the properties: (i) it is of deficiency 9, the forms of the integrals of the first kind being given in that Example; (ii) the coordinates of points of the curve are expressible as single valued quadruply-periodic functions of two variables, the variables being connected by a fixed relation (the equation of the plane determining the curve as a section of the hyperelliptic surface); (iii) there are two integrals of the first kind for the curve which reduce to hyperelliptic integrals of four columns of periods, these being the arguments of the quadruply-periodic functions. This case therefore furnishes a very exact example of the general theory considered in the previous chapter of this volume, in virtue of the property (ii).

Note. It may be remarked that if the equation of § 72 be rendered homogeneous by writing $z = 1 + \frac{1}{2}(ex + fy)$, it takes the form

$$(z^2 - \phi_2)^2 = 4xy\,(ax + by)\,(cx + dy),$$

where ϕ_2 is homogeneous of the second degree in x, y, representing a quartic curve of which four bitangents are concurrent; that this geometrical property is a necessary and sufficient condition, in the case of a plane quartic, for a defective elliptic integral of rank 2, is proved directly by Kowalevski from the transcendental result here obtained in § 71; the curve is a projection of the space curve intersection of the quadric surface

$$z^2 - \phi_2 = xt,$$

and the cubic cone $\quad xt^2 = 4y\,(ax + by)\,(cx + dy)$;

the elliptic integral of a plane section of the latter is the defective integral of the text. The equation $z^4 = x^4 + y^4$ of § 74 is, geometrically, a particular case.

See further, Appendix to Part II., Note IV.

CHAPTER IX.

PROPOSITIONS FOR RATIONAL FUNCTIONS.

EXPRESSION OF A GENERAL PERIODIC FUNCTION BY THETA FUNCTIONS.

77. In what follows we have in mind the theorem, formulated by Kronecker (*Werke*, II. (1897), p. 275 ff.) that the points $(z_1, z_2, \ldots, z_n)$ satisfying any set of polynomial relations

$$G_1(z_1, \ldots, z_n) = 0, \ldots, G_m(z_1, \ldots, z_n) = 0,$$

are those belonging to a certain number of irreducible algebraical constructs, each of these constructs being represented by a set of equations of the form

$$f(y, x_1, \ldots, x_{n-k}) = 0, \quad x_{n-k+1} = \frac{\phi_{n-k+1}}{f'}, \ \ldots, \ x_n = \frac{\phi_n}{f'};$$

herein $x_1, x_2, \ldots, x_n$ are independent general linear functions of $z_1, \ldots, z_n$, to be used to replace these in the original equations and so eliminate any accidental want of parity in the way in which $z_1, \ldots, z_n$ enter into the original equations, the function f is a rational polynomial in y with coefficients rational in $x_1, \ldots, x_{n-k}$ which is irreducible in this form, and f' denotes $\partial f/\partial y$, while $\phi_{n-k+1}, \ldots, \phi_n$ are polynomials in y with coefficients rational in $x_1, \ldots, x_{n-k}$. Points $(x_1, \ldots, x_n)$ for which simultaneously $f=0$ and $f'=0$ do not arise for all values of $x_1, \ldots, x_{n-k}$, but only when these are connected by relations, and thus are given, in the arrangement here taken, by equations of the form above with k changed into $k+1$; in other words the algebraical construct above, until conventions as to its limiting points are introduced, is an open aggregate. To place the result in a clearer light we reproduce the proof in outline.

Having introduced the variables $x_1, \ldots, x_n$ in place of $z_1, \ldots, z_n$, take

$$y = u_1 x_1 + \ldots + u_n x_n,$$

where $u_1, \ldots, u_n$ are constants, to be retained as explicit *indeterminates** in

* For Kronecker's insistence on the significance of Gauss's introduction of such quantities, see *Werke*, II., p. 355. The discussion of the distinction to be made between them and numerical quantities is a matter of interest. One striking illustration of their use is in the problem of the theory of Groups, of finding a function unaltered by a specified sub-group but altered by any transformation of the fundamental group which does not belong to this sub-group; it may sometimes be easy to find such a function involving explicit indeterminates while difficult to specify precise numerical values which may replace these and leave the property of the function unimpaired. In the paper referred to, Kronecker gives other illustrations; and in the theory of irreducibility a theorem of Hilbert's, *Crelle*, CX. (1892), p. 121, may be cited.

the succeeding work. Thereby, after multiplication by a proper power of u_n, replace the original equations by polynomials in $y, x_1, \ldots, x_{n-1}$ and $u_1, \ldots, u_n$; each of these may be supposed decomposed by rational processes into a product of irreducible polynomials in y, whose coefficients are rational in $x_1, \ldots, x_{n-1}, u_1, \ldots, u_n$; and, of any one of these irreducible factors, entering into any one of the polynomial equations, all powers higher than the first may be removed. The original equations are then replaced by a set of equations

$$H_1(y, x_1, \ldots, x_{n-1}) = 0, \ldots, H_m(y, x_1, \ldots, x_{n-1}) = 0,$$

in each of which the left side is a product of first powers of irreducible polynomials; all points $(z_1, \ldots, z_n)$ satisfying the original equations satisfy these, and conversely.

If now these polynomials $H_1, \ldots, H_m$ have a common rational irreducible factor, let it be $F_1(y, x_1, \ldots, x_{n-1})$, and let H_r/F_1 be K_r; the points satisfying the original equations thus satisfy, either,

$$F_1(y, x_1, \ldots, x_{n-1}) = 0,$$

or, all the equations

$$K_1(y, x_1, \ldots, x_{n-1}) = 0, \ldots, K_m(y, x_1, \ldots, x_{n-1}) = 0,$$

and conversely. Consider now the latter equations; form from these the two

$$\lambda_1 K_1 + \ldots + \lambda_m K_m = 0, \quad \mu_1 K_1 + \ldots + \mu_m K_m = 0,$$

wherein $\lambda_1, \ldots, \lambda_m, \mu_1, \ldots, \mu_m$ are undetermined multipliers; from these two the variable x_{n-1} can be rationally eliminated, and the result arranged as a polynomial in the $2m$ quantities $\lambda_1, \ldots, \lambda_m, \mu_1, \ldots, \mu_m$, whose coefficients, say $L_1, L_2, \ldots$, are rational integral polynomials in $y, x_1, \ldots, x_{n-2}$. Any set of values of $y, x_1, \ldots, x_{n-1}$ which satisfies all the equations $K_1 = 0, \ldots, K_m = 0$ gives then a set of values of $y, x_1, \ldots, x_{n-2}$ which makes every one of these coefficients $L_1, L_2, \ldots$ vanish; conversely every solution of the system

$$L_1(y, x_1, \ldots, x_{n-2}) = 0, \quad L_2(y, x_1, \ldots, x_{n-2}) = 0, \ldots,$$

taken with an appropriate value of x_{n-1}, independent of $\lambda_1, \ldots, \lambda_m, \mu_1, \ldots, \mu_m$, gives a set of solutions of the equations $K_1 = 0, \ldots, K_m = 0$.

We can then proceed with the equations $L_1 = 0, L_2 = 0, \ldots$ precisely as we did with the equations $H_1 = 0, \ldots, H_m = 0$; obtaining first a single equation

$$F_2(y, x_1, \ldots, x_{n-2}) = 0,$$

and then a set of polynomial equations in $y, x_1, \ldots, x_{n-3}$; and so on.

Eventually the original system of equations is replaced by a set

$$F_k(y, x_1, \ldots, x_{n-k}) = 0, \qquad (k = 1, 2, \ldots, n),$$

wherein any one or more of the n equations $F_k = 0$ may be absent; any solution of the original equations gives rise to a solution of one of these equations, and conversely, any solution of the equation $F_k = 0$, coupled with appropriate values of the k variables $x_{n-k+1}, \ldots, x_n$, gives a solution of the original equations. These appropriate values are determinable at once. For let $f(y, x_1, \ldots, x_{n-k})$ be a factor of F_k which is rational in $y, x_1, \ldots, x_{n-k}$ and irreducible in this form; the equation $f=0$, wherein the indeterminates $u_1, \ldots, u_n$ enter, may be written more at length in the form

$$f(u_1 x_1 + \ldots + u_n x_n, x_1, \ldots, x_{n-k}, u_1, \ldots, u_n) = 0;$$

we seek the solutions $x_1, \ldots, x_n$ independent of $u_1, \ldots, u_n$; we may then differentiate in regard to u_{n-k+r}, and so obtain

$$\frac{\partial f}{\partial y} x_{n-k+r} + \frac{\partial f}{\partial u_{n-k+r}} = 0,$$

or say
$$x_{n-k+r} = \frac{\phi_{n-k+r}}{f'}, \qquad (r = 1, 2, \ldots, k).$$

The original set of equations is thus replaced by a series of sets of equations each set of the form

$$f(y, x_1, \ldots, x_{n-k}) = 0, \quad x_{n-k+1} = \frac{\phi_{n-k+1}}{f'}, \ldots, x_n = \frac{\phi_n}{f'}.$$

If there are points, independent of the indeterminates $u_1, \ldots, u_n$, satisfying the equations

$$f(y, x_1, \ldots, x_{n-k}) = 0, \quad \frac{\partial f}{\partial y}(y, x_1, \ldots, x_{n-k}) = 0,$$

these will also satisfy an equation, obtainable by elimination of x_{n-k} from these, of the form

$$F(y, x_1, \ldots, x_{n-k-1}) = 0,$$

from which as before the appropriate associated values of $x_{n-k}, \ldots, x_n$ are deducible.

By the foregoing any set of equations connecting $x_1, \ldots, x_n$ is replaceable by the single equation obtained by setting equal to zero the product of a set of factors of the form $f(y, x_1, \ldots, x_{n-k})$. For example the three equations

$$y - z^2 = 0, \quad yz - x = 0, \quad xz - y^2 = 0,$$

which represent a cubic curve in the space (x, y, z), are replaceable by the single equation

$$f(t, x) \equiv (t - xu)^3 - 3vwx(t - xu) - x(v^3 x + w^3) = 0,$$

where
$$t = ux + vy + wz,$$

from which the appropriate values of y and z are obtainable. It is found here that the two equations

$$f(t, x) = 0, \quad \frac{\partial f}{\partial t}(t, x) = 0$$

are only satisfied when

$$v^3 t = w^2 (wu - v^2),$$

which gives no point independent of u, v, w. Or again the two equations

$$z + ax^2 + by^2 + 2gzx = 0, \quad z + a'x^2 + b'y^2 = 0$$

are replaceable by the single equation

$$f(t, x) \equiv \{(t - ux)(b - b' - 2gb'x) + (ba' - b'a) wx^2\}^2 + x^2v^2 (b - b' - 2gb'x)(a - a' - 2ga'x) = 0,$$

and here, by eliminating x between the equations

$$f(t, x) = 0, \quad \frac{\partial f}{\partial t}(t, x) = 0,$$

we arrive at

$$t\,[4g^2a't - 2g(a - a')u + w(a - a')^2] = 0,$$

of which the former factor gives the double point $x = 0$, $y = 0$, $z = 0$ of the curve, and the latter factor the point

$$x = \frac{a - a'}{2ga'}, \quad y = 0, \quad z = -\frac{(a - a')^2}{4g^2a'}.$$

But this replacement, of a set of equations connecting $x_1, \dots, x_n$, by a single equation such as $f(y, x_1, \dots, x_{n-k}) = 0$, or $\Pi f(y, x_1, \dots, x_{n-k}) = 0$, is dependent on the retention of the indeterminate quantities $u_1, \dots u_n$. A single irreducible algebraic construct of dimension $n - k$, in space of n dimensions $x_1, \dots, x_n$, is not necessarily representable by k equations connecting $x_1, \dots, x_n$, without indeterminates; that is, any k such equations may be such that they necessarily represent other constructs beside that which they are constructed to define. For example*, consider in three dimensions a quintic curve having a chord which cuts it in four points. It is known that no quadric surface contains this curve; if we seek to define it by the intersection of two surfaces these must at lowest be cubics, and will have a further intersection; if we seek to define it by three surfaces of orders $\mu + 3$, $\nu + 3$, $\rho + 3$ passing through it, these will have other points common, in fact of number

$$\mu\nu\rho + 3(\nu\rho + \rho\mu + \mu\nu) + 4(\mu + \nu + \rho),$$

which number vanishes only when all the surfaces are cubics; but three cubics do not define the curve since, being met by the four-point-secant in four points, they all contain this secant. It is thus impossible to assign three surfaces containing the curve which have no other common point; and four surfaces are necessary. And in general the theorem is stated by Kronecker that to define a construct, or system of constructs, of whatever dimension, in space of n dimensions, $n + 1$ polynomial equations are sufficient, and may be necessary†.

78. Let $f(y, x)$ be an irreducible rational equation of order k in y. Consider the aggregate of all rational symmetric functions of n arbitrary unconnected pairs $(x_1, y_1), \dots, (x_n, y_n)$, each function being rational in the

* Vahlen, *Crelle*, CVIII. (1891), p. 346.

† For a proof, see Molk, *Acta Math.*, VI. (1885), p. 159.

$2n$ quantities $x_1, \ldots, x_n, y_1, \ldots, y_n$, and symmetric both in regard to $x_1, \ldots, x_n$ and in regard to $y_1, \ldots, y_n$. Particular cases of such functions are the coefficients of the powers of θ in the product $(\theta + x_1)(\theta + x_2) \ldots (\theta + x_n)$, namely

$$\xi_1 = x_1 + \ldots + x_n, \quad \xi_2 = x_1x_2 + \ldots + x_{n-1}x_n, \ldots, \xi_n = x_1x_2 \ldots x_n.$$

It is known, if $x = c$ be an arbitrarily taken particular value of x, that rational functions $g_1(x, y), \ldots, g_{k-1}(x, y)$ can be chosen, unconnected by any equation

$$u_0 + u_1g_1(x, y) + \ldots + u_{k-1}g_{k-1}(x, y) = 0$$

in which $u_0, u_1, \ldots, u_{k-1}$ are rational functions of x, becoming infinite for no (finite or infinite) value of x other than $x = c$, in terms of which all other rational functions of x and y, which become infinite only for the points at which $x = c$, can be expressed, in the standard form

$$P_0 + P_1g_1(x, y) + \ldots + P_{k-1}g_{k-1}(x, y),$$

where P_a denotes an integral polynomial in $(x-c)^{-1}$; every function of the form

$$[A + A_1g_1(x, y) + \ldots + A_{k-1}g_{k-1}(x, y)]/(x - x_1),$$

wherein $A, A_1, \ldots, A_{k-1}$ are constants and x_1 is not equal to c, must then become infinite for some one of the (k or less) places at which $x = x_1$, since otherwise, being then only infinite for $x = c$, it would be capable of expression in the previous standard form (see the author's *Abel's Theorem*, Chapter IV.). Let $p_1, \ldots, p_{k-1}$ be any such integers that

$$(x-c)^{p_1}g_1(x, y), \ldots, (x-c)^{p_{k-1}}g_{k-1}(x, y)$$

all vanish for every place $x = c$. Take undetermined constants $\lambda_1, \ldots, \lambda_{k-1}$, and put

$$H(x, y) = \lambda_1(x-c)^{p_1}g_1(x, y) + \ldots + \lambda_{k-1}(x-c)^{p_{k-1}}g_{k-1}(x, y);$$

then $$\eta = H(x_1, y_1) + \ldots + H(x_n, y_n)$$

is also a rational symmetric function of the n places $(x_1, y_1), \ldots, (x_n, y_n)$.

It is clear that any rational function of $\xi_1, \ldots, \xi_n, \eta$ is a rational symmetric function of $(x_1, y_1), \ldots, (x_n, y_n)$; we proceed to shew conversely that any rational symmetric function of $(x_1, y_1), \ldots, (x_n, y_n)$ is rationally expressible by $\xi_1, \ldots, \xi_n, \eta$.

To any value of x belong k values of y, which, save for a finite number of values of x, are different; thus when $\xi_1, \ldots, \xi_n$ are assigned, and thereby the set $x_1, \ldots, x_n$, there correspond k^n values of η, say $\eta^{(1)}, \eta^{(2)}, \ldots$; the product of the k^n factors

$$(\theta - \eta^{(1)})(\theta - \eta^{(2)}) \ldots$$

is then rational in $\xi_1, \ldots, \xi_n$, and there exists an equation

$$F(\eta, \xi_1, \ldots, \xi_n) = 0,$$

of order k^n in η, rational in $\xi_1, \ldots, \xi_n, \eta$. We proceed to shew that it is not the case that there exist equalities between the values of η which are the roots of this equation for all values of $\xi_1, \ldots, \xi_n$ and $\lambda_1, \ldots, \lambda_{k-1}$.

For any two of the k^n values of η are of the form

$$H(x_1, y_1^{(i)}) + \ldots + H(x_n, y_n^{(j)}); \quad H(x_1, y_1^{(I)}) + \ldots + H(x_n, y_n^{(J)}),$$

where, of the n couples, $(i, I), \ldots, (j, J)$, not every one can consist of two equal integers; suppose $i \neq I$; the difference of these values of η is

$$\begin{aligned}&\lambda_1 (x_1 - c)^{p_1} [g_1(x_1, y_1^{(i)}) - g_1(x_1, y_1^{(I)})] + \ldots \\ &\qquad + \lambda_{k-1}(x_1 - c)^{p_{k-1}} [g_{k-1}(x_1, y_1^{(i)}) - g_{k-1}(x_1, y_1^{(I)})] \\ &+ \ldots\ldots\ldots\ldots\ldots\ldots \\ &+ \lambda_1 (x_n - c)^{p_1} [g_1(x_n, y_n^{(j)}) - g_1(x_n, y_n^{(J)})] + \ldots \\ &\qquad + \lambda_{k-1}(x_n - c)^{p_{k-1}} [g_{k-1}(x_n, y_n^{(j)}) - g_{k-1}(x_n, y_n^{(J)})];\end{aligned}$$

if these were equal for all values of $x_1, \ldots, x_n$ they would be so for $x_2 = c, x_3 = c, \ldots, x_n = c$, and therefore

$$\begin{aligned}&\lambda_1 (x_1 - c)^{p_1} [g_1(x_1, y_1^{(i)}) - g_1(x_1, y_1^{(I)})] + \ldots \\ &\qquad + \lambda_{k-1}(x_1 - c)^{p_{k-1}} [g_{k-1}(x_1, y_1^{(i)}) - g_{k-1}(x_1, y_1^{(I)})]\end{aligned}$$

would vanish for all values of x_1 and all values of $\lambda_1, \ldots, \lambda_{k-1}$; for all values of x_1 we should then have

$$g_1(x_1, y_1^{(i)}) = g_1(x_1, y_1^{(I)}), \ldots, g_{k-1}(x_1, y_1^{(i)}) = g_{k-1}(x_1, y_1^{(I)});$$

suppose this were so, taking a value of x_1 for which the corresponding values of y_1 are all different; denote $g_r(x_1, y_1^{(i)})$ by a_r; we can choose $A_1, \ldots, A_{k-1}$ so that the $k-2$ expressions

$$A_1 [g_1(x_1, y_1^{(s)}) - a_1] + \ldots + A_{k-1} [g_{k-1}(x_1, y_1^{(s)}) - a_{k-1}],$$

for s equal in turn to the values from $1, 2, \ldots, k$ other than i and I, are all zero: then the function

$$G = A_1 [g_1(x, y) - a_1] + \ldots + A_{k-1} [g_{k-1}(x, y) - a_{k-1}]$$

would vanish for all the k places at which $x = x_1$, and the function $G/(x - x_1)$ would not be infinite for $x = x_1$. We have seen that this is impossible.

We can therefore give particular numerical values to $\lambda_1, \ldots, \lambda_{k-1}$ such that the integral polynomial in $\xi_1, \ldots, \xi_n$ obtained by elimination of η between $F = 0$ and $\partial F/\partial\eta = 0$ is not identically zero. And if ζ be any rational symmetric function of the n places $(x_1, y_1), \ldots, (x_n, y_n)$, and μ be an undetermined constant, the function of $\eta + \mu\zeta$ satisfies a rational equation

$$F_1(\eta + \mu\zeta, \xi_1, \ldots, \xi_n, \mu) = 0,$$

for which $\quad F_1(\eta, \xi_1, \ldots, \xi_n, 0) = F(\eta, \xi_1, \ldots, \xi_n);$

thus we have

$$\zeta \frac{\partial F_1}{\partial \eta} + \frac{\partial F_1}{\partial \mu} = 0, \quad \zeta = -\left(\frac{\partial F_1}{\partial \mu}\right)_{\mu=0} \Big/ \frac{\partial F}{\partial \eta},$$

whereby ζ is expressible rationally in terms of $\xi_1, \dots, \xi_n, \eta$, for all values of these other than those for which $F=0$, $\partial F/\partial\eta = 0$ are both satisfied. It may be remarked also that the function $F(\eta, \xi_1, \dots, \xi_n)$, regarded as an integral polynomial in η with coefficients rational in $\xi_1, \dots, \xi_n$, is irreducible; for y_1 is known* to be a monogenic function of x_1; thus η is a monogenic function of x_1, and therefore also of $x_1, \dots, x_n$, and therefore also of $\xi_1, \dots, \xi_n$; thus if there be two or more rational factors of $F(\eta, \xi_1, \dots, \xi_n)$ they must be identical and F must be a perfect power; we have however seen that the values of η are in general different.

Consider now the correspondence between the set of places $(x_1, y_1), \dots, (x_n, y_n)$ on the Riemann surface, and the place $(\xi_1, \dots, \xi_n, \eta)$ of $F(\eta, \xi_1, \dots, \xi_n) = 0$. When $(x_1, y_1), \dots, (x_n, y_n)$ are given, the place $(\xi_1, \dots, \xi_n, \eta)$ is determined without ambiguity by means of $\xi_1 = x_1 + \dots + x_n, \dots, \xi_n = x_1 x_2 \dots x_n$ and $\eta = H(x_1, y_1) + \dots + H(x_n, y_n)$. When $\xi_1, \dots, \xi_n$ are given, the set $x_1, x_2, \dots, x_n$ is determined; and, if r be any positive integer, the function

$$x_1^r y_1 + \dots + x_n^r y_n,$$

which is rational and symmetrical in $(x_1, y_1), \dots, (x_n, y_n)$, is, by what we have proved, rational in $\xi_1, \dots, \xi_n, \eta$, so that we may write

$$x_1^r y_1 + \dots + x_n^r y_n = P_r(\eta, \xi_1, \dots, \xi_n); \qquad (r = 0, 1, \dots, (n-1));$$

from these n equations y_1 is determined rationally in terms of $x_1, \xi_1, \dots, \xi_n, \eta$. The place $(\xi_1, \dots, \xi_n, \eta)$ thus determines uniquely a set of places $(x_1, y_1), \dots, (x_n, y_n)$.

79. Let $\xi_1, \dots, \xi_n$ be independent variables, and η an algebraic function of these, determined by an irreducible polynomial equation $F(\eta, \xi_1, \dots, \xi_n) = 0$. Consider a certain infinite aggregate of rational functions of $\xi_1, \dots, \xi_n, \eta$, not including necessarily all rational functions, but such that any rational function of two or more of the elements of the aggregate, with constant coefficients (belonging to the assumed rationality-domain), also belongs to the aggregate.

It is then evident that any $n+1$ functions of the aggregate are connected by a rational relation, but it may be that a rational relation always connects a certain less number of the functions. Let μ be the greatest integer such that there are μ of the functions unconnected by a rational relation ($\mu \leqq n$), and $\phi_1, \dots, \phi_\mu$ be μ functions of the aggregate not so connected; then every $\mu+1$ functions of the aggregate are connected by one or more rational relations; thus if ψ be any function of the aggregate other than $\phi_1, \dots, \phi_\mu$ we have an equation $(\psi, \phi_1, \dots, \phi_\mu) = 0$, and, if, in this, for $\psi, \phi_1, \dots, \phi_\mu$ are substituted their rational values in terms of $\xi_1, \dots, \xi_n, \eta$, the equation is either satisfied identically for all values of $\xi_1, \dots, \xi_n, \eta$, or, if not, the result contains η and, when arranged as a polynomial in η, divides

* Cf. § 52 above, and *Proc. Lond. Math. Soc.* IV. (1906), p. 116.

by $F(\eta, \xi_1, \ldots, \xi_n)$. We can suppose the equation $(\psi, \phi_1, \ldots, \phi_\mu) = 0$ arranged as a polynomial in ψ; if it be not irreducible let it be arranged as a product of irreducible polynomials in ψ with coefficients rational in $\phi_1, \ldots, \phi_\mu$; two such polynomials which are not identical cannot both vanish identically in virtue of $F(\eta, \xi_1, \ldots, \xi_n) = 0$, or there would exist a rational relation connecting $\phi_1, \ldots, \phi_\mu$ only; contrary to hypothesis. Similarly there cannot be any other relation $\{\psi, \phi_1, \ldots, \phi_\mu\} = 0$ independent of $(\psi, \phi_1, \ldots, \phi_\mu) = 0$. There is thus one irreducible relation $[\psi, \phi_1, \ldots, \phi_\mu] = 0$, of which every other rational equation connecting $\psi, \phi_1, \ldots, \phi_\mu$ is an identical rational consequence.

Consider now the equations

$$\phi_1 = a_1, \ \ldots, \ \phi_\mu = a_\mu, \ F(\eta, \xi_1, \ldots, \xi_n) = 0,$$

for independent undetermined values of $a_1, \ldots, a_\mu$. These equations may be satisfied by points or constructs which do not vary when $a_1, \ldots, a_\mu$ vary, or for which one or more of the functions $\phi_1, \ldots, \phi_\mu, F$ is indeterminate; such solutions we do not consider: we desire to make it clear that the solutions of these equations, variable with $a_1, \ldots, a_\mu$, and holding independently of any relation connecting the values of these, which give definite values to each of the functions $\phi_1, \ldots, \phi_\mu, F$, consist of constructs of $(n - \mu)$ (complex) dimensions. The first equation $\phi_1 = a_1$, coupled with $F = 0$, has for solution, variable with a_1, one or more constructs of $(n - 1)$ complex dimensions; the points of such a construct which give to ϕ_2 a determinate value will not, unless further conditioned, render ϕ_2 equal to a_2 for any value of a_2; thus the points to be considered which satisfy both $\phi_1 = a_1$, and $\phi_2 = a_2$, are upon one or more constructs of $(n - 2)$ complex dimensions. And so on*. Let then N be the number of irreducible algebraic constructs of $(n - \mu)$ dimensions satisfying the equations, variable with $a_1, \ldots, a_\mu$. Any function ψ, rational in $\xi_1, \ldots, \xi_n, \eta$, is capable of taking every complex value upon such a construct unless it is constant upon the construct: by hypothesis we are now only considering functions ψ such that there exists a unique irreducible rational equation $[\psi, \phi_1, \ldots, \phi_\mu] = 0$; the values of ψ, for points $(\xi_1, \ldots, \xi_n, \eta)$ giving definite values $a_1, \ldots, a_\mu$ to $\phi_1, \ldots, \phi_\mu$ and variable with these values, are therefore finite in number: we infer therefore that the function ψ is constant upon each of the N constructs given by $\phi_1 = a_1, \ldots, \phi_\mu = a_\mu, F = 0$. There is thus an upper limit N, *independent of* ψ, for the order in ψ of the equation $[\psi, \phi_1, \ldots, \phi_\mu] = 0$, though this limit may not be reached.

* Or thus: if F be of order k in η, and $\phi_1^{(r)}$ denote $\phi_1(\eta^{(r)}, \xi_1, \ldots, \xi_n)$, the product $(\sigma - \phi_1^{(1)}) \ldots (\sigma - \phi_1^{(k)})$ is manifestly rational in $\xi_1, \ldots, \xi_n$, and thus ϕ_1 satisfies an equation $f(\phi_1, \xi_1, \ldots, \xi_n) = 0$. If not irreducible this is a power of an irreducible polynomial; for an equation

$$f_1[\phi_1(\eta, \xi_1, \ldots, \xi_n), \ \xi_1, \ldots, \xi_n] = 0,$$

satisfied by one root η of $F(\eta, \xi_1, \ldots, \xi_n) = 0$, is satisfied by all roots. Thus the equations above lead to irreducible equations $H_1(a_1, \xi_1, \ldots, \xi_n) = 0, \ldots, H_\mu(a_\mu, \xi_1, \ldots, \xi_n) = 0$, which, excluding rational functional relations connecting $a_1, \ldots, a_\mu$, are independent.

We may then take for ψ a function, among the aggregate of rational functions of $\xi_1, \dots, \xi_n, \eta$ under consideration, for which the order in ψ of the relation $[\psi, \phi_1, \dots, \phi_\mu] = 0$ reaches the highest value, say M, which is attained for any of these functions: the values of ψ upon the N constructs, if $M < N$, are then repetitions of N different values, which we may denote by $b_1, b_2, \dots, b_M$; we call a set of one or more of these constructs upon which ψ has the same value a ψ-range. Now let χ be any other rational function of the aggregate under consideration; as before it is constant upon each of the N algebraic constructs; we can prove that its value is the same upon all the constructs constituting any ψ-range. For let the different values which it takes upon the N constructs be denoted by $c_1, c_2, \dots$, and let λ be a constant not equal to any one of the finite number of quantities $(b_i - b_j)/(c_p - c_q)$; consider the function $\psi - \lambda\chi$. In virtue of the restriction upon the value of λ, this function, $\psi - \lambda\chi$, cannot have the same value for two constructs not belonging to the same ψ-range, for upon these constructs the values of ψ are different; it has then at least M different values upon the N fundamental constructs, and it will have more than M values unless it have the same value for all the constructs of every ψ-range; but, by hypothesis, there is no function of the aggregate considered with more than M different values upon the fundamental N constructs. The function $\psi - \lambda\chi$, and therefore also χ, has thus the same value over every ψ-range. If then $e_1, e_2, \dots, e_M$ be the values of $\psi - \lambda\chi$ for the various ψ-ranges, there being, possibly, equalities among these values, the function $\psi - \lambda\chi$ satisfies an equation $H_1 = \{\psi - \lambda\chi, \phi_1, \dots, \phi_\mu, \lambda\} = 0$, whose roots, when $\phi_1 = a_1, \dots, \phi_\mu = a_\mu$, are $e_1, \dots, e_M$, and we have

$$\{\psi, \phi_1, \dots, \phi_\mu, 0\} = [\psi, \phi_1, \dots, \phi_\mu], = H, \text{ say.}$$

Hence we have

$$-\chi \frac{\partial H_1}{\partial \psi} + \frac{\partial H_1}{\partial \lambda} = 0, \quad \chi = \left(\frac{\partial H_1}{\partial \lambda}\right)_{\lambda=0} \div \frac{\partial H}{\partial \psi}.$$

Thus every rational function of $\xi_1, \dots, \xi_n, \eta$, belonging to the aggregate considered, is rationally expressible by $\phi_1, \dots, \phi_\mu$ and ψ. This is the result we desired to establish.

80. We are now in a position to establish clearly the theorem, which was one of the main objects of the Second Part of this volume, that *the most general single-valued multiply-periodic meromorphic function is expressible by theta functions.*

Let $\phi(U_1, \dots, U_n)$ be such a function, with period system ϖ. As shewn in Chapter VII. (p. 199), we can obtain a Riemann surface, of deficiency p, upon which there is a defective system of integrals of the first kind, of number $n \leqq p$, whose period system at the period loops, Π, is expressible in the form

$\Pi = \varpi h$, where h is a matrix of integers of type $(2n, 2p)$; these integrals being denoted by $u_1^{x,c}, \ldots, u_n^{x,c}$, the congruences

$$\begin{array}{l} u_1^{x_1, a_1} + \ldots + u_1^{x_n, a_n} \equiv U_1, \\ \ldots\ldots\ldots\ldots\ldots\ldots\ldots\ldots \\ u_n^{x_1, a_1} + \ldots + u_n^{x_n, a_n} \equiv U_n, \end{array} \quad (\text{Mod. } \Pi),$$

wherein $(a_1), \ldots, (a_n)$ are arbitrary places upon the Riemann surface, are satisfied by a finite number of sets of places $(x_1), \ldots, (x_n)$, whose number we have found (p. 250). The function $\phi(U_1, \ldots, U_n)$, considered under the form

$$\phi(u_1^{x_1, a_1} + \ldots + u_1^{x_n, a_n}, \ldots\ldots, u_n^{x_1, a_1} + \ldots + u_n^{x_n, a_n}),$$

is a rational function of each of the places $(x_1), \ldots, (x_n)$, as we have already remarked, and is symmetrical in regard to these. It may then, as proved in this chapter (p. 279), be regarded as a rational function of $n+1$ variables $\xi_1, \ldots, \xi_n, \eta$, which are connected by a rational equation $F(\eta, \xi_1, \ldots, \xi_n) = 0$. Any single-valued meromorphic function of $U_1, \ldots, U_n$ with the periods ϖ, is similarly rationally expressible by $\xi_1, \ldots, \xi_n, \eta$; and any rational function of two such meromorphic functions with these periods is equally a single-valued meromorphic function with these periods. The aggregate of single-valued meromorphic functions of $U_1, \ldots, U_n$ with the periods ϖ is thus such a corpus of rational functions of $\xi_1, \ldots, \xi_n, \eta$ as that considered in § 79 (p. 280); and from among them a certain number, $\mu + 1$, of periodic functions, themselves connected by an irreducible rational equation $[\psi, \phi_1, \ldots, \phi_\mu] = 0$, can be selected, in terms of which all others are rationally expressible, the number μ being $\gtreqless n$. And in particular, a single-valued meromorphic function of $U_1, \ldots, U_n$ which is periodic with a system ϖ_0 in terms of which the system ϖ is expressible in the form $\varpi = \varpi_0 H$, where H is a matrix of integers, even though ϖ_0 may not be similarly expressible by ϖ, is expressible rationally by $\mu + 1$ functions with period-system ϖ; for it too has ϖ as a period-system.

This result is in itself of great interest. To apply it to the case in hand, it will be clearest to use the notations previously employed (p. 225); we had

$$\varpi = \varpi' g, \quad \varpi' c = (\varpi_1', 0), \quad \varpi_1' = \mu(1, \sigma) f, \quad f = \begin{pmatrix} rd^{-1}, & 0 \\ 0, & 1 \end{pmatrix} G,$$

where g is a unitary matrix of type $(2n, 2n)$, ϖ_1' is a matrix of type $(n, 2n)$ and $(\varpi_1', 0)$ of type $(n, 2p)$ of which the last $(2p - 2n)$ columns consist of zeros, f is a matrix of integers and G a unitary matrix of integers of type $(2n, 2n)$; we thus have

$$\frac{\mu^{-1}}{r} \varpi_1' = \frac{1}{r}(1, \sigma) \begin{pmatrix} rd^{-1}, & 0 \\ 0, & 1 \end{pmatrix} G = \left(d^{-1}, \frac{\sigma}{r}\right) G.$$

Therefore a function $\phi(U, \varpi)$, of $U_1, \ldots, U_n$, with periods ϖ, is a function with periods ϖ' and conversely; it therefore has periods ϖ_1', and, by what has been proved above, is expressible rationally in terms of functions $\psi(U, \varpi_1')$, with periods ϖ_1', though the converse is probably not the case; putting

$$V = \frac{\mu^{-1}}{r} U,$$

a function $\psi(U, \varpi_1')$ becomes a function of $V_1, \dots, V_n$ with periods $(d^{-1}, \sigma/r)\, G$, and therefore with periods $(d^{-1}, \sigma/r)$, since G is unitary; a function $\psi(U, \varpi)$ is thus expressible rationally by functions of $V_1, \dots, V_n$ with periods $(d^{-1}, \sigma/r)$, and therefore by functions $\chi(V;\, 1, \sigma/r)$, with periods $(1, \sigma/r)$, though the converse does not hold. We have previously shewn (p. 227) that we can form theta functions $\Theta(V;\, \sigma/r)$, with quasi-periods $(1, \sigma/r)$, and from these we can form periodic functions with periods $(1, \sigma/r)$. It appears thus that the functions $\phi(U, \varpi)$ are expressible rationally in terms of functions

$$\chi\left(V;\, 1, \frac{\sigma}{r}\right), \text{ or } \chi\left(\frac{\mu^{-1} U}{r};\, 1, \frac{\sigma}{r}\right),$$

which can be formed from theta functions $\Theta\left(\frac{\mu^{-1} U}{r};\, 1, \frac{\sigma}{r}\right)$. And this is the result*

81. The theorem established in this chapter that any single-valued meromorphic function of n variables with $2n$ sets of periods (obeying the necessary relations, see p. 224), can be expressed by means of theta functions, may be obtained in other ways. We give some account of two.

For the first† it is necessary to prove the following theorems:

(A) If $\phi_1, \dots, \phi_n$ be n such functions, whose Jacobian $\partial(\phi_1, \dots, \phi_n)/\partial(u_1, \dots, u_n)$ is not identically zero, there exist sets of n constants $a_1, \dots, a_n$, such that the solutions of the equations $\phi_1 = a_1, \dots, \phi_n = a_n$ which vary with $a_1, \dots, a_n$ and give definite values to all the functions $\phi_1, \dots, \phi_n$, consist only of isolated points, at each of which the Jacobian $\partial(\phi_1, \dots, \phi_n)/\partial(u_1, \dots, u_n)$ has a definite finite non-vanishing value. Let the number of these points in any period cell be N.

(B) If then ϕ_{n+1} be another such function, having the periods of the functions $\phi_1, \dots, \phi_n$ as primitive periods, we can form from ϕ_{n+1} a single-valued meromorphic function with these periods, whose values, at the N solutions of $\phi_1 = a_1, \dots, \phi_n = a_n$ lying in any period cell, are all different.

(C) The functions $\phi_1, \dots, \phi_n, \phi_{n+1}$ are connected by a rational relation; in terms of them any single-valued meromorphic function with the periods in question can be rationally expressed.

* The steps indicated by Weierstrass (*Werke*, III. (1903), p. 113) are different from those used here.

† Wirtinger, *Monatshefte für Math. u. Physik*, 1895 (Jahrgang VI., p. 69).

(D) Such a set of $(n+1)$ functions is furnished by a function ψ, having the periods as primitive periods, and its first partial derivatives.

(E) A linear aggregate with undetermined coefficients of the second partial logarithmic derivatives $\wp_{rs}(u)$ of a theta function $\vartheta(u, \tau)$, has the period $(1, \tau)$ as primitive periods.

(F) Such a linear aggregate is expressible rationally in terms of theta functions.

The proof of (A) may be carried through on lines similar to those we have previously adopted for the equations $f_1 = x$, $F_2 = 0, \ldots, F_n = 0$ (pp. 199 ff.). Or may be made to depend on the fact that each of $\phi_1, \ldots, \phi_n$ and the Jacobian Δ may be regarded as a rational symmetric function of n places upon a Riemann surface; there is thus a rational irreducible equation $(\Delta, \phi_1, \ldots, \phi_n) = 0$ giving the values of Δ when $\phi_1 = a_1, \ldots, \phi_n = a_n$. But the theorem would seem to be true of any single-valued meromorphic functions, whether periodic or not. For (B), if $u^{(1)}$, $u^{(2)}$ be two incongruent solutions of $\phi_1 = a_1, \ldots, \phi_n = a_n$, while we may have $\phi_{n+1}(u^{(1)}) = \phi_{n+1}(u^{(2)})$, not every differential coefficient of ϕ_{n+1} can have the same value at $u^{(1)}$ and $u^{(2)}$, since the difference $u^{(1)} - u^{(2)}$ is not a period of the function ϕ_{n+1}. Let ϕ'_{n+1} be a differential coefficient for which $\phi'_{n+1}(u^{(1)})$ is not equal to $\phi'_{n+1}(u^{(2)})$. Taking another pair of points satisfying $\phi_1 = a_1, \ldots, \phi_n = a_n$ we can similarly find a differential coefficient ϕ''_{n+1} not having the same value at these points; and so on. A linear aggregate of such differential coefficients is such a function as is desired. Denoting it by ϕ, we have then an irreducible rational equation $(\phi, \phi_1, \ldots, \phi_n) = 0$ of order N in ϕ, and if χ be another function with the periods considered, we similarly have $\{\phi + \mu\chi, \phi_1, \ldots, \phi_n, \mu\} = 0$ with $\{\phi, \phi_1, \ldots, \phi_n, 0\} = (\phi, \phi_1, \ldots, \phi_n)$. Differentiating $\{\phi + \mu\chi, \phi_1, \ldots, \phi_n, \mu\} = 0$ in regard to μ we obtain the expression of χ in terms of $\phi, \phi_1, \ldots, \phi_n$, postulated in (C). The theorem (D) depends on the facts that the Jacobian of the first n partial derivatives of ψ is not identically zero, while the values of ψ for the solutions of $\partial\psi/\partial u_1 = a_1, \ldots, \partial\psi/\partial u_n = a_n$ are different, if $a_1, \ldots, a_n$ be suitably taken. Theorem (E) is very easy to prove, and theorem (F) is obtained by taking second logarithmic derivatives of such a formula as expresses $\vartheta(u+v)\,\vartheta(u-v)$ in terms of theta functions of u and v (for example, *Abel's Theorem*, pp. 457, 516).

A second method of proof is of an entirely different character. It can be proved directly that a single-valued meromorphic function of n variables with $2n$ systems of periods is expressible as the quotient of two integral functions, having no common zeros save where the given function is indeterminate; and that these integral functions have the property that their second logarithmic partial derivatives are periodic functions with the original $2n$ sets of periods. An integral function with this property can be directly proved (as in the next chapter) to be expressible by theta functions. The writer may be allowed, for the proof of the first of these statements, to refer to his own papers, *Proceedings London Mathematical Society,* Ser. 2, Vol. I. (1903), p. 14 and *Cambridge Philosophical Transactions*, Vol. XVIII. (1899), p. 431; these are based upon the papers of Poincaré, *Acta Math.* II. (1883), *Acta Math.* XXII. (1898), *Acta Math.* XXVI. (1902), and of Kronecker, *Werke*, I., p. 198 (of date 1869)—Kronecker's paper deals with the problem of extending theorems of Cauchy to functions of more than one variable, with the use of integrals, and is in close connexion, not only with the theory of multiple potential but also with his theory of Characteristics for systems of rational equations, dimly foreshadowed by Sylvester* (*Collected Papers*, Vol. I., p. 528).

* For the theorem that a meromorphic function is expressible as a quotient of two integral functions, the reader should also consult Appell, *Liouville*, sér. 4, VII. (1891), p. 157; and an important paper by Cousin, *Acta Math.* XIX. (1895). In connexion with the closely connected theorem of the necessary relation among the periods of a single-valued meromorphic multiply periodic function see also Wirtinger, *Acta Math.* XXVI. (1902), p. 133, and Poincaré, *ibid.*, p. 43.

CHAPTER X.

THE ZEROS OF JACOBIAN FUNCTIONS.

82. CONSIDER a single valued integral function $f(u)$ of n variables $u_1, \ldots, u_n$, such that its second partial logarithmic derivatives have $2n$ systems of primitive periods, of matrix ϖ; no one of these derivatives being expressible by less than n linear functions of the variables, or having therefore (p. 203) any column of infinitesimal periods. The periods must, as follows from preceding investigations (p. 224), be subject to certain bilinear relations, with integral coefficients, and obey certain corresponding inequalities, say of the form

$$\varpi H \overline{\varpi} = 0, \qquad - i \varpi H \overline{\varpi}_0 x_0 x > 0,$$

where H is a skew symmetrical matrix of integers and x denotes a set of n arbitrary quantities, the suffix zero denoting the conjugate complex quantity; it is of importance for what follows that we assume the periods to allow only one such bilinear relation and corresponding inequality.

From the periodic derivatives we can as previously (Chap. VII.) deduce a Riemann surface, say of deficiency p, upon which $u_1, \ldots, u_n$ may be regarded as integrals of the first kind, forming a defective system if $n < p$; we use the same notation as before, putting

$$\Pi = \varpi h, \quad ghm = c, \quad \varpi = \varpi' g, \quad \varpi' c = (\varpi_1', 0) = \Pi m, \quad \Pi = \varpi_1' k,$$

so that in k, which is of type $(2n, 2p)$, the determinants of order $2n$ are coprime, and we denote the matrix ϖ_1' by a. Then from

$$\Pi \epsilon_{2p} \overline{\Pi} = 0, \quad - i \Pi \epsilon_{2p} \overline{\Pi}_0 x_0 x > 0,$$

we have

$$a k \epsilon_{2p} \bar{k} \bar{a} = 0, \quad - i a k \epsilon_{2p} \bar{k} \bar{a}_0 x_0 x > 0,$$

which are the bilinear relations and inequalities in question.

The periods ϖ_1', or a, are sums of integral multiples of the periods ϖ, and the second partial logarithmic derivatives of the function $f(u)$ have the quantities a as periods; if then $a^{(j)}$ denote one of the $2n$ columns of the matrix a, we have equations of the form

$$f(u + a^{(j)}) / f(u) = \exp. 2\pi i \left[b^{(j)} (u + \tfrac{1}{2} a^{(j)}) + c^{(j)} \right], \qquad (j = 1, \ldots, (2n)),$$

where $b^{(j)}$ denotes a column of n constants, and $c^{(j)}$ a definite constant; from these equations we infer

$$f(u+a^{(1)}+a^{(2)})/f(u) = \exp.\, 2\pi i\,\{[b^{(1)}+b^{(2)}][u+\tfrac{1}{2}a^{(1)}+\tfrac{1}{2}a^{(2)}] \\ + c^{(1)}+c^{(2)}+\tfrac{1}{2}[b^{(1)}a^{(2)}-b^{(2)}a^{(1)}]\},$$

and therefore, since the right side must be unaltered by interchange of the exponents 1 and 2, the quantity $b^{(1)}a^{(2)}-b^{(2)}a^{(1)}$ must be an integer; thus if b denote the matrix of type $(n, 2n)$ whose j-th column is $b^{(j)}$, the skew symmetrical matrix $\bar{b}a-\bar{a}b$, of type $(2n, 2n)$, must consist of integers. We shall put

$$A=\begin{pmatrix} a \\ b\end{pmatrix}, \text{ so that } \Delta=\bar{b}a-\bar{a}b=(\bar{b},\,-\bar{a})\begin{pmatrix} a \\ b\end{pmatrix}=(\bar{a},\,\bar{b})\begin{pmatrix} 0, & -1 \\ 1, & 0\end{pmatrix}\begin{pmatrix} a \\ b\end{pmatrix}=\bar{A}\epsilon_{2n}A.$$

From the fact that $\bar{b}a-\bar{a}b$ consists of integers it can be shewn at once* by induction that the separate formulae lead, if m denote any row of $2n$ integers, to

$$f(u+am)=e^{2\pi i H}f(u),$$

where $$H=bm\,(u+\tfrac{1}{2}am)+cm-\tfrac{1}{2}\sum_{i<j}\Delta_{i,j}m_i m_j, \qquad (i, j=1, \dots, (2n)).$$

It can further be shewn, without recurring to the Riemann surface, if z denote any $2n$ quantities not all zero, satisfying $az=0$, and z_0 their conjugate complexes, that

$$-i\Delta z z_0 > 0;$$

if $z=\zeta+i\zeta'$, since Δ is skew symmetrical and $\Delta\zeta^2=0$, this is the same as

$$-i\Delta\,[\zeta(-i\zeta')+i\zeta'\zeta]=2\Delta\zeta'\zeta>0,$$

or, as $\Delta=\bar{b}a-\bar{a}b$, and $az=0$, it is the same as

$$-i\,(az\,.\,bz_0-az_0\,.\,bz)=iaz_0\,.\,bz>0,$$

the quantity on the left being in each case real.

As will be seen, if we assume the determinant of Δ, or A, not to vanish, this inequality is deducible by use of the Riemann surface. But as, conversely, an independent proof enables us to infer $|\Delta|\neq 0$, a fact important to us, we reproduce the following remarkable proof due to Frobenius, *Crelle*, XCVII. (1884). We cannot simultaneously have $az=0$, $az_0=0$, since the latter is the same as $a_0 z=0$, and we should have the determinant $\begin{vmatrix} a \\ a_0\end{vmatrix}$, of type $(2n, 2n)$, zero, contrary to the hypothesis of the non-existence of infinitesimal periods. If v be any set of n arguments, t a single complex quantity, $w=c+\bar{b}v$, and $\xi=tz_0+t_0z$, we have at once, identically, in virtue of $az=0$,

$$e^{-i\pi t^2 az_0\,.\,bz_0-2\pi it\,(w-w_0)\,z_0}\,f(v+taz_0)=e^{-i\pi tt_0\Delta zz_0}\,e^{2\pi i\,(tw_0z_0+t_0wz)}\,L \ldots\text{(A)}$$

* For instance, *Abel's Theorem*, p. 582.

where $$L = e^{-2\pi i b\xi (v + \frac{1}{2}a\xi) - 2\pi i c\xi} f(v + a\xi);$$
consider now L as a function of the $2n$ real quantities ξ for variable values of these, denoting it by $L(\xi)$; we find at once, in virtue of the property of $f(u)$, if m denote any $2n$ integers, that
$$L(\xi + m) = e^H L(\xi),$$
where $$H = -\pi i (\Delta\xi m + \overset{i<j}{\Sigma} \Delta_{i,j} m_i m_j),$$
so that $L(\xi + m)/L(\xi)$ is of modulus unity; when every element of ξ is positive (or zero) and less than unity, the function $L(\xi)$ is, by its definition above, manifestly finite; thus a real positive quantity G is assignable such that, whatever finite values z and t may have,
$$| e^{2\pi i (t w_0 z_0 + t_0 w z)} L | < G;$$
recurring to the equation (A) however, and regarding v and z as fixed, the function of t on the left side,
$$\chi(t) = e^{-i\pi t^2 a z_0 \,.\, b z_0 - 2\pi i t (w - w_0) z_0} f(v + t a z_0),$$
is an integral function; it must then be capable of becoming infinite when t is infinite, and so therefore, if ρ denote the real quantity $-i\pi\Delta z z_0$, must the quantity $e^{\rho t t_0}$; but if ρ were zero or negative this would be impossible. Thus we have as desired
$$-i\Delta z z_0 > 0.$$

This assumes that $\chi(t)$ is not independent of t; we have, however, if $\chi(t) = \chi(0)$,
$$e^{-i\pi t^2 a z_0 \,.\, b z_0} \frac{f(v + t a z_0)}{f(v)} = e^{2\pi i t (w - w_0) z_0},$$
wherein, since $a z_0$ cannot be zero, the left side is a function of v, the quantities t and z being regarded as constant; on the right however the quantity $(w - w_0) z_0$, which is equal to $(\bar{b} v - \bar{b}_0 v_0) z_0$ or $b z_0 \,.\, v - b_0 z_0 \,.\, v_0$, if a function of v, is a linear function—differentiation of this equation would then shew that $t a z_0$ is a system of periods for the second partial logarithmic derivatives of $f(v)$, and as t can be taken arbitrarily small this is impossible, these functions having no column of infinitesimal periods.

Having then $-i\Delta z z_0 > 0$ or $i a z_0 \,.\, b z > 0$ when $a z = 0$, it follows that we cannot simultaneously satisfy the $2n$ equations $a z = 0$, $b z = 0$; thus the determinant of A or $\begin{pmatrix} a \\ b \end{pmatrix}$, and therefore also of Δ or $\bar{A}\epsilon_{2n} A$, is other than zero.

This being so we infer from $\Delta = \bar{A}\epsilon_{2n} A$, first $\Delta^{-1} = -A^{-1}\epsilon_{2n}\bar{A}^{-1}$, and then
$$-\epsilon_{2n} = A\Delta^{-1}\bar{A} = \begin{pmatrix} a \\ b \end{pmatrix} \Delta^{-1} (\bar{a}, \bar{b}) = \begin{pmatrix} a\Delta^{-1} \\ b\Delta^{-1} \end{pmatrix} (\bar{a}, \bar{b}) = \begin{pmatrix} a\Delta^{-1}\bar{a}, & a\Delta^{-1}\bar{b} \\ b\Delta^{-1}\bar{a}, & b\Delta^{-1}\bar{b} \end{pmatrix},$$
and therefore $$a\Delta^{-1}\bar{a} = 0, \quad a\Delta^{-1}\bar{b} = 1, \quad b\Delta^{-1}\bar{b} = 0,$$
while, if x denote a set of n arbitrary quantities, and we take $2n$ quantities

z subject to $az=0$, $bz=x$, or say $z=A^{-1}(0, x)$, and write ϵ for ϵ_{2n}, we have, in virtue of

$$A^{-1}=\Delta^{-1}\bar{A}\epsilon, \quad \bar{A}_0^{-1}\Delta=\epsilon A_0,$$

$$\begin{aligned}-i\Delta zz_0 &= -i\bar{A}_0^{-1}\Delta A^{-1}(0, x)(0, x_0) = -i\epsilon A_0 A^{-1}(0, x)(0, x_0)\\ &= -i\epsilon A_0\Delta^{-1}\bar{A}\epsilon\,(0, x)(0, x_0)\\ &= iA_0\Delta^{-1}\bar{A}\,(-x, 0)(-x_0, 0) = -iA\Delta^{-1}\bar{A}_0(-x_0, 0)(-x, 0)\\ &= -i\begin{pmatrix} a\Delta^{-1}\bar{a}_0, & a\Delta^{-1}\bar{b}_0\\ b\Delta^{-1}\bar{a}_0, & b\Delta^{-1}\bar{b}_0\end{pmatrix}(-x_0, 0)(-x, 0) = -ia\Delta^{-1}\bar{a}_0 x_0 x,\end{aligned}$$

and the condition $-i\Delta zz_0>0$ is thus equivalent with

$$-ia\Delta^{-1}\bar{a}_0x_0x>0,$$

where x denotes a set of n arbitrary quantities not all zero.

Let R be the positive integer which is the first invariant factor of the matrix Δ, namely the determinant of Δ divided by the highest common factor of the first minors of Δ, so that $R\Delta^{-1}$ is a matrix of integers whose elements have no common factor other than unity; comparing then the equations

$$ak\epsilon_{2p}\bar{k}\bar{a}=0, \quad aR\Delta^{-1}\bar{a}=0,$$

and recalling that the periods are subject only to one set of bilinear relations with integral coefficients, we can infer that, if m be the highest common positive divisor of the elements of the matrix $k\epsilon_{2p}\bar{k}$, we have $k\epsilon_{2p}\bar{k}=\pm mR\Delta^{-1}$; comparing further the inequalities

$$-iak\epsilon_{2p}\bar{k}\bar{a}_0x_0x>0, \quad -ia\Delta^{-1}\bar{a}_0x_0x>0,$$

we can infer that the sign is positive, or

$$k\epsilon_{2p}\bar{k}=mR\Delta^{-1},$$

while, by the way, we see that, save perhaps for a $\pm$ sign, the relation $-i\Delta zz_0>0$ could in fact have been inferred from $-ia\Delta^{-1}\bar{a}_0x_0x>0$.

83. In what has preceded we have regarded the Jacobian function as given, and the Riemann surface as derived by means of it. But we may take another point of view. Suppose we have any Riemann surface of deficiency p upon which are n integrals of the first kind forming a defective system, the period matrix Π of these integrals being expressible by a matrix of $2n$ columns a, in the form $\Pi=ak$, where, in k, which is of type $(2n, 2p)$, the determinants of order $2n$ are co-prime; then we may consider integral functions of n variables whose second partial logarithmic derivatives have the periods a. That such functions always exist is clear from p. 227; they can be formed by the help of theta functions. The matrix $k\epsilon_{2p}\bar{k}$, and the number m, which is the highest common factor of the elements of the matrix $k\epsilon_{2p}\bar{k}$, will then be determined by the Riemann surface; but the matrix $\Delta=\bar{b}a-\bar{a}b$, though containing, in the case of all the functions considered, the same matrix a, may vary from function to function, and therewith also the number R, the first invariant factor of Δ, while $R\Delta^{-1}$, $=\frac{1}{m}k\epsilon_{2p}\bar{k}$, will be the same for all.

Taking this point of view, consider n Jacobian functions $f_1(u), \ldots, f_n(u)$; we proceed to prove that the equations

$$f_1(u-e^{(1)})=0, \ldots, f_n(u-e^{(n)})=0$$

have a number of sets of simultaneous solutions given by

$$N = R_1 R_2 \ldots R_n (n!)/\sqrt{|R\Delta^{-1}|},$$

and that, if $(u_1^{(\lambda)}, u_2^{(\lambda)}, \ldots, u_n^{(\lambda)})$ be one of these sets,

$$\frac{1}{N}\sum_{\lambda=1}^{N} u_\alpha^{(\lambda)} = \frac{1}{n}\sum_{\mu=1}^{n} e_\alpha^{(\mu)} + C_\alpha, \qquad (\alpha = 1, \ldots, n),$$

where C_α is independent of $e^{(1)}, \ldots, e^{(n)}$, and vanishes, save for Nth parts of periods, when each of the functions $f_1, \ldots, f_n$ is either even or odd.

Consider, first, one of the Jacobian functions, which we shall denote by $f(u)$. If we put $\zeta_\alpha(u) = \partial \log f(u)/\partial u_\alpha$, and regard $u_1, \ldots, u_n$ as integrals of the first kind upon the Riemann surface, the number of zeros of $f(u-e)$ upon the surface is the value of the integral

$$\frac{1}{2\pi i}\int d\log f(u-e), = \frac{1}{2\pi i}\int [\zeta_1(u-e)\,du_1 + \ldots + \zeta_n(u-e)\,du_n],$$

taken round the edges of the period loops. When however the arguments u are respectively increased by the elements of one of the columns of the matrix Π, $= ak$, the functions $\zeta_1(u-e), \ldots, \zeta_n(u-e)$ are increased by the elements of the corresponding column of the matrix $2\pi i bk$; thus, if we put $U = bk$, the value of the integral above is

$$\sum_{j=1}^{p} [U^{(j)}\,\Pi^{(j+p)} - U^{(j+p)}\,\Pi^{(j)}],$$

or

$$\sum_j (\bar{U}\Pi - \bar{\Pi}U)_{j,\,j+p},$$

that is

$$\sum_j [\bar{k}(\bar{b}a - \bar{a}b)\,k]_{j,\,j+p},$$

or

$$\sum_j (\bar{k}\Delta k)_{j,\,j+p}.$$

Now, if k be any matrix of type $(2n, 2p)$, and Δ any skew symmetrical matrix of type $(2n, 2n)$, we have

$$\sum_{j=1}^{p} (\bar{k}\Delta k)_{j,\,j+p} = \tfrac{1}{2}\sum_{\sigma=1}^{2n} (\Delta k\epsilon_{2p}\bar{k})_{\sigma,\sigma};$$

for $(\bar{k}\Delta k)_{\mu,\nu} = \sum_{\rho,\sigma} k_{\rho,\mu}\Delta_{\rho,\sigma}k_{\sigma,\nu} = \sum_{\rho,\sigma}\Delta_{\rho,\sigma}k_{\mu,\mu}k_{\sigma,\nu} = \sum_{\rho,\sigma}^{\rho<\sigma}\Delta_{\rho,\sigma}(k_{\rho,\mu}k_{\sigma,\nu} - k_{\sigma,\mu}k_{\rho,\nu})$,

so that
$$\sum_{j=1}^{p} (\bar{k}\Delta k)_{j,j+p} = \sum_{\rho,\sigma}^{\rho<\sigma} \Delta_{\rho,\sigma} \sum_{j=1}^{p} (k_{\rho,j}k_{\sigma,j+p} - k_{\sigma,j}k_{\rho,j+p})$$
$$= -\sum_{\rho,\sigma}^{\rho<\sigma} \Delta_{\rho,\sigma} (k\epsilon_{2p}\bar{k})_{\rho,\sigma} = \sum_{\rho,\sigma}^{\rho<\sigma} \Delta_{\sigma,\rho} (k\epsilon_{2p}\bar{k})_{\rho,\sigma}$$
$$= \tfrac{1}{2} \sum_{\rho,\sigma} \Delta_{\sigma,\rho} (k\epsilon\bar{k})_{\rho,\sigma} = \tfrac{1}{2} \sum_{\sigma=1}^{2n} (\Delta k\epsilon\bar{k})_{\sigma,\sigma},$$
the identity, for $\rho < \sigma$,
$$-(k\epsilon_{2p}\bar{k})_{\rho,\sigma} = \sum_{j=1}^{p} (k_{\rho,j}k_{\sigma,j+p} - k_{\sigma,j}k_{\rho,j+p}),$$
being at once obvious (cf. Appendix to Part II, Note III).

In our case we have
$$k\epsilon_{2p}\bar{k} = mR\Delta^{-1},$$
and the number of zeros is
$$\tfrac{1}{2} \sum_{\sigma=1}^{2n} (\Delta \,.\, mR\Delta^{-1})_{\sigma,\sigma} = mRn.$$

If these zeros be at (x_1), (x_2), ..., the sum
$$u_a^{x_1, a} + u_a^{x_2, a} + \dots$$
is (cf. p. 234) the value of
$$-\frac{1}{2\pi i} \int du_a \log f(u - e),$$
taken round the period loops, save for a sum of integral multiples of the elements of the αth row of the matrix Π, that is, save for a sum of integral multiples of the αth row of the matrix a. When the arguments u are increased by the elements $\Pi^{(j)}$ of the jth column of Π, the function $\log f(u-e)$ is increased, save possibly for integers, by
$$2\pi i U^{(j)} (u - e + \tfrac{1}{2}\Pi^{(j)}) + 2\pi i c k^{(j)} - \pi i K^{(j)},$$
where $K^{(j)}$ is a certain integer; the portion of the integral under consideration which contains $e_1, \dots, e_n$ is thus
$$\sum_{j=1}^{p} \sum_{\beta=1}^{n} e_\beta (U_{\beta,j}\Pi_{a,j+p} - U_{\beta,j+p}\Pi_{a,j}),$$
or*
$$\sum_{\beta=1}^{n} e_\beta (\Pi\epsilon_{2p}\bar{U})_{a,\beta},$$
or
$$\sum_{\beta=1}^{n} e_\beta (ak\epsilon_{2p}\bar{k}\bar{b})_{a,\beta},$$
$$= Rm \sum_{\beta} e_\beta (a\Delta^{-1}\bar{b})_{a,\beta},$$

---

* For if $\Pi = (\Pi_1, \Pi_2)$, $U = (U_1, U_2)$, where Π_1, etc. are of type (n, p), we have
$$(\Pi_1, \Pi_2) \begin{pmatrix} 0 & -1 \\ 1 & 0 \end{pmatrix} \begin{pmatrix} \bar{U}_1 \\ \bar{U}_2 \end{pmatrix} = (\Pi_2, -\Pi_1) \begin{pmatrix} \bar{U}_1 \\ \bar{U}_2 \end{pmatrix} = \Pi_2\bar{U}_1 - \Pi_1\bar{U}_2,$$
and the (a, β)th element of this is
$$\sum_j [(\Pi_2)_{a,j} (U_1)_{\beta,j} - (\Pi_1)_{a,j} (U_2)_{\beta,j}] = \Pi_{a,j+p}\, U_{\beta,j} - \Pi_{a,j}\, U_{\beta,j+p}.$$

and, as we have seen that $a\Delta^{-1}\bar{b} = 1$, this is

$$Rme_a.$$

Thus if $(a_1), (a_2), \ldots$ be the zeros of $f(u)$ and $(x_1), (x_2), \ldots$ the zeros of $f(u-e)$ we have

$$\sum_{\lambda=1}^{mRn} u_a^{x_\lambda, a_\lambda} = mRe_a, \qquad (\alpha = 1, \ldots, n).$$

It follows in the same way that if f be any function of position on the Riemann surface, which is capable of expression about every point of the surface by a converging series of positive and negative, but *integral*, powers of the parameter for the point of the surface; but has only poles and no essential singularities, so that the number of negative powers of the parameter is finite in every such series; and the function be single valued on the dissected surface; and its value $f^{(j)}$ on the left side of the jth period loop ($j = 1, \ldots, (2p)$) be equal to $fe^{2\pi i H^{(j)}}$, where f is its value on the right side and $H^{(j)}$ is of the form

$$Qbk^{(j)}[u^{x,a} - q] + R^{(j)},$$

where Q is a single number independent of j, q a set of n numbers independent of j, $R^{(j)}$ is a quantity independent of x and q, and $bk^{(j)}$ denotes the elements of the jth column of the matrix bk, or U, previously occurring, then the difference between the number of zeros x_1', x_2', ... and of poles x_1'', x_2'', ... of the function is

$$QmRn,$$

and we have $$\sum_\lambda u^{x'_\lambda} - \sum_\mu u^{x''_\mu} = QmRq + A,$$

where A is independent of q. We use this result in what follows.

Considering s places $(x_1), \ldots, (x_{s-1}), (x)$, we shall denote the value of the integral of the first kind at these places, with definite lower limits, by $u_1, u_2, \ldots, u_{s-1}, u$ respectively. When we have a set of s equations

$$f_1(u_1 + \ldots + u_{s-1} - e_1) = 0, \ldots, f_r(u_1 + \ldots + u_{s-1} - e_r) = 0,$$

$$f_{r+1}(u_1 + \ldots + u_{s-1} + u - e_{r+1}) = 0, \ldots, f_s(u_1 + \ldots + u_{s-1} + u - e_s) = 0,$$

in the s variables $(x_1), \ldots, (x_{s-1}), (x)$, wherein $f_1, \ldots, f_s$ are, as has been explained, Jacobian functions, with the same quasi-periods of matrix a, of which it will be noticed the first r equations do not contain (x), we shall say that we have the case (s, r). The case $(s, 0)$ is then that in which the s variables enter into each of the s functions; the case (s, s) would be that in which the variable x does not enter at all, and does not arise; thus we may have $r = 0, 1, \ldots, (s-1)$. For simplicity we write e_k, instead of $e^{(k)}$, to denote a row of n constants.

This set of equations determines sets of solutions for $(x_1), \ldots, (x_{s-1}), (x)$, and hence determines positions for (x). We proceed to shew that the total number of positions for (x) is

$$N_{s,r} = m^s R_1 \ldots R_s \frac{n!}{(n-s+1)!}(s-r)(n-s+r+1),$$

and that the sum of the values of the integral u at these positions is

$$S_{s,r} = m^s R_1 \ldots R_s \frac{(n-1)!}{(n-s+1)!}\{-(s-r)(e_1+\ldots+e_r)+(n-s+r+1)(e_{r+1}+\ldots+e_s)\},$$

save for periods and quantities independent of $e_1, \ldots, e_s$, the last equation standing of course for n equations.

In particular for the case $(s, 0)$, where all the s variables enter into all the functions, and enter symmetrically, the number of positions for (x) will be s times the number of sets of positions of $(x_1), (x_2), \ldots, (x_{s-1}), (x)$ which satisfy the equations. The number of such sets will thus be

$$m^s R_1 \ldots R_s \frac{n!}{(n-s)!},$$

and, if $(x_1'), \ldots, (x'_{s-1}), (x')$ denote such a set,

$$\Sigma(u^{x_1'} + \ldots + u^{x'_{s-1}} + u^{x'}) = m^s R_1 \ldots R_s \frac{(n-1)!}{(n-s)!}(e_1+e_2+\ldots+e_s),$$

save for quantities independent of $e_1, \ldots, e_s$.

We prove these results by induction, shewing that the formulae for the case (s, r) are deducible from those for the cases $(s, r+1)$ and $(s-1, 0)$, and in particular the formulae for the case $(s, s-1)$ are deducible from those for the case $(s-1, 0)$. As they have been proved for the case $(1, 0)$, they therefore hold in general.

Consider the $s-1$ equations

$$f_1(u_1+\ldots+u_{s-1}-e_1)=0, \ldots, f_r(u_1+\ldots+u_{s-1}-e_r)=0,$$
$$f_{r+1}(u_1+\ldots+u_{s-1}+u-e_{r+1})=0, \ldots, f_{s-1}(u_1+\ldots+u_{s-1}+u-e_{s-1})=0,$$

obtained from the original equations by omitting the last of these; regard them as equations for $(x_1), \ldots, (x_{s-1})$ only, in terms of (x); this is then a case $(s-1, 0)$; there will be a number of sets of solutions given by

$$m^{s-1} R_1 \ldots R_{s-1} \frac{n!}{(n-s+1)!},$$

and, if such a set be denoted by $x_1^{(\lambda)}, \ldots, x^{(\lambda)}_{s-1}$, we shall have

$$\sum_{\lambda}(u_1^{(\lambda)} + \ldots + u^{(\lambda)}_{s-1}) = m^{s-1} R_1 \ldots R_{s-1} \frac{(n-1)!}{(n-s+1)!}[\Sigma e - (s-r-1)u] + A,$$

where λ has a number of values equal to the number of sets, Σe denotes $e_1 + \ldots + e_{s-1}$, and A is independent of (x), and of $e_1, \ldots, e_{s-1}$, and of e_s.

Consider now the function of (x) given by the product

$$P = \prod_{\lambda} f_s [u_1^{(\lambda)} + \ldots + u^{(\lambda)}_{s-1} + u - e_s]:$$

in passing from a position of (x) on the right of the period loop (a_j), where $j = 1, \ldots, (2p)$, to the corresponding position on the left of this loop, the integrals u are increased by the elements of the jth column of Π, say, u is increased by $\Pi^{(j)}$, or $ak^{(j)}$, where $k^{(j)}$ denotes the jth column of k, and the set $x_1^{(\lambda)}, \ldots, x^{(\lambda)}_{s-1}$ is changed to another set of solutions, say $x_1^{(\mu)}, \ldots, x^{(\mu)}_{s-1}$, and at the same time the sum

$$u_1^{(\lambda)} + \ldots + u^{(\lambda)}_{s-1}, \; = W^{(\lambda)}, \text{ say,}$$

is changed to $W^{(\mu)} + \Pi t_\mu$, where t_μ denotes a set of integers, depending on j as well as λ; from the equation above (p. 293) giving $\sum_{\lambda} W^{(\lambda)}$, wherein A does not depend upon (x), we then infer that

$$\sum_{\lambda} \Pi t_\mu = - m^{s-1} R_1 \ldots R_{s-1} \frac{(n-1)!}{(n-s+1)!} (s - r - 1) \Pi^{(j)};$$

this equation is of the form

$$a (kt^{(j)} + Hk^{(j)}) = 0,$$

where $t^{(j)} = \sum_{\lambda} t_\mu$, and H is real; an equation $a\xi = 0$, wherein ξ denotes a set of $(2n)$ real quantities, involves also $a_0 \xi = 0$, where a_0 is the matrix whose elements are the conjugate complexes of those of a, and hence $\xi = 0$, since the determinant $\begin{vmatrix} a \\ a_0 \end{vmatrix}$ does not vanish; we therefore have here

$$kt^{(j)} + Hk^{(j)} = 0,$$

and hence $\displaystyle \sum_{\lambda} b_s kt_\mu = - m^{s-1} R_1 \ldots R_{s-1} \frac{(n-1)!}{(n-s+1)!} (s - r - 1) b_s k^{(j)}$,

wherein we shall, as previously, denote $b_s k^{(j)}$ by $U_s^{(j)}$. Now we have

$$f_s (u_1^{(\mu)} + \ldots + u^{(\mu)}_{s-1} + u + \Pi t_\mu + \Pi^{(j)} - e_s) / f_s (u_1^{(\mu)} + \ldots + u^{(\mu)}_{s-1} + u - e_s)$$

equal to $e^{2\pi i H_\mu}$, where

$$H_\mu = (b_s kt_\mu + b_s k^{(j)}) (u_1^{(\mu)} + \ldots + u^{(\mu)}_{s-1} + u - e_s) + B_\mu,$$

and B_μ is independent of (x) and $e_1, \ldots, e_s$, but may depend on j; thus the function of (x) denoted by P has at the period loop (a_j) the factor $e^{2\pi i H^{(j)}}$ where

$$H^{(j)} - \sum_{\lambda} b_s kt_\mu \,.\, W^{(\mu)} - \sum_{\lambda} B_\mu$$

$$= \sum_{\lambda} b_s kt_\mu (u - e_s) + U_s^{(j)} \sum_{\lambda} W^{(\mu)} + m^{s-1} R_1 \ldots R_{s-1} \frac{n!}{(n-s+1)!} U_s^{(j)} (u - e_s),$$

which, if we put

$$N_s = m^{s-1} R_1 \ldots R_{s-1} \frac{(n-1)!}{(n-s+1)!},$$

is the same as

$$-N_s U_s^{(j)}(s-r-1)(u-e_s)+U_s^{(j)}\{N_s[\Sigma e-(s-r-1)u]+A\}+N_s n U_s^{(j)}(u-e_s),$$

or $$N_s U_s^{(j)}\{[n-2(s-r-1)]u+\Sigma e-[n-(s-r-1)]e_s\}+U_s^{(j)}A.$$

Consider next the function of (x) denoted by the product

$$Q=\prod_\lambda f_s(u_1^{(\lambda)}+\ldots+u^{(\lambda)}_{s-1});$$

by precisely the same reasoning its factor for the passage of the period loop (a_j) is $e^{2\pi i H_0^{(j)}}$, where

$$H_0^{(j)}=\sum_\lambda b_s k t_\mu \,.\, W^{(\mu)}+C,$$

and C is independent of (x) and $e_1, \ldots, e_s$.

If then finally we consider the function of (x) denoted by P/Q, its factor for the period loop (a_j), save for a multiplier independent of (x) and $e_1, \ldots, e_s$, will be

$$\exp.\ 2\pi i N_s U_s^{(j)}\{[n-2(s-r-1)]u+\Sigma e-[n-(s-r-1)]e_s\};$$

and hence, recalling the remark of p. 292, the difference between the numbers of zeros of the functions of (x) denoted by P and Q will be

$$N_s[n-2(s-r-1)]mR_s n,$$

and, if the zeros of P be $z_1', z_2', \ldots$, and of Q be $z_1'', z_2'', \ldots$, we shall have

$$\sum_\sigma u^{z'_\sigma}-\sum_\rho u^{z''_\rho}=N_s\{[n-(s-r-1)]e_s-\Sigma e\}mR_s,$$

save for quantities independent of $e_1, \ldots, e_s$.

The product-function of (x)

$$P=\prod_\lambda f_s(u_1^{(\lambda)}+\ldots+u^{(\lambda)}_{s-1}+u-e_s)$$

has for zeros the places (x) which, with appropriate associated positions of $x_1, \ldots, x_{s-1}$, satisfy the equations

$$f_1(u_1+\ldots+u_{s-1}-e_1)=0, \ldots, f_r(u_1+\ldots+u_{s-1}-e_r)=0,$$

$$f_{r+1}(u_1+\ldots+u_{s-1}+u-e_{r+1})=0, \ldots, f_s(u_1+\ldots+u_{s-1}+u-e_s)=0;$$

consider the zeros of the product

$$Q=\prod_\lambda f_s(u_1^{(\lambda)}+\ldots+u^{(\lambda)}_{s-1}):$$

these are manifestly the places (x) which, with appropriate positions for $(x_1), \ldots, (x_{s-1})$, satisfy the equation $f_s(u_1+\ldots+u_{s-1})=0$ and the $(s-1)$ equations which determined the sets $x_1^{(\lambda)}, \ldots, x^{(\lambda)}_{s-1}$ from (x); we are then to consider the s equations

$$f_1(u_1+\ldots+u_{s-1}-e_1)=0, \ldots, f_r(u_1+\ldots+u_{s-1}-e_r)=0,\ f_s(u_1+\ldots+u_{s-1})=0,$$

$$f_{r+1}(u_1+\ldots+u_{s-1}+u-e_{r+1})=0, \ldots, f_{s-1}(u_1+\ldots+u_{s-1}+u-e_{s-1})=0;$$

these are a case $(s, r+1)$; the number of positions for (x) is therefore

$$m^s R_1 \dots R_s \frac{n!}{(n-s+1)!}(s-r-1)(n-s+r+2),$$

or

$$N_s m R_s n\,(s-r-1)(n-s+r+2),$$

while, if $z_1'', z_2'', \dots$ denote these positions, the sum $\sum\limits_\rho u^{z''_\rho}$ is given by

$$\sum_\rho u^{z''_\rho} = N_s m R_s \{-(s-r-1)(e_1+\dots+e_r)+(n-s+r+2)(e_{r+1}+\dots+e_{s-1})\}+E,$$

where E is independent of $e_1, \dots, e_s$.

And it is important for the induction to notice, and easier to notice at this stage, that this argument in regard to Q holds equally when r is $s-1$; the equations from which we start out are then

$$f_1(u_1+\dots+u_{s-1}-e_1)=0, \dots, f_{s-1}(u_1+\dots+u_{s-1}-e_{s-1})=0,$$
$$f_s(u_1+\dots+u_{s-1}+u-e_s)=0;$$

the sets $x_1^{(\lambda)}, \dots, x^{(\lambda)}_{s-1}$ are determined in terms of (x) from the first $s-1$ of these equations, that is they are all independent of (x), and the function Q does not depend upon (x); and the formulae for Q both become evanescent.

Adding now the number of zeros for Q to the number obtained for the difference of the numbers of zeros of P and Q, we have, for the number of zeros of P,

$$N_s m R_s n\,\{n-2(s-r-1)+(s-r-1)(n-s+r+2)\}$$
$$= N_s m R_s n\,(s-r)(n-s+r+1)$$
$$= m^s R_1 \dots R_s \frac{n!}{(n-s+1)!}(s-r)(n-s+r+1),$$

as originally stated; and, adding the value just found for the sum $\sum\limits_\rho u^{z''_\rho}$ to the value previously found for the sum $\sum\limits_\sigma u^{z'_\sigma} - \sum\limits_\rho u^{z''_\rho}$, we have

$$\sum_\sigma u^{z'_\sigma} = N_s m R_s \{(n-s+r+1)e_s - \Sigma e - (s-r-1)(e_1+\dots+e_r)$$
$$+(n-s+r+2)(e_{r+1}+\dots+e_{s-1})\}$$
$$= N_s m R_s \{-(s-r)(e_1+\dots+e_r)+(n-s+r+1)(e_{r+1}+\dots+e_s)\}$$
$$= m^s R_1 \dots R_s \frac{(n-1)!}{(n-s+1)!}\{-(s-r)(e_1+\dots+e_r)$$
$$+(n-s+r+1)(e_{r+1}+\dots+e_s)\},$$

also as originally stated.

The result is then established, and therewith the formulae for a case $(s, 0)$, as originally remarked—and therefore finally, for a case $(n, 0)$, the n equations

$$f_1(u_1+\dots+u_{n-1}+u_n-e_1)=0, \quad \dots, \quad f_n(u_1+\dots+u_{n-1}+u_n-e_n)=0$$

are proved to have a number of sets of solutions given by

$$m^n R_1 \ldots R_n (n\,!),$$

and, if $(x_1^{(\lambda)}, \ldots, x_n^{(\lambda)})$ denote one of these sets, we have

$$\sum_\lambda u^{x_1^{(\lambda)}} + \ldots + u^{x_n^{(\lambda)}} = m^n R_1 \ldots R_n [(n-1)\,!] (e_1 + \ldots + e_n),$$

save for quantities independent of $e_1, \ldots, e_n$.

We have however previously shewn that (p. 250) if $U = (U_1, \ldots, U_n)$ be n arbitrary variables, the n equations represented by

$$u_1 + \ldots + u_n \equiv U \qquad (\text{mod. } \Pi)$$

are satisfied by $H = (|k\epsilon_{2p}\bar{k}|)^{\frac{1}{2}}$ sets of positions of $(x_1), \ldots, (x_n)$ upon the Riemann surface. Consider then the n equations

$$f_1(U - e_1) = 0, \ldots, f_n(U - e_n) = 0\,;$$

to any set of values for U satisfying these, correspond H sets of positions for $(x_1), \ldots, (x_n)$; the number of sets of values for U is thus

$$\frac{1}{H} m^n R_1 \ldots R_n (n\,!)\,;$$

but we have $k\epsilon_{2p}\bar{k} = mR\Delta^{-1}$, and $|k\epsilon_{2p}\bar{k}| = m^{2n} |R\Delta^{-1}|$; this number can therefore also be written

$$T = (|R\Delta^{-1}|)^{-\frac{1}{2}} R_1 \ldots R_n (n\,!),$$

where $R_1\Delta_1^{-1} = R_2\Delta_2^{-1} = \ldots.$ And, if $U^{(\lambda)}$ denote one of the sets of positions,

$$\sum_\lambda U^{(\lambda)} = (|R\Delta^{-1}|)^{-\frac{1}{2}} R_1 \ldots R_n [(n-1)!] (e_1 + \ldots + e_n),$$

or

$$\sum_\lambda U^{(\lambda)} = \frac{T}{n} (e_1 + \ldots + e_n) + A,$$

where A is independent of $e_1, \ldots, e_n$.

In the case where every one of the functions $f_1, \ldots, f_n$ is even or odd, we have $A = 0$. For considering then the case where $e_1 = 0, \ldots, e_n = 0$, we have if $f_a(U) = 0$ also $f_a(-U) = 0$; thus the sets of solutions are in pairs of opposite sign, and the sum is zero, and therefore also A. It is therefore zero for all values of $e_1, \ldots, e_n$, save of course for a sum of integral multiples of the periods Π, or a—these forms of the statement being identical in virtue of the equations $\Pi = ak$, $(a, 0) = \Pi m$ of pp. 226, 230.

The foregoing investigation is, in its essential idea, derived from a paper by W. Wirtinger, *Monatsh. f. Mathematik u. Physik*, VII. Jahrg. (1896), pp. 1—25. The present writer cannot sufficiently express his admiration for it. The idea of obtaining the number of simultaneous solutions of a set of theta functions of arbitrary orders, and of expressing the sum of the values of the solutions, was however first entertained by Poincaré; his method of investigation is essentially different from the above: see Poincaré, *Bull. d. Sc. Math.*

d. France, XI. (1883), p. 132; *American Journal*, VIII. (1886), p. 334; *Compt. Rend.* 4 Fév. 1895; *Liouville*, 5me Sér. t. I. (1895), p. 222; *Acta Math.* XXVI. (1902), p. 95: see also Kronecker, *Werke*, I. (1895), p. 200 (*Berlin. Monats.* 1869).

84. The function $f(u)$ is easily reduced to the theta functions belonging to the Riemann surface. We can in fact find a unitary matrix of integers of type $(2n, 2n)$ such that

$$\gamma R\Delta^{-1}\bar{\gamma} = \begin{pmatrix} 0 & -e \\ e & 0 \end{pmatrix}, \text{ so that } \bar{\gamma}^{-1}\Delta\gamma^{-1} = R\begin{pmatrix} 0 & e^{-1} \\ -e^{-1} & 0 \end{pmatrix} = K \text{ say, or } \Delta = \bar{\gamma}K\gamma,$$

where e denotes a diagonal matrix whose diagonal consists of positive integers $e_1, e_2, \ldots, e_n$ such that e_{a+1}/e_a is an integer; as then every element of the matrix $R\Delta^{-1}$ is a linear function, with integral coefficients, of the integers $e_1, \ldots, e_n$, and the elements of $R\Delta^{-1}$ are co-prime, it follows that $e_1 = 1$. Further each of R/e_a is an integer. Putting then (cf. p. 286)

$$a = (\omega, \omega')\gamma, \qquad b = (\beta, \beta')\gamma,$$

$$(\omega, \omega') = \Omega, \qquad (\beta, \beta') = H,$$

if m denote any row of $2n$ integers, and $\mu = \gamma m$, we have

$$bm(u + \tfrac{1}{2}am) = H\mu(u + \tfrac{1}{2}\Omega\mu),$$

while
$$\Delta_{ij} = \sum_{k,l} K_{k,l}\gamma_{k,i}\gamma_{l,j},$$

$$\Delta_{ij}m_i m_j = \sum_{k,l} K_{k,l}\gamma_{k,i}\gamma_{l,j}m_i m_j = \sum_{k<l} K_{k,l}(\gamma_{k,i}\gamma_{l,j} - \gamma_{l,i}\gamma_{k,j})m_i m_j$$

$$\equiv \sum_{k<l} K_{k,l}(\gamma_{k,i}\gamma_{l,j} + \gamma_{l,i}\gamma_{k,j})m_i m_j, \qquad (\text{mod. } 2)$$

and

$$\sum_{i<j}\Delta_{i,j}m_i m_j \equiv \sum_{k<l} K_{k,l}\Big(\sum_{i<j}\gamma_{k,i}\gamma_{l,j}m_i m_j + \sum_{i<j}\gamma_{l,i}\gamma_{k,j}m_i m_j\Big)$$

$$\equiv \sum_{k<l} K_{k,l}\Big(\sum_{i<j}\gamma_{k,i}\gamma_{l,j}m_i m_j + \sum_{i>j}\gamma_{l,j}\gamma_{k,i}m_i m_j\Big), \qquad (\text{mod. } 2)$$

so that

$$\sum_{i<j}\Delta_{i,j}m_i m_j + \sum_{k<l} K_{k,l}\sum_i \gamma_{k,i}\gamma_{l,i}m_i^2 \equiv \sum_{k<l} K_{k,l}\mu_k\mu_l,$$

or, as $m_i^2 \equiv m_i$ (mod. 2), if we put

$$\sum_{k<l}\gamma_{k,i}\gamma_{l,i}K_{k,l} = F_i,$$

we have
$$\sum_{i<j}\Delta_{i,j}m_i m_j \equiv \sum_{k<l} K_{k,l}\mu_k\mu_l - Fm. \qquad (\text{mod. } 2)$$

Thus

$$bm(u + \tfrac{1}{2}am) + cm - \tfrac{1}{2}\sum_{i<j}\Delta_{i,j}m_i m_j \equiv H\mu(u + \tfrac{1}{2}\Omega\mu) + C\mu - \tfrac{1}{2}\sum_{k<l} K_{k,l}\mu_k\mu_l,$$
(mod. 1)

where
$$C\mu = cm + \tfrac{1}{2}Fm,$$

namely
$$C = \overline{\gamma^{-1}}(c + \tfrac{1}{2}F).$$

Now we have

$$R\begin{pmatrix}0 & e^{-1}\\ -e^{-1} & 0\end{pmatrix} = \bar{\gamma}^{-1}(\bar{b}a - \bar{a}b)\gamma^{-1} = \bar{H}\Omega - \bar{\Omega}H = \begin{pmatrix}\bar{\beta}\\ \bar{\beta}'\end{pmatrix}(\omega,\ \omega') - \begin{pmatrix}\bar{\omega}\\ \bar{\omega}'\end{pmatrix}(\beta,\ \beta')$$

$$= \begin{pmatrix}\bar{\beta}\omega - \bar{\omega}\beta & \bar{\beta}\omega' - \bar{\omega}\beta'\\ \bar{\beta}'\omega - \bar{\omega}'\beta & \bar{\beta}'\omega' - \bar{\omega}'\beta'\end{pmatrix},$$

so that $\bar{\beta}\omega = \bar{\omega}\beta, \quad \bar{\beta}'\omega' = \bar{\omega}'\beta', \quad \bar{\beta}\omega' - \bar{\omega}\beta' = Re^{-1}$;

also

$$0 < -iaR\Delta^{-1}\bar{a}_0 x_0 x = -i\Omega\gamma R\Delta^{-1}\bar{\gamma}\bar{\Omega}_0 x_0 x = -i(\omega,\ \omega')\begin{pmatrix}0 & -e\\ e & 0\end{pmatrix}\begin{pmatrix}\bar{\omega}_0\\ \bar{\omega}_0'\end{pmatrix}x_0 x$$

$$= -i(\omega' e,\ -\omega e)\begin{pmatrix}\bar{\omega}_0\\ \bar{\omega}_0'\end{pmatrix}x_0 x = -i(\omega' e\bar{\omega}_0 - \omega e\bar{\omega}_0')x_0 x = -i(\omega' e\xi_0 x - \omega_0' e\xi x_0),$$

where $\xi = \bar{\omega}x$; thus ω is of non-vanishing determinant, or we could choose x so that $\xi = 0$; if then $\rho = R(\omega e)^{-1}\omega'$, $e\xi = t = e\bar{\omega}x$, we have

$$0 < -i(\omega e\rho t_0 x - \omega_0 e\rho_0 t x_0) = -i(\bar{\rho}tt_0 - \bar{\rho}_0 t_0 t) = -i(\bar{\rho} - \rho_0)tt_0,$$

and $$0 = aR\Delta^{-1}\bar{a} = \omega' e\bar{\omega} - \omega e\bar{\omega}' = \frac{1}{R}\omega e(\rho - \bar{\rho})e\bar{\omega};$$

thus ρ is a symmetrical matrix, and for arbitrary t, if $\rho = p + iq$, $t = u + iv$,

$$0 < -i(\rho - \rho_0)tt_0 < -i(2iq)(u^2 + v^2) < 2q(u^2 + v^2),$$

so that for real $u_1, \ldots, u_n$, the form $i\rho u^2$ has its real part negative*, while $|q| \neq 0$.

---

* If we put, κ and λ being any constants,

$$\delta = \begin{pmatrix}\lambda e & 0\\ 0 & 1\end{pmatrix} J \begin{pmatrix}\kappa e^{-1} & 0\\ 0 & 1\end{pmatrix}\gamma,$$

where $J\epsilon_{2n}\bar{J} = \epsilon_{2n}$, so that J is a matrix of integers belonging to a linear transformation, we find

$$\delta R\Delta^{-1}\bar{\delta} = \kappa\lambda\begin{pmatrix}0 & -e\\ e & 0\end{pmatrix}.$$

Thence, taking $(\omega,\ \omega') = (v,\ v')\delta\gamma^{-1}$, $a = (v,\ v')\delta$, we find as before that the determinant formed by the first n columns of $(\omega,\ \omega')\gamma\delta^{-1}$, namely, if $J = \begin{pmatrix}\alpha & \beta\\ \alpha' & \beta'\end{pmatrix}^{-1}$, of

$$(\omega,\ \omega')\begin{pmatrix}\frac{1}{\kappa}e & 0\\ 0 & 1\end{pmatrix}\begin{pmatrix}\alpha & \beta\\ \alpha' & \beta'\end{pmatrix}\begin{pmatrix}\frac{1}{\lambda}e^{-1} & 0\\ 0 & 1\end{pmatrix},$$

is not zero; that is the determinant of $\omega e\alpha + \kappa\omega'\alpha'$, and therefore of

$$\alpha + c\rho\alpha',$$

is not zero, c, replacing $\frac{\kappa}{R}$, being any constant; in particular $|\omega'| \neq 0$. The preceding work is identical in form with that given p. 227. We have in fact

$$\begin{pmatrix}Re^{-1} & 0\\ 0 & 1\end{pmatrix}\gamma R\Delta^{-1}\bar{\gamma}\begin{pmatrix}Re^{-1} & 0\\ 0 & 1\end{pmatrix} = R\begin{pmatrix}0 & -1\\ 1 & 0\end{pmatrix},$$

and $a = (\omega,\ \omega')\gamma = (\nu,\ \nu')\begin{pmatrix}Re^{-1} & 0\\ 0 & 1\end{pmatrix}\gamma$, if $\nu = \frac{1}{R}\omega e$, $\nu' = \omega'$, so that $\rho = \nu^{-1}\nu'$.

Take now $P = -\frac{1}{2}\beta\omega^{-1}$, which by the above is a symmetrical matrix, of type (n, n), and multiply $f(u)$ by $e^{2\pi i P u^2}$; then

$$P[(u+am)^2 - u^2] = P[(u+\Omega\mu)^2 - u^2] = 2P\Omega\mu \,.\, u + \bar{\Omega}P\Omega\mu^2,$$

and, if $f_1(u) = e^{2\pi i P u^2} f(u)$, we have $f_1(u+am)/f_1(u) = e^{2\pi i T}$ where

$$T = 2P\Omega\mu \,.\, u + \bar{\Omega}P\Omega\mu^2 + H\mu\,(u + \tfrac{1}{2}\Omega\mu) + C\mu - \tfrac{1}{2}\sum_{k<l} K_{k,l}\mu_k\mu_l.$$

Herein, since

$$2P = -\beta\omega^{-1} = -\overline{\omega^{-1}}\bar{\beta}, \quad \bar{\omega}(\beta' - \overline{\omega^{-1}}\bar{\beta}\omega') = -Re^{-1},$$

we have, if $\mu = (M, M')$,

$$2P\Omega\mu \,.\, u + H\mu \,.\, u$$
$$= [(-\beta, -\overline{\omega^{-1}}\bar{\beta}\omega')\,\mu + (\beta, \beta')\,\mu]\,u = (0, \beta' - \overline{\omega^{-1}}\bar{\beta}\omega')\,\mu \,.\, u = -R\overline{\omega^{-1}}e^{-1}M' \,.\, u$$
$$= -Re^{-1}\omega^{-1}u \,.\, M' = -RvM',$$

if $v = (\omega e)^{-1} u$;

while

$$\bar{\Omega}P\Omega\mu^2 + \tfrac{1}{2}H\mu \,.\, \Omega\mu$$
$$= -\tfrac{1}{2}R\overline{\omega^{-1}}e^{-1}M' \,.\, (\omega M + \omega' M') = -\tfrac{1}{2}Re^{-1}\omega^{-1}(\omega M + \omega' M')\,M'$$
$$= -\tfrac{1}{2}Re^{-1}MM' - \tfrac{1}{2}\rho M'^2,$$

since

$$\rho = R(\omega e)^{-1}\omega' = Re^{-1}\omega^{-1}\omega';$$

also, since

$$K = R\begin{pmatrix} 0 & e^{-1} \\ -e^{-1} & 0 \end{pmatrix},$$

we have

$$-\tfrac{1}{2}\sum_{k<l} K_{k,l}\mu_k\mu_l = -\tfrac{1}{2}Re^{-1}MM';$$

thus on the whole

$$T = -RM'\left(v + \frac{1}{2}\frac{\rho}{R}M'\right) - Re^{-1}MM' + C\mu;$$

now let $C = (q, q')$, and take $Q = -\overline{\omega^{-1}}q$, so that

$$Q(u+am) - Qu = -\overline{\omega^{-1}}q \,.\, \Omega\mu = -\omega^{-1}(\omega M + \omega' M')\,q = -(M + \omega^{-1}\omega' M')\,q;$$

then, as $C\mu = (qM + q'M')$, we have

$$Q(u+am) - Qu + C\mu = q'M' - \frac{1}{R}e\rho M'q = q'M' - \frac{1}{R}\rho eqM';$$

and thus, if

$$f_2(u) = e^{2\pi i Pu^2 + 2\pi i Qu} f(u),$$

we have, since

$$e^{-2\pi i Re^{-1}MM'} = 1,$$

$$f_2(u+am) = e^{-2\pi i RM'\left(v + \frac{1}{2}\frac{\rho}{R}M'\right) + 2\pi i\left(q' - \frac{1}{R}\rho eq\right)M'} f_2(u);$$

which, if

$$w = v - \frac{1}{R}\left(q' - \frac{1}{R}\rho eq\right), = (\omega e)^{-1}\left(u + \frac{1}{R}\omega' eq - \frac{1}{R}\omega eq'\right),$$

is the same as

$$f_2(u+am) = e^{-2\pi i RM'\left(w + \frac{1}{2}\frac{\rho}{R}M'\right)} f_2(u);$$

we have

$$(\omega e)^{-1}(u+am)=v+\left(e^{-1},\ \frac{\rho}{R}\right)(M,\ M')=v+e^{-1}M+\frac{\rho}{R}M';$$

putting then $f_2(u)=F(w)$, we have

$$F\left(w+e^{-1}M+\frac{\rho}{R}M'\right)=e^{-2\pi iRM'\left(w+\frac{1}{2}\frac{\rho}{R}M'\right)}F(w);$$

we have however previously shewn (Part I. p. 21) that an integral function satisfying this equation is expressible in the form

$$\sum_h B_h\Theta\left(Rw,\ \rho\ \middle|\ \begin{matrix}\frac{1}{R}eh\\ 0\end{matrix}\right),$$

where h denotes the n integers $h_1, \ldots, h_n$ in which $0 \leqq h_a < \frac{R}{e_a}$, so that this is a sum of $R^n/e_1e_2\ldots e_n$ functions, namely, as $\Delta=R\bar{\gamma}\begin{pmatrix}0 & e^{-1}\\ -e^{-1} & 0\end{pmatrix}\gamma$, of $\sqrt{|\Delta|}$ functions.

And we notice, if $\nu=\frac{1}{R}\omega e$, that

$$Rw=\nu^{-1}\left(u+\frac{\omega' eq-\omega eq'}{R}\right).$$

Compare this work with that given on p. 227. We have denoted by R the first invariant factor of the matrix Δ, namely the determinant of Δ divided by the highest common factor of the first minors of Δ; denote similarly by r the first invariant factor of the matrix $k\epsilon_{2p}\bar{k}$; we have denoted by m the last invariant factor of $k\epsilon_{2p}\bar{k}$, namely the highest common factor of the elements of $k\epsilon_{2p}\bar{k}$, taken positive; denote similarly by M the highest common factor of the elements of Δ. The equation

$$\gamma R\Delta^{-1}\bar{\gamma}=\begin{pmatrix}0 & -e\\ e & 0\end{pmatrix},$$

gives

$$\Delta=\bar{\gamma}\begin{pmatrix}0 & Re^{-1}\\ -Re^{-1} & 0\end{pmatrix}\gamma,$$

and therefore, as γ is unitary,

$$M=\frac{R}{e_n}, \qquad R=\frac{R}{e_1}=R;$$

but from

$$k\epsilon_{2p}\bar{k}=mR\Delta^{-1}$$

we have

$$\gamma k\epsilon_{2p}\bar{k}\bar{\gamma}=m\begin{pmatrix}0 & -e\\ e & 0\end{pmatrix},$$

and hence

$$r=me_n;$$

thus

$$Mr=mR.$$

If then we put, as on p. 227 (cf. Appendix to Part II, Note II)

$$Gk\epsilon_{2p}\bar{k}\bar{G} = \begin{pmatrix} 0 & -d \\ d & 0 \end{pmatrix},$$

where G is unitary, we may take $\gamma = G$, $d = me$, and

$$a = (\omega, \omega')\gamma = (\mu, \mu')\begin{pmatrix} rd^{-1} & 0 \\ 0 & 1 \end{pmatrix} G$$

gives

$$\omega = \mu r d^{-1}, \quad \omega' = \mu',$$

$$\frac{\rho}{R} = (\omega\epsilon)^{-1}\omega' = \frac{m}{r}\mu^{-1}\mu' = m\frac{\sigma}{r},$$

while

$$e^{-1} = md^{-1}$$

and

$$(\omega e)^{-1}u = m\frac{\mu^{-1}u}{r}.$$

A Jacobian function in arguments $(\omega e)^{-1}u$ with quasi-periods $\left(e^{-1}, \frac{\rho}{R}\right)$ is thus a Jacobian function in arguments $m \cdot \frac{\mu^{-1}u}{r}$ with quasi-periods $m\left(d^{-1}, \frac{\sigma}{r}\right)$. The function upon which the expression of the periodic functions was shewn to depend was (p. 283) a function in arguments $\frac{\mu^{-1}u}{r}$ with quasi-periods $\left(d^{-1}, \frac{\sigma}{r}\right)$.

85. *Remark.* Considering as before a Jacobian function $f(u)$ on the Riemann surface, let $\zeta_a(u)$ denote $\partial \log f(u)/\partial u_a$; if u be regarded as an integral of the first kind on the Riemann surface, depending on the place (x), the function $\zeta_a(u)$ is an integral of the second kind with poles at the mRn zeros of $f(u)$, having for the passage of the period loop (a_j) the increment $2\pi i U_{a,j}$. We may consider such a function as

$$Z_j = \sum_{a=1}^{n}\left[U_{a,i}u_a - \frac{1}{2\pi i}\Pi_{a,i}\zeta_a(u)\right], \qquad (j = 1, \ldots, 2p);$$

at the jth period loop this function has the increment

$$\sum_{a=1}^{n}(U_{a,i}\Pi_{a,j} - \Pi_{a,i}U_{a,j}),$$

which is

$$(\bar{U}\Pi - \bar{\Pi}U)_{i,j}, \text{ or } (\bar{k}\Delta k)_{i,j};$$

assuming provisionally that the matrix $\bar{k}\Delta k$ is not of vanishing determinant, the $2p$ functions

$$Y = (\bar{k}\Delta k)^{-1}Z$$

are such that all the $2p$ periods of Y_j are zero except that at the loop (a_j), which is unity. If then $v_1, \ldots, v_p$ be the normal integrals of the first kind, the function

$$R_k = -v_k + Y_k + \tau_{k,1}Y_{p+1} + \ldots + \tau_{k,p}Y_{2p}, \qquad (k = 1, \ldots, p),$$

has all its periods zero, namely is a rational function on the Riemann surface.

APPENDIX TO PART II.

NOTE I.

THE REDUCTION OF A MATRIX TO ONE HAVING ONLY PRINCIPAL DIAGONAL ELEMENTS.

LET a be a matrix of integers of m rows and n columns; consider the bilinear form

$$ayx = \sum_{\alpha=1}^{m} \sum_{\beta=1}^{n} a_{\alpha,\beta} x_\alpha y_\beta ;$$

if we put $x = \bar{g}x'$, $y = hy'$, where g is a matrix of integers, of type (m, m), whose determinant is positive or negative unity, and h a matrix of integers, of type (n, n), whose determinant is positive or negative unity, we obtain

$$ahy' \,.\, \bar{g}x' = gahy'x', = a'y'x', \text{ say,}$$

where $a' = gah$; it is to be shewn that the matrices g, h can be chosen so that

$$a'y'x' = c_1 x_1' y_1' + c_2 x_2' y_2' + \ldots + c_l x_l' y_l' ,$$

where $c_1, \ldots, c_l$ are positive integers, and each of c_{r+1}/c_r is an integer.

If in ayx we put $x_\alpha = x'_{\alpha'}$, $x_{\alpha'} = x'_\alpha$, for a particular pair of suffixes α, α', every other x being equal to the corresponding x', the form $a'y'x'$ obtained will have $a'_{\alpha,\beta} = a_{\alpha',\beta}$, $a'_{\alpha',\beta} = a_{\alpha,\beta}$, namely we shall interchange the rows α and α' of the matrix. Similarly we can interchange any two columns by a similarly simple unitary substitution upon the variables $y_1, \ldots, y_n$. If we put $x_\alpha = -x'_\alpha$, for a particular value of α, we shall change the sign of one row, and we can equally change the sign of any one column by a transformation for $y_1, \ldots, y_n$. If we put for a particular pair α, α'

$$x_\alpha = x'_\alpha + mx'_{\alpha'}, \quad x_{\alpha'} = x'_{\alpha'},$$

all other x's being unaltered, we shall have

$$a_{\alpha,\beta} x_\alpha + a_{\alpha',\beta} x_{\alpha'} = a_{\alpha,\beta} x'_\alpha + (a_{\alpha',\beta} + m a_{\alpha,\beta}) x'_{\alpha'},$$

namely $$a'_{\alpha,\beta} = a_{\alpha,\beta}, \quad a'_{\alpha',\beta} = a_{\alpha',\beta} + m a_{\alpha,\beta},$$

so that we thereby add to the row α', the row α, multiplied by m. Similarly, by a unitary substitution, we can add any multiple of any column to any other column.

Taking now the matrix a, first divide all its elements $a_{\alpha,\beta}$ by their greatest common (positive) divisor; then, by interchange of rows and columns, put the (absolutely) smallest element which is not zero, or one of these, in the first place of the first row, and by change in the sign of the first row, if necessary, take this smallest element positive; then, by adding suitable multiples of the first row to all other rows, and suitable multiples of the first column to all other columns, make all elements of the first row and column less in absolute value than the first element. By repeating these steps we shall be able to arrive at a matrix in which the first element of the first row is positive unity and all other elements in the first row and column are zeros.

After this, deal with the matrix obtained by ignoring the first row and column in a similar way, making substitutions only for the variables other than the first x and the first y; and so on. The bilinear form will thus take a shape

$$c_1\{x_1'y_1' + k_2[x_2'y_2' + k_3(x_3'y_3' + \dots)]\},$$

or say

$$c_1x_1'y_1' + \dots + c_lx_l'y_l',$$

where $k_2 = c_2/c_1$, $k_3 = c_3/c_2$, ... are positive integers, and the matrix has a form

$$\begin{pmatrix} c_1, & 0, & 0, & 0, & 0, & 0, & . \\ 0, & c_2, & 0, & 0, & 0, & 0, & \\ 0, & 0, & c_3, & 0, & 0, & 0, & . \\ 0, & 0, & 0, & c_4, & 0, & 0, & \\ . & . & . & . & . & . & . \end{pmatrix},$$

there being $n - l$ columns of zeros on the right, and $m - l$ rows of zeros below. Here the greatest common divisor of determinants of order r is $c_1c_2 \dots c_r$, and the invariant factors, or elementary divisors, are $\dots, c_3, c_2, c_1$; the form is thus unique. The number l, characterised by the fact that all minors of the matrix a of more than l rows and columns have a vanishing determinant, is the rank of the matrix. Denoting the inverses of the square unitary matrices g, h by G, H we may write the result

$$a = G\begin{pmatrix} c & 0 \\ 0 & 0 \end{pmatrix}H = G_1cH_1,$$

where G_1, of type (m, l), is constituted by the first l columns of G, and is unitary in the sense that the determinants of it of l rows and columns have unity as their greatest common divisor, and H_1, of type (l, n), is constituted by the first l rows of H, and is similarly unitary.

For a simple instance take the matrix

$$a = \begin{pmatrix} 1, & 2, & 3, & 4 \\ 5, & 6, & 7, & 8 \end{pmatrix},$$

which can be changed in turn into the following forms:

$$\begin{pmatrix} 1, & 0, & 0, & 0 \\ 5, & -4, & -8, & -12 \end{pmatrix}, \quad \begin{pmatrix} 1, & 0, & 0, & 0 \\ 0, & -4, & -8, & -12 \end{pmatrix}, \quad \begin{pmatrix} 1, & 0, & 0, & 0 \\ 0, & -4, & 0, & 0 \end{pmatrix},$$

the bilinear form

$$ayx = x_1y_1 + 2x_1y_2 + 3x_1y_3 + 4x_1y_4 + 5x_2y_1 + 6x_2y_2 + 7x_2y_3 + 8x_2y_4$$

being $$x_1(y_1 + 2y_2 + 3y_3 + 4y_4) + x_2(5y_1 + 6y_2 + 7y_3 + 8y_4),$$

or $$x_1y_1' + x_2(-4y_2' + 5y_1'),$$

or $$(x_1 + 5x_2)\,y_1' - 4x_2y_2',$$

that is $$x_1'y_1' + 4x_2'y_2',$$

where $$(x_1', x_2') = \begin{pmatrix} 1, & 5 \\ 0, & -1 \end{pmatrix}(x_1, x_2)$$

and
$$(y_1', y_2', y_3', y_4') = \begin{pmatrix} 1, & 2, & 3, & 4 \\ 0, & 1, & 2, & 3 \\ 0, & 0, & 1, & 0 \\ 0, & 0, & 0, & 1 \end{pmatrix}(y_1, y_2, y_3, y_4),$$

giving
$$(y_1', y_2') = \begin{pmatrix} 1, & 2, & 3, & 4 \\ 0, & 1, & 2, & 3 \end{pmatrix}(y_1, y_2, y_3, y_4).$$

We give three applications of the result.

(α) If a be a matrix of integers of m rows and n columns, with $m < n$, the determinants of order m from this not being all zero, we can determine $n - m$ other rows of integers which, put with a, give a matrix of n rows and columns, with determinant equal to the greatest common divisor of the determinants of order m in a: in particular if a be unitary the additional $n - m$ rows can be found so that the resulting determinant is unitary.

For taking the notation as before, we have $l = m$, and

$$a = G(c, 0)\,H,$$

where G is of type (m, m); consider the matrix product

$$\begin{pmatrix} G, & 0 \\ 0, & 1 \end{pmatrix}\begin{pmatrix} c, & 0 \\ 0, & 1 \end{pmatrix}H,$$

where each factor is of type (n, n), the unity denoting in each case a diagonal matrix whose $n - m$ elements in the diagonal are all unities and other elements zero, the zero denoting a matrix whose elements are zero, of type $(m, n - m)$, or $(n - m, m)$, according to its position. This is the same as

$$\begin{pmatrix} Gc, & 0 \\ 0, & 1 \end{pmatrix}H, = \begin{pmatrix} GcH_1 \\ H_2 \end{pmatrix}, = \begin{pmatrix} a \\ H_2 \end{pmatrix},$$

where H_1, as before, is constituted by the first m rows of H, and H_2 by the remaining $n-m$ rows. The determinant of this matrix is

$$|Gc|\;|H|, \;=c_1c_2\ldots c_m,$$

and this matrix is therefore such a matrix as desired.

(β) In the same case, $m<n$, the rank of the matrix a being m, we have as before

$$a=GcH_1, \;=fk, \text{ say,}$$

where f, $=Gc$, is of type (m, m), and k, $=H_1$, is of type (m, n) *and is unitary*, in the sense that its determinants of order m have unity for highest common factor. The question arises whether the matrix a is capable of the form

$$a=f_1k_1,$$

in which f_1 is of type (m, m), and k_1 is of type (m, n) *and is unitary*, in other ways. We prove that this is only possible by the obvious change

$$f=f_1\gamma, \quad k=\gamma^{-1}k_1,$$

wherein γ, of type (m, m), is unitary.

For, form the matrix of type (n, n), of determinant unity, whose first m rows are constituted by the matrix k, as we have just shewn possible (under (α)); let m denote the inverse of this matrix, so that

$$km=(1,\ 0),$$

where 1 denotes a diagonal matrix of type (m, m), having unities in the diagonal but its other elements zero, and 0 denotes a zero matrix of type $(m, n-m)$; the equation

$$fk=f_1k_1$$

then gives

$$f(1,\ 0)=f_1k_1m,$$

and if we put

$$k_1m=(\gamma,\ \lambda),$$

where γ is of type (m, m) and λ of type $(m, n-m)$, this is the same as

$$f=f_1\gamma, \text{ with } 0=f_1\lambda;$$

the former gives

$$f_1\gamma k=f_1k_1,$$

which, since by hypothesis the determinant of f_1 is not zero, leads to

$$k=\gamma^{-1}k_1,$$

as stated above.

If instead of the numbers m, n we have respectively the even numbers $2n$, $2p$, as is the case in the applications made in the text of this volume, and if, as there, ϵ_{2p} denote a matrix of type $(2p, 2p)$ whose elements are zero save the elements $(r, p+r)$, each of which is -1, and the elements $(p+r, r)$, each of which is 1, we have the result that a matrix of integers a, of type $(2n, 2p)$, and rank $2n$, can be written in the form

$$a=fk,$$

wherein f is of type $(2n, 2n)$, and k is of type $(2n, 2p)$, and is *unitary*, and in whatever way this be done, the matrix, of type $(2n, 2n)$,

$$k\epsilon_{2p}\bar{k}$$

has the same determinant. The number expressed by this determinant, which was called the *multiplicity* in the text, is thus uniquely determined by the matrix a.

(γ) A third simple application is to determine the number of integers representable in the form ax, where a is a square matrix type (n, n), of non-vanishing determinant, $(m = n = l)$, and x is a row of rational fractions, two rows whose difference consists of n integers being counted equivalent. Take, as before,

$$a = GcH;$$

then

$$ax = z,$$

where z is a row of n integers, is the same as

$$c\xi = \zeta,$$

where

$$Hx = \xi, \quad G^{-1}z = \zeta,$$

so that when z consists of integers, so does ζ, and conversely, and when $x' - x$ consists of integers, so does $\xi' - \xi = H(x' - x)$, and conversely. The problem is then of the number of integers representable by $c\xi$, that is by

$$(c_1\xi_1, c_2\xi_2, \ldots, c_n\xi_n),$$

and of these the suitable solutions are manifestly

$$c_1\xi_1 = 0, 1, \ldots, c_1 - 1; \quad c_2\xi_2 = 0, 1, \ldots, c_2 - 1; \ldots,$$

of which the number is $c_1c_2 \ldots c_n$, equal to the determinant of the matrix a.

NOTE II.

THE COGREDIENT REDUCTION OF A SKEW-SYMMETRIC MATRIX OF INTEGERS.

Consider a bilinear form in the m variables $x_1, \ldots, x_m$ and the m variables $y_1, \ldots, y_m$, having the shape

$$ayx = \Sigma a_{i,j}(x_iy_j - x_jy_i),$$

where the coefficients $a_{i,j}$ are integers; we proceed to shew how, by cogredient unitary substitutions

$$x = g\xi, \quad y = g\eta,$$

where g is a matrix of integers of type (m, m) of determinant unity, the form can be reduced to the shape

$$d_1(\xi_{n+1}\eta_1 - \xi_1\eta_{n+1}) + d_1d_2(\xi_{n+2}\eta_2 - \xi_2\eta_{n+2}) + \ldots,$$

in which the couplets of variables occurring are of the forms

$$\xi_1\eta_{n+1}-\xi_{n+1}\eta_1,\quad \xi_2\eta_{n+2}-\xi_{n+2}\eta_2,\quad \dots,\quad \xi_n\eta_{2n}-\xi_{2n}\eta_n,$$

or say $(1, n+1),\quad (2, n+2),\quad \dots,\quad (n, 2n),$

in which no two couplets involve the same suffix, and the total number of variables ξ is even, $=2n$, as of variables η, while $d_1, d_2, \dots, d_n$ are positive integers.

(α) In the first place, we can, by unitary substitutions, change the original form to one in which the only couplets such as $(i, j) = x_iy_j - x_jy_i$ which occur are

$$(1, 2),\ (2, 3),\ (3, 4),\ (4, 5),\ \dots,\ (m-1, m),$$

in which any two consecutive couplets have a common suffix; we may describe such a form as a *linked* form.

For consider any two couplets

$$a(x_iy_j - x_jy_i) + b(x_iy_k - x_ky_i);$$

let m be the greatest common divisor of a and b, and ρ, σ, without common factor, be integers chosen so that

$$a\sigma - b\rho = m;$$

putting $\dfrac{a}{m}x_j + \dfrac{b}{m}x_k = x_j', \qquad \dfrac{a}{m}y_j + \dfrac{b}{m}y_k = y_j',$

$$\rho x_j + \sigma x_k = x_k', \qquad \rho y_j + \sigma y_k = y_k',$$

the other variables (than x_j, x_k) being unchanged, this being a unitary substitution, the two couplets become

$$m(x_iy_j' - x_j'y_i),$$

and instead of two couplets (i, j), (i, k) we have now only one couplet (i, j). Thus, considering the aggregate of the couplets involving x_1 and y_1 in the original form, namely

$$a_{1,2}(x_1y_2 - x_2y_1) + a_{1,3}(x_1y_3 - x_3y_1) + \dots + a_{1,m}(x_1y_m - x_my_1),$$

we can first replace the two first couplets by a single couplet

$$c_{1,2}(x_1y_2' - x_2'y_1),$$

this requiring a substitution, of x_2' and x_3' in place of x_2 and x_3 (and of y_2' and y_3' in place of y_2 and y_3) which does not affect any other of the couplets involving x_1 and y_1; the number $c_{1,2}$ is a divisor of $a_{1,2}$, being the greatest common divisor of $a_{1,2}$ and $a_{1,3}$; taking next the couplets

$$c_{1,2}(x_1y_2' - x_2'y_1) + a_{1,4}(x_1y_4 - x_4y_1),$$

we can by a substitution replacing x_2', x_4 by x_2'', x_4' (and similarly y_2', y_4 by y_2'', y_4'), replace these couplets by a single couplet $c_{1,3}(x_1y_2'' - x_2''y_1)$, where

$c_{1,3}$ is a divisor of $c_{1,2}$ and therefore a divisor of $a_{1,2}$. Proceeding thus the form is reduced to

$$\alpha (x_1 \eta_2 - \xi_2 y_1) + H,$$

where H is a skew-symmetric form in $m-1$ pairs of variables $\xi_2, \eta_2, \xi_3, \eta_3 \ldots$, not involving x_1, y_1, and α is a divisor of $a_{1,2}$. By applying a similar process to H, we can, by a unitary substitution which does not affect x_1, y_1 or ξ_2, η_2, reduce this to a form

$$\beta (\xi_2 \eta_3' - \xi_3' \eta_2) + K,$$

where K is a form not involving the variables x_1, y_1, or ξ_2, η_2. And so on. The original form is thus reduced, say, to

$$b_{1,2}(X_1 Y_2 - X_2 Y_1) + b_{2,3}(X_2 Y_3 - X_3 Y_2) + \ldots + b_{m-1,m}(X_{m-1} Y_m - X_m Y_{m-1}).$$

(β) From this it appears at once that integer values of $x_1, y_1, \ldots, x_m, y_m$, can be chosen which will make the original form equal to the greatest common divisor of all the coefficients $a_{1,2}, a_{1,3}, \ldots, a_{2,3}, \ldots, a_{m-1,m}$.

For, the linked form just written, with coefficients $b_{i,j}$, being obtained from the original by unitary substitutions, the greatest common divisor of its coefficients $b_{i,j}$ is necessarily the same as for the original form. Suppose, for a time, this factor divided out, so that we may regard $b_{1,2}, b_{2,3}, \ldots, b_{m-1,m}$ as having only unity as common divisor. We can then obtain integers $p_2, p_3, \ldots, p_m$, without common factor, to make

$$b_{1,2} p_2 + b_{2,3} p_3 + \ldots + b_{m-1,m} p_m = 1;$$

take then $$X_1 = X_2 = \ldots = X_m = 1,$$

and $$Y_1 = q_1,\ Y_2 = q_2,\ \ldots,\ Y_m = q_m,$$

so that $$Y_2 - Y_1 = p_2,\ Y_3 - Y_2 = p_3,\ \ldots,\ Y_m - Y_{m-1} = p_m,$$

which is satisfied, for instance, by

$$Y_1 = 0,\ Y_2 = p_2,\ Y_3 = p_2 + p_3,\ \ldots,\ Y_m = p_2 + p_3 + \ldots + p_m;$$

then, for these values, the linked form has the value unity. Let the corresponding values of $x_1, \ldots, x_m$ and $y_1, \ldots, y_m$, obtained from these by the unitary substitutions, be denoted respectively by $a_1, \ldots, a_m$ and $b_1, \ldots, b_m$; for these the original form has also the value unity; and as the two matrices

$$\begin{pmatrix} a_1, & a_2, & \ldots, & a_m \\ b_1, & b_2, & \ldots, & b_m \end{pmatrix}, \quad \begin{pmatrix} 1, & 1, & \ldots, & 1 \\ q_1, & q_2, & \ldots, & q_m \end{pmatrix}$$

are obtained from one another by unitary substitutions, and the binary determinants from the latter (which are, in part, the numbers $p_2, p_3, \ldots, p_m$) have unity as common factor, the same is true of the former matrix.

The statement is therefore proved in the case when the coefficients of the form have unity for common factor. It then follows at once in the case when they have a common factor greater than unity.

(γ) Hence, the original form can be changed to one in which the coefficient of the first couplet, (1, 2), is equal to the highest common factor of all the coefficients.

Suppose this highest common factor to be unity, and, as in (β), let

$$x_1 = a_1, \ \ldots, \ x_m = a_m, \qquad y_1 = b_1, \ \ldots, \ y_m = b_m$$

be values of the variables reducing the original form to unity. We can then, as proved in Note I (p. 305), since the binary determinants $a_i b_j - a_j b_i$ have unity for highest common factor, determine a matrix of integers of determinant unity whose first two rows are respectively $a_1, \ldots, a_m$ and $b_1, \ldots, b_m$, say

$$P = \begin{pmatrix} a_1, & a_2, & \ldots, & a_m \\ b_1, & b_2, & \ldots, & b_m \\ c_{3,1}, & c_{3,2}, & \ldots, & c_{3,m} \\ \cdots & \cdots & \cdots & \cdots \\ c_{m,1}, & c_{m,2}, & \ldots, & c_{m,m} \end{pmatrix};$$

putting then

$$(x_1, \ldots, x_m) = \overline{P}(\xi_1, \ldots, \xi_m), \quad (y_1, \ldots, y_m) = \overline{P}(\eta_1, \ldots, \eta_m),$$

we obtain

$$ayx = Pa\overline{P}\eta\xi,$$

wherein the coefficient of the couplet $\xi_1\eta_2 - \xi_2\eta_1$ is

$$(Pa\overline{P})_{1,2} = \sum_{r=1}^{m} P_{1,r}(a\overline{P})_{r,2} = \sum_{r,s}^{1\ldots m} a_{r,s}(P_{1,r}P_{2,s} - P_{1,s}P_{2,r})$$

$$= \sum_{r,s}^{1\ldots m} a_{r,s}(a_r b_s - a_s b_r) = 1,$$

as was desired. When the coefficients of the original form have a common factor greater than unity, the corresponding transformed form is one in which the coefficient of the couplet $\xi_1\eta_2 - \xi_2\eta_1$ is this factor.

(δ) Still supposing the coefficients in the form to have unity as common factor, and the form to have been reduced, as in (γ), to a form

$$\xi_1\eta_2 - \xi_2\eta_1 + \ldots$$

in which the first couplet has unity as coefficient, let this form be transformed, as in (α), to a linked form,

$$X_1Y_2 - X_2Y_1 + \beta_{2,3}(X_2Y_3 - X_3Y_2) + \ldots + \beta_{m-1,m}(X_{m-1}Y_m - X_mY_{m-1}),$$

in which $X_1 = \xi_1$, $Y_1 = \eta_1$, and the first coefficient, being the common divisor of all the coefficients, is unity. Herein put

$$X_1 - \beta_{2,3}X_3 = X_1', \qquad Y_1 - \beta_{2,3}Y_3 = Y_1',$$

as a transformation for X_1, Y_1, the other variables being unaltered; thereby we get

$$X_1'Y_2 - X_2Y_1' + M,$$

where

$$M_1 = \beta_{3,4}(X_3 Y_4 - X_4 Y_3) + \ldots + \beta_{m-1,m}(X_{m-1} Y_m - X_m Y_{m-1}),$$

involves only $m-2$ variables $X_3, \ldots, X_m$ and $m-2$ variables $Y_3, \ldots, Y_m$. Let similar reasoning be applied to the form M_1 after division of all its coefficients by their highest common factor, and so on. If d_1 denote the highest common factor of the coefficients of the form as originally given, we thus see that this form can be changed to the shape

$$d_1\{(1, 2) + d_2[(3, 4) + d_3((5, 6) + \ldots)]\},$$

or

$$d_1(x_1'y_2' - x_2'y_1') + d_1 d_2(x_3'y_4' - x_4'y_3') + \ldots + d_1 d_2 \ldots d_n(x'_{2n-1}y'_{2n} - x'_{2n}y'_{2n-1}),$$

wherein $d_1, d_2, \ldots, d_n$ are positive integers, and $2n$, an even integer, is not greater than m; putting now

$$x'_{2k-1} = -\xi_k, \quad x'_{2k} = \xi_{n+k}, \quad y'_{2k-1} = -\eta_k, \quad y'_{2k} = \eta_{n+k}, \qquad (k = 1, 2, \ldots, n),$$

this is the same as

$$d_1(\xi_{n+1}\eta_1 - \xi_1\eta_{n+1}) + d_1 d_2(\xi_{n+2}\eta_2 - \xi_2\eta_{n+2}) + \ldots + d_1 d_2 \ldots d_n(\xi_{2n}\eta_n - \xi_n\eta_{2n}).$$

In other words there exist unitary transformations from the original form, say

$$x = g\xi, \quad y = g\eta,$$

such that

$$ayx = \bar{g}ag\eta\xi = \begin{pmatrix} 0 & -d & \lambda \\ d & 0 & \mu \\ \lambda' & \mu' & \nu \end{pmatrix}\eta\xi,$$

or

$$\bar{g}ag = \begin{pmatrix} 0 & -d & \lambda \\ d & 0 & \mu \\ \lambda' & \mu' & \nu \end{pmatrix},$$

where 0 denotes a matrix of n rows and columns of which every element is zero, d denotes a matrix of n rows and columns having every element zero except those in the diagonal which are in turn $d_1, d_1 d_2, \ldots, d_1 d_2 \ldots d_n$, while $\lambda, \mu, \nu, \lambda', \mu'$ are matrices consisting wholly of zeros, of respective types $(n, m-2n)$, $(n, m-2n)$, $(m-2n, m-2n)$, $(m-2n, n)$, $(m-2n, n)$. Of the whole matrix, the minors of $1, 2, 3, 4, \ldots, 2n$, rows and columns have, for the greatest common divisor, respectively,

$$d_1, d_1^2, d_1^3 d_2, d_1^4 d_2^2, \ldots, d_1^{2n-1} d_2^{2n-3} \ldots d_n, d_1^{2n} d_2^{2n-2}, \ldots, d_n^2,$$

so that the corresponding invariant factors are

$$d_1, d_1, d_1 d_2, d_1 d_2, \ldots, d_1 d_2 \ldots d_n, d_1 d_2 \ldots d_n,$$

while all determinants of more than $2n$ rows and columns are zero. In particular if the original matrix a is of non-vanishing determinant we must have $m = 2n$, and there is a transformation such that

$$\bar{g}ag = \begin{pmatrix} 0 & -d \\ d & 0 \end{pmatrix}.$$

(ϵ) In the preceding reduction every step can be at once carried out for any given form. But the number of steps can be reduced, and the use of the so-called linked form avoided, if we establish in some other way that values of the variables can be found to render the original form equal to the greatest common divisor of its coefficients, which we have proved by the use of the linked form. This result being assumed, the form can be reduced, as in (γ), to the shape

$$d_1 F \equiv d_1 [\xi_1\eta_2 - \xi_2\eta_1 + \alpha_{1,3}(\xi_1\eta_3 - \xi_3\eta_1) + \ldots];$$

and then, instead of (δ), we may put

$$x_1' = \frac{\partial F}{\partial \eta_2} = \xi_1 - \alpha_{2,3}\xi_3 - \ldots, \quad y_1' = -\frac{\partial F}{\partial \xi_2} = \eta_1 - \alpha_{2,3}\eta_3 - \ldots,$$
$$x_2' = -\frac{\partial F}{\partial \eta_1} = \xi_2 + \alpha_{1,3}\xi_3 + \ldots, \quad y_2' = \frac{\partial F}{\partial \xi_1} = \eta_2 + \alpha_{1,3}\eta_3 + \ldots,$$

whereby the form reduces to

$$d_1 \{(x_1'y_2' - x_2'y_1') + N\},$$

where N is a form not containing the four variables x_1', x_2', y_1', y_2', for which then similar reduction is possible (Frobenius, *Crelle*, LXXXVI. and LXXXVIII.).

(ζ) Any form

$$a(x_1y_2 - x_2y_1) + b(x_3y_4 - x_4y_3) + c(x_5y_6 - x_6y_5) + \ldots,$$

in which no two couplets have a common variable, can be at once reduced to

$$d_1(\xi_1\eta_2 - \xi_2\eta_1) + d_1d_2(\xi_3\eta_4 - \xi_4\eta_3) + d_1d_2d_3(\xi_5\eta_6 - \xi_6\eta_5) + \ldots,$$

as follows. Take the pair of couplets

$$A(x_1y_2 - x_2y_1) + B(x_3y_4 - x_4y_3)$$

in which A, B have no common factor; find μ, ν so that $A\mu + B\nu = 1$; put

$$\begin{aligned} x_1 &= \mu x_1' - Bx_3', & y_1 &= \mu y_1' - By_3', \\ x_2 &= x_2' - B\nu x_4', & y_2 &= y_2' - B\nu y_4', \\ x_3 &= \nu x_1' + Ax_3', & y_3 &= \nu y_1' + Ay_3', \\ x_4 &= x_2' + A\mu x_4', & y_4 &= y_2' + A\mu y_4', \end{aligned}$$

which is a unitary substitution, giving, as we at once find,

$$A(x_1y_2 - x_2y_1) + B(x_3y_4 - x_4y_3) = x_1'y_2' - x_2'y_1' + AB(x_3'y_4' - x_4'y_3').$$

A repetition of this process suffices for the purpose.

(ι) Suppose the skew-symmetric matrix of integers, a, to be of type $(2n, 2n)$, and of non-vanishing determinant. Then as has been shewn, we can find a unitary matrix g, of integers, such that

$$\bar{g}ag = \begin{pmatrix} 0 & -d \\ d & 0 \end{pmatrix},$$

where d is a diagonal matrix of positive integer elements $d_1, d_2, \ldots, d_n$ for which each of $d_2/d_1, d_3/d_2, \ldots, d_n/d_{n-1}$ is integral. Let d^{-1} be the inverse matrix of d, a diagonal matrix of elements $d_1^{-1}, d_2^{-1}, \ldots, d_n^{-1}$; we have, if 1 denote the unit matrix of type (n, n),

$$\begin{pmatrix} rd^{-1} & 0 \\ 0 & 1 \end{pmatrix}\begin{pmatrix} 0 & -d \\ d & 0 \end{pmatrix}\begin{pmatrix} rd^{-1} & 0 \\ 0 & 1 \end{pmatrix} = \begin{pmatrix} 0 & -r \\ d & 0 \end{pmatrix}\begin{pmatrix} rd^{-1} & 0 \\ 0 & 1 \end{pmatrix} = \begin{pmatrix} 0 & -r \\ r & 0 \end{pmatrix} = r\begin{pmatrix} 0 & -1 \\ 1 & 0 \end{pmatrix};$$

if we take $r = d_n$, the first invariant factor of a, being the quotient of the determinant $(d_1 d_2 \ldots d_n)^2$, of a, by the highest common factor

$$d_1^2 d_2^2 \ldots d_{n-1}^2 d_n,$$

of its minors of order $2n - 1$, then

$$\begin{pmatrix} rd^{-1} & 0 \\ 0 & 1 \end{pmatrix}$$

is a matrix of integers. Conversely, if γ be any matrix of integers such that

$$\bar{\gamma}\begin{pmatrix} 0 & -d \\ d & 0 \end{pmatrix}\gamma = s\begin{pmatrix} 0 & -1 \\ 1 & 0 \end{pmatrix},$$

where s is an integer, and J, of type $(2n, 2n)$, given by

$$J = \begin{pmatrix} \alpha & \beta \\ \alpha' & \beta' \end{pmatrix},$$

be the most general matrix such that

$$\bar{J}\begin{pmatrix} 0 & -1 \\ 1 & 0 \end{pmatrix}J = \begin{pmatrix} 0 & -1 \\ 1 & 0 \end{pmatrix},$$

we have, from $$\begin{pmatrix} sd^{-1} & 0 \\ 0 & 1 \end{pmatrix}\begin{pmatrix} 0 & -d \\ d & 0 \end{pmatrix}\begin{pmatrix} sd^{-1} & 0 \\ 0 & 1 \end{pmatrix} = s\begin{pmatrix} 0 & -1 \\ 1 & 0 \end{pmatrix},$$

the equation $$\begin{pmatrix} 0 & -d \\ d & 0 \end{pmatrix} = s\begin{pmatrix} s^{-1}d & 0 \\ 0 & 1 \end{pmatrix}\begin{pmatrix} 0 & -1 \\ 1 & 0 \end{pmatrix}\begin{pmatrix} s^{-1}d & 0 \\ 0 & 1 \end{pmatrix},$$

and hence $$\bar{\gamma}\begin{pmatrix} s^{-1}d & 0 \\ 0 & 1 \end{pmatrix}\begin{pmatrix} 0 & -1 \\ 1 & 0 \end{pmatrix}\begin{pmatrix} s^{-1}d & 0 \\ 0 & 1 \end{pmatrix}\gamma = \begin{pmatrix} 0 & -1 \\ 1 & 0 \end{pmatrix},$$

so that $$\begin{pmatrix} s^{-1}d & 0 \\ 0 & 1 \end{pmatrix}\gamma = J,$$

or $$\gamma = \begin{pmatrix} sd^{-1} & 0 \\ 0 & 1 \end{pmatrix}\begin{pmatrix} \alpha & \beta \\ \alpha' & \beta' \end{pmatrix} = \begin{pmatrix} sd^{-1}\alpha & sd^{-1}\beta \\ \alpha' & \beta' \end{pmatrix};$$

now $d^{-1}\alpha$ differs from α in that its first row is divided by d_1, its second row by d_2, and so on; in order then that all the elements of $sd^{-1}\alpha$ and $sd^{-1}\beta$ should be integers each of the quantities $sd_1^{-1}, sd_2^{-1}, \ldots, sd_n^{-1}$ must be integral, or, if these be fractions with denominators $e_1, e_2, \ldots, e_n$, the last row of α must, after division by e_n, consist of integers, as must also the last row of β; we have however from the definition of J (cf. p. 314)

$$\alpha_{n,1}\beta'_{n,1} - \alpha'_{n,1}\beta_{n,1} + \alpha_{n,2}\beta'_{n,2} - \alpha'_{n,2}\beta_{n,2} + \ldots + \alpha_{n,n}\beta'_{n,n} - \alpha'_{n,n}\beta_{n,n} = 1;$$

thus $e_n = 1$ and s divides by d_n. In other words the most general matrix of integers, γ, for which

$$\bar{\gamma}\begin{pmatrix}0 & -d\\ d & 0\end{pmatrix}\gamma = s\begin{pmatrix}0 & -1\\ 1 & 0\end{pmatrix},$$

wherein s is an integer, is of the form

$$\gamma = \begin{pmatrix}sd^{-1} & 0\\ 0 & 1\end{pmatrix}J,$$

where J is a matrix for which

$$\bar{J}\begin{pmatrix}0 & -1\\ 1 & 0\end{pmatrix}J = \begin{pmatrix}0 & -1\\ 1 & 0\end{pmatrix},$$

and s necessarily divides by d_n, the first invariant factor of the matrix

$$\begin{pmatrix}0 & -d\\ d & 0\end{pmatrix}.$$

The matrix $$f = g\gamma$$
is then such that $$\bar{f}af = s\begin{pmatrix}0 & -1\\ 1 & 0\end{pmatrix},$$

and is the most general matrix of integers effecting this transformation, while s is necessarily equal to, or a multiple of, the first invariant factor of the matrix a.

NOTE III.

ON TWO FORMS OF EXPANSION OF A DETERMINANT.

If

$$a_1,\ a_2,\ \dots,\ a_n,\ a_1',\ a_2',\ \dots,\ a_n'$$
$$b_1,\ b_2,\ \dots,\ b_n,\ b_1',\ b_2',\ \dots,\ b_n'$$

be two rows, each of $2n$ quantities, the quantity

$$(a;\ b) = a_1b_1' - a_1'b_1 + a_2b_2' - a_2'b_2 + \dots + a_nb_n' - a_n'b_n$$

may be called the *combinant*, or the *splice* of the two rows. For instance if we have a matrix of $2n$ rows and columns such that

$$\begin{pmatrix}\alpha & \beta\\ \alpha' & \beta'\end{pmatrix}\begin{pmatrix}0 & -1\\ 1 & 0\end{pmatrix}\begin{pmatrix}\bar{\alpha} & \bar{\alpha}'\\ \bar{\beta} & \bar{\beta}'\end{pmatrix} = \begin{pmatrix}0 & -1\\ 1 & 0\end{pmatrix},$$

where 1 denotes the matrix unity of type (n, n), and each of $\alpha, \beta, \alpha', \beta'$ is also of type (n, n), namely such that

$$\begin{pmatrix}\beta\bar{\alpha} - \alpha\bar{\beta} & \beta\bar{\alpha}' - \alpha\bar{\beta}'\\ \beta'\bar{\alpha} - \alpha'\bar{\beta} & \beta'\bar{\alpha}' - \alpha'\bar{\beta}'\end{pmatrix} = \begin{pmatrix}0 & -1\\ 1 & 0\end{pmatrix},$$

then $$\alpha_{r,1}\beta_{s,1} - \alpha_{s,1}\beta_{r,1} + \dots + \alpha_{r,n}\beta_{s,n} - \alpha_{s,n}\beta_{r,n} = 0,$$
$$\alpha_{r,1}\beta'_{r,1} - \alpha'_{r,1}\beta_{r,1} + \dots + \alpha_{r,n}\beta'_{r,n} - \alpha'_{r,n}\beta_{r,n} = 1,$$

and so on, namely the splice of any two rows of the matrix

$$\begin{pmatrix}\alpha & \beta\\ \alpha' & \beta'\end{pmatrix}$$

is zero, except of rows of places r and $r + n$, when the splice is unity.

(α) If $$A = (\alpha, \alpha')$$
be a matrix of type $(2n, 2p)$, with $n \gtreqless p$, so that each of α, α' is of type $(2n, p)$, we have, with
$$\epsilon_{2p} = \begin{pmatrix} 0 & -1 \\ 1 & 0 \end{pmatrix},$$
wherein 1 denotes the unit matrix of type (p, p),
$$A\epsilon_{2p}\bar{A} = (\alpha, \alpha')\begin{pmatrix} 0 & -1 \\ 1 & 0 \end{pmatrix}\begin{pmatrix} \bar{\alpha} \\ \bar{\alpha}' \end{pmatrix} = (\alpha', -\alpha)\begin{pmatrix} \bar{\alpha} \\ \bar{\alpha}' \end{pmatrix} = \alpha'\bar{\alpha} - \alpha\bar{\alpha}',$$
a matrix of type $(2n, 2n)$, wherein the (r, s)th element is
$$\alpha'_{r,1}\alpha_{s,1} + \ldots + \alpha'_{r,p}\alpha_{s,p} - \alpha_{r,1}\alpha'_{s,1} - \ldots - \alpha_{r,p}\alpha'_{s,p},$$
which is the negative of the splice of the two rows
$$\alpha_{r,1}, \ldots, \alpha_{r,p}, \alpha'_{r,1}, \ldots, \alpha'_{r,p}$$
$$\alpha_{s,1}, \ldots, \alpha_{s,p}, \alpha'_{s,1}, \ldots, \alpha'_{s,p}$$
of the matrix (α, α'); denoting this by (r, s) we thus have
$$A\epsilon_{2p}\bar{A} = \begin{pmatrix} 0, & -(1,2), & -(1,3), & \ldots \\ (1,2), & 0, & -(2,3), & \ldots \\ (1,3), & (2,3), & 0, & \ldots \\ \cdot & \cdot & \cdot & \ldots \end{pmatrix}.$$

Thus in particular, when $n = p$, and A is a square matrix of type $(2n, 2n)$, by taking the square root of the determinant of both sides, we have
$$|A| = \text{the Pfaffian } \Sigma \pm (1, 2)(3, 4) \ldots (2n-1, 2n),$$
whereby any determinant of even order $2n$ is expressed as a Pfaffian involving $1 \,.\, 3 \,.\, 5 \ldots (2n-1)$ terms, each of which is a product of n splices from two rows of the determinant. For example, the determinant
$$\Delta = \begin{vmatrix} a_1, & b_1, & a_1', & b_1' \\ a_2, & b_2, & a_2', & b_2' \\ a_3, & b_3, & a_3', & b_3' \\ a_4, & b_4, & a_4', & b_4' \end{vmatrix},$$
if $$(r, s) = a_r a_s' - a_s a_r' + b_r b_s' - b_s b_r',$$
has the form $$\Delta = (1, 2)(3, 4) - (1, 3)(2, 4) + (1, 4)(2, 3).$$

(β) The same determinant of order $2n$ can be expanded as a sum of products of binary determinants. Divide the determinant mentally into pairs of columns, say the first and second, the third and fourth, in general the $(2h-1)$th and $2h$th. From the first pair of columns take the k_1th and k_2th rows, and let $[k_1, k_2]_1$ denote the binary determinant so obtained; from the second pair of columns take similarly the determinant $[k_3, k_4]_2$ involving elements from the k_3th and k_4th rows, and so on; we suppose $k_1 < k_2$, $k_3 < k_4$, and so on. Then the determinant can be written
$$\Sigma \pm [k_1, k_2]_1 [k_3, k_4]_2 \ldots [k_{2n-1}, k_{2n}]_n,$$

where the number of terms is

$$\binom{2n}{2}\binom{2n-2}{2}\cdots\binom{4}{2}, = (n!)\ 1\,.\,3\,.\,5\,.\,\ldots\,(2n-1),$$

and the sign is $\pm$ according as $k_1, k_2, k_3, k_4, \ldots$ is an order formed from the normal order 1, 2, 3, 4, ... by an even or odd number of inversions. For instance, for the determinant Δ we have the ordinary expansion of six terms

$$\Delta = (a_1b_2 - a_2b_1)(a_3'b_4' - a_4'b_3') + \ldots + (a_3b_4 - a_4b_3)(a_1'b_2' - a_2'b_1').$$

(γ) We can easily connect these two methods of expansion. Take the second method of expansion to be based upon a subdivision of the determinant into pairs of columns of which the first pair is constituted by the first and $(n+1)$th columns, the second pair by the second and $(n+2)$th columns, ..., the nth pair by the nth and $2n$th columns. Then the splice of the rth and sth rows of the determinant is, in the notation employed in (α) and (β),

$$(r, s) = [r, s]_1 + [r, s]_2 + \ldots + [r, s]_n,$$

where $[r, s]_h$ denotes a binary determinant formed from the hth pair of columns. Hence the Pfaffian expansion of the determinant, formed as in (α), is

$$\Sigma \pm \{[1, 2]_1 + [1, 2]_2 + \ldots + [1, 2]_n\}\{[3, 4]_1 + \ldots + [3, 4]_n\}\{\ldots\ldots\ldots\}$$

or

$$\begin{aligned} &\Sigma \pm [1, 2]_1 [3, 4]_2 [5, 6]_3 \ldots \\ +&\Sigma \pm [3, 4]_1 [1, 2]_2 [5, 6]_3 \ldots \\ +&\ldots \\ +&\Sigma \pm [1, 2]_1 [3, 4]_1 [5, 6]_3 \ldots \\ +&\ldots\ldots\ldots\ldots\ldots\ldots\ldots\ldots\ldots\ldots, \end{aligned}$$

wherein, in each of the first $(n!)$ rows, which are formed from one another merely by permutation of the suffixes 1, 2, ..., n, there are no two suffixes equal, while in each of the remaining rows two suffixes (at least) are equal. Such a row, for example, as

$$\Sigma \pm [1, 2]_1 [3, 4]_1 [5, 6]_3 \ldots,$$

arises, however, associated with others which, together with it, make the expansion, in binary determinants, of a determinant in which the second pair of columns is the same as the first pair, that is of a vanishing determinant. The Pfaffian expansion thus gives the expansion in binary determinants; and the form of the latter is at once deducible from the form of the former by permutation of the factors of the terms. For instance, for $n = 2$, the Pfaffian expansion is

$$(1, 2), (3, 4) - (1, 3)(2, 4) + (1, 4)(2, 3),$$

and the expansion in binary determinants is

$$\begin{aligned} &[1, 2]_1 [3, 4]_2 - [1, 3]_1 [2, 4]_2 + [1, 4]_1 [2, 3]_2 \\ +&[3, 4]_1 [1, 2]_2 - [2, 4]_1 [1, 3]_2 + [2, 3]_1 [1, 4]_2. \end{aligned}$$

NOTE IV.

SOME CURVES LYING UPON THE KUMMER SURFACE, IN CONNEXION WITH THE THEORY OF DEFECTIVE INTEGRALS.

1. Upon the hyperelliptic surface $\Psi(x, y, \xi) = 0$, expressing the relation connecting the functions $x = \wp_{22}(u)$, $y = \wp_{21}(u)$, $\xi = \wp_{222}(u)$, the two integrals (p. 44)

$$u_2 = 4\int\frac{\Delta_{13}dx - \Delta_{12}dy}{\xi\partial\Delta/\partial z}, \quad u_1 = 4\int\frac{-\Delta_{12}dx + \Delta_{11}dy}{\xi\partial\Delta/\partial z},$$

beside being everywhere finite, are single valued save for their additive periods, and are thus among the everywhere finite integrals belonging to any algebraic curve upon $\Psi = 0$; every such curve of deficiency greater than 2 thus possesses defective integrals.

But upon the Kummer surface, these integrals, of which the integrand involves rational functions of x, y, z multiplied by the ambiguous quantity ξ, though still everywhere finite, are capable of change of sign, and are therefore not in general among the ordinary everywhere finite integrals of a curve upon this surface.

Any plane (algebraic) curve possesses, in addition to its ordinary single valued integrals of the first kind, everywhere finite integrals similarly capable of change of sign. For example, on the curve

$$y^2 = \prod_{i=1}^{5}(x - a_i),$$

the integral
$$\int(x - a_i)^{\frac{1}{2}}\frac{dx}{y}$$

is everywhere finite; and, on the curve

$$x^4 + y^4 = 1,$$

the integral
$$\int(1 - x^2)^{\frac{1}{2}}\frac{dx}{y^3}$$

is everywhere finite; in general if, upon any plane curve of deficiency p, the adjoint polynomial of $2p - 2$ zeros associated with an ordinary integral of the first kind, v, be denoted by ϕ, and Φ, Ψ denote such adjoint polynomials each with the peculiarity of having $p - 1$ repeated zeros, the integral

$$\int\frac{dv}{\phi}(\Phi\Psi)^{\frac{1}{2}}$$

is everywhere finite. These integrals are single valued upon the associated Riemann surface dissected by the period loops which render the ordinary integrals single valued, but the relation connecting the values of an integral at the two sides of any such loop is of the form

$$u' = (-1)^g u + \Omega,$$

where Ω is a constant for that loop, and g, also constant for that loop, is 0 or 1; with each such integral there is thus a set of $2p$ numbers g, and it can be proved that, for each of the $2^{2p}-1$ possible sets of such $2p$ numbers, the number of linearly independent integrals is $p-1$ *.

For the case of a plane quartic curve, $f=0$, with $p=3$, there are, associated with any set of 6 numbers g, twelve † bitangents, forming a so-called Steiner system, breaking into couples x_1, ξ_1, x_2, ξ_2, ..., x_6, ξ_6, such that, for $i=3, \ldots, 6$, we have

$$\sqrt{x_i \xi_i} = A_i \sqrt{x_1 \xi_1} + B_i \sqrt{x_2 \xi_2},$$

where A_i, B_i are constants; and the corresponding integrals‡ are

$$\int \sqrt{x_1 \xi_1} \frac{dx}{f'(y)}, \quad \int \sqrt{x_2 \xi_2} \frac{dx}{f'(y)}.$$

On the Kummer surface, the factor under the integral sign, in the integrals u_2, u_1, which is not rational in x, y, z, is ξ; or, since the ratios $\xi : \eta : \zeta : \tau$ are rational in x, y, z, it may be taken to be any linear form $l_0\xi + l_1\eta + l_2\zeta + l_3\tau$; we have (Ex. 7, p. 152) the identities

$$\theta\phi\xi + (\theta+\phi)\eta + \zeta = 2\sqrt{P_\theta P_\phi P_{\theta\phi}},$$

$$\theta\phi\psi\xi + (\theta\phi + \theta\psi + \phi\psi)\eta + (\theta+\phi+\psi)\zeta + \tau = 2\sqrt{P_{\theta\phi} P_{\theta\psi} P_{\phi\psi}},$$

wherein θ, ϕ, ψ are roots of the fundamental quintic; the sign of the square root under the integral sign may thus be expressed in terms of any one of the 20 radicals of these forms, of which any two have a rational ratio; these 20 radicals are all expressible linearly in terms of four of them, for example in terms of

$$\sqrt{P_{\theta\phi} P_{\theta\psi} P_{\phi\psi}}, \quad \sqrt{P_\theta P_\phi P_{\theta\phi}}, \quad \sqrt{P_\theta P_\psi P_{\theta\psi}}, \quad \sqrt{P_\phi P_\psi P_{\phi\psi}}.$$

This suggests at once the relations among the square roots of the products of two bitangents of a plane quartic curve. To see how, in the case of a plane section of a Kummer surface, these radicals reduce to square roots of products of two bitangents, consider any plane passing through the two points at infinity

$$\frac{x}{1} = -\frac{y}{\theta} = \frac{z}{\theta^2} = \infty, \quad \frac{x}{1} = -\frac{y}{\phi} = \frac{z}{\phi^2} = \infty,$$

* A proof is given in the author's *Abel's Theorem*, Chap. XIV. See p. 420.

† *loc. cit.*, p. 381.

‡ A very general case of such factorial integrals, and theta functions formed with them, is considered by Wirtinger, *Untersuchungen über Thetafunctionen* (Leipzig, 1895), pp. 73—125.

where θ, ϕ are *not* necessarily roots of the fundamental quintic; the equation of the plane may therefore be taken to be

$$x\theta\phi + y(\theta+\phi) + z - \frac{F(\theta,\phi) - 2\Theta\Phi}{4(\theta-\phi)^2} = m,$$

or say $P_{\theta\phi} = m$; if we put

$$a = \frac{(\phi-\psi)\Theta}{(\theta-\phi)(\theta-\psi)}, \quad b = \frac{(\psi-\theta)\Phi}{(\phi-\psi)(\phi-\theta)}, \quad c = \frac{(\theta-\phi)\Psi}{(\psi-\theta)(\psi-\phi)},$$

where ψ, like θ and ϕ, is any quantity, and

$$\Theta^2 = f(\theta), \quad \Phi^2 = f(\phi), \quad \Psi^2 = f(\psi),$$

and put also $\quad X = P_{\phi\psi}, \quad Y = P_{\psi\theta}, \quad Z = P_{\theta\phi}$,

we have* the identity

$$[\theta\phi\psi\xi + (\theta\phi+\theta\psi+\phi\psi)\eta + (\theta+\phi+\psi)\zeta + \tau]^2$$
$$= 4XYZ + a^2X^2 + b^2Y^2 + c^2Z^2 - 2bcYZ - 2caZX - 2abXY;$$

from this identity, taking $\psi = \infty$, we have

$$[\theta\phi\xi + (\theta+\phi)\eta + \zeta]^2 = 4P_\theta P_\phi P_{\theta\phi} + (\theta-\phi)^{-2}(\Theta P_\phi - \Phi P_\theta)^2,$$

where $P_\theta = y + \theta x - \theta^2$, and θ, ϕ are arbitrary; while, taking ψ to be any root of the fundamental quintic, so that $c = 0$, we have, still with θ and ϕ arbitrary,

$$[\theta\phi\psi\xi + (\theta\phi+\theta\psi+\phi\psi)\eta + (\theta+\phi+\psi)\zeta + \tau]^2 = 4P_{\theta\psi}P_{\phi\psi}P_{\theta\phi} + (aP_{\phi\psi} - bP_{\theta\psi})^2;$$

thus when $P_{\theta\phi} = m$ we have

$$\theta\phi\psi\xi + (\theta\phi+\theta\psi+\phi\psi)\eta + (\theta+\phi+\psi)\zeta + \tau = \{4mP_{\theta\psi}P_{\phi\psi} + (aP_{\phi\psi} - bP_{\theta\psi})^2\}^{\frac{1}{2}};$$

now we know that the cubic function in x, y, z, obtained by squaring the left side, gives, when equated to zero, a surface touching the Kummer surface wherever it meets it; the right side therefore represents the square root of the product of two double tangents of the plane quartic obtained by the section of the Kummer surface with the plane $P_{\theta\phi} = m$. For this plane quartic the square root under the integral sign, in the two surface integrals u_2, u_1, is thus reduced, as regards its sign, to any one of the six radicals obtained by taking ψ equal in turn to all the roots of the fundamental sextic†; and of these radicals all are expressible linearly by any two of them, since we have

$$\sum_{1,2,3} (\psi_i - \psi_j)\{4mP_{\theta\psi_i}P_{\phi\psi_i} + (a_iP_{\phi\psi_i} - b_iP_{\theta\psi_i})^2\}^{\frac{1}{2}} = 0.$$

* We know (p. 152) that the terms of the third order in x, y, z, on the two sides, agree; and it is easily found that the cubic surface obtained by equating the right side to zero has nodes at $(X, Y, Z) = (0, 0, 0)$, $(0, ca, ab)$, $(bc, 0, ab)$, $(bc, ca, 0)$, as on p. 143; for $P_{\phi\psi} = bc$ is the same as $P_{\phi\psi} = \Phi\Psi/(\phi-\psi)^2, = E'_{\phi\psi} - E_{\phi\psi}$; putting $X_1 = -aX + bY + cZ$, $Y_1 = aX - bY + cZ$, $Z_1 = aX + bY - cZ$, $T_1 = 2abc - aX - bY - cZ$, the surface reduces to $X_1^{-1} + Y_1^{-1} + Z_1^{-1} + T_1^{-1} = 0$.

† Thus the 28 double tangents of the plane section $P_{\theta\phi} = m$ are determined, consisting of the

When the plane $P_{\theta\phi} = m$ becomes a tangent plane of the Kummer surface we have $m = 0$, or $m = ab$, corresponding to the two tangent planes through the chord (θ, ϕ) at infinity; in either case the radical

$$\{4mP_{\theta\psi}P_{\phi\psi} + (aP_{\phi\psi} - bP_{\theta\psi})^2\}^{\frac{1}{2}}$$

becomes rational in x, y, z, and the integrals u_2, u_1 become ordinary integrals of the first kind upon the section, which is now a hyperelliptic quartic curve of deficiency 2.

In general, upon any algebraic curve on the Kummer surface, in order that the integrals u_2, u_1 of the surface should be integrals of the first kind for this curve, it is clearly necessary and sufficient that, upon this curve, $\xi, = \wp_{222}(u)$, should be expressible rationally by the coordinates x, y, z of the point of this curve. Consider, with the Kummer surface, the surface $\Psi(x, y, \xi) = 0$; we have $\xi = \sqrt{R(x, y, z)}$, where R is a rational function, and, to any point (x, y, z) of a curve upon the Kummer surface, correspond two

---

16 intersections of the plane with the singular tangent planes, and the 12 determined in the text, which form a Steiner system. The pairs of this system intersect in the six points such as $P_{\theta\psi} = 0$, $P_{\phi\psi} = 0$, $P_{\theta\phi} = m$; the plane $P_{\theta\psi} = 0$ is the polar plane of $x/1 = -y/\theta = z/\theta^2 = \infty$ in the linear complex associated with the root ψ (whose form is given p. 74; see p. 105), and the six points $P_{\theta\psi} = 0$, $P_{\phi\psi} = 0$, $P_{\theta\phi} = m$ are the poles of the plane $P_{\theta\phi} = m$ in the six linear complexes; they lie on a conic, as follows from the identity $\Sigma(\Gamma_1 xx')^2 = 0$ (p. 174); cf. Klein, *Math. Annal.* II. (1870), p. 216.

Conversely, given any plane quartic curve, there can be drawn through it ∞^4 Kummer surfaces. We have in various ways, in this volume, reduced the equation of a Kummer surface to a form containing three explicit constants (*e.g.* p. 153); adding the 15 constants of a general projective transformation we have 18 constants; making the surface pass then through 14 ($= 4 . 4 - 3 + 1$) points of an arbitrary quartic curve, there remain 4 constants. The theorem is proved by Kummer (*Berlin. Monatsber.* 1864, p. 256), by identifying the irrational form of the quartic curve with the section, by its plane, of the Kummer surface taken in irrational form. The quartic curve being regarded as the envelope of the conic $\psi^2 U + \psi V + W = 0$ (Salmon, *Higher Plane Curves* (1879), p. 226), there are six values of ψ for which this conic represents two straight lines; the six points of intersection of these pairs are easily shewn to lie upon a conic, S; dividing these six points into two triangles in one of the ten possible ways, there exists a unique conic, Σ, of which these are self-polar triangles; taking two arbitrary non-intersecting straight lines through the two points in which this unique conic, Σ, cuts one side of one of the two triangles, these lines and the conic Σ determine a ruled quadric; it is then easy to determine six linear complexes, every two in involution, in which the poles of the given plane, of the quartic curve, are the angular points of the two inscribed triangles of the conic S. Hence the Kummer surface can be found as desired (Ciani, *Ann. di Mat.* 3rd Series, t. II. (1899), p. 93). The six complexes being $\Gamma_1, \ldots, \Gamma_6$ (cf. p. 168), the two arbitrarily assumed lines are the directrices $\Gamma_1 \pm i\Gamma_2$, and the quadric is $\Gamma_1 \Gamma_2^{-1} \Gamma_3 (x)^2 = 0$ (cf. p. 81); the involutory transformation $(x') = \Gamma_2^{-1} \Gamma_1 (x)$ may be defined by drawing from (x) the secant of $\Gamma_1 \pm i\Gamma_2$, and taking the fourth harmonic point (x'); the six linear complexes are obtained by the sequence of such a transformation and reciprocation in regard to the quadric surface (cf. Hudson, *Kummer's Quartic Surface*, p. 41). Finally, the construction in the text enables us to obtain the Kummer surface, as the locus of nodes of a certain cubic surface with four nodes, which touches its tritangent plane at the points of contact, with the given plane quartic curve, of one of the bitangents of this curve. The conic $\psi^2 U + \psi V + W = 0$ lies on this cubic surface.

points (x, y, ξ), $(x, y, -\xi)$ of the associated curve upon $\Psi(x, y, \xi)=0$; if, however, upon this curve, $R(x, y, z)=[U(x, y, z)]^2$, where U is a rational function, the associated curve upon $\Psi(x, y, \xi)=0$ breaks up into two curves, one satisfying $\xi=U(x, y, z)$, the other satisfying $\xi=-U(x, y, z)$, where, on the right, z is to be replaced by its rational expression in x, y and ξ. Of this the tangent plane section of the Kummer surface forms the handiest example; if in the identity

$$[\theta\phi\xi+(\theta+\phi)\eta+\zeta]^2=4P_\theta P_\phi P_{\theta\phi}+(\theta-\phi)^{-2}[\Theta P_\phi-\Phi P_\theta]^2,$$

we put (p. 38)

$$\theta+\phi=x', \quad \theta\phi=-y', \quad E_{\theta\phi}=z',$$

$$\frac{\Theta-\Phi}{\theta-\phi}=\xi', \quad \frac{\theta\Phi-\phi\Theta}{\theta-\phi}=\eta', \quad \frac{\theta^2\Phi-\phi^2\Theta}{\theta-\phi}=-\zeta',$$

we have

$$(-\xi y'+\eta x'+\zeta)^2-(-\xi' y+\eta' x+\zeta')^2$$
$$=4[(x-x')(xy'-x'y)-(y-y')^2][xy'-x'y+z'-z],$$

and thus, upon the tangent plane of the Kummer surface, which, with fixed (x', y', z'), is expressed by

$$xy'-x'y+z'-z=0,$$

we have* $\quad -\xi y'+\eta x'+\zeta=+(-\xi' y+\eta' x+\zeta'),$

or $\quad -\xi y'+\eta x'+\zeta=-(-\xi' y+\eta' x+\zeta'),$

of which the former is the same as

$$\xi=\frac{1}{4}\frac{1-y'\Delta_{11}+x'\Delta_{12}+\Delta_{13}}{-y\xi'+x\eta'+\zeta'},$$

where Δ_{11}, etc., are the minors in the determinant Δ (p. 41).

Besides the tangent planes there is an infinite number of curves upon the Kummer surface upon which the integrals of the surface are integrals of the first kind; if C be the cubic polynomial in x, y, z obtained by squaring any function of the form $l_0\xi+l_1\eta+l_2\zeta+l_3\tau$ (cf. pp. 139—150), and P, Q be any two integral polynomials in x, y, z, any surface $CQ^2=P^2$ cuts the Kummer surface in such a curve; the surface $CQ^2=P^2$ is one which touches the cubic surface $C=0$ at all their common points.

If we consider any birational transformation of the Kummer surface whereby to a point P corresponds a point P', we may associate with P the integrals of the surface belonging to P'; these will be single valued, as well as finite, on an algebraic curve of the surface containing P, if the integrals of the surface are single valued on the corresponding curve containing P'.

* This may be easily obtained also by applying the converse of Abel's Theorem to the equation $u=v+u^{t,a}$ (cf. p. 121).

In particular, the transformation from a point to its satellite point enables us to associate with the points of any curve on the surface the integrals (p. 78)

$$\int \frac{Q_1 d\xi + Q_2 d\eta + Q_3 d\zeta}{\sqrt{\sigma Q_3}}, \quad -\int \frac{Q_1 d\eta + Q_2 d\zeta + Q_3 d\tau}{\sqrt{\sigma Q_3}},$$

which are single valued on a curve upon which σQ_3 is expressible as the square of a homogeneous rational function of ξ, η, ζ, τ of effective dimension 3. For instance the curve of intersection of the Weddle surface with the quadric cone

$$x_0 Q_1 + y_0 Q_2 + z_0 Q_3 + P_4 = 0,$$

where (x_0, y_0, z_0) are the coordinates of any point of the Kummer surface, or of the Kummer surface $\Delta = 0$ with the cubic surface

$$x_0 \frac{\partial \Delta}{\partial x} + y_0 \frac{\partial \Delta}{\partial y} + z_0 \frac{\partial \Delta}{\partial z} + \frac{\partial \Delta}{\partial t} = 0,$$

this being the locus of the points satellite to those of a tangent section of the Kummer surface (p. 76), is a curve upon which the above integrals are integrals of the first kind. We have considered in this volume a group of 32 birational transformations; these are made up however by combining the process of passing to the satellite point, just considered, with the process of adding a half period to the integrals of the surface.

2. We proceed now to consider a particular curve upon the Weddle surface, of which the corresponding curve upon the Kummer surface is one of the principal asymptotic curves (cf. Exx. 18—20, p. 162); it will be seen to be of deficiency 5 and to have five integrals of the first kind reducible to elliptic integrals; it is the curve of contact of a tangent cone from a node, of which the points are expressible by single valued periodic functions; it thus furnishes a good example of Chapter VII.; and, like the plane quartic curves of four concurrent bitangents, it lies upon cubic cones, whose elliptic integrals give the defective integrals of the curve.

Let x, y, z be homogeneous coordinates in a plane, and

$$C = yza\,(yc' - zb') + zxb\,(za' - xc') + xyc\,(xb' - ya'),$$
$$Q = bcx\,(y - z) + cay\,(z - x) + abz\,(x - y),$$
$$P = x\,(b - c) + y\,(c - a) + z\,(a - b),$$

where $\quad a' = 1 - a, \quad b' = 1 - b, \quad c' = 1 - c;$

the sextic curve $\quad F \equiv C^2 - 4xyzPQ = 0$

has cusps at the angular points of the triangle of reference and at the points $(1, 1, 1)$, (a, b, c), and is of deficiency 5; it touches the join of every two cusps. The five cuspidal tangents, of which two are

$$a'\,(b - c)\,x + b'\,(c - a)\,y + c'\,(a - b)\,z = 0,$$

$$a'\,(b - c)\,\frac{x}{a} + b'\,(c - a)\,\frac{y}{b} + c'\,(a - b)\,\frac{z}{c} = 0,$$

meet in one point,

$$\frac{xa'}{a} = \frac{yb'}{b} = \frac{zc'}{c},$$

which lies on the curve, and on the conic

$$bcx(y-z) + cay(z-x) + abz(x-y) = 0,$$

which is the conic containing the five cusps, the conic and sextic having the same tangent at this point, namely

$$a'^2(b-c)\frac{x}{a} + b'^2(c-a)\frac{y}{b} + c'^2(a-b)\frac{z}{c} = 0.$$

We have

$$xF_1 + yF_2 + zF_3 = 0,$$
$$dx\,F_1 + dy\,F_2 + dz\,F_3 = 0,$$

where $F_1 = \partial F/\partial x$, etc.; and hence

$$\frac{ydz - zdy}{F_1} = \ldots = \ldots = \frac{x'(ydz - zdy) + y'(zdx - xdz) + z'(xdy - ydx)}{x'F_1 + y'F_2 + z'F_3},$$

where x', y', z' are arbitrary, and if this be denoted by $d\omega$, the integrals of the first kind are of the form

$$\int \Omega\, d\omega,$$

where $\Omega = 0$ is a cubic curve through the five cusps. In particular a cubic curve can be drawn through one cusp to touch, at the remaining four cusps, the joining lines of these to the first cusp; and these 5 cubic curves are linearly independent; for instance the curve

$$\Omega_0 \equiv cxyP - zQ = 0,$$

or $$(c-a)x(bz^2 + cy^2) + (b-c)y(cx^2 + az^2) + 2(a-b)cxyz = 0,$$

can easily be seen to be such a cubic for the cusp $x = 0$, $y = 0$, touching the lines $x = 0$, $y = 0$, $x - y = 0$, $xb - ya = 0$ at the remaining cusps. Taking correspondingly $x' = 0$, $y' = 0$, there is an integral of the first kind

$$\int \frac{\Omega_0(xdy - ydx)}{\partial F/\partial z};$$

we find however on calculation that there is for points on the sextic the identity

$$\left(\frac{\partial F}{\partial z}\right)^2 = 16(1-a)(1-b)xy(x-y)(bx-ay)\Omega_0^2;$$

the above integral is thus a constant multiple of the elliptic integral

$$\int \frac{dt}{\sqrt{t(1-t)(b-at)}},$$

and there are four other linearly independent integrals of the first kind also similarly each reducing to an elliptic integral.

Take now the equation to a Weddle surface referred to four of its nodes as corners of tetrahedron of reference, the other two nodes being $(a, b, c, 1)$ and $(1, 1, 1, 1)$, and regard $t = 0$ as the plane at infinity; this equation is (cf. *Proc. Lond. Math. Soc.* Ser. 2, Vol. I. 1903—4, p. 250)

$$xyzP + C + Q = 0,$$

and the tangent cone from the origin $(0, 0, 0)$ is

$$C^2 - 4xyzPQ = 0,$$

containing the plane curve considered above. Any point (x, y, z) of the surface projects, from the origin, to a point of the surface of coordinates $\left(\frac{x}{H}, \frac{y}{H}, \frac{z}{H}\right)$ (*loc. cit.* p. 257), where H is a function capable, in virtue of the equation of the Weddle surface, of the forms

$$H = \frac{zx\,(z'a' - x'c')}{ca'z'x - c'azx'} = \frac{xy\,(x'b' - y'a')}{ab'x'y - a'bxy'} = \frac{xyzP}{Q},$$

where $x' = 1 - x$, $a' = 1 - a$, etc.; thus the curve of contact of the Weddle surface with the sextic tangent cone from the node $(0, 0, 0)$ is characterised by $H = 1$, and lies on the cubic cones

$$ab'x'y - a'bxy' = xy\,(x'b' - y'a'), \qquad \text{(i)}$$

$$ca'z'x - c'azx' = zx\,(z'a' - x'c'), \qquad \text{(ii)}$$

as well as on the surfaces

$$xyzP = Q, \quad C + 2Q = 0;$$

supplying a fourth coordinate $t\,(= 1)$ the two cones (i), (ii) are

$$t^2\,(xa'b - yab') + 2t\,(a - b)\,xy + xy\,(a'y - b'x) = 0, \qquad \text{(i')}$$

$$t^2\,(xa'c - zac') + 2t\,(a - c)\,xz + xz\,(a'z - c'x) = 0, \qquad \text{(ii')}$$

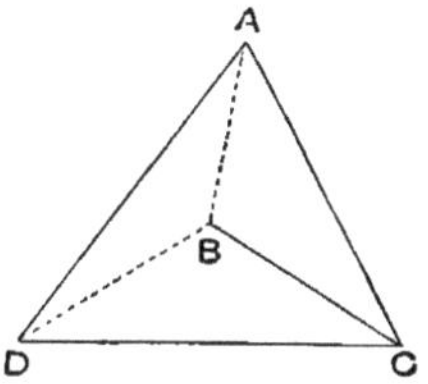

of which the former, with vertex at C, has DCB and DCA for tangent planes, and the latter, with vertex at B, has DBC and DBA for tangent planes. The two cubic cones, with a common generator along which they touch, have therefore, as residual intersection, a space curve *of order* 7, of which DA is the tangent at A. As we see from its projection upon the plane ABC, previously considered, its *deficiency is* 5. In accordance with general considerations, this may also be seen by drawing a quadric surface $(2 = 3 + 3 - 4)$ to touch the plane DBC along BC; such a quadric is of the form

$$x\,(Ax + By + Cz + Dt) + t^2 = 0,$$

containing $p=5$ terms; as the space curve touches DA at A, and the nodes are symmetrical, the space curve touches DB at B and DC at C, and hence touches the quadric at B and C; the Weddle surface contains the line of intersection of DBC with the plane $yc'-zb'=(b-c)t$, which joins A to the nodes $(a, b, c, 1)$, $(1, 1, 1, 1)$, and contains the line BC; thus DBC is a tangent plane of the Weddle surface, at the point $t=0$, $x=0$, $yc'=zb'$, and the space curve passes through this point, and has its tangent line in the plane DBC, and therefore also touches the quadric at this point; there are thus $2.7-6=8=2(p-1)$ further intersections of the quadric and the space curve, as should be the case. Further it may be remarked that not only are the tangent lines of the space curve at the five nodes, other than D, concurrent in D, but the osculating planes at these meet in one line, namely $\frac{xa'}{a}=\frac{yb'}{b}=\frac{zc'}{c}$, which is the tangent of the curve at D.

The integral of the first kind associated with the cubic curve in the plane $z=0$ which is given by the cone (i′) is

$$\int (xdy-ydx)/[t\,(xa'b-yab')+(a-b)\,xy],$$

the denominator being obtained by differentiation in regard to t, and being in fact, when equated to zero, the quadric cone containing the lines which join the node C to the other five nodes; in virtue of (i′) this denominator is capable of the form

$$[(a-b)^2 x^2 y^2 - xy\,(xa'b-yab')\,(a'y-b'x)]^{\frac{1}{2}},$$

or

$$[a'b'xy\,(x-y)\,(bx-ay)]^{\frac{1}{2}},$$

so that we come back to the defective integral previously considered for the plane sextic in $t=0$; *the space curve has thus five integrals of the first kind each of which reduces to an elliptic integral; to find any one it is only necessary to draw the cubic cone joining one of the five nodes, other than D, to the curve, and to put down the elliptic integral associated with a plane section of this; our previous discussion of the plane sextic, in the plane* $t=0$, *shews that the integrals so obtained are linearly independent, each being associated with a cubic cone whose vertex is D having a particular geometrical description.*

In the notation used in this volume the space septic is given by

$$\sigma\,(2u)=0,$$

or

$$2u \equiv u^{t,\,a},$$

this being the consequence of supposing two satellite points, for which

$$2v \equiv u^{t_1,\,u}+u^{t_2,\,u}, \quad 2w \equiv u^{t_1,\,u}-u^{t_2,\,a},$$

to coincide; the homogeneous coordinates of the points of the curve may thus be taken to be

$$\wp_{222}(\tfrac{1}{2}u^{t,\,a}) : \wp_{221}(\tfrac{1}{2}u^{t,\,a}) : \wp_{211}(\tfrac{1}{2}u^{t,\,a}) : \wp_{111}(\tfrac{1}{2}u^{t,\,a}),$$

which are single valued periodic functions of variables whose number is less than the deficiency. The reduction of the integrals arises from the fact that the curve is on cones whose plane sections are of lower deficiency than the curve, each generator of any one of these cones being a multiple secant of the curve. The 32 birational transformations of the Weddle surface, arising by projections from the nodes, reduce in the case of a point on the space-septic to 16, obtained by adding half-periods to the arguments of the functions $\wp_{222}(\frac{1}{2}u^{t,a})$, etc. In fact, if (1) denote the node $(1, 1, 1, 1)$ and (a) denote the node $(a, b, c, 1)$, any point $(x, y, z, 1)$ of the curve gives rise to the eight points (*Proc. Lond. Math. Soc.* 1903, p. 257), also on the curve,

$$(x, y, z) = (x, y, z), \quad (A1a) = (BC) = \left(x, \frac{b}{y}, \frac{c}{z}\right),$$

$$(A) = \left(\frac{a}{x}, y, z\right), \quad (B1a) = (CA) = \left(\frac{a}{x}, y, \frac{c}{z}\right),$$

$$(B) = \left(x, \frac{b}{y}, z\right), \quad (C1a) = (AB) = \left(\frac{a}{x}, \frac{b}{y}, z\right),$$

$$(C) = \left(x, y, \frac{c}{z}\right), \quad (1a) = (ABC) = \left(\frac{a}{x}, \frac{b}{y}, \frac{c}{z}\right),$$

and also to the eight points obtained by writing here throughout, (x_1, y_1, z_1) respectively for (x, y, z), where

$$x_1 = \frac{ax'}{a-x}, \quad y_1 = \frac{by'}{b-y}, \quad z_1 = \frac{cz'}{c-z},$$

the point (x_1, y_1, z_1) being that obtained by projection from the node (1). The integral of the first kind we have written at length,

$$\int \frac{xdy - ydx}{xa'b - yab' + (a-b)\,xy},$$

has thus the same value at the four points

$$(x, y, z), \quad \left(x, y, \frac{c}{z}\right), \quad \left(\frac{a}{x}, \frac{b}{y}, z\right), \quad \left(\frac{a}{x}, \frac{b}{y}, \frac{c}{z}\right).$$

In the notation used in this volume, the two planes joining the node $(1, -b, b^2, -b^3)$ respectively to $(0, 0, 0, 1)$, $(1, -\theta, \theta^2, -\theta^3)$ and to $(0, 0, 0, 1)$, $(1, -\phi, \phi^2, -\phi^3)$ are

$$x \equiv b\theta\xi + (b+\theta)\,\eta + \zeta = 0, \quad y \equiv b\phi\xi + (b+\phi)\,\eta + \zeta = 0,$$

and the quadric cone whose vertex is $(1, -b, b^2, -b^3)$ containing the other five nodes is

$$Q_1 - bQ_2 + b^2 Q_3 = 0;$$

thus the general form of the defective integrals is

$$\int \frac{\eta d\zeta - \zeta d\eta - b\,(\zeta d\xi - \xi d\zeta) + b^2\,(\xi d\eta - \eta d\xi)}{Q_1 - bQ_2 + b^2 Q_3},$$

where b is in turn the five roots of the fundamental quintic.

It does not appear that the integrals of the surface are single valued upon the curve.

ADDITIONAL BIBLIOGRAPHICAL NOTES.

P. 10. The integral $R_{z,c}^{x,a}$ and the polynomial $F(x, z)$ are given in Weierstrass's lectures, *Werke*, Bd. IV. (1902), pp. 273, 274. They may be obtained directly from a formula given by Abel, *Œuvres Complètes* (1881), vol. I. p. 49 ; as in the author's *Abel's Theorem* (1897), p. 195.

P. 20. The conception of a theta function of order r goes back at least to Hermite ; cf. *Compt. Rend.* t. XL. (1855), and a letter from Brioschi to Hermite, *ibid.* t. XLVII. (1858), and Schottky, *Abriss einer Theorie der Abel'schen Functionen von drei Variabeln* (Leipzig, 1880).

P. 36. This particular deduction of the algebraic form of the zeta functions was given in the author's *Abel's Theorem*, p. 320. See also Bolza, *Gött. Nachr.* 1894, p. 268, *Amer. Journ.* XVII. (1895).

P. 38. The equations $\wp_{22} = x_1 + x_2$, $\wp_{21} = -x_1 x_2$, $\wp_{11} =$ etc., are given by Brioschi, *Ann. di Math.* Ser. 2, t. XIV. (1887), p. 298.

P. 39. For the forms for the squares of the functions $\wp_{222}$, etc., see *Proc. Camb. Phil. Soc.* vol. IX. part IX, 1898, p. 517 ; also *ibid.* vol. XII. part III. 1903, p. 219, and *Acta Math.* t. XXVII. (1903), p. 135. That such expressions should exist follows from the general theorem of p. 21.

Pp. 41–54. See the references of the preceding Note. The algebraic deduction of the differential equations here given is probably the most elementary that can be given ; but it would appear that a development is required on the lines that are possible for the differential equation of the elliptic function $\wp(u)$; the functions $\wp_{22}(u)$, etc. are single valued meromorphic quadruply periodic functions whose infinity construct is the repetition of that expressed by $u = u^{t,a}$ (pp. 34, 96). And there is, besides, an algebraic problem : putting down the five equations $\wp_{2222} - 6\wp_{22}^2 = A_1\wp_{22} + B_1\wp_{21} + C_1\wp_{11} + D_1$, to determine directly the possible forms for the 20 coefficients $A_1, \ldots, D_5$ in order that these five equations should be consistent, under the hypothesis that $\wp_{22}$, $\wp_{21}$, $\wp_{11}$ are the second partial derivatives of a single function (cf. § 12, p. 49).

P. 50. As remarked in Ex. 16, p. 162, the linear transformation for the functions $\wp_{22}$, $\wp_{21}$, $\wp_{11}$ is the most general linear homogeneous transformation leaving unaltered the form $\wp_{22}\wp_{11} - \wp_{21}^2$.

P. 77. The formulae

$$\frac{\xi}{s_1' - s_2'} = \frac{-\eta}{s_1't_2' - s_2't_1'} = \frac{\zeta}{s_1't_2'^2 - s_2't_1'^2} = \frac{-\tau}{s_1't_2'^3 - s_2't_1'^3},$$

are cited by Hudson, *Kummer's Quartic Surface*, p. 172, as having been given by Mr H. W. Richmond. See also H. Bateman, *Proc. Lond. Math. Soc.* vol. III. (1905), p. 229.

P. 82. For the 32 birational transformations of the Kummer surface and the six linear complexes a paper of Klein, *Math. Annal.* II. (1870), p. 213 is fundamental.

Pp. 83–97. The results of this chapter were obtained in 1898; see the references in the Note to p. 39. *Linear* partial differential equations for the theta functions of two variables, involving differentiations in regard to the roots of the fundamental quintic, are given by Brioschi, *Ann. di Mat.* Ser. 2, t. XIV. (1887), p. 300, and applied by him to the expansions of the functions. For the case of the even functions he returns to the matter in *Gött. Nachr.* 1890, p. 236, and his results are developed by Bolza, *Amer. Journ. of Math.* vol. XXI. (1898), where many references will be found. Writing, for an even function,

$$\sigma = 1 + \tfrac{1}{2} S_1 + \tfrac{1}{24} S_2 + \dots,$$

Bolza obtains, after Brioschi, the equation

$$S_n = D(S_{n-1}) + (4n-3) S_1 S_{n-1} - 12(n-1)(2n-3)(\alpha\beta)^4 a_u{}^2 \beta_u{}^2 \,.\, S_{n-2},$$

where D is a complicated operator in regard to the roots of the two cubic factors of $a_u{}^6$ with which the particular function considered is associated. The result obtained is that all the coefficients are integral polynomials in 9 covariants of these two cubics. The reader may also consult, besides the papers of Klein and Burkhardt on the theory of the hyperelliptic sigma functions (*Math. Annal.* XXVII. XXXII. XXXV.), Wiltheiss, *Crelle*, XCIX.; *Math. Annal.* XXIX. XXXI. XXXIII. XXXVI.; Pascal, *Ann. di Mat.* Ser. 2, t. XVII. XVIII. XIX.

The procedure of the text is less simple in theory than that considered by these authors, in that it expresses any term in the expansion in terms of all preceding terms, and is applicable, in the form given, only to functions of two variables. For these, however, it would seem to be in practice much simpler, as not involving differentiations in regard to the coefficients of the fundamental sextic. It is much to be desired that the differential equations for the hyperelliptic functions of three variables, and the associated algebraic constructs, should be studied on the lines here followed for the case of two variables; a beginning is made in the papers given in the note to p. 39.

P. 100. The formula for $\sigma(u+v)\,\sigma(u-v)/\sigma^2(u)\,\sigma^2(v)$ was obtained in the author's *Abel's Theorem*, p. 333; and a method for obtaining the corresponding formula for any hyperelliptic case is worked out in detail *Amer. Journ. of Math.* vol. XX. (1898), p. 384. But materials for the formula were already at hand; it is easy to shew, and it is shewn by Humbert, *Liouville*, Ser. 4, t. IX. (1893), p. 112, that $\sigma(u+v)\,\sigma(u-v)=0$ represents a tangent section of the Kummer surface, and it was known (Klein, *Math. Annal.* II. (1870)), that the tangent section is associated with a linear complex (cf. p. 76 of this volume).

P. 107. For orthogonal matrices of theta functions cf. Brioschi, *Ann. di Mat.* XIV. (1887), p. 343; Caspary, *Crelle*, XCVI. (1884), pp. 182, 324; Frobenius, *ibid.* p. 100; Weierstrass, *Berlin Sitzungsber.* 1882, I-XXVI. p. 506.

P. 108. The identity of Ex. 7, p. 152, gives also, if θ, ϕ, ψ_1, ψ_2, ψ_3 be the roots of the fundamental quintic,

$$(\psi_2-\psi_3)\sqrt{P_{\theta\psi_1}P_{\phi\psi_1}} + (\psi_3-\psi_1)\sqrt{P_{\theta\psi_2}P_{\phi\psi_2}} + (\psi_1-\psi_2)\sqrt{P_{\theta\psi_3}P_{\phi\psi_3}} = 0.$$

P. 113. For the geometrical behaviour of the asymptotic lines, see a drawing given by Rohn, *Math. Annal.* XV. (1879), p. 340.

P. 147. For a similar identity see Humbert, *Liouville*, IX. (1893), p. 98.

P. 173. The simplified forms of the linear complexes are those used by Klein, *Math. Annal.* II. (1870).

P. 181. This proof of the converse of Abel's Theorem utilises Riemann's normal elementary integral of the third kind. The proof given in Weierstrass's Lectures (*Werke*, IV. (1902), pp. 417–419) is different in form; but, I think, not essentially different in substance.

P. 185. Another proof of the inequality is obtainable from the complex integral of p. 17.

P. 187. A proof of Weierstrass's implicit function theorem derived from Cauchy's complex integral is given in Picard, *Traité d'Analyse*, t. II. (1893), p. 245, after Simart.

P. 193. The theorem here proved is quoted by Weierstrass, *Werke*, III. (1903), p. 79, as belonging "to the elements of the Theory of Functions"; the proof given in the text is modified from that which applies to the case of rational functions, given later p. 273; see also Blumenthal, *Math. Annal.* LVII. (1903), p. 356.

Pp. 199–204. The reader will naturally consult Weierstrass's papers on functions of several variables (*Gesamm. Werke*). See also the references given p. 285 of this volume.

Pp. 205–215. This account is given in Weierstrass's posthumous paper, *Werke*, III. (1903), pp. 71–104. The reader should compare Wirtinger's paper, *Monatsh. für Math. u. Physik*, Jahrgang VI. (1895), p. 69, which proceeds on similar lines. The references given in this last paper seem worth repeating here: (1) Hermite, in the Appendix to Edition 6 of Lacroix, *Traité des calcul differ. et integ.* Paris, 1861; Deutsch von Natani, 1863; (2) Weierstrass, *Berlin Monatsber.* 1869, 1876, *Crelle*, LXXXIX. (1880); (3) Hurwitz, *Crelle*, XCIV. (1883); (4) Poincaré et Picard, *Compt. Rend.* (1883), t. XCVII. p. 1284; (5) Laurent, *Traité d'Analyse*; (6) Appell, *Liouville*, Ser. 4, t. VII. (1891); to these may be added also the references given p. 285 of this volume.

P. 217. The argument of § 60 is not given by Weierstrass, and is possibly in need of further examination. The conclusion of Weierstrass's posthumous paper referred to is brief, and relies on Hurwitz's paper quoted on p. 202 of this volume. The argument constructed in Chap. IX. of this volume has seemed clearer.

P. 229 ff. This chapter, as stated in the text, is capable of much further development, both on the transcendental side and the geometrical side. As to the former we may instance the points referred to in the footnotes of pp. 241, 255 and 267; cf. Wirtinger, *Untersuchungen über Thetafunctionen*, II. Teil; as to the latter, the geometrical properties of curves in a plane, and in space, possessing defective integrals, seem worthy of further study. Cf. the case considered Appendix to Part II. Note IV.

P. 245. References as to complex multiplication are given in the author's *Abel's Theorem*, chap. XXI.

P. 267. The letter of Gauss to Olbers quoted at the beginning of this volume (p. iv.) is said to refer to the general theorem of which a particular case is here used.

P. 280. The theorem of § 79 suggests the corresponding question for a corpus of rational functions of n independent variables; if an aggregate of rational functions of n independent variables be taken, not necessarily all rational functions, but such that any rational function of functions of the aggregate also belongs to the aggregate, can a set of n

(or less) functions of the aggregate be found in terms of which all other functions of the aggregate are rationally expressible? The theorem has been proved for $n=1$ and $n=2$; for $n=1$ see Lüroth, *Math. Annal.* IX. (1876), p. 163; for $n=2$ see Castelnuovo et Enriques, *Math. Annal.* XLVIII. (1897), p. 313. I have here to make an acknowledgment; I had constructed, as part of this chapter, a proof that the theorem is true for any value of n; Prof. W. Burnside, F.R.S., who was kind enough to read it, pointed out to me that this was not in general valid.

P. 285. See also Hartogs, *Über neuere Untersuchungen auf dem Gebiete der analytischen Funktionen mehrerer Variablen*, Jahresber. d. Deut. Math. Ver. XVI. (1907), p. 223, and the references there given.

P. 303 ff. For the subject matter of Notes I. and II see Frobenius's papers, *Crelle* LXXXVI. LXXXVIII. (1879, 1880).

INDEX OF AUTHORS.

GENERAL INDEX.

CAMBRIDGE: PRINTED BY JOHN CLAY, M.A. AT THE UNIVERSITY PRESS.

ImTheStory.com

Personalized Classic Books in many genre's

Unique gift for kids, partners, friends, colleagues

Customize:

- Character Names
- Upload your own front/back cover images (optional)
- Inscribe a personal message/dedication on the inside page (optional)

Customize many titles Including

- Alice in Wonderland
- Romeo and Juliet
- The Wizard of Oz
- A Christmas Carol
- Dracula
- Dr. Jekyll & Mr. Hyde
- And more...

Lightning Source UK Ltd.
Milton Keynes UK
UKHW02f2018260218
318522UK00004B/115/P

9 781313 880541